Hightower Baptist Church, Cherokee County, Georgia:

An Early History Woven with a Strong and Abiding Faith in Jesus Christ, 1834-1950

Joyce Milford Hutchins

For Hightower Baptist Church

Copyright © 2015

All rights reserved

Library of Congress Control Number: 2015951234

ISBN: 978-1-943529-13-1

Additional copies of this book may be obtained from:

Hightower Baptist Church

3444 Hightower Road

Ball Ground, Georgia 30107

Published by Yawn's Publishing

198 North Street

Canton, Georgia 30114

678.880.1922   www.yawnspublishing.com

Front cover photograph of Hightower Baptist Church by David Akoubian

Author's note: Unless otherwise noted, the pictures in this book are from my personal collection.

Contents

Preface	5
Reflection	6
Dedication	7
Organization of Chapters and Disclaimer	8
Chapter 1. Overview of Hightower Baptist Church	9
Chapter 2. Pre-1834	17
Chapter 3. 1834-1881	24
Chapter 4. 1882-1902, Minutes and Membership Roll, Book One	34
Chapter 5. 1903-1909, Minutes and Membership Roll, Book Two	81
Chapter 6. 1910-1923, Minutes and Membership Roll, Book Three	103
Chapter 7. 1924-1938, Minutes and Membership Roll, Book Four	142
Chapter 8. 1939-1950, Minutes and Membership Roll, Book Five	174
Chapter 9. Beliefs and Worship Services	198
Chapter 10. Church Leadership, Pastors and Deacons	207

Chapter 11. Hightower Highlights, Family Connections, Places and Events   235

Chapter 12. Cemetery Records   323

Appendix

    A. Membership data   390

    B. Deeds/ land lot information   392

    C. Military veterans at HBC   398

    D. Identification of Persons Named on Stained Glass Windows   402

References   408

Index   413

Preface

"Remember them which have the rule over you, who have spoken unto you the word of God: whose faith follow, considering the end of their conversation. Jesus Christ the same yesterday, and to day, and for ever." Hebrews 13: 7 and 8. The following quote is from the book *Story of Georgia Baptist*, by B. D. Ragsdale: "He who will not look into the past to see the way our forebearers have traveled cannot with certainty interpret the present nor with clarity chart the future."

In a spirit of admiration and respect, this work is an effort to record and share the rich history of the first century and more of the people and place known as Hightower Baptist Church (HBC). As I reflect on my connection with HBC, my memories are rich with many beloved people and events of this dear place. As the youngest of four children to a deacon and church clerk father (Robert Milford), and a Sunday school teacher mother (Cleo Heard Milford), I grew up with this church being a major part of my life. The most significant event for me at Hightower happened on the third Sunday in February 1966, after Brother Paul's (Thompson) sermon and in the presence of many (including my parents and grandparents Joel and Birddie Heard); I accepted Christ as my personal Savior.

Throughout my youth, I admit that I had little interest in the rich history of Hightower. Unlike my childhood friend, Coy, who recently shared that he thought Hightower must have been named for some unknown tower high on a hill, I did not question the beginning of this place of worship. As time moved on, I found myself in discussions with loved ones like Nettie Lee Lovelace and my mother. By the 1990s, we contemplated "helping" each other research and write the history of HBC. Regretfully, the project was not initiated at that time. Words cannot express the great loss endured by this church and the families at the passing of our leader and historian, Nettie Lee. Sensing the nudges of the spirit, I dedicated myself to the task of recording the history of HBC by setting regrets aside and going forth. I committed to a plan in 2013. I found comfort and direction from these words from Charles Stanley's website: http://www.intouch.org

> "How can we accomplish what God wants us to do? An individual's lack of talent or ability never hinders God's purposes; that is why a believer should never say, 'I can't possibly do that!' If the Lord has called us to a particular task or service, He's already preparing us to accomplish it. The Spirit gives each of us spiritual gifts—divine capabilities chosen by Him to enable us to fulfill our callings. When we exercise these gifts in the fullness of His power, He accomplishes His work through us."

Borrowing from the words of John Lummus (personal interview: September, 2013) when asked about worship beliefs at HBC that have not changed very much over time, he said "all of the basic fundamentals are still there [at Hightower] that you find anywhere in a church that is successful and that is founded on the rock." The rock is Jesus Christ, the risen Lord and Savior. May those beliefs continue to carry us throughout all generations. The time I have spent on this book has been a labor of love, and it is my wish that many will be uplifted by the ***strong and abiding faith*** that has been woven throughout the long history of this church.

Entry from a former pastor:

May 1, 2015

Reflection of the Great Church, Hightower Baptist Church

While I have known about Hightower all of my life and recall a lot of wonderful remarks about it being a spirit-filled church, my personal ministry as pastor spans the years of 1974 to 1981, and later when I was recalled the second time from 1993 to 2013. I was blessed to serve as the pastor of Hightower for a total of 27 years.

Rather than the building itself, it is all the members of the church that truly make up the church. However, I want to say that the members care deeply about keeping the building up-to-date with several remodels and updates making the church building a beautiful place for members and visitors to come and worship our good Lord.

As I reflect on the past times at Hightower, I cannot begin calling names because every member who walked into the church building is dear to my heart. However, what I remember the most is how the entire church supported me both times I served as their pastor, and what a joy it was to worship together.

I am very thankful for all the revivals we had at Hightower. I will never forget the night that the lights went out just as the altar call was given. Several souls were saved that night; I remember there were eleven saved.

Vacation Bible Schools (VBS) were also special to me. I enjoyed all of them and am thankful for all the souls that were saved. I especially remember the Thursday service in 1995 when there were twenty-four who professed Jesus as their Savior. What a meeting!

All of the deacons, choir, VBS staff, youth, home preachers, song leaders, and every member will always be remembered and appreciated for all you do for the Lord Jesus Christ.

What a great church to reflect upon and remember how the Lord has used you. However, the past is over, but the future looks great for all who will follow the good Lord. My sincere prayer for Hightower is to hold to the principles of God's Word.

May God Bless You!

In Christ,

Brother Gerral Richards

("Numps" to some)

Dedication

To the memory of those faithful pioneers who founded, organized, chartered and/or constituted Hightower Baptist Church. Records do not exist to verify their names, but it is believed that they founded with a desire to worship their God in the best way they knew how. They had strong beliefs in right and wrong and left a heritage that is priceless.

Special Thanks

My Mother, Cleo Heard Milford (in spirit), has been with me every step of the way in the writing of this book. She was an historian, ahead of her time but without the technology that is now available. The many loose notes, writings, conversations and certainly her personal daily diary (from 1934-2004) have aided in the records found herein. The love that both my parents (my dad, Robert) had for their church and family was more than can be described. In short, without my mom, I would have lacked the interest to pursue the writing of this book. So to my mom, thanks and I love you forever! Nettie Lee Lovelace is another, among many, at HBC that blazed the trail for such a project as this to be successful. She was a mentor to many and a valuable asset to HBC.

I am grateful to the deacons for their trust in me as they approved this project. To the current clerk, Edwin Wilkie, and also to Reverends Gerral Richards, John Lummus and Ronnie McCormick, your help is appreciated. Dr. Jimmy Orr provided a review of the historical information, which was a great help. Regina Groover went the extra mile with her help on the list of veterans.

For the research piece, many have willingly helped. I am appreciative of all those who provided information about their families, and most of all, the pictures. An effort to list your names is in the reference list at the end of this book. Thanks to all! To Rev. Gerral Richards: thanks for recommending Ken Wyatt who provided a wealth of his own research and has supported me along this journey. A special thanks to Ken's wife, Emily, for proofreading the draft. To the family at Yawn's Publishing in Canton: your guidance and support have been tremendous. To Mitchell Collins (Mt. Tabor), Carolyn Bates (Liberty Grove), Joey Wallace (New Harmony), and others who have authored their respective church history books: thanks for the wonderful examples of your efforts to record church histories. To Mary Helen Cissell: you were and continue to be an inspiration for recording local history. Special thanks to Judy Northington, my personal friend and photographer, and also to David Akoubian, professional photographer.

Finally, I am grateful for the encouragement and understanding from my relatives, including my siblings: Joe, John and Judy. Most of all, to my husband, David, my son, Andrew, my daughter-in-law, Lindsay, and granddaughter, Madelyn, thanks for your constant love and support.

Organization of chapters

This book is targeted not only for current members and extended families, but also as a historical reference for family researchers. Since no national, state or associational membership list exists in the Baptist denomination, records from individual churches such as those at Hightower Baptist Church are a valuable part of a family history. Therefore, great effort was extended in this work to include names of members from the church rolls and/or minutes. The existing records (unfortunately a few pages are missing) were carefully transcribed. Readers must be aware that errors, omissions and misspelled names do exist in the original records, in spite of the obvious and honest efforts of the church clerks. Over the years, committees were formed to review and revise the records as noted in the minutes; yet, some errors still exist.

The first chapters are a chronological review of HBC from its earliest days through 1950, including the existing church records. HBC continues to be an active and strong church, with an abundance of recent written records. However, a decision was made to end this book at 1950, allowing for some measure of privacy for the current members and helping manage the anticipated size of this book. The chapters are aligned with the dates found in the existing church records (ledger books) containing membership rolls and minutes of monthly business sessions. While the rolls were divided alphabetically, the entries for each letter are predominately chronological. There is value in noting how and when the names were recorded on the membership rolls, the records of which can be compared with existing U.S. Census lists to support family history studies.

The later chapters present a variety of topics of interest including information about pastors, deacons, family stories and cemetery records. Anecdotal remarks from personal interviews and personal diaries are added throughout the chapters to provide the personal touch and emotion felt so strongly at this place.

Several abbreviations used include Hightower Baptist Church (HBC), Baptist Church (BC), Baptist Association (BA), experience (exp), buried (bur), letter (let) and County (Co). Counties are often referred to by their present names, even if they had not yet been formed. All geographical locations are or were in what is now Georgia, unless designated otherwise.

Disclaimer:

This book represents a glimpse into the history of a place and its people. Any reference to race or ethnicity is a reflection of the terms used during the era in discussion and are not meant in any discriminatory manner. Mistakes are easily made when researching and writing a history. Some information found about people, places and dates had conflicting information. Transcribing old documents that are almost illegible, in addition to the many versions of spellings of names was a difficult task. Often, dates are misaligned by a year or more. As this book is read, errors will be found. Please forgive, and be assured that none are intentional.

Chapter 1: Overview of Hightower Baptist Church

A message from the current pastor:

I am the way, the truth, and the life

From the humble beginnings of Hightower Baptist Church, this passage has been and always will be the life blood of the church. John 14:6, "I am the way, the truth, and the life: no man cometh unto the father, but by me."

Jesus is the way!

There was no other way for God to erase the effect of sin except by blood. The shedding of Christ's blood indicated that the penalty for sin had been paid; a perfect sinless life had been sacrificed for the lives of all who have sinned. "Without the shedding of blood, there is no forgiveness of sins" (Hebrews 9:22). Therefore, Christ has made a way for us through his sacrificial death at Calvary.

Jesus is the truth!

If something is true, it is true for all people, in all places, at all times. No matter where you live in the world, 1+1=2 no matter who you are, or where you are, it is the same. Jesus is truth even in a world that disagrees about Him or has no concept of who He is. He is still absolute truth.

Jesus is life!

John 10:10 states, "the thief cometh not, but for to steal, and to kill, and to destroy: I am come that they might have life, and that they might have *it* more abundantly."

To be saved, a man must confess that Jesus is Lord, while acknowledging in his heart that Christ must have full rule over his life. This confession of Christ as Lord assumes that it is Christ who will work and fulfill His own righteousness within man, as man is unable to attain righteousness of his own accord. Jesus calls this experience the "new birth." He told Nicodemus: "Except a man be born again, he cannot see the Kingdom of God" (John 3:3).

I invite you now to receive the Lord Jesus Christ as your personal Savior. "But as many as received Him, to them gave He power to become the sons of God, even to them that believe on His name" (John 1:12). Romans 10:9 says, "That if you confess with your mouth Jesus as Lord, and believe in your heart that God raised Him from the dead, you will be saved." Because of Jesus' death on our behalf, all we have to do is believe in Him, trusting His death as the payment for our sins - and we will be saved!

Will you let Jesus be the way, the truth, and the life of your life?

In Christ our Lord,

Ronnie McCormick, Pastor

May 2015

From the past, into the present and going forward into the future, the message of salvation like the one presented by Pastor Ronnie McCormick is of universal importance to this church and its people. Understanding the scope of the message enables a reader of this book to gain a greater appreciation of the strong and abiding faith of all the church members throughout the ages. Ultimately, it is hoped that the messages from this church will serve as a witness to others in their pursuit of salvation.

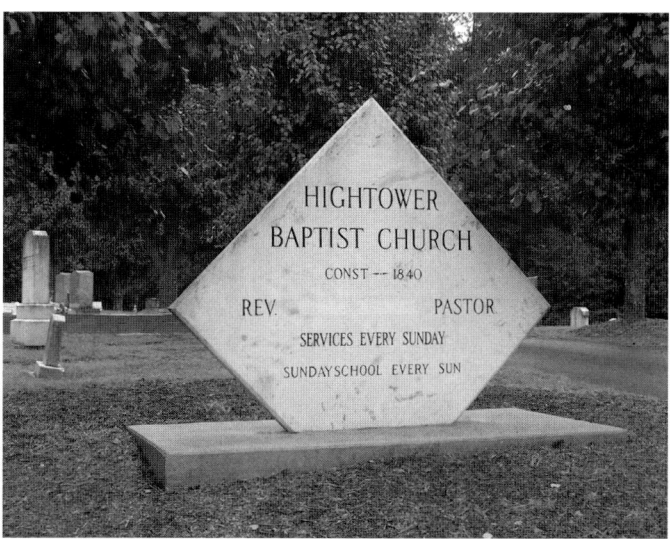

These things are known:

- Hightower Baptist Church (HBC), also referred to as "Old" Hightower, is located at 3444 Hightower Road, (State Highway 369), Ball Ground, Georgia, in the rural setting of the Free Home Community, Northeast Cherokee County, Georgia, about two miles west of the Cherokee/Forsyth County line. Additional information can be found at www.hightowerbaptistchurch.com.

- The church property is listed as about 22 acres, which are portions of Land Lots 535 and 536, Third District, Second Section of Cherokee County Georgia. The Global Positioning System (GPS) coordinates for the address are: Latitude: 34.288038 | Longitude: -84.28146.

- The structures include a framed white church, complete with steeple and attached rooms for Sunday school classes, adjacent fellowship hall with a basement including space for Sunday school classes, a pavilion, and an outdoor baptismal pool.

- The cemetery grounds are believed to contain upwards of 900 graves; the tombstone with the oldest legible burial date is July 1844, that of Dr. Bedney Franklin of the Franklin Gold Mine Family.

- The clapboard-like sign attached high on the front of the church states:

    "Hightower Baptist Church, Oct. 1, 1882"

- The diamond shaped marble sign located on the church property states: "Hightower Baptist Church; Const. – 1840"

    Pastor:

    Services Every Sunday /Sunday school Every Sun.

- The membership roll and church minutes (recorded in ledger books), currently in possession of the church, begin on June 17, 1882. Transcriptions of the first five books, 1882-1950, are included in subsequent chapters of this book. Earlier records were either not recorded or lost; therefore, written information prior to 1882 is scarce. However, some early information about HBC was recorded in Hightower Association minutes.

- On October 3, 1982, the congregation held a celebration recognizing 100 years of occupying the same worship building.

What is the origin of the name Hightower?

Until and unless additional evidence is discovered, the exact beginnings of the HBC, including the original "meeting house," may never be known to those who call this church their home. This work presents available facts along with some possibilities about the founding of this place of worship. Great effort is extended to respect any conflicting information found in existing church and association minutes and from other researchers. It is believed that all have presented information as accurately as possible for the era in which the research was conducted.

No information has been found to indicate a <u>tower</u> located on a <u>high</u> hill or mountain in the North Georgia area. However, sources such as Goff (1975, p. 64) and Krakow (1975, p. 108) explain that the name of Hightower is the settler's pronunciation for the Indian word Etowah. Many place-names of Georgia are those of Indian origin. Dialects were seldom easily translated word-for-word; therefore, often several interpretations and pronunciations were given for similar names. Etowah River and Hightower River are names used interchangeably. Goff further explains that, "The name Hightower is a corruption of the Indian word itawa which the white people also turned into the present Etowah. It was a common practice for those of British origin to add the letter h in front of place names beginning with a vowel. In the cases of Hightower and Hiawassee, the h remains. In other cases such as Hocony/Oconee, the h was eventually dropped. The significance or meaning of the name itawa, or Etowah, is not known" (p. 397). Found in *Georgia Place Names*, in Krakow's opinion, the name Hightower is derived from the Cherokee word, etawaha, meaning "deadwood," or loaned from the Creek word, italwa, or "town". The name was corrupted or changed to "Hightower". Other sources, such as Wikipedia, describe "the Etowah River as a 164-mile-long waterway that rises northwest of Dahlonega, Georgia, north of Atlanta. Its name is the Cherokee version of the original Muskogee word Etalwa, which means a "trail crossing". Don Shadburn of nearby Forsyth County is a writer and local expert on area history. In his work *Unhallowed Intrusion*, Shadburn (1993) claims that "the name Hightower is a corruption of the Indian word I'ta'wa – meaning deadwood place. In other words, Hightower grew from a colloquial term of speech of many Europeans who settled in the region. As Itawa gradually evolved into Hightower through phonetics, so the spelling underwent changes to justify pronunciation: Itowa, Etowa(h), High'towa(h)', Hightower and High'tow'er. The adopted spelling of Hightower, within a few short decades became rather commonplace in most people's speech and written usage" (Shadburn, p. vii). During the research for this book, numerous spellings have been found for Hightower and Etowah. While these examples contribute to the difficulty of this study, ironically these variations also provide an insight to the connections. Examples of spellings include: Hightower, High'to'wa, High'to'wer, Hightowah, It-towah, Itawa, Itawaor, Italwa, Etowah, Etowwah, Etowa, Edahwah, Heytower, Howtower, High Tower, High Towers, Hightowers, Etalwa, Etower, Etowee, Edawah, Eightowen, and Etowah River, Hightower Creek, Hightower Crossroads, Hightower District, Hightower River and Hightower Trail (Cashin, 1994; Krakow, 1975; Goff, 1975).

Where was Hightower?

The following examples show that determining the location of Etowah or Hightower was as confusing as determining the spelling. One early location for the village of Hightower (Ca: 1780s; from aboutNorthGeorgia.com, accessed online) was present day Rome, Georgia. Later, the village of Hightower moved east along the Etowah to present day Cartersville, Georgia. The name, "Hightower Trail," refers to a historically important trading route from the early Augusta, Georgia, area to the territory in the northwest part of Georgia and on to Tennessee. Hightower and Itawa of Forsyth Co. Georgia were two separate places about a mile apart. Hightower was a crossroads township and Itawa an Indian Village. Hightower was also known as Frog Town. On Matthew Carey's 1795 map, the river was labeled "High Town River." On later maps, such as the 1839 Cass County map, it was referred to as "Hightower River," a name that was used in most early Cherokee records. Hightower, as a surname (or last name of a family), was found in Virginia, and North and South Carolina in the late 1700s and early 1800s, per early marriage and census records.

In summary, the research of the name "Hightower" proved to be difficult. While many different possibilities exist, it is most likely that the name of Hightower Church was chosen from the nearby river named Etowah and/or Hightower.

Brief history of Hightower Baptist Church

The beginning of a church is often marked by the date it was organized, chartered or constituted. While the exact date to mark the beginning of HBC remains in question, it is clear that HBC was definitely among one of the first churches in Cherokee County, Georgia (*Men and Missions Vol. II*: Ararat BC, 1833, also known as Baptist Church at Cherokee Courthouse, eventually became First Baptist of Canton and Mt. Zion BC 1834). Evidence does indicate that a congregation called Hightower Baptist Church, assembled at least by 1834, and belonged to the Chattahoochee Association (Chattahoochee Association Records). Nearby churches, such as Friendship (1840) and Mt. Tabor (1833), have recorded in their history books that their congregations met for a period of time, maybe a year or so, before they "petitioned for admission into the Hightower Association" (McConnell, p. 41; Collins and Collins, p. 1). If that pattern of meeting for a couple of years prior to applying to an association was also true for HBC, that would give reason for the suggestions that HBC "appears to have been organized in 1832 or earlier" (*Men and Missions Vol. II*, p. 184). A particular legend, that has existed with HBC people for years, is a story of the possible beginning of the cemetery. Although no date is noted, the story says that in the spring of the year, a group of travelers came by and camped at a spring behind the Lovelace (Stephens) home place. While there, a child died and a decision was made to bury the child up on the hill. A fascinating connection to this story was made during the study of the history of HBC. Upon a review of a topographical map of the property of HBC, it was noted that the area of highest altitude correlates with the location of graves in the cemetery that are believed to be the oldest burials. Could this indeed be a connection with this long told story of the child's burial and the highest point on the hill? No grave marker has been found to verify this legend; however, numerous graves exist in this area and are unmarked. It is only a guess that the child's burial was possibly in the era of 1820-1835.

The marker above the current front porch of the sanctuary says, "Hightower Church, October 1, 1882." It is believed that this date reflects the age of the inner portion of the current church building. Even though the next picture is from the funeral service of Rev. Robert W. Roper in 1939, it shows the front of the church before the addition of the first porch. The picture on the right is of Brother Bob Buffington, also before the porch addition, and was taken during the time of coal heaters, as evidenced by the coal shed shown in the background left of the church building. Several additions and remodeling efforts have taken place over time.

Picture of church, courtesy of Bobby Roper

Picture of Mr. Buffington in front of church, courtesy of Ken Wyatt

The marble/granite nameplate located near the front drive says the church was constituted in 1840. The dilemma continues to exist about the term constituted. While several records note that HBC was constituted in 1840, one Hightower Association record states it was constituted in 1845! Could the year 1840 reflect when the church officially recognized a charter/rules of decorum/etc.? Possibilities exist that the congregation met in private homes before the construction of the first church building. Could 1840 possibly reflect the date of the construction of the log-hewn structure known as the meeting house? Or could HBC indeed have been constituted earlier than most records show? The determination of the 1840 date is unclear; however, it is possible that the congregation did, in fact, establish a constitution or covenant at that time. This date could also coincide with the beginning of the pastorate of Rev. Alfred Webb. One may surmise that if indeed Indians were worshiping at HBC, the "congregation" would have withstood a severe transition during the late 1830s with the "Trail of Tears" and could have "reorganized" in 1840. Even though these items note a beginning in the early 1830s, further study is needed to clarify the precise dates.

Two previously recorded histories of HBC: By Nettie Lee Lovelace, and by Randy Wilkie

(1) A four page historical sketch was sent to the Hightower Baptist Association in preparation for *Men and Missions, Vol. II, Churches* (original submission was neither dated nor signed). A similar version to this sketch, and authored by Nettie Lee Lovelace was included in the 2003 HBC Membership Directory. It is likely that Nettie Lee also wrote the entry for the association; however, the authorship has not been confirmed. The portions noted in italics below show items edited for publication in Hightower Baptist Association's *Men and Missions, Vol. II, Churches,* pages 183 and 184.

Nettie Lee Lovelace
Photo courtesy of Chris Chandler

Historical Sketch: HIGHTOWER BAPTIST CHURCH, Highway 369, Ball Ground, Georgia, 30107, believed written by Nettie Lee Lovelace.

The Hightower Baptist Association minutes of 1835 listed Hightower Baptist Church as one of the churches making up the association. Only three years earlier the Hightower community was a part of the Cherokee Indian Territory. Cherokee County was established in 1832. The minutes showed Alfred Webb as the pastor. ... *but other records show that Elder Solomon Peak was the pastor when the Hightower Association was formed in 1835 at Silver Springs Baptist Church. Elder Peak is shown in the 1835 Hightower Minutes as one of the delegates from Hightower Baptist Church.* There were 32 members listed separately as male and female, from 1848-1875 members were also listed by race: white and colored. Some sources have recorded the church as constituted in 1840; however, other records do not support that date. According to the available data it appears to have been organized in 1832 or earlier.

A large well-kept cemetery surrounds the church. Several gravestones are for people born in Cornwallis, England, in the early 1800s. According to information passed down through generations, slaves and Indians are also buried there.

The church was built in the Hightower community, a part of the Cherokee Indian Territory, near the Hightower River, which is now known as the Etowah River. The first building was made of hand-hewn logs. Hightower School was near the church, but later was moved to Andrews Chapel Methodist Church about a mile east. Andrews Chapel Cemetery, now overgrown with trees and vines, is the only vestige of the church or school.

The second building, which was called the meeting house, was built in 1882. It was a frame rectangular building with two front doors and large field rocks for steps. It was heated by two potbellied stoves and lit by kerosene lamps mounted on the wall in front of tin reflectors, which were later replaced by gas lights, then electric lights when electricity became available. Water was brought in buckets from a nearby spring and placed on a table. Everyone drank from the same dipper. During the church service, men sat on the left side of the church and the women sat on the right, which is probably the reason for two front doors.

Today in 2003, there is such a contrast between the first (log-hewn) and the second (wooden-framed) buildings. Many of the younger generation who worship at Hightower probably do not realize the age of the second building that was erected in 1882. The present structure is a beautiful sanctuary that was built around the second building. After several renovations, additions and much improvement, the present building has central heat, air conditioning, modern plumbing, Sunday school rooms, a pastor's office, carpeted floors, padded pews, chandeliers, stained glass windows and a steeple.

Additional structures and other improvements have been added on the church site. Among these are a fellowship hall with additional classrooms connected to the main building by a breezeway, a pavilion for "dinner on the ground," family reunions and other activities. Landscaping, a paved parking area, and cemetery maintenance have improved the church grounds. Several acres of land adjacent to the church property have been purchased for expansion of activities and future needs.

For many years, worship services were held on the third Sunday each month, with conference on Saturday before the third Sunday. In 1957, the first Sunday service was added. In 1974, the Women's Missionary Union was organized and sponsored a fifth Sunday service with the offering going to support the WMU. After some effort to go full-time, in 1982 the church did vote to do so. Some had doubts concerning going full-time for fear that attendance would be poor and could not support a full time ministry financially. Both premises were proven wrong; attendance improved, and the church was blessed financially.

Pastors serving the church since 1832 were: Alfred Webb, E. W. Allred, Thad Pickett, A. S. Sheffield, H. T. Ingram, Elias Cochran, J. R. Allen, E. A. Cochran, C. A. Wallis, A. J. Henderson, J. R. Stone, R. A. Roper, P. W. Tribble, John Lummus, Jack Sutton, Elbert Majors, Paul Thompson, Lealon Ellis, T. W. Henderson, Robert Martin, Harold Thompson, Ronnie McCormick, and Gerral Richards. *Additional information about former pastors can be found in Men and Missions, Vol. II.*

Various groups that make the church strong and active are: 1) the Board of Deacons, 2) the Women's Missionary Union, 3) Sunday school, 4) Vacation Bible School, 5) the Adult Choir, 6) the Children's Choirs, and 7) the Youth Groups. All improvements and work of the various groups are a reflection of the spiritual commitment of the membership.

Although many changes have taken place and the membership has increased from thirty-two in 1832 to more than seven hundred in 2003, one constant thread is woven throughout the history of the church. A <u>strong and abiding faith</u> in Jesus Christ and His cause and love for each other has been that constant.

Randy Wilkie
Photo courtesy of Brian Wallace

Revivals: A spring revival usually runs in late March or early April. Services are held for three nights. The summer revival begins on the 3rd Sunday in July. Morning services are at 10:45, and evening services are held through Saturday night at 7:45 PM.

Missions: The church supports the Southern Baptist Convention's Cooperative Program, the Women's Missionary Union, Sunday school and an outstanding youth program.

.....

(2) Below is the script from the presentation by Randy Wilkie, History of Hightower, published in DVD format on *Hightower Baptist Church: History and Memories,* August 2010, Editor/Producer/Videographer: Brian Wallace; Associate Producers: Debbie and Randy Boles. (Randy Wilkie is current chairman of deacons).

History of Hightower: My name is Randy Wilkie and I am a member and deacon of Hightower Church. I've been in this church all my life; my parents brought me here. I was saved here in 1964 and I've raised my family here; my grandkids are being raised here now. This church has been an integral part of my life. I hope to pass it down for many generations to come and I hope we will hand it to the next generation in as good of a condition as it was handed to us.

This church has been here for a long time. Our records that we have, the church minutes go back to 1882/1883. We know that the building, the original part of it was constructed about that time. It was a rectangular building, no porch, no Sunday School rooms, no choir and it started in 1883 and we have minutes or records from that point on up to date but the church has been here much longer than that. We have heard that there was a church [building] across the road that burned, but we have bits and pieces of evidence that I will share that tells us that this church has been around much longer than 1883.

In the 1883 minutes, our record of the church acknowledges a former pastor, his name was Alfred Webb. He had just recently died [as recorded in the 1883 minutes] and he was being remembered. It says that he was a former pastor who pastored the church for upwards of forty years. If you look at 1882 and look at him being here for forty years before, and we don't know how long the time was between when he left the church and the time he died, but that easily takes us back to the 1840s.

We have records of the land purchase in 1845. A man by the name of Daniel Stephens sold this church two acres of land. I have looked in the cemetery and I have found a grave where a person was buried here in 1844 [Bedney Franklin: 1815-1844]. That is the oldest one I could find. Of course, there are many unmarked graves, but of those with monuments that are dated, we know that one was buried here at least in 1844. That dates the church back to at least one year before the land purchase. According to one of the signs, it says constituted in 1840. I'm not sure where that firm figure came from but it is possible the church goes back to the 1830s, maybe around the time of the land lotteries and when the Indians were marched out. The whites were coming in; the land was being surveyed out, and given to the people - the new settlers.

For a little bit of history on this side of 1883, we know that we had the original building then, but if you go on down about fifty-six years later after the original building was constructed, Sunday school was organized and the choir section was built in 1938. This was probably about the time the church got electricity, but I don't have exact figures of when power was installed in this church. Sunday school was held in the main part of the sanctuary. Since there were no individual Sunday school rooms, the different classes met in the main sanctuary and divided into groups and had class. It wasn't too long, just a few years on down the road in 1957 when the Sunday school rooms were built and three years before that, in 1954, the porch was added to the church.

As time went on and when the people got the means to do so, they added on to the church just as we have done in our lifetime a few times. Since that time, we've seen some other things happen. To touch on those briefly, in 1967, additional Sunday school rooms were added and indoor plumbing and indoor restrooms were installed. Up until then, the old outhouses were used, as a matter of fact, the structures of the old outhouses are still here. But we really got "uptown" in 1967 with indoor plumbing, which was a great luxury. The first air conditioning was installed in 1969, they were window units. Up until then, you just came to church in the summertime and you were hot. We used the funeral home fans (hand fans) and tried to cool off the best you could. Later on, 1973, stained glass windows were installed. In 1974, the Women's Missionary Union (WMU) was organized and central heat and air conditioning was put in. That was really a nice addition because the window units were noisy. In 1977, the parking lot was paved. Up until then, it was gravel and dusty dirt, and sometimes mud when you came into the building if you weren't careful. In 1984/1985 the fellowship hall was built. During that time, several other churches were building these additions. We tossed around the idea, took a vote, and the majority voted to build a fellowship hall. The original thought was just for the main floor, but once we got started, the land was steep enough for us to put in a basement. So as an afterthought, we ended up with the fellowship hall and additional Sunday School rooms in the basement.

In 1989, a steeple was added on to the church. In 1992, the main sanctuary was extended. Attendance had increased and we got to the point that we were having a packed church pretty regularly so we took a vote and added on to the church.

Always here at Hightower, we usually have some members with the necessary skills for construction so we pitch in and help do the work. It seems we have less and less free time, but we still do a lot of the work ourselves and enjoy it. It is a good chance for fellowship. In 1996, the fellowship hall was expanded.

One of the most recent ventures was the purchase of an adjacent piece of property in 2002. We had a chance to buy the land, it was fifteen plus acres. The church voted to do that and the church pulled together to get it paid for in about four or five years. So now, we have room to grow and hope someday we will need that. Since we bought that, we have installed a playground and a building for the youth group.

Time goes on, we keep growing, keep changing, but the main thing is that no matter what we do here at this church, the main thing is Jesus Christ, and that we promote the gospel. The main thing includes providing a place for our families and our community to come hear Jesus Christ preached and taught. Most of all our community needs to see us live out Jesus Christ. My hope and prayer for this church is that this generation will pull together, keep growing, keep promoting Christ and hand this church down to our children and grandchildren and give them the opportunity to hand it on down to the next generations."

.....

Summary: Both Nettie Lee Lovelace and Randy Wilkie provided remarks about the worship and fellowship that continues into the 2000s, long after those beginning days of the early 1800s. No doubt, current members are dedicated to sustaining that strong and abiding faith in Jesus Christ that has been a part of this congregation for many years.

Chapter 2: Pre-1834

Through research and preparation for this publication of the history of HBC, the following statements are believed to be accurate at the time of this printing. Continued studies may provide further insights to the earliest days as records are scarce and often difficult to link.

- Community
    - Creek Indian Land until 1755, followed by occupation of Cherokee Indians
    - 1828 - Benjamin Parks is credited with discovery of gold; Gold Rush of 1829-31, the ensuing immigration of settlers
    - By 1830, the Cherokee Nation consisted of most of Northwest (NW) Georgia (including lands west of the Chattahoochee River)
    - By 1831, Cherokee Nation (NW Georgia) becomes Cherokee County
    - Gold Land Lottery of 1831 and 1832
    - 1832 - the large and original Cherokee County is divide into 10 smaller counties; the HBC area became Cross Roads District of Cherokee County
    - Land lots were bought and sold from the lottery winners of the 1832 Gold Lottery

- Religion/Baptists
    - 1733 - Baptists were likely on the ship with Oglethorpe upon arrival in Savannah, Georgia
    - 1772 - Kiokee BC near Augusta, Georgia, was formed, believed to be the first Georgia BC that is still in existence today
    - 1799 - Sarepta BA was founded in northeast Georgia
    - 1820s - Baptist missionaries preached and organized schools in Cherokee Indian lands, some may have been near HBC
    - 1832 - possible founding date for HBC, although this date appears to be circumstantial
    - 1833 - Mount Tabor (Forsyth Co.), Liberty (Dawson Co.) and Ararat (Cherokee Co., later became First BC in Canton) were founded
    - 1833 - two other area churches were formed. Hightower _may_ have been one of those?

- Occupations: farmers, gold miners, blacksmiths, grist mill operators

- Transportation: oxen or horse and wagon, walking, horseback, crossed streams or rivers by fords or ferries

- Cemetery: Undetermined if burials began at HBC before the church was established in 1834

The silhouette above is a portion of a sign atop a gate to a field near current Hightower church. The historical timeline depicts the events of the Hightower community with the first two shown above: Cherokee Indians and gold miners.

Pre-1834:

During the late 1700s and into the early 1800s, the North Georgia area was the Cherokee Nation and home to the Cherokee Indians. Several critical events took place that directly impacted the likely founding of HBC. The influx of Baptist missionaries, the discovery of gold that prompted an influx of the European Settlers, the Georgia Land Lottery System and the eventual "Trail of Tears" are all incidents that left their mark on the early people who became worshipers at HBC.

Early Baptist Missionaries and HBC

Before the surge of whites into North Georgia, missionaries worked among the Cherokees and the earliest white settlers to bring the good news of religion. Marlin (1933) describes that the Cherokees "possessed originally a full set of creation-myths and sun-worshiping rites, they later turned in large numbers to the teachings of the missionaries who worked among the Cherokees as early as 1803 and who formed a civilizing influence on them" (p. 10).

In 1808, the Cherokee people were well-organized and well-governed. They even had laws that protected the rights of widows and orphans. An 1809 census of the Cherokee Nation counted 12,395 Cherokee, 583 Negro slaves and 314 Europeans. In an 1824 Cherokee Census: 15,000 Cherokee lived in the nation, owning about 1,000 slaves, 22,400 cattle, 7,600 houses, 40,000 pigs, and 3,000 sheep. There were 12 saw mills, 20 grist mills and 55 blacksmith shops. They had accumulated many wagons, plows, and spinning wheels and were continuing to be influenced by the life of the new settlers.

During the time of 1800 – 1830, a few white families likely found their way into the bottom lands of the Etowah River near Board Tree Creek in the shadows of the current day Hightower Church. Possibly those newcomers, as well as the resident Cherokees, were the recipients of the missionary work of early Baptists, such as Humphrey Posey, Duncan O'Bryant, William Manning, Jeremiah Reeves and Evan Jones who were bringing the good news of religion. Each of these missionaries has traces of connections to HBC! Letters, diaries and stories about

O'Bryant, Jones and others are discussed in length in the work of Robert G. Gardner: *Cherokees and Baptists in Georgia*. Several references closely place these early missionaries in and near current day HBC. Place names also indicate locations or communities near HBC. While further study is needed to clarify the facts, the possibilities of involvement with HBC definitely spark an interest and are worth mentioning.

Photo from: *History of the Baptist Denomination in Georgia: with Biographical Compendium and Portrait Gallery of Baptist Ministers and other Georgia Baptists.*

Humphrey Posey (1780-1846) was an early missionary to the Cherokees. In 1817, Posey was appointed by the Triennial Convention (the forerunner of the Southern Baptist Convention) as one of the first Baptist missionaries to work among the Cherokee people of North Georgia and Western North Carolina. His ministry among the Cherokees produced a number of churches and Christian schools that greatly benefited those he served. Humphrey Posey was greatly loved and respected among the Cherokee. Robert Fleming, in his *Sketch of the Life of Elder Humphrey Posey,* included a letter written by Alfred Webb (well-known HBC pastor for "upwards of forty years" in the mid-1800s). In 1809 or 1810, Posey visited the home of Webb's parents in North Carolina when Webb was about nine or ten years old. Webb described Posey as: "a laborer who aided in the conversion of many sinners, taught school and helped to establish many churches." The 1828 records of The Catawba River Baptist Association meeting in North Carolina held at Bill's Creek Church in Rutherford County, state that the introductory sermon was by Humphrey Posey with Elder Alfred Webb as the moderator. No doubt Posey was a mentor to Webb and could have been influential in Webb's move to Georgia in 1837.

Duncan O'Bryant (1785/1786-1834) - A congregation of worshipers possibly existed in the Hightower area prior to the organization of HBC because of the work of missionary Duncan O'Bryant. A school and church had been established at Tinsawattee on the Etowah River. In 1824, the Rev Duncan O'Briant/O'Bryant/Bryant became the teacher/preacher who taught an average of twenty students a year until 1829 when the school moved to Hickory Log, eight miles to the south on the same river. Most of his church members and students were probably of mixed ancestry or whites married to Cherokees. O'Bryant is credited for erecting a school building in Cherokee County, and also holding services in private residences in the areas of current day Cherokee, Dawson, and Forsyth Counties. Huddleston states in *From Heretics to Heroes* that "in 1827, A Cherokee Indian Baptist Church was organized under O'Bryant at Tinsawattee with 15 members which were located near Hightower Baptist Church in Cherokee County." No information is given to define "near" and the exact location of the Tinsawatee congregation is difficult to pinpoint. Tinsawatee is said to have been a meeting house in Dawson County, now believed to be located near Mill Creek and Etowah River in lower Dawson County (Don Shadburn, personal interview July 23, 2013). The area or community was referred to as Savannah or Big Savannah. The records of the Chattahoochee Association in 1827 state that "Tensewattee, one of the churches which joined this year, had been organized in the Cherokee Nation, and was represented by Duncan O'Briant, a missionary, who labored several years among the Cherokees." Goff in *Placenames of Georgia* concurs with this suggested location of Tinsawattee. Goff notes that "Tinsawattee is also known as or spelled as Tensawattee, Tinswatte, Tensawatie, Tensaw Watee, Tansaw-Wattee, Tensau water, Tennessewater, etc." Goff further states, "Tinsawattee was a Cherokee settlement or town connected with the Big Savanah, located in current lower Dawson County with fine bottomlands found on the north or on the right side of the Etowah River. Sometime in the 1820s, the Baptists established a missionary station at Tensawattee under the stewardship of the Reverend and Mrs. Duncan Bryant. The church did not remain long at the site before it was removed to Hickory Log Town, near today's Canton." Feeling the hostility from President Andrew Jackson and land-hungry Georgians, O'Bryant was prompted to lead the group of about twenty-eight (plus his wife and eight of their children) to join a larger traveling party early in 1831/1832 and head for "the Arcansaw Contary" (in the territory that is now in Eastern Oklahoma). Unfortunately, his untimely death in 1834 or 1835 ended his missionary work among the Cherokees. These references to HBC and meetings in private residences between southern Dawson Co. and Canton in Cherokee Co. provide exciting theories about a congregation near HBC before the believed beginning in 1834, but without proof, they remain as speculations.

Commissioned by the Georgia Baptist Convention, Rev. Jeremiah Reeves (1772-1837) and Rev. William Manning (1797-1871) were sent as missionaries to North Georgia for the purpose of forming much needed churches. A report of the Georgia Baptist Convention in May of 1834 states that Rev. Reeves had aided in the constitution of five churches in 1833. Three of those are believed to be Mount Tabor (Forsyth Co.), Liberty (Dawson Co.) and Ararat (Cherokee Co., now First Baptist of Canton), (Collins and Collins, 1999, p. 2). Collins states: "the identity of the other two churches is presently unknown." Considering the fact that the location of HBC is between those churches and the dates are aligned, it is possible that HBC was one of those unidentified churches that Manning and Reeves established (*Men and Missions, Vol. II*, p. 252). An interesting insight about Jeremiah Reeves recorded by Campbell (1874) and accessed online states, "While a resident in Jackson County, he received an appointment from the Georgia Baptist Convention. His field of labor was mostly confined to the Cherokee country (note country which referred to Indian lands, not county). He traveled two years through that section, part of the time on his own account, and part under appointment of the Convention; met with and encountered many hardships, as the country was wild and just settling up. He was one of the first pioneers to that section of the state, aided in constituting several churches, ordained deacons, formed temperance societies, and inculcated the missionary spirit wherever his lot was cast." Manning served as moderator of the Chattahoochee Baptist Association in 1832 and continued to serve with the association for the next few years (Chattahoochee BA history).

Evan Jones (1788-1882) is believed to have worked among the Cherokee people for fifty-two years (Gardner, 1989, p. 101). Even though he was not among the earliest missionaries to work in the Cherokee territory, his work was documented in various personal journals and letters of correspondence. The HBC connection is from an entry in Jones' journal of March 25, 1837. While this occurs after the believed beginning of HBC, it is interesting to note that a missionary was still working among the Native Americans in the nearby area. Found in *Cherokees and Baptists in Georgia,* Gardner states that "in March and December of 1837, Jones and Bushyhead (Jones' interpreter) enjoyed success at the home of Nooche (or Noo-tsee), near 'Nelson's' – probably close to the site of the Hightower Baptist Church in eastern Cherokee County" (p. 198).

Found in *Heritage of Cherokee*, a sketch of John Daniel Nelson: "A Journal of the Baptist Rev. Evan Jones for 1837 records that he stopped at 'Nelson's' on his circuit-riding trip through the Cherokee Territory. It was located 'four miles up the Etowah from Long Swamp' on a map published in *American Baptist Magazine* in 1837" (p.439).

Also found in *Cherokees and Baptists in Georgia*, Gardner notes: "the location would have been where the Broad Tree [i.e., Boardtree] Creek joins the Etowah, a mile north of Hightower Baptist Church and about a half-mile west of the old Franklin Gold Mine" (p. 199). He also explains that Nelson's is not believed to be the same as present day Nelson, Georgia, in Pickens County. Krakow supports this with information that says Nelson was incorporated in 1891 (Krakow, 1975).

Summary

In summary, Humphrey Posey may have influenced Alfred Webb to move to Georgia. Maybe Duncan O'Bryant met in "private residences" near HBC in the early to mid-1820s. Pictured below is a private home currently located near HBC that was built many, many years ago and likely similar to the private residences where early congregations met. As Jeremiah Reeves and William Manning were establishing churches in the Forsyth and Cherokee County areas, could HBC have been one of those unnamed ones that began in 1833? In 1837, Evan Jones may have assembled with a number of Indians where Board Tree Creek joins the Etowah River just prior to the infamous 1838 "Trail of Tears." While these early connections cannot be established as proven fact, the links certainly provide exciting theories about the founding of HBC.

This picture of a "private residence" could be a replica of where the first few families gathered to worship which led to the establishment of HBC. The house is known as the Fowler family home place and is located in the HBC community. It is constructed of logs, and the stacked-stone foundation is visible in the photo. This home was noted as a "better" home as the logs shown on the porch wall have been smoothed on all four sides as opposed to round logs with notched ends. Round logs indicated a quicker build and likely a more temporary residence.

Community

No doubt, the years just before and just after 1834 were a most dynamic time for the people of Northeastern Cherokee County. Knowledge of gold mining opportunities spread quickly after 1828; the state government of Georgia and the U.S. government were on the move to decide how and when to go forth with removal of the Cherokee Indians; the formation of county boundaries changed with the 1831 and 1832 surveys; and the gold land lottery of 1832 brought new people with curiosities and excitement about gold. In the midst of these changes, survival and rearing a family were often difficult. Providing food, shelter and clothing were concerns that occupied the time and efforts of the settlers. Most importantly to many, religion likely played a role in how the newcomers dealt with all the changes.

Gold Mining and Land Lotteries

Gold had been discovered in 1828 and some believe that the Indians and mixed bloods in the area already knew of the value of gold and had mined gold earlier than that date. The State of Georgia divided the area where gold was thought to most likely exist into 40 acre lots and the non-gold potential areas into 160 acre lots. Georgia gave away the Cherokee Nation East in the 6th or 1832 Land Lottery. Scouts had been in the area looking for places where gold already had been found. Georgia had troops in the area to try to stop the illegal poaching of the gold. The speculators had riders ready when the lots were drawn, and as soon as one of the good gold lots were matched with the lottery winner, the riders would go to the winner's residence to try to purchase the lot. This was a race between the speculators fast horses and smooth talking buyers to see who could get there and close the deal first. As with any boom to a new area, there was an influx of all kinds of people: speculators, lawyers, merchants, gold miners, camp followers, and thieves. In addition, the preachers and teachers and the ordinary farmers also came, and North Georgia started with a mixture of people. Some stayed and some moved on, but it was an exciting time.

Cherokee County, Georgia, can continue to argue that it has two different birth dates. The first named Cherokee County, Georgia, was established on Dec. 26, 1831, as the entire area west of the Chattahoochee and north of the Carroll County line. On Dec. 3, 1832, the area was cut into ten smaller counties: Cherokee, Forsyth, Lumpkin, Union, Cobb, Gilmer, Murray, Cass (now Bartow), Floyd, and Paulding. Other divisions have resulted in additional county formations over time.

In the HBC area, one of the most notable lottery winners was a widow from Clark County, Georgia, Mary G. Franklin. She won land lot 466 in the third district, in the second section of Cherokee County. She established the successful Franklin Gold Mines. At her passing in 1858, she was buried at HBC Cemetery (See story in Chapter 11: "Mary Franklin"). The mining industry continued for a number of years under different business names such as Pascoe, Franklin and McDonald, Creighton, and others. In 2015, the historical marker located at the Cherokee County Courthouse, Canton, Georgia, references the gold mining operations of the past.

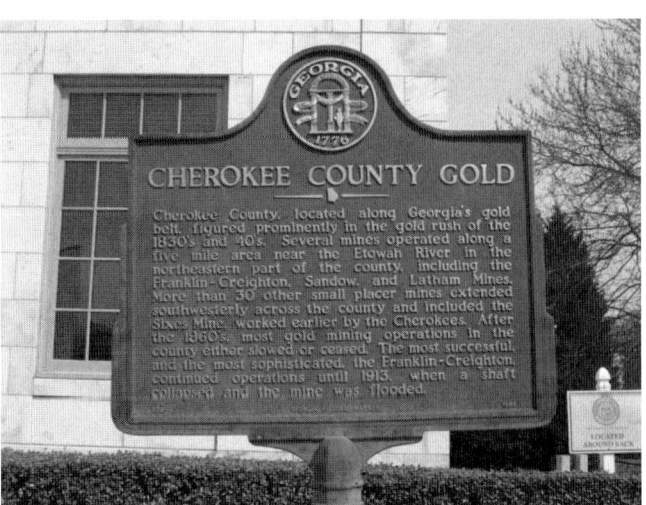

Cherokee County Gold

"Cherokee County, located along Georgia's gold belt, figured prominently in the gold rush of the 1830s and 40s. Several mines operated along a five mile area near the Etowah River in the northeastern part of the county, including the Franklin-Creighton, Sandow, and Latham Mines. More than 30 other small placer mines extended southwesterly across the county and included the Sixes Mine, worked earlier by the Cherokees. After the 1860s, most gold mining operations in the county either slowed or ceased. The most successful, and the most sophisticated, the Franklin-Creighton, continued operations until 1913, when a shaft collapsed and the mine was flooded."

The following picture is of an original deed from the 1832 Gold Land Lottery and signed by the Governor Wilson Lumpkin. Even though the location of this lot is not in the HBC community, the deed is of interest because it matches the design of the 1832 deeds, including the beeswax seal.

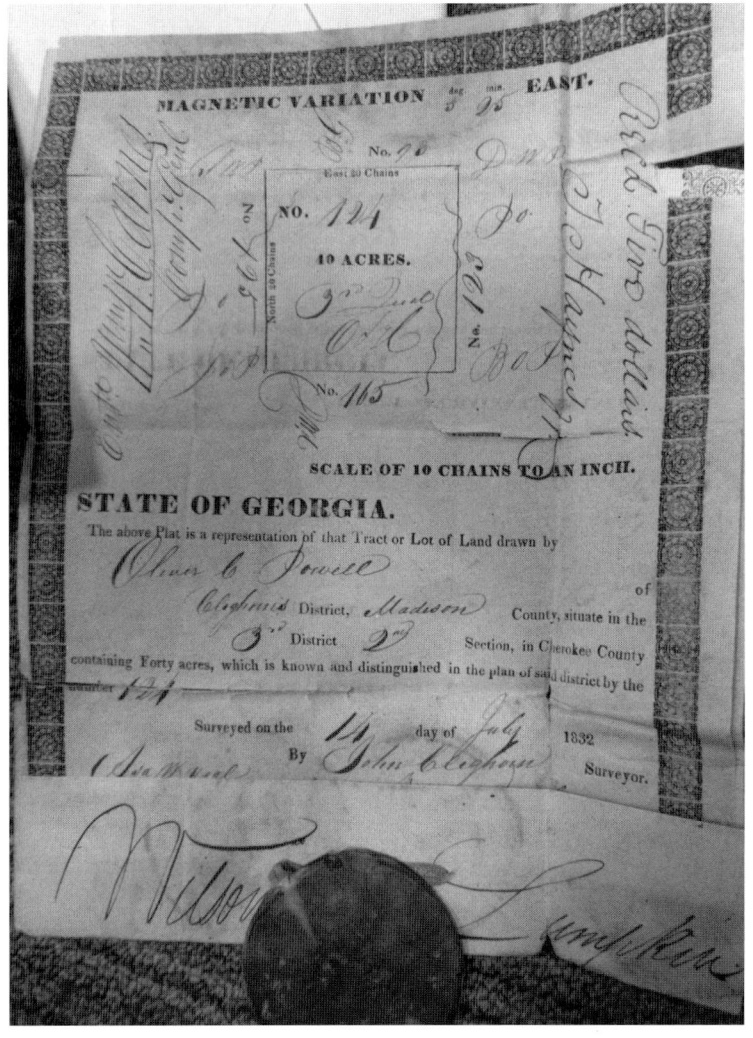

Livelihood of Settlers and Preachers

Since no records of the beginning of HBC have been located, one could guess that the founding of HBC may be similar to that of Ararat BC, the forerunner to First Baptist Church in Canton, Georgia. Typical for the era of time and found in the records of their church history, Ararat was established on August 23, 1833, by twelve people at the Cherokee County Courthouse with the help of Rev. Jeremiah Reeves and William Manning, missionaries for the Georgia Baptist Convention. A presbytery was selected, a constitution presented, and the people received it. Rev. Manning led a prayer, and Rev. Reeves gave the charge. The church body then went into conference and voted on when to hold conference meetings going forth, and appointed a church clerk. Also noted in the history of Ararat, on June 1837, Alfred Webb was elected as pastor "for a small sum." Webb remained at that church through 1840 (Roberts, 1933). Could this be a link to Webb's possible beginning at HBC in 1840? The answer to that question remains undetermined.

The livelihood of a local preacher was at best a challenge. Alfred Webb was among one of the first pastors of HBC, and his tenure likely paralleled the work of Rev. John E. Rives. Since a description of Webb's early preaching days has not been found, this narrative of Rives could aptly describe the beginnings of HBC as well as a similar livelihood of Alfred Webb. Sybil Wood McRay wrote in *This 'n That, History of Hall County, Georgia,* the recollections of a pioneer preacher, John E. Rives (1802-1895) who lived in Hall and later in Dawson Counties. Rives crossed the Chattahoochee (River) at Shallow Ford in March of 1821. At that time, the Cherokee Indians held the lands west, and the whites east, of the Chestatee River. Rives noted that "Liberty Church, now in Dawson County, was organized in a log dwelling about 1833 and all denominations worshipped there. As a minister, I (Rives) used to work five days in the week, then start early Saturday morning to attend my churches – some of them nineteen miles distant. I rode to the churches when I had a horse, and walked when I did not have one. In those days we carried our Bible and hymn book in saddle wallets, thrown over the shoulder or across the saddle. Stock then was not so plentiful and conveyances, except wagons, were seldom in the country. The women, clad in goods of their own make, walked to meeting barefoot, till within sight of the church, and then sitting down on the roadside or by some rippling brook, dusted and dressed their feet. No churches in that day and time had preaching every Sunday. Most of them had preaching one weekend a month, a business session and preaching service on Saturday and the regular worship service on the following Sunday." Rev. John E., also known as Jackie, Rives was the great grandfather of HBC's Birddie Godfrey Heard (1887-1972). Alfred Webb and the other early pastors at HBC likely experienced similar conditions as described above by Rives.

Rev. John Rives

The way of life for the settlers was likely similar to the following sketch. Pierce (1956) writes of pioneer life of Methodists, yet likely the story was the same for area Baptists as representatives from both denominations were attempting to connect with the settlers. The hardships of pioneer life included challenges for survival as well as challenges for the church during the time between the 1820s and 1860s. "It was a time of isolation, long hours of toil, heart breaking failure of crops prompting another move, illness with the uncertainty of any medical care, danger of wild beast, and sometimes wilder man. Pioneer surroundings seemed to have a bad effect even upon many who had previously had religious training and experiences. Many succumbed to the new environment and quickly released themselves not only from all pious impulses but even from all ethical restraints. Lawlessness and rowdyism of various sorts and degrees became rampant; Sabbath desecration, gambling, swearing, drinking, fighting, and other more reprehensible sins became too common for comment."

Travel, at best, was often difficult. In the early days, there were few, if any, bridges. To get to the other side of a stream, the waterway had to be forded. The shallowest place in the stream was selected for the ford, and the roads were laid out to these particular spots. Normally, the fords were rather safe, but when it rained and the water level rose, it could get quite dangerous. Occasionally, lives of persons and animals, as well as equipment, were lost in the swift water (Dawson Co. Heritage: Bridges).

Surely it was a time when strength to endure was encouraged by searching fellowship with those of similar faith. The role of the early church in the survival of the settlers no doubt provided an important anchor in the community.

Chapter 3: 1834-1881

- Community
    - During the 1830s, some Cherokees remained in the area while others began the removal westward, which continued until the final removal in 1838, known as the "Trail of Tears"
    - Many people continued to relocate here from the Carolinas and elsewhere in Georgia
    - In 1856, there was a local company named the Hightower Mining Company
    - Post office names included Leonards and Board Tree until 1869, and Ophir from 1869-1892 (which was very near HBC)
    - Hightower School was nearby in the late 1800s, specific location undetermined

- Religion/Baptists
    - 1834 - HBC was accepted as a member of Chattahoochee BA
    - 1835 - HBC was dismissed from Chattahoochee BA to unite with other churches in forming a new association to the west of Hall County. HBC was one of eleven original churches that formed the Hightower BA
    - Church congregations met once monthly; ministers were scarce and often pastored three or four churches during the same year
    - 1858 - McKinney Purcell ordained at HBC as preacher
    - 1873 - Great Revival time at Sharp Mountain BC, Ball Ground ,77 baptized and HBC baptized 34

- Occupations: Farmers and miners; Soldiers during the early 1860s

- Transportation
    - Horse/mule and wagon, walking, horseback
    - Public roads were scarce for the first fifty years after Indians were removed from Cherokee County
    - In 1879, the Marietta and North Georgia Railroad reached Canton

- Cemetery
    - The section for the first burials at HBC was in the front of the current church building, extending

toward current State Highway 369. Apparently, the oldest portion is closest to the current church, and evidence exists of a number of burial sites both with and without stones. It is in this section, nearer to the tree line, where legend says that slaves and Indians were buried. In the *Heritage of Cherokee County, 1831-1998*, Nettie Lee Lovelace reported that "according to information passed down through generations, slaves and Indians are buried among the white settlers in the large well-kept cemetery that surrounds HBC."

- It has been told that the first grave at HBC was that of a young child whose family had temporarily camped at a spring near Boardtree Creek, and while there the young child died. The family buried the child at the top of the hill.
- The first marked date of death at HBC cemetery is 1844, which indicates that the cemetery began before the church took possession of the property. The first deed that has been located is from Daniel Stephens to HBC in 1845 (see appendix).

1834

The first fifty years (more or less) of HBC were definitely filled with dramatic changes. Since no current church records exist from that era, other sources such as association minutes, neighboring church records and U.S. Census, etc. were consulted. Relocation, gold mining, land lotteries, the Civil War, reconstruction, etc. were events that surely tested the faith of the early members and each event had an impact on the ways of life of the people at the newly established HBC.

Chattahoochee Association

The Chattahoochee Association formed in Hall Co. in 1826 and began with eight member churches. Tensawattee was one of the churches that joined in 1827. Tensawattee had been organized in the Cherokee Nation and was represented by Duncan O'Briant, a missionary. The Association met in 1834 at Yellow Creek BC in Hall Co. where Antioch, Hightower, Goshen and Silver Springs Churches united.

The earliest evidence found of the beginning of HBC is the acceptance into the Chattahoochee Baptist Association of **1834**. As was the custom, a congregation would begin their worship "meetings" in a place of residence or under a shade tree once a month. Upon agreement to go forth, the church would select a few leaders, and members from neighboring churches would meet to form a presbytery to aid in the organization of the new church. At some point in time after forming, the congregation could apply to become a member of an association. Therefore, HBC may have begun as early as 1832 or 1833.

No photo evidence survives of the early HBC church buildings. It is likely that the structure was similar to the log building to the left. It is known that during the 1800s, church buildings were not very attractive or comfortable. They were described as being in the open forest, a shell of a house, unceiled, unplastered within, shutters would not shut, doors that hung by a hinge, benches narrow, openings here and there in the weatherboarding or between the logs. Some of the buildings, which were described as meeting houses, served a community for multiple functions, such as a school or for worship centers for several denominations. The first deed to HBC dates 1845 and references the meeting house and graveyard (see appendix, deeds). Hawke (1988) further describes a meeting

This personal photo taken Feb. 8, 2014 at Calloway Gardens of a restored log cabin from the early 1800s.

house as the single place for country people where almost everyone met more or less regularly. Men went to the grist mill or attended court days, but the entire family traveled to church. The Sabbath offered everyone a break from the routine of everyday life and the chance for all to renew ties with the neighborhood. With the guidance and help from the Lord, HBC began to make a difference in the lives of the settlers in a mighty way. The results of the work of the earliest pioneers contributed to the successful survival of HBC throughout the many years.

1846: Cold State

1840 is the date accepted as the possible year that HBC was constituted. Likely, this date found the people at HBC excited about the newness of the church. However, by 1845 the excitement of the new church must have declined. Interesting notations found in Hightower BA minutes in 1846 described the "condition" of member churches during that year. The name of each church was listed followed by a statement such as: in a prosperous condition; is somewhat refreshed and is at peace among themselves; has had some additions during the year but is now in a cold state; in a cold state but at peace; etc. Hightower Church is listed as "in a cold state." If data is accurate, the cold state could have been because of the decrease in members from 1846 to 1847. The data in 1846 showed that three were baptized and membership was 51. By 1847, no baptisms were listed and total membership was 38 (3 were received by letter, 11 were dismissed and 3 excluded). By 1848, the total membership was 48, with 8 baptisms and 12 received by letter. One can only guess what happened and if the 11 that were dismissed in 1847 were among the 12 received in 1848. Neither can the cold state be fully understood just by a comparison of membership numbers.

1850s

Holbrook Campground, in a neighboring community, began yearly revival services in 1838. By 1853, other locations were holding similar campmeeting services: Bethlehem (west of Cumming), Concord (north of Cumming) and Sharp Mountain (north of Canton). Members were not only laboring with crops for survival but also dealing with medical uncertainties noted by numerous deaths and burials at HBC in the 1850s. Stories have survived that typhoid fever was one of those perils that tested the faith of those in the HBC community (see additional story in Chapter 11: Illness, Tragedy and Death).

1860s

By 1860, Alfred Webb had been the pastor for at least twenty years; the membership was noted as 82, with 70 whites and 12 colored; Abraham Lincoln was the new U.S. President, and Joseph E. Brown (from Canton) was the governor of Georgia. Yet, the life of those around HBC suffered a major change within the next few years that would take a tragic toll on those early church members. Rev. Webb became a delegate from Dawson County to the meeting in Milledgeville where Georgia voted to secede from the Union. While no known battle of the Civil War is believed to have taken place near the HBC area, the effects of the war were no less damaging to those who lived in Northeast Cherokee County. The lack of communication regarding the events taking place throughout the states no doubt contributed much fear. The military draft began in 1862 with demands for healthy men between ages of eighteen and thirty-five, but as the war continued, the draft age was extended to range between seventeen and fifty. Also in 1862, a terrible drought brought crop failure that added to the misery of families trying to endure without salt, leather, or thread to clothe themselves and their children. Women and young children struggled to make their crops, and survival was challenged. Recent publications speak of the effects on Cherokee County citizens and many who were divided as to which "side" to support. By the end of the war, local residents had to endure the hardships from the Union army, Confederate army, and the Home Guard taking their supplies and livestock indiscriminately (*Cherokee County Civil War Sesquicentennial Committee*, p. 52). While at least six grave markers at HBC read CSA (Confederate States of America), one is marked as Union Soldier (See Veterans in appendix). An account of the impact of the Civil War on the people of HBC is described in the story, "It Was Just Pitiful Times" (see Chapter 11, Hightower Highlights). The Hightower BA holds minute books from 1845 and forward, but some are missing during the 1860s when Association meetings were not held due to the war. Probably more than ever before, the faith of the HBC people was pushed to the limit.

Reconstruction

Data about HBC found in HBA records indicate that the war years certainly contributed to a decrease in the male membership. In 1867, HBC had 66 white members, 18 male and 48 female. In 1868, ten new members were baptized and seven joined by letter, boosting the membership to 92. Family units were splintered as a result of the war years. Numbers of women were left widowed and some with small children. It was not uncommon to find listings in the censuses of 1870 and 1880 with blended families. Reconstruction after the Civil War was likely a trying time on the faithful members of HBC. However, apparently a few prospered as noted in the Georgia Tax Digests of the Cross Roads District with several landowners having large acreage of farms. Surely the strength of the fellowship of the country church helped its people to recover from the devastation of the recent past.

African Americans and HBC Membership

The Hightower BA records include membership data showing various numbers that must be loosely interpreted as the totals do not always calculate correctly. Of interest from 1847 until 1875, the HBC data from some of those years show the number of members with listings for whites, males, females, and colored. The 1870 U.S. Census included identification as to color (white, black and mulatto) and indicates that people of color lived near the white families. In the case of a long-time resident of the area, Wiley Petty is listed as white and a farmer. Listed near the Wiley Petty home are two additional homes, the heads of each household was Phoebe Petty and James Petty and the race was listed as black. Both were listed as farm laborers. (HBC membership book one includes Wiley Petty, died in 1899 and also Pheba Petty, died Feb. 3, 1889.) It is likely that Phoebe and Pheba Petty were the same person. From these records, it is apparent that the black neighbors were welcomed at HBC. However, in the 1870s, some black families in the community may have chosen to attend Mount Fair (near Pool's Mill) or Ebenezer (near Orange) which were established by black families after the Civil War. These two churches and others joined to form the Sawnee Mountain Baptist Association. From information found in the *Heritage of Forsyth County* (p. 98), Sawnee Mountain Baptist Association was founded by Rev. Levi Greenlee in the 1870s. The association was located about three miles west of Cumming on what is now Kelly Mill Road near the Old Kelly Mill Pond. Rev. Greenlee was ordained as a preacher by the white Baptist Church in Cumming and was always invited to sit with the white ministers at quarterly meetings and the Hightower BA when held at the Cumming white Baptist Church. While the family legends of HBC families and descendants include that "slaves" are believed to have been buried at HBC, burials of African Americans may have continued long after the Civil War. There is no record to prove the burial of Phoebe Petty at HBC, but since the date of death is clearly recorded in the membership roll, one could guess that Phoebe Petty may be among those interred at HBC.

HBC at Ophir, Georgia

From the Hightower BA minutes, HBC was listed with the post office at Ophir from 1869-1891. Before 1869, the post office noted was Lennard's or Board Tree. After 1891, the post office was Creighton or Boling until 1905 when postal service began from Ball Ground. In 1876, Ophir was a postal village of Cherokee County twelve miles from the county seat, thirty miles from Marietta and thirty miles from Gainesville. The community north of the Etowah River that became Ophir did not begin at that location until after the church was established in 1877; the post office there in early years was McConnell's. The businesses at Ophir as found in the 1876-1877 Georgia State Directory included: Postmaster: J. A. Donald; General Store: W. H. Haskins; Teacher at High Tower School: R. B. Allen; Mine: H. H. Ham. In later years, the Ophir Post Office was located in the Wilkie Country Store and postmaster was George Washington Wilkie.

Membership milestone: 1873 HBC had 35 baptisms and for the first time the membership totaled over 100.

1880 occupations

From the U.S. census of the mid to late 1800s, the majority of persons listed as heads of household were male and were either farmers (which meant landowner) or farm laborers (which meant rented from landowner or a sharecropper). In addition to farming, a few other occupations found in the area in the 1880 census include: blacksmith (Andrew J. White); country merchant (Jonathan L. Coggins); miner (Abraham Wyatt); miller (Henry T. Drummond); house servants (Phoebe and Flora Petty, in the Wiley Petty household); shoemaker (Earl Mosteller); blacksmith (William J. Boling); milling (James M. Boling); country merchant (John W. Cannon); schoolteachers (Francis M. Phillips, Lucy Frasier and Mary E. Bills); cobbler (George Wilkie, age 82).

Mary Franklin of the Franklin Gold Mine Co. died in 1858. During the war years, mining efforts were likely hindered, and by 1867 the mine was sold and became Franklin and McDonald Gold Mining Co. Later the Franklin mines were sold to J. M. Creighton in 1883. Over the years, many different company names would represent mining efforts, including the name of Hightower Mining Company, not believed to have any connection with the church.

Methodists

A possibility exists that a Methodist congregation may have shared the HBC "meeting house" as a place of worship. Two factors linking this possibility include grave markers at HBC noting Methodist membership and typical use of "meeting houses" explained by Rev. Charles Jones (Personal interview, May 16, 2013, Rev. Charles Jones, director of Historical Commission Archives and Museum at Georgia Baptist Convention, Duluth, GA). While reviewing the inscriptions on grave markers, in what appears to be the oldest section of the cemetery, there are three distinct recordings of Methodist church memberships. While it is possible that these people were members of a Methodist congregation at another site, it is a possibility shared by Jones that the meeting house at HBC may have been used on alternate Sundays for worship of other denominations.

Fire!

At some point in the late 1870s, it is thought that the "meeting house" was destroyed by fire. This story has survived through the years, but the exact location of that church building remains a question. Many members repeat that they have heard that the building was located on the other side of the road. Regardless, those members exhibited their strong and abiding faith by going forth with plans for a new church building, as evidenced in the news article below, as well as by the sign on the current building that simply states October 1, 1882.

Cherokee Advance, Cherokee Co., GA; 1/23/1880 - Vol. 1; 1/30/1880

Ophir Inklings

The farmers have begun seeding oats and we fear too soon, as the spring freezes may prove too fatal for such crops.

Efforts are being strenuously made to build a new church at Hightower.

The strong and abiding faith of those hard working country folks around HBC helped launch a new era by the construction of a church building that would serve as a focus of worship for generations to come. With the effects of the war and reconstruction behind them, these survivors had a tremendous vision and even though no records exist about the project, much cooperation among members would have been required. By 1880, the church membership had reached 151, and even without the tragic fire, a larger church was needed.

Whether a coincidence or by design, the written records (in possession of the church in 2015) began in 1882, the same year that the new church building was occupied. Materials (paper and pen) would have been difficult to maintain throughout the early 1800s; perhaps no HBC records were ever kept before 1882. Or, the possibility certainly exists today that logically says if older written records were kept, they were destroyed in the church fire. Regardless, HBC celebrates the efforts of the written records that began in 1882.

Plant Church?

Several families that were likely members at HBC in the late 1870s, became charter members at nearby Mt. Pisgah BC on October 18, 1881, in Forsyth County, Georgia. In 2015, the term "plant church" would apply to Mt. Pisgah, perhaps. Other reasons may have occurred to drive the founding of Mt. Pisgah, but there was a definite connection to HBC. Charter members included families of: Dr. M. L. Pool, G. W. Fowler, John S. Hawkins, Street Hawkins, and John Wyatt (*Men and Missions, Vol. II*).

1834-1881, Names of HBC delegates found in Association Minutes

Year	HBC Delegates to Association
Before 1834?	
1834 Chattahoochee Association	S (Solomon) Peak, J (Jesse) George, H Holcomb (15 members)
1835 Hightower Association founded.	J George, S Peak, L J Hudson
1835, Baptist Registry (published in 1836 in Philadelphia)	S. Peak, Jas L Hutson, 4 baptized; 32 members
1836 -1844	(no data for HBC)
1845	S Elrod, Z (Zebulon) Williams
1846	D (Daniel) Stephens, J (John) Nix
1847	D Stephens, Z Williams
1848	Z Williams, J (James) Persell
1849	J Persell, J (Dr. John) Burns
1850	J Pursell, Z Williams
1851	D Stephens, J Pursell
1852	J Pursell, J Burns
1853	J Pursell, M (Moses?) Ledbetter
1854	J Pursell, M Ledbetter

Year	HBC Delegates to Association
1855	J Pursell, J Burnes
1856	J Pursell, J Burns
1857	Joseph Underwood, J. Purcell
1858	J Pursell, M Purcell (McKinney?)
1859	J Pursell, E Dean
1860	J Pursell, E Dean
1861	J. Purcell, W. Fowler
1862	J. Purcell, Martin Roberts
1863-1866	(no data for HBC)
1867	M Pursell, J L Coggins
1868	M Pursell, J L Coggins
1869	M Pursell, M L Pool
1870	M Pursell, M L Pool
1871	M Pursell, M L Pool
1872	M Pursell, M L Pool
1873	M Purcell, J B Richards
1874	M Pursell, M L Pool
1875	M Pursell
1876	J B Richards, Elias Nix; 3rd Dist. at Hightower, July
1877	C S Hawkins, M L Pool
1878	M L Pool, J B Richards
1879	C S Hawkins
1880	J B Richards C S Hawkins
1881	John B Richards, C S Hawkins, M L Pool

Possible Early Membership (1834-1881)

Who were the possible "Charter Members?" Since there is no record of the beginning of HBC, it is impossible to locate the charter members. The 1834 Chattahoochee Association minutes list HBC as having fifteen members. It is only a guess that the delegates S. Peak, J. George and H. Holcomb and their families were most of that fifteen. In an effort to reconstruct a list of possible early members, numerous sources have been reviewed such as the 1834, 1840, and later decades of the U.S. Censuses of Cherokee, Forsyth, Pickens, Dawson, and Hall Counties; the 1882 HBC membership roll; Hightower Baptist Association minutes; Chattahoochee Baptist Association minutes; grave records; family history notes; etc. This effort must be respected as a logical guess, and is not intended to be the actual membership roll. Some names are included because family members and/or descendants were found on the 1882 HBC membership roll or because family members are known to be buried at HBC. Some names listed indicate early membership, even though they may be listed in book one of HBC rolls. With each name below, remarks are noted to explain reasons for inclusion in this list. A delegate denotes representation from HBC to HBA meetings that were held yearly with other churches in the association. It is believed that only a member would be selected as a delegate; therefore, those listed as delegates would be members, but adding the family members of delegates is circumstantial.

Last name	First name	Middle name	*Remarks, (maiden name, spouse, birth-death, buried at Hightower BC – HBC, etc.)*
Peak	S.		*ca 1771-1858; Rev. Solomon; 1834 & 1835 delegate*

Last name	First name	Middle name	*Remarks, (maiden name, spouse, birth-death, buried at Hightower BC – HBC, etc.)*
Peak	Rachel		*1775-1850; wife of Solomon Peak*
George	J. Jesse		*b ca 1799 – died bet 1870-1882 in Arkansas, 1834 delegate*
George	Katherine		*1813-aft 1880; or 1812-1882; wife of Jesse George*
George	Isaac		*ca 1774-ca 1861; father of Jesse George, 1860 census with Jesse and family*
George	Martha	Hambright	*Died bef 1860; wife of Isaac George*
George	Allen	Solomon	*Brother of Jesse George*
George	Anna	Elizabeth Ingram	*Wife of Allen George, marriage in 1835 in Cherokee Co. Ga.*
Holcomb	H. Henry Jr.		*1768-1852; 1834 delegate; listed as a deacon and charter member of Conns Creek BC in 1847*
Holcomb	Priscilla	Dooly	*1772-? Wife of Henry Holcomb*
Holcomb	Henry	Dooly	*1793-? Son of Henry Holcomb*
Hudson	L.	J.	*1789-1843; Lemuel James; 1835 pastor at HBC; Member?*
Hudson	Mourning	Raines	*Wife of L. J. Hudson; Member?*
Franklin	Mary	Graves	*1782-1858; moved to area ca 1833; bur HBC; tombstone says member of the Baptist Church for 51 years, unknown if she transferred letter to HBC*
Franklin	Bedney		*1815-1844; bur HBC; son of Mary Franklin*
Burns	John (Dr.)		*1794-1858; in Cherokee Co. in 1840; 1849 delegate (+ add'l yrs); bur HBC;*
Burns	Lucy		*1796-1877; wife of John Burns; bur HBC*
Burns	Catherine	B.	*1766-1849; mother of John Burns; bur HBC*
Burns	Warren	M.	*1831-1847; son of John and Lucy Burns; bur HBC*
Burns	Melmoth	W.	*1833-1847; son of John and Lucy Burns; bur HBC*
Coffee	James	Calton	*1819-1913; in Cherokee 1840-1860; buried in Arkansas*
Coffee	Adaline	Burns	*1801-1889; wife of James C. Coffee*
Coffee	James	E.	*1836-1852; bur HBC; son of James C. and Adaline Coffee*
Leonard	Jesse J. Sr.		*Descendants bur HBC; he may have been a Methodist? Local storeowner in 1833 and first area post office, "Lennard's"*
Petty	Major	Wiley	*1805-1892; member Book 1; early land owner near HBC; bur HBC*
Petty	Martha	Bailey Nix	*1811-1871; wife of Wiley Petty; bur HBC*
White	James		*1776-1848; bur HBC*
White	Mary	Barker	*Ca 1780-1853; wife of James White; bur HBC*
White	Elizabeth		*1795-?; dau of James & Mary White*
White	Jane	McClure	*1801-1855; dau of James & Mary White*
Elrod	S.		*1845 delegate*
Williams	Zebulon		*1799-1879; Delegate many times; bur HBC*
Williams	Ollie	Barker	*1806-1883; wife of Zebulon Williams; bur HBC*
Stephens	Daniel		*1802-1852; Delegate; bur HBC; sold land to HBC in 1845, first deed for church*

Last name	First name	Middle name	*Remarks, (maiden name, spouse, birth-death, buried at Hightower BC – HBC, etc.)*
Stephens	Sela		*1799-1852; wife of Daniel Stephens; bur HBC*
Stephens	William		*1830-1852; son of Daniel Stephens, bur HBC*
Stephens	Samuel		*1832-1852; son of Daniel Stephens, bur HBC*
Stephens	Miley	J.	*1834-1852; dau of Daniel Stephens, bur HBC*
Stephens	John	H.	*1828-1863; son of Daniel Stephens, died in Savannah, Ga.*
Nix	J		*1806-1879; John? 1846 delegate?*
Hester	Mary Williams		*1812-1887; sister of Zebulon Williams, a widow with several children, moved near HBC about 1851; member Book 1*
Kemp	Aaron		*1779-1865? bur HBC*
Kemp	Sarah		*1785-1865? bur HBC*
Kemp	Harry/Harvy		*1821-1849; bur HBC*
Kemp	M.	L.	*1825/28-1851; bur HBC*
Hawkins	John	Samuel	*1817-1888; young dau. bur HBC 1852; helped charter Mt. Pisgah 1881*
Hawkins	Samantha / Sarah	M. Kemp	*1827-1913; wife of John S. Hawkins*
Boling	William		*1804-1880; his 1st wife is buried HBC*
Boling	Mary		*1808-1852; 1st wife of William; bur HBC*
Boling	James	A.	*1827-1853; son of William Boling; bur HBC*
Boling	William	H.	*1829-1853; son of William Boling; bur HBC*
Boling	John	R.	*1832-1853; son of William Boling; bur HBC*
Boling	Floyd	T.	*1842-1862, son of William Boling; bur HBC; likely a memorial marker, died Richmond, VA*
Persell	J		*1797-1882; James Purcell; in Cherokee Co. in 1840; Delegate many times; bur HBC*
Purcell	Mary		*1805-1876; wife of James Purcell; bur HBC*
Purcell	Benjamin		*1827-1899; son of James Purcell; bur HBC*
Purcell	Elizabeth	Boling	*1831-1853; wife of Benjamin Purcell; bur HBC; dau of William Boling*
Ledbetter	M		*1813-1855; Moses; delegate 1853 & 1854*
Ledbetter	Mary		"Polly" Wife of Moses
Fowler	Fannie	Ledbetter	*d 1870, dau. of Moses; 1st wife of Phillip Fowler*
Cochran	Francis	Sarah Nix	*1824-1853; mother of E. A. and R. W. Cochran; 1st wife of T. B. Cochran; bur HBC; tomb says Sarah Cochran, member of HBC*
Cochran	Terrell	B.	*1817-1868; his 1st wife bur HBC*
Cochran	Nevels	Holcomb	*1815-1863; bur HBC*
Cochran	Altiney J.	Griffin	*1818-1855; bur HBC*
Underwood	Joseph		*Ca 1799- 1875; 1857 delegate; also a physician*
Underwood	Ann		*1810-?; 2nd wife of Joseph Underwood*
Purcell	M		*1830-1905; James "McKinney;" Delegate many times; In 1857, he was ordained at HBC to preach*

Last name	First name	Middle name	Remarks, (maiden name, spouse, birth-death, buried at Hightower BC – HBC, etc.)
Purcell	Mary G.	Creamer	1831-1904; wife of McKinney Purcell
Dean	E		1819-1907; Elijah?; 1859 & 1860 delegate; later moved to Woodstock
Dean	Eliza	Fowler	1825-1904; wife of Elijah
Fowler	James		1797-1876; bur HBC, family notes say he joined HBC 1848
Fowler	Sarah		1804-1875; bur HBC beside James, wife of James Fowler, likely joined HBC 1848
Fowler	W.	T.	William Thomas? 1841-1869; bur HBC; son of James and Sarah Fowler
Fowler	W		1803-1884; William?; Delegate in 1861; (William and wife Lucinda were dismissed by letter from Mt. Tabor in 1857)
Fowler	Lucy		1808-1902; wife of William
Roberts	Martin		1807-1864; delegate 1862
Roberts	Sarah A.	Williamson	Ca 1815-1873; 2nd wife of Martin Roberts
Coggins	J	L	1815-1890; Jonathan L.; delegate 1867 & 1868
Coggins	Elizabeth		1808-1874; wife of J. L. Coggins
Pool	M	L	1825-1895; Dr. Marcus Lafayette Pool; Delegate many times; became a charter member in 1881 at Mt.Pisgah
Pool	Lucy C.	Mangum	1826-1883; wife of M. L. Pool; became a charter member in 1881 at Mt.Pisgah
Fowler	Martha J.	Pool	1845-1863; dau of M. L. Pool; bur HBC
Lipscomb	Laura T.	Pool	1859-1875; dau of M. L. Pool; bur HBC
Pool	Nancy	A.	became a charter member in 1881 at Mt.Pisgah
Richards	J	B	1839-1920; John Bedney; Delegate many times; also HBC clerk
Richards	Laura	Strickland	1846-1909; wife of J. B. Richards
Nix	Elias		? delegate 1876
Nix	Valentine		1822-1894; delegate to Union mtg.; bur HBC
Nix	Cynthia		1822-1896; wife of Valentine; bur HBC
Wist	Joseph		? Delegate to union meeting, 1876
Hawkins	C	S	1847-1928; Cicero Street; Delegate many times; Licensed and ordained at HBC as preacher
Hawkins	Eliza	Pascoe	1843-1903; wife of C. S. Hawkins
Pursell	A	J	1832-1910, Andrew Jackson; OR 1850-1942, Andrew Jackson; delegate, and clerk (1879-1881); it is unclear which A. J. Purcell was at HBC, or if indeed both?
Pursell	Nancy L.	Holcomb	? Wife of A. J. Pursell (1832-1910)
Pursell	Josephine	White	? 1849-1926; wife of A. J. Pursell (1850-1942)
Wyatt	Joseph		1831-1910; 1st wife bur HBC; numerous descendants at HBC; he joined Ophir 1877
Wyatt	Mary C.	Pascoe	1837-1884; 1st wife of Joseph Wyatt; bur HBC

Chapter 4: 1882-1902, Minutes and Membership Roll, Book One

- Community
    - Post office names include Ophir, Creighton and Boling
    - School at Andrew's Chapel

- Religion/Baptists/HBC
    - 1884 - deacon ordination
    - March 17, 1888 - HBC organized Sunday school
    - February, 1898 - HBC voted to have preaching two times per month and organized Sunday school
    - 1890 - deacon ordination
    - June 14, 1890 - HBC organized a Sabbath School (again)
    - April 15, 1893 - request was made to the clerk to bring the minute book to next conference. May 20, 1893, clerk called the roll.
    - Nov. 20, 1897 - Granted Professor Fowler leave to teach a singing school provided he will be responsible for any damages
    - Wyatt/Buffington family reported that in late 1800s, a huge baptizing was held at the Petty Dam on Board Tree Creek (38 were baptized in 1898, maybe the baptizing at the Petty's?)
    - 1900 - deacon ordination

- Occupations
    - Farmers, farm laborers and day laborers
    - Mining jobs: machinist, foreman, chemist, civil engineer
        - (1896: 85 employees were working 2 shifts @ 12 hours each; wages $.75 - $2.50 per day. In 1896, five mine shafts were present. The mines were worked for 70 continuous years.)
    - Skilled laborers: blacksmith, carpenter
    - Physicians and teachers

- Transportation
    - Walking, horse and buggy, mule and wagon
    - 1882, Marietta and North Georgia Railroad reach Ball Ground, Georgia

- Cemetery
    - The location of the burials was in section one in the front of the current church building and gradually extended toward current state Highway 369, now labeled section two (sections as noted in appendix: "Cemetery")

Pictured above is C. A. Milford (1869-1920) and a great uncle of Robert Milford (1915-1988). C. A. was a member of nearby Zion Hill BC. This picture shows a team of mules or horses with wagon in tow that would have been similar to those used to travel to "meeting day" at HBC each third Sunday.

New church

Everyone loves a new house. Surely, members were proud of their new church home believed to be occupied on October 1, 1882, where worship in the new sanctuary was on the third Saturday and Sunday of each month. As travel permitted, HBC folks visited other nearby churches. Many of these churches were listed in the minutes of book one when HBC would invite the neighboring churches to join HBC for services. Found in *Men and Missions of Hightower Association: Vol. II, Churches,* the following list shows the Sunday of the month each church held worship, and the date in parentheses denotes the year each church was organized:

1st: New Harmony (1855), Chalcedonia (1873), Ophir (1877), Concord (1837), Bethlehem (1836), Sharp Mountain (1836)

2nd: Mt. Zion (1834), Yellow Creek (1884), Mt. Tabor (1833), Conns Creek (1847), Friendship (1840)

3rd: Hightower

4th: Macedonia (1873), Hopewell (1851), Mt. Pisgah (1881), Mt. Vernon (1840)

Area Methodist churches were also attended, especially for Sunday school. However, as indicated in the HBC minutes, joining the Methodist Church was frowned upon within the Baptist church. Charges were brought against those joining the Methodist, with claims of "departing the faith" or "joining another church of a different faith and order." The results were expulsion from the Baptist Church roll.

New jobs

New jobs were offered at the gold mines as the gold properties were brought together in 1882 under the management of a group of northern capitalists and the company chose the name Franklin & McDonald Mining and Manufacturing Company. In 1883, the vice-president of the company, Mr. J. M. Creighton, a wealthy railroad official from Philadelphia, purchased the remaining interest from the other stockholders. The name was changed to the Creighton Mine and later Creighton Road was named for Mr. Creighton. Legend says that the "shingle house" (on the left) was constructed during the late 1800s, and it is one of the few remaining structures visible in 2015 from the Franklin/Creighton Gold mining era.

While many may think of cotton as a plantation and pre-civil war era crop, it must be realized that cotton farming was essential to the livelihood of many North Georgia families into the early 1900s. Cherokee County was a rich agricultural district in the areas outlying Canton, which led to the development of the town as a market and trading center, especially after the railroad arrived in 1879. Canton Textile Mills was founded in 1899, by R. T. Jones. Within a few years, the mill was producing indigo-dyed denim (Cherokee County Historical Society, 1981). The marble industry became an important addition to employment opportunities. The railroad line reached a community north of Canton by 1882, leading to the founding of the town of Ball Ground, Georgia.

During the time of HBC minutes and membership roll in book one, two U.S. Censuses would have been taken. Unfortunately, The Eleventh Census of the United States (1890) was destroyed or severely damaged by fire at the Commerce Department in Washington, D. C. in 1921. Very few records were salvaged, and none have been found of Cherokee County, Georgia. The 1900 U.S. Census of Cherokee County, Cross Roads District enumerates again many farmers, farm laborers and day laborers. Mining operations continued, and several jobs reflected work in that field: civil engineers, machine runners, foremen at mines, chemists, blacksmiths at mines, etc. Of local community interest was the mention in the 1900 Census in Cross Roads of a farmer/principal by the name of Delany or Delavan Lively. He was the person credited with the beginning of Free Home community. He was 59 at the time.

School

Most likely the school nearest HBC was Andrew's Chapel. Rev. W. S. Norton is listed in the 1900 census, Cross Roads District, as a teacher (See additional information, Chapter 11: Schools near HBC). Also, W. S. Norton was ordained as a preacher at HBC on April 14, 1900. He reportedly suffered a case of the mumps and died in 1903, with burial following at HBC. The picture is of the restored Conns Creek School located in the community of the same name, just north of HBC. Logically, the schools in the Hightower community were similar to the one-room style, common for the era of the late 1800s and early 1900s.

Cherokee Advance…

Rev. H. T. Ingram of Laredo wrote in the *Cumming Baptist Leader* and reported in the *Cherokee Advance,* "Hightower is one among the oldest churches in the country, like the fruitful vine, has gathered to her clusters annually such as the Lord, by grace, has saved until she now numbers above two hundred and fifty faithful workers in the Lord's vineyard, composed mostly of young, and middle aged members. Major Petty and brother Pinson are perhaps the oldest brethren" (*Cherokee Advance;* November 20, 1891; Page 3 Column 4).

Membership milestones

In 1888, HBC for the first time noted a membership over 200. The HBA records for that year report 203 members, 80 males and 123 females. By 1901, HBC had 316 members, marking the first record of membership over 300. Of those, 138 were males and 178 were females.

Church minutes

A monthly business session was held usually on each Saturday before the third Sunday, with the pastor serving as moderator. This service began with a few songs, followed by a sermon, also called preaching. The business meeting followed, and the clerk recorded the events which became known as the church minutes. The following are the items of business:

1. Invite visitors and brothers to seats with us. (Also known as invite visitors to sit with us in council; Tradition of welcoming "male" brethren from other churches who were invited to help in the organizing and in continuing the gospel. They were welcome to speak at a session, but could not vote.)

2. Reference. Reading of the minute of the past conference; Corrections, amendments, adopting the same.

3. Call for peace and fellowship of the church. Opportunity to present a charge or record in peace.

4. Open the door of Hightower Church for the reception of members. Sang a verse of a song, usually without music, if a person was presented, vote to be received: 1) by letter from another church of same faith and order 2) under watch care until letter can be obtained or 3) as candidate for baptism and 4) by restoration. In very early years, some persons joined by statement; one presents to join, but former church of same faith and order is no longer in existence or no records exist. If no one is presented, recorded as none offered.

5. Call for general business.

The minutes of a particular church serve as an excellent source of history. Often the name(s) of the preacher(s) are listed and occasionally the biblical texts for the sermon. The reception/dismissal of members certainly gives record to the time and place of individuals and families. The earliest records of HBC show very little information concerning the finances. Money was collected upon need (for wine, association minutes, etc.) rather than routine monthly collections. When a project was approved, a finance committee was chosen to solicit members for donations for the designated project.

HBC minutes, that are available, begin in 1882 and were recorded by the church clerk. The clerk was elected yearly to serve as record keeper and treasurer. The chapters that follow include transcriptions of minutes from 1882-1950. One HBC clerk's name was found in the HBA minutes before 1882. Clerks willing to assume this role are remembered with the upmost of respect and appreciation for their writings. These were brave men who gave their best effort, in spite of misspellings and some omissions. Some recordings are written in pencil. Some dates do not follow a logical order. Dates listed for conferences must have been guesses – sometimes the date indicates a weekday, maybe calendars weren't accessible? Sometimes the date indicates a conference on Sunday, which could be possible as the church can "enter into conference" when needed. Often months are skipped or omitted – it is certainly possible that conference was not held every month, especially when weather limited transportation. The records by the same clerk are often in different handwriting, indicating other persons actually wrote in the minute book. What is most important for this publication is that these records are appreciated, celebrated, and shared with respect.

Church discipline: For many readers, an interesting record is that of the peace and fellowship of the church, or as sometimes referred to as "what were they turned out for this month". As Baptist churches were established in North Georgia in the 1800s, the practice of holding members to a strict morality was universal. The same was true for earlier Baptist churches in North and South Carolina, the former home of many Georgia settlers. Church discipline was not just a practice at Hightower, but common to many area churches. This was a practice that continued well into the early 1900s. The church conferences or business meetings almost served as a court. Church members had to appear before the group to answer charges. If the person being charged was not present, a committee would be appointed to go and see the brother or sister who was accused of misdeeds and direct him or her to attend the next meeting. Witnesses would give testimony, and the accused person could give his side of the story. If guilty and a confession was made, usually the church members accepted an apology. Sometimes, the records indicate that the church would bear with the accused, as if to give them a chance to improve their behavior. If no apology or "acknowledgement" was expressed, the person would be turned out or excluded from the church, (his or her name stricken from the church membership roll) which was a mark of disgrace in those days. Also, it was unfavorable for a member to join a church of another denomination without first withdrawing membership. This charge for "departing the faith" was the most common reason for exclusion that continued into the middle 1900s.

Due to the sensitive nature of the charges and the chance a descendant might recognize his or her ancestor, the names of individuals charged and/or excluded have been omitted from the transcription of the minutes for this book. Also omitted are the names of individuals who made acknowledgements and were restored to full membership.

Minutes, 1882-1902

Each entry:

Date, Minister(s) who preached on that date,

Any of the items that had activity on that given date

Items:

1. Invited visiting brethren to seats with us
2. Called for the fellowship of the church
3. Called for reference

4. Opened the door of the church for the reception of members

5. General Business

Moderator, Church Clerk

June Term 1882, Bro. E. W. Allred. 5. Elected Brethren J. B. Richards, E. Cochran and J. L. Williams as delegates to the Association. Also, elected J. B. Richards, Clerk of this Church. E. W. Allred, Mod., J. B. Richards C.C.

July 15, 1882, The Baptist Church of Christ at Hightower, after preaching by Bro. J. H. Lathem followed by Bro. E. W. Allred met into conference. 5. Made up for minutes, $1.00. E. W. Allred, Mod., J. B. Richards, C.C.

Aug. Term, Bro. E. Cochran and Bro. W. L. Howard. 4. Received by experience Bro. Ransom Fowler. W. L. Howard, Mod. Pro Tem, John Richards, C.C.

September Term (September 16, 1882), Bro. A. W. Richards and Bro. E. W. Allred. 4. Received by experience, Bro. J. L. Anderson and Dora Fowler and Sister Sarah Porter by letter. E. W. Allred, Mod., John B. Richards, C.C.

Oct. 14, 1882, Bro. J. R. Westbrook and Bro. E. W. Allred. 5. Granted letters of dismission to Sister Porter and daughter. E. W. Allred, Mod., John B. Richards, C.C.

Nov. Term, 1882, Bro. E. Cochran and Bro. E. W. Allred. 5. Re-elected Bro. E. W. Allred as pastor of the church for the year 1883. Granted letters of dismission to Bro. Henry Ellis and Sister Neomia Lindsey. E. W. Allred, Mod., John B. Richards, C.C.

Dec. Term, 1882, Bro. E. W. Allred. 4. Received by letter Sister Susan Harden and Sister Susan Hardy. 5. Granted letters of dismission to Amanda Southern and daughter and Bro. William Porter and wife.

March 16, 1883, Bro. W. L. Howard and Bro. E. W. Allred. 2. A Sister having joined another church of a different faith and order. Moved and carried that her church letter be called in. 4. Received by letter Bro. W. L. Howard as a licensed preacher and Bro. Harvey Waldrep. 5. Granted letters of dismission to W. N. Howard and wife. E. W. Allred, Mod., John B. Richards, C.C.

No date, but recorded on page between March 16, 1883, and April Term 1883; Bro. E. W. Allred from Psalms 3:6. 4. Received by letters Bro. J. M. White and wife.

April Term, 1883, Bro. E. Cochran and Bro. W. L. Howard. 2. On a motion, a charge was brought against a sister for having joined another church of a different faith and order. Took up the charge and excluded her from the fellowship of this church. 4. Rec'd Bro. J. M. White and wife, M. J. White. 5. Granted letters of dismission to Bro. R. S. Richardson and W. L. D. Howard and wife. Moved and carried that the following churches be invited to commence with us at our May Meeting: Macedonia, Conns Creek, Ophir, Mt. Tabor, Friendship, and New Harmony. W. L. Howard, Mod. Pro Tem, John B. Richards, C.C.

May 20, 1883, Bro. W. L. Howard and A. W. Richards. 4. Received by letter sister Rachel E. Howard. 5. Granted letters of dismission to Sister Matilda Bobo, Bro. T. J. Jones, B. P. Jones, M. H. Tidwell and Susanah Jones. A. W. Richards, Mod. Pro Tem, John B. Richards, C.C.

June 16, 1883, E. Cochran and Bro. E. W. Allred. 2. On motion, appointed a committee consisting of Brethren Richards, Biddy and Pursell to investigate the report against a sister, and report at our next regular meeting. 5. Elected as delegates to the association: Brethren Richards, Cochran and J. L. Williams. E. W. Allred, Mod.; John B. Richards C.C.

July 14, 1883, Bro. D. J. Maddox from Paul's 1st letter to Cor. 6-9, and Bro. Cochran. 3. Call for reference and continued case against a sister. 5. Granted letters of dismission to Sister Fannie Blackstock and Sister Ella Bailey. D. J. Maddox, Mod. Pro Tem, John B. Richards, C.C.

August, 1883, Bro. J. B. Parham from Paul's letter to Titus, 2-11 and Bro E. W. Allred. 2. Preferred a charge against a sister for fornication, taken up the charge and excluded her from the fellowship of the church. Also preferred a charge against a brother and wife for having declared non-fellowship with the church – taken up the charge and excluded them from fellowship of the church. 5. Granted letters of dismission to Bro. J. M. Howard and daughters, and Mary H. Harbin, Tyra Harbin and wife and daughters and S. M. Harbin. E. W. Allred, Mod., J. B. Richards, C.C.

Sept. 17, 1883, Bro. E. Cochran from Matthew 5:20, and Bro. Allred. 4. Received by letter Bro. Durell Fowler, also Bro. M. R. C. McGullion and wife Margarett McGullion upon a profession of their faith recognizing their baptism as valid. 5. Granted letter of dismission to Bro. T. B. Jones. On motion went into the choice of a preacher for the year 1884, and called Bro. T. Pickett by acclamation. E. W. Allred, Mod., John B. Richards, C.C.

Oct. 20, 1883, Bro. Wade and Bro. Pickett. 4. Received by letter Bro. J. W. Fitts and Sister Missouria S. Castleberry. 5. Granted letters of dismission to J. R. Fowler, Mary Fowler, Dora Fowler, John G. McGuillian and B. J. Christopher and J. Umptrey, by order of the church. E. W. Allred, Mod., J. B. Richards, C.C.

Nov. 17, 1883, Bro. E. Cochran from Matthew 2:2. 4. Received Sisters Ruthey Springer and Niza Springer. 5. Granted letters of dismission to Bro W. L. Howard and Sister R. E. Howard and also to Sister Anna Smallwood. Rev E. Cochran, Mod. Pro Tem, John B. Richards, C.C.

In Memory of Bro. Alfred Webb.

Our church has never been called upon to mourn death of a brother more universally beloved than he whose name hereto this notice. He loved the church and the cause of Christianity. His intercession with his brethren in all the relations of life, and his communion with them illustrates his high appreciation of, and decoration to the cause of Christianity and the profession he made, in his daily walk and conversation he exhibited his high estimate of Christ Church here on earth, and added luster to its wisdom, strength and beauty. Honored and beloved by us, while living, let us while we record these lines, resolve to copy his virtues and embalm his memory in our hearts.

Resolved:

    1st. That in the death of Bro. Alfred Webb, the Baptist church has lost one of its most useful and beloved ministers, the community one of its best citizens and the country a long tried urbane and faithful citizens.

    2nd. That we bow submissively to the will of him who doeth all things well.

    3rd. That having faithfully served this church as pastor for upward of forty years: that a blank page in our record book be inscribed to his memory.

This Nov. 17th, 1883.

John B. Richards, Church Clerk

(In the minute book, the next page is blank)

Dec. 16, 1883, Bro. E. Cochran, from John 15 and 12. Item 5. Granted letters of dismission to Bro. J. D. Porter and wife P. J. Porter. E. Cochran, Mod. Pro Tem, John B. Richards, C.C.

Feb. 16, 1884, Bro. E. W. Allred from Ephesians 10-25. 4. Received by letter J. P. Rich. 5. Granted letters of dismissal to Bro. J. L. Anderson and Sister Mary Anderson.

March 15, 1884, Bro. John H. Lathem. 4. Received by letter Bro. Wesley Evans and wife, H. L. Evans and Sister Annie Ford. 5. Elected delegates to the union meeting, Brethren Richards, Cochran and Williams. John H. Lathem, Mod. Pro Tem, John B. Richards, C.C.

April 19, 1884, Bro. Pickett followed by Bro. Lathem. 2. Received acknowledgement from a brother. 4. Received Brethren B. F. Pruitt, J. W. Harbin and Sister M. H. Pruitt and Mary H. Harbin and Sister Newel Williams. 5. Moved and carried that on our next regular meeting, the church invite our sister churches to commune with us. Called Bro. T. Pickett as our supply for the balance of the year, 1884. Granted a letter of dismissal to Bro. W. P. Fowler. E. W. Allred, Mod., J. B. Richards C.C.

May 17, 1884, Bro. J. H. Henson from John 6th: 64, followed by Bro. Pickett. 2. Brought a charge against a sister for having left her husband and married again. Took up the charge and excluded her from the fellowship of the church. 5. Granted letters of dismissal to Bro. Slaughter and Sister Mason.

June 16, 1884, Bro. T. Pickett. 2. Received an acknowledgement by a brother for drinking too much. Preferred charge against a brother and his wife for having joined another church of a different faith and order and excluded them from the church. 5. Elected delegates to the association: J. B. Richards, J. L. Williams, and E. Cochran. Appointed the following brethren as a searching preaching committee: J. L. Williams, H. C. Boling, R. Purcell, E. Cochran and F. Hawkins. Granted a letter of dismissal to Sister Sarah Howard. T. Pickett, Mod., J. B. Richards, C.C.

July 19, 1884, Bro. E. Cochran. 4. Rec'd by experience Thomas N. Smith and wife J. A. Smith. 5. Made up for minutes, $1.65. T. Pickett, Mod., J. B. Richards, C.C.

Sept. 21, 1884, Bro. T. Pickett from Paul's letter to Titus. 4. Received by letter, Sister M. F. Burgess. 5. Granted letter of dismissal to Sister Nancy Cox. T. Pickett, Mod., John B. Richards, C.C.

Oct. 19, 1884, Bro. Maddox, followed by Bro. Pickett. 4. Received by experience G. Pas. 5. Took up collection and paid Bro. Pickett $100.00 for this years' service. Moved and carried that at our next regular meeting, Bro. E. A. Cochran be ordained and set apart to the full work of the ministry. Presbytery to be composed by Brethren Pickett, Hays, Ray, Ingram and Harris. Also elected J. L. Williams and Thomas N. Smith as Deacons to be ordained at the same time. T. Pickett, Mod., J. B. Richards, C.C.

Oct. 20, 1884, Bro. W. L. Ray. 3. Called for reference and the ordination of Bro. E. Cochran to the ministry; J. L. Williams and T. N. Smith as deacons. Being in order, the following brethren was organized as a presbytery: Eld. W. L. Ray, J. H. Hairson, J. D. Harris, J. D. Devore, and T. Pickett, Chairman. Brother J. B. Richards sequestered to act as Secretary. On motion by Bro. Pickett, Bro. Richards presented the candidates to the Presbytery. Examination by Brethren Ray and Pickett. Prayer by Brethren Harris and Pickett. After services closed, Bro. Cochran was presented to the Church as an Ordained Minister fully set apart for the work. Brethren J. L. Williams, T. N. Smith as Deacons was then presented to the church. 4. Rec'd by letter Bro. J. E. Turner and wife E. M. Turner. 5. Granted letters of dismission to Brethren E. Smallwood, T. M. Williams, Bro. B. F. Burgess and wife, J. M. Williams, Abi Williams, Rebecca Williams, Sarah Williams and John Holt. T. Pickett, Mod., John B. Richards, C.C.

March 14, 1885, Bro. W. L. Howard from Luke 17:26. 4. Rec'd by letter Sister Manervia Holt. 5. Granted letters of dismission to Bro. H. P. Mashburn and wife and Sister Martha Fowler. Elected the following brethren as delegates to the union meeting: H. C. Boling, T. N. Smith and R. J. Purcell. W. L. Howard, Mod., Pro Tem, W. E. Evans, C.C. Pro Tem.

May 16, 1885, Bro. T. Pickett, followed by Bro. Cochran. 5. Granted letters of dismission to Bro. W. J. Nix, Sister Bell Hogan and Caroline Gilstrap. T. Pickett, Mod., John B. Richards, C.C.

June 16, 1885, Bro. E. Cochran from Cor. 1st ch. 5. Granted letters of dismission to Bro. W. T. Crenshaw and wife, Sister Hulda Reaves, Lausenda Reaves, Melzournence Castleberry, Emeline Smallwood, Sarah Harden and Bro. G. Pass and wife. Elected delegates to association: J. B. Richards, J. L. Williams and E. Cochran and Z. Smith alternates. E. Cochran, Mod. Pro Tem, John B. Richards, C.C.

June 20, 1885, Bro. T. Pickett from Phil. 1st and 27. 2. Preferred a charge against a brother and his wife for the account of adultery. On motion taken up the charge and referred it until our next regular conference. 4. Rec'd. by letter Sister Bell Dowda and Sister F. A. Wilkie. 5. Granted a letter of dismission to Violet Scudder. T. Pickett, Mod., John B. Richards, C.C.

Aug. 15, 1885, Bro. T. Pickett. 3. Reference, taken up the case of a brother and wife and after hearing the acknowledgement of the sister, she was retained in our fellowship. Referred the case of the brother until our next regular meeting. 5. Granted letters of dismission to Sister Allice Newhouse, Sarah Holcombe and Cyntha Cox. T. Pickett, Mod., John B. Richards, C.C.

Sept. 19, 1885, Bro. J. W. Wooten from Numbers 10-23. Item 3. Reference, and taken up the case of a brother and excluded him from the fellowship of the church for the offence of adultery. J. W. Wooten, Mod. Pro Tem, John B. Richards, C.C.

Oct. 16, 1885, Bro. Pickett. 2. On motion, the letter granted to a brother was called in, and a charge preferred against him for stealing. Taken up the charge and excluded him from the fellowship. On motion, a charge was brought against a brother for having departed from the faith and joined another church of a different faith and order and was excluded from the fellowship of this church. 5. On motion, called Bro. A. Sheffield as our pastor for the ensuing year by acclamation. T. Picket, Mod., John B. Richards, C.C.

Dec. 20, 1885, Bro. E. Cochran. 5. Granted a letter of dismission to Sister Julia Howard. E. Cochran, Mod., John B. Richards, C.C.

(*missing: Jan., Feb., and Mar. 1886*)

Apr. 17, 1886, Bro. A. Sheffield. 2. Preferred a charge against a sister for adultery. Taken up the charge and excluded her from the fellowship of this church. Preferred a charge against a brother for lying, taken up the charge and excluded him from the fellowship of this church. 5. Granted letters of dismission to Bro. B. F. Pruett and wife. A. Sheffield, Mod., W. E. Evans, C.C. Pro Tem.

May 17, 1886, Bro. A. Sheffield. 4. Received by letter Bro. D. R. Hitt and wife, M. J. A. Hitt. 5. Appointed the following brethren as delegates to the union meeting, John B. Richards, Joseph Hester, John L. Williams, James M. Richards and Thomas N. Smith. A. Sheffield Mod., John B. Richards, C.C.

Jun. 18, 1886, Brother Robinson ? from John 1st & 2nd, followed by Bro. Harden? 5. On motion of John L. Williams, elected the following Brethren as delegates to represent this church at the next Hightower Baptist Association to wit: John B. Richards, E. Cochran and John L. Williams; James M. Richards, Alternate. A. Sheffield, Mod., John B. Richards.

July 1886, Bro. A. Sheffield. 5. On motion of John L. Williams, elected the following brethren as delegates to represent this church in the next Hightower Association to wit: John B. Richards, E. Cochran and John L. Williams; James M. Richards alternate. A. Sheffield, Mod., John B. Richards, C.C.

Aug. 15, 1886, Brother A. Sheffield. 5. Granted letters of dismission to Sister Pass and Brother J. W. Fitts. A. Sheffield, Mod., John B. Richards, C.C.

Oct. 20, 1886, Bro. D. J. Maddox from Cor. 13:13, followed by Bro. A. Sheffield. 2. Received an acknowledgement from a sister for swearing. 4. Received by letter Bro. T. J. Warren, Henry T. Warren and Sister Martha Warren and Chalcedonia Warren. 5. Granted letters of dismission to Bro. Fed Hawkins and wife [*M. E. Hawkins*]. A. Sheffield, Mod., John B. Richards, C.C.

Nov. 20, 1886, Bro. A. Sheffield. 2. Received acknowledgement from a brother for swearing. 4. Received by letter Sister Feba C. Mason. A. Sheffield, Mod., John B. Richards, C.C.

Feb. 19, 1887, Bro. E. W. Allred from Roms. 1-8. 2. Preferred a charge against a sister for having abandoned her husband and carrying away goods that did not belong to her. On motion, the charges was taken up and excluded her from the fellowship of this church. After hearing acknowledgements of another sister for having joined another church of a different [faith] and order, she was restored to fellowship. 5. Granted letter of dismission to Sister Hitt and Hodges. E. W. Allred, Mod., John B. Richards, C.C.

Jun. 18, 1887, Bro. E. Cochran from Gal. 3-29. 5. Appointed as delegates to the union meeting of the fourth district: Brethren John B. Richards, B. H. Howard, J. W. Eaton, J. M. Richards, A. J. White, H. C. Boling and A. J. Pursell, and elected the following Brethren as delegates to Hightower Association: John B. Richards, J. M. Richards, E. Cochran and J. L. Williams as alternate. E. Cochran, Mod., John B. Richards, C.C.

Jul. 16, 1887, Bro. Cochran followed by Allred. 2. Preferred a charge against a brother for swearing. Took up the charge and excluded him from the fellowship of the church. On motion, a committee was appointed to cite a brother to the church for drinking to an excess. Also appointed a committee to cite another brother to the church for drinking. 4. Received a brother by restoration by rescinding the action of the church so far as his exclusion. E. W. Allred, Mod., John B. Richards, C.C.

Aug. 20, 1887, Bro. W. H. Dean followed by Bro. E. W. Allred. 2. Received an acknowledgement from a brother for drinking to an excess. E. W. Allred, Mod., John B. Richards, C.C.

Sep. 18, 1887, Brother E. Cochran from 1st Cor. 1-12. 2. Preferred a charge against a sister for disorderly conduct. Took up the charge and excluded her from the fellowship of the church. 4. Received by letter Jane Mason and W. H. Burton by experience. 5. Made choice of E. W. Allred as supply for the year 1888 and E. W. Cochran [*probably E. A. Cochran*] as joint supply. Mod. Pro Tem, John B. Richards, C. C.

Oct. 15, 1887, E. W. Allred followed by Bro. E. Cochran. 4. Received by letter, Sister E. E. Lyle. 5. Granted letters of dismission to J. M. Odum, Hester A. Odum, J. P. Rich and Martha Stephens. E. W. Allred, Mod., John B. Richards, C.C.

Nov. Term, 1887, E. W. Allred. *[no business under any item]* E. W. Allred, Mod., John B. Richards, C.C.

Dec. Term, 1887, Bro. E. W. Allred followed by E. Cochran. *[no business under any item]*. E. W. Allred, Mod., John B. Richards, C.C.

Jan. Term, 1888, Bro. E. W. Allred. *[no business under any item]* E. W. Allred, Mod., John B. Richards, C.C.

Feb. 1888, Bro. Blackwell from Acts 17: 10-30. 4. Received by letter Bro. M. H. Hardy and wife M. A. Hardy. 5. Appointed delegates to union meeting to wit: J. L. Williams, J. B. Richards, J. B. Lawson, K. H. Fletcher and A. T. Hester. E. W. Allred, Mod., John B. Richards, C.C.

Mar. 17, 1888, Bro. E. Cochran, followed by E. W. Allred. 4. Received by letter Sister Caroline Gilstrap. 5. Granted a letter of dismission to Bro. Henry Pursell. Organized a Sunday School with the following officers to wit: J. B. Lawson, Supt., John Halcombe, Assist. Supt., H. K. Fletcher, Secty. E. W. Allred, Mod., John B. Richards, C.C.

April Term, 1888, Bro. Blackwell from Mat. 15:13, followed by Bro. Stephens. 2. Received acknowledgements from a brother for using profane language. Preferred a charge against a sister for adultery. Took up the charge and excluded her from the fellowship of the church. 4. Received by letter Brethren Henry Grimes, H. K. Fletcher and Sister Myra Fletcher. E. W. Allred, Mod., John B. Richards, C.C.

May Term, 1888. Bro. E. W. Allred. *[no business under any item]*. E. W. Allred, Mod., John B. Richards, C.C.

June Term, 1888, Bro. E. W. Allred. *[no business under any item]*. E. W. Allred, Mod., John B. Richards, C.C.

July Term, 1888, Bro. E. W. Allred. 5. Elected the following brethren as delegates to association: John B. Richards, Thomas N. Smith, and Ansil Williams. E. W. Allred, Mod., John B. Richards, C.C.

Aug. 18, 1888, Bro. E. Cochran from John 14-15. 2. Preferred a charge against a brother for drinking to an excess and cited him to the church to answer the church. 4. Received by letter S. E. Jones, Bro. John S. Wyatt and wife J. P. Wyatt and Sister L. Baker by experience. E. Cochran, Mod. Pro Tem, John B. Richards, C.C.

Oct. 20, 1888, Bro. Allred. 3. Received an acknowledgement from a brother for drinking. 5. Granted a letter of dismission to Brother [W. A.] Collins. E. W. Allred, Mod., John S. Wyatt, C.C. Pro Tem.

Nov. 17, 1888, E. Cochran. 5. Granted a letter of dismission to Mary Rainwaters. Amount made up for Pastor $22.50. E. Cochran, Mod. Pro Tem, John B. Richards, C.C.

Dec. 15, 1888, Bro. H. Ingram, pastor from St. John, 21st chapt. 5. Granted letters of dismission to Bro. W. E. Evans and wife. Amount made up for Pastor $5.50. Henry Ingram, Mod., J. W. McGullion, C.C. Pro Tem.

Jan. 19, 1889, Bro. H. Ingram from Paul's letter to the Romans, c. 4 and 20 ?. 2. Received acknowledgements of a brother for getting drunk. 4. Received G. B. Fletcher by letter. 5. Granted letters of dismission to Bro. Frank Barnwell and wife and Bro. Lowery Boling and Sister Pheba C. Mason and Sister Mary Crow. Also elected Bro J. W. McGuillion as C.C. Henry Ingram, Mod., H. C. Boling, C.C. Pro Tem.

Apr. 20, 1889, Bro. H. Ingram from Hebrews, 12 chapt, 1st and 2nd verses. 2. Preferred a charge against a brother for false swearing. Referred until next meeting and appointed Brethren J. S. Wyatt, J. M. White and G.W. Wilkie to notify the brother of the charge. 5. Granted letter of dismission to Sister Jane Wilson. H. T. Ingram, Mod., J. W. McGuillion, C.C.

Sunday morning, Apr. 21, 1889, Bro. H. T. Ingram. Moove and second, went into conference. Moove and second, withdrew the charge against a brother for false swearing and referred to a committee to settle. The Mod. elected the committee Brethren J. B. Richards, T. N. Smith, and J. L. Williams. H. T. Ingram, Mod., J. W. McGuillion, C.C.

May 18, 1889, Bro. Edd Hudson followed by Bro. E. Cochran. 5. Granted a letter of dismission to Sister Martha Hyde. E. Cochran, Mod., J. W. McGuillion, C.C.

Jun. 15, 1889, Bro. West, followed by Bro. E. Cochran. 3. Recended the act of withdrawing the charge against a brother for false swearing, the charge to stand as preferred and he be sited to next meeting for trial by the same committee. 5. Appointed delegates to the union meeting to be held at Mount Tabor embracing the 4th Sunday in July next: Bro. B. Fletcher, Bro. J. S. Wyatt, Bro. H.C. Boling, Bro. J. W. McGullion and J. M. Richards. Also elected delegates to the Association at Macedonia embracing the 2nd Sunday in August next and elected Brethren E. Cochran, J. B. Richards and J. L. Williams and R. J. Pursell as alternate. E. Cochran, Mod., J. W. McGullion, C.C.

Jul. 20, 1889, Bro. S. C. Harris from Rom, 8th cha., 2nd and 3rd v. followed by Bro. H. T. Ingram. 3. Taken up the charge against a brother and excluded him from the fellowship of the church. 5. Read the letters to the association and union meeting. H. T. Ingram, Mod., J. W. McGuillion, C.C.

Aug. 1889, Bro. H. T. Ingram from Rev. 3rd chap, 4th v. followed by Bro. W. W. West. *[no business under any item]*. H. T. Ingram, Mod., J. W. McGuillion, C.C.

Sep. 14, 1889, Bro. E. Richards from Gal. 6th chap., and 8th v. followed by Bro. H. T. Ingram. 4. Received by letter Sisters Rebeca White and Mattie Whitener. H. T. Ingram, Mod., J. S. Wyatt, C.C. Pro Tem.

Oct. 19, 1889, Bro. H. T. Ingram from Matt. 24 ch. and 14 v. 4. Received by letter Peter Martin and wife Cary E. Martin. 5. Elected Pastors for ensuing year: Bros. H. T. Ingram and E. Cochran, supply. Elected to the Sunday

School Association to be held at Friendship Church Saturday before the 1st Sunday in Nov. next: J. S. Wyatt and J. W. McGullion, H. K. Fletcher, alternate. H. T. Ingram, Mod., J. W. McGuillion, C.C.

Dec. 14, 1889, Bro. E. Cochran. 5. Granted letters of dismission to John L. Williams, Mary A. Williams, G. B. Williams, A. M. Williams, Mary C. Burton and Wm. Burton. Paid Pastors $30.50 for services rendered. H. T. Ingraim, Mod., J. W. Eaton, C.C. Protem.

Jan. 18, 1890, Bro. E. Cochran. 5. Granted letters of dismission to Bro. Joel Williams and wife, Rebecka White and Lou White. E. Cochran, Mod., J. W. McGullion, C.C.

Feb. 1890, Bro. H. T. Ingram. 5. Appointed delegates to the union meeting: Bros. J. W. McGullion, E. Cochran, J. S. Wyatt, J. M. Richards and R. J. Pursell. H. T. Ingram, Mod., J. W. McGullion, C.C.

Mar. 15, 1890, Bro. E. Cochran. 5. referd election of deacons to next meeting. Adopted the letter prepared for the union meeting. H. T. Ingram, Mod., J. W. McGullion, C.C.

Apr. 19, 1890, Bro. E. Cochran from 1st John, Chapter 2, 14th verse. 2. Received acknowledgement from a brother for drinking to much. 5. Elected J. M. Richards and J. S. Wyatt, Deacons. Invited the Eldership of the following churches for Presbatery to ordain deacons elect at next meeting: Macedonie, New Harmony, Mt. Tabor, Friendship, Ophir. E. Cochran, Mod., H. C. Boling, C.C. Pro Tem.

May 17, 1890, Bro. J. H. Lathem, followed by Bro. H. T. Ingram. 5. Went into the Election of a deacon and nominated Bros. J. S. Hester and G. B. Fletcher. Bro. G. B. Fletcher receiving the highest was duly elected. By move and second, Hightower Church with visiting Brethren formed the Presbytery for the examination of Bros elect, for deacons to wit: J. S. Wyatt and G. B. Fletcher. The Presbytery formed was Rev. John H. Lathem, Rev. H. T. Ingram. Rev. E. Cochran, Rev. Levi Stephens, A. C. Conn, Joseph Wyatt, A. Cornelison, F. Nix, J. B. Richards and Thomas Smith. The Bros. elect was examined and found orthodox and worthy of ordination as deacons of this church which duty was performed by the Presbytery. H. T. Ingram, Mod., James W. McGullion, C.C.

Jun. 14, 1890, Bro. E. Cochran from Jonah 2nd chapter and 9th verse. 5. Elected delegates to the association to wit: Bros. J. B. Richards, Joe Hester, T. N. Smith and J. W. McGullion. Granted letters of dismission to W. T. Elliott, Margrett Elliott, Mattie Elliott, Minnie Elliott, Lura Roggers, A. J. Thomas and James Howard. By move and second, organized a Sabbath School and the officers elected were: G. B. Fletcher, Supt., J. S. Wyatt, Assistant Supt., J. W. McGullion, Sec. E. Cochran, Mod., J. W. McGullion, C.C.

Jul. 1890, Bro. G. Biddy and H. T. Ingram. 5. Adopted the Letter to the Association as our work for the last year. H. T. Ingram, Mod., James W. McGullion, C.C.

Aug. 16, 1890, Bro. E. Cochran and H. T. Ingram. 2. Preferred charges against a brother for profane language and for drunkenness. 4. Received by experience Miss Josia Cordell. 5. Read acknowledgement of a brother. Granted letters of dismission to Bro. J. D. Carnes and wife. Also to J. B. Richards and family. Appointed a committee of one to meet at Friendship Church of Friday before 2nd Sunday in Oct. for the purpose of reporting and subscribed for the erection of a High School House to wit: J. S. Wyatt. Appointed a committee of five to solicit subscriptions to build said house to wit: J. S. Wyatt, J. W. McGullion, E. Cochran, H. C. Boling, and R. J. Pursell. H. T. Ingram, Mod., James W. McGullion, C.C.

Sep. 20, 1890, Bros. M. G. Wilkie and H. T. Ingram. 3. Taken up the charges against a brother for drunkenness and profane language and acquitted him. 4. Received by letter Sisters Lou Stoyles and Hassie Hardin. 5. Granted letters of dismission to Bro. J. F. Dowdie and wife. Elected Bro. H. T. Ingram as Pastor for the ensuing year. E. Cochran, Mod., James W. McGullion, C.C.

Oct. 18, 1890, Bros. Elias Cochran and Eliga Roper. 5. Granted letter of dismission to Sister Sallie Carnes. By motion organized Sabath School and elected J. W. McGullion, Supt.; J. S. Wyatt, Assistant Supt.; A. H. Wilkie, Sec.

Paid pastors $8.65. H. T. Ingram, Mod., James W. McGullion, C.C.

Nov. 16, 1890, Bro. H. T. Ingram. 5. Granted a letter of dismission to Sister Laura Humphrey. Paid pastor $16.00. H. T. Ingram, Mod., James W. McGullion, C.C.

Dec. 20, 1890, Bros. E. Cochran and H. T. Ingram. 2. Preferred a charge against a brother for using profane language. Referd the charge to next meeting and appointed Bros. T. N. Smith and W. E. Evans to notify the brother of the charge preferred. Receipts: Two Dollars. H. T. Ingram, Mod., James W. McGullion, C.C.

Feb. 14, 1891, Bros. H. L. Stephens and H. T. Ingram. 2. Preferd a charge against a brother for swearing and referd it to next meeting. Prefered charges against another brother for drinking and swearing, and referd it to next meeting. 3. Taken up the charge against a brother *[from Dec. 1890 for using profane language]* and excluded him from the fellowship of the church. 5. Granted a letter of dismission to Sister Allice [*White*] Wofford. H. T. Ingram, Mod., H. C. Boling, C.C. Pro Tem.

Mar. 14, 1891, Bro. E. Cochran. 2. A brother made acknowledgement for drunkness. Preferd a charge against another brother for profanity and referd same to next meeting. Rec'd acknowledgement of another brother for profanity. 3. Referd charge against a brother until next meeting. Taken up a charge against another brother for drunkness and rec'd acknowledgement for the same. 5. Granted letters of dismission to Sister Laura Humphrey. Elias Cochran, Mod. Protem, J. S. Wyatt, C. C. Protem.

Apr, 1891, Bros. H. T. Ingram and Elias Cochran. 3. Taken up the charge against a brother and excluded him from the fellowship of the church. Also the charge against another brother and excluded him. 5. collected $1.00 to buy wine. Volunteers to invite sister churches to communion. Ophir: J. W. McGullion, New Harmony: A. T. Hester. Conns Creek: H. K. Fletcher. Friendship: J. N. Hardy. H. T. Ingram, Mod., James W. McGullion, C.C.

May 16, 1891, Bros. E. Cochran and H. T. Ingram. [*no business under any item*]. H. T. Ingram, Mod., H. K. Fletcher, C.C. Protem.

Jun. 19, 1891, Bro. J. L. Wyatt. 4. Received by letter Bro. Wm. Wooten and wife. 5. Elected delegates to the association to wit: E. Cochran, T. N. Smith, R. J. Pursell, J. S. Wyatt and J. S. Hester. J. L. Wyatt, Mod. Protem, W. E. Evans, C.C. Protem.

Jul. 18, 1891, Bros. H. T. Ingram and E. Cochran. 2. Preferd a charge against a brother for drunkness and referd till next meeting. 5. Elected delegates to the union meeting to wit: J. S. Wyatt, J. W. Eaton, A. T. Hester, J. W. McGullion, and A. J. White. For minutes: $1.03. H. T. Ingram, Mod., James W. McGullion, C.C.

Aug. 15, 1891, Brothers E. Cochran and H. T. Ingram. 2. Took up a charge of a brother and received his acknowledgement. 4. Rec'd. by letter Leana Leonard, R. A. Ramsey and Ann Ramsey. 5. Granted letters of dismission to W. T. Crenshaw and Martha Crenshaw. H. T. Ingram, Mod., H. K. Fletcher, C.C. Protem.

Sep. 19, 1891, Bro. E. Cochran. 2. Preferd a charge against a brother for swearing and referd same to next meeting and appointed a committee to see him: J. R. Biddy and J. M. Richards. 4. Received by experience J. D. Ray, and N. M. White by letter. 5. Elected Eliga Roper, pastor for the ensuing year and appointed a committee to notify him of his election to wit: J. W. Eaton and J. M. Richards. Dismissed by letter S. L. Richards and Wm. Mason. H. T. Ingram, Mod., James W. McGullion, C.C.

Oct. 17, 1891, 3. Taken up the charge against a brother for swearing and excluded him. 4. Received by letter J. J. Holcombe, Lou Holcombe and J. P. Rich. 5. Herd report of com. on pastor and Bro. Roper could not attend. Elected J. R. Allen, Pastor and appointed Bro. W. E. Evans to notify him of his election. Collections for pastor $16.50. H. T. Ingram, Mod., G. B. Fletcher, C.C. Protem

Mar. 19, 1892, After singing, went into conference. 2. Preferd charges against two bros. for drunkness, taken up the charges and excluded them from the fellowship. Received an acknowledgement from a bro. for drinking and using profane language and excused him. Also from another brother and excused him. Also from an additional brother and excused him. A sister presented herself for restoration and the matter was referd to next meeting. 5. Dismissed by letter Lydia Collins and L. A. Nix. J. B. Richards, Mod. Protem, J. W. McGullion, C.C.

April, 1892, Bro. G. L. Barnwell and J. R. Allen. 3. Taken up a case against a sister and refused to restore her to fellowship. 5. Received an invitation from Ophir Baptist Church to Communion. Appointed brethren to invite sister churches to our Communion. J. R. Allen, Mod., J. S. Wyatt, C. C. Protem.

May Term, 1892, Bros. Stripling and J. R. Allen. 2. Preferd a charge against a brother for drunkness and referd same until next meeting. Also preferd charge against another brother for drunkness and deferd same. J. R. Allen, Mod., J. S. Wyatt, C. C. Protem.

June Term, 1892, 3. Received an acknowledgement from a brother on the charge preferd and aquited him. Another brother's case was carried over til next meeting. 5. Elected delegates to the Association to wit: Thos. Smith, J. S. Wyatt, J. M. Richards, Elias Cochran and R. J. Pursell. Elected delegates to the union meeting to wit: J. B. Chastain, Thos. Smith, J. R. Biddy, J. S. Wyatt, and B. H. Williams. J. R. Allen, Mod., J. S. Wyatt, C.C. Protem.

July 16, 1892, Bros. E. A. Cochran and J. R. Allen. 2. Preferred a charge against a sister for profanity and excluded her. 3. Taken up the case against a brother for drunkness and excluded him from the church. 5. Read and adopted letters to the union meeting and association. Moved and carried that we elect a preaching committee. Elected as committee: H. C. Boling, J. S. Wyatt, R. J. Purcell, J. M. Richards and T. N. Smith. J. R. Allen, Mod., J. S. Wyatt, C.C. Protem.

August Term, 1892, Bros. E. A. Cochran and J. R. Allen. 5. Granted letters to the following: Bro. W. M. Dobson and wife and Sara Smith, also J. D. Ray. Moved and carried that we elect a clerk. Elected Brother R. B. Pursell. J. R. Allen, Mod., J. S. Wyatt, C. C. Protem.

Sep. 17, 1892, Bros. J. R. Allen and W. W. West. 2. Received acknowledgements of a brother. 4. Received by experience, Sister N. A. Chastain. 5. Granted request of New Harmony to meet with her in the ordination of Bro. Harris. The church had the rules of order read. Moved to have the 11th item inserted viz. no member shall be allowed to absent himself during conference without leave of the Moderator. By motion, instructed clerk to get up the old rules of Decorum by next conference. Granted letter to Sister S. A. Dobson. J. R. Allen, Mod., R. B. Purcell, C.C.

Oct. 15, 1892, After singing, met in conference; Elected Bro. J. S. Wyatt as Moderator. 4. Received by letter Sister Margarett Chastain. 5. Went into the election of a pastor for the ensuing year. Elected by acclamation, Bro. J. R. Allen. J. S. Wyatt, Mod. Protem, R. B. Purcell, C.C.

Nov. 19, 1892, Bro. Lee and J. R. Allen. 2. Move and second to prefer a charge against a brother for drunkness, carried. Moved that we refer the case of the brother till next conference. Another brother makes his acknowledgements for getting into a row at the election. His acknowledgements was received. Moved that we prefer a charge against another brother for drunkness. Carried. Moved and second to pass the case of this brother till next meeting. Carried. Moved and second to prefer a charge against a brother for contempt. Carried. Moved and second to take up the charge. Carried. Moved to exclude him. Carried. 5. Brother Allen accepted the call of Hightower Church for another year. Paid Brother J. R. Allen as pastor of Hightower Church $8.90. J. R. Allen, Mod., R. B. Purcell, C.C.

Feb. Term, 1893, Bro. E. A. Cochran; Elected Bro. E. A. Cochran, Moderator. 3. Received acknowledgement of a brother. Referred the charge of another brother till next conference. E. A. Cochran, Mod. Protem, R. B. Purcell, C.C.

Apr. 15, 1893, Bros. J. R. Allen and E. A. Cochran. 3. Moved that we bear with a brother till next meeting. 5. Invitations from the following churches to their communion: Ophir, Mt. Tabor, Friendship, and New Harmony.

Collected $0.65 for to buy wine with. Bro. J. R. Allen called for volunteers to invite the following churches to communion with us. Ophir, Mt. Taber, Friendship, Conns Creek and New Harmony. Granted letters to Brother J. H. Morgan and also Bro. John Webster. Request the clerk to bring the minute book next conference. J. R. Allen, Mod., R. B. Purcell, C.C.

May 20, 1893, Bro. E. A. Cochran and J. R. Allen. 3. Took up the case of a brother and received his acknowledgements. 5. Bro. E.A. Cochran announced that all was ready for communion. Clerk called the roll. J. R. Allen, Mod., R. B. Purcell, C.C.

Jun. 17, 1893, Bros. W. W. West and E. A. Cochran; Elected Bro. E. A. Cochran, Mod. 2. Received acknowledgements of a brother for getting drunk, also received acknowledgement of two additional brothers for getting drunk. Preferred a charge against a brother for swearing, carried the charge over till next meeting. 5. Went into the election of delegates to the union meeting. Elected the following brethren: J. S. Wyatt, J. R. Biddy, T. J. Warren, R. J. Purcell, J. B. Chastain. Moved and second that the second offence of drunkness be excluded hereafter, carried. Granted letters of dismission to Sister Synthia Wilkie, also Brother Parks Wilkie. Moved that we lay the acknowledgement of a brother over till next meeting, Carried. Went into an election of delegates to the association. Elected the following brethren: G. B. Fletcher, R. J. Purcell, J. B. Chastain, J. S. Wyatt, and E. A. Cochran. E. A. Cochran, Mod. Protem, R. B. Purcell, C.C.

Jul. 15, 1893, Bros. Martin Green and J. R. Allen. 3. Took up the reference case of a brother for swearing and bore with him. Also another brother and restored him. 5. Granted a letter of dismission to Bro. M. G. Wilkie. Clerk read the letter to the association. Moved and seconded that we recend action taken by the church at last meeting regarding drunkness. Carried. Took up collection for minutes. Collected $1.25. J. R. Allen, Mod., R. B. Purcell, C.C.

Aug. 19, 1893, Bro. E. A. Cochran; Elected Bro. E. A. Cochran, Mod. 5. Granted a letter of dismission to Sister L. Thomas. Collected $0.75 to buy oil and can with. E. A. Cochran, Mod. Protem, R. B. Purcell, C.C.

Sep. 16, 1893, Bros. Wm. Cagle and J. R. Allen. 4. Received by letter Bro. John Holcomb and wife and daughter and by experience Joseph B. Chastain. 5. Received an invitation from Friendship to their communion the 2nd Sunday in October. Moved and carried that we postpone the case of a brother till next meeting. J. R. Allen, Mod., R. B. Purcell, C.C.

Oct. 14, 1893, Bros. W. J. Hyde and J. R. Allen. 2. Preferred charge against a sister for commiting of adultery. Took up the charge and excluded her from the fellowship of the church. Also preferred charge against two other sisters for commiting adultery. Took up the charges and excluded them. 5. Granted a letter of dismission to Sister Lena Baker. Went into election of a preacher for another year. Elected Bro. J. R. Allen. J. R. Allen, Mod., R. B. Purcell, C.C.

Feb. 17, 1894, After singing and prayer, met in conference. Elected Bro. M. D. Greene, Mod. *[no business under any item]*. M. D. Greene, Mod. Protem, R B. Purcell, C.C.

Apr. 18, 1894, Bro. J. R. Allen. 4. Received by letter Sister S. M. White. 5. Accepted an invitation from Conns Creek, also Ophir and Mt. Tabor to their communions in May. Called for volunteers to invite the following churches to be with us at our communion in May: Cons Creek, Ophir, Mt. Tabor, Friendship. Collected 60 cts. to buy wine. Went into an election of delegates to the union meeting. Elected the following Bros: J. S. Wyatt, H. K. Fletcher, R. J. Purcell, John Holcomb and R. W. Cochran. J. R. Allen, Mod., R. B. Purcell, C.C.

Jun. 16, 1894, Bros. M. D. Greene and J. R. Allen. 3. Prefered charge against a brother for swindling took up the charge and excluded him from the fellowship of the church. 4. Received by letter Sisters Sarah Wyatt and Fannie Purcell. 5. Postponed the communions till July meeting. Went into election of delegates to the association. Elected the following Brethren: J. S. Wyatt, J. B. Chastain, John W. Holcomb, R. J. Purcell and T. N. Smith. J. R. Allen, Mod., R. B. Purcell, C.C.

Jul. 14, 1894, Bro. J. R. Allen. Received acknowledgements of a brother. Also received acknowledgements of another brother for drinking. 5. Granted letter to Bro. J. P. Rich. Granted letter to Bro. Harbin and wife. J. R. Allen, Pro. Mod., R. B. Purcell, C.C.

Aug. 18, 1894, Bros. R. W. Cochran and F. C. Hawkins; Elected Bro. R. W. Cochran, Mod. 2. Received acknowledgements of a brother for drunkness and swearing, also another brother for drunkness. 5. Granted letters of dismission to Bro. Peter Martin and wife, also Sisters Sally Logan and Mary Cagle. The church licensed Bro. R. W. Cochran to preach. R. W. Cochran, Mod. Pro, R. B. Purcell, C.C.

Sep. 15, 1894, Bro. F. C. Hawkins and E. A. Cochran; Elected Bro. E. A. Cochran, Mod. 2. Preferred a charge against a brother for drunkness, refered the charge till next meeting. 5. Granted a letter of dismission to Sister Mattie Petty. Went into election of a preacher for another year. Elected Bro. E. A. Cochran. Moved and carried that preaching commence at 11 o'clock hereafter Saturday and Sunday. E. A. Cochran, Mod., R. B. Purcell, C.C.

Oct. 20, 1894, Bros. C. S. Hawkins, M. D. Greene and E. A. Cochran. 3. Took up the case against a brother for drunkness and bore with him. 5. Granted a letter of dismission to Sister Susan Gibson. Collected $1.00 for Bro. Allen also .45 cts for Bro. West. Appointed a committee of 6 to correct the roal [roll]. They were as follows: Bros. Ben Howard, J. M. Richards, R. J. Purcell, J. S. Wyatt, C. B. Fowler and H. C. Boling. E. A. Cochran, Mod., R. B. Purcell, C.C.

Nov. 17, 1894, Bros. E. A. Cochran and R. W. Cochran. 5. Received report of committee on the roll. E. A. Cochran, Mod., R. B. Purcell, C.C.

Dec. 15, 1894, Bros. E. A. Cochran and R. W. Cochran. 2. Preferred a charge against two brethren for drunkness. Referred the cases till next meeting. 5. Granted letters of dismission to Bros. Harris Nelson, J. N. Hardy and C. R. Hardy and Sisters M. H. Hardy [*membership roll shows Susan Hardy dbl on this date?*] and F. I. Gilstrap. E. A. Cochran, Mod., R. B. Purcell, C.C.

Jan. 19, 1895, Bros. R. W. Cochran and E. A. Cochran. 3. Took up the case of a brother and bore with him, also took up the case of another brother and excluded him from the fellowship of the church. E. A. Cochran, Mod., R. B. Purcell, C.C.

Mar. 16, 1895, Bros. Martin D. Greene and Elias A. Cochran. 5. Elected the following named brethren to the union meeting: T. N. Smith, R. W. Cochran, J. R. Biddy, A. J. White, R. J. Purcell. E. A. Cochran, Mod., R. B. Purcell, C.C.

Apr. 20, 1895, R. W. Cochran and E. A. Cochran. 5. Granted letters of dismission to Bro. J. E. Hosey and daughter. Received invitations from Cons Creek and Friendship to their communion. Appointed Bro. J. S. Wyatt, Treasury. Called for volunteers to invite Cons Creek, Ophir, Mt. Tabor, Friendship, New Harmony to our communion the 3rd Sunday in May. E. A. Cochran, Mod., R. B. Purcell, C.C.

May 18, 1895, Bros. E. A. Cochran and C. S. Hawkins. 2. Preferred charge against a brother for drunkness, carried the charge till next conference. Preferred charge against another brother for drunkness, referred the charge till next conference. 5. Granted letters of dismission to Bro. S. H. Pinson and wife. Moved and carried that we always turn a case over a month. Moved and carried that we rescend the above act. E. A. Cochran, Mod., R. B. Purcell, C.C.

Jun. 15, 1895, Bros. R. W. Cochran and E. A. Cochran. 3. Took up charge against a brother for drunkness, preferred charges against him for contempt. Took up the charge and excluded him from the fellowship of the church. Took up the case of another brother for drunkness and bore with him. 5. Went into the election of delegates. Elected the following to the Association: E. A. Cochran, J. S. Wyatt, John Holcomb, R. J. Purcell, H. C. Boling, and R. W. Cochran. E. A. Cochran, Mod., R. B. Purcell, C.C.

Jul. 20, 1895, Bros. R. W. Cochran, C. S. Hawkins and E. A. Cochran. 5. Read the letter to the association. E. A. Cochran, Mod., R. B. Purcell, C.C.

Aug. 17, 1895, Bro. E. A. Cochran and R. W. Cochran. 5. Granted a letter of dismission to Bro. E. Smallwood. E. A. Cochran, Mod., R. B. Purcell, C.C.

Sep. 14, 1895, Bros. Elias Biddy and William West. 5. Granted letters of dismission to Bro. Elbert Ledbetter and wife, also to William Fowler, also Bro. A. H. Lee and wife. Went into election for a pastor for another year. Elected Bro. J. L. Wyatt. Appointed Bros. J. B. Chastain and R. J. Purcell to see if he would attend out church. E. A. Cochran, Mod., R. B. Purcell, C.C.

Oct. 19, 1895, Bro. E. A. Cochran. 5. Granted letters of dismission to Sister Odem, also Bro. Wm. Jones and wife, also Sisters Lydia, Lucy and Sally Fowler's, also Bro. Tank Fowler. E. A. Cochran, Mod., R. B. Purcell, C.C.

Oct. 20, 1895, J. L. Wyatt and C. A. Wallis. Called conference, elected Bro. J. L. Wyatt, Mod. Went into the election of a pastor for another year. Elected Bro. C. A. Wallis. J. L. Wyatt, Mod., R. B. Purcell, C.C.

Nov. 16, 1895, Bro. C. A. Wallis. 5. Granted a letter of dismission to Bro. Mc. Baker. C. A. Wallis, Mod., R. B. Purcell, C.C.

Dec. 14, 1895, Bros. C. A. Wallis and C. S. Hawkins. 2. Preferred charge against a sister for adultery. Took up the charge and excluded her. Also preferred charge against a brother for drunkness and profanity. Took up the charge and excluded him from the fellowship of the church. C. A. Wallis, Mod., R. B. Purcell, C.C.

Jan. 18, 1896, Bros. C. A. Wallis and R. W. Cochran. [*no business under any item*]. C. A. Wallis, Mod., R. B. Purcell, C.C.

Feb. 15, 1896, Bros. M. D. Greene and J. J. Hardin. 2. Received acknowledgements of a brother for drunkness. 5. Granted Sister Dora Fowler a letter of dismission of account of having had her other misplaced. J. J. Hardin, Mod. [*protem*], R. B. Purcell, C. C.

Mar. 14, 1896, Bro. C. A. Wallis. 5. Moved and carried that Bro. G. R. Fowler have a duplicate letter. Granted a letter of dismission to Sister Mattie Whitner. Went into election of delegates to the union meeting. Elected Brethren: R. J. Purcell, John Holcomb, T. N. Smith, J. R. Biddy, J. S. Wyatt and H. C. Boling, Alt. C. A. Wallis, Mod., R. B. Purcell, C.C.

Apr. 18, 1896, Bros. J. H. Milton, M. D. Greene and C. A. Wallis. 4. Received by letter Sister Fannie Bryant. 5. Church agreed to commune at our next regular meeting, it being the regular time. Invited Cons Creek, Ophir, Mt. Tabor, Mt. Pisgah, Friendship and New Harmony Churches to be with us. Elected delegates to the union meeting. Elected Brethren: H. K. Fletcher, R. J. Purcell, H. C. Boling, J. M. Richards and J. R. Biddy. C. A. Wallis, Mod., R. B. Purcell, C.C.

May 16, 1896, Bros. C. A. Wallis and C. S. Hawkins. [*no business under any item*]. C. A. Wallis, Mod., R. B. Purcell, C.C.

Jun. 20, 1896, Bros. W. W. West and C. A. Wallis. 2. Preferred a charge against a brother for abuse of his wife and separation. Referred the charge till next conference. Appointed Bros. H. C. Boling, J. M. Richards and E. A. Cochran to go and [see] the bro. 5. Election of delegates to the Association. Appointed Bros. R. J. Purcell, T. N. Smith, J. S. Wyatt, A. T. Hester, R. W. Cochran and H. C. Boling, Alt. Elected a delegate to the North Ga. Convention, elected Bro. E. A. Cochran, and T. N. Smith, alt. C. A. Wallis, Mod., R. B. Purcell, C.C.

Jul. 18, 1896, Bros. C. A. Wallis and R. W. Cochran. 2. Received acknowledgements of a brother for drunkness. Took up the report that another brother has been drunk, preferred the charge against him, refered the charge till next conference. 3. Took up the case of a brother for abuse and separation. Refered the case till next conference.

5. Elected delegates to the union meeting. Elected Bros. H. C. Boling, R. B. Purcell, J. B. Chastain, J. M. Richards and Thos. Bryant, Alt. C. A. Wallis, Mod., R. B. Purcell, C.C.

Aug. 15, 1896, Bro. C. A. Wallis. 2. Preferred a charge against another brother for drunkness, took up the charge and excluded him from the fellowship of the church. Preferred a charge against an additional brother for drunkness, referred the charge until next conference. Preferred a charge against a brother for profanity, layed the charge over till next conference. 3. Took up the charge against a brother for drunkness and received his acknowledgements. Also took up the charge against a brother for abuse and separation of his wife, took up the charge and excluded him from the fellowship of the church. 5. Granted Lindy Fowler a letter of dismission, also granted Bros. J. J. Warren and H. T. Warren letters, also Sisters Martha Warren, Callie Warren and Donie Warren letters of dismission. Liberated Bro. R. J. Purcell to talk and express his feelings here and elsewhere, also Bro. C. B. Fowler. C. A. Wallis, Mod., R. B. Purcell, C.C.

Sep. 19, 1896, Bros. R. Waters and C. A. Wallis. 3. Took up and layed over the charge against a brother till next conference on account of sickness. Took up the charge against another brother for profanity, received his acknowledgement. 5. Granted Sister Caroline Gilstrap a letter of dismission. Went into election of pastor for another year, elected Bro. C. A. Wallis. C. A. Wallis, Mod., R. B. Purcell, C.C.

Oct. 18, 1896 (Sunday?) Bro. R. J. Purcell and C. A. Wallis. 3. Took up the charge against a brother for drunkness and received his acknowledgements. 5. Accepted an invitation from Mt. Pisgah to be at their communion, also from Friendship. C. A. Wallis, Mod., R. B. Purcell, C.C.

Nov. 14, 1896, Bros. R. W. Cochran and C. A. Wallis. 2. Preferred a charge against a sister for fornication. Took up the charge and excluded her from the fellowship of the church. 4. Received by letter Bro. G. B. Haygood and wife. 5. Election of delegates to union meeting. Elected: Bro. G. B. Haygood, R. J. Purcell, H. C. Boling, R. B. Purcell and J. M. Richards. C. A. Wallis, Mod., R. B. Purcell, C.C.

Dec. 19, 1896, Bro. Eligah Roper and C. A. Wallis. 2. Preferred charge against a brother for profanity. Took up the charge and excluded him. 4. Received by letter Bro. Mc. Baker. 5. Election of delegates to the union meeting. Elected: Bros. John Holcomb, J. F. Dowda, J. M. Richards, H. C. Boling and G. B. Haygood. C. A. Wallis, Mod., H. C. Boling, C.C. Protem.

Jan. term, 1897, Bro. C. A. Wallis. 2. Preferred a charge against a brother for drunkness and profanity. Took up the charge and excluded him from the fellowship of the church. C. A. Wallis, Mod., R. J. Purcell, C.C. Protem.

Mar. 20, 1887, Bros. C. A. Wallis and R. W. Cochran. 2. Preferred a charge against a brother and wife for separation. Referred the charge till next conference. 4. Received by letter Bro. J. H. Ellis and wife. C.A. Wallis, Mod., R. B. Purcell, C.C.

Apr. 17, 1897, Bros. R. W. Cochran and C. A. Wallace. 3. Took up the charge against a brother and his wife for separation. Acquitted the brother of the charge, excluded the sister from the fellowship of the church. 5. Elected delegates to union meeting. Elected Bros. John W. Holcomb, J. B. Haygood, Henry Ellis, J. R. Biddy, H. C. Boling, and R. B. Purcell, alt. C. A. Wallace, Mod., R. B. Purcell, C.C.

May 15, 1897, Bros. J. M. Anderson and C. A. Wallace. 2. Received the acknowledgements of a brother. 4. Received by letter Bro. Perry Andrews and wife, Catharine J. Andrews. 5. Called for the next annual union meeting. C. A. Wallace, Mod., R. B. Purcell, C.C.

Jun. 19, 1897, James L. Wyatt. 4. Received by letter Sister Nancy Dawson. 5. Elected the following brethren to represent us in the Association: J. S. Wyatt, J. F. Dowda, H. C. Boling, R. W. Cochran, J. W. Holcomb, and G. B. Haygood, alternate. James L. Wyatt, Mod., R. B. Purcell, C.C.

Jul. 17, 1897, Bros. R. J. Purcell and C. A. Wallace. 5. Collected $1.00 for minutes. C. A. Wallace, Mod., R. B.

Purcell, C.C.

Aug. 14, 1897, Bros. McKinney Pursell and C. A. Wallace. *[no business under any item].* C. A. Wallace, Mod., R. B. Purcell, C.C.

Sep. 18, 1897, Bro. H. T. Ingraim. 5. Elected a preaching committee: G. B. Haygood, H. C. Boling, J. S. Wyatt, J. R. Biddy, J. M. Richards. Elected a finance committee: J. S. Wyatt, G. B. Fletcher, H. C. Boling, A. T. Hester, G. B. Hagood. Elected Bro. C. A. Wallis to attend us as pastor another year. Granted Sister Smallwood a duplicate letter. Granted Sister Sarah Holcomb a letter of dismission. C. A. Wallis, Mod., R. B. Purcell, C.C.

Oct. 16, 1897, Bros. C. S. Hawkins and C. A. Wallis. 5. Granted a letter of dismission to Bro. M. R. C. McGullion. Elected delegates to union meeting. Elected Brethren: G. B. Haygood, R. B. Pursell, H. K. Fletcher, A. T. Hester and B. H. Howard. C. A. Wallis, Mod., R. B. Pursell, C.C.

Nov. 20, 1897, Bros. R. W. Cochran and C. A. Wallis. 2. Preferred charge against a brother for fornication. Appointed C. B. Fowler, G. B. Haygood and G. B. Fletcher to see him. 4. Received by recantation, a Brother. 5. Granted Professor C. B. Fowler leave to teach a singing school provided he will be responsible for any damages. C. A. Wallis, Mod., R. B. Pursell, C.C.

Dec. 18, 1897, Bros. C. A. Wallis and R. W. Cochran. 3. Took up the charge against a brother and excluded him from the fellowship of the church. C. A. Wallis, Mod., R. B. Pursell, C.C.

Feb. 19, 1898, Bros. R. W. Cochran and C. A. Wallis. 2. Preferred charge against a brother for drunkness. Referred the charge till next conference. 5. Granted a letter of dismission to Sister Christopher. Motion carried to have preaching twice a month. Organized a Sunday School. Elected Bro. John W. Holcomb, Supt., and J. H. Ellis Assist. Supt., Elected R. B. Pursell, Sec. C. A. Wallis, Mod., R. B. Pursell, C.C.

Mar. 19, 1898, Bros. M. D. Greene and C. A. Wallis. 3. Took up the charge against a brother for drunkness and received his acknowledgments. 5. Granted letters of dismission to Sister Lula Sewal and Mary Sparks. C. A. Wallis, Mod., R. B. Pursell, C.C.

Apr. 16, 1898, Bros. J. M. Anderson and C. A. Wallis. 5. Called for volunteers to invite Conns Creek, Ophir, Mt. Tabor, New Harmony, Friendship and Mt. Pisgah to be at our communion. Received invitations from Conns Creek and Friendship. C. A. Wallis, Mod., R. B. Pursell, C.C.

May 14, 1898, Bros. Elias Biddy and C. A. Wallis. 2. Preferred a charge against a brother for drunkness and profanity. Referred the charge till next conference. 4. Received by experience Bro. John B. Pruitt. 5. Moved and carried that the old Bible be kept with the church records. C. A. Wallis, Mod., R. B. Pursell, C.C.

Jun. 18, 1898, Bros. C. B. Fowler and C. A. Wallis. 3. Took up the charge against a brother for profanity and bore with him. 4. Received by experience Sister Annie L. Cochran. 5. Elected delegates to union meeting. Elected Brethren: J. S. Wyatt, H. K. Fletcher, G. B. Hagood, J. W. Holcomb, J. F. Dowda, John A. Boling, R. J. M. Pursell and J. H. Ellis, alt. Elected delegates to association. Elected Brethren: John W. Holcomb, J. H. Ellis, J. S. Wyatt, R. W. Cochran, G. B. Hagood. E. A. Cochran. C. A. Wallis, Mod., R. B. Pursell, C.C.

Jul. 16, 1898, Bros. C. A. Wallis and C. B. Fowler. 5. Read the letters to the union meeting and the association. C. A. Wallis, Mod., R. B. Pursell, C.C.

Aug. 20, 1898, Bros. C. A. Wallis and J. L. Hitt. 4. Received by letter Bro. John Williams. 5. Granted letters of dismission to Brethren and Sisters Perry Andrews and wife, Newton Bailey and wife, T. G. Fowler, Annie Ford, and Joanna Cape. C. A. Wallis, Mod., R. B. Pursell, C.C.

Sep. 17, 1898, Bros. R. W. Cochran, M. D. Greene and C. A. Wallis. 4. Received by experience Bro. John T. Dawson. 5. Called a preacher to attend us another year, called Bro. Henry T. Ingram. Motion carried that we ask Bro. Wallis to come back and be with us all he can. Granted a letter of dismission to Bro. John F. Wheeler. C. A. Wallis, Mod., R. B. Pursell, C.C.

Oct. 15, 1898, Bro. A. G. Hembree. Elected Bro. R. W. Cochran, Moderator. 5. Granted letters of dismission to Bro. C. B. Fowler and wife, also to Bro. Clark Stoyles and wife, also to Bro. George Wheeler. R. W. Cochran, Mod. Pro., R. B. Purcell, C.C.

Nov. 19, 1898, Bros. H. T. Ingram and C. A. Wallis. [*No business under any item*]. H. T. Ingram, Mod., R. B. Purcell, C.C.

Jan. 14, 1899, Bro. Elias Biddy. Elected Bro. Clayborne A. Wallis, Moderator. [*No business under any item*]. C. A. Wallis, Mod. Pro., R. B. Purcell, C.C.

Apr. 15, 1899, Bro. H. T. Ingram. 5. Granted letter of dismission to Bro. Joseph B. Chastain. Invited Ophir, Conns Creek, New Harmony, Mt. Pisgah, Friendship, and Mt. Tabor to our communion by volunteers. H. T. Ingram, Mod., R. B. Purcell, C.C.

May 20, 1899, Bros. E. A. Cochran and C. A. Wallis. 2. Preferred a charge against a brother for lying. Moved not to sustain the charge, carried.

Jun. 17, 1899, Bros. H. T. Ingram and E. A. Cochran. 2. Preferred charge against a brother for giving another brother the lie. Excluded him. 5. Appointed Bro. R. J. Pursell, Treasurer. Granted Bro. Louis Nelson a letter of dismission. Election of delegates to association. Elected Brethren: R. J. Pursell, G. B. Hagood, J. W. Holcomb, G. B. Fletcher, Jas. M. Richards and J. R. Biddy, alt. Elected Brethren: J. A. Cantrell, Henry Ellis, F. C. Dowda, Silas Chastain, J. R. Biddy and H. C. Boling, alt. to the union meeting. H. T. Ingram, Mod., R. B. Purcell, C.C.

Jul. 15, 1899, J. L. Wyatt and J. H. Lathem. Elected R. W. Cochran, Mod. 1. Excepted J. L. Wyatt as a visiting brother 2. Motion to receive the acknowledgment of a brother withdrawn until the door of the church is open. Received the acknowledgment of another brother for giving a brother the lie. Received the acknowledgments of an additional brother for drunkness. 4. Received a brother by restoration. 5. Granted Bro. J. S. Wyatt a letter of dismission. R. W. Cochran, Mod. Pro, R. B. Purcell, C.C.

Aug. 19, 1899, Bros. C. S. Hawkins and E. A. Cochran. Elected C. S. Hawkins, Moderator. 2. Received acknowledgements of a brother for stepping aside. 4. Received by letter Sister Leannie Pinson. 5. Granted a letter of dismission to Bro. Will Bryant. C. S. Hawkins, Mod. Pro., R. B. Purcell, C.C.

Sep. 16, 1899, Bro. H. T. Ingram. 4. Received by experience Bro. R. A. Dunigan. 5. Went into the election of a preacher for another year. Elected Bro. Henry T. Ingram. Granted a letter of dismission to Sister Lizzie Durham, also to Bro. Durell Fowler a letter of dismission. Henry T. Ingram, Mod., R. Benj. Pursell, C.C.

Oct. 14, 1899, Bros. R. W. Cochran and C. S. Hawkins. 4. Received by letter Sister H. A. Odem; by a brother by restoration. H. T. Ingram, Mod., R. B. Pursell, C.C.

Nov. 18, 1899, Bro. H. T. Ingram. 4. Received by letter Sister Sarah Greene and Etta Wilkie. 5. Granted Bro. Joseph A. Wyatt a letter of dismission. Granted Sister Lucy Nix a duplicate letter. H. T. Ingram, Mod., R. B. Pursell, C.C.

Dec. 16, 1899, After prayer by Bro. R. W. Cochran, elected Bro. R. W. Cochran, Mod. 2. Preferred a charge against a sister for denying the Baptice Faith by joining the Methodis. Excluded her. Preferred a charge against a brother for drunkness, excluded him. Preferred a charge against another sister for adultery, excluded her. Preferred a charge against another brother for a report of drunkness, referred the charge till next conference. Preferred a charge against an additional brother for drunkness, referred charge till next conference. 5. Appointed a committee of 3 to look after the surveying between two Bros. Appointed Bros. J. W. Holcomb, G. B. Haygood and T. N. Smith. R. W. Cochran, Mod. Pro., R. B. Pursell, C.C.

Jan. 20, 1900, Bro. Elias A. Cochran, Elected E. A. Cochran, Mod. 3. Took up the charge against a brother, and received his acknowledgements. Also received acknowledgements from another brother. E. A. Cochran, Mod. Pro., R. B. Pursell, C.C.

Mar. 17, 1900, Bro. W. S. Norton, Elected W. S. Norton, Mod. 2. Preferred charges against Brethren (seven males) and sisters (five females) for dancing or taking part. Appointed Bros. G. B. Fletcher, G. B. Hagood, and J. J. Holcomb to notify the brethren and sisters of the charges against them. Preferred a charge against a brother for stealing, took up the charge and excluded him. 5. Granted Bedia Wilkie a letter of dismission. W. S. Norton, Mod. Pro., R. B. Pursell, C.C.

Apr. 14, 1900, Bro. H. T. Ingram. 2. Preferred charges against six brethren for swearing, layed them over till next conference. Received the acknowledgements of two brethren for swearing. Received the acknowledgements of another brother for swearing and drunkness. 3. Took up charge against six brethren, and five sisters, received their acknowledgements. Took up the charge against one brother and excluded him. 5. Motion carried to set apart Bro. W. S. Norton for ordination. Received invitations from Conns Creek and Friendship to be at their communion. Set apart Saturday before 3rd Sunday in May for the Ordination. Invited the eldership of Conns Creek, Ball Ground, Massadonia, Mt Pisgah, New Harmony, Friendship to form a presbatery. Invited Conns Creek, Ball Ground, Massadonia, New Harmony, Friendship, Mt. Pisgah to be at our communion, 3rd Sunday in May. H. T. Ingram, Mod., R. B. Pursell, C.C.

May 19, 1900, Bro. W. S. Norton, took intermission of 30 minutes, met in conference. 2. Preferred a charge against a sister for dancing, layed over the charge till next conference. 3. Took up the charge of a brother and excluded him from the fellowship of the church. Took up the charge against another brother and received his acknowledgements. Took up the charge against another three brothers and layed over the charges till next conference and received the acknowledgements of another brother. 5. Granted Sister Ameda Petty a letter of dismission. Went into the examination of Bro. W. S. Norton for Ordination. Appointed Bro. John W. Holcomb, spokeman of the church. Organized a presbatry of the following ministers: John. H. Lathem, John Biddy, Elias Biddy, H. T. Ingram, C. A. Wallis. The following deacons being present: S. L. Coker, A. C. Sewell, T. N. Smith, G. B. Fletcher, J. L. Williams. Elected Bro. Johnny Lathem, Mod. or Chairman. Elected R. B. Pursell, clerk. W. S. Norton, elect for Minister was duly examined by the Presbatery and found worthy of Ordination as minister and was duly performed. Appointed Bro. H. T. Ingram to write out the credentials for Brother W. S. Norton. H. T. Ingram, Mod., R. B. Pursell, C.C.

Jun. 16, 1900, Bro. E. A. Cochran, Elected E. A. Cochran, Moderator. 3. Received acknowledgements of two brethren; Layed over the charges against another brother; took up the charge against a sister and excluded her. 4. Brother A. G. Hembree came forward with a letter, but withdrew. 5. Elected delegates to union meeting as follows: Bros. G. B. Hagood, J. F. Dowda, J. J. Holcomb, J. H. Ellis, and J. W. Holcomb. Elected delegates to Association as follows: J. W. Holcomb, E. A. Cochran, G. B. Hagood, J. F. Dowda and W. S. Norton. Granted W. E. Evans and wife a letter of dismission. E. A. Cochran, Mod. Pro., R. B. Pursell, C.C.

Jul. 14, 1900, Bros. R. W. Cochran and H. T. Ingram. 3. Took up the charge against a brother for profanity and excluded him. Layed the charge of another brother over till next conference. H. T. Ingram, Mod., R. B. Pursell, C.C.

Aug. 18, 1900, Bro. W. S. Norton, Elected W. S. Norton, Mod. 3. Layed over the charge against a brother till next conference. 4. Received by letter Bro. D. M. B. Dobson and wife, Sister Jane Dobson. 5. Granted Bro. M. B. Pruitt a letter of dismission. W. S. Norton, Mod. Pro., R. B. Pursell, C.C.

Sep. 15, 1900, Bros. John Biddy and H. T. Ingram. 3. Took up the charge against a brother for profanity, excluded him. 4. Received by letter Sisters Neely Norton and S. A. Dobson. Restored a brother to the fellowship of the church. 5. Granted Bro. W. D. Davenport a letter of dismission. Elected Bro. H. T. Ingram pastor for another year. Appointed J. F. Dowda on the finance committee. Appointed Bro. T. N. Smith on the preaching committee. H. T. Ingram, Mod., R. B. Pursell, C.C.

Oct. 20, 1900, Bro. H. T. Ingram. 4. Received by letter Bro. J. S. Andrews and wife Sister Jane Andrews. Henry T. Ingram, Mod., R. B. Pursell, C.C.

Dec. 15, 1900, Bro. H. T. Ingram. 5. Granted J. H. Loggins, Samuel Loggins and Robert Loggins and Sisters Lucy Loggins, Mirandy Loggins and Maggie Loggins letters of dismission. H. T. Ingram, Mod., R. B. Pursell, C.C.

Jan. 19, 1901, Bro. E. A. Cochran. 5. Conns Creek invited the eldership of this church to be at the ordination of Bro. A. T. Holcomb Friday before the second Sunday in February. H. T. Ingram, Mod., R. B. Pursell, C.C.

Feb. 16, 1901, Bro. C. A. Wallis, Elected Bro. C. A. Wallis, Moderator. 5. Appointed Brethren R. J. Pursell, J. J. Holcomb, J. M. Richards, H. C. Boling, R. B. Pursell, and W. S. Norton delegates to the Union Meeting at Conns Creek the 5th Sunday in Mch. Commencing Friday before. C. A. Wallis Mod. Pro., R. B. Pursell, C.C.

Apr. 20, 1901, Bro. W. S. Norton, Elected Bro. W. S. Norton, Moderator. 2. Received the acknowledgement of a brother for drunkness. Preferred a charge against another brother for drunkness, referred the charge till next conference. 5. Collected 55 cts. for towels. Invited Conns Creek, Ophir, Mt. Tabor, Mt. Pisgah, Friendship and New Harmony. W. S. Norton, Mod. Pro., R. B. Pursell, C.C.

May 18, 1901, Henry T. Ingram. 3. Took up the charge against a brother for drunkness, received his acknowledgements. 5. Collected 75 cts. to pay for wine. Collected $2.80 for Sister Mason. H. T. Ingram, Mod., R. B. Pursell, C.C.

Jun. 15, 1901, R. W. Cochran and C. B. Fowler, Elected R. W. Cochran [moderator]. 5. Elected Brethren: R. J. Pursell, R. W. Cochran, J. M. Richards, B. F. Howard, J. H. Ellis and J. F. Dowda delegates to the association. R. W. Cochran, Mod. Pro., R. B. Pursell, C. C.

Jul. 20, 1901, Bros. H. T. Ingram and C. B. Fowler. 5. Collected 60 cts. for minutes. Henry T. Ingram, Mod., R. B. Pursell, C.C.

Aug. 17, 1901, 2. Preferred a charge against a sister for fornication, excluded her from fellowship of the church. 5. Set Bro. R. W. Cochran apart for ordination to the full work of the ministry. Invited the eldership of Conns Creek, Ophir, Mt. Tabor, Mt. Pisgah, Friendship, New Harmony, Macedonia and Liberty to be at the ordination Saturday before the 3rd Sunday in Sept. Elected R. J. Pursell, spokesman for the church. J. H. Lathem, Mod Protem., R. B. Pursell, C.C.

Sep. 14, 1901, Bro. H. T. Ingram. 5. Went in to the examination for ordination of Bro. R. W. Cochran. Organized a presbytery as follows: H. T. Ingram, lead in questions, A. T. Holcomb, C. S. Hawkins, C. A. Wallis, Wm. West, J. H. Lathem, Mod. John Biddy, W. S. Norton, A. G. Hembree, Elias Biddy, E. A. Cochran. Elected John Biddy, Moderator and R. B. Pursell, Clerk. R. W. Cochran, elect for ordination as minister was duly examined by the presbytery and found worthy of ordination and was duly performed. Appointed W. S. Norton to write the credentials. Called a preacher for another year, called A. J. Henderson. H. T. Ingram, Mod., R. B. Pursell, C.C.

Oct. 19, 1901, Bro. H. T. Ingram. 4. Received by letter Bro. J. M. Leonard. H. T. Ingram, Mod., R. B. Pursell, C.C.

Nov. 16, 1901, A. J. Henderson. *[No business under any item].* Andrew Henderson, Mod., R. B. Pursell, C.C.

Jan. 19, 1902, Bro A. J. Henderson. 5. Granted Sister Lyle a letter of dismission. A. J. Henderson, Mod., H. C. Boling, C.C. Pro.

Apr. 19, 1902, Bros. A. J. Henderson and John Biddy. 5. Invited Conns Creek, Ophir, Mt. Tabor, Mt. Pisgah, Friendship, New Harmony and Liberty to be with us at our communion the 3rd Sunday in May. Received an invitation from Conns Creek to be at their communion the 2nd Sunday in May. Collected 71 cts. to buy wine. Andrew J. Henderson, Mod., R. B. Pursell, C.C.

May 17, 1902, Bro. R. A. Dunigan and R. W. Cochran.5. Elected delegates to union meeting. Elected Brethren: B. F. Howard, G. B. Hagood, R. A. Dunigan, James Richards, R. J. Pursell and J. H. Ellis. R. W. Cochran, Mod. Pro., R. B. Pursell, C.C.

Jun. 14, 1902, Bros. J. L. Wyatt and A. J. Henderson. 4. Received by letter Bro. Robert Warren and wife. 5. Elected delegates to the association. Elected Brethren: R. J. Pursell, J. H. Ellis, G. B. Hagood, R. W. Cochran, H. C. Boling and R. B. Pursell. Collected $2.50 for Bro. J. F. Dowda. A. J. Henderson, Mod.

Jul. 19, 1902, Bros. R. W. Cochran and A. J. Henderson. 5. Collected 30 cts. for minutes. A. J. Henderson, Mod., R. B. Pursell, C.C.

Aug. 17, 1902, Bros. R. W. Cochran and A. J. Henderson. 4. Received a brother by restoration. 5. Granted a letter of dismission to Bros. I. C. T. Cox, John Williams and John Nelson. Collected 1.84 for Bro. Andrews/Anderson? A. J. Henderson, Mod., R. B. Pursell, C.C.

Sep. 20, 1902, T. J. Clayton, Elected Bro. T. J. Clayton, Mod. 5. Went into election of a pastor for another year. Suspended the regular order of business and elected Bro. A. J. Henderson by acclamation. Collected for pastor $9.50. T. J. Clayton, Mod. Pro., R. B. Pursell, C.C.

Oct 19, 1902, Bro. A. J. Henderson. 5. Collected for pastor $3.75. A. J. Henderson, Mod., R. B. Pursell, C.C.

Book 1; 1882 – 1902 Membership

t in first column indicates person was still a member in 1903 and name was <u>transferred</u> to book two

* Information following any asterisk indicates information was listed in minutes, but not in roll.

Last name in () indicates maiden name; Abbreviations include Let/Letter; Exp/Experience; m/married; w/o wife of; h/o husband of; s/o son/of; d/o daughter/of; bur/buried; b/born; d/died

	Last name	First name	Middle name	How/when Received, Other Info	How/when Dismissed, Other Info	*Annotated Remarks; items not listed in church roll (full/maiden name; spouse; birth-death; buried at HBC)*
	Anderson	J.	L.	*Exp Sep 1882	Let Feb 16, 1884	
	Anderson	Mary	A.		Let Feb 16, 1884	
	Andrews	Mary			Dead	
	Andrews	Perry		Let May 15, 1897	Let Aug 20, 1898	*Wilburn Perry*
	Andrews	Catherine	J.	Let May 15, 1897	Let Aug 20, 1898	*w/o Perry, middle name: Jane*
t	Andrews	J.	S.	Let Oct 20, 1900	Deacon, Died	*Died Dec 1902*
t	Andrews	Jane		Let Oct 20, 1900		*w/o J.S Andrews*
t	Andrews	Lou	A	Exp Aug 1902		
t	Andrews	Mattie	M.	Exp Aug 1897		*(Green) 1880-1951, bur HBC*
t	Biddy	Richards				*John Richard, 1841-1927 m Susan Hardin*
	Blackstock	Fannie			Let Jul 14, 1883	*Dead*
	Burton	Mary	V.		Let Dec 14, 1889	*1865-1958*
	Boling	Lowery		Let	Let Jan 19, 1889	
t	Boling	H.	C.			*Henry Clay, 1839-1910, bur HBC*

	Last name	First name	Middle name	How/when Received, Other Info	How/when Dismissed, Other Info	Annotated Remarks; items not listed in church roll (full/maiden name; spouse; birth-death; buried at HBC)
t	Boling	E.	R.			Emily Rebecca (Green), 1847-1909 w/o Henry Clay Boling, bur HBC
t	Boling	M.	A. Richards	Exp Aug 1884		M (Mabel) A Boling married ? Richards
	Burgess	D.?	F.	Exp Aug 1884		
	Bredges ?	W.	M	Exp Aug 1884		
	Barnwell	D.	M.	Exp	Dead	Drury Madison, 1852-1888
t	Barnwell	E. ~~Elbert~~ or Eliza	J.	Exp Aug 19, 1887		Elbert? Or Eliza Jane (Watson) Barnwell, 1858-1951
	Biddy	S.	E.	Exp Aug 19, 1887	Died Jul 4, 1901	Susan Elizabeth, 1845-1900/01
	Bailey	Newton		Let Aug 5, 1888	Let Aug 20, 1898	Abt 1858-
	Bailey	Ella		Let Aug 5, 1888	*Let Jul 14 1883 Let Aug 20, 1898	1855-1912, w/o Newton Bailey
t	Bryant	Thomas		Let Aug 5, 1888		1851-1923, bur HBC
t	Bryant	Lucy		Let Aug 5, 1888		Lucy Ann (Garrett), 1856-1922, bur HBC, w/o Thomas Bryant
	Baker	L., *Lena		Exp Aug 18 1888?	Let Oct 1893; dead?	"Sister"
	Burton	W. / Wm.	H.	Exp Sep 18, 1887	Let Dec 14, 1889	William, 1867-1942
	Barnwell	Benj	F. Frank		Let Jan 19, 1889	Benjamin Frank
	Barnwell	Sarah	S.		Let Jan 19, 1889	w/o Frank Barnwell
	Biddy	J.	M.	Exp Sep 15, 1889	Died Sep 5, 1892	
	Brady	W.	W.	Exp Sep 15, 1889		
t	Bryant	J.	T.	Exp Aug 31, 1890		John T., 1871-1914, wife: Fannie E. (Kelley), bur HBC
t	Bryant	G.	M.	Exp Aug 31, 1890		George Mansell
	Bryant	W.	A.	Exp Aug 31, 1890	Let Aug 19, 1899	William Andrew
t	Bryant	Vena	Dooly	Exp Aug 31, 1890		Margaret Louvenia (Bryant) m Mr. Dooly
t	Boling	W.	T.	Exp Aug 31, 1890		William Thompson, 1868-1929, bur HBC
t	Boling	J.	L.	Exp Aug 31, 1890		Joseph Lowery, 1872-1926, bur HBC
	Bryant	F.	E.	Exp Aug 31, 1890	See Durham	Frances Elizabeth (Bryant) Durham
t	Biddy	George		Exp Sep 15, 1889		
	Biddy	John	Thomas	Exp Sep 1893		
t	Boling	R.	Jackson	Exp Sep 1893		Reuben Jackson
t	Bryant	Susan	E.	Exp Sep 1893	See Kelly	Susan Eveline "Evie"(Bryant) b 1880 - m Robert A.E. Kelly
	Baker	Laura			dead	

	Last name	First name	Middle name	How/when Received, Other Info	How/when Dismissed, Other Info	*Annotated Remarks; items not listed in church roll (full/maiden name; spouse; birth-death; buried at HBC)*
	Baker	Mc			Let Nov 19, 1895	
t	Baker	Mrs.				
t	Brady	Sally		Exp Sep 1894	Priest	
t	Bryant	Fannie		Let Apr 18 1896		*Fannie (Kelly) m John T. Bryant*
t	Baker	Mc		Let Nov 1896		*Bro Mac*
t	Baker	Eliza		Let Aug 1897		
t	Boling	Pruid		Exp Aug 1892		*Mary Prude (Green) Boling 1877-1924 Bur HBC, wife of John Franklin Boling*
t	Boling	John	F.	Exp Aug 1897		*John Franklin, 1873-1926, bur HBC*
t	Boling	Martha		Let Aug 1899		
t	Biddy	Lula		Exp Sep 1899		
t	Biddy	John		Let Aug 1900		
t	Biddy	Elisabeth		Let Aug 1900		*Sarah Elizabeth Biddy*
t	Biddy	Nicie	L.	Let Aug 1900		*1877-1960*
t	Biddy	A.	R.	Let Aug 1900		*1875-1910*
t	Biddy	A.	L.	Let Aug 1900		*? transferred to book 2 ?*
t	Biddy					*Emory?*
	Biddy	John	Thomas		Died May 13, 1901	
t	Biddy	M.	Alma	Exp Sep 1900		*Martha Alma (1887-1965) m. Fletcher Bryant*
t	Boling	Nettie	R.	Exp Sep 1900	See Pearson	*m. Edgar Pearson, 1882-1950 bur HBC*
t	Bryant	Fletcher	A.	Exp Sep 1900		*1884-1949*
t	Bloodworth	G.	Milton	Exp Sep 1900		*George Milton, 1884-1944*
t	Bryant	F.	Belle	Exp Sep 1900		*Fannie Belle (Price) m. George Mancel Bryant*
t	Bryant	H.	Jackson	Exp Aug 1902		
t	Brooks	Joseph	W.	Exp Aug 1902		
t	Brooks	Richard		Exp Aug 1902		*1882-1956, m. Adeline ?*
	Crenshaw	W.	T.		Let Jun 20 1885	*William T. Crenshaw, 1852-? m. Martha ?*
	Carnes	J.	D.		Let Aug 16 1890	*Jefferson D. 1861-1943, m. Caleba (Bobo)*
t	Cochran	E.	A.		Ordained Minister, Nov 1884	*Elias A. 1845-1931, bur HBC*
	Cox	Nancy			Let *Sep 21, 1884? Jun 18, 1885?	*1884 in minutes, 1885 in roll*

	Last name	First name	Middle name	How/when Received, Other Info	How/when Dismissed, Other Info	*Annotated Remarks; items not listed in church roll (full/maiden name; spouse; birth-death; buried at HBC)*
	Carnes	Calebia	D.		Let Aug 16 1890	*Caleba (Bobo) 1863-1933, m. J.D. Carnes*
	Christopher	*B	*J		Let Oct 20, 1883	*listed as B J in minutes*
	Carnes	Sally			Let Oct 18, 1890	
	Cox	Syntha			*Let Aug 15,1885 or Let Sep 4, 1885	*Cyntha*
	Castleberry	Missouria	S.	Let Oct 20, 1883	Let Jun 16, 1885	
t	Cochran	R.	W.	Exp	Ordained Minister	*Robert W., d. Aug 24, 1937, bur HBC*
	Christopher	B.	J.		Let May 17, 1886	
t	Cochran	M.	M.			*Matilda M. m. R.W. Cochran, d 07 Nov 1925, bur HBC*
t	Chastain	J.	B.	Let Jul 16, 1887		*Joel Benjamin or Benny 1853-1928?*
	Crow	Mary		Let Aug 19, 1887	Let Jun 19, 1889	
	Collins	W.	A.	Exp Aug 19, 1887	Let Oct 20, 1888	*Bro.*
	Cagle	Mary		Exp Sep 15, 1889	Let Aug 18, 1894	
	Collins	Lydia		Exp Sep 15, 1889	Let Mar 19, 1892	
t	Cordell	Josia		Exp Aug 24, 1890		
t	Chastain	N, Sister	A	Exp Sep 1892		*1852-1917, Nancy Adaline, m J. Ben Chastain*
t	Chastain	J.	F.	Exp Sep 1892		*John Franklin*
	Chastain	Margaret		Let Oct 15, 1892	Let Nov 1901	
	Chastain	Joseph	B.	Exp Sep 1893	Let Apr 15, 1899	*Joe Brown, 1875-1958*
	Chastain	J.	Silas		Let Nov 1901	*1873-1905*
t	Cantrell	M	O. "Tavy"	Exp Aug 1897		*Mary Octavia "Tavie" Cantrell 1882-1974*
t	Cochran	Julia	J.	Exp Aug 1897	See Dawson in D	*1879-1970, m John T. Dawson*
t	Chastain	A.	Bennie	Exp Aug 1897		*Alford Bennie, 1884-1926*
	Cochran	Sarah	Emmie		Died Jun 30, 1901	*Sarah Emmaline (Fowler), 1834-1901, 2nd w/o Rev. E.A. Cochran*
t	Chastain	O.	Agathy	Exp Aug 1897		*m. John Franklin Chastain*
	Cantrell	R.	M.	Let Sep 1897		*Raymond*
t	Cantrell	J.	A.	Let Sep 1897		*James Alfred*
t	Cantrell	G.	A.	Let Sep 1897		*Georgia*
t	Cochran	Annie	L.	Exp Jun 18, 1898	See Haygood	
t	Chastain	Elijah	C.	Exp Aug 1899		*Elijah Coleman, 1886-1948*
t	Cannon	Lesom		Exp Aug 1899		
t	Cannon	Florence		Exp Aug 1899		

	Last name	First name	Middle name	How/when Received, Other Info	How/when Dismissed, Other Info	*Annotated Remarks; items not listed in church roll (full/maiden name; spouse; birth-death; buried at HBC)*
t	Cannon	Elmore	L.	Exp Sep 1900		*1887-1957, Elmer Cranston, h/o Minnie Thacker*
t	Cannon	F.	Edna			*1886-1970, Florence Edna (Cannon) m. Joseph Carl Thacker in 1908*
t	Chastain	George	B.			
t	Cantrell	R.	M.			*Raymond Marion, 1879-1940, bur HBC, s/o Alfred and Georgia Cantrell;*
t	Collier	Nancy	J.	Exp Sep 1901		
t	Collier	Mary		Exp Sep 1901		
t	Cantrell	Lula		Exp Sep 1899		*Lula Viola (Hester), 1883-1954, m Raymond Cantrell, bur HBC*
t	Collier	Linie	A.	Aug 1902		
	Cox	I.	C. T.	Aug 17 1902	Let Aug 17, 1902	*Bro.*
t	Crow	Ader	L	Exp Aug 1899		*Ada Lucinda (Nelson)*
t	Cape	Eveline		Let Mar 1898		
	Dowda	Bellymay		Let Jul 20, 1885	Let Sep 20, 1890	*1862-1901, bur HBC, Ellemanda B. (Mitchell) m John F. Dowda*
	Dowda	J.	F.	Exp Aug 20, 1885	Let Sep 20, 1890	*John Franklin, 1865-1902, Bur HBC*
	Dobson	William		Let	Let Aug 1892 By death Oct 26, 1950	*1861-1950, William Monroe Dobson, bur HBC*
	Dobson	M.	E.	Exp Aug 19, 1887	Let Aug 1892	
	Davenport	David		Let Aug 20, 1890		
t	Davenport	Sarah	J.	Let Aug 20, 1890		*Sarah J. (Heygood)*
	Dobson	S.	A.	Exp Aug 31, 1890	Let Sep 17, 1892	
	Dowda	Bellyuray		Let Aug 1897	Died Feb 24, 1901	*Bell, bur HBC, m. John Franklin Dowda*
	Dowda	J.	F.	Let Aug 1897	Died Sep 26, 1902	*John Franklin, bur HBC*
t	Dawson	Nancy		Let Jun 19, 1897		
t	Dawson	John	T.	Exp Sep 1898		
t	Dawson	Julia	J.	Exp Aug 1897		
t	Dooly	Vena		Exp Aug 31, 1890		*(Bryant)*
	Durham	F.	Elizabeth	Exp Aug 31, 1890	Let Sep 16, 1899	*"Lizzie" (Bryant)*
	Dunigan	Raymond		Exp Sep 16, 1899		*1877-1929, Raymond Aulelua Dunigan*
	Dunigan	Mary		Exp Sep 16, 1899		*Mary L (Hester), 1879-1951*
	Dobson	D.	M. B.	Let Aug 14, 1900 Ordained Deacon	Let Nov 15, 1902	*David Miles Berry Dobson, 1851-1909*

	Last name	First name	Middle name	How/when Received, Other Info	How/when Dismissed, Other Info	*Annotated Remarks; items not listed in church roll (full/ maiden name; spouse; birth-death; buried at HBC)*
	Dobson	Jane		Let Aug 14, 1900	Let Nov 15, 1902	*Sarah Jane (Hogan), 2nd wife of David Dobson*
t	Dobson	S.	Ader	Let Sep 15, 1900		*Susan Adia, 1876-1961*
	Davenport	David			Let Sep 1900	**W. D.*
t	Dowda	Ida	B.	Exp Sep 1900		
t	Dowda	William	D.	Exp Sep 1900		
t	Dobson	J.	Simeon	Exp Sep 1900		*1878-1943, Jesse Simeon, m. Lou Dora Watson*
t	Dobson	W.	Neely	Exp Sep 1900		*1881-1975, William Neely*
t	Eaton	Jesse	W.			*Jesse Washington, 1855-1927*
	Evans	Wesley		Let Mar 15,1884	Let Dec 15, 1888 *Let Jun 16 1900	
	Evans	H.	L.	Let Mar 15, 1884	Let Dec 15, 1888 *Let Jun 16 1900	*Harriett, *w/o Wesley Evans*
	Eaton	A.	J.	Let Aug 20, 1885	Dead	*Andrew Jackson, 1833-1890, CSA, bur HBC*
	Elliott	Thomas		Let Aug 19, 1887	Let Jun 14, 1890	*W. Thomas*
	Elliott	Margaret		Let Aug 19, 1887	Let Jun 14, 1890	
t	Eaton	Sylpha		Let Aug 19, 1887		*Or Zilphia, 1857-1928, m. Jessie W. Eaton*
	Elliott	Minnie		Let Aug 19, 1887	Let Jun 14, 1890	
	Elliott	M.	J.	Exp Aug 1888	Let Jun 14, 1890	**Mattie*
	Eaton	Ovelene		Exp Aug 31, 1890	See Harden	*m. Larkin Harden*
t	Ellis	J.	H.	Let Mar 20, 1897		*J. Henry, 1862-1926, bur HBC*
t	Ellis	Catharine		Let Mar 20, 1897		*1866-1948, Mary Catharine (Haygood), m J. Henry Ellis*
t	Ellis	Rosanna	M.	Exp Aug 1897	See Pruitt	*Mary Rosanna Ellis m. John B. Pruitt*
t	Eaton	Rachel	E.	Exp Aug 1897		*(Speer) 1879-1971*
t	Ellis	John	B.	Exp Aug 1899		*John Barry, 1885-1915*
t	Ellis	J.	Elbert	Exp Sep 1900		*James Elbert, 1888-1932, bur HBC*
t	Eaton	L.	Daisy	Exp Sep 1901	Let Jul 1904	
	Fowler	C.	B.	Liberated Aug 15, 1896 Tombstone says joined HBC by experience 1888	Let Oct 15, 1898	*Charlie, 1855-1925, m. Georgia Campbell, bur HBC, Tombstone says joined HBC by experience 1888*
	Fowler	Wiley			Let	*m. Martha Young?*
	Fowler	T.	G.		Let Aug 20, 1898	
	Fowler	C.	A.			
	Fowler	W.	P.		Let Apr 19, 1884	*Wiley Petty Fowler?*

	Last name	First name	Middle name	How/when Received, Other Info	How/when Dismissed, Other Info	*Annotated Remarks; items not listed in church roll (full/ maiden name; spouse; birth-death; buried at HBC)*
t	Fowler	C.	R.			*Bro. or G. R.?*
t	Fowler	Ransom		*Exp Aug 1882		
	Fowler	Sarah	Emaline		See Cochran	*1834-1901, m. E.A. Cochran, Bur HBC*
	Floyed	Mary			Let Oct 20, 1883	*in minutes, listed as Mary Fowler?*
t	Fowler	Margaret				*(Sando)*
t	Freeman	Charity				
t	Fowler	Lucy		Charley's Mother		*1808-1902, Lucinda "Lucy" Elizabeth, w/o William M. Fowler*
t	Fowler	Mary	M.			
	Fowler	Lydia			Let Oct 19, 1895	
t	Fowler	Mary	E.			*See Bryant?*
	Fowler	Martha			Let Mar 14, 1885	
	Fowler	E.	C.	Emma Cochran	Died Jun 30, 1901	*?*
	Fowler	Dora		Exp Sep 1882	Let Oct 20, 1883	*add'l copy of let Feb 17, 1896*
	Fowler	Jane		Jane Cochran	Died	*1st w/o E.A. Cochran, 1830-1888, bur HBC*
	Fowler	Durell		Let Sep 15, 1883	Let Sep 1899	
	Fitts	J.	W.	Let Oct 20, 1883	Let Aug 15, 1886 *Let Apr 1910	*Jesse W., m. Mary Jane (Green)*
	Fowler	J.	R.		Let Oct 20 1883	
	Ford	Annie		Let Mar 15, 1884	Let Aug 20, 1898	
t	Floyed	Thomas		Exp Aug 1884		*Also Floyd*
	Floyed	M.	J.	Exp Aug 1884		*Mary Jane (Purcell ?) Bates, m Thomas R. Floyd on 13 Apr 1871 in Cherokee Co GA, Mary Jane was sister to McKinney Purcell*
	Fowler	S.	F.?	Exp Aug 1884	Let Oct 19, 1895	*Sally*
	Fowler	William		Exp Aug 20, 1885	Let Sep 14, 1895	
t	Fletcher	G.	B.	Let Jan 19, 1889	Deacon	*George Barto "Bart," 1862-1932, bur HBC, m. 1st: Sallie Ledbetter 2nd: Rhoda J.?*
t	Fletcher	H.	K.	Let Apr, 1888		*Hezekiah Kelly, 1860-1926, bur HBC, m. Augusta (Hester)*
t	Fletcher	Myra		Let Apr, 1888	See Hogan	*1821-1908*
	Fowler	W.	A.	Exp Aug 31, 1890		*Will*
t	Fowler	G.	C.	Exp Aug 31, 1890		*George*
	Fowler	Mary		Exp Aug 1891	See Sparks?	
	Fowler	Lular		Exp Aug 1891	Let Mar 1898	*? m William Washington Fowler?*
	Fowler	Joannar		Exp Aug 1891	Let Aug 1898	

	Last name	First name	Middle name	How/when Received, Other Info	How/when Dismissed, Other Info	*Annotated Remarks; items not listed in church roll (full/ maiden name; spouse; birth-death; buried at HBC)*
	Fowler	Lucey		Exp Aug 1891	Let Oct 19, 1895	
	Fowler	Tank		Exp Aug 1891	Let Oct 19, 1895	
	Fowler	Wiley		Exp Aug 1891		
	Fowler	George		Exp Sep 1893		
t	Fletcher	Augusta	H.	Exp Aug 1887		*Augusta Azalee (Hester), 1870-1949, m Hezekiah K. Fletcher, bur HBC*
	Fowler	Lindia			Let Aug 15, 1896	*Lindy*
t	Fowler	Sallie	L.	Exp Aug 1897		
t	Fuller	Savilla	R.	Exp Aug 1897		*(Martin), 1880-1973, m William Fuller*
t	Fuller	W.	I. Zeir	Exp Aug 1897		*William Isaiah, Zear, 1873-1930*
t	Fowler	William		Let Aug 1897		
t	Fowler	Theodocia		Let Aug 1897		
t	Fletcher	Sally	A.	Exp Aug 17, 1887		*Sarah Azalee (Ledbetter), 1869-1903, 1st w/o G Barto Fletcher, bur HBC*
	Fowler	Georgia	Ann		Let Oct 15, 1898	*1853-1924, bur HBC, (Campbell m Charley B Fowler) Tombstone says joined HBC by experience 1887*
t	Floyd	Sidney	W.	Exp Aug 1899		
t	Floyd	Lydia		Exp Aug 1899		
t	Floyd	Nettie		Exp Aug 1899		*B abt 1884*
t	Floyd	Armanda		Exp Aug 1899		*m George "Floyd" Roper*
t	Fowler	Annie	L.	Exp Sep 1900		
t	Fowler	Johnny	A.	Exp Sep 1900		
t	Fowler	W.	Thomas	Exp Sep 1900		*William? Thomas*
t	Floyd	Cora	L.	Exp Sep 1900		
t	Fitts	Charley	F.	Exp Sep 1900		
t	Floyd	Amanda	S.	Let Sep 1900		*Sis?*
t	Green	Thomas	E.			*Edward, bur HBC, m Elizabeth?*
t	Green	Joseph	E.			
	Green	Martha			Died Jul 17, 1899	
t	Green	Nancy	L.			*m Joseph Green, 1850-1928, bur HBC*
	Gibson	S.	A.		Dead	
	Gibson	A.				
t	Green	Mary	Jane		see Fitts new book	*m Jesse W Fitts*
t	Green	Elizabeth				
	Garrett	W.	A.	Exp Aug 19 1887		

	Last name	First name	Middle name	How/when Received, Other Info	How/when Dismissed, Other Info	*Annotated Remarks; items not listed in church roll (full/ maiden name; spouse; birth-death; buried at HBC)*
t	Gilliland	O.	I.	Exp Aug 5 1888	See Richards	*Octavy I (Gilliland)*
t	Grimes	Henry		Let Apr 1888		
t	Greene	Pruid		Exp Aug 1889	See Boling	*Mary Prude (Green) Boling 1877-1924, bur HBC, w/o John Franklin Boling*
	Greene	E.	O.	Exp Sep 1892		*Bro Ed*
	Gilliland	S.	Lula	Exp 1893		
t	Greene	Mattie	M.	Exp Aug 1897	See Andrews	*(Green) 1880-1951, bur HBC by W.J. Andrews*
t	Greene	Mary	E.	Exp Aug 1897		
t	Greene	Mary	E. (babe)	Exp Aug 1897		
t	Greene	Parillee		Let Aug 1885		*Perry Lee (Richards), 1866-1918, m Jesse Green*
t	Greene	Sarah		Let Nov 1899		
t	Greene	Maud	M.	Exp Sep 1900		
t	Groover	Will	J.	Exp Sep 1900		*William, 1851-1926, 1st m Judy, 2nd m Sarah*
t	Gillstrap	L.	Daisy	Exp Sep 1900		
t	Greene	Lou		Sep 1900		
	Grimes	Martha			Let Sep 1901	
t	Howard	Elisha				
	Howard	B.	H.		Died Jan 8, 1901	*Benjamin Harrison*
t	Howard	B.	F.			*Benjamin Franklin, "Bud"*
	Hawkins	F.	L.		Let Oct 20, 1886	**Bro Fed*
	Hester	Joseph	S.			*1846-1906, bur HBC*
t	Hester	A.	T.			*Andrew Thomas? 1847-1910, m Elizabeth Davis?*
	Howard	W.	L.	*Let Mar 16, 1883, Licensed preacher	Let Nov 17, 1883	*1857-1929, W L D, Lic Preacher*
t	Howard	L.	H.			
	Holcombe	Sarah			*Let Aug 1885 Let Sep 1897	
	Howard	Jane			Died June 13, 1900	*w/o Benjamin H Howard*
t	Howard	Mary			See Harbin	
	Hawkins	M.	E.		Let Oct 20, 1886	*w/o F L/Fed, Mary Elizabeth (Cobb)*
	Hester	Mary			dead	*1812-1887?*
t	Hester	E.	J.			*Eliza Jane (Jefferson) m Joseph B Hester, 1819-1936*
	Howard	Anna	C.			

	Last name	First name	Middle name	How/when Received, Other Info	How/when Dismissed, Other Info	*Annotated Remarks; items not listed in church roll (full/maiden name; spouse; birth-death; buried at HBC)*
	Hogan	Bell			Let May 16, 1885	
t	Harden	S.	A.			
t	Howard	Victoria			Bud's wife	*Harriett Victoria (Cole) Howard*
t	Hester	E.	C.			
	Hardy	Susan		Let Dec 1882	Let Dec 1894	
t	Harden	Susan		Let Dec 1882		
	Howard	Susie	E. McDaniel			
	Howard	R.	E.		Let Nov 17, 1883	*Sister*
	Howard	Sarah		Let	Let Jun 16, 1884	
	Howard	Julia			*Let Dec 20, 1885	
	Harbin	J.	W.	Let Apr 19, 1884	Let Jul 1894	
	Harbin	Mary	H.	Let Apr 19, 1884	*Let Aug 1883 Let July 1894	*m J W Harbin*
	Holt	John	W.	Exp Aug 19, 1884	Let Oct 20, 1884	
	Holt	Jasper		Exp Aug 19, 1884	Let Oct 20, 1884	
	Hosey	S.	E.	Exp 1884	*Let Apr 20, 1895	
	Holt	Manerva		Let Mar 14 1885	died	*m John*
	Hosey	J.	E.	Exp Aug 1884	*Let Apr 20, 1895	*April 20, 1895 J. E. Hosey and daughter, dismissed by letter*
t	Holt	Lena		Let Aug 1891		
	Hosey	M.	M.	Exp Aug 20, 1885		
	Howard	M.	L.	Exp Aug 20, 1885	Died Aug 14, 1896	
t	Harden	J.	D.	Exp Aug 20, 1885		
	Howard	J.	C.	Let Jun 14, 1890	Let	
	Hitt	D.	K.	Let May 17, 1886 Let Apr 17, 1886		
	Hitt	M.	J. A.	Let May 17, 1886		**w/o D K Hitt*
	Hodgeas	Mrs.			Let Feb 17, 1887	*"Sister"*
	Hester	A.	A.	Exp Aug 19, 1887	See Fletcher	*Augusta Azalee (Hester) m Hezikiah K Fletcher Bur HBC*
	Hardy	M.	H.	Let Oct 1887 Let Feb 1888	Let Aug 16, 1890	
	Hardy	M.	A.	Let Oct 1887 Let Feb 1888	Let Aug 16, 1890	*w/o M H Hardy*

	Last name	First name	Middle name	How/when Received, Other Info	How/when Dismissed, Other Info	*Annotated Remarks; items not listed in church roll (full/maiden name; spouse; birth-death; buried at HBC)*
	Hardin	Eliza		Exp	Died Apr 23, 1889	
t	Hardin	T.	J.	Exp Sep 15, 1889		*Thomas J. m Mary Elizabeth Stephens*
	Hardin	R.	L.	Exp Sep 15, 1889		*Robert Lee, 1874-1960*
	Hardy	J, Bro	N.	Exp Sep 15, 1889	Let Dec 1894	*"Bro"*
	Hardy	F, Sister	I.	Exp Sep 15, 1889	(Gilstrap) Let Dec 1894	
t	Hardy	C.	A.	Exp Aug 31, 1890		
t	Haygood	S.	G.	Exp Aug 31, 1890		*1876-1935, Seldon/Sellivan Green Haygood/Hagood, m Mattie Wallace, bur HBC*
t	Hamilton	J.	B.	Exp Aug 31, 1890		
	Hamilton	Sarah		Exp Aug 31, 1890		
t	Hester	Ellen	White	Exp Aug 31, 1890	See White	*1872-1933, Ellen Clara (Hester) m John Bullock White*
t	Hester	Mattie		Exp Aug 31, 1890	See Pursell	*1875-1951, "Martha A." m Thomas Benjamin Pursell*
t	Hardin	Ida		Exp Aug 31, 1890		*m J. H. Farmer*
	Holcombe	Martha	Martin	Exp Aug 31, 1890	See Martin	
t	Holcombe	J.	J.	Let Oct 17, 1891		*James J., 1864-1937, bur HBC*
t	Holcombe	Lou		Let Oct 17 1891		*Louise, 1862-1927, bur HBC, shares grave marker with J J Holcombe*
	Hardy	C, Bro.	R	Exp Aug 1892	Let Dec 1894	*"Bro"*
t	Haygood	J.	E.	Exp Aug 1892		*James Elmer, 1881-1931, bur HBC by 2 wives: Annie and May*
	Haygood	J.	S.	Exp Aug 1892		*John Sullivan, 1878-1944, m Tommy Etta, bur HBC*
t	Holcomb	S.	D. "Bud"	Exp Sep 1893		*Sherman Davis "Bud", m Alice Dora Wilkie, 1878-1962, bur HBC*
t	Holcomb	John	W.	Let Sep 1893		
t	Holcomb	S.	D. "Mony"	Let Sep 1893	See Howard	*Monie Holcomb Howard*
t	Holcomb	Cansady		Let Sep 1893		*(Haygood) 1844-1927, m John W Holcomb, bur HBC*
t	Hardin	Charley		Exp 1893		
t	Howard	Emma	D.	Exp Aug 1902		
t	Howard	L.	May	Exp Aug 1902		
t	Holcomb	Bertha	S.	Exp Aug 1902		
t	Haygood	Annie	L	Exp Jun 18, 1898		*(Cochran)*

	Last name	First name	Middle name	How/when Received, Other Info	How/when Dismissed, Other Info	*Annotated Remarks; items not listed in church roll (full/ maiden name; spouse; birth-death; buried at HBC)*
t	Hester	Laura	J.	Exp Sep 1900		*1881-1954, Laura Jane (Hester) m Joseph Aaron Wyatt*
t	Hester	William	H.	Exp Sep 1900		*1879-1905*
t	Herring	A.	Webb	Exp Sep 1900		*b 1881*
t	Howard	G.	Walter	Exp Sep 1900		
	Hawkins	Maud	M.	Exp Sep 1900		*Maude b abt 1887*
t	Hester	May		Let Aug 1898		*May Swinford (Hester) Thrasher*
t	Hester	Lula		Exp Sep 1899	See Cantrell	*Lula Viola (Hester), 1883-1954, m Raymond Cantrell*
t	Hester	Joseph	S.			*Died 1906*
t	Higgins	Mamie		Exp Aug 1899		
t	Higgins	Lizzie		Exp Aug 1899		
	Holcomb	Homer	L.	Exp Aug 1899		
t	Holcomb	W	Henry	Exp Aug 1899		
t	Holcomb	Cora	L.	Exp Aug 1897		*(White)*
t	Haygood	Lizzie		Exp Aug 1897		*Died Jan 24, 1903*
t	Holcomb	John	T.	Exp Aug 1897		
t	Hester	L.	Dora	Exp Aug 1885		*Dora (Wheeler) 1866-1937, bur HBC with John Hester, 1869- 1916*
t	Howard	S.	D. "Mon-ie"	Let Sep 1893		*(Holcomb)*
t	Hogan	Myria		Apr 1888		*1821-1908, Susanna Myra Brady Fletcher m William Hogan, bur HBC*
t	Hardin	Ovelene		Exp Aug 1890		*(Eaton), m Larkin Hardin*
t	Hester	Mary	E.	Exp Aug 1897	See Greene	
t	Harden	Annie	O.	Exp Aug 1897		*See Holcomb?*
t	Harden	F.	Olie	Exp Aug 1897		*(Green)*
t	Hagood	I.	Lizzie	Exp Aug 1897		*Died Jan 24, 1903*
t	Haygood	G.	B.	Let Nov 1896		*1848-1925, Bro Greene B, bur HBC*
t	Haygood	Soushannah		Let Nov 1896		*1844-1922, Suseana (Mosteller) bur HBC, w/o G B Haygood*
t	Ingraim	J.	L.	Exp Aug 1892		*James Lewis, s/o James J. Ingraim*
t	Ingraim	J.	J.	Let Aug 1892		*James Jeff Ingraim*
t	Ingraim	Farriba		Let Aug 1892		*m James J Ingraim*
t	Ingraim	T.	G. W.	Exp Aug 1892		*Thomas, s/o James J. Ingraim*
	Jones	T.	B.		Let Sep 17, 1883	*Bro*
	Jones	Susan	E.	Let Aug 19, 1888	Let Oct 19, 1895	*m Wm Jones*
	Jones	Wm		Exp Aug 31, 1890	Let Oct 19, 1895	
t	Kemp	Mary	D.	Exp Aug 19, 1884		*See Law/Low*

	Last name	First name	Middle name	How/when Received, Other Info	How/when Dismissed, Other Info	*Annotated Remarks; items not listed in church roll (full/maiden name; spouse; birth-death; buried at HBC)*
t	Kelly	Susan	E.	Exp Sep 1893		*Susan Eveline "Evie"(Bryant) b 1880 - m Robert A.E. Kelly*
	Lindsey	Thomas	M.		Dead	*1858-1887*
	Ledbetter	J.	E.		Let Sep 18, 1895	*Bro Elbert/Elmer, b 1857, h/o Ellen Josephine Sewell*
	Long	Rosa			Dead	
	Lathem	Jane	Smith			*1859-1899, Sarah "Jane" Sandow, m 1st William Lathem, m. 2nd T. N. Smith*
	Lee	Nancy			Let Sep 14, 1895	*w/o A. H. Lee*
	Ledbetter	Sarah	E.	Exp Aug 19, 1884	Dead	
	Lawson	J.	B.	Exp Aug 19, 1884		
	Lyle	F, Sister	J.	Exp Aug 19, 1884		*Sis*
	Lyle	A, Sister	M.	Exp Aug 19, 1884		
t	Ledbetter	S.	A.	Exp Aug 19, 1884	See Fletcher	*Sarah/Sallie Asalee, 1869-1903, m G. B. Fletcher*
t	Leonard	Leanna		Let Aug 18, 1891		*1824-1913, m Jesse J Leonard in 1845, bur HBC, he was in Civil War, she drew widow's pension*
	Lee	A.	H.	Exp Aug 1892	Let Sep 14, 1895	*Bro.*
	Ledbetter	Virgil	W.	Exp	*Let Aug 1913	
t	Leonard	Ida		Exp Aug 1897		*m William B Turner ? 03 Jan 1904*
	Logins	Samuel		Let Aug 1897	Let Dec 15, 1900	
	Logins	James		Let Aug 1897	Let Dec 15, 1900	*J H, 1844-1939, father of Charley H Loggins*
	Logins	Robert		Let Aug 1897	Let Dec 15, 1900	
	Logins	Maggie		Let Aug 1897	Let Dec 15, 1900	*1870/1873-1944*
	Logins	Lucy		Let Aug 1897	Let Dec 15, 1900	
	Logins	Martha		Let Aug 1897	Let Dec 15, 1900	*Mirandy*
t	Little	Lilly	A.	Exp Sep 1900		*(Little) Williams*
	Lathem	Victoria	E.	Exp Sep 1900	Died Sep 21, 1902	*m John W Lathem*
t	Leonard	John	M.	Let Oct 19, 1901		
t	Little	Tom		Exp Aug 1902		*Thomas E, 1874-1951*
t	Little	Senie		Exp Aug 1902		*Mary Senie, m Tom Little, 1878-1915*
t	Little	Lou	Cindia	Exp Aug 1902		*? Lucinda Eulline (Little), 1890-1955, m Elijah Dobson, bur HBC*
t	Little	Dock		Exp Aug 1902		*1886-1961, m Lillie Montana (Hester), bur HBC*
	Mashburn	H.	P.		Let Mar 14, 1885	
	McGuillion	James				*1853-1905, m Martha Josephine (Wilkie)*

	Last name	First name	Middle name	How/when Received, Other Info	How/when Dismissed, Other Info	Annotated Remarks; items not listed in church roll (full/maiden name; spouse; birth-death; buried at HBC)
	McGuillion	John			Let Oct 20, 1883	
	Morgan	J.	H.		Let Apr 15, 1893	
	McGuillion	Lucinda			Died Mar 25, 1893	
t	Mason	Martha				
	Mashburn	M.	L.		Let Mar 14, 1885	w/o H P Mashburn
	McGuillion	M. Matthew	R. C.	Profession of faith, Sep 15, 1883	Let Oct 16, 1897	Brother
	McGuillion	Margaret		Profession of faith, Sep 15, 1883		
	Mason	J.	E.	Exp Aug 20, 1885		
	Mason	Fheba		Let Nov 20, 1886	Let Jan 19, 1889	Sis Feba, Pheba
t	Mason	Jane		Let Sep 1887		
t	McDonald	Martha		Let Aug 29, 1890		
	Mason	W.	H.	Exp Aug 31, 1890	Let Sep 19, 1891	*Wm.
	Martin	Peter		Let Oct 19, 1889	Let Aug 18, 1894	
	Martin	Cary E. *Mrs.		Let Oct 19, 1889	Let Aug 18, 1894	Cary Evaline m Peter Martin
	Mason	Dora	J. (Babe)	Exp Aug 1897	See Price in "P"	
t	Mason	John	W.	Exp Aug 1897		
t	Martin	Martha	(Scrap)	Exp Aug 1890		
t	McGuillion	Mattie	J.	Exp Aug 19, 1887	Death 1951	1875-1951, Mattie (Wilkie) w/o James McGullion, bur HBC
t	Maddox	R.	V.	Exp Aug 1897		
t	Mason	S.	Ida	Exp Aug 1899		
t	Mason	Dora		Exp Sep 1900		
t	Mason	Cora	E.	Exp Sep 1900		
t	Mason	Mary		Let Sep 1900		(Nix)
t	Mason	Celia		Exp Aug 1902		
	Nash	Lucinda				
	Nix	Lucy	A.		Let Mar 19, 1892 *Copy of let Nov 1899	
	Newhouse	E.	A.		Let Aug 12, 1885	*Allice
†	Nix	Mary	F			
	Nix	M.	J. E.		Died Feb 1900	
	Nesbit	Margarett		Exp Aug 19, 1884		
	Nickleson	Mary		Exp Sep 15, 1889		
	Nelson	J.	H.	Exp Aug 31, 1890	Let Dec 1894	Bro Harris

	Last name	First name	Middle name	How/when Received, Other Info	How/when Dismissed, Other Info	*Annotated Remarks; items not listed in church roll (full/maiden name; spouse; birth-death; buried at HBC)*
	Nelson	Louis		Exp Sep 1893	Let Jun 17, 1899	
t	Nelson	Maiden	J.	Exp Aug 1897		
	Nelson	John		Exp Aug 1897	Let Aug 1902	*B abt 1880*
	Nelson	Ader	L.	Exp Aug 1899	See Crow	*B abt 1884*
t	Norton	W.	S.	Let Jul 1899	Ordained Minister May 19, 1900	*1866-1903, William Samuel, bur HBC*
t	Norton	Neely		Let Sep 15, 1900		*Sis Cornelia Norton, w/o W. S. Norton*
t	Nix	Meary		Let Sep 15, 1900	See Mason	
t	Norton	Pearl	M.	Exp Aug 1902		*d/o W S and Cornelia Norton*
t	Odum	W. / Wyley	F.			
	Odum	J.	M.		Let Oct 15, 1887	*James Marcus*
	Odum	H.	A.		*Let Oct 15, 1887 Let Oct 19, 1895	*Sis Hester Ann (Kemp?), m James M Odum*
t	Odum	S.	J.			*Susan/Sara Jane "Abi"*
	Odum	Caroline			Let May 16, 1885	*Abt 1862- 1939, m Henry Bruce Gilstrap*
	Odum	L.	M.			*Bro Margers/Marquis*
	Odum	Ida		Exp Aug 20 1885		
t	Odum	L.		Exp Aug 19 1887		*Lettie, "Lindy"?*
	Odum	Grover	C.	Exp Aug 1897		*Cleveland*
t	Odum	H.	A.	Let Oct 14, 1899		*Sis Hester Ann*
t	Odum	L.	M.			
	Porter	J.	D.		Let Dec 16, 1883	*Joseph*
t	Pursell	R.	J.		liberated Aug 15, 1896	*Reuben James, 1852-1927*
	Petty	Wiley			Died Aug 1899	
	Pass	Martha			Let Jun 20, 1885	
t	Pursell	Elisabeth	M.			*(Jackson), w/o Reuben James Purcell*
	Pursell	Tressa	S.		Died Apr 27, 1889	*Susan Theresa Purcell, 1844-1889, bur HBC, dau of James and Mary Purcell*
	Pursell	Josephine				*Josephine (White), 1849-1926, m Andrew Jackson Purcell*
t	Pursell	Luiza				*Louiza; Louisa Ann Jones? 2nd w/o Benjamin Purcell?*
t	Petty	A.				*Atlantic, 2nd wife of Wiley, 1826-1898*

	Last name	First name	Middle name	How/when Received, Other Info	How/when Dismissed, Other Info	*Annotated Remarks; items not listed in church roll (full/ maiden name; spouse; birth-death; buried at HBC)*
t	Priest	Rutha		Nov 17, 1883		B 1837, (Ruthey Springer), m Epson Priest
	Porter	P.	J.		Let Dec 16, 1883	Patsy, m J D Porter
	Pruett	B.	F.	Let Apr 19, 1884	Let Apr 17, 1886	Benjamin Franklin, b 1842 *Apr 1886, B F Pruett and wife dbl
	Pruett	M.	H.	Let Apr 19, 1884	Let Apr 17, 1886	Sister Mary H (Redmond), m B F Pruett?
	Pruett	N.	H.	Exp Aug 20, 1885	dead	Norman?
	Petty	Pheba			Died Feb 3, 1889	
	Pinson	S.	H.		Let May 18, 1895	Bro. Street Henry, 1814-1902
	Pinson	Martha			Let May 18, 1895	(Williams), m S H Pinson
	Pruett	M.	B.	Exp Aug 19, 1887	Let Aug 18, 1900	
	Petty	W./U.	M.	Exp Aug 19, 1887		Bro.
	Petty	M. *Mattie	D.	Exp Aug 19, 1887	Let Sep 15, 1894	Sis Mattie Dow Harris Petty
t	Pearson	J.	H.	Exp Aug 5, 1887		
t	Prewitt	M.	E.	Exp Aug 5, 1887		
t	Pascoe	Samuel		Let Feb 1888		Samuel Washington Pascoe, 1855-1937
t	Pascoe	John		Let Feb 1888		John Jackson Pascoe
t	Pascoe	Mrs.		Let Feb 1888		Ella (Stephens) m Samuel Pascoe, 1864-1904
t	Pascoe	Mrs.		Let Feb 1888		Effie (Stephens) m John Jackson Pascoe
	Petty	James		Let May 17, 1890	Died Feb 7, 1900	
	Petty	Ameda		Let May 17, 1890	Let May 19, 1900	Amanda?
t	Purcell	R.	Benjamin	Exp Aug 24, 1890		Reuben Benjamin Purcell, b 1876, h/o Fannie Edwards
t	Purcell	Rufus	J. M.	Exp Aug 24, 1890		h/o Daisy L.Nix
		??		Exp Aug 24, 1890		
t	Pierce	Martha		Let Aug 24, 1890		Martha Mayberry (Wilkie), 1864-1936, m Henry Harrison Pierce
t	Pierce	William		Exp Aug 1890		1880-1921, s/o H H and Martha Pierce
t	Purcell	Fannie	M.	Let Jun 16, 1894		m Reuben Ben Purcell
t	Pierce	Arastus		Exp Sep 1894		R. Erastus Pierce
	Pinson	S.	H.	Let Aug 1895	Died Apr 1902	Street Henry Pinson
	Pinson	Martha		Let Aug 1895	Died 1901	
t	Priest	Ella				(Stephens), m George W Priest

	Last name	First name	Middle name	How/when Received, Other Info	How/when Dismissed, Other Info	*Annotated Remarks; items not listed in church roll (full/ maiden name; spouse; birth-death; buried at HBC)*
t	Pearson	Edgar		Exp Aug 1897		*1880-1935, Edd H, bur HBC*
t	Purcell	J.	Luther	Exp Aug 1897		*James Luther Purcell*
t	Purcell	Mattie		Exp Aug 1890		*Martha "Mattie" (Hester), 1875-1951, w/o Thomas Benjamin Purcell*
t	Pruitt	John	B.	Exp Jun 1898		*Abt 1877-1925*
t	Pruitt	Roseanna	Mary	Exp Aug 1897		*Abt 1884*
t	Purcell	W	Louis	Exp Aug 1899		*1886-?, h/o Laura Maddox*
t	Pinson	Leannie		Let Aug 19, 1899		
t	Price	F.	Belle	Exp Sep 1900	See Bryant	*Fannie Belle (Price) m George Mancel Bryant*
t	Price	Lilly	M.	Exp Sep 1900		*(Price) m Mason*
t	Price	W.	O. "Dick"	Exp Sep 1900		*W Oscar "Dick"*
t	Price	W.	H. "Sampson"	Exp Sep 1900		*"Sampson or Samp"*
t	Price	M.	Odella	Exp Sep 1901	See Purcell	*Minnie Odella, m James Luther Purcell*
t	Price	Dora	J.	Exp Aug 1897		*1880-1946*
t	Purcell	M	Odella	Exp Sep 1901		*Minnie Odella (Price), m James Luther Purcell*
t	Purcell	Lela	B.	Exp Aug 1902		*Liller; d/o Reuben J and Elizabeth Purcell*
t	Price	J.	Milton	Exp Aug 1902		*James Milton, 1880-1957*
t	Pearson	Nettie	R.	Exp Sep 1900		*1882-1950, Nettie (Boling) m Edgar Pearson, bur HBC*
t	Priest	Sallie		Exp Sep 1894		*Sallie (Brady)*
	Richards	John	B.	Exp Oct 19, 1869	Let Aug 16, 1890	
	Richards	Ida	B.		Let Aug 16, 1890	
	Reaves	Rebeca			Let	
	Reaves	Lucinda			Let Sep 1885 *Let May 1885	
	Reaves	Wiley			dead	
	Reaves	Hulda			Let Sep 1885 *Let May 1885	
	Richards	Laura		Exp Oct 19, 1869	Let Aug 16, 1890	*Laura (Strickland), m John B Richards*
t	Reynolds	M.	J.			
	Rich	J.	P.	Let Feb 16, 1884	Let Oct 15, 1887	*Jepthins /Jepthius/Jeptha, 1818-1901, m Winnie?*
	Rainwater	Mary		Exp Aug 19, 1884/5	Let Nov 17, 1888	

	Last name	First name	Middle name	How/when Received, Other Info	How/when Dismissed, Other Info	*Annotated Remarks; items not listed in church roll (full/maiden name; spouse; birth-death; buried at HBC)*
	Robinson	T.	F.	Exp Aug 19, 1884/5		*Thomas Franklin*
	Roper	J.	R.	Exp Aug 19, 1884/5		*Jack?*
	Roper	Sarah		Exp Aug 19, 1884/5		
	Robinson	F.	D.	Exp Aug 19, 1884/5		*Febia/Phebia, m Thomas F Robinson*
t	Robinson	Ida		Exp Aug 19, 1884/5		*1871-*
t	~~Richards~~	~~J.~~	Jr.	Wilkie		*??*
	Richards	S.	L.	Exp Aug 19, 1884/5	Let Sep 19, 1891	
t	Richards	J.	M. S.	Let Aug 19, 1884/5		
	Richards	Marion		Let Aug 19, 1884/5	Died Apr 11, 1901	
t	Richards	M.	A.	Let Aug 19, 1884/5		*Book 2 as Mabel A. Richards*
t	Richards	Paralee		Let Aug 19, 1884/5	Greene	*Perry Lee (Richards)1866-1918, m Jesse Brown Green*
	Rogers	Laura		Let Aug 19, 1887	Let Jun 14, 1890	
	Richards	J.	B. Jr.	Exp Aug 19, 1887	Let Aug 16, 1890	*John B Richards, Jr.*
	Richards	L.	A.	Exp Aug 19, 1887	Let Aug 16, 1890	*Laura Alice Richards*
t	Ramsey	R.	A.	Let Aug 15, 1891		*Rice A. Ramsey, 1850-1925, bur HBC*
t	Ramsey	Ann		Let Aug 15, 1891		*Susan Ann (Leonard), w/Rice Ramsey, 1856-1939, bur HBC*
	Ray	J.	D.	Exp Sep 19, 1891	Let Aug 1892	
	Rich	J.	P.	Let Oct 17, 1891	Let Jul 14, 1894	*Jepthins /Jepthius/Jeptha, 1818-1901, m Winnie?*
	Richards	John	H.	Exp Aug 1885		
t	Rich	Victoria		Exp Aug 1897	death	*Victoria (Sandow), 1874-1954, m Elisha Grant Rich*
t	Richards	Mabel	A.	Exp Aug 1884		*Mabel(Boling)*
t	Richards	Octavy	I.	Exp Aug 1888		*Octavia (Gilliland)*
t	Smallwood	J.	M.			*James M?*
	Smith	Z.	T.			
	Smallwood	E.			Let Oct 1884	*Brother*
	Southern	A.*Amanda			Let Dec 1882	
	Strickland	Louis			Died Mar 24 1885	

	Last name	First name	Middle name	How/when Received, Other Info	How/when Dismissed, Other Info	*Annotated Remarks; items not listed in church roll (full/maiden name; spouse; birth-death; buried at HBC)*
	Springer	Martha				
t	Sando	Margarett	Fowler		See Fowler	*w/o Fowler*
	Smallwood	E.			Let Aug 1895	*Bro Elijah?*
t	Stephens	Mary				*Mary (Petty), 1823-1902, aka "Aunt Polly," m Larkin Stephens, bur HBC*
t	Smallwood	M.	S.			
	Smallwood	Elvinia			Let Sep 8, 1888	
t	Stephens	Ella	Pries		See Priest	*1866-1943, m George Priest*
t	Southern	Eliza				
	Smallwood	Anna			Let Nov 17, 1883	
	Springer	Niza		Let Nov 17, 1883		
	Seabolt	Ella		Exp Aug 19, 1884	Let	
	Sewell	E.	J. Ledbetter	Exp Aug 19, 1887	Let Sep 1895	*Ellen Josephine (Sewell), w/o Elbert Ledbetter*
t	Stephens	M.	J.	Exp Aug 19, 1887		
t	Stephens	R.		Exp Aug 19, 1887		
t	Smith	T.	N.	Exp Jul 19, 1884	deacon	*Thomas Nathan, 1857-1919, m Joanna Angeline, deacon on Nov 1884, bur HBC*
	Smith	J.	A.	Exp Jul 19, 1884	Died 1889	*Joanna Angeline, "Angie," 1861-1889, m Thomas Nathan Smith, bur HBC*
	Smith	Sarah		Exp Sep 15, 1889	Let Aug 1892	
t	Smith	Oby	Odum	Exp Sep 15, 1889		*(Smith), m? Odum*
	Sears	Joe		Exp Aug 31, 1890	Died Apr 1899	
	Stoyle	W.	C.	Exp Aug 31, 1890	Let Oct 15, 1898	*Bro Clark*
t	Stephens	J.	H.	Exp Aug 31, 1890		*John H. Stephens*
t	Stephens	Laura		Exp Aug 31, 1890		
	Stoyles	Lou		Let Sep 20, 1890	Let Oct 15, 1898	
	Speer	Rachael	E.	Exp Aug 1897	See Eaton	
	Smith	Jane			Died Dec 10, 1899	*Sara "Jane" Sandow Lathem Smith, 1559-1899, bur HBC*
	Smith	Alice		Exp Aug 1888		
	Sparks	Mary		Exp Aug 1891/92	Let Mar 19, 1898	*Mary (Fowler) Sparks*
t	Sandow	M.	Viola	Exp Sep 1893		*Viola Minerva (Wilkie) Sandow, 1879-1969, m Sherman Sandow in 1898, bur HBC*
t	Swinford	May		Let Aug 1898	See Hester	*May (Swinford) Hester Thrasher*
t	Smith	A "Gussie"	F.	Exp Sep 1899		*Augustus Franklin Smith*
t	Smith	Millie	A.	Let Sep 1900		*w/o Colonel Smith*
t	Smith	Colonel	N.	Exp Sep 1900		*Colonel Nathan Smith*

	Last name	First name	Middle name	How/when Received, Other Info	How/when Dismissed, Other Info	Annotated Remarks; items not listed in church roll (full/maiden name; spouse; birth-death; buried at HBC)
t	Smith	Octavia	A.	Exp Aug 1902		
	Sandow					
t	Tippens	Caroline				
t	Tomblin	Nancy				
t	Tippens	Nancy	M.			
t	Tippens	Virginia				
	Thomas	Lucy		Let	Let Aug 1893	
	Turner	J.	E.	Let Nov 1884		John E
	Turner	E.	M.	Let Nov 1884		m John E Turner
	Thomas	A.	J.	Exp	Let Jun 14, 1890	
t	Thompson	James	M.	Aug 1897		
t	Thompson	Mary	J "Tack"	Exp Aug 1897		
t	Thompson	Minnie	D.	Exp Aug 1897		
t	Thompson	Jessie	M.	Exp Aug 1897		
t	Thompson	Judge	N.	Exp Aug 1899		
t	Thompson	Lilly	M.	Exp Sep 1900		
	Williams	J.	L.		Let Dec 14, 1889	John Lewis, Deacon Oct 19, 1884
	Williams	J.	M.		Let Oct 20, 1884	
t	White	A.	J.			Andrew Jackson, 1833-1904
	Williams	T.	Jack		Let Oct 20, 1884	Thomas Jefferson?
	Williams	Joel	L.		Let Jan 18, 1890	
	Williams	Ansel			Let Dec 14, 1889	Ansel Monroe Williams, 1867-1915
	Waldrep	Henry/ Harvey		Let Mar 16, 1883		
	White	John	M.			1845-1930
t	Wilkie	D.	O. B.			
	White	Rebecca			Died Aug 1893	m A J White
	Williams	Rebecca			Let Oct 20, 1884	1836-1906
	Williams	Sarah			Let Oct 20, 1884	1939-1905
t	Wilkie	Margaret				
	Williams	A.	A.		Let Oct 20, 1884	Abi Altzaney
	Williams	Margaret			Let Oct 20, 1884	
t	Willson	Nancy	J.			
t	White	N.	J.			
	Williams	Nevel		Let Apr 19, 1884	Let Jan 18, 1890	Sis
	Williams	G.	B.	Exp Aug 19, 1884	Let Dec 14, 1889	
	Williams	M.	A.	Exp Aug 19, 1884	Let Dec 14, 1889	
	Watson	M.	A.	Exp Aug 18, 1884	Let Aug 19, 1884	

	Last name	First name	Middle name	How/when Received, Other Info	How/when Dismissed, Other Info	*Annotated Remarks; items not listed in church roll (full/ maiden name; spouse; birth-death; buried at HBC)*
	White	Alice		Exp Aug 19, 1884	Let Feb 14, 1891	*Alice (White) m. *Wofford*
t	Wilkie	F.	A.	Exp Jul 20, 1885		*Sister Fannie?*
t	Wilkie	H.	F.	Exp Aug 20, 1885		
	Wheeler	S., Sister	V.	Exp Aug 20, 1885		*Sister Victoria?*
t	Wheeler	Dora	Hester	Exp Aug 20, 1885	See Hester	*(Wheeler), 1866-1937, Bur HBC with John Hester 1869- 1916*
t	Wilkie	H.	N.	Exp Aug 20, 1885		
	Warren	T.	J.	Let Oct 20, 1886	Let Aug 15, 1896	*Bro*
	Warren	H.	T.	Let Oct 20, 1886	Let Aug 15, 1896	**Henry*
	Warren	Martha		Let Oct 20, 1886	Let Aug 15, 1896	
	Warren	Chalcedonia		Let Oct 20, 1886	Let Aug 15, 1896	*Donie*
	Wimbish	A.	L.	Let	*Let Jan 16, 1915 Dead	
	White	Alice	Smith	Exp Aug 5, 1888	See Smith	
	Wilson	F.	A.	Exp Aug 19, 1887		
	Wilkie	M.	J.	Exp Aug 19, 1887	See McGullion	*Mattie, Martha, 1874-1951, bur HBC*
t	Williams	B.	H.	Exp Aug 19, 1887		*Berry Hawkins Williams, "Bud," 1846-1940*
t	Williams	L.	A.	Exp Aug 19, 1887		*Loucinda (Davis), m B H Williams;*
	Wyatt	John	S.	Let Aug 18, 1888		*Deacon on May 17 1890, John Samuel Wyatt, bur HBC*
	Wyatt	J.	P.	Let Aug 18, 1888	Died Mar 30, 1893	*Julia (Hawkins), m John S. Wyatt, bur HBC*
	White	Mary	L.	Let Aug 20, 1889	Let Jan 18, 1890	*Mary Lou*
	White	Rebeca		Let Sep 14, 1889	Let Jan 18, 1890	**Rebecka*
	Whitner	Mattie		Let Sep 14, 1889	Let Mar 14, 1896	
	Wyatt	Mary		Exp Sep 15, 1889	See White	*m William A White, 1877-1961, bur HBC*
	Wilkie	M.	G.	Let Aug 23, 1890	*Let Jul 15, 1893 Hand minister	*Bro. Mason George? 1844-1913*
	Wilkie	Homer		Let Aug 23, 1890		
	Wilkie	Synthia		Let Aug 23, 1890	Let Jun 17, 1893	*2nd wife of Mason George Wilkie*
	Wheeler	G.	W.	Exp Aug 31, 1890	Let Oct 1898	*George Washington Wheeler*
t	Wilkie	J.	H.	Exp Aug 31, 1890		*John Harrison Wilkie, 1871-1949, bur HBC*
t	Wilkie	H.	Glenn	Exp Aug 31, 1890		*Hiram Glenn, 1877-1956, Ordained as deacon July 1904, bur HBC*
	Wilkie	J.	P.	Exp Aug 31, 1890	Let Jun 17, 1893	*Bro J Parks Wilkie*

	Last name	First name	Middle name	How/when Received, Other Info	How/when Dismissed, Other Info	*Annotated Remarks; items not listed in church roll (full/maiden name; spouse; birth-death; buried at HBC)*
t	Williams	J.	R.	Exp Aug 31, 1890		*Jessie R*
t	Wallace	Lydia		Exp Aug 31, 1890	dead	
	Wooten	William		Let Jun 19, 1891		
	Wooten	Sarah		Let Jun 19, 1891	Died Jul 9, 1893	*w/o William Wooten*
t	White	Nancy	M.			
	Warren	Callie		Exp	Let Aug 1896	
	White	Julius		Exp		*1875-1915*
	Webster	John			Let Apr 15, 1893	
t	Wilkie	M	Viola	Exp Sep 1893	See Sandow	*Viola Minerva (Wilkie) Sandow, 1879-1969, m Sherman Sandow*
	Wyatt	Sarah		Let Jun 16, 1894	Died Sep 9/10, 1897	*bur HBC, Bk 1 says Sep 10, tombstone says Sep 9.*
t	White	S.	M. Mrs.	Let Apr 18, 1894		*Sis Margaret*
t	Williams	Jack	L.	Let	Deacon	*Ordained Nov 1884*
t	Williams	Mary	A.	Let		*Mary Ann Wooten Williams*
t	Williams	Azzalee		Let		
t	Wilkie	G.	H.			*Can't find in book 2*
t	Wilkie	Lee				*Henry "Lee"? 1867-1936, bur HBC*
t	Wilkie	TheODocia		Exp Aug 1902		*(Stancil), 1873-1957, w/o John Harrison Wilkie, bur HBC*
t	Wilkie	Georgia	Ann	Exp Aug 1902		*1890-1965, m R. E. Lovelace*
t	Warren	Delcy		Let Jun 1901/1902		*Delsie, w/o Robert Warren, HBC minutes RBL Jun 14, 1902*
t	Warren	Robert		Let Jun 1901/1902		*HBC minutes RBL Jun 14, 1902*
t	Wallis	Mattie	L.	Exp Sep 1900		*Martha Lou "Mattie" (Wallace), 1888-1945, w/o Edward Forrest Wilkie*
t	Wright	Conrad	A.	Exp Sep 1900		
t	Wilkie	G.	Neel	Exp Sep 1900		
t	Wilkie	Myrtie	J.	Exp Sep 1900		*Myrtie Jewell Wilkie, 1887-1977, bur HBC*
t	Wilkie	Etta				
t	Wallace	Jessie	W.	Let Jan 1900		
	Wilkie	Etta		Let Nov 18, 1899		
t	Wilkie	Alice		Exp Sep 1899		*1884-1968, m Sherman Holcomb, bur HBC*
	Wyatt	John	S.		Let Jul 1899; Deacon	
	Wheeler	John	F.		Let Sep 17, 1898	
	Williams	John		Let Aug 20, 1898	Let Aug 17, 1902	

	Last name	First name	Middle name	How/when Received, Other Info	How/when Dismissed, Other Info	*Annotated Remarks; items not listed in church roll (full/ maiden name; spouse; birth-death; buried at HBC)*
t	White	John	W.			
t	White	Joseph	W.	Exp Aug 1897		
	White	Mary		Exp Sep 1889	Let Sep 1900	
t	White	Ellen		Exp Aug 1890		? 1872-1933, Ellen Clara (Hester) w/o John Bullock White
t	White	Cora	L.	Exp Aug 1897	See Holcomb	m Henry Holcomb, 1878-1936
t	Wilkie	Lula	P.	Exp Aug 1897		Lula (Jones) Wilkie, 1879-1962, bur HBC
t	Williams	Ollie	T.	Exp Aug 1897		
t	Wallace	M.	Jane	Exp Aug 1897		
t	Wyatt	Joseph	A.	Exp Aug 1897	*Let Nov 18, 1899	m Laura Jane Hester
	Young	Rebecca			Died	Died, 1899
	Yancy	Milton			dead	
	Young	R.	V.	Exp Aug 31, 1890	See Maddox	
*1	Bailey	Ella			Let Jul 14, 1883	
*1	Bobo	Matilda			Let May 1883	
*1	Burgess	B. (Bro)	F. and wife		Let Oct 20, 1884	
*1	Burgess	M (Sister)	F.	Let Sep 1884		
*1	Cape	Joanna			Let Aug 20, 1898	
*1	Christopher	Sister			Let Feb 19, 1898	
*1	Crenshaw	E.	T.		Let Aug 16, 1891	
*1	Crenshaw	Martha			Let Aug 16, 1891	
*1	Crenshaw	Wife of W.	T.		Let Jun 20, 1885	
*1	Ellis	Henry			Let Nov 1882	
*1	Floyed	Jane				
*1	Fowler	Cap (Bro)				
*1	Fowler	G.	R.		Let Mar 14, 1896 (add'l copy)	
*1	Fowler	Mary			Let Oct 20, 1883	*listed in roll as Mary Floyed
*1	Fowler	Richard				
*1	Gibson	Susan			Let Oct 20, 1894	
*1	Gilmer	E, Sister	A.		Apr 1883	*Joined another church*
*1	Gilmer	Sister			Mar 1883	*Joined another church*
*1	Gilstrap	Caroline		Let Mar 17 1888	Let May 16, 1885 *Let Sep 19, 1896	*recorded on roll as Caroline Odum

	Last name	First name	Middle name	How/when Received, Other Info	How/when Dismissed, Other Info	*Annotated Remarks; items not listed in church roll (full/ maiden name; spouse; birth-death; buried at HBC)*
*1	Gilstap	F., Sister	Hardy		Let Dec 1894	
*1	Harbin	Tyra, wife and daughters			Let Aug 1883	
*1	Harbin	S.	M.		Let Aug 1883	
*1	Harden	Sarah			Let Jun 16, 1885	
*1	Hemphill	Lucindy, Mrs.				
*1	Hitt	Sister			Let Feb 17, 1887	
*1	Howard	Anna/ wife of WLD			Let Apr 1883	
*1	Howard	J.	M. & daughters		Let Aug 1883	
*1	Howard	James			Let Jun 14, 1890	
*1	Howard	Rachel	E.	Let May 1883		
*1	Howard	W.	L. D.		Let Apr 1883	
*1	Howard	W.	N.		Let Mar 16, 1883	
*1	Howard	W., Wife of	N.		Let Mar 16, 1883	
*1	Humphrey	Laura			Let Nov 16, 1890 Let Mar 14, 1891	
*1	Hyde	Martha			Let May 15, 1889	
*1	Jones	B.	P.		Let May 1883	
*1	Jones	Susanah			Let May 1883	
*1	Jones	T.	J.		Let May 1883	
*1	Lindsey	Neomia			Let Nov 1882	
*1	Lyle	E., Sister	E.	Let Oct 15, 1887		
*1	Lyle	Sister			Let Jan 19, 1902	
*1	Mason	Sister			Let May 1884	
*1	Nelson	Lula				
*1	Nix	W.	J.		Let May 16, 1885	
*1	Pass	G.		Exp Oct 19, 1884	Let Jun 20, 1885	
*1	Pass	Sister			Let Aug 15, 1886	
*1	Pool	C.	J.			
*1	Porter	Sarah		Let Sep 1882		
*1	Porter	Sister and daughter			Let Oct 14, 1882	
*1	Porter	William			Let Dec 1882	
*1	Porter	Wife of William			Let Dec 1882	

	Last name	First name	Middle name	How/when Received, Other Info	How/when Dismissed, Other Info	*Annotated Remarks; items not listed in church roll (full/ maiden name; spouse; birth-death; buried at HBC)*
*1	Pursell	A.	J.			
*1	Pursell	Henry			Let Mar 17 1888	
*1	Richardson	R., Bro.	S.		Let Apr 1883	
*1	Scudder	Violet			Let Jun 20, 1885	
*1	Sewell	Lula			Let Mar 19, 1898	
*1	Slaughter	Bro			Let May 1884	
*1	Smallwood	Emeline			Let Jun 16, 1885	
*1	Smallwood	Sister			Let Sep 18, 1897 add'l copy	
*1	Southern	Andrew	J.		*Let Apr 1913	
*1	Southern	Amanda, Dau. of			Let Dec 1882	
*1	Springer	Ruthey		Let Nov 17, 1883		*See Priest*
*1	Stephens	Martha			Let Oct 15, 1887	
*1	Tidwell	M.	H.		Let May 1883	
*1	Umphrey	J.			Let Oct 1883	
*1	White	J.	M.	Let Apr 1883		
*1	White	Jack				
*1	White	N.	M.	Exp Sep 19, 1891		
*1	White	M.	J.	Let Apr 1883		
*1	White	W.	J.			
*1	Williams	T. (Bro)	M.		Let Oct 20, 1884	
*1	Wilkie	Bedia, Sister			Let Mar 17, 1900	
*1	Wilson	Jane			Let Apr 20, 1889	
*1	Wofford	Alice	(White)		Let Feb 14, 1891	

Chapter 5: 1903-1909, Minutes and Membership Roll, Book Two

- Community
    - Andrew's Chapel school burned, and the Creighton Mining Company supplied space for the school to continue. In 1907, school was known as Creighton School.

- Religion/Baptists
    - 1904, deacon ordination

- Occupations
    - Farming
    - Gold mining, pyrite mining

- Transportation
    - Roads were still dirt, wagons were still most popular mode of travel to church
    - 1908, Henry Ford began making the Model T

- Cemetery
    - Burials continued in sections one and two

Ed Lovelace, Photo courtesy Chris Chandler

Chapter five is aligned with membership and minute book two (1903-1909) and holds records of only a short seven years of church history. One can guess that the second ledger book that was retained had a fewer number of pages than book one, prompting a third book in less than a ten year span. The community was noting some changes. Surely there was excitement about the future of vehicle transportation even though it would still be several years away for this community. While some mining continued to exist, farming was still the most common occupation. Corn was always a consistent crop and was produced not only for food but for support of the livestock as well. Robert Ed Lovelace is shown with his mules, Dan and Charlie, possibly as he was laying by his crop.

George Washington "Wash" Wilkie was photographed many years ago by the edge of his field. He was a successful farmer and large landowner of his day, and father-in-law to Ed Lovelace. Wash and Francis Green Wilkie were parents to eleven children; many descendants still attend HBC.

Photo courtesy Chris Chandler

The Lightner Leander West family moved to their home on Ball Ground Road in Free Home about 1900. The farm structures pictured are still surviving on the farm once owned by the West family. The corn crib on the left was essential to the farm life of the members at HBC as the new century arrived. Lightner was not only a farmer but also a skilled carpenter and craftsman.

Photo courtesy Milford family

Transportation to and from the monthly church meetings continued to be by wagon. At an old-timer's day celebration at HBC about 1986, an effort was made to remind churchgoers of a time when travel was quite difficult. E. W. Cochran (pictured in the hat) as well as some members of his family rode to church in a two-horse wagon.

Photo courtesy of Regina Groover

Minutes, 1903-1909

Each entry:

Date, Minister(s) who preached on that date.

Any of the items that had activity on that given date.

Items:

1. Invited visiting brethren to seats with us
2. Called for the fellowship of the church
3. Called for reference
4. Opened the door of the church for the reception of members
5. General Business

Moderator, Church Clerk

Apr. 18, 1903, Bro. A. J. Henderson and C. B. Fowler. 5. Granted Bro. Joe Fowler a letter of dismission. Invited New Harmony, Mt. Pisgah, Mt. Tabor, Friendship, Conns Creek, Ophir and Liberty to be at our communion, the 3rd Sunday in May. Collected 45 cts. to buy wine. A. J. Henderson, Mod., R. B. Purcell, C.C.

May 19, 1903, Bros. R. W. Cochran and A. J. Henderson. *[no business under any item].* A. J. Henderson, Mod., R. B. Purcell, C.C.

Jun. 19, 1903, Bro. A. J. Henderson. 4. Received by letter Sister Martha J. Richards. 5. Appointed delegates to union meeting, Brethren: H. K. Fletcher, R. J. Purcell, J. M. Richards, J. R. Biddy, J. H. Ellis, J. W. Holcomb and John Pruitt. Appointed delegates to association, Brethren: R. J. Purcell, J. W. Holcomb, J. M. Richards, J. H. Ellis, H. K. Fletcher, R. B. Purcell and J. R. Biddy. A. J. Henderson, Mod., R. B. Purcell, C.C.

Jul. 18, 1903, C. D. McCurley, Johnny Lathem and A. J. Henderson. 5. Read and adopted letters to union meeting and association. A. J. Henderson, Mod., R. B. Purcell, C.C.

Aug. 15, 1903, Bro. A. J. Henderson. 2. Preferred a charge against a sister for denying the faith, took up the charge and excluded her from the fellowship of the church. 5. Granted letters of dismission to Sisters Ader Crow and Maiden Nelson and Bro. Milton Bloodworth. Collected $2.50 for Sister Floyd. A. J. Henderson, Mod., R. B. Purcell, C.C.

Sep. 19, 1903, Bro. A. J. Henderson. 5. Suspended the regular order of business and elected Bro. A. J. Henderson, Pastor for another year by acclamation. Collected $3.00 for pastor. A. J. Henderson, Mod., R. B. Purcell, C.C.

Nov. 14, 1903, Bros. C. B. Fowler and A. J. Henderson. 5. Collected for Bro. Henderson $8.15. A. J. Henderson, R. B. Purcell, C.C.

Mar. 1904, Bro. Henderson. 2. A charge preferred against a sister and brother, excluded. Also preferred against another brother against his father, charge taken up, referred until next meeting. A. J. Henderson, Mod., H. G. Wilkie, Temporary Clerk.

Apr. 16, 1904, Bros. R. W. Cochran and McKinny Purcell. Elected R. W. Cochran, moderator. 2. Preferred a charge against a brother for drunkness, referred the charge till next conference. Preferred a charge against a brother for deserting his wife, drunkness, and excluded him. Preferred a charge against a sister for fornication, excluded her. 3. Took up the charge against a brother for mistreating his father and excluded him from the fellowship of the church. 5. Collected 50 cts. to buy wine. Received an invitation from Conns Creek to their communion. Granted Sister Mary Thrasher a letter of dismission. Macedonia invited the eldership of this church to be at the ordination of deacons. Invited Mt. Pisgah, New Harmony, Ophir, Mt. Tabor, Conns Creek and Liberty to be at our communion. R. W. Cochran, Mod. Pro, R. B. Purcell, C.C.

May 14, 1904, Bros. A. J. Henderson and Elias Biddy. 2. Preferred a charge against a brother for profanity, referred the [charge] till next conference. 3. Passed the charge against a brother till next conference. 4. Received by letter Bro. Valley Loggins and wife. 5. Set apart Bros. H. G. Wilkie, J. H. Ellis and G. B. Hagood for ordination of deacons on 3rd Sat. in July. Invited the eldership of New Harmony, Macedonia, Conns Creek, Ophir, Liberty and Mt. Pisgah to be at the ordination of our deacons. Let the letter of Bro. W. M. Dobson and wife stand over till next conference. A. J. Henderson, Mod., R. B. Purcell, C.C.

Jun. 18, 1904, Bros. A. J. Henderson and Elias Biddy. 3. Received the acknowledgements of a brother for drunkness, also received the acknowledgements of another brother for swearing. 4. Received by letter Sister Warren, also received the letters of Bro. W. M. B. Dobson and wife, also received a brother's acknowledgements. 5. Granted Bro. W. M. B. Dobson and wife [*Mary E.*] letters of dismission. Layed aside regular order of business and elected delegates to the association. Elected by nomination, Bros. R. J. Purcell, J. H. Ellis, J. J. Holcomb, Thos. N. Smith, J. L. Williams, H. G. Wilkie, R. A. Dunigan and R. W. Cochran. Elected Brethren R. L. Warren, H. K. Fletcher, Milton Price, J. H. Ellis and H. G. Wilkie as delegates to the union meeting. New Harmony invited the eldership of this church to be at the ordination of Bro. McKiney Purcell on Friday before the first Sun. in Aug. Elected Bro. T. N. Smith spokesman of the church. A. J. Henderson, Mod., R. B. Purcell, C.C.

Jul. 16, 1904, Bro. A. J. Henderson. 4. Received by letter Bro. J. N. Wiginton. 5. Granted Bro. Mack Baker and wife letters of dismission, also Bro. Jesse Eaton and family.

The following deacons were ordained, Brethren: G. B. Hagood, H. G. Wilkie, and J. H. Ellis. The Presbytery was formed of Calaway Nix, James Daniel, James S. Cook, T. N. Smith, J. L. Williams, G. B. Fletcher, and Ministers Elias Biddy, C. S. Hawkins and R. W. Cochran. Bro. Holcomb was elected spokesman of the church and Bro. Henderson to conduct the ordinational examination, Bro. Hawkins to deliver the charge to the deacons, Bro. Biddy to lead the ordinational prayer. This work was finished and Bro. E. A. Cochran's name was inserted as delegate to the association. A. J. Henderson, Mod., J. F. McCluney, C.C. Protem.

Sep. 17, 1904, Bro. A. J. Henderson and 10 minutes intermission, met in conference. 2. Preferred a charge against a brother for drunkness, referred the charge till next conference. Appointed Bros. T. N. Smith, R. A. Dunigan, and G. B. Fletcher to try to settle the difference between two brethren. 4. Received a sister by restoration. 5. Suspended the regular order of business and elected Bro. Henderson, pastor for another year by acclamation. Elected Bro. J. H. Ellis on preaching committee in place of R. J. Purcell. Bro. A. J. Henderson accepted the call of the church. Granted Bro. J. B. Chastain and family letters of dismission. A. J. Henderson, Mod., R. B. Purcell, C.C.

Oct. 15, 1904, Bros. C. S. Hawkins and A. J. Henderson. 3. A charge against a brother, layed over. 5. Granted letters of dismission to Bro. Bud Williams, wife, and three children and Oveline Hardin. A. J. Henderson, Mod., R. B. Purcell, C.C.

Nov. 20, 1904, Bro. H. T. Ingram. Referred a charge against a brother for drunkness, layed over till next conference and J. J. Holcomb to notify. 3. Took up a charge against a brother, received his acknowledgments. 5. Granted Bro. Mark Odem and wife letters of dismission. Bro. A. J. Henderson resigned the care of Hightower Church. Received his resignation. H. T. Ingram, Mod. Pro., R. B. Purcell, C.C.

Mar. 18, 1905, Bro. A. J. Henderson. 3. Passed over the charge against a brother till next conference. 5. Granted letters of dismission to Bro. Neel Wilkie and Sister Rachel Eaton, also Bro. John Chastain and wife, also Lesom Cannon and wife. Elected delegates to union meeting by appointment, Brethren: John Mason, J. W. Holcomb, Bud Holcomb, R. W. Cochran, Jas. Holcomb, were appointed. A. J. Henderson, Mod., R. B. Purcell, C.C.

May 20, 1905, Bro. A. J. Henderson. 2. Preferred a charge against a brother for profanity, layed it over till next conference. 3. Took up the charge against a brother, received his acknowledgements. 5. Granted Bro. Bud Howard and wife and 3 children letters of dismission. Read the Rules of Order. A. J. Henderson, Mod., R. B. Purcell, C.C.

Jun. 17, 1905, Bro. A. J. Henderson and N. E. Mulkey. 3. Received the acknowledgements for a brother for drunkness and also received acknowledgements for swearing. 4. Received by letter Sister Dizie Warren.

Sep. 16, 1905, Bro. Elias Biddy, elected Bro. Biddy, Mod. 4. Received a brother by acknowledgements also received by experience, Bro. Bob Kelly. 5. Granted letters of dismission to Bros. Johnny Fowler, C. A. Fowler, Gustis Smith, Sisters Margarett Fowler and Sallie Fowler. Elected Bro. Geo. R. Brown as pastor for another year. Elected Bros. T. N. Smith and G. B. Hagood to notify him. Elias Biddy, Mod. Pro., R. B. Purcell, C.C.

Oct. 14, 1905, Bro. T. Pickett. 5. Granted Sister Dora Anderson a letter of dismission. Layed aside the regular order of business and elected Bro. J. R. Allen, pastor for another year by acclamation. Liberty Church invited the eldership of this church to the ordination of Bro. James Cowart the 5th Sunday in Oct. R. W. Cochran, Mod., R. B. Purcell, C.C.

Apr. Term, 1906, 4. Granted Bro. Henry Grimes a letter of dismission. Also granted Sister L. M. White a letter of dismission. Elected delegates to union meeting. Elected: Bros. G. B. Hagood, G. B. Fletcher, R. L. Warren, R. A. Dunigan, T. N. Smith. J. R. Allen, Mod., H. G. Wilkie, C.C. Pro.

May 19, 1906, Bros. E. A. Cochran and C. S. Hawkins. 4. Received by letter Bro. L. L. West, Sisters Mrs. West, Nettie West, Ella West and Adeline Brooks. 5. Granted Bro. Thos. Fowler a letter of dismission. J. R. Allen, Mod., R. B. Purcell, C.C.

Jun. 16, 1906, Bro. J. R. Allen and E. A. Cochran. 5. Suspended the regular order of business and appointed delegates to association, Brethren T. N. Smith, E. A. Cochran, R. J. Purcell, R. W. Cochran, G. B. Hagood, Jas. Richards, J. H. Ellis, alternates: R. L. Warren and H. C. Boling. Granted Bro. Simeon Dobson a letter of dismission. J. R. Allen, Mod., R. B. Purcell, C.C.

Aug. 18, 1906, Bro. J. R. Allen. 4. Received by letter Bro. John Wallace and wife. 5. Granted Bro. Jas. Cantrell a letter of dismission. J. R. Allen, Mod., H. G. Wilkie, C.C. Pro.

Sep. 15, 1906, Bro. E. A. Cochran, after 20 minutes intermission, elected Bro. E. A. Cochran, Mod. 2. Preferred a charge against a brother for drunkness and swearing, excluded him. Preferred a charge against another brother for murder, excluded him. 5. Granted Bro. Charley Fowler a letter of dismission. Went into election of a preacher for another year. Suspended the regular order of business and elected Bro. J. R. Allen by acclamation. E. A. Cochran, Mod. Pro., R. B. Purcell, C.C.

Dec. 1906, Bro. R. W. Cochran. 3. Preferred a charge against a brother for deserting his wife. Laid over the charge till next conference. 5. Took up a collection for Bro. Allen. R. W. Cochran, Mod. Pro., H. G. Wilkie, Clerk, Pro.

Jan. 20, 1907, Bro. R. W. Cochran. 3. Taken up the charge against a brother and rescinded the charge against him. 5. Granted Bro. Marion Richards and wife letters of dismission. All sow elected Bro. H. G. Wilkie as their churches clerk for the remaining part of this year. R. W. Cochran, Mod. Pro., H. K. Fletcher, C.C. Pro.

Apr. 1907, Hightower Baptis Church of Crist at Hightower, Bro. J. R. Aline. 4. Sister Sarah Cloud came forward by letter and was united as a member in full fellowship with us. 5. Appointed the following to invite sister churches: G. B. Haygood, Ophir; H. Ellis, Pisgue; R. W. Cochran; H C. Boling; J. M Richards; J. B. Biddy; to be with us on the

3rd Sunday and Saturday before in May. Also collected eight dollars and fifteen cts. for visiting ministers. J. R. Aline, Mod., H. G. Wilkie, C.C.

May 18, 1907, Hightower Babtis Church of Christ at Hightower after preaching by Bro. R. A. Dunigan followed by J. R. Aline. 5. Granted Sister Saviller Fuller a letter of dismission. Al sow elected the following brethren to attend the union meetings wit: Bros. T. N. Smith, G. B. Fletcher, R. A. Dunigan, J. M. Richards, R. L. Warren, H. C. Bolling. Collected fifty cents for church expenses. J. R. Aline, Mod., H. G. Wilkie, C.C.

Jun. 15, 1907, Bro. A. T. Holcomb. 5. Appointed the following brethren to attend the association: T. N. Smith, R. A. Dunigan, H. C. Boling, Bud Heggwood, James Holcomb, Jessie Wallace, alternate. Granted Sister Ida Williams a letter of dismission. A. T. Holcomb, Mod. Pro., H. G. Wilkie, C.C.

Jul. 20, 1907, Bro. J. R. Aline. 4. Received Sister Maggie Chasteen by letter. 5. Collected for minutes. J. R. Aline, Mod., H. G. Wilkie, C.C.

Aug. 17, 1907, Bro. R. A. Dunigan. 2. Received acknowledgements from a sister. 5. Granted Nettie Pearce/Pearson a letter of dismission. Appointed a commity to raise the money to cover our church house. R. A. Dunigan, Mod., H. K. Fletcher, C. Pro tem.

Sep. 14, 1907, Bro. R. W. Cochran. 5. Granted letter of dismission: Bro. Will Grover, Bro. Ras E. Pearce, Sisters: Josia Cordell, Thomas Floyd. All so suspended the regular order of business and elected J. R. Aline as pastor of Hightower Church for another year. All so elected H. G. Wilkie, Clerk. R. W. Cochran, Mod. Pro., H. G. Wilkie, C.C.

Oct. 19, 1907, Bro. Bennett, Cochran and Aline. 5. Granted letters of dismission: J. J. Pasco, S. W. Pasco and Effie Pasco. Collected sixteen dollars and twenty-five cts. for pastor. J. R. Allen, Mod., H. G. Wilkie, C.C.

Nov. 1907, Bro. J. R. Allen. 4. Received by letter Sister Clair Bell Holcomb. 5. Collected for pastor for the past year, forty-eight dollars. J. R. Allen, Mod., H. G. Wilkie, C.C.

Mar. 14, 1908, Bro. R. W. Cochran and J. R. Allen. 5. Granted G. B. Chastain letter of dismission. All so accepted invitations for the eldership of Hightower to be with Mt. Puisgue on Saturday before 5th Sunday to assist in ordination of deacons. J. R. Allen, Mod., H. G. Wilkie, C.C.

May, 1908, Bro. J. R. Allen and C. B. Fowler. 5. Suspended the regular order of business and appointed the following members as delegates to the union meeting to be held at Ophir Church on Friday before the third Sunday in July to wit: J. H. Ellis, H. K. Fletcher, R. L. Warren, T. N. Smith, J. M. Loggins, Jno. White. J. R. Allen, Mod., H. G. Wilkie, C.C.

Jun. 1908, Bro. R. A. Dunigan and J. R. Allen. 5. Elected by appointments the following brethren as delegates to the association to be held at Concord beginning on Thursday before the second Sunday in Aug. to wit: G. B. Hagood, T. N. Smith, J. H. Ellis, E. A. Cochran, J. J. Holcomb, R. L. Warren, H. K. Fletcher, alternate. All so collected 15 cts. for minutes. J. R. Allen, Mod., H. G. Wilkie, C.C.

Jul. Term, 1908, Bros. C. S. Hawkins and R. W. Cochran. 5. Submitted to reading of associational letter and adopted same. R. W. Cochran, Mod. Pro., H. G. Wilkie, C.C.

Aug. Term, 1908, Bros. J. D. Harris and J. R. Allen. 2. Received acknowledgements from a brother. 5. Granted Letter of dismission to Bro. H. T. Warren. J. R. Allen, Mod., H. K. Fletcher, Clerk Pro.

Sep. 19, 1908, Bros. J. R. Stone and E. A. Cochran. 5. Granted letters of dismission: Sisters Daisy Clark and Ida Dowda. All sow distributed minutes of the association for the past years work. All sow collected $1.00 to by a new church book for Hightower church. The church gives Bro. Stone till Sunday to make up his decision as our pastor. Bro. J. R. Stone accepts the pastoral care of Hightower for the forthcoming year. J. R. Stone, Mod., H. G. Wilkie, C. C.

Oct. Term, 1908, Bro. J. R. Stone and E. A. Cochran. 2. Received acknowledgements of a brother for fighting, and for another brother for not living as he should. 4. Received by experience the following members to wit: Etta Herring, U Jene (Eugenia) Rider, May Christopher, Mary Bryant, Susia Green. 5. Bro. G. B. Fletcher moves that the church be assessed to raise money to meet her expenses, vote being taken 10 to sixteen in favor of assessment, then after an address by our pastor, this motion was withdrawn till next meeting. All sow that a presbatery meet at Hightower on Friday before the 3rd Sunday in Nov. for the purpose of ordaining Bro. R. A. Dunigan, and the eldership of the following churches are invited: Ophir, Conns Creek, New Harmony, Mt Puisgue, Masidonia, Liberty. All sow appointed G. B. Hegwood as spokesman for the church. Collected 24.00 for Rev. J. R. Allen. J. R. Stone, Mod., H. G. Wilkie, C.C.

Nov. 15, 1908, preaching by R. A. Dunigan and prayer by Elder H. T. Ingram, the church proceeded to organize a presbatery for the purpose of ordaining Bro. Dunigan to the full work of the ministry. On motion Br. J. R. Stone act as chairman, all sow that Bro. H. T. Ingram lead the question of the ordination, G. B. Fletcher, spokesman for the church, Bro. E. A. Cochran to lead the ordination prayer. All sow that H. G. Wilkie act as secretary and Bro. C. A. Wallace to deliver the charge. Names of the presbatery to wit:

Elders H. T. Ingram, C. A. Wallace, J. R. Stone, E. A. Cochran, J. L. Waight/ Wyatt, A. G. Hembree as ordained ministers.

Names of deacons to wit: S. L. Coker, W. I. Sewell, J. M. Smith, J. D. Parker/ Pasco, G. B. Fletcher, J. H. Ellis, I. T. Bennett

Bro. J. L. Wight/Wyatt to deliver Bro. Dunigan to the church. Moved that H. T. Ingram write the credentials for Bro. Dunigan after a song and the delivery to the church. Then the presbatery adjourned. J. R. Stone, Mod., H. G. Wilkie, Sect., J. M. Smith, Assistant Sec.

Nov., 1908, Bro. J. R. Stone. 5. Received for Pastor J. R. Allen $100 for the past years work. Paid on house nine dollars. R. A. Dunigan, R. L. Warren, John Wallace. J. R. Stone, Mod., H. G. Wilkie, C.C.

Feb. 20, 1909, J. R. Stone. 2. A brother makes acknowledgements for drinking, the church accepts his acknowledgement. 4. Received by letter G. W. Little. 5. Moved and carried the finance commity in charge of the work of repairing the church are hereby dismissed with the thanks of the church. Suspended the regular order of election and elected by appointment the following brethren as delegates to the union meeting to be held with the church of Concord in Forsyth Co. on Friday before first Sunday in April and the following brethren to attend to wit: G. B. Hegwood, T. N. Smith, J. H. Ellis, R. L. Warren, H. K. Fletcher, and H. G. Wilkie, alternate. All so granted Sister Evey Kelly a letter of dismission. J. R. Stone, Mod., H. G. Wilkie, C.C.

Mar. 20, 1909, Rev. J. R. Stone. 5. Granted R. E. Kelley a letter of dismission. All so adopted the letter to the union meeting. J. R. Stone, Mod., H. G. Wilkie, C.C.

April Term, 1909, J. R. Stone. 5. Collected 1.45 to buy wine for the communion. Received an invitation to commune with New Harmony and Liberty on the first Sunday in May. J. R. Stone, Mod., H. K. Fletcher, Clerk of the Pro Tem.

May Term, 1909, J. R. Stone. [*No business under any item*]. J. R. Stone, Mod., H. G. Wilkie, C.C.

June Term, 1909, 5. Suspended the regular order of election and elected by appointment the following members to be present at Union Hill on Thursday before the second Sunday in Aug. to be at the association to be held with that church: T. N. Smith, R. L. Warren, J. M. Richards, J. W. Holcomb, E. A. Cochran, H. G. Wilkie. Granted Marian Broks/ Brooks a letter of dismission. J. R. Stone, Mod., H. G. Wilkie, C.C.

June Term, Rev. J. R. Stone. Same as above, but the addition of R. J. Pursell as a delegate to the association.

July Term, 1909, Rev. J. R. Stone. 5. Moved and carried that report of the church be read, the same being adopted by the church. Granted Sister Martha Pearce a letter of dismission. Taken up collection for minutes, received $1.05. J. R. Stone, Mod., H. G. Wilkie, C.C.

Aug. 14, 1909, R. W. Cochran, elected R. W. Cochran, moderator. 5. Moved and carried that the moderator of this conference appoint a commity to revise and draw off the names of this church and place them on the new book. The commity is as follows: G. B. Hegwood, T. N. Smith, Thos. Briant, H. K. Fletcher, H. G. Wilkie. All sow that we appoint a finance committee in lue of the deacons to assist in the financial needs of the church and the support of the ministry, the same being approved by the church and appointed by the moderator, namely: John B. Ellis, J. T. Briant, J. M. Richards, H. K. Fletcher, L. L. West, G. W. Little. Moved and carried that church rolls be called and the same is here submitted. All sow granted Sister Mary Gabrell a letter of dismission. R. W. Cochran, Mod., H. G. Wilkie, C.C.

Sept. Term, 1909, Rev. J. R. Stone. 2. Preferred a charge against a sister for adultery, moved and carried that the church withdraw fellowship from her. All sow moved and carried the church withdraw fellowship from a brother for desertion of his family. All sow moved and carried the church withdraw fellowship from another sister for living in adultery. Moved and carried that the church prefer a charge against another brother for fighting, taken up the charge and excluded him from the fellowship of the church. 4. Received the acknowledgement of a brother and restored him back to the fellowship of the church. 5. Moved and carried that the church go into the election of a pastor for another year. Moved and carried that we suspend the regular order of business and elect by eclimation. Moved and carried that Bro. Stone be nominated as our pastor. The church then voting and unanimously elected Bro. Stone as our pastor for another year and the same being accepted by him. Taken up collection for our pastor, received fifteen dollars, forty-five cts. Paid previous $12.60, total $28.05. J. R. Stone, Mod., H. G. Wilkie, C.C.

Book 2: 1903-1909 Membership, by order of entry

* Information found only in minutes

1 by the name indicates person also listed in book 1.

	Last name	First name	Middle name	How/when received, Other info	How/when dismissed, Other Info	*Remarks; items not listed in church roll (maiden name; spouse; birth-death; buried at HBC)*
1	Andrews	J.	S.	Let Oct 20, 1900	Died Dec 1902 Deacon	
1	Andrews	Jane		Let Oct 20, 1900	Death, time unk.	*w/o J. S. Andrews*
1	Andrews	Lou	A.	Exp Aug 12, 1902	Deceased	
1	Andrews	Mattie	M.	Exp Aug 1897	Death, time unk.	*(Green) 1880-1951, bur HBC with W.J. Andrews*
	Anderson	Dora		Exp Aug 1900	Let Oct 14, 1905	
1	Biddy	Richards				*John Richard, 1841-1927 m. Susan Hardin*
1	Boling	H.	C.			*Henry Clay, 1939-1910, bur HBC, also Bowling in Bk 3.*
1	Boling	Emily	R.		Died Oct 14, 1909	*Emily Rebecca (Green), 1847-1909 wife of Henry Clay, bur HBC, also Bowling in Bk 3*
1	Bryant	Thomas		Let Aug 5, 1888		*1851-1923, bur HBC*

	Last name	First name	Middle name	How/when received, Other info	How/when dismissed, Other Info	*Remarks; items not listed in church roll (maiden name; spouse; birth-death; buried at HBC)*
1	Bryant	Lucy		Let Aug 5, 1888		*Lucy Ann (Garrett), 1856-1922, bur HBC, w/o Thomas Bryant*
1	Bryant	John	T.	Exp Aug 31, 1890		*1870-1914, h/o Fannie E (Kelley) Bryant, bur HBC*
1	Bryant	G.	Mats	Exp Aug 31, 1890		*George Mansell*
1	Boling	W.	Thompson	Exp Aug 31, 1890		*William Thompson, 1868-1929, bur HBC*
1	Boling	J.	Loury	Exp Aug 31, 1890		
1	Biddy	George		Exp Sep 15, 1889		
1	Boling	Reuben	J.	Exp Sep 15, 1893		*Reuben Jackson*
1	Baker	Mrs.				
1	Bryant	Fannie		Let Apr 18, 1896		*Fannie (Kelly) Bryant, w/o John T Bryant*
1	Baker	Mc		Let Nov 1896	Let Jul 1904	*Bro Mac*
1	Baker	Eliza		Let Aug 1897	Let Jul 1904	*w/o Mack*
1	Boling	Pruid		Exp Aug 1892	Death, time, unk.	*Mary Prude (Green) Boling, 1877-1924, bur HBC, w/o John Franklin Boling*
1	Boling	John	F.	Exp Aug 1897		*John Franklin, 1873-1926, bur HBC*
1	Boling	Martha		Let Aug 1899		
1	Biddy	John		Let Aug 1900	Let Oct 1909	
1	Biddy	Elisabeth		Let Aug 1900	Let Oct 1909	*Sarah Elizabeth/Elisabeth*
1	Biddy	Nicie	L.	Let Aug 1900	Let Oct 1909	*1877-1960*
1	Biddy	A.	R.	Let Aug 1900	Let Oct 1909	*1875-1910*
1	Biddy	A.	L.	Let Aug 1900	Let Oct 1909	
1	Biddy	Emory		Let Aug 1900	Let Oct 1909	*"Emory" not listed in book 1, only the last name…*
1	Biddy	Lula		Exp Sep 1899	Let Oct 1909	
1	Biddy	Elma		Exp Sep 1900	Let Oct 1909	*M. Alma w/o Fletcher Bryant*
1	Bryant	Fletcher	A.	Exp Sep 1900	Let Oct 1909	*1884-1949*
1	Bryant	F.	Belle	Exp Sep 1900	Death time unknown	*Fannie Belle (Price) m. George Mancel Bryant*
1	Bloodworth	G.	Milton	Exp Sep 1900	Let Aug 1903	*George Milton, 1884-1944*
1	Bryant	H.	Jackson	Exp Aug 1902	Let 1909	
1	Brooks	Richard		Exp Aug 1902	Let Oct 1909	*1882-1956, m. Adeline?*
1	Brooks	Joseph	W.	Exp Aug 1902		*m. Missouri?*
1	Barnwell	Elbert	J.	Exp Aug 1884 or 1887		
	Bryant	Lewis		Exp Aug 1904	Deceased, time unknown	

	Last name	First name	Middle name	How/when received, Other info	How/when dismissed, Other Info	*Remarks; items not listed in church roll (maiden name; spouse; birth-death; buried at HBC)*
	Brooks	Adeline		Let May 1906	Let Oct 16, 1909	*1885-1979*
	Bryant	Posey		Exp Aug 1906		
	Boling	James		Exp Aug 1907		
	Boling	Maud		Exp Aug 1907	Died Jun 25, 1909	
	Bryant	Lula		Let Aug 23, 1908?		
	Bryant	Viola		Exp Aug 20, 1908		
	Bryant	Mary		Exp Aug 20, 1908		
	Bryant	Mary	J.	Exp Oct 17, 1908		
1	Cochran	Elias	A.		Deceased, time unknown; Ordained Minister	*1845-1931, Ordained on Nov 1884* *bur HBC with 3 wives*
1	Cochran	Robert	W.	Exp Aug 1885	Deceased, time unknown; Ordained Minister-	*1852-1937, bur HBC*
1	Cochran	Matilda	M.			*Matilda M.w/o R.W. Cochran, d 07 Nov 1925, bur HBC*
1	Chastain	J.	Benj	Let Jul 1887	Let Sep 1904	*Joel Benjamin or Benny 1853-1928?*
1	Chastain	N.	A.	Exp Sep 1892	Let Sep 1904	*Sister Netty? 1852-1917, Nancy Adaline, w/o J. Ben Chastain*
1	Chastain	John	F.	Exp Sep 1892	Let Mar 1905	*John Franklin*
1	Cantrell	M.	O. "Tavy"	Exp Aug 1897	Let Oct 1906	*Mary Octavia "Tavie" Cantrell*
1	Chastain	A.	Bennie	Exp Aug 1897	Let Sep 1904	
1	Chastain	O.	Agathy	Exp Aug 1897	Let Mar 1905	*m. John Franklin Chastain*
1	Cantrell	J.	Alfred	Let Sep 1897	Let 1906	*James Alfred*
1	Cantrell	Georgia	A.	Let Sep 1897	Let Oct 1906	
1	Chastain	Elijah	C.	Exp Aug 1899	Let Sep 1904	*Elijah Coleman, 1886-1948*
1	Cannon	Lesom		Exp Aug 1899	Let Mar 1905	
1	Cannon	Florence		Exp Aug 1899	Let Mar 1905	
1	Cannon	Elmore	L.	Exp Sep 1900	Death 1957	*1887-1957, Elmer Cranston, h/o Minnie Thacker*
1	Cannon	F.	Edna	Exp Sep 1900	Death	*1886-1970, Florence Edna Cannon m. Joseph Carl Thacker in 1908*
1	Chastain	George	B.	Exp Sep 1900	Let Mar 14, 1908	
1	Cantrell	Raymond	M.		Deceased, time unknown	*Raymond Marion, 1874-1940, s/o Alfred and Georgia Cantrell, bur HBC*
1	Collier	Nancy	J.	Exp Sep 1901		

	Last name	First name	Middle name	How/when received, Other info	How/when dismissed, Other Info	*Remarks; items not listed in church roll (maiden name; spouse; birth-death; buried at HBC)*
1	Collier	Mary		Exp Sep 1901		
1	Collier	Linie	A.	Exp Aug 1902		
1	Crow	Ader	L.	Exp Aug 1899	*Let Aug 15 1903	*Ada Lucinda (Nelson)*
1	Cape	Eveline		Let Mar 1898		
	Cochran	E.	Virgil	Exp Aug 1903	Death	*Elias Virgil, 1883-1954, s/o R W Cochran;*
	Cochran	I.	Elisabeth	Exp Aug 1897	Death	*Ina Elizabeth, 1886-1962, w/o Virgil Cochran*
1	Cantrell	Lula		Exp Sep 1899	Deceased, time unknown	*Lula Viola (Hester), 1883-1954, m Raymon Cantrell*
1	Cordell	Josia		Exp Aug 1890	Let Sep 14, 1907	
	Cloud	Sarah		Let Apr 1907		
	Chastain	Maggie		Let Jul 20 1907		
	Clark	Daisy		Exp Aug 1907	Let Sep 1908	
	Collier	John		Exp Aug 1907		
	Christopher	May		Exp Oct 17 1908		
1	Davenport	Sarah	J.	Let Aug 20 1890		*Sarah J. (Heygood)*
1	Dawson	Nancy		Let Jun 19 1897		
1	Dawson	John	T.	Exp Sep 1898	Deceased time unk	
1	Dawson	Julia	J.	Exp Aug 1897		*Julia J (Cochran), 1879-1970, w/o John T Dawson*
1	Dooly	Vena		Exp Aug 31, 1890		*Or Viennan (Bryant)*
1	Dunnigan	R.	Aulelia	Exp Sep 16, 1899		*Raymond Aulelua Dunagan*
1	Dunnigan	Mary		Exp Sep 16, 1899		*Mary Laura (Hester)*
1	Dobson	S.	Ader	Let Sep 15, 1900		*Sis Susan Adia, 1876-1961*
1	Dowda	Ida	B.	Exp Sep 1900	Let Sep 19, 1908	
1	Dowda	William	D.	Exp Sep 1900		
	Dobson	J.	Simeon	Exp Sep 1900	Let Jun 16, 1906	
	Dobson	W.	Neely	Exp Sep 1900		
1	Dobson	Loucidia		Exp Aug 1902	Let Sep. 1940	*? 1880-1953, bur HBC, Lucinda Eulline (Little) w/o Elijah Dobson*
	Dowda	A.	Eary E.	Exp Aug 1903		
1	Dawson	Nancy		Exp Aug 1903		
	Dobson	E.	W.	Exp Aug 1906	Let Sep. 1940	*Elijah W, 1878-1958, h/o Loucinda (Little), bur HBC*
	Drummond	Texie		Exp Aug 1906	Dead	*(Hester), 1874-1913, 1st w/o George W Drummond*
1	Eaton	Jessie	W.		Let Jul 1904	*Bro Jessie Washington, 1855-1927*

	Last name	First name	Middle name	How/when received, Other info	How/when dismissed, Other Info	*Remarks; items not listed in church roll (maiden name; spouse; birth-death; buried at HBC)*
1	Eaton	Sylphia		Let Aug 19, 1887	Let Jul 1904	*Zillie, w/o Jessie Eaton, Or Zilphia, 1857-1928*
1	Ellis	J.	Henry	Let Mar 20, 1897	Deceased time unk. Deacon, July 1904	
1	Ellis	Catherine		Let Mar 20, 1897		*1866-1948, Mary Catharine (Haygood), w/o J. Henry Ellis*
1	Eaton	Rachael		Exp Aug 1897	Let Mar 1905	*Rachael E (Speer), 1879-1971*
1	Ellis	John	B.	Exp Aug 1899		*John Barry, 1885-1915*
1	Ellis	J.	Elbert	Exp Sep 1900		*James Elbert "Elb", 1888-1932, bur HBC*
1	Eaton	L.	Daisy	Exp Sep 1901	Let Jul 1904	
	Ellice	Ida	O.	Let Aug 22, 1907		*Ida Wallace Ellis, 1883-1968*
	Ellice	Omie		Exp Aug 1907		*Oma Mae Ellis?*
1	Fowler	Margarett			Let Sep 16, 1905	*(Sandow?)*
1	Floyd	Thomas		Exp Aug 14, 1884	Let Sep 14, 1907	
1	Fletcher	G.	Bartow	Exp Jan 1886 *Bk 1: RBL Jan 1889	Deceased, time unk. Deacon 1890	*George Bartow "Bart", 1862 – 1932, bur HBC*
1	Fletcher	H.	Kelly	Let Apr 1888		*H K, Hezekiah Kelly Fletcher, 1860-1926, h/o Augusta (Hester)*
1	Fowler	George	C.	Exp Aug 31, 1890		
1	Fletcher	Augusta	A.	Exp Aug 1887		*Augusta Azalee (Hester), 1870-1947, w/o Hezekiah K. Fletcher, bur HBC*
1	Fowler	Sallie	L.	Exp Aug 1897	Let Sep 16, 1905	
1	Fowler	William		Let Aug 1897		
1	Fowler	Theodocia		Let Aug 1897		
1	Fuller	Savilla	R.	Exp Aug 1897	Let May 18, 1907	*(Martin), 1880-1973, w/o William Fuller*
1	Fuller	W.	I. "Jeir"	Exp Aug 1897		*Or Zeir, William Isaiah, Zear, 1873-1930*
1	Floyd	Sidney	W.	Exp Aug 1899		
1	Floyd	Lydia		Exp Aug 1899		*1896-1926, w/o A J Fowler*
1	Floyd	Nettie		Exp Aug 1899	Died Aug 1903	
1	Floyd	Armandia	Jr.	Exp Aug 1899	See Roper	*w/o George "Floyd" Roper*
1	Fowler	Annie	L.	Exp Sep 1900	See Speer	
1	Fowler	Johnny	A.	Exp Sep 1900	*Let Sep 16, 1905	
1	Fowler	W.	Thomas	Exp Sep 1900	Let Apr 1906	*William? Thomas*
1	Floyd	Cora	L.	Exp Sep 1900		
1	Fitts	Charley	F.	Exp Sep 1900		*Also Charlie*

	Last name	First name	Middle name	How/when received, Other info	How/when dismissed, Other Info	*Remarks; items not listed in church roll (maiden name; spouse; birth-death; buried at HBC)*
1	Floyd	Armandia	Sr.	Let Sep 1900/01		
1	Fletcher	Sallie	A.	Exp Aug 1887	Died Nov 18, 1903	*Sarah Azalee, 1869-1903, (Ledbetter), 1st w/o G Bartow Fletcher, bur HBC*
	Farmer	Ida		Exp Aug 1890		
1	Fowler	C.	R.		Let	
1	Fowler	Ransom		*Exp Aug 1882		
1	Freeman	Charity			Died Feb 13, 1904	
1	Fowler	Lucy			Died	*Charley's mother, 1808-1902, Lucinda "Lucy" Elizabeth, w/o William M. Fowler*
1	Fowler	Mary	M.			
1	Fowler	Mary	E.			
1	Fitts	Mary	J.			*Mary Jane (Green), w/o Jesse W. Fitts*
	Fowler	Sarah	E.			
1	Fowler	C.	A.		Let Sep 1905	
	Fletcher	Evlee		Exp Aug 1907		*Myra Evalee Fletcher Richards, w/o James Washington Richards, bur HBC* *dbl Aug. 21, 1937, rejoined Aug. 1938*
	Fowler	Mattie	L.	Exp Aug 26, 1908		*See Mason*
	Fowler	Newton		Exp Aug 26, 1908		
1	Greene	Thomas	E.			*Thomas Edward, 1848-1922, bur HBC, h/o Elizabeth Arwood*
1	Greene	Joseph	E.			
1	Greene	Nancy	L.			*w/o Joseph Green*
1	Greene	Elisabeth				
1	Greene	Mary	E.	Exp Aug 1897	See Speer	
1	Greene	Mary	E. "babe"	Exp Aug 1897		
1	Greene	Parilee		Let Aug 1885		*Perry Lee (Richards)1866-1918, w/o Jesse Brown Green*
1	Greene	Sarah		Let Nov 1899	Died Aug 13, 1908/1909	*bur HBC*
1	Greene	Lou				
1	Greene	Maud	M.	Exp Sep 1900		*Maudie, 1886-1913, bur HBC*
1	Gilstrap	L.	Daisy Holbrook	Exp Sep 1900		*m. Holbrook*
1	Groover	Will	J.	Exp Sep 1900	Let Sep 14, 1907	*William, 1851-1926, 1st m Judy, 2nd m Sarah*

	Last name	First name	Middle name	How/when received, Other info	How/when dismissed, Other Info	*Remarks; items not listed in church roll (maiden name; spouse; birth-death; buried at HBC)*
	Gibson	A.				
1	Grimes	Henry		Let Apr 1888		
	Green	May	Adams?	Exp Aug 20, 1908		
	Green	Susia		Exp Oct 17, 1908		*Susie Green Pearson, 1888-1963, bur HBC*
	Green	W.	P.	Exp Oct 1908		
1	Howard	Elisha				
1	Howard	Bud	F.		Let *May 20, 1905	*Benjamin Franklin, "Bud"*
1	Hester	A.	T., Scott			*Andrew Thomas? 1847-1910, m Elizabeth Davis?*
1	Holt	Lena	Rite	Let Aug 1891	See Rite? / Wright?	*d/o John and Manerva Holt*
1	Harden	Thomas	J.	Exp Sep 1889		*Thomas J Hardin, m Mary Elizabeth Stephens*
	Hagood	Sullivan	G.	Exp Aug 31, 1890		*1876-1935, Seldon/Sellivan Green m Mattie Wallace; bur HBC*
	Hagood	J.	Elmer	Exp Aug 1892		
1	Hamilton	J.	B.	Exp Aug 31, 1890	Dead	
1	Holcomb	James	J.	Let Oct 17, 1891		*James J, 1864-1937, bur HBC*
1	Holcomb	Lou		Let Oct 17, 1891		*Louise, 1862-1927, bur HBC, shares grave marker with J J Holcombe*
1	Holcomb	S.	D. "Bud"	Exp Sep 1893	Deceased, time unk	*Sherman Davis "Bud", m Alice Dora Wilkie, 1878-1962, bur HBC*
	Harden	Hassie		Let Sep 1890		
	Holcomb	John	W.	Let Sep 1893		
1	Holcomb	Cansady		Let Sep 1893		*Canzady (Haygood), 1844-1927, m John W Holcomb, bur HBC*
1	Howard	S.	D. "Monie"	Let Sep 1893		*(Holcomb)*
1	Hardin	Charley		Exp Sep 1893		
1	Hagood	Greene	B.	Let Nov 1896		*1848-1925, Bro Greene B., bur HBC*
1	Hagood	Soushannah		Let Nov 1896		*1844-1922, Suseana (Mosteller) bur HBC, w/o Greene Hagood*
1	Hagood	J.	Elmer	Exp Aug 1903		*J Elmer, 1881-1931, bur HBC with 2 wives, Annie and May*
1	Hardin	F.	Ollie	Exp Aug 1897		*(Green)*
1	Hardin	Annie	O.	Exp Aug 1897	See Holcomb	
1	Holcomb	John	T.	Exp Aug 1897		
1	Hagood	Lizzie		Exp Aug 1897	Died Jan 24 1903	

	Last name	First name	Middle name	How/when received, Other info	How/when dismissed, Other Info	*Remarks; items not listed in church roll (maiden name; spouse; birth-death; buried at HBC)*
1	Holcomb	Cora	L.	Exp Aug 1897		*(White) 1878-1936*
1	Hester	L.	Dora	Exp Aug 1885	Deceased, time unk	*(Wheeler), 1866-1937, bur HBC by John Hester 1869- 1916*
1	Hardin	Oveline		Exp Aug 31, 1890	Let Oct 15, 1904	*(Eaton) w/o Larkin Hardin*
1	Hogan	Myria		Let Apr 1888	dead	*1821-1908, bur HBC, Susanna Myra Brady Fletcher Hogan, m William Hogan*
1	Howard	L.	H.	Let		
1	Hester	Joseph	S.		Died Jul 1906	
1	Hagood	Annie	L.	Exp Jun 18, 1898		*(Cochran)*
1	Hester	May		Let Aug 1898	See Thrasher	*May (Swinford) Hester Thrasher*
1	Holcomb	W.	Henry	Exp Aug 1899	Deceased, time unk	
1	Higgins	Mamie	L.	Exp Aug 1899	Deceased time unk	
1	Higgins	Lizzie		Exp Aug 1899		
1	Howard	G.	Walter	Exp Sep 1900	*Let May 1905	*1884-1945*
1	Herring	A.	Webb	Exp Sep 1900		*Alfred Webb Herring, B 1881*
1	Hester	William	H.	Exp Sep 1900	dead	*1879-1905*
1	Hester	Laura	J.	Exp Sep 1900	See Wyatt	*1881-1954, Laura Jane m Joseph Aaron Wyatt*
1	Howard	Emma	D.	Exp Aug 1902	*Let May 1905	
1	Howard	L.	May	Exp Aug 1902	*Let May 1905	*Lillie May*
1	Holcomb	Bertha	S.	Exp Aug 1902		
	Holcomb	J.	Atley	Exp Aug 1903	dead	
1	Harbin	Mary				*(Howard)*
1	Howard	Victoria			*Let May 1905	*Harriett Victoria (Cole), w/o Bud; 1865-1946*
1	Hester	E.	J.			*Eliza Jane (Jefferson), w/o Joseph B Hester, 1849-1936*
1	Hester	E	C.			
1	Harden	Susan		Let Dec 1882		
1	Harden	S.	A.			
1	Hosey	M.	M.	Exp Aug 1885		
1	Harden	J.	D.	Exp Aug 1885		
1	Hardy	C.	A.	Exp Aug 31 1890		
	Howard	Celia		Exp Aug 1902		
	Howard	Millard		Let Aug 1905		
	Hawkins	O.	W.	Exp Aug 1906		
	Hester	C.	C.	Exp Aug 1906		*Christopher Columbus? 1881-1946, bur HBC*

	Last name	First name	Middle name	How/when received, Other info	How/when dismissed, Other Info	*Remarks; items not listed in church roll (maiden name; spouse; birth-death; buried at HBC)*
	Hester	Mattie		Exp Aug 1906	Deceased time unk	
	Hester	Mattie	Miss	Exp Aug 1906		
	Hester	Lillie		Exp Aug 1906	See Little	*1883-1979, w/o Dock Little, bur HBC*
	Hester	Daisy		Exp Aug 1907		*1889-1957, w/o Henry Scott*
	Hegwood	W.	D.	Exp Aug 1907		
	Hegwood	Sally	M.	Exp Aug 1907		
	Hall	Molly		Exp Aug 1907		
	Holcomb	Clair	Bell	Let Nov 1907		
	Herring	N.	F.	Let Aug 20, 1908		*Newton F, 1860-1926, h/o Josephine Herring*
	Herring	May		Exp Aug 20, 1908		*Maybell*
	Herring	Pearl		Exp Aug 20, 1908		*Nancy Pearl*
	Hall	Bessie		Exp Aug 20, 1908		
	Herring	Etta		Exp Oct 17, 1908		*Mary Etta*
	Howard	W. L.	D.	Let May 16, 1909		
	Howard	Anna		Let May 16, 1909		*Anner, 1860-1940, bur HBC*
1	Ingram	J.	Lewis	Exp Aug 1892		*James Lewis, s/o James J*
1	Ingram	Thomas	G. W.	Exp Aug 1892		*Thomas, s/o James J*
1	Ingram	Jeff	J.	Let Aug 1892		*James Jeff*
1	Ingram	Farriba		Let Aug 1892		*m James Jeff*
1	Kelly	Susan	E.	Exp Sep 1893		*Susan Eveline "Evie"(Bryant), b 1880 –w/o Robert A. E. Kelly*
	Kemp	Mary	D.	Exp Aug 19, 1884	See Law/Low	
	Kelly	Robert		Exp Sep 1905	Let Mar 20, 1909	*Bob*
1	Kelley	Evia			Let Feb 1909	*Susan Eveline "Evie"(Bryant), b 1880 – w/o Robert A. E. Kelly*
1	Leonard	Leannie		Let Aug 15 1891		*1824-1913/18, bur HBC, w/o Jesse Leonard, he was in Civil War, she drew widow's pension*
1	Leonard	Ida		Exp Aug 1897	See Turner, d Jan. 12, 1905	*m William B Turner*
1	Leonard	John	M.	Let Oct 19, 1901		
1	Little	Lillie	A.	Exp Sep 1900	See Williams	
1	Little	Tom		Exp Aug 1902		*Thomas E, 1874-1951*
1	Little	Senie		Exp Aug 1902		*Mary Senie, w/o Tom Little, 1878-1915*
1	Little	Dock		Exp Aug 1902	Deceased, time unk	*1886-1961, h/o Lillie Montana Hester bur HBC*
	Loggins	Mirandy		Let Aug 1904		*1877-*

	Last name	First name	Middle name	How/when received, Other info	How/when dismissed, Other Info	*Remarks; items not listed in church roll (maiden name; spouse; birth-death; buried at HBC)*
	Loggins	Robert		Let Aug 1904		*1879-*
	Loggins	Lucy		Let Aug 1904		*1850-*
	Loggins	Maggie		Let Aug 1904		*1873*
	Loggins	James	H.	Let Aug 1904		*1844-1939*
	Loggins	Valley		Let May 1904		*Bro, 1870*
	Loggins	Susan		Let May 1904		*w/o Valley Loggins*
	Loggins	?	No name listed	Exp Aug 1906		
	Leonard	Ethel		Exp Aug 1906	See Boling	*w/o James Boling*
	Leonard	Sinie		Exp Aug 1906	See Barrett	
	Little	Henry		Exp Aug 1906		
	Loggins	Julie		Let Aug 24, 1907		*1890-1961, bur HBC*
	Little	Harvey		Exp Aug 1907		
	Little	Millie		Let Aug 17, 1908		
	Little	Frank		Exp Aug 20, 1908		
	Little	Callia		Exp Aug 20, 1908		*Callie*
	Lenard	Lula		Exp Aug 1908	*Let Nov 1913	*(Cochran?)*
	Little	Geo	W.	Let Feb 1909	Deceased time unk	
	M & N pages MISSING					
	Nelson	Maiden			*Let Aug 15, 1903	*1882-*
	Odem	L.	Marquis		Let Nov 20, 1904	
	Odem	Hester	Ann	Let Oct 14, 1899	Let Nov 20, 1904	
	Odem	Oby		Exp Sep 15, 1889		*(Smith)*
1	Odem	Wyley	F.			
1	Odem	S.	J.			*Susan/Sara Jane "Abi"*
1	Odem	L.		Exp Aug 1887	Dead	*Lettie, "Lindy"*
1	Odem	Marques		Let Aug 1907		*Bro. Margers/Marquis*
1	Odem	Hester	Ann	Let Aug 1907		*Sis*
1	Odem	Grover	C.	Exp Aug 1907		*Grover Cleveland*
1	Purcell	Reuben	J.			*Reuben James, 1852-1927, liberated Aug 15, 1896*
1	Purcell	Elisabeth	M.			*Or Pursell, (Jackson), w/o Reuben James Purcell*
	Purcell	Louiza			Dead	

	Last name	First name	Middle name	How/when received, Other info	How/when dismissed, Other Info	*Remarks; items not listed in church roll (maiden name; spouse; birth-death; buried at HBC)*
1	Priest	Rutha		Let Nov 17, 1883	Let	*1838-1916, (Ruthey Springer), w/o Epson Priest*
1	Prewitt	Mont	E.	Exp Aug 5, 1887		
1	Pascoe	John		Let Feb 1888	Let Oct 19, 1907	*John Jackson, 1855-1921*
1	Pascoe	Samuel		Let Feb 1888	Let Oct 19, 1907	*Samuel Washington, 1855-1937*
1	Pascoe	Mrs.		Let Feb 1888	Let Oct 19, 1907	*Effie (Stephens), w/o John Jackson Pascoe*
1	Pascoe	Mrs.		Let Feb 1888		*Ella (Stephens), 1864-1904, w/o Samuel W Pascoe*
1	Purcell	R.	Benj	Exp Aug 24, 1890		*Reuben Benjamin Purcell, h/o Fannie Edwards?*
1	Purcell	Rufus	J. M.	Exp Aug 24, 1890	Death	*h/o Daisy Nix*
1	Pierce	William		Exp Aug 24, 1890	Death	*1880-1921, s/o H H and Martha Pierce*
1	Pierce	Martha		Let Aug 24, 1890	*Let Jul 1909	*Martha Mayberry (Wilkie), 1864-1936, w/o Henry Harrison Pierce*
1	Purcell	Fannie	M.	Let Jun 16, 1894		
1	Pierce	R.	Erastus	Exp Sep 1894	Let Sep 14, 1907	
1	Priest	Ella				*(Stephens), 1866-1943, w/o George W. Priest*
1	Pearson	Edgar		Exp Aug 1897	Dead	*1880-1935, Edd H, bur HBC*
1	Purcell	J.	Luther	Exp Aug 1897		*James Luther Purcell*
1	Purcell	Mattie		Exp Aug 31, 1890		*Martha "Mattie" (Hester), 1875-1951, w/o Thomas Benjamin Purcell*
1	Pruitt	John	B.	Exp Jun 1898		*1877-1925*
1	Pruitt	Rosanna	M.	Exp Aug 1897		*Roseanna Mary (Ellis), 1883-1963, *w/o J B Pruitt*
1	Purcell	W.	Louis	Exp Aug 1899		*1886-?, h/o Laura Maddox*
1	Pinson	Leannie		Let Aug 19, 1899		
1	Price	Lillie	M.	Exp Sep 1900	See Mason	
1	Price	W.	Oscar	Exp Sep 1900		*"Dick"*
1	Price	W.	H. "Samp"	Exp Sep 1900		*"Sampson"*
1	Price	Dora	J.	Exp Aug 1897		*(Mason) 1880-1946*
1	Purcell	M.	Odella	Exp Sep 1901	(Price)	*Minnie Odella (Price), w/o James Luther Purcell*
1	Purcell	Lela	B.	Exp Aug 1902		*Liller*
1	Price	J.	Milton	Exp Aug 1902		*James Milton, 1880-1957*
1	Pearson	Nettie	R.	Exp Sep 1900		*1882-1950, (Boling) w/o Edgar Pearson, bur HBC*
1	Priest	Sallie		Exp Sep 1894		*(Brady)*
	Price	Dortha		Exp Aug 1903		*Dorthy*

	Last name	First name	Middle name	How/when received, Other info	How/when dismissed, Other Info	*Remarks; items not listed in church roll (maiden name; spouse; birth-death; buried at HBC)*
	Pierce	Marietta		Exp Aug 1903	See Thompson	
1	Petty	A.			Dead	*? Atlantic, 2nd wife of Wiley Petty, 1826-1898*
1	Pearson	J.	H.	Exp Aug 5, 1887		
	Priest	E.	M.	Exp Aug 1906		*Epson/Epty, 1846-1923*
	Pearce	Rocksey		Exp Aug 1907		*Roxana Pierce*
	Parker	Almer		Exp Aug 1908		*Almer (Parker) Brooks*
	Richards	J.	Marion	Let Aug 1885	Let Jan 20, 1907	
1	Richards	James	M.	Let Aug 19, 1885		*James M Richards, Sr.*
1	Ramsey	R.	A.	Let Aug 15, 1891		*Rice, 1850-1925, bur HBC*
1	Ramsey	Ann		Let Aug 15, 1891		*(Leonard) w/o Rice Ramsey, m in 1879, 1856-1939, bur HBC*
1	Rich	Victoria		Exp Aug 1897	Death Aug 1, 1954	*1874-1954, (Sandow), bur HBC?*
1	Richards	Mabel	A.	Exp Aug 19, 1884		*(Boling)*
1	Richards	Octavy	I.	Exp Aug 5, 1888		
	Richards	Martha	J.	Let Jun 19, 1903		
1	Reynolds	M.	J.			
	Robertson	Ida		Exp Aug 19, 1885		*1871-*
	Rider?	UJenia		Exp Oct 17, 1908		
1	Smith	Thomas	N.	Exp Jul 1884	Deacon	*Thomas Nathan, 1857-1919, m 1st J. Angeline, m 2nd Jane, ordained as deacon on Nov 1884, bur HBC*
1	Stephens	John	H.	Exp Aug 1890		
1	Stephens	Laura		Exp Aug 1890		
1	Sandow	M.	Viola	Exp Sep 1893	Death	*Viola Minerva (Wilkie) Sandow, 1879-1969, m Sherman Sandow*
1	Smith	A.	F "Gussie"	Exp Sep 1899	Let Sep 18, 1905	*Agustis*
1	Smith	Millie	A.	Let Sep 1900		
1	Smith	Colonel	N.	Exp Sep 1900		
1	Smith	Octavia	A.	Exp Aug 1902		
	Speer	Annie		Exp Sep 1900		
1	Smallwood	J.	M.			*James M.?*
	Smallwood	E.				
1	Smallwood	M.	S.			
1	Stephens	Mary				*1823-1902; aka "Aunt Polly"; m Larkin Stephens; bur HBC*
1	Southern	Elisa				
1	Stephens	M.	J.	Exp Aug 1887		
1	Stephens	R.		Exp Aug 1887		
1	Speer	Mary	E.	Exp Aug 1887		*(Greene)*

	Last name	First name	Middle name	How/when received, Other info	How/when dismissed, Other Info	*Remarks; items not listed in church roll (maiden name; spouse; birth-death; buried at HBC)*
	Smith	Nettie		Exp Aug 1906		
	Speer	Charley	C.	Exp Aug 1907		
	Smith	E.	J.	Let Aug 17, 1908		
	Smith	Sarah	E.	Let Aug 17, 1908/1909	death	*Sarah Elizabeth Smith; Mrs. E. J. Smith*
	Southern	Amanda		Let May 16, 1909		
1	Thompson	James	M.			
1	Thompson	Mary	J. "Tack"	Exp Aug 1897		
1	Thompson	Minnie	D.	Exp Aug 1897		
1	Thompson	Jessie	M.	Exp Aug 1897		
1	Thompson	Judge	N.	Exp Aug 1899		*1850*
1	Thompson	Lillie	M.	Exp Sep 1900		
1	Tippens	Caroline			Dead	
1	Tippens	Nancy	M.		Dead	
1	Tippens	Virginia				
1	Tomblin	Nancy			Dead	
	Turner	Ida		Exp Aug 1897	Died Jan 12, 1905	*(Leonard)*
	Thompson	Marietta		Exp Aug 1903		*(Pierce)*
1	Thrasher	May		Let Aug 1898	Let Apr 1904	*(Hester) Listed in census as Thornton? not Thrasher?*
	Thompson	Sarah		Let Aug 17, 1908		
	Umphrey	E.	C.	Let Mar 1898		
1	White	A.	Jack		Died Aug 1904	*Andrew Jackson, 1833-1904, bur HBC?*
1	Williams	B.	H. "Bud"	Exp Aug 17, 1887	Let Oct 1904	*Berry Hawkins Williams, "Bud", 1846-1940*
1	Williams	Loucindia	A.	Exp Aug 17, 1887	Let Oct 1904	*Loucinda (Davis), w/o B H Williams*
1	Wilkie	J.	Harrison	Exp Aug 1890	death	*John Harrison, 1871-1949, bur HBC*
1	Wilkie	H.	Glenn	Exp Aug 1890	Death; deacon	*Hiram Glenn, 1877-1956, Ordained deacon July 1904, bur HBC*
1	Williams	Jessie	R.	Exp Aug 1890	Let Oct 1904	
1	Wallace	Lydia		Exp Aug 1890	dead	
1	White	Julius		Exp Aug 1890		
1	White	S.	Margarett	Let Apr 18, 1894	Let Apr 1906?	*Mrs. Margaret White*
1	Williams	Jack	L.	Let Aug 1894		*Ordained as deacon, Nov 1884*
1	Williams	Mary	A.	Let Aug 1894	Dead	*Mary Ann (Wooten), w/o J L Williams*
1	Williams	Azzalee		Let Aug 1894		
	Wyatt	Joseph	A.	Exp. Aug 1897	Let 1899	

	Last name	First name	Middle name	How/when received, Other info	How/when dismissed, Other Info	*Remarks; items not listed in church roll (maiden name; spouse; birth-death; buried at HBC)*
1	Wallace	M	Jane	Exp Aug 1897		
1	Williams	Ollie	T.	Exp Aug 1897	Let Oct 1904	
1	Wilkie	Lula	P.	Exp Aug 1897	Death 1962	*Lula Pearl (Jones), 1879-1962, bur HBC, w/o Glenn Wilkie*
1	White	Ellen		Exp Aug 31, 1890		*1872-1933, Ellen Clara (Hester) w/o John Bullock White*
1	White	Joseph	W.	Exp Aug 3, 1897	Death	
1	White	John	W.			
1	Wilkie	Alice		Exp Sep 1899	Death Mar 20 1968 See Holcomb	*1884-1968, w/o Sherman Holcomb; bur HBC*
1	Wallace	Jessie	W	Let Jan 1900		
1	Wilkie	Etta			Let Mar 1905	
1	Wilkie	Myrtie	J.	Exp Sep 1900	Death 1978	*Myrtie Jewell Wilkie, 1887-1977, bur HBC*
1	Wilkie	G	Neel	Exp Sep 1900	Let Mar 1905	
1	Wright	Conrad	A.	Exp Sep 1900		
1	Wallace	Mattie		Exp Sep 1900	See Wilkie	*Martha Lou "Mattie" (Wallace), 1888, w/o Edward Forrest Wilkie*
1	Warren	Robert		Let Jun 1901		
1	Warren	Delcy		Let Jun 1901		*Delsie; w/o Robert Warren*
1	Wilkie	Georgia	A.	Exp Aug 1902	See Lovelace	*Georgia Ann (Wilkie), 1890-1965, m Robert Edgar Lovelace, bur HBC*
1	Wilkie	TheOdocia		Exp Aug 1902	Death 1957	*(Stancil), 1873-1957, m John Harrison Wilkie, bur HBC*
1	Wilkie	D.	O. B.			
1	Wilkie	Margarett				
1	Willson	Nancy	J.			
1	White	N.	J.			
1	Wilkie	Fannie	A.	Exp Jul 1885		
1	Wilkie	H.	F.	Exp Aug 1885		
1	Wilkie	H.	N.	Exp Aug 1885		
1	Willson	F.	A.	Exp Aug 19, 1889		
1	White	Nancy	M.			
1	Wilkie	Lee			death	*Henry "Lee"? 1867-1936, bur HBC*
	Wyatt	Laura	J.	Exp Sep 1900		*(Hester)*
	Williams	Lillie	A.	Exp Aug 1900		
	Warren	Dizie	E.	Let Jun 17, 1904/5		*Dizzie*
	Williams	S.	Ida	Exp Aug 1899	Let Jan 15, 1907	
	Wiginton	J.	N.	Let Jul 1904		*Wigginton*

	Last name	First name	Middle name	How/when received, Other info	How/when dismissed, Other Info	*Remarks; items not listed in church roll (maiden name; spouse; birth-death; buried at HBC)*
	West	L.	L.	Let May 1906		*Lightner Leander West, 1863-1927, bur HBC*
	West	Mrs. L.	L.	Let May 1906		*Josephine McDaniel West, 1857-1928, w/o L L West, bur HBC*
	West	Nettie		Let May 1906	See Hester	*1888-1946, m Thad Hester*
	West	Ella		Let May 1906		*1884-1962; bur HBC*
	Wilkie	Mattie	L.	Exp Sep 1900	Death	
	Warren	Johnny		Exp Aug 1906		
	Warren	Ethel		Exp Aug 1906		
	Wallace	John		Let Aug 18, 1906		
	Wallace	Ethel		Let Aug 18, 1906		*Ethel Dunagan, 1897-1934, w/o Truman Wallace*
	Williams	J.	J.	Let Aug 21, 1907		
	Warren	Henry	J.	Let Aug 21, 1907		
	Wallice	Bessie		Exp Aug 20, 1908		
*2	Brooks	Marian			Let Jun 19, 1909	
*2	Dobson	Mary	E.	Let Jun 18, 1904	Let Jun 18, 1904	*w/o W M B Dobson*
*2	Dobson	W.	M. B.	Let Jun 18, 1904	Let Jun 18, 1904	
*2	Fowler	Charley			Let Sep 15, 1906	
*2	Fowler	Joe			Let Apr 18, 1903	
*2	Gabrell	Mary			Let Aug 14, 1909	
*2	Mason	Johnny				
*2	Nelson	Maiden			Let Aug 15, 1903	
*2	Pearce	Nettie			Let Aug 17, 1907	
*2	Pearson	Maud				
*2	Richards	Marion & wife			Let Jan 20, 1907	
*2	Warren	H.	T.		Let Aug 1908	

Chapter 6: 1910-1923, Minutes and Membership Roll, Book Three

- Community
    - Industrial revolution
    - World War I

- Religion/Baptists,
    - Assessing members for money to support the church
    - Increasing church property
    - Baptismal pool built Aug. 1918
    - 1920 - deacon ordination

- Occupations
    - Farmers
    - Pyrite miners
    - Cotton mill employees

- Transportation
    - Wagons
    - Cars

- Cemetery
    - Section one and two
    - Addition of section three and four

As the U.S. endured World War I, several men from HBC were soldiers during that war, as noted in the list of military records in the appendix of this book. Pictured is Emory West who served his country. On the home front, the area of HBC was isolated from the world in many ways; however, the products of the second industrial revolution (mid 1800s until World War I) gradually trickled into the community. The railroad to Ball Ground, the news of petroleum or gas-powered engines (cars!) and eventually electricity, promised to improve life as it was known. It would be years before these items were common place, but the news of the possibilities of making farming easier, of travel improvements and of comfort in homes were vital for renewed hope of successful futures. In the meantime chores, such as milling sugar cane, continued to be a slow process. Pictured below is a young George H. Lovelace (born 1909) with two of the family mules, Charlie and Dan, at a syrup mill on the family farm.

Robert "Emory" West
Photo courtesy of Tim Perkins

George H. Lovelace
Photo courtesy of Chris Chandler

In 1914, HBC minutes note that the church approved funds for buying new tools to dig graves. The practice of church members volunteering to dig graves for the deceased continued for a number of years, likely into the 1940s and 50s, until companies took over the task. By 1915, the needs of the church led to an assessment of each member for funds. A motion was brought before the church to pass a resolution for every member of HBC to donate 5 cents every 3 months towards bearing the expense of the church. Also, a motion was presented to the church for every male member to pay 5 cents a month. By 1917, a motion carried to abolish the "anvalorem" system of the church. (Possibly this reference was meant as Ad valorem, which usually refers to an expected amount to pay for a particular purpose.)

It is thought that the location for baptisms in the early years of HBC was in the nearby Etowah River. In August, 1918, a baptismal pool was built on Lovelace property just east of the current church. This project must have been completed before funds were available because the minutes state that in January, 1919, the church decided to borrow money to finish paying for the pool that was built in August, 1918.

The 1910 census for Cross Roads District, Cherokee Co. continued to enumerate farmers and farm laborers as the most common occupation. The farmers were the landowners and the laborers were the tenants and workers on the farms. Often included as laborers were children; one child laborer listed was only eight years old! Other jobs indicated work at the pyrite mines, including engineers, laborers, blacksmiths, etc. Sherman Sandow was a bookkeeper at the mines, Dr. George C. McClure was the general practice physician and Clara B. White was listed as the public school teacher. The cotton industry not only employed the local farmers, but some folks began moving to the "city" of Canton to be near the cotton mill. Canton Textile Mills was continuing to prosper, and in early 1923, Mill Number Two was constructed. The plants continued to operate until the 1960s. Plant Number One closed in 1969. After his stint in the military, Mr. Emory West of HBC returned home and was photographed in a cotton field. It seems this was a staged picture as he was rather well dressed for picking cotton! Mr. Emory later operated the Free Home General Store for many years.

Ford, General Motors and Chrysler began making cars in the early 1900s. By the 1920s, more affordable models were available. The transition on the church grounds of tethering the horses and mules to clearing more land for parking the automobiles had begun; even though this was likely a slow process for the local people. Wagon transportation continued for a number of years for many at HBC. Shown below is a picture of common wagon travel with dirt roads being the common path. The couple in the picture is Clarence and Inez Coltrane, relatives of Emmett and Mary Lee Cochran.

Robert "Emory" West
Photo courtesy of Mary Helen Cissell

Photo courtesy of Brenda Curtis

Another example from horse and buggy days is the young boys below, believed to be L-R: Thomas Edward Green (1900-1984), Edwin "Dennis" Wilkie (1905-1994) and James "Harrison" Wilkie (1900-1985). Photo was taken possibly at the Green family home. Photo courtesy of Ken Wyatt

For the first time since the deed of 1845, HBC expanded the church property in 1914. In the HBC minutes of January, 1914, a report was given on buying land for burying ground. Deed 2 (1914) and Deed 3 (1920) were recorded during this era. It was likely that needed expansion of the burial ground was the reason for the transaction (see Appendix). These deeds correspond with the portion of land in the triangle near the current highway; for this book the portion is labeled section three. The first year of death recorded on a tombstone in this section is 1915, with the exception of a few memorial markers showing an earlier date. Additional property was soon secured, noted on Deed 4 (March, 1923) between Mrs.

Georgia Lovelace and HBC which preserved a ½ acre adjacent and behind or south of the church building, noted as section four for this book. On Nov. 24, 1923, HBC minutes note: "Granted permission to remove the pines in the church yard." Those with a vision for the future were making plans for the increased need for parking vehicles.

During 1918-1919, many people suffered from the Spanish flu epidemic, and numbers of people died. According to the *Heritage of Cherokee County, Ga.*: "People in rural areas who had no access to an undertaker 'laid-out' their dead and did their own burials." Many may have died from flu in rural areas and never reported the cause of death. Thirteen burials are recorded at HBC in 1918 and 1919, with six of those in November of 1918, and five of those six were age eleven and under. This listing cannot confirm a connection with the flu epidemic, but that was certainly a possibility. The following list includes those buried at HBC, in 1918: Effie Viola Dobson, age 3; Marie Green, age 3; Olin Green, age 11; Jewell Mae Hester, age 17; Lizzie Wright Jones, age 45; Mary E. Leonard, age 71; Oscar Pearson, age 36; Edward M. Porter, age 2; John Anthony Sandow, Jr. age 55; Wade Sheffield, age 6; and Flonnie Myrtle Wilkie, age 11. In 1919, the list of burials includes: Clifton Bryant, age 10; and Dorothy Cannon, age 8 months.

Membership milestones: From 1901, HBC membership was at or near 300 for a number of years, and then began to rise to the mid-300s by 1915. It was in the year of 1920 when the membership first totaled over 400. The last year that the data showed male/female membership was in 1907.

Minutes, 1910-1923, Book 3

Each entry:

Date, Minister(s) who preached on that date.

Any of the items that had activity on that given date.

Items:

1. Invited visiting brethren to seats with us

2. Called for the fellowship of the church

3. Called for reference

4. Opened the door of the church for the reception of members

5. General Business

Moderator, Church Clerk

Oct. 1909, Bro. J. R. Stone. 4. Received by letter Sister Jane Collit, Sister Vader Ellis 5. Granted letters of dismission to: Richard Brooks and wife Adeline Brooks, Luther J. Pursell and wife Deller (Odella) Pursell. Received eight dollars for pastor. J. R. Stone, H. K. Fletcher, C. Pro.

Nov. Term, 1909, J. R. Stone. 5. Granted Bro. Colonel Smith and wife [*Millie*] letters of dismission. All sow granted J. J. Holcomb and family [*wife: Louise, daus: Bertha, Clara Belle*] letters of dismission. Accepted an invitation to Ball Ground Baptis church to be with them to ordain some deacons. A request was made by a brother for restoration of his wife, was referred till next meeting. J. R. Stone, Mod., R. B. Pursell, C. Pro.

Jan. 19, 1910, J. R. Stone. 2. Moved and carried that the church appoint a committee to see a brother and report at next conference. 3. Received the acknowledgements of a sister. 5. Granted letters of dismission: R. B. Pursell and wife [*Fannie Edwards Pursell*] and R. J. Pursell and wife [*Elizabeth*] and J. S. Parker and wife [*Sallie*] and Almer [*Alma*] Parker Brooks. J. R. Stone, Mod., H. G. Wilkie, C.C.

Feb. 16, 1910, Rev. J. R. Stone. 3. Restored a brother back to the church, preferred a charge against his wife for leaving her husband. 5. Appointed delegates to union meeting as follows: Bro. Green B. Heggood, W. O. Price, G. M. Bryant, Jesse Wallace, Johnie Ellis. J. R. Stone, Mod., W. O. Price, C. of Pro.

Mar. 19, 1910, Pastor J. R. Stone. 3. Taken up the reference case against a sister and excluded her. 5. On motion the church ordered the finance committee to raise money to paint the church. J. R. Stone, Mod., H. K. Fletcher, C. of Pro.

Apr. Term, 1910, Rev. E. A. Cochran. 5. Granted the following brethren letters of dismission: J. N. Wigginton, Jess Fitts. E. A. Cochran, Mod. Pro T., H. G. Wilkie, C.C.

May 14, 1910, 5. Collected four dollars twenty cents for church repairs. All sow elected another member on the finance committee, Bro. Thomas Bryant. J. R. Stone, Mod., H. G. Wilkie, C.C.

Jun. 17, 1910, C. S. Hawkins and E. A. Cochran. 5. Elected delegates to the association to be held at New Harmony on Tuesday before second Sunday in July. Names to wit: T. N. Smith, Rev. E. A. Cochran, W. L. D. Howard, J. W. Holcomb, R. L. Warren, G. W. Little, alt. J. R. Stone, Mod., W. O. Price, C.C.

July Term, 1910, Rev. J. R. Stone. 5. Submitted to the reading of the letter of the sociation, the same being approved. Collected sixty-five cts. for minutes. Moved and carried that the letter of Bro. H. C. Bowling being adopted to the brotherin and sisters that compose the church at Hightower: "I think of you all often and wood be glad to be with you all and injoy your presants. In love I no I love you all. I hav tride to have any ?___. I no I was converted over thirty years ago. I hav never douted my conversion. I hope you will pray for me in my lonely our. I all ways tride to be at conference when I was able. I wood like to sea any of you any time. Your presence wood cheer mee up. I now my time is short and I must soon pass out and joine the heavenly host above. The Lords will bee don not mine. I think I hav got a minute of the association for the last 20 years. May God bless Bro. Stone. For fear I worry you patience, I close. Remember mee, H. C. Bolling" [*Henry Clay Boling, b Oct 15, 1839, d Oct 25, 1910, bur HBC*]

Aug. 20, 1910, R. W. Cochran. 5. Moved and carried that the finance comitty consult the members and community next week in reguard to painting the church. All sow moved and carried that Bro. G. M. Bryant be in charge of looking after the lamps during the meeting. R. W. Cochran, Mod. Prot., H. G. Wilkie, C.C.

Sep. 17, 1910, Pastor J. R. Stone. 5. Granted Sister Larrah J. Wyatt a letter of dismission. Went into the election of a pastor for the next year. Motion taken to nominate Bro. John R. Stone as our pastor. Motion carried, then the church voting on the same and unanimously elected him as our pastor for the coming year and the same is accepted by him. Taken up collection for our pastor, received seven dollars and fifty cnts. All sow elected H. G. Wilkie as clerk of the church for the coming year. J. R. Stone, Mod., H. G. Wilkie, C.C.

Oct. 15, 1910, Bro. J. R. Stone. 5. Granted Bro. Arthur Heggood a letter of dismission. On motion, ordered the committee to go ahead and paint the church and the church pay for it. Collected $7.25 for our pastor, $2.50 for painting the house. J. R. Stone, Mod., W. O. Price, C. of Prot.

Nov. 19, 1910, Rev. J. R. Stone. 2. Taken up the letter ritten by a brother, on motion the church preferred charge against the brother for contempt of the church. Taken up the charge and excluded him from the church. All so motion carried to prefer charge against a sister for contempt, excluded her. 5. Taken up collection for our pastor, received 4.50 cts. Received for painting the church house, one dollar and 50 cts. J. R. Stone, Mod., H. G. Wilkie, C.C.

Dec. 1910, Rev. J. R. Stone. 5. Collected 15.00 for our pastor. J. R. Stone, Mod., H. G. Wilkie, C.C.

Jan. 1911, our pastor. 5. Taken up collection for our pastor, received 17.25. Nothing else under the head of general business, we close. J. R. Stone, Mod., H. G. Wilkie, C.C.

Feb. 1911, After preaching by our pastor, meeting adjourned, no conference. Preaching Sunday.

March, 1911, our pastor. 5. Elected delegates to the union meeting to wit: Bros. G. B. Haygood, W. O. Price, J. H. Ellis, J. W. Wallace, J. M. Richards. Also received an invitation from Canton Church for the eldership of the church to ordain Bro. Cutts to preach. J. R. Stone, Mod., H. K. Fletcher, Clerk Pro.

Apr. 14, 1911, Bro. Gustis Smith, Elected R. A. Dunigan as moderator. [*No business under any item*]. R. A. Dunigan, Mod. Pro., J. W. [*Wallace?*], clerk of the Prot.

May 20, 1911, Rev. J. R. Stone. 4. Sister Isabel White came forward by letter and was united with the church. 5. Granted Bro. J. W. Wallace a letter of dismission. Took up collection for Sister Odem, received $1.25. J. R. Stone, Mod., H. G. Wilkie, C.C.

Jun. 18, 1911, Bro. J. R. Stone. 4. Received Abraham Covington by letter. 5. On motion, elected delegates to association, on motion, suspended regular order of business and elected by acclamation the following brethren to association, Bros: T. N. Smith, L. L. West, J. H. Ellis, R. L. Warren, E. A. Cochran, and alternate H. K. Fletcher. Oscar Price on motion to employ a sexton to employ, keep the house in order. J. R. Stone, Mod., R. A. Dunagan, C. Prot.

Jul. 15, 1911, Pastor J. R. Stone. 4. Received Bro. G. W. Wehunt, deacon and wife as members in full fellowship with us. 5. On motion, to call for the next session of the Hightower Association to be held with the church at Hightower. Motion carried. Collected for minutes, one dollar and thirty cts. All sow submitted to the reading of the letter to the association, the same being adopted. Collected 35 cts. to buy a water picher. J. R. Stone, Mod., H. G. Wilkie, C.C.

Aug. 19, 1911, Bro. E. A. Cochran. 5. Motion taken to receive the work of painting the house. Motion carried. Motion taken up for collection for painting house, received 6.00 dollars. On motion, granted letters to Sister Octa Smith, Sister Maggie Smith. Taken up collection to by oil, received 50 cts. J. R. Stone, Mod., R. A. Dunagan, C. Pro.

Sep. 16, 1911, J. R. Stone. 5. Granted Sister Bessie Wallace a letter of dismission. Motion before the church to elect as our pastor for another year. Suspended the regular order by eclimation, motion carried. Bro. Stone being nominated and elected him for another year. Invitation from Bro. Wilson to invite the eldership of this church to be with Liberty Church on Friday before the first Sunday in Oct. to assist in the ordination of a deacon. Invitation accepted. J. R. Stone, Mod., H. G. Wilkie, C.C.

Oct. 14, 1911, Bro. J. R. Stone. 4. Sister Ida Fowler and Sister Sallie came forward. 5. Collected $17.00 dollars for our pastor. J. R. Stone, Mod., Oscar Price, C.C. Prot.

Nov. 18, 1911, J. R. Stone. 5. Collected 17.00 for the pastor. J. R. Stone, Mod., Oscar Price, C. of P.

Dec. 16, 1911, R. W. Cochran, Elected R. W. Cochran as moderator. 5. Taken up collection for our pastor, received $7.00. All sow received $3.00 for painting the house. R. W. Cochran, Mod., H. G. Wilkie, C.C.

Jan. 20, 1912, Bro. R. W. Cochran. The pastor being absent, elected Bro. Cochran as moderator, also elected H. K. Fletcher as clerk. 5. Granted letters of dismission to Bro. Robert Warren, Sister Warren and Johnie Warren. R. W. Cochran, Mod. Protem, H. K. Fletcher, Clerk Protem.

Feb. 17, 1912, J. R. Stone, Pastor. 2. Received a letter from a sister, by move and second to appoint a committee to investigate the matter and bring it in proper shape to the church. Committee: L. L. West, G. B. Haygood, J. H. Ellis. J. R. Stone, Mod., H. K. Fletcher, Clerk of Protem.

Mar. 16, 1912, Bro. J. R. Stone. 3. Taken up the charge against a sister, motion to accept her written acknowledgement. 5. Granted Bro. J. L. Williams and daughter [Azalee] a letter of dismission. Paid Bro. Stone 8 dollars. J. R. Stone, Mod., H. G. Wilkie, C. C.

May 18, 1912, Bro. J. R. Stone. 5. Granted Bro. Robert Loggins and wife letter of dismission. Appointed a committee on arrangements of the association: T. N. Smith, L. L. West, J. H. Ellis, H. G. Wilkie, R. W. Cochran, W. O. Price, Ramon Cantrell, J. M. Richards, Thomas Bryant, John Bryant. J. R. Stone, Mod., H. K. Fletcher, C. Prot.

Jun. 15, 1912, Not having any preaching, met in conference. The pastor being absent, the Church proceeded and elected R. W. Cochran as moderator. 5. Motion carried to elect delegates to the association at Hightower by appointment. Their names as follows: T. N. Smith, G. B. Heggood, L. L. West, Rev. E. A. Cochran, J. H. Ellis, R. W. Cochran, H. K. Fletcher, alternate. Also motion carried to elect delegates to the union meeting to be held with the church at Mt. Vernon, commencing on Friday before the fourth Sunday in July, their names are as follows: H. K. Fletcher, T. N. Smith, Oscar Price, Luther Wallace, G. M. Bryant. Also motion carried to grant J. Elmer Heggood and wife Annie L. Heggood a letter of dismission, also motion carried to grant Annie L. Speer a letter of dismission. R. W. Cochran, Mod. Prot., H. G. Wilkie, C.C.

Jul. 20, 1912, R. W. Cochran, R. W. Cochran elected moderator. 3. Motion carried to write a sister in reguard to her membership. 4. Recieved by letter Sister Lucy Dawson. 5. Motion carried to appoint a committee to see the land owners and get their consent to prohibit the selling of lemonade. Luther Wallace, J. T. Bryant, H. G. Wilkie. Also submitted to the reading of the letter to the union meeting, also to the association. The same being approved. Rev. Cochran, Mod. Prot., H. G. Wilkie, C.C.

Aug. 17, 1912, R. A. Dunagan, elected R. W. Cochran as moderator. 5. Motion carried to take up a collection for paying Bro. T. N. Smith for supplying the people with water during the association. Motion carried to grant Bro. Henry Holcombe a letter of dismission. Collect $1.20 toward covering the debt of Bro. Smith. R. W. Cochran, Mod. P., H. G. Wilkie, C.C.

Sep. 14, 1912, Bro. J. A. McClure, elected J. A. McClure as moderator. 2. Received from a brother, acknowledgements. Also motion carried to erase a sister's name from our church book. 4. Bro. John West came forward by experience and the church extended him the right hand of fellowship. 5. Motion carried to grant Bro. V. Loggins and wife Susan a letter of dismission. Also motion before the church to elect a pastor for another year. On motion to nominate Bro. Stone, also motion carried to suspend the regular order of elections and elect by acclamation the same being adopted, the church taken a vote and unanimously elected Bro. J. R. Stone for our pastor for another year. J. A. McClure, M. P., H. G. Wilkie, C.C.

Nov. 16, 1912, pastor, J. R. Stone. 5. Took up collection for the pastor, collected $10.00. J. R. Stone, Mod., H. K. Fletcher, C. Prot.

Dec. 14, 1912, J. R. Stone. 5. Collected $2.50 for our pastor. J. R. Stone, Mod., H. K. Fletcher, C. Prot.

Feb. 15, 1913, Bros. E. A. Cochran and J. R. Stone. 5. Motion carried to grant Bro. E. J. Smith and wife [Sarah] a letter of dismission. Received $6.50 for our pastor. J. R. Stone Mod., H. G. Wilkie C.C.

Mar 1913, pastor, J. R. Stone. 5. Taken up collection to pay T. N. Smith supplying the association with ice and water. Received $1.25. J. R. Stone, Mod., H. G. Wilkie, C.C.

May, 1913, J. R. Stone. 4. Received Bro. Jacob Padgett and wife Francis as members in full fellowship. J. R. Stone, Mod., H. G. Wilkie, C.C.

Jun. 1913, J. R. Stone. 5. Went into the lection of delegates to attend the association to be held with the church at Massadonia. Suspending the regular order of business and elect by appointment, motion carried. The names as follows: T. N. Smith, G. B. Heggood, H. G. Wilkie, J. T. Bryant, Thomas Bryant, R. W. Cochran as mesingers. All sow elected delegates to the union meeting by appointment, their names as followes: W. L. D. Howard, Luther Wallace, Jessie Wallace, J. H. Ellis, Henry Howard, W. E. Pearse. J. R. Stone, Mod., H. G. Wilkie, C.C.

Jul. 19, 1913, R. W. Cochran, elected R. W. Cochran as moderator. 5. Taken up collection for minutes, collected fifty-five cents. Also submitted to the reading of the letter to the union meeting, also to the association, same being adopted by the church. R. W. Cochran, Mod. Prot., H. G. Wilkie, C.C.

Aug. 16, 1913, Bro. J. R. Stone and R. W. Cochran. 4. Two joined by letter, Sister Nancy Long and Sister Martha Long. 5. Granted letters of dismission to Virgil Ledbetter, also Sister Lizzie Southern. J. R. Stone, Mod., H. K. Fletcher, C.C. Prot.

Sep. 19, 1913, J. R. Stone. 1. To invite visiting Bros. and sisters to seats with us. 5. Motion carried to go into the election of a pastor for another year. Motion carried to suspend the regular order of election and elect by acclamation. Also motion carried to nominate Bro. J. R. Stone, the same being unanimously elected. Granted J. M. Thompson and 2 daughters letters of dismission. Collected $14.05 for pastor. J. R. Stone, Mod., H. G. Wilkie, C.C.

Nov. 15, 1913, Bro. J. R. Stone and R. W. Cochran. 1. Invite bros. and sisters to seats with us. 5. Granted letters of dismission to Sister Lula Leonard, also to Sister Stelly Dispain. Taken up collection for pastor, received $10.00. J. R. Stone, Mod., R. W. Cochran, C.C. Prot.

Dec. 20, 1913, Bro. R. W. Cochran and J. R. Stone. 1. Invite bros. and sisters to seats with us. 4. Received Sister Emma Hester by letter. 5. Moved and second to appoint a committee to see about getting more land for burying ground. Committee: T. N. Smith, L. L. West, Henry Ellis, R. W. Cochran. Made up to get some coal and stove pipe. J. R. Stone, Mod., R. M. Cantrell, C.C. Prot.

Jan. 18, 1914, Bro. J. R. Stone. 1. Invite visiting bros. to seats with us. 2. Preferred a charge against a brother for drunkenness. Layed charge over till next conference. 5. Granted letters of dismission to Sisters Pearl and Cornelia Norton. Received the report of committee on the buying of the land for burying ground. Motion made for pastor to appoint a committee to raise the money to pay for same. Committee: Henry Howard, Paul Cochran, Oma Ellis, Mertie Wilkie. J. R. Stone, Mod., H. K. Fletcher, Clerk Prot.

Feb. 1914, no meeting

Mar. 14, 1914, R. L. Warren, elected Bro. Warren as mod. 2. Motion carried to prefer charge against a sister and a brother for adultery, motion carried to take up the charge and exclude the same. 3. Motion carried to accept a brother's written statement. Charges taken up and the church bore with him in his written statement. 5. Granted Bro. R. A. Dunigan and wife, Mary letters of dismission. Elected delegates to the union meeting at Four Mile. R. L. Warren, Mod. P., H. G. Wilkie, C.C.

Apr. 18, 1914, Bros. E. A. Cochran and J. R. Stone. 2. Motion before the church to prefer a charge against a brother. Charge preferred. Motion to withdraw fellowship from him, motion carried. 5. Collected $2.00 for land purchase, also .65 cents to buy wine. Also elected delegates to invite the churches to commune with us. Also motion carried to grant Bro. Andrew Southern a letter of dismission. J. R. Stone, Mod., H. G. Wilkie, C.C.

Jun. 20, 1914, Bro. A. F. Smith, and J. R. Stone. 5. Went in to the election of delegates to the association. Suspended the regular order and elected by acclamation: R. W. Cochran, J. H. Ellis, T. N. Smith, Ed Pearson, H. K. Fletcher, H. G. Wilkie. J. R. Stone, Mod., H. G. Wilkie, C.C.

Jul., 1914, Bros. Gaddis and Cochran. 5. Motion carried to put E. A. Cochran in R. W. Cochran's place and L. L. West in H. G. Wilkie's place [*delegates to association*]. Collected 60 cents for minutes. R. W. Cochran, Mod., H.

G. Wilkie, C.C.

Aug. 15, 1914, J. R. Stone, and prayer by R. W. Cochran. 5. Motion carried to restore a sister to the fellowship of the church. All so grant Maudia Hawkins a letter of dismission. J. R. Stone, Mod., H. G. Wilkie, C.C.

Sep. 19, 1914, After singing and prayer by Bro. W. L. D. Howard, the church elected Thomas N. Smith as moderator. 2. Received acknowledgements of a brother for drunkness. 5. Went into the election of a pastor for the next year. Motion carried to nominate Bro J. R. Stone. Elected by ballot: J. R. Stone 32, Johnie Miller 1, Bro. Stone being duly elected as our pastor for the coming year. All sow granted letter of dismission to Sister Alice Fowler. All so appointed Johnie Wallace and G. M. Bryant on the finance committee. T. N. Smith, Mod. Prot., H. G. Wilkie, C.C.

Oct. 17, 1914, R. W. Cochran and J. R. Stone. 5. Paid Bro. Stone $9.00. Bro. Stone agreed to remain our pastor. Moved and carried to appoint a committee to repair windows. Committee: Bros. Haggood, Stevens, Wallace and Fletcher. Also moved and carried to buy a set off tools to dig graves. Same committee to collect money and do the buying and work. This the work of the day. J. R. Stone, Mod., R. M. Cantrell, C. Prot.

Jan. 16, 1915, J. R. Stone. 2. A motion to prefer a charge against a sister for adultery. Motion carried to exclude her from the fellowship of the church. 4. Motion to accept the letters of Bro. Dunagan and wife back to our church. 5. Motion carried to grant Bro. Abraham Covington a letter of dismission. Also granted letters of dismission to Bro. A. L. Wimbish and wife. Also granted a letter of dismission to Isabel Wyatt. Collected for our pastor $11.25. Motion carried to organize Sunday school at Hightower Church. Elected Bro. W. E. Pierce as Supt. and H. G. Wilkie as Sectary. J. R. Stone, Mod., H. G. Wilkie, C.C.

Feb. 19, 1915, Bro. J. R. Stone. 2. Motion carried to appoint a committee to see a brother in regard to drunkness. Committee H. G. Wilkie and John Holcombe. 5. Collected 75 cents for the pastor. J. R. Stone, Mod., H. G. Wilkie, C.C.

Apr. 17, 1915, Bros. J. R. Stone and R. W. Cochran. 3. Taken up the reference charge against a brother, motion carried to appoint a committee to see him in person before next conference. 5. Collected 95 cents to buy wine. Invited the following churches to commune with us on the 3rd. New Harmony, T. N. Smith; Mt. Pisgah, W. E. Pierce; Mt. Tabor, Henry Ellis; Liberty, H. G. Wilkie; Ophir, W. E. Pierce; Conns Creek, Henry Ellis. Motion carried to appoint 4 male members and 4 female members on the finance committee to wit: Lizzie Cochran, Mattie Hester, Bell Bryant, Mertie Wilkie, J. M. Stevens, G. M. Bryant, J. H. Wilkie, W. E. Pierce, R. W. Cochran. J. R. Stone, Mod., H. G. Wilkie, C.C.

May 16, 1915, J. R. Stone. 3. Motion carried to receive the acknowledgements of a brother. 4. Received by letter Bro. J. A. Satterfield and wife Sallie, Ella, Bula, Bomer and Milledge as members in full fellowship with us. 5. Motion carried to grant Sister Dessie and Bertha Gaddis a letter of dismission. Taken up collection for the orphans home and state mission, $7.00. Also received 4.25 for our pastor on last year. J. R. Stone, Mod., H. G. Wilkie, C.C.

June Term, 1915, Bro. J. R. Stone. 2. Motion carried to prefer a charge against a sister for dancing. The Faith taken up the charge and excluded her from the fellowship of the church. All so reading the statement of another sister, motion carried to prefer a charge against a brother for in sulting language in her presence. Prefered charge till next meeting and appointed Bro W. E. Pearce, H. G. Wilkie, Johnie Wallace to notify the brother of the charge. 4. Received by letter Bro. Gatewood Southern and wife Lilla Southern. 5. Elected the following members as delegates to the association to wit: L. L. West, T. N. Smith, R. W. Cochran, W. E. Pearce, H. G. Wilkie, J. H. Loggins, C. C. Hester, alternate. Also motion carried to liberate Bro. W. F. Pearce as a licensed minister to exercise hear and elsewhere. All sow instructed the clerk to rite out his license which is ritten and delivered to Bro. W. E. Pearce. Received $1.80 for missions. J. R. Stone, Mod., H. G. Wilkie, C.C.

Jul. 17, 1915, Pastor J. R. Stone. 3. Taken up the charge against a brother, referred till next meeting. 5. Collected $1.75 for orphans home. Brother Milton Price and wife called for letters of dismission and the church granted the same. Read letter to the association and adopted the same. J. R. Stone, Mod., R. M. Cantrell, C.C. Prot.

Aug. 14, 1915, Bro. W. E. Pierce and J. R. Stone. 3. Taken up the reference against a brother, motion carried to bear with him. 4. Received by letter Bro. J. S. Parker and wife Sally. 5. Motion carried to accept Bro. West work in regard to lighting the house, also to instruct the finance committee to collect money and pay for same. Motion carried to appoint Bro. Johnie Wallace church sexton during the meeting. Also motion to grant Danilla Low a letter of dismission. Collected $1.15 for lighting expenses. J. R. Stone, Mod., H. G. Wilkie, C.C.

Sep. 18, 1915, Bros. Hawkins and Stone. 4. Received by letter Bro. McPherson and wife. 5. Went into election for a pastor for another year. Motion to suspend the regular order of election and elect by acclamation. Motion before the church to nominate Bro. Stone. Bro. Stone elected as nominee. The church taken a rising vote and elected Bro. Stone as pastor for another year. Also motion before the church to pass a resolution for every member of Hightower Church to donate 5 cents every 3 months toward bearing the expense of the church. Also motion before the church for every male member to pay 5 cents a month. Motion withdrawn till next conference. Motion to hear from Bro. Stone if he would accept the pastorial chair if Hightower Church does her duty. Also motion to grant Sister Vashti Price a letter of dismission, the same being granted. Collected 12.50 for the pastor. Azzriah McPherson, Mod., Prot., H. G. Wilkie, C.C.

Oct. 16, 1915, J. R. Stone. 4. Received Ellen Sikes by letter, also Bro. John H. Richards came forward and talked to the church and was received in full fellowship. 5. W. T. Boling and wife were granted letters of dismission. Received $12.25 for pastor. J. R. Stone, Mod., R. M. Cantrell, C. Prot.

Nov. 20, 1915, J. R. Stone. 2. Preferred a charge against a brother for contempt of church, taken up and withdrew fellowship from him. 4. Received the letter of Bro. Henry Holcombe as a member in full fellowship with us. 5. Received 4.50 for our pastor. J. R. Stone Mod., H. G. Wilkie, C.C.

Dec. 18, 1915, No service.

Jan. 1916, J. R. Stone, no conference.

Feb. 19, 1916, Preaching by our pastor on Saturday and Sunday, now [no] conference.

Mar. 18, 1916, J. R. Stone. 5. A motion before the church to vote the an vilorom sistem to this church. Motion carried 29-14 in favor of the above system. Motion to elect J. M. Steavens as assistant secretary, motion carried. Received for our pastor in all to date $67.50. Total on the 5 cts fund: $3.75. Motion before the church to dismiss the present finance committee: motion carried. The church all so elected T. N. Smith, R. M. Cantrell, J. M. Steavens as the new finance committee, this being no other business, conference closed. J. R. Stone, Mod., H. G. Wilkie, C.C.

Apr. 15, 1916, Our pastor, J. R. Stone. 2. A brother states to the church that he has been swaring and ask the church bair with him and the request is granted. 5. Motion before the church to grant Rev. E. A. Cochran and wife Cansire Cochran letters of dismission. Letters granted. Received for our pastor $1.50. J. R. Stone, Mod., H. G. Wilkie, C.C.

May 20, 1916, Bro. J. R. Stone. 5. Granted J. S. Parker and wife letters of dismission. J. R. Stone, Mod., H. G. Wilkie, C.C.

Jun. 17, 1916, J. R. Stone. 2. Accepted the acknowledgement of a brother for in sulting language. 5. Appointed the following delegates to the union meeting at Union Hill on Thursday before the 3rd Sunday in July as follows: L. L. West, H. K. Fletcher, T. N. Smith, Johnie Wallace, Turner White. All sow appointed delegates to the association at Conns Creek on Tuesday before the 2nd Sunday in August to wit: T. N. Smith, L. L. West, H. K. Fletcher, G. B. Heggood, Tomas Bryant, J. H. Ellis, alternate. J. R. Stone, Mod., H. G. Wilkie, C.C.

Jul. Term, 1916, Our pastor. 2. A brother states that report as to his drinking is [his] fault, the church excepts his statement.

Aug. 19, 1916, Bro. R. W. Cochran, church elects R. W. Cochran as moderator. 2. On motion, the church prefers a charge against a brother for braking the peace between man and wife. Taken up the charge and excluded him. 5. The church donates $1.00 toward the erection of a monument of Bro. Hayes of Friendship. R. W. Cochran, Mod. Prot., H. G. Wilkie, C.C. [*Rev. Samuel L. Hayes, 1836-23 Nov. 1915*].

Sep. 16, 1916, Our pastor. 2. Church preferred a charge against a sister for contempt of the church, taken up the charge and excluded her. All sow motion to prefer charge against a brother for drinking, motion carried. 4. Received the letters of the bairers/*bearers* Bro. R. L. Harden and wife, O. V. Harden and Dallia May Harden and Etta Harden as members. 5. Granted letters of dismission to Sister May Adams, Bro. Golden Price, Bro. Seldon G. Hegwood, Sister Mattie Purcell, Sister Jane Ingram, Bro. James Bolling and wife Ethell Bolling, Sister Essia Henderson. Went into the election of a pastor. On motion Bro. J. R. Stone and Bro. C. A. Wallace was nominated. Elected under the regular order of business, 10 to 25 in favor of Bro. Stone and Bro. Stone excepted the call to serve the church another year. Received $15. 64 for Bro. Stone. Received $8.40 for R. W. Cochran. J. R. Stone, Mod., H. G. Wilkie, C.C.

Oct. 14, 1916, Bro. R. W. Cochran, 2. Prefer a charge against a sister, taken up the charge and withdrew fellowship from her. 5. Granted Bro. J. B. Pruitt and wife [*Rosannah*] letters of dismission, also granted Sister Ida Ellis letter of dismission. R. W. Cochran, Mod. Prot., R. M. Cantrell, C.C. Prot.

Nov. 1916 – Feb. 1917: No report

Mar. 17, 1917, Bro. J. R. Stone. 2. Motion before the church to prefer charge against a brother for using profane language. Motion to refer charge to next meeting. Taken up a charge against another brother for drinking, referred case to next meeting. 5. Paid pastor $2.37, received on 5 cent fund: $2.25. J. R. Stone, Mod., H. G. Wilkie, C.C.

Apr. 14, 1917, our pastor. 2. Taken up case of a brother. The brother arose to address the church as to his conduct. Motion carried to defer the report to general business. 3. Taken up in a brothers case, received his acknowledgements. Also received the acknowledgements of another brother for swearing while in a state of anger. 5. Taken up the report of a brother and referred same till next meeting. Also motion carried to invite the sister churches to commune with us on the 3rd Sunday in May. Allso motion carried to employ J. V. Price to do the concrete work on the Franklin monuments. Also motion carried to reject the resignation of Bro. Stone. Also motion carried to abolish the anvaloraum system of the church. Motion carried. J. R. Stone, Mod., H. G. Wilkie, C.C.

May 12, 1917, our pastor. 3. By motion and second except the statement of a brother and bair with him. 4. Received by letter Sisters Lula Groover, also received as a candidate for baptism Bro. Hommer Little. 5. Distributed the minutes. Collected for Bro. Stone $26.25. Granted Ellis Wadkins letter of dismission.

Jun. 17, 1917 [*Sunday?*] Our pastor. 5. Went into the election of delegates to the association to be held at Mount Zion Church commencing on Thursday before the 2nd Sunday in Aug. to wit: Thomas N. Smith, H. K. Fletcher, J. M. Loggins, G. W. Little, Jr., J. T. Wallace, W. E. Pearce, alternate. All so elected the following to attend the union meeting at Oak Grove in Milton Co. L. L. West, H. K. Fletcher, W. E. Pearce, C. C. Hester, H. G. Wilkie. J. R. Stone, Mod., H. G. Wilkie, C.C.

Jul. 14, 1917, Bro. J. R. Stone. 5. Collected 95 cents for minutes. J. R. Stone, Mod., R. W. Cantrell, C.C.

Aug. 18, 1917, Bro. McPherson followed by R. W. Cochran. 4. Received Bro. J. M. Chumbler and wife as members. 5. Granted the following letters of dismission: Moses Dispain, Martha, Pearl and Stella Sissom. Received to buy oil and gas 20 cents. R. W. Cochran, Mod. Prot., H. G. Wilkie, C.C.

Sep. 15, 1917, Bro J. L. Hitt. 5. Granted Sister Hester Ann Odem a letter of dismission. J. L. Hitt, Mod. Prot., H. G.

Wilkie, C.C.

Nov. 17, 1917, Bro. J. R. Stone. 5. Collected for pastor $8.50. J. R. Stone, Mod., W. E. Pierce, C.P.

Feb. 19, 1918 [*Jan. 19 or Sat. Feb. 16?*], E. A. Cochran and J. R. Stone. 4. Received Steve Dean and wife. 5. Collected for repairs 1.60. J. R. Stone, Mod., H. G. Wilkie, C.C.

Mar. 16, 1918, Bro. E. A. Cochran. 5. Motion carried to meet Sunday morning at 9:30 to organize a Sunday School. J. R. Stone, Mod., R. M. Cantrell, C. Prot.

Apr. 20, 1918, Rev. J. R. Stone and Rev. E. A. Cochran. 5. Taken up collection to buy wine, rec'd 1.05. Appointed the following members to invite the sister churches to commune with Hightower Church on the 3rd Sunday in May: Steve Dean, Fred Long, H. G. Wilkie, and Henry Ellis. J. R. Stone, Mod., H. G. Wilkie, C.C.

May 18, 1918, Rev. E. A. Cochran and Rev. J. R. Stone. 5. Granted letter of dismission to Miss Leyoma [*Leoma*] Wimpee. Church accepts the invitation to commune with Mica Church on the fourth Sunday in May. J. R. Stone, Mod., H. G. Wilkie, C.C.

Jun. 15, 1918, Rev. E. A. Cochran and J. R. Stone. 4. Received by letter Rev. E. A. Cochran and wife Kansas as members in full with us. 5. Regular order of election suspended and delegates elected by appointment to attend the association held with Friendship Baptist Church to wit: Rev. E. A. Cochran, H. G. Wilkie, T. N. Smith, C. C. Hester, Joseph White. Also appointed the following to represent our church at the union meeting to be held with Amicalola Baptist Church on Thursday before the second Sunday in July. J. M. White, Edgar Pearson, Joe White. J. R. Stone, Mod., H. G. Wilkie, C.C.

Aug. 17, 1918, Rev. E. A. Cochran, elected Rev. R. W. Cochran as moderator. 5. Granted Sister Willie and Estelle Groover letters of dismission. Motion carried for Bro. Hanson [*James H. Hanson?*] to assist Bro. J. R. Stone in meeting. R. W. Cochran, Mod. Pro., H. G. Wilkie, C.C.

Sep. 14, 1918, Rev. E. A. Cochran and Pastor J. R. Stone. 5. Letter of Sister Emma Porter read and accepted as member of this church. Motion carried to elect pastor for following year. Elected Bro. J. R. Stone. Received entire vote. Granted Leoree Dispain and wife letter of dismission. J. R. Stone, Mod., H. G. Wilkie, C.C.

Oct. 19, 1918, J. R. Stone. 5. Received on the pool $13.75. Also collected for pastor $40.00. Brother Stone also agrees to be pastor of Hightower Church for another year if same church will do her full duty. J. R. Stone, Mod., H. G. Wilkie, C.C.

Nov. 1918, Bro. J. R. Stone. No conference.

Jan. 1919, Pastor J. R. Stone. 5. Granted the following letters of dismission: Bro. Homer Long and wife, Bro. Ben Long and wife, also Sisters Martha and Ethel Long. Also the church decides to borrow money and finish paying for the pool built in August, 1918. J. R. Stone, Mod., H. G. Wilkie, C.C.

Feb. 1919, No meeting.

Mar. 1919, Rev. E. A. Cochran and J. R. Stone. No conference. J. R. Stone, Mod., H. G. Wilkie, C.C.

April 1919, Our pastor followed by R. W. Cochran. 5. Granted Sister Sinia Barrett letter of dismission. Collected $10.70 on the pool and .95 to buy wine. J. R. Stone, Mod., H. G. Wilkie, C.C.

May, 1919, E. A. Cochran, J. R. Stone. 4. Bro. Mancel Bryant [*recorded on membership roll as Edd Bryant*] came to talk to the church and after hearing his statement the church moved to except him as a candidate for baptism, motion carried. 5. Collected $13.75 on the pool, this pays all except $4.50. J. R. Stone, Mod., H. G. Wilkie, C.C.

June, 1919, Bro. Holcomb and our pastor, J. R. Stone. 5. Went into the election of delegates to the association at

Juno on Tuesday before the 2nd Sunday in Aug. The church suspended the regular order of elections and elect by appointment as follows: E. A. Cochran, H. G. Wilkie, R. M. Cantrell, G. C. Little, J. T. Wallace, E. H. Pearson. Also this church is invited to Conns Creek on Saturday before 2nd Sunday to assist in the ordination of deacons. J. R. Stone, Mod., H. G. Wilkie, C.C.

Aug. 1919, Rev. E. A. Cochran. *[no business under any item].* E. A. Cochran, Mod. Prot., H. G. Wilkie, C.C.

Nov. 1919, J. R. Stone. 5. Granted Bro. George Mason and wife letters of dismission. Received $2.00 for our pastor. J. R. Stone, Mod., H. G. Wilkie, C.C.

Dec. 1919, no meeting. **Jan. 1920,** no meeting.

Feb. 15, 1920, E. A. Cochran and J. R. Stone. 5. Granted Sister Mattie Parker a letter of dismission and also Sister Thad Hester. Paid the pastor $3.50. Motion for H. G. Wilkie to see about buying some windows, motion carried. J. R. Stone, Mod., H. G. Wilkie, C.C.

March, no meeting. **April,** no meeting.

May 15, 1920, J. R. Stone. 5. Granted Louisa Bryant a letter of dismission. Collected $2.95 for the expense of the church. J. R. Stone, Mod., H. G. Wilkie, C.C.

Jun. 16, 1920, Rev. J. R. Stone. 5. Elected the following brethren to attend the Hightower Association: Rev. E. A. Cochran, J. T. Wallace, R. M. Cantrell, J. H. Wilkie, Jr., H. G. Wilkie, S. D. Dean, alternate. J. R. Stone, Mod., H. G. Wilkie, C.C.

Jul. 15, 1920, Pastor J. R. Stone. 4. Received by letter Bro. J. A. Wyatt and wife Larrah J. as members of the church in full fellowship. 5. Read and adopted the letter to the association. J. R. Stone, Mod., H. G. Wilkie, C.C.

Aug. 16, 1920, Bro. D. L. Haggood and Rev. E. A. Cochran. 5. Granted Sister O. V. [*Ovolena*] Hardin and daughter Dallie, letters of dismission. J. R. Stone, Mod., H. G. Wilkie, C.C.

Sep. 18, 1920, our pastor. 4. Received by letter Sister Velvia Holcomb. 5. Granted Bro. G. N. Wilkie and wife [*Henrietta*] letters of dismission. All so Sister Ader Dobson. All so nominated and set apart the following brethren to be ordained as deacons: Bro. R. M. Cantrell, Bro. H. T. White, Bro. Jess L. Wilkie, the time set for the ordination at our next regular meeting. Went into the election of a pastor for the coming year. Rev. J. R. Stone being the nominee the church unanimously voting and elected Bro. J. R. Stone as pastor for the coming year. Collected $33.75 for Bro. Stone. Collected $5.75 to pay on the work at the church on removing the pieces and covering some. J. R. Stone, Mod., H. G. Wilkie, C.C.

Oct. 16, 1920, After preaching by Rev. J. R. Stone, the church adjourned for dinner then reassembled and went into conference. 3. Taken by motion of the reference of the candate for the ordination of deacons. Rev. E. A. Cochran present the candates to the church. Rev. E. A. Cochran to examine the same before a presbetery. The presbetery as follows: J. R. Stone, moderator of the presbetery; Rev. E. A. Cochran, to lead the questions and examine the candates; Rev. J. W. Miller to leede the ordination prayer; After which Rev. J. R. Stone to deliver the church; By motion Rev. R. W. Cochran to deliver the candates back to the church. The presbetery is as follows: Rev. J. R. Stone, moderator, E. A. Cochran, J. W. Miller, R. W. Cochran, C. C. Hawkins, Deacons: C. E. Right, S. L. Coker, W. D. Heggood, W. C. Turner, W. B. Wofford, S. W. Riding, J. D. Parker, J. H. Ellis, H. G. Wilkie. By motion the church presides in the ordination by prayer and the laying on of hands. Followed by the laying on of the hand of the presbetery. 5. By motion, received the invitation to be with Liberty Grove. All so granted Sister Burtha Hamby letter of dismission. Received $14.50 for our pastor. J. R. Stone, Mod., H. G. Wilkie, C.C.

Apr. 16, 1921, our pastor. 5. Collected one dollar and 25 cts to buy wine. All so 1.10 on the repairing of the windows lights. J. R. Stone, Mod., H. G. Wilkie, C.C. [*window lights thought to be windowpanes*].

May 15, 1921, Rev. Henderson and Bro. J. R. Stone. 5. Granted the following letters of dismission: Sister Lula Groover, J. A. Bolling and wife Ethell. All so reading of the church discipling and rules commity to revise the books. H. G. Wilkie, R. M. Cantrell, J. L. Wilkie, J. H. Ellis, Ed Priest. J. R. Stone, Mod., H. G. Wilkie, C.C.

Jun. 18, 1921, Rev. E. A. Cochran and J. R. Stone. 5. Motion to suspend the regular order of election and appointed the following bro. as messengers to the sociation to be held at Alphrete: No. 1: E. A. Cochran, 2: H. G. Wilkie, 3: R. M. Cantrell, 4: J. H. Little, 5: Jess T. Wilkie, 6: J. H. Ellis. All so elected by appointment R. E. Ellis, E. C. Priest, Felton Dean, G. Southern and W. C. Wallace as delegates to the union meeting at Ophir. All so taken up a collection for minutes, 80 cts.

Jul. 19, 1921, our pastor and Bro. Goss. 5. Granted sister Bulla Wadkins letter of dismission. All so submitted to reading of the letter to the association, the same being adopted. All so granted Ed Priest and wife Eliza Priest letter of dismission. J. R. Stone, Mod., H. G. Wilkie, C.C.

Aug. 19, 1921, Bro. D. L. Heggood *[no business under any item]*. Rev. D. L. Heggood, Mod. Prot., R. M. Cantrell.

Sep. 17, 1921, our pastor. 5. By motion, granted Bro. Henry Warren a letter of dismission. All so by motion and second went into the election of a pastor for the coming year. Elected by ballot Bro. J. R. Stone as our pastor for the next year, he receiving 67 to 1 for Rev. W. H. Smith. Bro. J. R. Stone excepts the pastoral cair *[care]* of the church for the coming year. Collected for our pastor to date: $34.75. By motion, the church sets 11 o'clock to begin service time. J. R. Stone, Mod., H. G. Wilkie, C.C.

Oct. 1921, W. D. Heggood as moderator. 5. Went into the election of a pastor for the coming year. By motion and second nominated Rev. R. A. Roper and unanimously elected him to the pastoral cair *[care]* of Hightower church for the coming year and Bro. Roper excepts the church. W. D. Heggood, Mod. Pro, H. G. Wilkie, C.C.

Nov. 1921, our pastor, Rev. R. A. Roper. 5. Collected 20 dollars for Bro. Stone. Rev. R. A. Roper, Mod., H. G. Wilkie, C.C.

Dec. 1921, Rev. E. A. Cochran and R. A. Roper. 5. Granted Luther Wallace letter of dismission. Rev. R. A. Roper, Mod., H. G. Wilkie, C.C.

Feb. 24, 1922, R. A. Roper. 2. By motion and second the church preferred a charge against a sister. Deferred the charge till next meeting. All so by motion and second preferred charge against a brother for drinking. Deferred charge till next meeting. All sow preferred charge against another brother for drinking. Charge denide and motion withdrawn. Rev. R. A. Roper, Mod., H. G. Wilkie, C.C.

Mar. 25, 1922, Bro. J. I. Holbrook. Elected J. I. Holbrook as moderator. 3. Taken up the referrance against a sister and excluded her from the church. All so by motion and second the church taken up the charge against a brother, he making acknowledgements to the satisfaction to the church. All so by motion, the church withdraw a charge against another brother for drinking. 4. Received by letter Sister Maudie Brackett Hester as member of Hightower Church. J. I. Holbrook, Mod. Prot., H. G. Wilkie, C.C.

April, 1922, Rev. R. W. Cochran and R. A. Roper. 5. Motion and second, granted Bro. G. M. Bryant and wife Bell letter of dismission. Collected 1.00 for common purpose. R. A. Roper, Mod., H. G. Wilkie, C.C.

May, 1922, Pastor R. A. Roper *[no business under any item]*. Rev. R. A. Roper, Mod., H. G. Wilkie, C.C.

Jun. 24, 1922, E. A. Cochran. 5. Suspend the regular order of election and appointed the following messengers *[to association]*: 1. R. E. Loveless, 2. R. M. Cantrell, 3. H. G. Wilkie, 4th E.A. Cochran, 5th E. H. Pearson, [6] C. C. Hester and Jess L. Wilkie, alternate. Rev. R. A. Roper, Mod., H. G. Wilkie, C.C.

Jul. 23, 1922, Bro. R. A. Roper. 4. Received by letter Rev. A. A. Roper and Sister Louise Roper as members in full fellowship with us. R. A. Roper, Mod., H. G. Wilkie, C.C.

Aug. 1922, Bro. A. A. Roper. 4. Received by letter Bro. J. S. Wyatt and Sister Octavia as members in full fellowship with us, Bro. J. S. Wyatt as a deacon of Hightower. 5. Granted the following letters: Sister Hesie Harden, Bro. C. C. Speer, letters of dismission. By motion, the [*church*] moves to erase the name of a sister from the church book. A. A. Roper, Mod. Prot, H. G. Wilkie, C.C.

Sep. 23, 1922, Rev. R. A. Roper. 4. Sister Lizzie Wyatt by exp. Sister Ella Green, Sister Mrs. Hattie Green, Sister Etta Drummond as members in full fellowship with us. 5. Received Bro. J. S. Wyatt as a deacon of Hightower Church. Went into the election of a pastor. By motion, suspended the regular order of elections and excepted by nomination. By motion and second, nominated Bro. R. A. Roper, their being no others, the nomination closed after which the church voted and elected Bro. R. A. Roper as pastor of Hightower Church for the coming year. Received for Bro. Roper 49.75. R. A. Roper, Mod., H. G. Wilkie, C.C.

Oct. 1922, Rev. R. A. Roper. 5. Taken up 10.00 for our pastor. R. A. Roper, Mod., H. G. Wilkie, C.C.

Nov. 25, 1922. Bro. D. L. Haggood and by pastor. 2. By motion and second, preferred a charge against a brother for drunkness. By motion and [*second*] referred charge till next regular conference. All so by motion and second preferred a charge against another brother for drunkness, deferred charge till next reg. conference. 5. Collected 6.35 to by cole [*coal*]. R. A. Roper, Mod., H. G. Wilkie, C.C.

Dec. 23, 1922, our pastor. 3. By motion and second, taken up the reference of a brother, after reading the letter, the church deferred charge till next conference. Also taken up the charge of drunkness against another brother and by motion and second, we withdraw fellowship from him. 5. Collected 2.75 to by [*buy*] church book. For Bro. Roper $4.50. R. A. Roper, Mod., H. G. Wilkie, C.C.

Jan. 25, 1923, our pastor, Rev. R. A. Roper. 2. By motion and second, the church preferred a charge against a sister for living in adultery. By motion and second the church withdraws fellowship from her. All so by motion and second the church prefers charge against a brother for living in adultery. Taken up the charge and excluded him from the fellowship of the church. 3. By motion and second, taken the reference against a brother for drunkness, by motion and second, the church withdraws fellowship from him. 4. Received by letter Rev. R. A. Roper and wife Sister Martha Jane Roper and Sister Emma Roper as members in good standing with us. Also received under the watch cair Bro. Hallmond and Colmond Roper, under the watch cair of Hightower Church. 5. Collected for our pastor 2 dollars. R. A. Roper, Mod., H. G. Wilkie, C.C.

Feb. 25, 1923, Pastor R. A. Roper. 5. By motion and second the church appointed a commity to by [*buy*] some more land for church purposes. Committy as follows: L. L. West, J. S. Wyatt, R. E. Loveless, H. G. Wilkie, A. A. Roper, E. G. Rich. R. A. Roper Mod., H. G. Wilkie, C.C.

Mar. 24, 1923, Bro. R. Dunagan? followed by our pastor Bro. R. A. Roper. 2. By motion and second the church preferred charge against a brother for cursing and unseeming [*unseemly*] talking. Deferred charge till next meeting. 5. Report of committee on buying more land and adopted. Collected $14.90 on the payment of same. R. A. Roper, Mod., H. G. Wilkie, C.C.

Apr. 1923, Bro. Dean. Elects J. S. Wyatt as moderator. 2. The church excepts the acknowledgements of a brother for drunkness and bairs with him. 3. Taken the reference of a brother and by motion and second the church moves to withdraw fellowship from him. 5. Collected money to pay off the land and H. G. Wilkie to get the deed to same and have it recorded. J. S. Wyatt, Mod. Prot., H. G. Wilkie, C.C.

Jun. 22, 1923, Rev. R. A. Roper. 3. Taken the referrance against a brother for drunkness. The brother makes his acknowledgements and the church received them and bore with him. 4. Received Bro. Hallmond and Collmond Roper by letter. Elected messengers to represent Hightower in the association to wit: Rev. R. A. Roper, R. M. Cantrell, R. E. Loveless, E. G. Rich, E. H. Pearson, A. A. Roper as messengers from Hightower. Collected $2.10 cts. for minutes. All so by motion, the church never to use the money in the treasury to pay for the housekeeper. R. A. Roper, Mod., H. G. Wilkie, C.C.

Various financial records and other information noted at end of book 3, names as listed:

Aug. 18, 1909. For pastor: W.N. Martin, L. L. West comm.[*committee*], Aug. 19, J. T. Bryant Comm,

March 1910, received for orphans home, 2.50, for building and repairs, 2.00

Nov. 20, 1915: J. M. Richards, W. E. Pierce and wife, J. T. Wallace and wife. Mrs. G. Mattie Hester, R. M. Cantrell and wife, J. P. Green, G. B. Haggood

Feb. 19, 1916: Mrs. G. W. Little, J. H. Ellis, Eulee Richards, C. L. Logins

April 15, 1916: J. H. Wilkie, R. W. Cochran, Walter Herring, W. E. Pearce, H. K. Fletcher and wife, G. M. Bryant, J. M. Steavens, Gatewood Southern and wife, Azriath McFerson

1922, dismist by letter? Excluded 1, Died Sister Bryant in April, Died T. E. Green June 21, 1922

Financial record for pastor, no date: H. G. Wilkie, J. T. Wallace, J. H. Ellis, Steve Dean, J. M. Richards, Viola Sandow, Mrs. J. M. Richards, G. W. Little, Oscar Hester, Mrs. S. P. Porter, Mrs. Nancy Green, Lum Hester, J. L. Wilkie, Mrs. Francis Padgett, Mrs. Fannie Wilkie, W. T. Fowler, Grady Fowler Sr., J. H. Wilkie Jr., Raul Green, Roy Green

Book 3; 1910-1923 Membership

* Information found only in minutes

	Last name	First name	Middle Name/ married name	How/when received, other info	How/when dismissed, Other Info	Remarks; items not listed in church roll (maiden name; spouse; birth-death; buried at - HBC; etc.)
3	Andrews	Jane			Let	
3	Andrews	Lou	A.		Let Aug 1956	
3	Andrews	Mattie	M.		Death Dec 23, 1951	(Green) 1880-1951, bur HBC by W.J. Andrews
3	Adams	May		Exp Aug 1908	Let Sep 1916	
3	Andrews	Gusta		Exp Aug 1915	death	
3	Andrews	Minnie		Exp Aug 1919	Death Jul 22, 1980	Minnie Pearl, 1903-1980, m Edgar Cronan, bur HBC
3	Biddy	J.	R.		Died Jun 30, 1910	? John Richard, "Rusty", b Dec 01 1841
3	Bowling	H.	C.		Died Oct 25, 1910	Boling, 1839-1910, bur HBC
3	Bowling	Emily	R.		Died Oct 1909	Emily Rebecca Green Boling, 1847-1909, bur HBC
3	Bryant	Thomas		Let Aug 5, 1888	Died 1923	1851-1923, bur HBC
3	Bryant	L.	A.	Let Aug 5, 1888	Died Apr 1922	Lucy Ann (Garrett), 1856-1922, bur HBC, w/o Thomas Bryant
3	Bryant	J.	T.	Exp Aug 1890	Died Jul 24, 1914	John T. 1871-1914, bur HBC, s/o Thomas and Lucy Bryant
3	Bryant	G.	Mansel	Exp Aug 1890	Let *Apr 1922	George Mancel Bryant
3	Boling	W.	T.	Exp Aug 1890	Let Oct 1915	William Thompson, 1868-1929, bur HBC
3	Boling	J.	Lowry	Exp Aug 1890	Death	Joseph Lowery, 1872-1926, bur HBC
3	Boling	Reuben	J.	Exp Sep 1893	death	
3	Bryant	Fannie		Let Apr 1896	Let Jul 20, 1929 death	
3	Boling	Pruid		Exp Aug 1892	Died 1922 or 24	Mary Pruid (Green) Boling; 1877-1922, bur HBC
3	Boling	John	F.	Exp Aug 1897	death	1873-1926, bur HBC
3	Boling	Martha		Let Aug 1899	Let Oct 1915	*w/o W T Boling
3	Biddy	John		Let Aug 1900	Let Sep 1909	
3	Biddy	Elizabeth		Let Aug 1900	Let Sep 1909	Sarah Elzabeth
3	Biddy	Nicie	L.	Let Aug 1900	Let Sep 1909	
3	Biddy	A.	R.	Let Aug 1900	Let Sep 1909	
3	Biddy	A.	L.	Let Aug 1900	Let Sep 1909	
3	Biddy	Emory		Let Aug 1900	Let Sep 1909	
3	Biddy	Lula		Exp Aug 1899	Let Sep 1909, dead	

	Last name	First name	Middle Name/ married name	How/when received, other info	How/when dismissed, Other Info	*Remarks; items not listed in church roll (maiden name; spouse; birth-death; buried at - HBC; etc.)*
3	Biddy	Elma		Exp Aug 1900	Let Sep 1909	
3	Bryant	F.	A.	Exp Aug 1900		
3	Bryant	F.	Belle	Exp Aug 1900	Let	
3	Bryant	J.	H.	Exp Aug 1902	Let	*? Jackson*
3	Brooks	Richard		Exp Aug 1902	Let Oct 1909	
3	Brooks	Jas	W.	Exp Aug 1902	Let Mar 1914	
3	Bryant	Lewis		Exp Aug 1904	Let 1930	*h/o Lula Bryant*
3	Brooks	Adeline		Let May 1906	Let Oct 1909	*1885-1979*
3	Bryant	Posey		Exp Aug 1906		
3	Boling	James		Exp Aug 1907	Let Sep 1916 *Let May 1921	*1921: J A Bolling and wife Ethell*
3	Bryant	Mary	E.	Exp Oct 17, 1908	Let	
3	Boling	Ethel	(Leonard)	Exp Aug 1906	Let Sep 1916 *Let May 1921	*w/o James Boling*
3	Barrett	Sinia /Siney	(Leonard)	Exp Aug 1906	*Let Apr 1919 Let Aug 1920	
3	Bryant	Gordon		Exp Aug 1906	Let Nov. 1924	
3	Bryant	Martha		Exp Aug 1911	Let Apr 1947	
3	Bryant	Louvenia		Let Aug 1916	Let 1919	*Margaret Louvenia "Venie"*
3	Buffington	Drusiller, Mrs.		Exp Aug 1916		*1867-1948, Mrs. Drucilla Dunagan Buffington*
3	Buffington	Robert		Exp Aug 1918	Dead	*1891-1952, bur HBC*
3	Barker	Floyd		Exp Aug 1919	Let 1928	
3	Bryant	Edd		Exp 1919		
3	Bowles	Allie, Miss		Exp Aug 26, 1921	Let Sep 19, 1925	
3	Bolling	Edith, Miss		Exp Aug 1922	Dead	
3	Cochran	E.	A. Rev.	*Let June 1918	Let Apr 1916 Let 1919 Minister	*Elias, 1845-1931, bur HBC*
3	Cochran	R.	W.	Exp Aug 1885	Let May 1928	*Robert Wiley, 1852-1937, bur HBC*
3	Cochran	Matilda	M.		Death	*(Leonard), 1863-1925, bur HBC, w/o R. W. Cochran*
3	Cannon	Elmore	L.	Exp Sep 1900	Death	
3	Cantrell	Ramon	M.		Death 1940, deacon	*Raymond Marion, 1879-1940, bur HBC*
3	Collier	Nancy	J.	Exp Sep 1901		
3	Collier	May, Mary		Exp Sep 1901		

	Last name	First name	Middle Name/ married name	How/when received, other info	How/when dismissed, Other Info	*Remarks; items not listed in church roll (maiden name; spouse; birth-death; buried at - HBC; etc.)*
3	Collier	Lena, Linie	A.	Exp Aug 1902		
3	Cape	Eveline		Let Mar 1898		
3	Cochran	E.	Virgil	Exp Aug 1903	Let Sep 16, 1927	*Elias Virgil, 1883-1954*
3	Cochran	I.	Elizabeth	Exp Aug 1897	Let Sep 17, 1927	
3	Cantrell	Lula		Exp Sep 1899	death	*Lula Viola (Hester), 1883-1954, w/o Raymon Cantrell, bur HBC*
3	Cloud	Sarah		Let Apr 1907	death	
3	Chastain	Maggie		Let Jul 7, 1907	Let 1931	
3	Christopher	May		Exp Oct 1908	Let Aug 1924	
3	Croy	Lydia		Exp Aug 1899	Let Nov 1937 dead	
3	Croy	L.	O.	Exp Aug 23, 1909	Let Nov 1937	*Lewis O Croy?*
3	Chasteene	William	B.	Exp Aug 23, 1909	Let Jul 28, 1923	
3	Chasteene	Thomas		Exp Aug 23, 1909		
3	Christopher	Coria, Cora	A.	Exp Aug 23, 1909		
3	Christopher	Bell		Exp Aug 23, 1909		
3	Collit	Jane		Let Oct 1909		
3	Chastain	Ida	M.	Exp 1910?		
3	Covington	Abraham		Let Jun 18, 1911	Let 1915	
3	Cox	Albert		Exp Aug 1913		
3	Cochran	Paul		Exp Aug 1913	Let Aug 1923	
3	Cape	Delia		Exp Aug 1915		
3	Collit	Thurman		Exp Aug 1915		
3	Chumbler	Nelia		Exp Aug 1917		
3	Chumbler	J.	M.	Let Aug 1917		*? James M.; bur HBC*
3	Chumbler	L.	E.	Let Aug 1917		*? Emma Lee? bur HBC*
3	Chumbler	Robert		Exp Aug 1919	Let Oct 15, 1938	*R. C., Robert Calton*
3	Davenport	Sarah	J.	Let Aug 1890	Dead, w/o Dave	*Sarah J. (Heygood)*
3	Dawson	J.	F.	Exp Sep 1898		
3	Dawson	Julia	J.	Exp Aug 1897		
3	Dawson	Nancy		Exp Aug 1903		
3	Dunnigan	R.	Aulelia	Exp Sep 1899 Let Jan 16, 1915	Minister Let Mar 14, 1914 Let Dec 1924	*Raymond Aulelia Dunagan, Ordained at HBC Nov 15, 1908, 1877-1929*
3	Dunnigan	Mary		Exp Sep 1899 Let Jan 16, 1915	Let Mar 14, 1914 Let Dec 1924	*Mary Laura (Hester) Dunagan, 1879-1951*

	Last name	First name	Middle Name/ married name	How/when received, other info	How/when dismissed, Other Info	*Remarks; items not listed in church roll (maiden name; spouse; birth-death; buried at - HBC; etc.)*
3	Dobson	S.	Ada	Let Sep 1900	*Let Sep 1920	*Susan Adia, 1876-1961, ? Dbl, Feb 1912, Sister S A Dobson*
3	Dowda	W.	D.	Exp Sep 1900	Let	
3	Dobson	W.	Neely	Exp Sep 1900	Let Apr 1947	*William Neely, 1881-1975, m Jane Mason*
3	Dobson	Lucinda		Exp Aug 1902	Let	
3	Dowda	A.	Eary E.	Exp Aug 1903	Let Sep 1916	
3	Dobson	E.	W.	Exp Aug 1906		
3	Drummond	Texas		Exp Aug 1906	dead	*(Hester), 1874-1913, bur HBC, 1st w/o George W Drummond*
3	Dispain	Nettie		Let Aug 23, 1911	Let	
3	Dispain	Moses		Let Aug 23, 1911	Let 1917	*1866-1943*
3	Dispain	Martha		Let Aug 23, 1911	Let 1917	*1866-1956*
3	Dispain	Pearl		Exp Aug 1912	Let 1917	
3	Dispain	Pearl	Odum		Let	*Pearlie, Purley, 1893-1971*
3	Drummond	J.	L.	Exp Aug 1913	Jess Drummond Let Jul 15, 1934	
3	Dean	W.	M.	Exp Aug 1913	Let Aug 1924	*W. Milton, "Milt" Dean*
3	Dawson	Maudia		Exp Aug 1914	Let Apr 17, 1926	
3	Dispain	Leeory, Mr.		Exp Aug 1914	Let * Sep 1918	*Leora, Leola, 1889-1976*
3	Dunigan	Pearl		Exp Aug 1914	Let Aug 20, 1927	
3	Dean	Lila	May	Exp Aug 1915		
3	Dispain	Stella		Let Aug 1915	*Let Nov 1913 Stelly; Let Aug 1917	**1917 Stella Sissom*
3	Dunigan	Oliver		Exp Aug 1916	Let Dec 1924, dead	
3	Dean	Steve		Let 1918	Let Nov 1924	*S D? 1870-1952, bur HBC*
3	Dean	Sarah		Let 1918	Let Nov 1924	*1876-1948, bur HBC*
3	Dean	Mattie		Exp Aug 1917	Let Dec 1936	
3	Dean	Felton		Exp Aug 1917	Let 1933	*James Felton*
3	Dobson	Della		Exp Aug 1917	Let Aug 1939	*Della Dobson Scott*
3	Dobson	Dora		Exp Aug 1917	Let Jul 1923	*1898-*
3	Dobson	Ethel		Exp Aug 1917		
3	Dobson	Early		Exp Aug 1917		*Jessie Earley Dobson, 1896-1986*
3	Dobson	Lemur		Exp Aug 1917	Died Mar 1983	*Lemur Washington Dobson, bur HBC*
3	Dobson	Rufus		Exp Aug 1917		*Rufus David Dobson, 1904-1986*

	Last name	First name	Middle Name/ married name	How/when received, other info	How/when dismissed, Other Info	*Remarks; items not listed in church roll (maiden name; spouse; birth-death; buried at - HBC; etc.)*
3	Dobson	Cora		Exp Aug 1917	Dead Nov 27, 2001	*m Cowart, 1907-2001*
3	Dobson	Halmon		Exp Aug 1918	Let Nov 17, 1962	
3	Dobson	W.	M.	Let Aug 22, 1919	dead	*William Monroe Dobson, 1861-1950, bur HBC*
3	Dobson	Martha		Let Aug 22, 1919	death	*Martha (Blackwell) Dobson, 1869-1940, w/o William M Dobson, bur HBC*
3	Dobson	Dorah		Let Aug 22, 1919		*Dora*
3	Dobson	Clinton		Exp Aug 1919	Let Aug 1948	*James Clinton Dobson, 1901-1966*
3	Dean	Mary		Let 1919	Let Aug 25, 1924	
3	Dean	Della		Exp 1920	Let Nov 1924	
3	Dean	Marron, Mr.		Aug 26, 1921	Let Oct 20, 1934	*Marion Dean*
3	Dean	Albert		Aug 26, 1921	Death May 1982	
3	Dean	Mary		Aug 26, 1921		
3	Dean	Liley		Exp Aug 22, 1922		*Miss*
3	Drummond	Etta		Exp Sep 1922	Let Jul 15, 1933	*Miss Drummond m Eason*
3	Ellis	J.	Henry	Let Mar 1897	Death 1926 Deacon	*John Henry, 1863-1926, bur HBC*
3	Ellis	Mary	C.	Let Mar 1897	Death 1948	*Mary Catherine, 1866-1948, bur HBC*
3	Ellis	John	B.	Exp Aug 1899	dead	*John Barry, 1885-1915*
3	Ellis	J.	Elbert	Exp Sep 1900	dead	*James Elbert,"Elb", 1888-1932, bur HBC*
3	Ellis	Ida	O.	Let Aug 1907	Let 1916	*Ida Wallace Ellis, or Ellice, 1883-1968*
3	Ellis	Oma , Omie	Porter	Exp Aug 1908	Dead	*Oma Mae Ellis/Ellice Porter, 1893-1974, bur HBC*
3	Ellis	Euness		Exp Aug 23, 1909	Let Jul 20, 1929	*Emma Eunice Ellis, 1895-1971, m J. Samuel Cochran, bur HBC*
3	Ellis	Vader		Let Oct 1909	Let Jun 1937	*Vader/Vada Wallace Ellis, 1888-1973*
3	Ellis	R.	L.	Exp Aug 25, 1910	Let	*Robert Lee, "Bob", 1891-1975*
3	Ellis	Malia	B.	Exp Aug 25, 1910		*Mollie P. (Sewell), 1893-1975*
3	Eubanks	Herman		Exp Aug 1913	Dead 1917	*1894-1916, bur HBC*
3	Ellis	George		Exp Aug 1915		
3	Ellis	Irene		Exp Aug 1919	Death Oct 10, 1991	*m Sams*

	Last name	First name	Middle Name/ married name	How/when received, other info	How/when dismissed, Other Info	Remarks; items not listed in church roll (maiden name; spouse; birth-death; buried at - HBC; etc.)
3	Ellis	Willie		Exp Aug 1919	Let	
3	Evans	Maudie, Mrs.		Aug 1920		
3	Evans	Claud	A.	Aug 1920	Let Aug 1923	
3	Evans	Mary	A.	Aug 1920	Let Aug 1923	
3	Fletcher	G.	Bartow	Exp Jan 1886	Death 1932 Deacon	George Barto "Bart", 1862 – 1932, bur HBC , m. 1st Sallie Ledbetter, 2nd Rhoda J. Spears
3	Fletcher	H.	Kelley	Let Apr 1888	Death 1926	Hezekiah Kelly Fletcher, h/o Augusta (Hester), 1860-1926, bur HBC
3	Fletcher	Augusta	A.	Exp Aug 1887	Death 1947	Augusta Azalee (Hester), 1870-1947, m Hezekiah K. Fletcher, bur HBC
3	Fowler	Wm		Let Aug 1897	Let 1929	William Fowler
3	Fowler	Theodocia		Let Aug 1897	Death May 1924	
3	Floyd	Sidney	W.	Exp Aug 1899	Dead	
3	Fowler	W.	Thomas	Exp Sep 1900	Let Apr 1906	
3	Floyd	Cora	L.	Exp Sep 1900		
3	Fitts	Charlie		Exp Sep 1900	Dead Mar 1919	Charley F.
3	Farmer	Ida	(Hardin)	Exp Aug 1890		
3	Fowler	Ransom			Death	
3	Fowler	Mary	M.		Dead	
3	Fowler	Mary	E.		See Bryson	
3	Fitts	Mary	J.			Mary Jane (Green), w/o Jesse W. Fitts
3	Fowler	Sarah	E. Cochran		dead	Sarah Emaline "Emma" (Fowler), 1834-1901, 2nd wife of E. A Cochran
3	Fletcher	Evelee	Richards	Exp Aug 1907	Death 1951	Myra Evalee Fletcher Richards, w/o James Washington Richards, bur HBC

Dbl Aug. 21, 1937, rejoined Aug. 1938 |
3	Fowler	Mattie	L.	Exp Aug 1908	See Mason	Mattie Lou Fowler Mason?
3	Fowler	Newton		Exp Aug 1908	Let 1930	
3	Fowler	Odest		Exp Aug 1913	Let 1938	Odis?
3	Fowler	Alice		Exp Aug 1913	*Let Sep 1914

Let 1930 | m. Newton Fowler |
3	Fowler	Ella		Letter	Death	
3	Fletcher	Austin		Exp Aug 1915	Let 1929	
3	Fletcher	Harmon		Exp Aug 1915	Dead 1940	

	Last name	First name	Middle Name/ married name	How/when received, other info	How/when dismissed, Other Info	*Remarks; items not listed in church roll (maiden name; spouse; birth-death; buried at - HBC; etc.)*
3	Fletcher	Rhoda		Exp Aug 1915	Dead	*Rhoda J (Spears), 1876-1951, 2nd w/o George Bartow Fletcher, bur HBC*
3	Fowler	Dela?		Exp Aug 1915?		
3	Fowler	Grady	Jr.		Dead	
3	Fowler	Grady	Sr.	Exp Aug 1918		
3	Fowler	Hattie		Exp Aug 1918	Let 1930	
3	Fowler	Julie, Julia		Aug 1921	Let 1930	
3	Fowler	Minor		Let Aug 1918		
3	Fowler	Lussie		Let Aug 1918	Let Apr 1949	
3	Fletcher	Aubrey		Exp Aug 1918	Death 1961	
3	Fletcher	Vester		Exp Aug 1919	Death Jul 3, 1974	
3	Fletcher	Era		Exp Aug 1919	Let Sep 17, 1938	*Era Estelle Fletcher Tribble*
3	Fowler	Janey		Aug 1920		
3	Fowler	Julie, Miss		Aug 1921	Let 1930	
3	Fletcher	Jenie, Mrs		Let 1922	Let 1930/Oct. 1929	*Genia m Austin Fletcher*
3	Green	T.	E.	Exp	Died Jun 21, 1922	*Thomas E. Green/Greene, 1848-1922*
3	Green	Joseph	E.	Exp	Died Apr 26, 1916	*Joseph P. Green? 1858-1916, bur HBC*
3	Green	Nancy	L.		Death	*1850-1928? Bur HBC*
3	Green	Elizabeth			Death	*1853-1928? Bur HBC*
3	Green	Mary	E.	Ex Aug 1897	Let 1922?	*1878-1940? bur HBC*
3	Green	Paralee		Let Aug 1885	Dead 1919	
3	Green	S.	L.?		Died May 15, 1916	*Samuel L, 1855-1916, bur HBC*
3	Green	Maud	M		Dead 1913	*Maudie, 1886-1913, bur HBC*
3	Green	Susie		Exp Oct 1908	Death Apr 20, 1963	*m Pearson, 1888-1963*
3	Green	W.	E.	Exp Oct 1908	Death Jan 25, 1956	*William Edward, 1874-1956, bur HBC*
3	Green	F.	Ola	Exp Aug 1903	Death 1931	
3	Green	Nellia		Exp Aug 1910		*Nellie? B 1896, m Bret Watkins?*
3	Green	Josef	B.	Exp Aug 1911		
3	Gaddis	Dessie	V.	Exp Aug 1912	Let May 15, 1915	
3	Gaddis	Bertha	L.	Exp Aug 1913	Let May 15, 1915	
3	Gaddis	Amanda		Exp Aug 1913	Let Aug 1917	
3	Green	H.	N.	Exp Aug 1913	Death Jul 1968	*Henry Newton "Newt", 1883-1968, bur HBC*

	Last name	First name	Middle Name/ married name	How/when received, other info	How/when dismissed, Other Info	*Remarks; items not listed in church roll (maiden name; spouse; birth-death; buried at - HBC; etc.)*
3	Green	Rosalee		Exp Aug 1913	Death 1938	*Rossie Lee Hester Green, 1886-1938, w/o Newt Green*
3	Green	J.	R.	Exp Aug 1914	Died Feb 1915	*John R, 1876-1915, bur HBC*
3	Green	Tim		Exp Aug 1914	Death Mar 1971	
3	Good	Clide				
3	Groover	Estella		Aug 1915	Let Aug 17, 1918	*Estelle*
3	Groover	Lula		Let Jun 1917	Let 1918 *Let May 1921	
3	Groover	Willie		Exp Aug 1917	Let Aug 17, 1918	*"Sister"*
3	Green	Raul		Exp Aug 1918	Let Dec 17, 1949	
3	Green	Roy		Exp Aug 1918	Death 1933	
3	Green	Lois		Exp Aug 1919	Let Aug 20, 1927	
3	Green	Thomas	Jr.	Exp Aug 26, 1921	Death Dec 28, 1984; *Gatha Wheeler's brother; Newt Green's son;*	*Tom W., 1904-1984*
3	Green	Hattie	Lou	Exp Aug 1922 *Sep 1922	Death Dec 30, 1997	*Hattie Lou Turner Green, 1904-1997*
3	Green	Ela, Miss		Exp Aug 1922 *Sep 1922		*Ella? b 1903; m Shelvie Cornett*
3	Green	Hester Miss or Mrs.?		Exp Aug 1922		
3	Howard	Elisha			Dead 1913	*? Elijah, 1812-1913, bur HBC*
3	Hester	A.	T. Scott		Dead 1910	*Andrew Thomas "Scott," 1847-1910*
3	Hardin	F.	J.	Exp Sep 1889	Dead	
3	Haygood	Seldon	G	Exp Aug 1890	Let Sep 1916	*Green Seldon, 1876-1935, bur HBC*
3	Haygood	J.	Elmer	Exp Aug 1903	Let *Jun 1912	*James Elmer, 1881-1931, bur HBC with 2 wives: Annie and May*
3	Holcombe	James	J.	Let Oct 1891	Let Nov 20, 1909	*James Jackson Holcomb, J.J. Holcombe, 1864-1937, bur HBC*
3	Holcombe	Louise		Let Oct 1891	Let Nov 20, 1909	*Louise (Hogan) 1862-1927, bur HBC, w/o James J Holcombe*
3	Holcombe	S.	D.	Exp Sep 1893	Dead	*?? Sherman D/ Bud, 1878-1962, bur HBC*
3	Hardin	Hassie		Let Sep 1890	Let Sep 1922 *Let Aug 1922	
3	Holcombe	John	W.	Let Sep 1893	Died Mar 1917	*1842-1917, bur HBC*

	Last name	First name	Middle Name/ married name	How/when received, other info	How/when dismissed, Other Info	*Remarks; items not listed in church roll (maiden name; spouse; birth-death; buried at - HBC; etc.)*
3	Holcombe	Cansada		Let Sep 1893	Dead	*?Ganzady/Canzady (Haygood) 1844-1927, m John W Holcomb, bur HBC*
3	Howard	S.	Desdemona	Let Sep 1893	dead	*"Monie" Holcombe Howard*
3	Hardin	Charley		Exp 1893	dead	
3	Haygood	Green	B.	Let Nov 1896	Death, deacon	*Samuel Greenberry, G. B., 1848-1925, deacon, bur HBC*
3	Haygood	Susannah		Let Nov 1896	died	*Suseana (Mosteller) w/o G B Haygood, bur HBC, 1844-1922*
3	Holcombe	Annie	O.	Exp Aug 1897/ Exp Aug 1903		
3	Holcombe	Cora	L.	Exp Aug 1897/ Exp Aug 1903	dead	*(White)*
3	Hester	L.	Dora	Exp Aug 1885	Let Aug 1924	
3	Howard	D.	H.	Let		*Henry?*
3	Haygood	Annie	L.	Exp Jun 1898	*Let Jun 1912 Dead 1913	*1881-1913, bur HBC, 1st w/o James Elmer Haygood*
3	Holbrook	Daisy	L.	Exp Sep 1900		
3	Holcombe	W.	Henry	Exp Aug 1899	Let	*Or Holcomb, s/o James J?, dbl on Nov 1909?*
3	Herring	A.	Webb	Exp Sep 1900		*Alfred Webb Herring, born 1881*
3	Holcombe	Bertha	S.	Exp Sep 1902	Let Nov 20, 1909	*d/o James J Holcombe*
3	Harbin	Mary				
3	Hester	E.	J.			
3	Hester	E.	C.			
3	Howard	Celia		Exp Aug 1902		
3	Howard	Millard		Let Aug 1905		
3	Hawkins	O.	W.	Exp Aug 1906	Let 1912	
3	Hester	C.	Columbus	Exp Aug 1906	dead	*Christopher Columbus, 1881-1946, bur HBC*
3	Hester	Mattie	Mrs. C.C.	Exp Aug 1906	Died Jun 28, 1965	*Mattie J, w/o C.C. Hester, 1883-1965, bur HBC*
3	Hester	Mattie	Miss Stevens	Exp Aug 1906	Died 1968	
3	Haygood	W.	D.	Exp Aug 1907	Let Feb 1910	
3	Haygood	Sallie	M.	Exp Aug 1907	Let Feb 1910	
3	Hall	Mollie	L.	Exp Aug 1907	Let	
3	Holcombe	Clara	Belle	Let Aug 1908	Let Nov 20, 1909	*d/o James J Holcombe*
3	Herring	Newton	F.	Let Aug 1908		
3	Herring	May		Exp Aug 1908	dead	

	Last name	First name	Middle Name/ married name	How/when received, other info	How/when dismissed, Other Info	*Remarks; items not listed in church roll (maiden name; spouse; birth-death; buried at - HBC; etc.)*
3	Hall	Bessie		Exp Aug 1908	Death Apr 27, 1982	
3	Herring	Etta		Exp Oct 1908		*Mary Etta*
3	Howard	W.	L. D.	Let May 16, 1909	Death 1930	*1857-1928? Bur HBC*
3	Howard	Anna		Let May 16, 1909	death	*Anner, 1860-1940, bur HBC*
3	Hughes	Cora	(Mason)	Exp Aug 1900	Let Apr 1910	
3	Holcombe	Alice		Exp Sep 1899	Death Mar 20, 1968	
3	Hester	Nettie	(West)	Let May 1906	Died 1946	*1888-1946*
3	Howard	Henry		Exp Aug 23, 1909	Died 1919	
3	Haygood	Arthur		Exp Aug 23, 1909	Let Oct 1910	*In minutes as Arthur Heggood*
3	Howard	Burtha		Exp Aug 23, 1909	dead	
3	Howard	Mattia	D.	Exp Aug 8, 1910	dead	
3	Hester	Lee		Exp Aug 8, 1910	Death Feb 6, 1987; deacon	*1889-1987*
3	Howard	Flordia		Exp Aug 8, 1910	dead	*Flara, 1885-1930, bur HBC*
3	Hester	Dolley		Exp Aug 8, 1910	Death Jun 1970	*m. Darby*
3	Hester	Ader	Miss	Exp Aug 1911	Let Sep 1943 *Ada Coker	*Ada Hester Coker*
3	Herring	Dollie		Exp Aug 1912		
3	Howard	Effie		Exp Aug 1912	Let Apr 17, 1926	
3	Hester	George	Emery	Exp Aug 1933		
3	Hester	Emma		Let Dec 20, 1913	Death Jan 26, 1977	*Emma Whitfield Hester, 1896-1977, w/o Lee Hester*
3	Hawkins	Maudia			Let Jul 1914	
3	Herring	J.	W.	Exp Aug 1914		
3	Howard	Fannie		Exp Aug 1914	Let Apr 15, 1972	
3	Holcomb	Henry	H.	Let 1915	Death 1930?	
3	Herring	N.	F.		Death	
3	Harden	R.	L.	Let Sep 1916		
3	Harden	O., Mrs.	V.	Let Sep 1916	Let Aug 1920	
3	Harden	Dollia	May	Let Sep 1916	Let Aug 1920	
3	Harden	Etta		Let Sep 1916	Let Aug 1920	
3	Herring	Emma		Exp Aug 1917	Died Mar 1919	*1890-1919, bur HBC*
3	Hester	Oscar		Exp Aug 1918	*Death Dec 28, 1979*	

	Last name	First name	Middle Name/ married name	How/when received, other info	How/when dismissed, Other Info	*Remarks; items not listed in church roll (maiden name; spouse; birth-death; buried at - HBC; etc.)*
3	Hester	Boy		Exp Aug 1918		*Boy Cranston Hester, 1893-1969, bur HBC*
3	Hester	Boy, Mrs.		Exp Aug 1918	death	*Zenie/Zena (Cloud) Hester, w/o Boy C. Hester, 1900-1995, bur HBC*
3	Hester	Pauline		Exp Aug 1919		
3	Hester	Dora, Mrs.		Exp Aug 1919		
3	Hester	Guss		Exp Aug 1919		*Augustus, 1895-1982, bur HBC*
3	Holcomb	Velvia		Let Sep 18 1920	Let May 1924	*Miss*
3	Hester	Doley , Miss				
3	Hester	Gussie, Sister		Exp Aug 1922	Died Dec 2, 1966	*Flora Augusta, 1892-1966, bur HBC*
3	Hester	Edker		Exp Aug 1922	dead	*Thomas Edgar; 1895-1936; Bur HBC*
3	Hester	Hattie		Exp Aug 1922	Mrs. Tom Chumbler	
3	Ingram	J.	Lewis	Exp Aug 1892		*James Lewis*
3	Ingram	Thomas	G. W.	Exp Aug 1892		
3	Ingram	Jeff	J.	Let Aug 1892		
3	Ingram	Fariba		Let Aug 1892	death	
3	Jones	G.	C.	Exp Aug 1915	Let 1947	*Grover*
3	Jones	Dora		Exp Aug 1915	death	
3	Kinsey	Bessey		Exp Aug 24, 1910	Let 1918	
3	Kinsey	Allis, Mrs.		Exp Aug 24, 1910	Let 1918	
3	Kelly	R.	E.	Let Jun 19, 1911	Let Sep 19, 1925	
3	Kelly	Evvie		Let Jun 19, 1911	Let Sep 19, 1925	
3	Kelly	Belle		Let Jun 19, 1911	Let Sep 19, 1925	
3	Kinsey	Mattie		Exp Aug 1911	Let 1918	
3	Leonard	Leannie		Let Aug 1891	Dead Nov 1913	*1824-1913, bur HBC*
3	Little	Tom		Exp Aug 1902	Let Sep 1947	
3	Little	Senie		Exp Aug 1902		
3	Little	Dock				*1886-1961, bur HBC*
3	Little	Lily	(Hester)		Death Aug 1979	*1883-1979, bur HBC*
3	Loggins	Miranda		Let Aug 1904	Death 1949	*1878-1949, m. David T. Emory, bur HBC*
3	Loggins	Robert		Let Aug 1904	Let May 18, 1912	
3	Loggins	Lucy		Let Aug 1904	Let May 18, 1912	
3	Loggins	Maggie		Let Aug 1904		
3	Loggins	James	H.	Let Aug 1904	Dead 1939	*1844-1939, bur HBC*
3	Loggins	Valley		Let May 1904	Let Sep 1912	

	Last name	First name	Middle Name/ married name	How/when received, other info	How/when dismissed, Other Info	*Remarks; items not listed in church roll (maiden name; spouse; birth-death; buried at - HBC; etc.)*
3	Loggins	Susan		Let May 1904	May 1912 *Let Sep 1912	*w/o Valley Loggins*
3	Little	Henry		Exp Aug 1906		
3	Loggins	Julia		Let Aug 24, 1907	Death May 1961	*Julie C., 1890-1961, bur HBC, w/o Charley Loggins*
3	Little	Harvey		Exp Aug 1907	Let Aug 19, 1932 Death April 1975	
3	Little	Millie		Let Aug 17, 1908	Let 1932	
3	Little	Frank		Exp Aug 20, 1908	Let Aug 15, 1936 –Let to Frank and wife	
3	Little	Callie		Exp Aug 20, 1908	Let Aug 14, 1954	
3	Leonard	Lula		Exp Aug 20, 1908	Let Nov 15, 1913	
3	Little	G.	W.	Let Feb 1909	Dead	
3	Low	Mary	D.	Exp Aug 1888	Let	*Kemp in book 1 and 2*
3	Lovelace	Georgia	A. (Wilkie)	Exp Aug 1902	Death Aug 24, 1965	*Georgia Anne, 1890-1965, bur HBC*
3	Lathem	Ethel	(Warren)	Exp Aug 1906		
3	Little	Andrew		Exp Aug 23, 1909	Dead	*1891-1921; bur HBC*
3	Loggins	Maranda		Let May 1910		
3	Loggins	Charley		Exp Aug 23, 1910	Death May 24, 1921	*Bur HBC*
3	Little	James		Exp Aug 1916		
3	Little	George	Jr	Exp Aug 24, 1910	Death Apr 3, 1962	*George Henry, 1882-1962, bur HBC*
3	Little	Maudia		Exp Aug 24, 1910	Death 1949	*Maude Alice, 1890-1949, bur HBC*
3	Little	Mattie, Mrs.		Exp Aug 1911	Let Dec. 1936	*w/o Homer Little*
3	Long	Martha		Let Aug 16, 1913	Let Jan 1919	*"Sis"*
3	Long	Nancy		Let Aug 16, 1913	Dead	*1833-1915, bur HBC*
3	Long	B.	R.	Exp Aug 1913	Let Jan 1919	*Ben*
3	Long	W.	H.	Exp Aug 1913	Let Jan 1919	*Homer*
3	Long	Ethel		Exp Aug 1914	Let Jan 1919	
3	Long	Mattie, Mrs.		Exp Aug 1914	Let Jan 1919	
3	Little	Steller, Mrs.		Exp Aug 1914	Let Aug 18, 1932	*Stella Little, w/o Harvey Little*

	Last name	First name	Middle Name/ married name	How/when received, other info	How/when dismissed, Other Info	*Remarks; items not listed in church roll (maiden name; spouse; birth-death; buried at - HBC; etc.)*
3	Little	Maudia, Mrs.		Exp Aug 1914	Let Aug 15, 1936 Dead	
3	Loggins	May		Exp Aug 1914	Death 1934	*Miss May/Mary, m. Kuykendall*
3	Loggins	Lousey		Exp Aug 1914		*Miss*
3	Loggins	Hattie		Exp Aug 1914		
3	Landcaster	Callie		Exp Aug 1915		
3	Little	Homer	Jack	Exp Aug 1917	Let Dec 1936	
3	Little	Dollie		Exp Aug 1917	Let Aug 1948	
3	Landcaster	Clarance		Exp Aug 26, 1921		
3	Landcaster	Ader		Exp Aug 26, 1921		*Miss*
3	Loveless	R.	E.	Exp Aug 26, 1921	Death, Deacon	*Robert Edgar Lovelace, 1886-1938, bur HBC*
3	Little	Miron		Exp Aug 1933	Death June 21, 1991	
3	McDaniel	Martha		Aug 1890	Dead	
3	Mason	J.	E.	Exp Aug 1885	Dead	
3	Martin	Martha	J.	Exp Aug 1890		*Mrs.?*
3	McGullion	Mattie	J.	Exp Aug 1887	Dead	*Martha Josephine "Mattie" McGullion, 1874-1951, bur HBC*
3	Mason	Mary		Let Aug 1900		
3	McDaniel	Anne	E.			
3	Mason	Lillie	M.	Exp Aug 1900		
3	Mason	George		Exp Aug 1911	Let	
3	McCloud	W.	H.	Exp Aug 1913	Let Mar 1919	
3	McFierson	Azratt		Let Sep 1915	Ordained Minister, Death 1926	*Azariah "Asa" McPherson, 1849-1926*
3	McFierson	Mrs.		Let Sep 1915	Dead	*Lois Cansady Edwards McPherson, 1845-1931*
3	McFierson	Razzia		Exp 1916	Let 1917	
3	Maddox	Media		Exp Aug 1917	Let 1931	
3	McPherson	E.	T.	Let Aug 1918	Let	*Enoch?*
3	McPherson	S., Mrs.	M.	Let Aug 1918		*Mrs.*
3	McPherson	Thomas		Let Aug 1918	Let Sep 1933	
3	Norton	Cornelia		Let Sep 1900	Let Jan 18, 1914	*Mrs. Sis Cornelia Norton, w/o W. S. Norton*
3	Norton	Pearl	M.	Exp Aug 1902	Let Jan 18, 1914	*d/o W S and Cornelia Norton*
3	Odum	Marcus		Let Aug 1907	Died May 1911	
3	Odum	Hester	A.	Let Aug 1907	Let Sep 1917	*Hester Ann*
3	Odum	Grover		Let Aug 1907		

	Last name	First name	Middle Name/ married name	How/when received, other info	How/when dismissed, Other Info	Remarks; items not listed in church roll (maiden name; spouse; birth-death; buried at - HBC; etc.)
3	O'Bryant	Lela		Let Aug 23, 1908		
3	O'Bryant	Viola		Exp Aug 20, 1908		
3	O'Bryant	Mary		Exp Aug 20, 1908		
3	Odum	Marque	E. B.	Let Aug 22, 1909		
3	Odum	E.	Purl	Let Aug 22, 1909	See Dispain	DBL 1919
3	O'Bryant	Dimple	F.		Let Dec 16, 1939	Dimple (O'Bryant) Greene
3	Purcell	Reuben	J.		Let Jan 19, 1910	Reuben James, 1852/53-1927, liberated (licensed) Aug 15, 1896
3	Purcell	Elizabeth	M.		Let Jan 19, 1910	w/o Reuben James Purcell
3	Purcell	R.	B.	Exp Aug 1890	Let Jan 19, 1910	Reuben Ben?
3	Purcell	Rufus	J. M.	Exp Aug 1890	Let Jan 19, 1910	h/o Daisy L. Nix
3	Pierce	William		Exp Aug 1890	dead	W E Pearse?, licensed minister on June 1915, 1880-1921
3	Priest	Ella	(Stephens)		Let Nov 20, 1909	(Stephens), 1866-1943, m George W Priest
3	Pearson	Edgar		Exp Aug 1897	Let Apr 18, 1925	E H? 1880-1935, bur HBC
3	Purcell	Mattie	(Hester)	Exp Aug 1890	Let Sep 1917 *Sept 1916	
3	Pruitt	John	B.	Exp Jun 1898	Let 1917 *Oct 1916	1877-1925
3	Pruitt	M.	Rosannah	Exp Aug 1897	Let 1917 *Oct 1916	Mary Roseanna (Ellis), 1883-1963, *w/o J B Pruitt
3	Purcell	W.	Lewis	Exp Aug 1899		
3	Pinson	Leannie		Let Aug 1899	Dead	
3	Price	W.	Oscar	Exp Aug 1900	Aug 22, 1919	
3	Price	W.	H. Sampson	Exp Aug 1900		
3	Price	Dora	J.	Exp Aug 1897	Let * Jul 1915	1880-1946, w/o James Milton Price?
3	Purcell	M	Odella	Exp Sep 1901	Let Oct 17, 1909	Deller, w/o Luther J Pursell
3	Purcell	Lela	B. Cobb	Exp Aug 1902	dead	Lelia Bell Purcell Cobb, 1891-1927
3	Price	J.	Milton	Exp Aug 1902	Let * Jul 1915	
3	Pearson	Nettie	R.	Exp Sep 1900	Let Sep 19, 1925	1882-1950, (Boling), w/o Edgar Pearson, bur HBC
3	Priest	Sallie		Exp Sep 1894		
3	Price	Dortha		Exp Aug 1903	Let Aug 12, 1919	

	Last name	First name	Middle Name/ married name	How/when received, other info	How/when dismissed, Other Info	*Remarks; items not listed in church roll (maiden name; spouse; birth-death; buried at - HBC; etc.)*
3	Priest	Epsy	M.	Exp Aug 1906	Died 1923	
3	Pierce	Roxana		Exp Aug 1907	Let Sep 1938	
3	Parker	Alma		Exp Aug 1908	Let Jan 19, 1910	*Almer (Parker) Brooks*
3	Pierce	R.	E.	Let Aug 20, 1909	Let Jan 19, 1910	*R. Erastus Pierce?*
3	Parker	J.	S.	Let Aug 20, 1909	Let Jan 19, 1910 Let May 1916 Died 1917	
3	Parker	Sallia		Let Aug 20, 1909	Let Jan 19, 1910 Let May 1916	
3	Pursell	Luther	J.		Let Oct 1909	
3	Pursell	Fannie			Let Jan 19, 1910	
3	Price	James	A.	Exp Aug 1911		
3	Price	Beckie, Mrs		Exp Aug 1911	Let 1931	
3	Price	N	Vastie	Exp Aug 1911	Let Sep 1915	
3	Price	Golden		Exp Aug 1911	Let Sep 1916	
3	Payne	M., Mrs.	E.	Exp Aug 1911		
3	Porter	Omie	(Ellis)		Let 1930 Deceased	*Oma Mae (Ellis) Porter, 1893-1974, bur HBC*
3	Price	Carrie, Mrs.		Exp Aug 1914	Let 1953	
3	Paggett	J.	A.	Let May 1913	Dead 1918	*Jacob Padgett, 1855-1918*
3	Paggett	Frances		Let May 1913	Let 1930/31	*w/o Jacob Padgett*
3	Parker	J.	S.	Let Aug 14, 1915	Died 1917	
3	Parker	Sallie		Let Aug 14, 1915		*w/o J S Parker*
3	Prince	Emma		Exp Aug 1915/16		*d/o Martin & Lula Prince*
3	Prince	Lula		Exp Aug 1915/16		*(Smallwood) w/o Martin Prince*
3	Porter	Carl		Exp Aug 1918		
3	Porter	Ruby		Exp Aug 1918		
3	Price	Ida	Bell	Exp Aug 1918	dead	
3	Porter	Sam Mrs., *Emma		Let Aug 1918	Dead 1962	*Emma D, 1883-1962, bur HBC by Sam Porter*
3	Padgett	Zeddie		Exp Aug 1919	Let Jul 12, 1944	*Zed, s/o Jacob and Francis Padgett, 1903-1975*
3	Pearson	Winnie		Exp Aug 1919	Let Sep 19, 1925	
3	Priest	Edgar		Exp Aug 1919	Let Jul 19, 1921	*1921: Ed Priest and wife Eliza*
3	Priest	Elizia		Let 1919?	Let Jul 19, 1921	

	Last name	First name	Middle Name/ married name	How/when received, other info	How/when dismissed, Other Info	Remarks; items not listed in church roll (maiden name; spouse; birth-death; buried at - HBC; etc.)
3	Pearce	Estell		Exp Aug 24, 1921	Dead	*Miss*
3	Pew	Myrtle		Exp Aug 24, 1921	Death	*Pugh?*
3	Ramsay	R.	A.	Let Aug 1891	Death	*Rice A, 1850-1925, bur HBC*
3	Ramsay	Ann		Let Aug 1891	Death 1939	*Susan Ann (Leonard), w/o Rice Ramsey, m in 1879, 1856-1939, bur HBC*
3	Rich	Victoria		Exp Aug 1897	Death	*Victoria (Sandow) Rich, 1874-1954*
3	Richards	James	M.	Let Aug 1885	Death 1928	*1840-1927, bur HBC*
3	Richards	Octavia	I.	Exp Aug 1888	Dead	
3	Richards	Martha	J.	Let Jun 1903	Let Mar 17, 1928	
3	Rider	Eugenia	Nellson	Exp Oct 17, 1908		
3	Roper	Arminda	(Floyd)	Exp Aug 1899	Let Jul 1923	
3	Richards	Mattia	L.	Exp Aug 28, 1910	Let?	
3	Rich	Jane		Let Aug 28, 1910		
3	Rich	Maggie		Exp Aug 1911	Death Feb 22, 1985	*Maggie Rich Eubanks Hamilton, 1896-1985, bur HBC*
3	Rich	Nellie	Parker	Exp Aug 1912	dead	*Nellie (Rich) Parker*
3	Richards	John	H.		dead	
3	Richards	J.	W.	Exp Aug 1916	Let Aug 21, 1937	
3	Roper	Eula	J.	Exp Aug 1918	Let	
3	Richards	Henry, Mrs.		Let Jul 1922?	Let 1924	
3	Roper	A.	A.	Let Jul 1922	Let May 1928 Death Licensed Minister	*Alfred A. Roper*
3	Roper	Louise	Sister	Let Jul 1922	Let May 1928	
3	Rich	E.	G.	Exp Sep 25, 1922	Death Licensed Minister Ordained minister 1926	*Rev. Elias/Elisha "Grant" Rich, 1869-1941, bur HBC*
3	Roper	R., Rev.	A.	Let Jan 24, 1923	Death Ordained minster	*Robert Amos, 1865-1939, bur HBC*
3	Roper	Martha, Mrs.	Jane	Let Jan 24, 1923	Dead	*(Covington) 1867-1957, bur HBC, w/o R A Roper*
3	Roper	Emma	Sister	Let Jan 24, 1923	Death Apr 3, 1969	*Mattie Emma (Roper) Green, 1905-1969, bur HBC*

	Last name	First name	Middle Name/ married name	How/when received, other info	How/when dismissed, Other Info	Remarks; items not listed in church roll (maiden name; spouse; birth-death; buried at - HBC; etc.)
3	Roper	H.	Colmand	Let Jan 24, 1923	Died Mar 1965	*Claborn Coleman Roper*
3	Roper	Halmond		Let Jan 24, 1923	Died Jun 21, 1973 Licensed minister	*Henry Holmon Roper*
3	Smith	T.	N.	Exp Jul 1884	Died Jun 1919 Deacon	*Thomas Nathan, 1857-1919, m 1st J. Angeline, m 2nd Jane, ordained as deacon on Nov 1884, bur HBC*
3	Sandow	M.	Viola	Exp Sep 1893	Died Jun 19, 1969	*Viola Minerva (Wilkie) Sandow, 1879-1969, bur HBC*
3	Smith	Millie	A.	Let Sep 1900	Let Nov 20, 1909	*w/o Colonel Smith*
3	Smith	Colonel	N.	Exp Sep 1900	Let Nov 20, 1909	*Colonel Nathan*
3	Smith	Octa	A.	Exp Aug 1902	Let Aug 19, 1911	*Octavia A Smith*
3	Speer	Annie	L. (Fowler)	Exp Sep 1900	Let 1913/ *Let Jun 1912	
3	Smallwood	M.	Sarah			
3	Sparks	Mary	(Fowler)		dead	
3	Speer	Mary	E (Green)	Exp Aug 1897	dead	
3	Scott	Daisy	(Hester)	Exp Aug 1907	Let Sep 17, 1949	
3	Speer	Charlie	C.	Exp Aug 1907	Let Sep 1922 *Let Aug 1922	
3	Smith	E.	J.	Let Aug 17, 1908	Let 1913	*Edward Jasper Smith, 1832-1916, bur HBC*
3	Smith	Sarah	E.	Let Aug 17, 1908/1909	Let 1913	*Sarah Elizabeth, w/o E J Smith, 1835-? bur HBC*
3	Southern	Amanda		Let May 16, 1909	Let 1913, dead	
3	Smith	Maggie	A.	Exp Aug 23, 1909	Let Aug 19, 1911	*Maggie Alice, d/o T N and Jane Smith*
3	Sparks	T.	M.	Let Aug 25, 1910	Let 1923 Death 1932	
3	Smith	Bessey		Exp Aug 25, 1910	Let Apr. 17, 1926	*Bessie*
3	Sissom	Stella	Dispain	Let Aug 1915	Let Aug 1917	
3	Scott	Henry		Exp Aug 1911	Let 1949	
3	Stephens	Agie		Exp Aug 1912	death	
3	Stephens	Mattie		See Hester	Death 1965/1968	*Hester*
3	Steavens	J.	M.	Exp Aug 1914	Let Nov 1932	
3	Steavens	Mattie, Mrs.		Exp Aug 1914	Let Nov 1932	
3	Satifield	J.	A.	Let Jun 19, 1915	Death 1930	
3	Satifield	Sallie, Mrs.		Let Jun 19, 1915		*w/o J A Satifield*
3	Satifield	Eller	Watkins	Let Jun 19, 1915	Let Aug 1917	

	Last name	First name	Middle Name/ married name	How/when received, other info	How/when dismissed, Other Info	*Remarks; items not listed in church roll (maiden name; spouse; birth-death; buried at - HBC; etc.)*
3	Satifield	Bullar		Let Jun 19, 1915	Dead	*Bulah*
3	Satifield	Bomer		Let Jun 19, 1915	Let 1934	
3	Satifield	Milledge		Let Jun 19, 1915	dead	*M C Satterfield, 1885-1957, bur HBC*
3	Southern	Gatewood		Let Jun 19, 1915	Death Mar 1942	*G. W., 1872-1942, bur HBC*
3	Southern	Lilly, Mrs.		Let Jun 19, 1915	Death Jun 1964	*Lillie/Lillian/Lilly (Moore), w/o Gatewood Southern, 1875-1964, bur HBC*
3	Sikes	Elen		Let Oct 16, 1915/1916	Let 1931	
3	Sikes	Lumus		Exp Aug 1917	Death Mar 1975	*Loomus, 1900-1975*
3	Smith	Paralee		Exp Aug 1917	Let Nov 1944	
3	Smith	Sarah		Let Aug 22, 1919		
3	Southern	Mary	Lee	Exp Aug 1919	Dead	
3	Saterfield	Rufus		Exp Aug 1919	Dead	*Rufus C., 1904-1971, bur HBC*
3	Smith	Secil		Exp Aug 1922	Let May 17, 1941	*Cecil*
3	Smith	Grady		Exp Aug 1922	Let May 1943	
3	Thompson	James	M.		Let Sep 1913	
3	Thompson	Mary	J. (Jack)	Exp Aug 1897	Let Sep 1913	*d/o James Thompson*
3	Thompson	Minnie	D.	Exp Aug 1897	Let Sep 1913	*d/o James Thompson*
3	Thompson	Judge	N.	Exp Aug 1899	Death May 1923	
3	Thompson	Lillie	M.	Exp Sep 1900		
3	Thompson	Sarah?		Exp Aug 17, 1908	Died 1918	
3	Thompson	Jessie	M.	Exp Aug 1897	Let Apr. 1946	*Bro Jess*
3	Thacker	J.	C.	Let Aug 24, 1910		
3	Turner	Julius, Mrs.		Let Aug 1922	Let Jul 30, 1929 dead	*Dora Louisa (Wyatt), 1882-1968, w/o Julius Turner, bur HBC*
3	Umphrey	Eveline	C.	Let Mar 1898	Died 1915	
3	Umphrey	Babe, Mrs.			Let Jul 1918	
3	Vaughn	Pearl	(Herring)	Exp Aug 1908	Let Oct 18, 1952	
3	Wilkie	J.	Harrison	Exp Aug 1890	Death 1949	*John Harrison Wilkie, 1871-1949, bur HBC*
3	Wilkie	H.	Glenn	Exp Aug 1890	Death, deacon	*Hiram Glenn Wilkie, 1877-1956, bur HBC*
3	White	Julius		Exp Aug 1890	Died June 1915	*1875-1915*
3	Williams	J.	L.	Let Aug 1894	Let *Mar 16, 1912, Deacon	*John Lewis Williams* *Dbl: March 16, 1912*

	Last name	First name	Middle Name/ married name	How/when received, other info	How/when dismissed, Other Info	Remarks; items not listed in church roll (maiden name; spouse; birth-death; buried at - HBC; etc.)
3	Williams	Azalee		Let Aug 1894	Let *Mar 16, 1912	d/o John Lewis Williams
3	Wilkie	Lula	Pearl	Exp Aug 1897	Died May 31, 1962	Lula (Jones) Wilkie, 1879-1962, w/o Glenn Wilkie
3	Wilkie	G.	Washington	Exp Jul 1885	Died May 14, 1917	George Washington Wilkie, 1850-1917?
3	Wilkie	Gelina	(Richards)		Dead	Jeulyne?
3	White	Ellen		Exp Aug 1890	Dead	1872-1933, Ellen Clara (Hester), w/o John Bullock White
3	White	Joseph	W.	Exp Aug 1897	Dead	
3	White	John	W.		Death	
3	Wallace	Jesse	W.	Let Jan 1900	Let May 1911	
3	Wilkie	Mattie	(Wallace)	Exp Sep 1900	death	Martha Lou "Mattie" (Wallace), 1888-1945, w/o Edward "Eddie" Earnest Wilkie, bur HBC
3	Wilkie	Myrtie	J.	Exp Sep 1900	Death, Jul 1977	Myrtie Jewell Wilkie, 1887-1977, bur HBC
3	Wilkie	Theodocia	(Stancel)	Exp Aug 1902	Let Jul 1925, dead	w/o John Harrison Wilkie, 1873-1957, bur HBC
3	Warren	Robt	L.	Let Jun 1901	Let 1912	
3	Warren	Delcia		Let Jun 1901	Let 1912	Dora D/Delcy/Delsie, w/o Robert Warren
3	Wilkie	Fannie	A.	Exp Jul 1885	Died Aug 1919	Frances Ann Wilkie, 1850-1919 bur HBC
3	White	Nancy	M.	Exp Jul 1885	Dead Sep 1913	
3	Wilkie	H.	Lee		dead	Henry Lee?
3	Wyatt	Laura	(Hester)	Exp Sep 1900	Let Sep 1910	Larrah (Hester), *w/o J A Wyatt
3	Williams	Sielie?	A.	Exp Sep 1900		
3	Warren	Dizzie	E.	Let Jun 1904		
3	Wigginton	J.	N.	Let Jul 1904	Let Mar 1910	Or Let April 1910
3	West	L.	L.	Let May 1906	dead	Lightener Leander, 1863-1927, bur HBC
3	West	Josie	L.	Let May 1906	Dead	Josephine L (McDaniel), w/o L L West, 1857-1928, bur HBC
3	West	Ella		Let May 1906	Dead Sep 28, 1962	1884-1962, bur HBC
3	Warren	Johnnie		Exp Aug 1906	Let 1912	
3	Warren	Henry	J.	Exp 1907	Let 1921	
3	Wallace	John		Let Aug 1906	Let Jun 20, 1925, Dead	John T.
3	Wallace	Ethel		Let Aug 1906	Let Jun 20, 1925, Dead	

	Last name	First name	Middle Name/ married name	How/when received, other info	How/when dismissed, Other Info	Remarks; items not listed in church roll (maiden name; spouse; birth-death; buried at - HBC; etc.)
3	Williams	J.	J.	Let Aug 21, 1907	Dead	
3	Williams	Nettie J.	(Smith)	Exp Aug 1906	Let Oct 17, 1909	
3	Wallace	Bessie		Exp Aug 20, 1908	Let 1912 *Let Sep 1911	*In minutes, dbl Sep 1911*
3	Wright	Lena	(Holt)	Let Sep 1901		
3	Wilkie	George	W. Jr.	Exp Aug 23, 1909	dead	
3	Wallace	Truman		Exp Aug 23, 1909	dead	*1890-1934*
3	Wilkie	Rose	Etta	Let Jun 1910	Death Feb 19, 1978	*Rosetta E (Cape) Wilkie, 1889-1978, bur HBC*
3	Wilkie	Hellen	E.	Exp Aug 24, 1910	Death Aug 20, 1975	
3	Wilkie	Allia	B.	Exp Aug 24, 1910	dead	
3	Wilkie	G.	Neal	Let Aug 24, 1910	Let Sep 18, 1920	
3	Wilkie	Henrietta		Let Aug 24, 1910	Let Sep 18, 1920	
3	Wadkins	Sarrah	J.	Exp Aug 24, 1910	Let Feb 1942	*Seary Jane Watkins?*
3	White	Isabel		Let May 1911	Let Sep 1923	*1882-1928 w/o Julius White?*
3	Weehunt	G.	W.	Let Jul 15, 1911	Dead Aug 1915 Deacon	*George W Wehunt, 1847-1915, bur HBC, Marker: "a faithful union soldier"*
3	Weehunt	A., Mrs.		Let Jul 15, 1911		*Avey Eveline (Kelly) Wehunt, 1854-? w/o George Wehunt, bur HBC ? marker, no date of death*
3	Wallace	Luther		Exp Aug 1911	Let Dec 1921	
3	Wallace	Maudia, Miss		See Boling Exp Aug 1911?		
3	White	Turner		Exp Aug 1911	Let H. T. White May 20, 1934 Deacon	*Henry Turner White, 1881-1940*
3	Wyatt	Dorah, Miss		Exp Aug 1911	Dead	
3	Wheeler	Ernest		Exp Aug 1911	Death Nov 3, 1985	*Ernest Filmore Wheeler, 1893-1985, bur HBC*
3	Wallace	Bertha		Exp Aug 1913	Dead	
3	Wilkie	Johnie	L.	Exp Aug 1913	Dead	*John L, 1897-1940, bur HBC*
3	Wade	J.	N.	Exp Aug 1913		*John? Copy of let Jul. 19, 1941*
3	Wilkie	Gordon		Exp Aug 1913	Death Feb 11, 1968	*1899-1968, son of Lee Wilkie*
3	Wadkins	Lizzie		Exp Aug 1913		

	Last name	First name	Middle Name/ married name	How/when received, other info	How/when dismissed, Other Info	*Remarks; items not listed in church roll (maiden name; spouse; birth-death; buried at - HBC; etc.)*
3	Wilkie	Jessie	L.	Exp Aug 1914	Dead Deacon	*Jesse Lee, 1893-1947, bur HBC*
3	Wallace	Ethel, Mrs.		Exp Aug 1914	dead	
3	Wilkie	Samuel		Exp Aug 1915	Death Oct 1973	*Walter "Samuel" 1902-1973, bur HBC*
3	Wade	W.	R.	Exp Aug 1915	Let Aug 23, 1919	
3	Wade	Lou	Ida E.	Exp Aug 1915	Let Aug 23, 1919	
3	Wallace	Lee		Let Aug 1915	Let Sep 1934	
3	Wallace	Eula		Let Aug 1915	Let Sep 1934	
3	White	Lilion, Mrs.		Exp Aug 1916	Let May 20, 1934	*Lillian White, 1884-1976, w/o Henry Turner White*
3	Wimpee	Leona		Exp Aug 1917	Let *May 1918	
3	Williams	Brantley		Let Aug 1917	Let Sep 1933	
3	White	Pearl, Mrs.		Exp Aug 1918	Let dead	*Pearl Dunagan White? 1901-1972 w/o Milton Jasper White?*
3	Wallace	H.	T.	Exp Aug 1918	Died May 1865	*Henry Thad Wallace, 1898-1965, bur HBC*
3	Wilkie	J.	Harrison	Exp Aug 1918	Death Jul 12, 1985	*1900-1985, bur HBC*
3	Wilkie	Annie	Belle	Exp Aug 1918	Death Jan 14, 1990	*1903-1990, w/o Henry Thad Wallace, bur HBC*
3	Wofford	Willie		Exp Aug 1918	Death, time unknown	
3	Wilkie	Grace, Mrs.		Let 1918	Let 1956, dead	
3	Wallace	W.	C.	Let Aug 21, 1919	?	*William Cicero? 1856-1944, bur HBC*
3	Wallace	Josie ?		Let Aug 21, 1919	Dead Sep 4, 1920	*Jossie R Wallace, 1857-1920, bur HBC*
3	West	Linton		Exp Aug 1919	dead	*? Walter Linton, 1883-1928, bur HBC*
3	West	Emma, Mrs.		Exp Aug 1919	Death Jan 18, 1950	*Emma Elizabeth West, w/o Walter Linton West, 1884-1950, bur HBC*
3	Wilkie	Mae, Mrs.		Exp Aug 1919	Death 1974	
3	Wilkie	Jewell		Exp Aug 1919	Death Dec 19, 1985	
3	Wyatt	Joe	E.	Let Jul 1920	Death Sep 14, 1962	
3	Wyatt	Laura	J.	Let Jul 15, 1920	Dead	*Larrah J, w/o J A Wyatt ?*
3	Wilkie	Rosetta, Mrs.		Exp Aug 1921	Death Feb 19, 1978	
3	Wilkie	E.	Dennis	Exp Aug 26, 1921	Death Feb 11, 1994	*Edwin Dennis Wilkie, 1905-1994, bur HBC*

	Last name	First name	Middle Name/ married name	How/when received, other info	How/when dismissed, Other Info	Remarks; items not listed in church roll (maiden name; spouse; birth-death; buried at - HBC; etc.)
3	Wilkie	Robert		Exp Aug 26, 1921	Deceased May 5, 1984	Robert L Wilkie, 1905-1984, bur HBC
3	Wilkie	Doil		Exp Aug 26, 1921	Let Aug 1944	Doyle Wilkie, 1906-1980
3	Wilkie	W.	S. "Sam"	Exp Aug 27, 1921	dead	
3	Wilkie	Charley		Exp Aug 27, 1921	Death Jul 22, 1964	Charlie M Wilkie, 1903-1964, bur HBC
3	Williams	Janie, Miss		Exp Aug 27, 1921	Death Oct 30, 1985	
3	Williams	Mastor ?		Exp Sep 19, 1921		
3	Wyatt	Cleveland		Exp Aug 27, 1921	Let Apr 15, 1950	
3	Wyatt	J.	S.	Let Sep 1922 *Let Aug 1922	Death 1929 Deacon	John Samuel, 1856-1929, bur HBC
3	Wyatt	Octavia		Let Sep 1922 *Let Aug 1922		Octavia (Smith), Sister J S Wyatt, 1861-1946, bur HBC
3	Wyatt	S.	S.	Let Oct 1922	Death Nov 26, 1974 Deacon	Samuel Septamus, 1886-1974, bur HBC
3	Wyatt	Pearl		Let Oct 1922	Death Aug 1971	Sister Pearl, 1885-1971, bur HBC
3	Wyatt	Lizzie		Let Oct 1922 *Exp Sep 1922	Let Feb 1940	Miss Lizzie
3	Wade	May		Exp Aug 1922	Let Sep 1948	Miss May
*3	Cochran	Kansas or Cansire		Let Jun 1918	Let Apr 1916	w/o E A Cochran, bur HBC
*3	Dawson	Lucy		Let Jul 20, 1912		
*3	Dobson	Ada, Sister			Let Sep 1920	
*3	Fowler	Ida		Oct 14, 1911		
*3	Fowler	Sallie		Oct 14, 1911		
*3	Hamby	Burtha			Let Oct 1920	
*3	Henderson	Essia, Sister			Let Sep 16, 1916	
*3	Hester	Maudie	Brackett	Let Mar 1922		
*3	Holcombe	Henry			Let Aug 17, 1912	
*3	Ingram	Jane			Let Sep 1916	
*3	Loggins	Robert, Mrs.			Let May 18, 1912	

	Last name	First name	Middle Name/ married name	How/when received, other info	How/when dismissed, Other Info	*Remarks; items not listed in church roll (maiden name; spouse; birth-death; buried at - HBC; etc.)*
*3	Low	Danilla			Let Aug 1915	
*3	Parker	Mattie			Let Feb 15, 1920	
*3	Richards	Estell				
*3	Southern	Lizzie			Let Aug 1913	
*3	Wadkins	Bulla			Let Jul 1921	
*3	Wadkins	Ellis			Let May 1917	
*3	West	John		Exp Sep 14, 1912		
*3	Wimbish	A., Mrs.	L		Let Jan 16, 1915	
*3	Wyatt	Isabel			Let Jan 16, 1915	

Chapter 7: 1924-1938, Minutes and Membership Roll, Book Four

- Community
    - 1925 drought
    - Economic collapse (1929–1933)
    - New Deal (1933–1938)

- Religion/Baptists
    - 1926 - deacon ordination
    - Dec. 1937 - selected a building committee to improve church
    - Jan. 1938 - Addition to church almost finished (extension of choir and pulpit area to back of church)

- Occupations
    - Farmers
    - Salesmen
    - Teachers

- Transportation
    - Cars
    - Wagons

- Cemetery

1925 brought an extensive drought to the North Georgia area, and many crops were failures. While throughout the United States the economy was growing with items such as the radio, automobile and telephone and electricity was becoming more available, the same was not true for North Georgia farms. Even though The Great Depression in the U.S. was linked with the economic fall in 1929, it has been recorded that the terrible drought in the HBC Community started economic difficulties for the people in the area several years before 1929. The economic crisis that followed in the 1930s continued to take a toll on the Hightower area.

One could theorize that as the faith of the church members was tested during the depression, strength to endure the hard times was found at church services and in fellowship with the church family. Between 1929 and 1940, only one year (1934) recorded a number of new baptisms less than ten. The most baptisms was 51, in 1930 or possibly 1931. The total membership rose from the low 400s in the late 1920s to over 500 by 1937. A national plan to help the economy and provide jobs became known as the New Deal. The local community benefited from the New Deal by the new Etowah elementary school. It was built less than a mile away from HBC and was constructed with Works Progress Administration (WPA) funds. The land was donated by Myrtie Wilkie and Joe Wyatt. Lumber was donated by several patrons, and the first trustees were Mr. R. E. Lovelace (chairman), H. G. Wilkie, Sr., and S. S. Wyatt. All five of these persons listed were HBC members. (The school was closed in 1956 when consolidation with Free Home and Holbrook became necessary due to a severe drop in enrollment.)

The 1930 U.S. Census Data for Cherokee County does record a listing for Cross Roads district. Some records incorrectly identify this district as Waleska, when indeed it is Cross Roads. This leads one to think that many of the residents had moved to Reinhardt and most likely the Waleska notation was a mistake. In the 1930 census, Cross Roads District had 1,075 persons identified with 218 households. 262 workers reported their occupations as farmers. Myrtie Wilkie (pictured left) was a merchant at a dry goods store and nine others were also merchants. Six were salesmen at a general store, five were teachers (one was Pearl McClure, wife of Dr. G. C. McClure). Three or less persons listed one of the following occupations: mail carrier, livestock trader, stone cutter at the marble mill, blacksmith, poultry farmer, servant, or carpenter. The two Baptist clergymen listed were Hightower's R. A. Roper and E. G. Rich and a medical doctor was G. C. McClure.

Myrtie Wilkie and store
Photo courtesy of Darrell Cook

Wagons continued as a mode of transportation in the 1920s and even in later years when roads were impassable. Ruby Hester Milford (2014 interview) told that her Mama and Daddy (Lee and Emma Hester) had a surrey and a wagon. "Mama would drive the surrey and take us kids to Ball Ground to go shopping at the Hubbard's Store. I was always afraid to cross the river. On meeting day at HBC, Dad would drive the wagon because we would pick up anyone along the way who wanted to attend church with us. Dad put straw in the wagon and Mama put quilts over the straw and we sat on the quilts. Gradually, the wagons were replaced with cars."

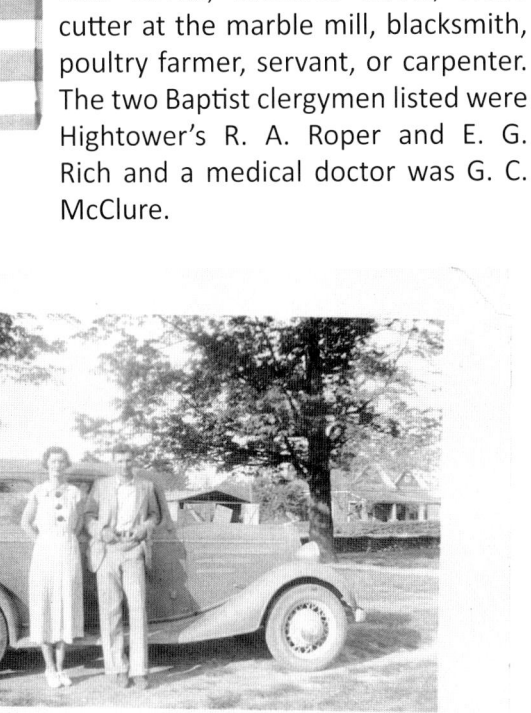

Buck and Jessie Pruitt

Buck and Jessie Pruitt are standing in front of a vehicle likely in the early 1930s. It is not known who owned the car, but Glenn W. Wilkie (2014 interview) recalls that Mr. Ed Lovelace was one of the first persons in the community to own a "new" car in 1929.

Sarah West and Mattie Heard,
ca 1930

Atholine Gilleland, sitting on car
Photo courtesy of Mitzi Chambers

Within a few years, many families began driving vehicles to provide transportation to and from church as well as other events. In the picture above, the two little church friends, Sarah West and Mattie Heard are standing in front of period cars. Both girls were born in 1925, so one could guess the year to be about 1930. In the second picture, young Atholine Gilleland is perched upon a fancy Chevrolet circa 1936 or 1937. It seems her family (shown in the background) was out for a ride in their family car, which was not considered a luxury convertible, and was impressed with the Chevy's enclosed cab. As told by Atholine (2014) the family wanted to take this picture because they thought this car was a special sight to see in rural northeast Cherokee County. The other children included Sam, Ed, Roger, Dorothy, Mary and Walton. All the Gilleland children attended HBC with their parents, Bunyan and Lillie Green Gilleland.

A few entries from the personal diaries of Cleo Heard Milford from 1938 include: Sunday, April 17, 1938, Homecoming at Hightower. Sunday school. Preaching by Tribble "Building a temple for the name of the Lord." Dedicated new part of church. July 24, 1938, 25 have joined, but baptizing has been put off until 1st Service in August, raining. August 7, 1938 Hightower (31) and Liberty (17) baptizing in afternoon together at Hightower (Liberty Church burned August 6, about 1:30 or 2:00 a.m.)

The special writings of two faithful HBC members, Ira (1912-2004) and Effie Hester (1916-2012) Cowart, wonderfully depict the "life and times" of this 1924-1938 era. The original stories summarized below were written in 1999 and shared for this book by a niece, Regina Groover.

Effie Cowart's History:

I was born in Cherokee County to Lee and Emma Whitfield Hester. We lived near Five Points and I attended a one room schoolhouse called Coker's Chapel through the seventh grade. I walked to Macedonia School for two years and finished ninth grade. We often washed clothes before walking to school. Clothes were washed between two planks in a trough with branch water running through the trough. Most of my time at home was spent helping my mother with the younger children and doing chores. I helped with cooking while my mother and Aunt Ida Wyatt quilted. Mother made all our clothes; some from feed sacks, flour sacks, and chicken feed sacks.

Effie and Ira Cowart
Photo courtesy of Regina Groover

Dad grew wheat and corn and went to the mill to grind the flour and meal. We always had plenty to eat because we raised hogs and had cows to milk and all kinds of fruit from fruit trees and vegetables from a garden. I helped mother can and cook, sometimes standing in a chair to make bread in the kitchen.

On weekends I went to church with our family in a two-horse wagon in my younger days. When I was older, Dad had a car so we could go to surrounding churches sometimes. I was saved at Liberty Baptist Church the same night my sister Ruby was also saved. We were baptized together at the place called the Mill Pond, where they ground corn for meal and wheat for flour.

My first date was at Ophir Church at a singing. Ira Cowart came out to my friend's car where I was sitting. Fannie asked Ira to sit down in her car on that rainy day, and we talked and that started our dating. We dated for about two years and were married on July 14, 1935. When we dated we liked to go to church and singings. I liked Ira after we met because he was a Christian and a singer.

When we married, I had a dress that cost $1.98 and a little white hat that cost $1.00. When we left to go home, Ira's Dad gave us 50 cents as a wedding gift. The next day, Ira went to the field to plow and I went to the branch to wash clothes.

When we could, we would go to Hightower Baptist Church where we both belonged. We are thankful for our 64 years together.

Ira Cowart's history:

I was born in Forsyth County in the northern part in a community called Mt. Tabor about one half mile east of Mt. Tabor Baptist Church. My Dad was William Cowart and my mother was Toma Cornett Cowart. We lived in that community about four years. I remember going to Mt. Tabor at age four. I also remember the pastor was Johnnie Stone; he spent the night with us. From there, my Dad moved a number of times from one farm to another. As a small boy, I remember when World War I ended. A neighbor, Ethel, was walking from the cotton field and my dad hollered to her to ask if she knew the war had ended. She said with a loud voice, "Thank the Lord, Johnie (her husband) won't have to go."

As a young boy, it was common for the young people to meet somewhere in the neighborhood and sing. I began to enjoy singing at about age eight or nine. I remember that 1925 was a very dry year. My dad only made enough cotton to pay for the fertilizer it took to grow the cotton. Cotton was the farmer's source of income back then. Some years, I worked on the farm for 50 cents a day (not an hour.) I mean I worked from early in the morning till late in the afternoon. My dad was a farm manager; he got $1.00 for two days work. That was called the depression days during the early thirties.

I found me a girlfriend in 1932; met her at a singing at Ophir Church. I liked Effie Hester pretty good and started going to see her. It was just about ten miles from where I lived [to her house]. I did not mind walking that far even if I had to come back at night. Sometimes if Dad was not going anywhere, he would let me drive his T Model Ford.

Finally, in 1935, Effie and I decided to get married. Effie set the date on 14th of July. I ordered me a blue all wool worsted suit from Sears for $9.95 and a neck tie that cost 50 cents. I think my shoes cost $1.98. Boy, was I dressed up. We got married on Sunday the 14th at 10 o'clock and went to Liberty Church for services. The Rev. Grant Rich did the wedding ceremony. We had lunch with Effie's family, went to my parent's for supper and then back and spent our honeymoon night with the Hester family. Got up on Monday, went back to Dad's house, caught "Ole Gray" out in the pasture and went to plowing cotton. Since I only had $2.50 to my name, we didn't have a "honeymoon." I worked a number of jobs over the years; farming, poultry business, Jones Mercantile Company in the grocery department and then for Big Apple Grocery in Roswell, GA.

I retired in 1977. I must say I never made much progress here in this life, nor fortune or fame, done nothing great, but do have a great name. As fast as time is going it won't be long until I will be as rich as anyone (in heaven). I do know one thing, I love everybody!

Minutes, 1923-1938, Book 4

Each entry:

Date, Minister(s) who preached on that date.

Any of the items that had activity on that given date.

Items:

1. Invited visiting brethren to seats with us

2. Called for the fellowship of the church

3. Called for reference

4. Opened the door of the church for the reception of members

5. General Business

Moderator, Church Clerk

Jul. 23, 1923, E. G. Rich, followed by our pastor. 3. Preferred a charge against a brother for contempt of the church. Taken up the charge and deferred same till our next regular conference. 5. Granted the following letters: Sister Armindy Roper, Bro. W. B. Chasteen, Sister Dorah McGuire. Rev. R. A. Roper, Mod., H. G. Wilkie, C.C.

Aug. 25, 1923, 2. The church hears a statement from a brother and bairs with him. 4. Received by experience Bro. Clinton Wyatt as candidate for baptism. 5. Granted the following letters of dismission: Bros. Paul Cochran, T. M. Sparkes, Claud Evans and Sister Mary Evans.

Sep. 24, 1923, R. W. Cochran followed by pastor. 3. Prefer charges against a brother for profanity, taken up the charge and withdrew fellowship from him. All so preferred charge against a brother for cursing, by motion the church withdraws fellowship from him. All so preferred charge against another brother for cursing, by motion the church withdraws fellowship from him. Apoint comity to investigate same. 5. by motion Sister Isabel White, letter of dismission. Went into the election of a pastor for the coming year. By motion, suspended the regular order of election and by eclimation, call Rev. Robert Roper as our pastor for the coming year. Collected $7.65 for Bro. Roper. Elected Bro. Bomer Satifield as housekeeper for the next year. Rev. R. A. Roper, Mod., H. G. Wilkie, C.C.

Oct. 24, 1923, Bro. E. G. Rich. 5. Heard the report of comity, same being received. Rev. R. A. Roper, Mod., H. G. Wilkie, C.C.

Nov. 24, 1923, Rev. R. A. Roper. 5. Granted permission to remove the pines in the church yard. Received for our pastor $74.85 + 15.50 = $90.35. Granted Bro. Joe White a letter of dismission.

Feb. 1924, Rev. R. A. Roper. 5. Collected $3.00 for house keeper. Appointed J. S. Wyatt, H. G. Wilkie to establish a line in front of the sanitary [cemetery], the same being done to the satisfaction of the church. Paid to our pastor one hundred and four dollars. Rev. R. A. Roper, Mod., H. G. Wilkie, C.C.

Mar. 22, 1924, pastor. 3. Received acknowledgements of a brother and the church bares with him. All so another brother, the church bares with him. Appointed Bro. A. A. Roper, R. E. Lovelace to investigate a report on a brother for drunkness. Apointed a commity to see another brother for drunkness, J. J. Turner, S. S. Wyatt, H. G. Wilkie, commity. 5. The church moves to paint the church. The following commity was appointed: L. L. West, H. G. Wilkie, R. E. Lovelace, S. S. Wyatt, Joe Wyatt, R. M. Cantrell, H. N. Green, J. J. Turner, Rev. R. A. Roper, J. H. Wilkie, A. A. Roper, E. G. Rich, commity. R. A. Roper, Mod., H. G. Wilkie, C.C.

Apr. 26, 1924, Rev. R. A. Roper. 3. Prefered a charge against a brother for cursing and misconduct around church. Taken up the charge and excluded him. 5. Granted Sister Ovilla Edwards letter of dismission. Collected 6.25 on the painting of the house. Rev. R. A. Roper, Mod., H. G. Wilkie, C.C.

May 24, 1924, Rev. R. A. Roper. 5. The church moved that the remainder of funds now on hand be turned into the treasure to be used as they might see fit. Rev. R. A. Roper, Mod., H. G. Wilkie, C.C.

Jun. 22, 1924, Bro. E. G. Rich, followed by our pastor. 5. Appointed the following members of Hightower to the union meeting of the 3rd week, meet with Marble Hill to wit: R. M. Cantrell, S. S. Wyatt, H. G. Wilkie, E. H. Pearson, R. E. Lovelace and E. G. Rich. All so by motion appointed the following messingers to the association to convene with Chalcedonia to wit: Bros. J. S. Wyatt, R. E. Lovelace, Rev. R. A. Roper, R. M. Cantrell, E. G. Rich, E. H. Pearson and H. G. Wilkie, alternate. Granted the following letters of dismission to Bro. Henry Holcomb, Sister Corra Holcomb, Sister Velvie Holcomb and Bro. George Tompson. Paid housekeeper 3 dollars for the quarter. The church has on hand to Jul. 26th a balance of 25 dollars and 5 cts. Rev. R. A. Roper, Mod., H. G. Wilkie, C.C.

Jul. 26, 1924, pastor. 5. Reading of the letter to association, the same being adopted. Collected $2.30 for minutes. Rev. R. A. Roper, Mod., H. G. Wilkie, C.C.

Aug. 23, 1924, Pastor R. A. Roper. 5. Granted the following letter of dismission: Bro. W. M. [William Milton "Melt"] Deane, Sister Mary Deane, Sister May Christopher. The church sets Friday before the 3rd Sunday in Sep. as the time for the ordination of Bro. A. A. Roper to the full work of the ministry. Invited the fowling eldership: Ophir, New Harmony, Mt. Pisgue, Conns Creek, Liberty, Macedonia to take part.

Sept. 19, 1924, Elder J. L. Wyatt from the third chapter of Timothy, church was dismissed for dinner, after which the eldership of Hightower and the sister churches met in the grove to organize a presbytery. The following ministers composing same. R A. Roper, Mod., J. L. Wyatt, E. A. Cochran, J. I. Holebrook, W. D. Hegwood, R. W. Cochran, J. W. Miller, J. L. Hitt, J. B. Holcomb, ordained ministers. All so the following deacons: G. B. Hegwood, B. F. Holcomb, W. B. Wofford, R. M. Cantrell, J. L. Wilkie, H. G. Wilkie, J. S. Wyatt, J. D. Porter, J. R. Ruddell, Bird Richards, Carter Wiginton, T. G. Tompson, J. H. Ellis, Pall Ward, S. L. Weehunt, deacons. Composed the presbytery after which the church met in conference. 5. General business: the ordination proceeds, Brother A. A. Roper the elect was presented to the body by Bro. E. G. Rich. Examination by Elder J. L. Wyatt. Ordination prayer led by Elder E. A. Cochran and laying on of hands. The charge by Elder J. I. Holebrooks. Rev. A. A. Roper being dewly examined and found worthy by the presbytery was delivered back to the church by Elder R. W. Cochran from which the hand fellowship was extended by the body. Rev. R. A. Roper, Mod., H. G. Wilkie, C.C.

Sep. 20, 1924, Rev. R. A. Roper. 5. Went in to election of pastor for another year. Suspended the regular order of election and by eclimation nominated Rev. R. A. Roper and the church unanimously elected Rev. R. A. Roper for another year. Motion and sec. to turn church house keys over to John Colwell. Received 2.00 for Bro. John Colwell for housekeeping. Received 11.25 for our pastor. R. A. Roper, Mod., H. G. Wilkie, Church Clerk.

Oct. 18, 1924, 3. Received acknowledgements from two brothers for drinking, the church bears with them. Also prefer a charge against another brother for drunkness, church to withdraw fellowship from that brother. 5. Collected the following amount for our pastor, $92.50. R. A. Roper, Mod., H. G. Wilkie, C.C.

Nov. 15, 1924, Rev. A. A. Roper and Rev. R. A. Roper. 3. Preferred a charge against a brother for drunkness, and church withdraws fellowship from him. 5. Granted the following letters of dismission, Bro. Gordon Bryant, Bro. Steve Deane and wife Sarah and Sister Della Deane. Contributes to our pastor $8.00. Total contributed to date $100.50. Amount on hand in the treasure $30.00. Rev. R. A. Roper, Mod., H. G. Wilkie, C.C.

Dec. 20, 1924, Rev. R. A. Roper. 3. Preferred a charge against a brother for drunkness. Deferred the charge till next meeting, the same being last. By motion and second the church withdraws fellowship from the brother. 5. Granted the following letters of dismission: Rev. R. A. Dunagan, Sister Mary Dunagan, and Bro. Oliver Dunagan. Rev. R. A. Roper, Mod., H. G. Wilkie, C.C.

Feb 14, 1925, Rev. R. A. Roper. 3. Preferred a charge against a brother for drunkness. By motion taken up the charge and the church withdrew fellowship from him. All so preferred a charge against a sister for departing from the faith. Withdrew fellowship from the sister. 5. Collected 3.70 for the housekeeper. Elected Bro. Amos Williams to keep for the house the rest of the year, 1925. Rev. R. A. Roper, Mod., H. G. Wilkie, C.C.

Apr. 18, 1925, pastor. 4. Received by letter Sister Winnie Rich. 5. Granted Bro. E. H. Pearson letter of dismission. Collected 75 cts to pay the housekeeper 45 cts. By motion the church move to draw from the treasure sufficient funds to by the wine for communion. Rev. R. A. Roper, Mod., H. G. Wilkie, C.C.

May 16, 1925, Rev. E. A. Cochran and Bro. E. G. Rich. 5. Motion that the painting comity finish the painting of the seats [sp.?] Rev. R. A. Roper, Mod., H. G. Wilkie, C.C.

Jun. 20, 1925, Bro. Lester Pagett and Rev. A. A. Roper. 3. Preferred a charge against a brother for drunkness. Deferred charge till next conference. 4. Received a brother by restoration, received by letter Bro. Eston Dobson from which the church extends to them the hand of church fellowship. 5. Granted Sister Mary Holcomb a letter of dismission. Elected delegates to the association by ballot as follows: Rev. R. A. Roper, H. N. Green, A. A. Roper, H. G. Wilkie, R. E. Loveless, R. M. Cantrell, Joe E. Wyatt, E. G. Rich. All so appointed delegates to the union meeting at Hightower on Thursday and Friday before the 4th Sunday in July as follows: R. M. Cantrell, R. E. Loveless, S. S. Wyatt, E. G. Rich, J. S. Wyatt, Linton West. All so appointed a commity to assign the places of the delegates: S. S. Wyatt, Linton West, Fulton Roper, commity. Granted Bro. J. T. Wallace and wife Ethell and son Clyde letter of dismission. A. A. Roper, Mod. Pro., H. G. Wilkie, C.C.

Jul. 1925, Rev. R. A. Roper. 2. Taken up the charge against a brother and received his acknowledgements and the church bore with him. 5. Granted Sister Theodocia Wilkie a letter of dismission. Collected $2.00 for minutes. Rev. R. A. Roper, Mod., H. G. Wilkie, C.C.

Aug. 15, 1925, Bro. E. G. Rich. 3. Preferred a charge against a brother for cursing, taken up the charge and the church withdrew fellowship from him. E. G. Rich, Mod. Prot., H. G. Wilkie, C.C.

Sep. 19, 1925, Rev. R. A. Roper. 5. Granted the following letters of dismission, Sister Nettie Pearson and daughter Winnie, and Bro. R. E. Kelly and wife and daughter, *[Evvie and Belle per membership roll, book 3]* Sister Alie Bowles. Went into calling of a pastor for the next year. By motion, suspended the regular order of elections and elect by eclimation. Nominated Rev. R. A. Roper and elected him for our pastor for the coming year. Received to date $77.00 for our pastor. Rev. R. A. Roper, Mod., H. G. Wilkie, C.C.

Oct. 16, 1925, our pastor. 4. Received by letter Sister Caroline Willson as a member in full fellowship with us. 5. By motion and second, the painting commity out until the house is finished and the church to stand by them. Collected to date for our pastor $90.50. R. A. Roper, Mod., H. G. Wilkie, C.C.

Nov. 1925, pastor. 5. Painting comity to meet Friday at 1 o'clock. R. A. Roper, Mod., H. G. Wilkie, C.C.

Dec. 15, 1925, Bro. E. G. Rich, the church elects Bro. E. G. Rich moderator in conference. 5. By motion the church draws from the treasure $8.75 to pay housekeeper. E. G. Rich, Mod. Pro., H. G. Wilkie, C.C.

Jan. 16, 1926, Bro. R. A. Roper. 5. Collected $3.50 for to pay housekeeper. R. A. Roper, Mod., H. G. Wilkie, C.C.

Feb. 20, 1926, Rev. R. A. Roper. (No business reported). Rev. R. A. Roper, Mod., H. G. Wilkie, C.C.

Mar. 16, 1926, Bro. E. G. Rich followed by the pastor. 2. Reference, by motion and second the church has saw fit to nominate and set forth Bro. R. E. Loveless, Bro. S. S. Wyatt and Bro. Fulton Roper for deacons of Hightower Church and as sat apart for ordination on Saturday before the 3rd Sunday in April. The eldership of the following churches are invited to assist in the work of the ordination: New Harmony, Mt Pisgue, Ophir, Mica, Ballground, Conns Creek, Liberty, Masidonia. By motion, the church takes from a brother his deaconship. Rev. R. A. Roper, Mod., H. G. Wilkie, C.C.

Apr. 17, 1926, W. L. D. Heywood, *[possibly Howard?]* the church dismist for dinner, after which they resembled to organize a presbytery by electing our pastor R. A. Roper moderator of the presbytery. Elder E. A. Cochran examined the candidates, ordination prayer led by W. L. D. Heygood, the charge given Bro. R. A. Roper, candidates presented by J. W. Wallace. Hightower Babtis Church in conference. 5. General business. Granted the following letters of dismission, Sister Efie Howard, Sister Maudie Davis, Sister Bessie Smith, Bro. Carl Roper. After examining the candidates to wit: Bro. R. E. Loveless, Bro. S. S. Wyatt, Bro. Fulton Roper, and finding worthy, the ordination as deacons of Hightower Church. The following ministers taking part in the ordination: Rev. R. A. Roper, E. A. Cochran, W. L. D. Heywood, A. A. Roper. All so the following deacons: Bro. J. W. Wallace, W. T. Ponder, C. H. C. Heard, B. F. Holcomb, G. J. Howell, R. G. Bell, J. S. Wyatt, J. H. Holcombe, R. M. Cantrell. Rev. R. A. Roper, Mod., H. G. Wilkie, C.C.

Jun. 20, 1926, Rev. A. A. Roper. 5. Went in to election of messengers to union meeting. Suspended the regular order of election, elected by appointment to wit: R. E. Lovelace, J. J. Turner, Osker Stewart, Sam Wilkie. Also appointed messengers to the association to be held with Shady Grove to wit: Rev. R. A. Roper, H. G. Wilkie, A. A. Roper, Osker Stewart, Sam Wilkie, J. J. Turner, Thomas Green, and Joe Williams, alternate. A. A. Roper, Mod. Prot., H. G. Wilkie, C.C.

Jul. 15, 1926, Rev. R. A. Roper. 5. Collected 2.50 for minutes, for our pastor 5.00. R. A. Roper, Mod., H. G. Wilkie, C.C.

Aug. 14, 1926, Bro. E. G. Rich. Elected E. G. Rich, moderator. 5. For minutes $2.50, for housekeeper 3.25, and on the painting 23.75. E. G. Rich, Mod. Prot., H. G. Wilkie, C.C.

Sep. 14, 1926, Bro. E. G. Rich and Rev. A. A. Roper. Elected Bro. A. A. Roper, moderator. 4. Received by experience Sister Viola Heggood as a candidate for baptism. 5. Went into the election of a pastor for the coming year. By motion, suspended the regular of election and elected by eclimation. Nominated Rev. R. A. Roper and by a unanimous vote the church elected Rev. R. A. Roper as the pastor for another year. By motion the commitys work on the painting of the church was excepted and they are dismist. Collected the following for Rev. R. A. Roper $2.75.

Oct. 15, 1926, E. G. Rich. 5. Collected the following for our pastor $23.50. R. A. Roper, Mod., R. E. Lovelace, C.C.

Nov. 13, 1926, Elder E. A. Cochran followed by Rev. R. A. Roper. 3. Preferred a charge against a sister for departing from the faith, church withdraws fellowship from her. 5. The church sets Friday before the 3rd Sunday in Dec. for the purpose of ordaining Bro. E. G. Rich to the full work of the ministry. Invited the eldership of the following churches to take part in the ordination: New Harmony, Mt. Pisgue, Ophir, Mica, Conns Creek, Ballground, Masidonia, Liberty, Sharp Mt. Collected for cole and lights $6.25, for our pastor $6.50. R. A. Roper, Mod., H. G. Wilkie, C.C.

Dec. 16, 1926, the church met in conference after preaching by Bro. E. G. Rich. In reading reference, was found necessary to go into ordination of Bro. E. G. Rich into the full work of the ministry. Bro. Rich was presented to presbytery by R. E. Lovelace, he was duly examined under leadership of Bro. C. A. Wallace. Bro. Rich being found sound in the faith to satisfaction of all. The ordination prayer was led by Bro. A. A. Roper, at close of prayer, presbytery proceeded by laying on of hands. The charge to Bro. Rich was ably given by Bro. J. B. Henderson after which Bro. Cowart gave charge to the church, after which Bro. T. M. Sewell tendered the Holy Book for Bro. Rich. Bro. Rich was duly received back by the church fully ordained. R. A. Roper, Moderator, R. E. Lovelace, Clerk.

Dec. 18, 1926, Rev. R. A. Roper. 4. Received the letter of Sister Margie Satifield as a member in full fellowship with us. 5. Collected for lights [and coal] $3.00, paid for housecair $2.95. R. A. Roper, Mod., H. G. Wilkie, C.C.

Jan. 15, 1927, Rev. E. G. Rich. Elected Bro. E. G. Rich, Moderator Prot. 3. Preferred a charge against a brother for drunkness and deferred same till our next regular conference. Received for pastor one dollar. E. G. Rich, Mod. Prot., H. G. Wilkie, C.C.

Feb. 19, 1927, Bro. Cowart, followed by our pastor. 2. Taken up the reference against a brother for drunkness, by motion the church withdraws fellowship from him. 3. The church received the acknowledgements of a brother and acknowledgements from another brother, and the church bairs with them. The church preferred a charge against another brother for drunkness, by motion, deferred the charge till next conference. Rev. R. A. Roper, Mod., H. G. Wilkie, C.C.

Mar. 16, 1927, our pastor. 3. Taken up the charge against a brother for drunkness, by motion, withdrew fellowship from him. All so preferred a charge against a brother for drunkness, and deferred same till next conference. 5. By motion and second, the church rules when a member is charged with drunkness, that he tell where he purchast or where's he got it. Rev. R. A. Roper, Mod., H. G. Wilkie, C.C.

Apr. 16, 1927, Bro. E. G. Rich, followed by our pastor. 2. Taken up the charge against a brother for drunkness and by motion of the church his acknowledgements were received and the church bairs with him. 5. Paid to Bro. Joe Williams $3.75 for cair of the house. All so rescinded the vote of the church in regards to a member missing 3 conferences. Rev. R. A. Roper, Mod., H. G. Wilkie, C.C.

May 15, 1927, our pastor. 3. By motion and second the preferred a charge against a brother for drunkness. Taken up the motion and withdrew fellowship from the brother. 5. Collected 2.75 for Bro. Joe Williams for care of the house. Rev. R. A. Roper, Mod., H. G. Wilkie, C.C.

Jun. 18, 1927, Rev. A. A. Roper and Rev. E. G. Rich. Elected A. A. Roper moderator. 5. Went in to the election of messengers to the union meeting to convene with the church at Concord beginning on Thursday after the 1 Sunday in August. By motion, suspended the regular order of election and elected by appointment as follows: H. G. Wilkie, R. E. Lovelace, Osker Stewart, Dennis Wilkie, J. J. Williams, Grady Cronan, alternate. To the association the following: Rev. R. A. Roper, H. G. Wilkie, A. A. Roper, R. E. Loveless, J. E. Wyatt, E. G. Rich, Dennis Wilkie, Alt. H. Grady Fowler. Rev. A. A. Roper, Mod. Prot., H. G. Wilkie, C.C.

Jul. 15, 1927, our pastor. 3. Received the acknowledgements of a brother for intoxication and the church bairs with him. 5. Granted Sister Nancy Doss Floyd a letter of dismission. Collected for minutes $2.00. Rev. R. A. Roper, Mod., H. G. Wilkie, C.C.

Aug. 20, 1927, R. W. Cochran, elected Bro. E. G. Rich moderator. 4. Received by letter Bro. Cart Wiginton and wife Clair Wiginton. [*Carter and Clara Wigginton*]. 5. Granted Sister Lois Green a letter of dismission and Sister Pearl Dunagan. E. G. Rich, Mod. Prot., H. G. Wilkie, C.C.

Sep. 16, 1927, our pastor. 4. Received sister Azey Fife Williams by letter. 5. Granted the following letters: Bro. Virgle Cochran and wife Sister Eliziebeth Cochran. By motion, church went into the election of a pastor for the coming year. By motion and second suspended the regular order of election and elected by eclimation. By motion, nominated Rev. R. A. Roper, their being no other nomination and by a rising vote, call Bro. Roper as our pastor for the coming year. Collected the following, for Bro. Williams 2.35, for clerk 3.10, for our pastor $12.00, Total 17.45. Rev. R. A. Roper, Mod., H. G. Wilkie, C.C.

Oct. 15, 1927, Pastor Rev. R. A. Roper. 5. Collected for our pastor $61.60. Rev. R. A. Roper, Mod., H. G. Wilkie, C.C.

Nov. 16, 1927, Rev. A. A. Roper, followed by Rev. R. A. Roper. 5. Received $5.00 for our pastor. Rev. R. A. Roper, Mod., H. G. Wilkie, C.C.

Dec. 17, 1927, Bro. A. A. Roper followed by Rev. R. A. Roper. 3. Preferred a charge against two sisters for fighting. Deferred the charge till next conference. On Sunday, 18th, by motion and second conference was opened under the head of reference, by motion the reference was taken up against a sister, she acknowledging to the charge and the church bears with her. The reference against the other sister deferred till next conference. 5. Granted Sister Viola Heggood a letter of dismission. Rev. R. A. Roper Mod., H. G. Wilkie, C.C.

Jan. 15, 1928, Rev. R. A. Roper. 2. A sister, making her acknowledgements to the satisfaction of the church and the church bears with her. 5. Received for our pastor 1.00. Rev. R. A. Roper, Mod., H. G. Wilkie, C.C.

Mar. 17, 1928, pastor. Elected Rev. R. W. Cochran, moderator. By motion and second rescinded the work of the call conference down to general business. Invite the following churches to our communion on May 3rd New

Harmony, Ophir, Conns Creek, Mica, Pisgue, Masidonia, Liberty. Granted Sister Martha J. Richards letter of dis. Collected 1.25 for communion purpose. 3.35 for Bro. Williams. Rev. R. A. Roper, Mod., H. G. Wilkie, C.C.

May 19, 1928, our pastor. After intermission, church met in conference. Elected Rev. R. W. Cochran moderator. 3. Received the acknowledgements of a brother for drunkness. All so received the acknowledgements of two other brothers for their grievances. 4. Received the acknowledgements of a brother and restored him to full fellowship. All so received by letter Bro. T. M. Mills. 5. Granted the following letters: Rev. R. W. Cochran, Rev. A. A. Roper and wife Sister Lou, Bro. Samuel, Bro. Vest and Sister Louise [*Alfred "Alf", wife Louise, son Samuel, son Vestus, and daughter Louise*]. Rev. R. W. Cochran, Mod. Prot., H. G. Wilkie, C.C.

Jun. 16, 1928, Pastor Rev. R. A. Roper. 5. Went in to the election of messengers to the association to convene with Ball Ground Babtis Church on August 7 and 8. By motion suspended the regular order of election and elected by appointment as follows: R. E. Loveless, Rev. R. A. Roper, J. E. Wyatt, H. G. Wilkie, Lee Hester, Fulton Roper, Joe Williams, alternate. All so elected the fowling messengers to the union meeting to convene with Sharp Mountain on Thursday and Friday before the 3 Sunday in July as follows: Rev. E. G. Rich, H. N. Green, Bro. Tim Green, Osker Stewart, Colman Roper, W. E. Green, G. C. Wilkie, alternate. Collected for minutes 85 cts. Rev. R. A. Roper, Mod., H. G. Wilkie, C.C.

Jul. 19, 1928, our pastor. 3. Received the acknowledgements of a brother, by motion restored him to the fellowship of the church. Rev. R. A. Roper, Mod., H. G. Wilkie, C.C.

Aug. 19, 1928, Rev. E. G. Rich. Elected Rev. E. G. Rich, Moderator. E. G. Rich, Mod. Prot., H. G. Wilkie, C.C.

Sep. 15, 1928, pastor. 5. Went into the election of a pastor for the coming year. By motion, suspended the regular order of ballot and elected by eclimation. Nominated Rev. R. A. Roper as our pastor. Their being no other nominated, by a rising vote of the church, Rev. R. A. Roper was elected to the pastoral cair of Hightower for the coming year. All so elected H. G. Wilkie as clerk. Granted Sister Olie Green and Bro. J. A. and Sister Satifield letters of dismission. Collected for our pastor $19.25 cts. Rev. R. A. Roper, Mod., H. G. Wilkie, C.C.

Oct. 28, 1928, E. G. Rich followed by pastor. 5. Granted letter to Bro. Luster Satterfield. Collected for our pastor $9.20. Rev. R. A. Roper, Moderator, H. G. Wilkie, C.C.

Dec. 16, 1928, Rev. E. G. Rich, followed by our pastor. 5. Collected 2.35 for housekeeper, 4.50 for our pastor. Rev. R. A. Roper, Mod., H. G. Wilkie, C.C.

Jan. 19, 1929, Rev. E. G. Rich. 5. For Bro. Joe Williams 3.75, for our pastor, 4.50. Total for our pastor $97.00. E. G. Rich, Mod. Prot., H. G. Wilkie, C.C.

Mar. 16, 1929, pastor. Collected for housekeeper $3.45. Rev. R. A. Roper, Mod., H. G. Wilkie, C.C.

Apr. 16, 1929, Pastor Rev. R. A. Roper. 5. Invited the following churches to commune with us: Ophir, Conns Creek, Mica, Mt. Pisgee, New Harmony, Macedonia, and Liberty. By motion and same the church at Hightower named that each male member contribute 25 cts. year to the finances of the church to be drawn on as the church see fit. Rev. R. A. Roper, Mod., H. G. Wilkie, C.C.

May 18, 1929, Rev. E. G. Rich followed by pastor Rev. R. A. Roper. [No business under any item]. Rev. R. A. Roper, Mod., H. G. Wilkie, C.C.

Jun. 15, 1929, Rev. J. P. Smith. 5. Elected by appointment the following members to attend the union meeting of the third district as follows: Rev. E. G. Rich, S. S. Wyatt, Joe E. Wyatt, R. M. Cantrell, Fulton Roper, and Lee Hester, alternate. Also elected by appointment the following members to attend the Hightower Association to convene with Providence Church in Milton Co. on Wednesday and Thursday after the first Sunday in August: H. G. Wilkie, Rev. R. A. Roper, Rev. E. G. Rich, B. V. Gilleland, J. H. Wilkie, C. C. Hester, Rev. E. A. Cochran, and G. H. Little, alternate. By action of the church granted Sister Izzie Saterfield a letter. R. A. Roper, Mod., H. G. Wilkie, C.C.

Jul. 20, 1929, Rev. E. G. Rich followed by our pastor. 5. Granted Sister Fannie Bryant and Sister Uness Ellis letter of dismission. All so granted Bro. J. J. Turner and wife Mrs. [Dora] Turner and daughters Miss Leo and Miss Ruby Turner letter of dismission. Rev. R. A. Roper, Mod., H. G. Wilkie, C.C.

Aug. 17, 1929, Rev. E. G. Rich. [No business under any item]. Rev. E. G. Rich, Mod. Pro., H. G. Wilkie, C.C.

Sep. 21, 1929, Rev. E. G. Rich followed by Pastor Rev. R. A. Roper. 4. Received the letter of Rev. R. W. Cochran as a member in full fellowship of the church. 5. Went into the election of our pastor, by motion and second suspended our regular order of election and elected by eclimation, nominated Rev. R. A. Roper as pastor for another year. R. A. Roper, Mod., H. G. Wilkie, C.C.

Oct. 1929, Rev. E. G. Rich followed by our pastor Rev. R. A. Roper. 5. Granted the following letters: Brother Austin Fletcher and Sister Gennie Fletcher. Rev. R. A. Roper, Mod., H. G. Wilkie, C.C.

Nov. 1929, Rev. J. H. Cowart. Elected E. G. Rich, Moderator Pro. 3. Preferred a charge against a brother for drunkness, the charge being taken up, he was excluded. 5. Collected $1.25 for our pastor. Rev. E. G. Rich, Mod. Pro., H. G. Wilkie, C.C.

Mar. 15, 1930, Rev. R. A. Roper. 3. Prefered a charge against a sister for misconduct, withdrew fellowship from her. Also preferred a charge against a brother for using profane language, deferred the same. 5. Collected $3.75 for R. E. Lovelace for care of the house. 50 cents. Rev. R. A. Roper, Mod., H. G. Wilkie, C.C.

Apr. 12, 1930, Rev. R. A. Roper, intermission then conference. 3. Taken up the charge against a brother for profanity, withdrew fellowship from him. Also referred a charge against another brother for drunkness, deferred the charge till next conference. 5. By motion, we rewrite Bro. Henry Worn [*Warren, dismissed by letter 1921*] a letter of dismission. Through an action of the church we the Baptist Church of Christ at Hightower do that day liberate and set apart our Brother Fulton Roper to the usage in as the Spirit might direct and this church pledges him this prayer and support in the great work and may the blessings of our great God be his guide. Rev. R. A. Roper, Mod., H. G. Wilkie, C.C.

May 17, 1930, Rev. G. B. Forrest, [*maybe Greenberry W. Forrest?*] followed by Rev. E. A. Cochran. 3. Received the acknowledgements of a brother for drunkness, the church bearing with him. R. A. Roper, Mod., H. G. Wilkie, C.C.

Jun. 14, 1930, Bro. Fulton Roper, Rev. E. G. Rich and Rev. R. A. Roper. 5. Elected the following messengers to the association: Elishy Cochran, Lee Hester, Joe Wyatt, Rev. E. A. Cochran, S. S. Wyatt, Fulton Roper, Rev. R. A. Roper. Also members to the union meeting: B. V. Gilleland, R. M. Cantrell, E. M. West, R. E. Lovelace, E. G. Rich, H. G. Wilkie, H. N. Green. Rev. R. A. Roper, Mod., H. G. Wilkie, C.C.

Jul. 19, 1930, Rev. R. A. Roper. 3. Preferred a charge against a brother for adultery, withdrew fellowship from him. Also preferred a charge against a brother for drunkness, withdrew fellowship from him. 5. Collected 1.74 cts. Rev. R. A. Roper, Mod., H. G. Wilkie, C.C.

Aug. 1930, Bro. Fulton Roper. Elected Bro. Fulton Roper, moderator. 4. Restored a brother to full fellowship. 5. Collected $2.50 for to buy oil to light the house. Br. Fulton Roper, Mod. Prot., H. G. Wilkie, C.C.

Sep. 20, 1930, Rev. E. G. Rich, followed by Rev. R. A. Roper. 5. Granted the following letters of dismission: Bro. Luis Bryant and wife Mrs. Lula Bryant, Bro. Newton Fowler and wife Mrs. Allice Fowler, Bro. William Fowler, Miss Hattie and Miss Julia Fowler and Sister Mattie Lou Mason. Went into the election of a pastor for the following year. By motion, suspended the regular order of election to elect by acclimation. Nominated Rev. R. A. Roper there being no other nominations, there was a motion to close. Motion caired. By a unanimous vote of the church, Rev. R. A. Roper was called as our pastor for coming year. Rev. R. A. Roper, Mod., H. G. Wilkie, C.C.

Oct. 18, 1930, Rev. E. G. Rich and Pastor Rev. R. A. Roper. 3. Preferred a charge against a brother for drunkness and profanity, deferred same till next conference. 4. Received acknowledgements of a brother. 5. Granted letter of dismission to Miss Vearie Calltrane [*Vera Coltrane*], Mrs. Oma Porter and Mrs. Esco Gilbert. Collected 34.00 for our pastor. Rev. R. A. Roper, Mod., H. G. Wilkie, C.C.

Nov. 18, 1930, Bro. Fulton Roper and Rev. E. G. Rich. 3. A brother came forward acknowledging to the charge preferred and the church bear with him. 5. Granted letters of dismission Miss Veara Calltrane, Mrs. Esco Gilbert, Mrs. Omma Porter. Collected for our pastor to this date $32.00. Rev. R. A. Roper, Mod., H. G. Wilkie, C.C.

Dec. 21, 1930, Rev. J. H. Cowart, Rev. E. G. Rich as moderator. 5. Collected for pastor $3.00, for housekeeper $2.25. Rev. E. G. Rich, Mod. Prot., H. G. Wilkie, C.C.

Jan. 17, 1931, Rev. R. A. Roper. 4. Received by letter Bro. Lee Ingram and wife Sister Pearl Ingram. 5. Granted the following letters of dismission: Sister Elline Sikes, Sister Maggie Chastain, Bro. Duffie Sparks, Sister Ella May Sary Sparks. Collected for housekeeper $1.50. Rev. R. A. Roper, Mod., H. G. Wilkie, C.C.

Feb. 15, 1931, Pastor Rev. R. A. Roper. 3. Preferred a charge against a brother for false testimony. Taken up the charge and withdrew fellowship. 4. Received Bro. Steve Dean and wife Sister Sarah Dean by letter. Also received by letter with the bearer Bro. J. A. Heard and wife Sister Bertie Heard and Bro. Archie Heard as members with us. Rev. R. A. Roper, Mod., H. G. Wilkie, C.C.

Mar. 15, 1931, Rev. R. A. Roper. Contributions to Sister Bolling $8.80 cts. Rev. R. A. Roper, Mod., H. G. Wilkie, C.C.

Apr. 18, 1931, Rev. R. A. Roper. 4. Received Sister Effie Hester and Ruby Lee Hester by letter as members in full fellowship with us. 5. Granted Sister Winnie Rich letter of dismission. Extended an invitation to New Harmony, Masidonia, Liberty, Mt. Pisgue and Conns Creek to commune with us on the 3rd. Rev. R. A. Roper, Mod., H. G. Wilkie C.C.

May 15, 1931, Bro. Fulton Roper followed by pastor. [Nothing recorded under any item]. Rev. R. A. Roper, Mod., H. G. Wilkie, C.C.

Jun. 20, 1931, Bro. Hubert Holbrook followed by Bro. Fulton Roper. 4. Received a brother by restoration. 5. Granted Bro. Holcomb a letter of dismission. By motion and second went in to the election of delegates to the association to be held with the Liberty Church in Dawson Co. on Wednesday and Thursday after the 1 Sunday in Aug. 1931. By motion, suspend the regular order of election and elected by appointment the following members as messengers. They are as follows: Fulton Roper, Bro. J. A. Heard, H. G. Wilkie, Rev. R. A. Roper, R. E. Loveless, G. H. Little, C. C. Hester, H. N. Green, and Rev. E. G. Rich, alternate. All so by motion elected the delegates to the union meeting to convene with Hightower Church on Thursday and Friday before the 4th Sunday in July. The following messengers: Fulton Roper, R. M. Cantrell, Tomas Heard, Halmond Roper, Tim Green, and J. A. Heard alternate. E. G. Rich, Mod., H. G. Wilkie, C.C.

Jul. 18, 1931, Rev. E. G. Rich followed by Bro. Fulton Roper. 5. Collected 1.25 for minutes. R. A. Roper, Mod., H. G. Wilkie, C.C.

Aug. 15, 1931, Bro. Joe Blackwell. Elected E. G. Rich, Mod. 4. Received Loyd Callwell as a candidate for baptism. 5. Voted to have day and night meeting. Rev. E. G. Rich, Mod. Prot., R. M. Cantrell, C.C. Prot.

Sep. 19, 1931, Rev. R. A. Roper. 4. Received by letter Sister Theodocia Wilkie and Sister Martha Williams. Also received by a brother by restoration. Received as a candidate for baptism Bro. Tom Willson. 5. Granted letters to Sister Medie [*Almeda/Meda*] Maddux, Sister Beckie Price, Bro. Gus Richards and wife Sister Dorrah Richards. Went into the election of a pastor for the coming year. By motion, nominated Bro. R. A. Roper there being no other nomination there was a motion that the nominations close. Elected by eclimation, motion carried and by a rising vote of the church, elected Bro. R. A. Roper, was called to the pastoral cair of Hightower Church for ensuing year. Rev. R. A. Roper, Mod., H. G. Wilkie, C.C.

Nov. 14, 1931, Rev. R. A. Roper followed by Fulton Roper. 5. Granted the following letter: Sister Frances Pagett, Nancie Dempsey and Margarett Dempsey. Collect $1.90 cts. to Roper's. Collected to date for our pastor $38.00. Rev. R. A. Roper, Mod., H. G. Wilkie, C.C.

Dec. 19, 1931, Rev. J. H. Cowart. 5. Collected for our pastor $6.00. Rev. R. A. Roper, H. G. Wilkie, C.C.

Jan. 16, 1932, Pastor Rev. R. A. Roper. 5. By motion and second we the Board of Deacons in conference refuse to receive the donation of the late Rev. E. A. Cochran and have notified Bro. Claud Wheeler of our action. Rev. R. A. Roper, Mod., H. G. Wilkie, C.C.

Feb. 20, 1932, Bro. Fulton Roper and Rev. E. G. Rich, followed by our pastor. [*No business under any item*]. Rev. R. A. Roper, Mod., H. G. Wilkie, C.C.

Mar. 19, 1932, Rev. R. A. Roper. [*No business under any item*]. Rev. R. A. Roper, Mod., H. G. Wilkie, C.C.

Apr. 16, 1932, Rev. R. A. Roper. 5. Collected $1.00 for communion purposes. Rev. R. A. Roper, Mod., H. G. Wilkie, C.C.

May 14, 1932, Bro. Fulton Roper. 3. Received the acknowledgements of a brother. 4. Received another brother by restoration. Rev. R. A. Roper, Mod., H. G. Wilkie, C.C.

Jun. 16, 1932, Rev. E. G. Rich followed by pastor. 5. Granted the following letters: Bro. R. D. Dobson and wife Sister Cary Dobson. By motion went in to the election of delegates to the association to convene with Sharp Mountain Church on Wednesday and Thursday before the fourth Sunday in Aug. 1932. By motion, suspended the regular order of election and elected by appointment as follows: S. S. Wyatt, Jess L. Wilkie, H. G. Wilkie, Rev. R. A. Roper, Joel Heard, Emory West, and alternates J. H. Wilkie and Joe E. Wyatt. All so went into the election of delegates to the union meeting to convene with Corinth Church in Pickens County on Thursday and Friday before the 4th Sunday in July as follows: Jess L. Wilkie, R. M. Cantrell, Lee Hester, E. G. Rich, W. M. Dobson, Joe E. Wyatt, Dewey Wyatt and alternate Osker Stewart.

Jul. 16, 1932, 5. Granted Sister Angie Porter letter of dismission. By motion, submitted to the reading of the letter to association, the same being approved. All so to the union meeting of the 3rd district, being accepted. Collected $1.60 cts. for minutes. Rev. R. A. Roper, Mod., H. G. Wilkie, C.C.

Aug. 20, 1932, Rev. E. G. Rich 3. Received the acknowledgements of six members and the church bear with them. 4. Received a brother by restoration, received by letter Bro. Monroe McPherson. 5. Motion carried to withdraw fellowship from a sister for contempt of the church by withdrawing fellowship from her by erasing her name from our church record. E. G. Rich, Mod. Prot., H. G. Wilkie C.C.

Sep. 1932, Rev. R. A. Roper. 3. Preferred a charge against a brother for contempt of the church. By motion, withdrew fellowship from him. 5. Went into the election of a pastor. By motion nominated Rev. R. A. Roper. By motion suspended the regular order of election, motion carried and elect by eclimation by a rising vote of the church. Rev. R. A. Roper was elected as pastor of Hightower for the coming year. All so granted the following letters of dismission, Bro. L. A. Ingram and wife Sister Pearl Ingram and daughter Sister Beatrice Ingram. All so through an action of the church each male member from 16 years up is to pay 1.00 dollar unto the church treasure for the purpose raising money to cover the church house. Received for our pastor $5.00. Rev. R. A. Roper, Mod., H. G. Wilkie, C.C.

Oct. 15, 1932, Rev. E. G. Rich followed by Rev. R. A. Roper. 5. The following members were appointed as commity to look after buying the shingles and the covering of the church as follows: H. G. Wilkie, R. E. Loveless, J. A. Heard, S. S. Wyatt, H. N. Green, Emory West. By motion of the church, December conference set as time to complete payment into the fund. Rev. R. A. Roper, Mod., H. G. Wilkie, C.C.

Nov. 19, 1932, pastor. 5. Granted Bro. J. M. Stevens and wife [*Mattie*] letter of dismission. Rev. R. A. Roper, Mod., H. G. Wilkie, C.C.

Jan. 14, 1933, 5. By motion of the church, extended the time of completing the collections due by those who has not paid till our conference in March.

Jan. 15, 1933, By motion of the church to have the timber removed from the crest of the old cemetery of which R. E. Loveless and H. N. Green…

… Date missing, possibly 1932 or 1933: Granted letter of dismission to Sister Bernice Cowart.

Jan. 21, 1933 or Feb.? or Apr. 20, 1933? 5. Granted letters to Sister Essie Blackwell, Bro. Ezra Blackwell, Viola Blackwell, Dorthey Blackwell. R. A. Roper, Mod., H. G. Wilkie, C.C.

May 17, 1933, Rev. E. G. Rich, followed by Pastor Rev. R. A. Roper. 3. Preferred a charge against three brethren for contempt of the church. Withdrew fellowship from the three brethren.

Jun. 17, 1933, Rev. E. G. Rich and Rev. R. A. Roper. 5. Granted Sister Azzie Williams letter. Also went into the election of messengers to the union meeting. Motion to suspend the order of regular election, elect by appointment, to the union meeting of 3rd district at Oak Grove Church Thursday and Friday before the 4th Sunday in July. Messengers as follows: Rev. E. G. Rich, R. E. Lovelace, J. A. Heard, S. S. Wyatt, Rev. R. A. Roper, R. E. West, and J. H. Wilkie, alternate. Also the following messengers to the association to be held Wednesday and Thursday after the 1st Sunday in August 1933 at Hopewell Church, now Fulton County. Messengers: J. A. Heard, J. A. Wyatt, Elias Cochran *[likely Elias Virgil Cochran]*, J. H. Wilkie, S. S. Wyatt, Rev. R. A. Roper, H. G. Wilkie, and Fulton Roper, alternate. This done in conference signed by an order of the church. R. A. Roper, Mod., H. G. Wilkie, C.C.

Jul. 15, 1933, Pastor. 5. Granted Sister Etta Drummond Eason a letter, all so Bro. Hubert Warren. Letter to the association read and adopted. Minutes fund to $1.50. Rev. R. A. Roper, Mod., H. G. Wilkie, C.C.

Aug. 19, 1933, Bro. Fulton Roper. Elected Bro. Fulton Roper, moderator. 4. Received two brethren by restoration. 5. Granted Bro. Ruff Satifield and Bro. Felt Dean letter of dismission. Bro. Fulton Roper, Mod. P. T., H. G. Wilkie, C.C.

Sep. 16, 1933, Rev. R. W. Cochran, followed by Bro. Moody. 3. Preferred a charge against a brother and two sisters for departing the faith, withdrew fellowship from them. 4. Received by letter Sister May Heggood and a brother by restoration. 5. Went into election of a pastor for the next year. By a motion and second, nominated Rev. R. A. Roper, there being no other nomination, nomination closed there was a move to suspend the regular order of election, motion caired and elect by eclimation and Rev. R. A. Roper was elected as moderator of Hightower Church for the coming year. Granted the following letters: Bro. Brantley Williams and Bro. Thomas McPherson. Rev. R. A. Roper, Mod., H. G. Wilkie, C.C.

Jan. 20, 1934, pastor. [No business under any item]. Rev. R. A. Roper, Mod., H. G. Wilkie, C.C.

Feb. 17, 1934, pastor. 3. Preferred a charge against a brother for drunkness, deferred same till our next regular conference. Rev. R. A. Roper, Mod., H. G. Wilkie, C.C.

Mar. 12, 1934, Rev. E. G. Rich followed by our pastor. 3. Deferred the charge against a brother till our next regular conference. 4. Received by motion of the church 1 dollar from a brother and restored him to the fellowship of the church. Also, restored another brother. Rev. R. A. Roper, Mod., H. G. Wilkie, C.C.

Apr. 21, 1934, pastor. 3. Taken the reference of a brother for drunkness, withdrew fellowship from him. 5. Invited Mt. Pisgue, New Harmony, Ophir, and Liberty to be with Hightower on 3 Sunday May. R. A. Roper, Mod., H. G. Wilkie, C.C.

May 20, 1934, Bro. Fulton Roper. 5. Granted Bro. H. T. White and wife Sister Lilian White letters of dismission. Through an action of the church purchased 50 song books for the church. All so by motion of the deacons, $13.00 from the treasure to pay for same. Rev. R. A. Roper, Mod., H. G. Wilkie, C.C.

Jun. 16, 1934, pastor. 3. A brother made acknowledgements to the church for drunkness and the church bore with him. Also preferred charge against another brother for drunkness, deferred same till next meeting. 4. Received by letter Sister Annie Buice. 5. Went into the election of messengers to the Hightower association to convene with the Baptist Church of Cumming Ga. on Wednesday and Thursday before the 1st Sunday in August. Names: Emmett Cochran, Tom Wilson, J. A. Heard, R. E. Loveless, E. G. Rich, H. G. Wilkie, R. A. Roper, G. W. Wilkie. All so elected the following to the union meeting to convene with Conns Creek on Thursday and Friday before the 4 Sunday in July. Names: Bud Heard, G. W. Wilkie, E. G. Rich, M. McPherson, R. E. Loveless, Elisha Cochran. Rev. R. A. Roper, Mod., H. G. Wilkie, C.C.

Jul. 15, 1934, pastor. 3. Taken up the charge against a brother for drunkness and deferred same till next regular conference. 5. Granted the following letters: Rev. Fulton Roper, Ruby Roper and Aubriene Roper and Bro. Jesse Drummond. Rev. R. A. Roper, Mod., H. G. Wilkie, C.C.

Aug. 18, 1934, Rev. E. G. Rich, elected E. G. Rich as moderator. 2. Received acknowledgement from a brother and the [church] bears with him. 5. Granted Bro. Harvey Little and wife [*Stella*] and daughters [*Myrtle and Marie*] letters of dismission. All so by motion to draw from the Treasure $2.50 pay for lighting the house. Rev. E. G. Rich, Mod. Prot., H. G. Wilkie, C.C.

Sep. 15, 1934, Bro. Fulton Roper. 3. Preferred charge against two sisters. 5. Went into the election of a pastor for the coming year. By motion and second nominated Rev. R. A. Roper. There being no other nomination, by motion and second to suspend the regular order of elections and elect by eclimation and by a rising vote, the church elected Rev. R. A. Roper as our pastor for coming year. All so granted the following letters of dismission: Bro. Lee Wallace and Mrs. Lee [*Eula*] Wallace and daughter [*Marie? or Kate?*]. To collection $6.75 for our pastor. Rev. R. A. Roper, Mod., H. G. Wilkie, C.C.

Oct. 20, 1934, pastor. 4. Received the following letters: Sister Bertie Roper and Sister Blanche Turner. 5. Granted the following letters of dismission: Sister Odessa Boling, Bro. Marion Dean. Collected $31.00 for our pastor. Rev. R. A. Roper, Mod., H. G. Wilkie, C.C.

Nov. 17, 1934, Rev. Fulton Roper. 5. Paid to our pastor eleven dollars. Total collection $94.75. R. A. Roper, Mod., H. G. Wilkie, C.C.

Dec. 15, 1934, our pastor. 5. Collected $5.00 for our pastor. Total $85.75. Rev. R. A. Roper, Mod., H. G. Wilkie, C.C.

Jan. 19, 1935, pastor. 5. Appointed a commity to solicit funds for Bro. Osker Stewart. Bro. Linton Wyatt and R. E. Lovelace, commity. Rev. R. A. Roper, Mod., H. G. Wilkie, C.C.

Feb. 16, 1935, Bro. E. G. Rich. Elected E. G. Rich Mod. Prot. [No business under any item]. E. G. Rich, Mod. Prot., H. G. Wilkie, C.C.

Mar. 16, 1935, Rev. A. A. Roper. [No business under any item]. Rev. R. A. Roper, Mod., H. G. Wilkie, C.C.

Apr. 20, 1935, E. G. Rich followed by Rev. R. A. Roper. 5. By motion, read the request of Bro. Seldon Heggood and the church bespended with an offering of 5 dollars. All so 40 cts for communion purposes. Invited the following churches to commune with us as follows: Liberty, Pisgue, New Harmony, Mica, Ophir. Rev. R. A. Roper, Mod., H. G. Wilkie, C.C.

May 18, 1935, Rev. R. A. Roper. [No business under any item]. Rev. R. A. Roper, Mod., H. G. Wilkie, C.C.

Jun. 15, 1935, Bro. Fulton Roper followed by our pastor. 5. Went into the election of delegates to the association to convene with Cole Mt. Baptist Church in Forsyth County. By motion, suspended the regular order of election and elected by appointment the following messengers to the association: J. A. Heard, Elisha Cochran, Lee Hester, Joe Wyatt, H. G. Wilkie, Emory West, G. H. Little, R. A. Roper. Also appointed the following delegates to the union meeting of the third district: Tom Heard, Dewey Wyatt, Rev. R. A. Roper, R. E. Lovelace, E. G. Rich, S. S. Wyatt, J. A. Heard. Rev. R. A. Roper, Mod., H. G. Wilkie, C.C.

July 13, 1935, Rev. R. A. Roper. 4. Received Bro. Isaiah Cowart as a member. 5. Collected for minutes $2.00. R. A. Roper, Mod., H. G. Wilkie, C.C.

Sep. 14, 1935, pastor. 4. Received letters of Mr. and Mrs. Wm. [*William E. and Toma Cara Cornett*] Cowart. 5. Granted Bro. Troy Holcombe a letter of dismission. By motion went into the election of a pastor for the coming year. By motion, nominated Rev. R. A. Roper, also by motion nominated Rev. Tyrie Sewell, by motion nominated

Bro. E. K. Padgett. Rev. A. A. Roper and Bro. Joe Wilkie to hold ballot. Rev. Roper receiving the majority was elected as our pastor of the coming year. Rev. R. A. Roper, Mod., H. G. Wilkie, C.C.

Oct. 19, 1935, Rev. R. A. Roper. 3. By motion, received from a brother his confession of wrong doing and the church bears with him and pray that he might walk in that straight and narrow pathway. 5. Granted the following letters: Miss Magalane Edwards, Mrs. Ollie [*Wilkie*] Bagwell, Mr. Maynard Edwards. Collected for our pastor to date $36.00, for repairs to house $3.35. Rev. R. A. Roper, Mod., H. G. Wilkie, C.C.

Dec. 14, 1935, pastor. 5. Collected for our pastor to date 46.00. Rev. R. A. Roper, Mod., H. G. Wilkie, C.C.

Mar. 21, 1936, pastor. Received by experience Mrs. Corrie Lee Dobson. R. A. Roper, Mod., H. G. Wilkie, C.C.

Apr. 18, 1936, Rev. A. A. Roper, E. G. Rich and Pastor. 5. The church extends to the sister churches a broad invitation to commune with Hightower on the 3rd Sun in May. Granted Sister Cinderella Bowers a letter of dismission. Rev. R. A. Roper, Mod., H. G. Wilkie, C.C.

May 16, 1936, pastor. [No business under any item]. Rev. R. A. Roper, Mod., H. G. Wilkie, C.C.

Jun. 20, 1936, Rev. E. G. Rich and pastor. 5. Went into the election of messengers to association. By motion, suspended the regular order of election and elected by appointment the following: E. G. Rich, R. E. Lovelace, Rev. R. A. Roper, G. C. Wilkie, H. N. Green, Lee Hester, Elisha Cochran. All so to the union meeting of the 3rd district, to meet at Chalcedonia on Thursday and Friday before the 4th Sunday in July, appointed following messengers: H. G. Wilkie, J. E. Wyatt, R. E. Loveless, H. N. Green, S. S. Wyatt, Rev. E. G. Rich, and R. M. Cantrell, alternate. Rev. R. A. Roper, Mod., H. G. Wilkie, C.C.

Jul. 18, 1936, Bro. A. A. Roper. 5. By motion and second of the church, "We your commity elected by the church to adopt a plan of financing the church and support of the ministry. We submit the following plan that we will endeavor to approach each member either by letter or otherwise asking them to pledge whatever an amount they feel like giving. Respectfully submitted. Beginning from the time this plan was accepted and continuing yearly. Commity, this done in conference." H. G. Wilkie, R. E. Lovelace, S. S. Wyatt, Deacons. Rev. R. A. Roper, Mod., H. G. Wilkie C.C.

Aug. 15, 1936, pastor. 5. Granted Bro. Frank Little and wife [*Maud?*] letter of dismission. Collected $2.75 on building the steps. Rev. Robert Roper, Mod., H. G. Wilkie, C.C.

Sep. 19, 1936, Rev. R. A. Roper. 5. Went into the election of a pastor for the coming year. By motion an second suspended the regular order of elections and elected eclimation. By motion, nominated Dr. Tribble and by a vote of the church, unanimously called Dr. Tribble as our pastor for the coming year. All so by motion, restored a brother to the fellowship of the church. Contributions for the support of our pastor for the past year $77.25. Balance in treasure $6.00. Rev. R. A. Roper, Mod., H. G. Wilkie, C.C.

Oct. 17, 1936, Rev. P. W. Tribble, pastor. 4. Restored two brethren to fellowship of the church. Received the following members by letter Sister Jewell and Mrs. Mirtle Colmond. 5. Granted Bro. Elias Rich Jr. a letter of dismission. Paid to our former pastor, Bro. R. A. Roper $92.25. Bal. in treasure $6.00. Rev. P. W. Tribble, Mod., H. G. Wilkie, C.C.

Nov. 21, 1936, Rev. P. W. Tribble. 5. Collected $6.00 to buy coal for the church. All so by motion and second appointed Bro. Frank Stewart as housekeeper for the next year. By motion the church pledges $12.00 for same. Collected $1.00 for our former pastor. Total $93.25. Rev. P. W. Tribble, Mod., H. G. Wilkie, C.C.

Dec. 19, 1936, Rev. P. W. Tribble. 5. Granted Bro. Homer Little and wife, Mrs. Mattie Little letters of dismission. Rev. P. W. Tribble, Mod., H. G. Wilkie, C.C.

Jan. 20, 1937, Rev. P. W. Tribble. [No business under any item]. Rev. P. W. Tribble, Mod., H. G. Wilkie, C.C.

Mar. 20, 1937, pastor. [No business under any item]. Rev. P. W. Tribble, Mod., H. G. Wilkie, C.C.

Apr. 17, 1937, Rev. P. W. Tribble. 4. Received the following by letter: Bro. J. J. Turner and wife Sister J. J. [*Dora Wyatt Turner*], Mrs. Leo Turner Boling and Bro. Paul Turner, all so by letter. 5. Taken up collection to pay the housekeeper for the past quarter the sum $3.00. Rev. P. W. Tribble, Mod., H. G. Wilkie, C.C.

May 15, 1937, Dr. P. W. Tribble. 5. Expenses for communion $1.50. Collected to purchase piano for the church $30.75. Rev. P. W. Tribble, Mod., H. G. Wilkie, C.C.

Jun. 1937, Rev. R. A. Roper. 5. Granted Sister Vader Ellis letter of dismission. All so appointed the following commity to select and purchase a piano for the church: H. G. Wilkie, Monroe McPherson, R. E. Lovelace, G. C. Wilkie, Elisha Cochran. The same having been purchased at a price of 60.00. Total collected on the piano $37.00. Total collected on the housekeeper 75 cts. Rev. R. A. Roper, Mod. Prot., H. G. Wilkie, C.C.

1937, By motion suspended the regular order of election and elected by appointment the following messengers to the association to convene with Concord Church of Cumming Ga. on Thursday and Friday after the first Sunday in Aug. as follows: R. E. Lovelace, J. A. Heard, Emory West, Rev. R. A. Roper, J. W. Richards, Henry Scott, Rev. E. G. Rich, R. M. Cantrell. All so to the union meeting of the 3 district to be held with Mt Pisgue Church on Thursday and [Friday] before the 4th Sunday in July as follows: H. G. Wilkie, E. G. Rich, J. W. Richards, Elisha Cochran, S. S. Wyatt, J. A. Heard, R. E. Lovelace, Lee Hester. Rev. R. A. Roper, Mod., H. G. Wilkie, C.C.

Jul. 17, 1937, Rev. P. W. Tribble. 5. Submitted to the reading of the letters to the association and to the union meeting, same being approved. Rev. P. W. Tribble, Mod., H. G. Wilkie, C C.

"The good old church at Hightower. A glorious revival. I wonder if Ruby [Hester], Nettie Lee [Lovelace] and I will ever be as close to one another in another meeting as we have for the last one. I hope so. I love them dearly." Entry in Cleo Heard Milford diary, July 31, 1937.

Aug. 21, 1937, Rev. E. G. Rich. 5. Granted following letters: Bro. J. W. Richards and wife Sister Euilee Richards and Aaron Richards. All so Sister Aline Stewart Sartor and Sister Irene Roper. Went into the election of a pastor of the coming year. By motion, suspended the regular order of election and elected by eclimation. Nominated Rev. P. W. Tribble and unanimously elected Bro. Tribble as our pastor another year. Rev. E. G. Rich, Mod. Prot., H. G. Wilkie, C.C.

Sep. 18, 1937, Rev. P. W. Tribble. 4. Received by letter with the bairer Sister Annie Wilkie and Sister Clara Wilkie, Bro. Spencer Wilkie and wife Sister FaeSeale under the watchcare of the church. 5. Granted Sister Martha Wilson a letter of dismission.

Oct. 16, 1937, pastor. Received by letter with bearer Bro. Hoyt Sewell. 5. Collected for our pastor $87.50, for housekeeper $3.00. Balance in treasure $4.00. Rev. P. W. Tribble, Mod., H. G. Wilkie, C.C.

Nov. 20, 1937, Rev. P. W. Tribble. 5. Granted Bro. L. O. Croy and wife Mrs. Carry L. [*Lydia*] Croy letters of dismission. Collected for our pastor $92.50. Rev. P. W. Tribble, Mod., H. G. Wilkie, C.C.

Dec. 1937, Rev. E. G. Rich followed by Rev. P. W. Tribble. Accepted the statement of a brother and the church bore with him. 4. Received the letter with bearer, Mrs. Mary Lee Cochran. 5. Went into the discussion of building on to the church. By motion appointed the following commity: Rev. E. G. Rich, Elisha Cochran, R. E. Lovelace, H. G. Wilkie, J. A. Heard. Rev. P. W. Tribble, Mod., H. G. Wilkie, C.C.

Jan. 15, 1938, Dr. P. W. Tribble. 4. Received by letter with the bearer Bro. Glen Smith. 5. Added to the finance commity Bro. J. H. Little, Bro. Oscar Stewart. Rev. P. W. Tribble, Mod., H. G. Wilkie, C.C.

Building committee met Jan. 19th, appointed R. E. Lovelace chairman of the building commity to get prices in the material that would be needed in the building. Same being bought and the addition all most finished. R. E. Lovelace, J. A. Heard, H. G. Wilkie, Elisha Cochran, Rev. E. G. Rich, commity.

Feb. 18, 1938 "worried about the money we haven't got to build church" Cleo Heard Milford Diary

Feb. 19, 1938, Dr. P. W. Tribble. 5. Finance commity reporting on finances for expense of the new addition to the church as follows: Miss Cleo Heard $6.75, Miss Annie Wilkie 29.12, Elisha Cochran 12.75, G. H. Little 3.25, Os Stewart 21.00, J. A. Heard 25.00, Dr. 1.00, 98.87, [other unidentified amounts]. Rev. P. W. Tribble, Mod., H. G. Wilkie, C.C.

Feb. 27, 1938, "Organized Sunday school at Hightower." Cleo Heard Milford Diary

Mar. 19, 1938, Dr. P. W. Tribble. 5. Granted the following letters of dismission: Bro. Richard Lathem and Bro. Johnie Pierce. Received on building fund R. E. West 1.00. Dr. P. W. Tribble, Mod., H. G. Wilkie, C.C.

April 16, 1938, Pastor [no business under any item] Rev. P. W. Tribble, Mod., H. G. Wilkie, C.C.

May 21, 1938, Rev. E. G. Rich and Dr. P. W. Tribble. 4. Received by letter with bearer Bro. Rienes [*William Raines*?]. 5. Granted Bro. Hollman Lovelace letter of dismission. Rev. P. W. Tribble, Mod., H. G. Wilkie, C.C.

Jun. 18, 1938, pastor. 5. Granted Sister J. E. Hegood a letter of dismission. Went into the election of messengers to the union meeting of the 3rd district. Suspended the regular order of election and elected by appointment, the following members: H. G. Wilkie, Joe Wyatt, Elisha Cochran, J. M. McPherson, S. S. Wyatt, Dewey Wyatt. All so to the association to meet with Macedonia Baptist Church on Wednesday and Thursday after the 1st Sunday in August the following messengers to attend: E. G. Rich, R. E. Lovelace, J. A. Head, S. S. Wyatt, R. M. Cantrell.

Jul. 16, 1938. Rev. P. W. Tribble. 4. Received by letter with the bearers: Sister Eulee Richards, Miss Gladys and Ethalee Richards and J. W. Richards as members with us. Rev. P. W. Tribble, Mod., H. G. Wilkie, C.C.

Aug. 20, 1938, Rev. E. G. Rich. 5. Went into the election of a pastor for the next year. By motion suspended regular order of election and by motion elected by eclimation Rev. P. W. Tribble as Pastor of Hightower Church for the coming year. All so granted Sister Carry Cannon letter of dismission. All so your present clerk tending his resignation as clerk that church have an appointment to elect a new clerk, same being laid over till next conference. Rev. E. G. Rich, Mod., Prot. H. G. Wilkie, C.C.

Sep. 17, 1938, Rev. P. W. Tribble. 4. Received by letter with the bearer Sister Auberine Scott. 5. Granted the following letters Sister Roxie Pierce, Sister Era [*Fletcher*] Tribble. Went into the election of a clerk and treasurer, by motion elected Bro. Linton Wyatt as clerk indefinitely. Contributed to our pastor $14.00. Rev. P. W. Tribble, Mod., H. G. Wilkie, C.C.

Oct. 15, 1938, Rev. P. W. Tribble. 5. Granted the following letters: Bro. Charles Ellington, Ode Fowler, R. C. Chumbler. Total $66.40, contributed to pastor $39.40. Rev. P. W. Tribble, Mod., Linton Wyatt, C.C.

Dec. 9, 1938: "Heard today of the shocking news of Mr. Ed Lovelace's death on Thursday night, Dec. 8. He's a man I loved and admired, especially as a Sunday school teacher and a prayer leader." Cleo Heard Milford Diary

Dec. 17, 1938, Rev. P. W. Tribble. [No business under any item]. Rev. P. W. Tribble, Mod., Linton Wyatt, C.C.

Book 4, 1924-1938 membership

* Information found only in minutes

	Last name	First name	Middle name	How/when received, *other info*	How/when dismissed, *other info*	*Remarks; items not listed in church roll (maiden name; spouse; birth-death; buried at HBC; etc.)*
4	Andrews	Homer "Peg"		Exp Aug 1929?	Death June 1982	
4	Andrews	Eva	Mae Pinkerton	Exp Jul 1937		
4	Adams	Thelma		Exp Aug 1925	Let 1926	
4	Andrews	Mary	Emmer Cronan	Exp Aug 1931		*Mary Emma Andrews m. Carl Cronan*
4	Bolles	Allie		Let Aug 1929	Let	*Bowles*
4	Bolles	Symanthy		Let Aug 1929	Let	*Bowles*
4	Bryson	Emma, Mrs.		Let Aug 30, 1924		
4	Boling	Desser, Mrs.		Exp Jul 1925	Let Oct 20, 1934	*Odessa Boling*
4	Buffington	Maud		Exp 1926	Death Oct 27, 1985	*Maude Pearson Buffington, 1891-1985, bur HBC*
4	Bryson	Onney		Exp 1928	Death	
4	Bannister	Harmon		Exp Aug 1930		
4	Blackwell	Essie		Exp Aug 1930	Let 1933	
4	Blackwell	Ezra		Exp Aug 1930	Let 1933	
4	Bruce	Hubert		Exp Aug 1930	Let Jun 19, 1948	
4	Bruce	Sadie		Exp Aug 1931	Let 1934 Let Oct 1940	
4	Blackwell	Viola		Exp Aug 1931	Let 1933	
4	Blackwell	Dorthy		Exp Aug 1931	Let 1933	
4	Buice	Annie, Mrs.		Let Jun 16, 1934		
4	Buffington	Winnie	Grace Wyatt	Exp Jul 1934	Death Aug 1, 2007	*Winnie (Buffington) Wyatt, 1918-2007, bur HBC*
4	Bowers	Cinderilla		Exp Jul 1934	Let Apr 18, 1936	
4	Buffington	Kate		Exp Jul 1935		*Kate (Buffington) Edwards, death 2013*
4	Bowers	Juanitta	Watkins	Exp Aug 1936	Let Aug 1956	*Juanita (Bowers) Watkins*
4	Bowers	J.	S.	Exp Aug 1936	Let Sep 18, 1948	
4	Baker	Roy		Exp Jul 1937	Let Apr 1946	
4	Brown	Howard		Exp Jul 1937		
4	Bailey	Elizabeth		Exp Aug 1, 1938		
4	Bailey	J.	W. Jr.	Exp Aug 1, 1938	Let Jul 19, 1967	
4	Bailey	E.	J.	Exp Aug 1, 1938	Let Dec 20, 1980	

	Last name	First name	Middle name	How/when received, *other info*	How/when dismissed, *other info*	*Remarks; items not listed in church roll (maiden name; spouse; birth-death; buried at HBC; etc.)*
4	Buffington	R.	L.		dead	
4	Chumbler	Thomas		Exp Aug 1923		
4	Cowart	Clay		Exp Jul 1934	Let Aug 14, 1954	
4	Cornett	Ella, Mrs.		Let Jul 1934		*Ella (Green) Cornett, 1903-1998*
4	Cowart	Isaiah		Let Jul 17, 1935	Death 1959	*1904-1959, bur HBC*
4	Cowart	Gilbert		Let Jul 17, 1935	Let 1936	
4	Cowart	Fay, Mrs.		Exp Jul 17, 1935		
4	Cowart	Fay		Exp Jul 1935	Let Dec 20, 1952	
4	Corn	Lilamae		Exp Jul 1935		
4	Cowart	Gilbert		Let Jul 1935	Let Dec 20, 1952	
4	Cowart	Dewey		Let Jul 1935	Death Jan 27, 1979, deacon, Licensed and Ordained Minister	*1908-1979, bur HBC*
4	Cowart	William		Let Jul 1935	Death Dec 24, 1973	*1889-1973, bur HBC*
4	Cowart	William, Mrs.		Let Jul 1935	Death Apr 14, 1982	*1891-1982, Toma Cara (Cornett) Cowart, bur HBC*
4	Corn	T.?	R.?	Exp Aug 1936		*Tom Corn? Coman for Coleman?*
4	Coleman				Let 1936?	*Irene? Charles H? 1893-1953, bur HBC*
4	Coleman	Jewall, Miss		*Let Oct 17, 1936	Let 1936?	
4	Coleman	Mrs.		*Let Oct 17 1936	Let 1936? Death Jul 1978	*Myrtle? 1894-1978, bur HBC*
4	Cronan	Geneva		Exp Jul 1937	Let Sep 1939	
4	Cloud	Gladys		Exp Jul 1937		
4	Cochran	Elbert		Exp Aug 1, 1938	Deacon	
4	Cowart	M.	H.	Exp Aug 1, 1938	Let Apr 19, 1969	
4	Coleman	Ted		Exp Aug 1, 1938	Let 1956, Death May 4, 1975	*bur HBC*
4	Cochran	Mary	Lee	Let Dec 1937	Death Jan 23, 2012	*1919-2012, bur HBC*
4	Crow	V. Miss	D.	Exp Aug 1925	Let Jul 1947	
4	Cronan	Eva, Miss		Exp Aug 1925	Let Jul 16, 1955	
4	Cronan	G.	G.	Exp Aug. 1926	Death Mar 1983	*George Grady, 1895-1983, bur HBC*
4	Cronan	F.	J.	Exp Aug 1926		*Fred Jackson? 1908-1993, bur HBC*
4	Cannon	Essie		Exp Aug 1928	Let Oct. 17, 1942	
4	Cannon	Maud		Let Aug. 1928	Let Oct 17, 1942	

	Last name	First name	Middle name	How/when received, *other info*	How/when dismissed, *other info*	*Remarks; items not listed in church roll (maiden name; spouse; birth-death; buried at HBC; etc.)*
4	Curby	Loura		Exp Aug 1928	Let Aug 1928	
4	Cornett	Shevie		Exp Aug 1929	Death Jul 1982	
4	Cochran	Elishy		Exp Aug 1929	Deacon Death Dec 26, 1970	*Elisha Cochran, 1884-1970, bur HBC*
4	Cochran	Emmett		Exp Aug 1929	Death Jun 23, 2003	*1915-2003, bur HBC*
4	Chumbler	Lou		Exp Aug 1929	Let Feb 16, 1952	
4	Collett	Joe		Exp Aug 1929	Let Jan 19, 1951	
4	Cochran	Geneva		Exp Aug 1930	Death Feb 8, 1982	*1916-1982, m Frank Wyatt, bur HBC*
4	Cornett	Lucile	Ray	Exp Aug 1930		
4	Collett	Lillie		Exp Aug 1930		
4	Cowart	Bernice		Exp Aug 1930	Let 1933	
4	Colwell	Margrett		Exp Aug 1930	Let Aug 1932	
4	Colwell	Nettie		Exp Aug 1930	Let Mar 20, 1954	
4	Cowart	Harlie		Exp Aug 1930	Death Feb 9, 1950	*Harley R, 1915-1950, bur HBC*
4	Coletrane	Vera		Exp Aug 1930	Let Oct 1930	
4	Cowart	James		Exp Aug 1930		
4	Cantrell	Willie	B.	Exp Aug 1931		
4	Cantrell	Ruby		Exp Aug 1931	Let Nov 19, 1949	
4	Calwell	Loyd		Exp Aug 1931	Aug 14, 1954	
4	Cloud	Loyd		Exp Aug 1933	Let Aug 14, 1954	
4	Cloud	Willie/Willis	Mae	Exp Aug 1933	Let Jun 20, 1953	
4	Cochran	E.	W.	Exp Jul 1934		*Edward Watson Cochran, 1922-2015, bur HBC*
4	Cannon	Roy		Exp Jul 1934	Dead	
4	Corn	Rudolf		Exp Jul 1934		
4	Dobson	Eston		Exp Aug 1923 Let Jun 20, 1925	*Let Aug 1945	
4	Dobson	Jane, Miss		Exp Aug 1923	dead	
4	Drummond	Edith	Wilkie	Exp Aug 1925	Death Nov 19, 1996	*m. Cleveland Wilkie*
4	Dobson	Louis		Exp Aug 1926	*Let Jul 17, 1948 dead	*Lewis*
4	Dean	Steve		Let Feb 15, 1931	dead	*1870-1952; bur HBC*
4	Dean	Sarah, Mrs.		Let Feb 15, 1931	dead	*Sarah Matilda (Crow) Dean, 1876-1948, bur HBC*

	Last name	First name	Middle name	How/when received, *other info*	How/when dismissed, other info	Remarks; items not listed in church roll (maiden name; spouse; birth-death; buried at HBC; etc.)
4	Dobson	R.	D.		Let Jun 1932	
4	Dean	Felt			Let Aug 19, 1933	
4	Dobson	Ceacle, Miss		Exp Aug 1936	Let Dec 20, 1952	
4	Dobson	G.	W.	Exp Aug 1936	Let 1948	
4	Dobson	Lonnie		Exp Jul 1937	Death Dec 2006	
4	Dobson	Wynelle		Exp Jul 1937	Let Mar 14, 1953	
4	Dean	Linton		Let Aug 1929	Death 1932	*1892-1932, bur HBC*
4	Drummond	Winell		Exp Aug 1930	Let Aug 14, 1954	
4	Drummond	Shelba	Stewart	Exp Aug 1930	Let Jun 19, 1954	*Shelby (Drummond) Stewart*
4	Dempsey	Nannie		Exp Aug 1930	Let Nov 1932	
4	Dobson	R.	D.	Exp Aug 1930	Feb 15, 1931 By letter	
4	Drummond	Wesley		Exp Aug 1931	Death Sep 1941	*1977-1941, George Wesley Drummond, bur HBC*
4	Drummond	Cora		Exp Aug 1931	Death Jun 1964	*Cora Bell Hester Drummond, 1888-1964, bur HBC*
4	Drummond	Joe	J.	Exp Aug 1932	Let Sep 1953	
4	Dean	Jenie	Bell Collier	Exp Aug 1932	Death Nov 9, 1999	*Gennie (Dean) Collier, 1915-1999, bur HBC*
4	Dean	George		Exp Jul 1934	Let Feb 19, 1983	
4	Dobson	Mark		Exp Jul 1934	Death Nov 11, 2004	
4	Dobson	Corrie, Miss	Lee	Exp 1936	Let Aug 1944	
4	Edwards	Ovella, Miss		Exp Aug 1923	Let Apr 26, 1924	
4	Edwards	Pawline		Exp Aug 1923		
4	Eubanks	Marie	Cloud	Exp Aug 1925		*Marie (Eubanks) Cloud, 1914-1998, bur HBC*
4	Edwards	Berry		Exp Aug 1932	dead	
4	Edwards	Maggaline		Exp Jul 1934	Let Oct 1935	
4	Edwards	Maynard		Exp Jul. 1934	Let Oct 1935	
4	Ellington	Charles		Exp Jul 1937	Let Oct 1938	
4	Epperson	Juanita		Exp Aug 1, 1938	Death Dec 2000	
4	Fowler	Florence		Exp Aug 1928		
4	Fowler	May		Exp Aug 1930		
4	Fletcher	Gennie		Exp Aug 1929	Let Oct 1929	
4	Foster	Susie, Mrs.	Mae	Exp Aug 1, 1938	Death Nov 2000	
4	Green	Lee	B.	Exp Jul 1937	Death Oct 6, 1986	
4	Green	Lee	Jessie	Exp Jul 1937	Let Dec 20 1952	

	Last name	First name	Middle name	How/when received, *other info*	How/when dismissed, *other info*	*Remarks; items not listed in church roll (maiden name; spouse; birth-death; buried at HBC; etc.)*
4	Green	Bill		Exp Jul 1937	Death Feb 25, 1981	*William Harold "Willie H." Green, 1919-1981, bur HBC*
4	Green	Blance		Exp Aug 1, 1938	Let May 20, 1944	*Blanche (Green) Swims*
4	Green	J. Jay	W.	Exp Aug 1, 1938		
4	Green	Tomas	E. Jr.	Exp Jul 1925	Deceased, Jan 6 1984	*h/o Hattie Turner Green, 1900-1984, bur HBC*
4	Green	Edd		Exp Aug 1925	Death	
4	Green	Carl		Exp Aug 1925	Let May 17, 1976	
4	Green	Hoyt		Exp Aug 1925	Death Jun 14, 1978	*Hoyt Axon Green, 1907-1978, bur HBC*
4	Green	Winnie, Miss		Exp Aug 1925		
4	Gilleland	Lilly, Mrs.		Exp Aug 1925	Death Nov 13, 1989	*Lillie (Green) Gilleland, 1898-1989, bur HBC*
4	Gilleland	Bunion		Let	Death Feb 21, 1968	*Bunion Vester Gilleland, 1886-1968, bur HBC*
4	Green	Garland		Exp Aug 1928	Death Oct 30, 1992	*Garland Luther Green, 1910-1992, bur HBC*
4	Gilbert	Esco		Exp Aug 1929	Let 1930	
4	Glover	Lorene		Exp Aug 1929	Let Aug 1930	
4	Green	Ruby		Exp Aug 1929	Death Dec 9, 1991	*Ruby (Green) Cowart; 1913-1991*
4	Green	Vester		Let Aug 1929	Death Mar 30, 1991	*Vester (Gilleland) Green, 1914-1991, bur HBC*
4	Gilleland	Etna		Exp Aug 1930		
4	Green	Grace		Exp Aug 1930	Let Dec 17, 1949	
4	Gazaway	May		Exp Aug 1931	Let Feb 18, 1939	
4	Green	Frank		Exp Aug 1932	Let Dec 20, 1952	
4	Green	Bonnie		Exp Jul 1934	Died 1983	*Bonnie Green, 1918-1983, bur HBC*
4	Green	Ella	Cornett		Death Jul 25, 1998	*Ella (Green) Cornett, 1903-1998*
4	Green	Lee		Exp Jul 1935	Death May 1975	
4	Green	Louise		Exp Jul 1935		
4	Gilleland	L.	J.	Exp Jul 1935	Death Apr 4, 1963	*1910-1963, bur HBC*
4	Green	Sally	Gatha	Exp Jul 1935	Death Feb 12, 2009	*Agatha "Sally" (Green) Wheeler, 1922-2009, bur HBC*
4	Green	Margaret		Exp Jul 1937	Let Jan 17, 1948	
4	Glover	Colleen		Exp Jul 1937		
4	Goodman	Eva		Exp Jul 1937		
4	Goodman	Beulah		Exp Jul 1937		
4	Goodman	Rufus		Exp Jul 1937		

	Last name	First name	Middle name	How/when received, *other info*	How/when dismissed, *other info*	*Remarks; items not listed in church roll (maiden name; spouse; birth-death; buried at HBC; etc.)*
4	Heard	Thomas		Exp Aug 1926	Let Aug 15, 1959	*Tom*
4	Holcomb	James	A.	Let Nov 1927		
4	Heard	Jessie	Pruitt	Exp Aug 1928	Death Apr 5, 2004	*Jessie (Heard) Pruitt, 1914-2004*
4	Heard	J.	A.	Let Feb 15, 1931	Deacon, Death Feb 28, 1968	*Joel Augustus Heard, 1886-1968*
4	Heard	J. Mrs.	A.	Let Feb 15, 1931	Death May 14, 1972	*Birddie Julie Godfrey Heard, 1887-1972*
4	Heard	Archie		Let Feb 15, 1931	Death 1933	*Arch Heard, 1909-1933*
4	Hawkins	Ollie	Mae	Exp Jul 1937		
4	Heard	Mattie		Exp Aug 1, 1938	Let Sep 1953	*Mattie (Heard) Turner*
4	Holcomb	N.	G.	Exp Aug 1938		
4	Hester	Grace		Exp Aug 31, 1924	Death, 1951	
4	Hensley	Sammuel		Exp Jul 1925		
4	Holcombe	Jake		Exp Aug 1925	Death Apr 1927	
4	Hester	Truman		Exp Aug 1925		
4	Hester	T.	P.	Exp Aug 1929	Death Dec 25, 1969	*Thaddeus Pickett Hester Sr.*
4	Hester	Toy		Exp Aug 1929	letter	
4	Heard	Cleo	Milford	Exp Aug 1929	Death Aug 11, 2007	*Cleo (Heard) Milford, 1917-2007, bur HBC*
4	Hendrix	Herman		Exp Aug 1930	Let Feb 1939	
4	Hester	Billie		Exp Aug 1930		
4	Heard	Lee		Exp Aug 1930		
4	Holiway	Mamie		Exp Aug 1930	death	
4	Holt	Glen		Exp Aug 1930	Death Jan 1940	
4	Hester	Effie	Cowart	Let Apr 1931	Death Dec 23, 2012	*Effie (Hester) Cowart, 1916-2012*
4	Hester	Ruby	Lee	Let Apr 1931	Let Jun 17, 1944 *Ruby Milford	*Ruby Lee (Hester) Milford*
4	Hamilton	Odos		Exp Aug 1931	Death Aug 1976	*Maynard Henry Hamilton, 1895-1976, bur HBC*
4	Holcomb	Troy		Exp Aug 1932	Let Oct 1935	
4	Heard	Bud, Master		Exp Aug 1933	Death Feb 24, 2007	*Lee "Bud" Heard, 1915-2007*
4	Hawkins	Clarence		Exp Jul 1934	Let Sep 1957	
4	Hawkins	Hunter		Exp Jul 1934		
4	Hawkins	Jewell		Exp Jul 1934		
4	Hester	Roy		Exp Jul 1934	Let Mar 15, 1969	
4	Heard	John		Exp Jul 1934	Death Feb 25, 1991	*Deacon, 1921-1991*
4	Heggood	G.	S.	Let Jun 18, 1934		

	Last name	First name	Middle name	How/when received, *other info*	How/when dismissed, *other info*	*Remarks; items not listed in church roll (maiden name; spouse; birth-death; buried at HBC; etc.)*
4	Haygood			Let Jul 1935		
4	Heggood	Ula, Mrs.		Exp Aug 1936	Death Jul 21, 1982	*Eula?*
4	Heggood	Isabell, Miss		Exp Aug 1936		
4	Hester	Edith	Cochran	Exp Aug 1936		*Edith (Hester) Cochran, 1922-2014, bur HBC*
4	Hill	Hazel		Exp Aug 1, 1938	Let Dec 20, 1975	*d/o Earl and Ollie Hill*
4	Ingram	Lee		Let Jan 17, 1930	Let Nov 1932	
4	Ingram	Pearl, Mrs.		Let Jan 17, 1930	Let Nov 1932	
4	Jones	Bert		Exp Aug 1930		
4	Jones	Ida		Exp Aug 1930		
4	Jones	Ed		Exp Aug 1932	Let Jul 1947	
4	Jones	Grover, Mrs.		Exp 1926	Death Jun 5, 1988	*Carrie Jones, 1897-1988, bur HBC*
4	Lovelace	George	Hollman	Exp Aug 31, 1924	Let May 1938 Deceased 1973	*George H. Lovelace, 1909-1973, bur HBC*
4	Lovelace	Fannie, Miss		Exp Aug 1925	Let Sep 1943	*Fannie (Lovelace) Wilson, 1912-1955, bur HBC*
4	Little	Dock, Bro.				*1886-1961, bur HBC*
4	Little	Broughton			Death Apr 9, 1969	*1910-1969, bur HBC*
4	Little	?				
4	Little	?				
4	Little	Jennie	Belle Wyatt	Exp 1928	Death Mar 23, 2004	*Jennie Belle (Little) Wyatt, 1911-2004*
4	Loggins	Jim		Exp 1928		
4	Lancaster	Velvie		Exp 1929	Let 1944	
4	Little	Bobbie	Grace Wyatt	Exp Aug 1930	Died	*Bobbie Grace (Little) Wyatt, 1917-2002, bur HBC*
4	Little	Ruby	Kate	Exp Aug 1930		
4	Little	Myrtle		Exp Aug 1930	Let Aug 18, 1932 death	
4	Little	Buren		Exp Aug 1930	Death 1956	*1912-1956, bur HBC*
4	Little	Marie		Exp Aug 1930	Let Aug 18, 1932	
4	Landcaster	Palline		Exp Aug 1931		
4	Lathem	Marie		Exp Aug 1931		
4	Little	Marron		Exp Aug 1932	Death 1974	
4	Lathem	Parnell		Exp Aug 1933		
4	Little	Bloomer		Exp Jul 1934	Death 1959	*John Bloomer Little, 1914-1959, bur HBC*
4	Lovelace	Nettie	Lee	Exp Jul 1934	Death Apr 18, 2010	*Nettie Lee Lovelace, 1919-2010, bur HBC*

	Last name	First name	Middle name	How/when received, *other info*	How/when dismissed, *other info*	**Remarks; items not listed in church roll (maiden name; spouse; birth-death; buried at HBC; etc.)**
4	Little	Kathryn	White	Exp Jul 1934		*Kathryn (Little) White*
4	Lathem	Richard		Exp Jul 1934	Let Mar 1938	
4	Little	Ruth		Exp Jul 1937	Let Oct 1940	
4	Lemby	Annie	Lee Hudgins	Exp Aug 1, 1938		
4	Little	C.	H.	Exp Aug 1, 1938	Death Apr 9, 1996	*Coleman?*
4	Mills	L., Mrs.		Exp Aug 31, 1924	Let Sep 1939	*Lily (Chumbler) Mills*
4	Mills	T., Bro.	M.	Let May 1928	Death Jul 1931	*Thompson Mills, 1861-1931, bur HBC*
4	Mills	Loma		Let Aug 1928	Death Jan 6, 1985	*Loma Mills, 1892-1985, bur HBC*
4	McPherson	Mary	Ellen	Exp Aug 1929	Let 1930 Or *Let Nov 18, 1944	
4	McPherson	J.	Monrow	Let Aug 1932	Let 1948?	
4	McPherson	Monroe			Let Mar 1949	*James Monroe, 1905-1992*
4	Nix	Harmon		Exp Aug 1929		
4	Nichols	Ila	Shoemake	Exp Aug 1930	Death May 16, 2004	*Ila (Nichols) Shoemake, 1914-2004, bur HBC*
4	Nichols	Cleodus		Exp Aug 1930		
4	Norrell	Ethel		Exp Aug 1, 1938	dead	
4	Nelson	Emmett		Exp Aug 1925		
4	Pierce	Johnie		Exp Aug 31, 1924	Let Mar 1938	
4	Pearson	Fay		Exp Aug 1930	Let Nov 19, 1949	*Fay (Pearson) Parris*
4	Pearson	Hazel		Exp Aug 1931	Let Sep 17, 1949, *Hazel Chadwick	*Hazel (Pearson) Chadwick*
4	Porter	Angie		Exp Aug 1931	Let Jul 1932	
4	Porter	Allen		Exp Aug 1933	Death 1989	
4	Phyfe	Rade		Exp Jul 1934	Death Jan 19, 1975	*Rade Phyfe, 1917-1975, bur HBC*
4	Patterson	Paul		Exp Jul 1934	Death Oct 1994	
4	Padget	Clarence		Exp 1937	Let Sep 1939	
4	Roper	Samuel		Exp Aug 25, 1923	Let Jun 1927 *Let May 1928	
4	Roper	Vester		Exp Aug 25, 1923	Let Jun 1927 *Let May 1928	
4	Roper	Palmer		Exp Aug 25, 1923		
4	Roper	Carl		Let Aug 29, 1923	Let Apr 1926	
4	Roebuck	Mattie, Miss	Ritchey	Exp Aug 1923	Death Jan 23, 1967	*Mattie (Roebuck) Ritchey, 1908-1967*

	Last name	First name	Middle name	How/when received, *other info*	How/when dismissed, *other info*	*Remarks; items not listed in church roll (maiden name; spouse; birth-death; buried at HBC; etc.)*
4	Roebuck	Ruth, Miss		Exp Jul 1925	Deceased Sep 16, 1984	
4	Roper	Louise, Miss		Exp Jul 1925	Let Jun 1927 *Let May 1928	
4	Rich	Hobert		Exp Aug 1925		
4	Rich	Otto		Exp Aug 1925	Let 1951	
4	Rich	Elias		Let Aug. 1925	Let Oct 1936	
4	Rich	Winnie, Miss		Let Aug 1925	Let Apr 1931 Let 1951	
4	Rich	Martha		Let Aug 1925	Let Oct 15, 1955	
4	Rich	Mrs. Olia		Let Aug 1928	Let Dec 1960	
4	Rich	Elias		Exp Aug 1932	Let Aug 18, 1951	
4	Rich	Hobert			Let Aug 20, 1966	
4	Roper	Auberine		Exp Aug 1929	Let Jul 15, 1934	
4	Roebuck	Alice	Green	Exp Aug 1929	Death Aug 1, 2004	*Alice (Roebuck) Green, 1911-2004, bur HBC*
4	Rich	Ruth		Exp Aug 1929		
4	Roper	Troy				
4	Reece	Balam		Exp Jul 1934		
4	Rich	Joe			Death, time unknown	
4	Roper	Bertie		Let Oct 1934	Death Nov 1, 1966	
4	Roper	Robert	Jr.	Exp Aug 1936	Let Oct 17, 1942	
4	Richards	Roy		Exp Aug 1936	Death Oct 24, 1978	*1918-1978, James Royston Richards*
4	Richards	Aron		Exp Aug 1936 *Let Jul 16, 1938	Let Aug 21, 1937	*1922-1960, Aaron Isaiah Richards, bur HBC*
4	Roper	Inez		Exp 1937	Let 1937	
4	Raines	W.		Let May 21, 1938	Let	*William?*
4	Roland	Eva		Exp Aug 1, 1938	Let Nov 1957	
4	Roland	Gladys		Exp Aug 1, 1938	Let Nov 15, 1997	
4	Roper	Clara	Mae	Exp Aug 1, 1938	Let 1944	
4	Rainey	D.	J.	Exp Aug 1, 1938	Let Nov 1951	
4	Rainey	D.	C.	Exp Aug 1, 1938	Let Jun 14, 1947	*Denver*
4	Roland	W.	E.	Let Aug 1938	Death 1948	
4	Roland	Georgia, Mrs.			Death, time unknown	
4	Richards	J.	W.	Let Aug 1938		*James Washington, 1899-1966, bur HBC*
4	Richards	Evlee, Mrs.		Let Aug 1938	*Let Aug 21 1937	*Myra Evalee (Fletcher) Richards, bur HBC*

	Last name	First name	Middle name	How/when received, *other info*	How/when dismissed, *other info*	*Remarks; items not listed in church roll (maiden name; spouse; birth-death; buried at HBC; etc.)*
4	Richards	Gladis, Miss		Let Aug 1938		
4	Satifield	R.		Exp Aug 31, 1924	Let Aug 19, 1933	*Ruff*
4	Satifield	Izie, Miss		Exp. Jul. 1925	Let 1929	
4	Stewart	Osker		Exp Aug 1925	Let Aug 1965	
4	Stewart	Pearl, Mrs.		Exp Aug 1925	Let Aug 14, 1954 Let Aug 1965	
4	Stewart	Veston, Master		Exp Jul 1925		
4	Satifield	Margrus / Margree Mrs.		Let Dec 1926	Died Nov 23, 1963	*Margie M. Satterfield, 1881-1963, bur HBC*
4	Scott	William		Let? Sep 1926		
4	Shipman	Margarett		Exp 1928	Let Nov 1931	
4	Scott	Claud			Let Jul 1942	
4	Scott	Clyde			Let Jul 1942	
4	Scott	Henry			Let Sep 17, 1949	
4	Scott	Myrtie, Miss		Exp Jul 1934	Let Sep 20, 1947	
4	Sewell	Birtha		Exp Aug 1936	Death Nov 11, 1995	*Bertha (Haygood) Sewell, 1912-1995, bur HBC*
4	Smith	Frank		Exp Aug 1929		
4	Stewart	Inez		Exp Aug 1929	Let Apr 1946	
4	Stewart	Frank		Exp Aug 1930	Let Aug 18, 1951	
4	Stewart	Alene		Exp Aug 1930	Let Aug 24, 1937	
4	Sparks	Duffie		Exp Aug 1930	Let Jan 17, 1931	
4	Sparks	Edna	Earl	Exp Aug 1930	Let Jan 17, 1931	
4	Sewell	Stonewall		Exp Aug 1930		
4	Sewell	Winnie	Lee	Exp Aug 1930	Let Apr 20, 1974	
4	Shoemake	Roy		Exp Aug 1930	Death Oct 1, 1982	*William Roy Shoemake, 1912-1982, bur HBC*
4	Staffice	Maud		Exp Aug 1930		
4	Shoemake	Lois		Exp Aug 1931	Death 1960	
4	Stewart	Nellie	Ruth	Exp Aug 1932	Let Nov 1951	
4	Strong			Let Jul 1935		*Thurlow Strong? Or Thurloe Strawn, baptized July 1935 per notes of Cleo H. Milford*
4	Strong	Lois		Exp 1937		*Lois Strawn*
4	Smith	Edith, Mrs.		Exp Aug 1, 1938	Death May 1998	
4	Smith	George		Exp Aug 1, 1938	Death Sep 6, 1974	
4	Scott	Auburine, Mrs.		Let Sep 1938	Let Jul 1942	

	Last name	First name	Middle name	How/when received, *other info*	How/when dismissed, *other info*	*Remarks; items not listed in church roll (maiden name; spouse; birth-death; buried at HBC; etc.)*
4	Sewell	Hoyt		Let Oct 16, 1937		*James Hoyt Sewell, 1914-1995, bur HBC*
4	Turner	J.	J.	Exp Aug 25, 1923	Let Aug 1929	
4	Turner	Lee		Exp Aug 25, 1923	Let Aug 1929	
4	Turner	Buster		Exp Aug 25, 1923	Dead	
4	Tompson	Harvey		Exp Aug 25, 1923		
4	Tompson	George		Exp Aug 25, 1923	Let Jun 1924	
4	Turner	Ruby, Miss		Exp Aug 1925	Let 1929	
4	Turner	Hubert		Exp Aug 1930		
4	Turner	Egbert		Exp Aug 1930		
4	Turner	Billy		Exp Jul 1934		
4	Turner	Blanche		Let Oct 1934	Death 1935	
4	Turner	J.	J.	Let Apr 1937	Death Mar 1962	*John Julius Turner, 1883-1962, bur HBC*
4	Turner	Sister		Let Apr 1937	Death Jun 26, 1968	*Louisa Dora Wyatt Turner, 1882-1968, bur HBC*
4	Turner	Paul		Let Apr 1937	Let Sep 1953	
4	Turner	Leo	Bolling	Let Apr 1937	Death Aug 1988	*Leo (Turner) Boling, 1907-1988, bur HBC*
4	Turner	Ozell		Exp 1937	Let Sep 1944	
4	Turner	Estee		Exp Aug 1, 1938	Death Oct 10, 1989	*Thomas Estee Turner, 1915-1989*
4	Wyatt	Clinton		Exp Aug 25, 1923	Let Sep 18, 1948	*Samuel Clinton, abt 1907-1974*
4	White	Mertie, Miss		Exp Aug 25, 1923	Death Sep 21, 1983	
4	White	Miss Naoma		Exp Aug 25, 1923	Death May 22, 1983	
4	Wilkie	Amos	F.	Exp Aug 25, 1923	Death Jan 19, 1972 Deacon	*Amos Felton Wilkie, 1908-1972, bur HBC*
4	Wilkie	G.	Cleveland	Exp Aug 25, 1923	Death Oct 30, 1997	
4	Wilkie	Myrtle	Mills	Exp Aug 25, 1923	Let Aug 14, 1976	
4	Williams	Pawlene	Satterfield	Exp Aug 25, 1923		
4	Wofford	Jenett		Exp Aug 25, 1923		
4	Wallace	Clide		Exp Aug 25, 1923	Let Jun 29, 1925	
4	Wyatt	Miss Annie		Exp Aug 25, 1923		
4	Wyatt	Mastor Dewey		Exp Jul 31, 1924	Death	*Mathel Dewey Wyatt, 1909-1995, bur HBC*
4	White	L.		Exp Jul 31, 1924	Let Apr 19, 1959	
4	White	O.		Exp Jul 31, 1924	Deceased Aug 11, 1985	*Oscar Oliver White, 1899-1985*
4	White	Miss Ruby		Exp Jul 31, 1924		

	Last name	First name	Middle name	How/when received, *other info*	How/when dismissed, *other info*	*Remarks; items not listed in church roll (maiden name; spouse; birth-death; buried at HBC; etc.)*
4	Wilkie	Clide		Exp Jul 31, 1924	Death Dec 14, 1979	
4	West	Ilar, Miss	Burns	Exp Jul 31, 1924	Death Oct 21, 1995	*Ila (West) Burns, 1906-1995*
4	Wyatt	Grady, Mastor		Exp Jul 1925	Death Aug 9, 1977	
4	Wyatt	Lealer, MIss		Exp Aug 1926	Death Nov 1, 1997	
4	Willson	Cairline, Mrs.		Let 1926		
4	Wyatt	Linton		Exp 1928	Death Nov 20, 2008 Deacon	*Arthur Linton Wyatt, 1914-2008, bur HBC*
4	Wyatt	Frank		Exp 1928	Death Jun 23,1984, Deacon	*Frank Wyatt, 1914-1984, bur HBC*
4	White	Brooke		Exp Jul 1934	Let Jul 20, 1968	
4	Wyatt	Toy		Exp Jul 1934	Death Oct 5, 1996	
4	White	Walton		Exp Jul 1934	Death Mar 21, 1990	
4	Wyatt	Samuel		Exp Jul 1934	Death Jul 14, 2004	
4	Wyatt	Jewell	Bannister	Exp Jul 1934	Let Oct 17, 1998	*Jewell (Wyatt) Bannister*
4	Wyatt	Wallace		Exp Jul 1937	Let Jun 1947	
4	Wilkie	Aaron		Exp Jul 1937		*s/o George W and Rosetta Wilkie*
4	Wyatt	Hazel		Exp Aug 1, 1938	Let Dec 17, 1949	*Hazel (Wyatt) Hasty*
4	Wilkie	Pearl	Gilleland	Exp Aug 1925	Let Oct 1935	*Pearl (Wilkie) Gilleland, 1912-2007, bur HBC*
4	Wilkie	Ollie	Bagwell	Exp Aug 1925	Let Oct 1935	*Ollie (Wilkie) Bagwell*
4	Woodall	Earnin		Exp Aug 1925		
4	West	J.	L.	Exp Aug 1925	Death Jan 7, 1973	
4	West	Walker			Death Nov 5, 2004	
4	West	Joseph			Let May 20, 1944	
4	West	Herbert			Let Sep 1952	
4	Wilkie	Josephine	Parker	Exp 1928	Death	*Josephine (Wilkie) Parker, 1917-2008, bur HBC*
4	Wilkie	L.	B.	Exp Aug 1930	Death Mar 24, 1988	*William Lee Broughton Wilkie, 1912-1988, bur HBC*
4	Wyatt	Broughton		Exp Aug 1930	Let Mar 1939	
4	West	Imogene	Cannon	Exp Aug 1930	Death Mar 2003	*Jewell Imogene (West) Cannon, 1916-2003, bur HBC*
4	Wilkie	Ola		Let Aug 1930	Death	
4	Williams	Myrtie	May	Exp Aug 1930	Let Apr 1942	
4	Warren	Hubert		Exp Aug 1930	Let 1933	

	Last name	First name	Middle name	How/when received, *other info*	How/when dismissed, *other info*	*Remarks; items not listed in church roll (maiden name; spouse; birth-death; buried at HBC; etc.)*
4	Wilkie	Grace		Exp Aug 1931	*Let Nov 17, 1953/6	*Grace Wilkie Blalock, 1925-2011*
4	Wilkie	Maggie	Lee	Exp Aug 1931	Death	
4	Wilkie	Weldon		Exp Aug 1932	Let Jul 19, 1967	*s/o George W and Rosetta Wilkie*
4	Wilkie	H.	G. Jr.	Exp Aug 1932	Let May 14, 1940	
4	Wilkie	Kate, Mrs.		Exp Aug 1932		
4	White	J.	L. Jr.			
4	Wilkie	H	S.	Exp Aug 1933	Hiram, death 1973	*Hiram Samuel Wilkie, 1921-1973, bur HBC*
4	Wilkie	Glenn	W.	Exp Jul 1934		*s/o George W and Rosetta Wilkie*
4	Wilkie	Alvin		Exp Jul 1934	Death?	
4	Wilkie	Clara		Exp Jul 1934	Let	
4	West	Frank		Exp Jul 1934	Death Apr 7, 2004	
4	Wilkie	Hazel, Miss		Exp Jul 1936	Let 1950	*1923-2013, d/o James Harrison and Ruby Wilkie, bur HBC: Hazel W. Cook*
4	White	H.	T.	Exp Jul 1936	Let Sep 1957	
4	White	Myrm, Miss		Exp Aug 1936		*Miriam White (Cleo Milford, personal notes)*
4	Wilkie	Wynelle		Exp Aug 1, 1938	Let Mar 19, 1966	
4	Wilkie	Annie, Miss		Let Sep 18, 1937	Death Feb 6, 1968	*Annie Francis Wilkie, 1905-1968, bur HBC*
4	Wilkie	Clair		Let Sep 18, 1937	Death Sep 14, 1963	*Clara J. Wilkie, 1907-1963, bur HBC*
4	Wilkie	Spencer, Mr.		Let Sep 18, 1937	Death Jul 2, 1974	*George Spencer Wilkie, 1913-1974*
4	Wilkie	Mrs. Faciel			Death Oct 9, 2000	*Fayceil (Turner) Wilkie, 1915-2000*
4	Woodall	Nellie	Grace McBrayer	Exp Aug 1938		
4	Wilkie	J.	T.	Exp Aug 1938		
4	White	E.	C. Charles	Exp Aug 1938	Let May 19, 1956	
4	Yother	Miss Hazel		Exp Aug 1925		
*4	Cannon	Carry			Let Aug 20, 1938	
*4	Dempsey	Margaret			Let Jun 20, 1931	
*4	Dobson	Cary			Let Jun 16, 1932	
*4	Floyd	Nancy	Doss		Let Jul 15, 1927	
*4	Fowler	Ella				

	Last name	First name	Middle name	How/when received, *other info*	How/when dismissed, *other info*	*Remarks; items not listed in church roll (maiden name; spouse; birth-death; buried at HBC; etc.)*
*4	Fowler	Julia			Let Sep 20, 1930	
*4	Green	Olie			Let Sep 15, 1928	
*4	Heggood	May		Let Sep 16, 1933	Let Jun 18, 1938	
*4	Heggood	Viola		Exp Sep 18, 1926	Let Dec 17, 1927	
*4	Hester	Oma, Mrs.			Let Oct 18, 1930	
*4	Holcomb	Corra			Let Jun 1924	
*4	Holcomb	Henry			Let Jun 1924	
*4	Holcomb	Hommer	H		Let Jun 20, 1931	
*4	Holcomb	Mary			Let Jun 20, 1925	
*4	Ingram	Beatrice			Let Sep 17, 1932	*d/o Lee and Pearl Ingram*
*4	Mason	Mattie	Lou		Let Sep 20, 1930	
*4	McGuire	Dorah			Let Jul 23, 1923	
*4	Richards	Dorrah			Let Sep 19, 1931	
*4	Richards	Ethalee		Let Jul 16, 1938		
*4	Richards	Gus			Let Sep 19, 1931	
*4	Roper	Fulton			Let Jul 15, 1934	
*4	Roper	Irene			Let Aug 21, 1937	
*4	Roper	Ruby			Let Jul 15, 1934	
*4	Satifield	J.	A.		Let Sep 15, 1928	
*4	Satifield	J. A., Mrs.			Let Sep 15, 1928	
*4	Satterfield	Luster			Let Oct 28, 1928	
*4	Smith	Glen		Let Jan 15, 1938	Let Aug 18, 1945	
*4	Sparks	Ella	Mary Sary		Let Jan 17, 1931	
*4	Wallace	C.	W.			
*4	Wallace	Daughter			Let Sep 15, 1934	*d/o Lee and Eula Wallace, Marie or Kate?*
*4	White	Joe			Let Oct 24, 1923	
*4	Wigginton	Carter		Let Aug 20, 1927		
*4	Wigginton	Clara		Let Aug 20, 1927		
*4	Wilkie	Theodocia		Let Sep 19, 1931		
*4	Williams	Azey	Fife	Let Sep 16, 1927		*w/o George A Williams*
*4	Williams	Azzie			Let Jun 17, 1933	
*4	Williams	Martha		Let Sep 19, 1931		
*4	Wilson	Martha			Let Sep 18, 1937	
*4	Wilson	Tom		Exp Sep 19, 1931		

Chapter 8: 1939-1950, Minutes and Membership Roll, Book Five

- Community
    - Ending of the Great Depression
    - World War II
    - Recovery

- Religion/Baptists
    - 1939 - deacon ordination
    - 1950 - deacon ordination

- Occupations
    - Farmers
    - Sawmillers
    - Few public jobs

- Transportation
    - Cars
    - Few wagons

- Cemetery
    - 1949, ½ acre lot purchased

The 1930s are remembered as one of the most difficult decades for this community. Many neighbors lived with the saying: "We really didn't realize how poor we were because no one else had anything either." Typical homes had no electricity, no running water, and no indoor bathrooms.

The New Deal (1933–1938) and the economic turnaround of the 1940s had an impact on the people of HBC to an extent, perhaps Gaddis (1993) reminds us best with these phrases: "Make do or do without; and good old times versus hard old times." Gaddis wrote columns titled "Cherokee in Days Gone By" and was mindful of local agricultural occupations: "Before Pres. Roosevelt, work days were often 12 hours per day, 6 days per week. Then began the 8 hour day, and minimum wage of $.75 per hour; however, the work rules have never applied to farmers." Even though the New Deal gradually brought electricity to rural areas through the Rural Electrification Administration of 1935, one could surmise now that it was slow to reach rural northeast Cherokee County, Georgia. Found in the diary of Cleo Heard Milford, on July 18, 1941, HBC members could state: "We have electric lights at church now."

Not until the United States entered World War II (1941) did the depression finally recede, but that came with a much different toll. The U.S. officially entered World War II on December 8, 1941 following an attack on Pearl Harbor, Hawaii. About a year before, in October 1940, President Roosevelt had signed into law the first peacetime selective service draft in U.S. history because of rising world conflicts. Multiple registrations held between November 1940 and October 1946 signed up more than 50 million American men aged 18–45 for the draft. Once again, the hearts and minds of the churchgoers at Hightower were drastically impacted by turmoil far away. The list of veterans of HBC found in the appendix of this book names at least twenty-seven soldiers of this war, likely there were many more. At least one, Thad Hester, Jr. (1924-1943) paid the ultimate sacrifice of his life for our freedom. To Mr. Hester and all the others, may HBC and its people never forget! In another diary entry of Cleo Milford, she wrote: "Sunday, March 17, 1946 – Sunday school, Special Program for Service Boys, Dr. Tribble preached." Shown below in uniform are:

John Heard with his younger sister Mattie.

E. W. Cochran
Photo courtesy of Regina Groover

From information found in the U.S. Census, 1940, Cherokee County, Cross Roads District, the occupation of workers remained predominantly farmers. Approximately 1,280 persons were enumerated with 271 homes. 247 were farmers followed by 21 saw millers, 12 persons worked jobs for public roads and 11 each worked for the cotton mill or were merchants. Miss Myrtie Wilkie was one of the merchants and Nettle Lee Lovelace was one of the five public school teachers. Other interesting jobs included three livestock dealers, three tufters at a bed spread house, three auto mechanics, four blacksmiths, two brick masons and one café waitress. One nearby road listed was the Creighton Mine Road. As shown right, many farmers

Emmett Cochran & Peggy
Photo courtesy Brenda Curtis

continued to use mule and plow as did Mr. Emmett Cochran. It appears that Mr. Cochran was getting double duty from the mule by allowing his first born, Peggy, to ride while he worked the field.

Trains and cars were common place, and even airline travel was available. However, the wagon still was useful. In 2014, Frankie Green Edge remarked: "I remember we went to church one time in the wagon, it had rained and rained and the roads were so bad. We lived down yonder on Julius Bridge Road, on the farm and that road, it was impassable and Papa Turner hitched up the mule and wagon and we all went to revival and they was several that had come in the wagons because the roads were so bad." (Frankie Green was baptized at HBC in July 1942.) Pictured right is the bridge over the Etowah River near Ball Ground. The bridge at the Etowah on Yellow Creek Road very near HBC was of similar construction. Dirt roads and one-lane bridges continued to be common into the 1950s.

On the HBC property, burials continued in the sections in front of the church building (sections one – three) but became more common in section four directly behind or south of the church. An additional half acre of property south of the church was acquired from Mrs. Georgia Lovelace, with the deed recorded in 1949 (see appendix, deed 4).

A few additional notable items from the minutes include: "February 19, 1949: On a motion and second, church decides to pay the pastor $25.00 per month," possibly the first decision to establish a salary for the pastor; "April 1949, voted to improve heating system and cover (new roof) the church; June 1949, disposed of coal heaters and pipe." The membership milestone of reaching six hundred members occurred in 1942. HBC records recorded a membership of 607.

Minutes, 1939-1950

Each entry:

Date; Minister(s) who preached on that date.

Any of the items that had activity on that given date.

Items:

1. Invited visiting brethren to seats with us
2. Called for the fellowship of the church
3. Called for reference
4. Opened the door of the church for the reception of members
5. General Business

Moderator, Church Clerk

Jan. 14, 1939, Rev. P. W. Tribble. 5. By motion to select four deacons for the church. By motion the following was selected, R. E. West, Joel Heard, Lee Hester, Elisha Cochran. By motion and second, appointed E. G. Rich, R. M. Cantrell, H. G. Wilkie, Newt Green, to invite other churches to the ordination. Rev. P. W. Tribble, Mod., Linton Wyatt, C.C.

Feb. 17, 1939, Ordination. Hightower Baptist Church met according to previous appointment for the purpose of ordaining deacons. Morning service preaching by Rev. J. S. Cochran. Dismission an hour for refreshments. The church met for the ordination service. The deacons named as following: Joel Heard, Elisha Cochran, Lee Hester, Emory West. Presbytery met and organized by electing Rev. P. W. Tribble, Mod., J. A. Sewell, clerk, R. M. Cantrell to present the candidates to the presbytery, T. M. Sewell to question the mouthpiece, H. G. McGinis to examine the candidates, A. A. Roper lead the ordination prayer, Fulton Roper to give the charge to the candidates, E. G. Rich to present the Bible, and to present the candidates back to the church. After preaching by Rev. P. W. Tribble, proceeded with the ordination, by prayer, and the laying on of hands and the hand of fellowship. Members that composed the presbytery, Ministers: R. A. Roper, A. A. Roper, J. W. Miller, R. F. Roper, T. M. Sewell, H. G. McGinis, E. G. Rich, J. S. Cochran, P. W. Tribble. Deacons: A. W. Sewell, J. J. Tims, S. S. Wyatt, R. M. Cantrell, H. G. Wilkie, Joe Wilkie, E. K. Padgett, J. A. Sewell. Rev. P. W. Tribble, Mod., J. A. Sewell, Clerk.

Feb. 18, 1939, Rev. P. W. Tribble. 5. Granted letters to Bro. Herman Hendrix and Sister Daphnamay Gazaway, also selected Bro. H. G. Wilkie as preacher committeeman. Rev. P. W. Tribble, Mod., Linton Wyatt, C.C.

Mar. 18, 1939, Rev. P. W. Tribble. 5. Granted Bro. Broughton Wyatt a letter of dismission. Rev. P. W. Tribble, Mod., Linton Wyatt, C.C.

Apr. 15, 1939, Rev. P. W. Tribble. 4. Received by letter Bro. Grady Heard and wife Minnie Heard. 5. By motion and second, deacons of Hightower Church received a check for one hundred dollars, will[ed] to the church by Sister Kansas S. Cochran. By motion and second, the fund will go for repairs of church. Rev. P. W. Tribble, Mod., Linton Wyatt, C.C.

May 20, 1939, Rev. E. G. Rich. 5. Collected $6.05 for paying expenses. E. G. Rich, Ass't. Mod., Linton Wyatt, C.C.

Jun. 17, 1939, Rev. P. W. Tribble. 5. Elected messengers to union meeting. Appointed were: S. S. Wyatt, H. G. Wilkie, R. B. Buffington, R. E. West, Shelvy Cornet. Allso to the Hightower Association to meet with Beaver Ruin Baptist Church on Wednesday and Thursday after the first Sunday in August. The following messengers are: J. A. Heard, E. F. Cochran, Newt Green, Joe Wyatt, Amos Wilkie, Monroe McPherson. Rev. P. W. Tribble, Mod., Linton Wyatt, C.C.

Jul. 1939, Rev. P. W. Tribble. 3. Received acknowledgements from a brother for drunkness, the church bearing with him. Dr. P. W. Tribble, Mod., Linton Wyatt, C.C.

Aug. 19, 1939, Rev. E. G. Rich. 4. Received by letter Bro. Taylor Whidby. 5. Granted the following letters: Sister Travis Lathem, Della [Dobson] Scott. By motion went into the election of a pastor for the coming year, by motion suspended regular order of election and by motion elected by acclimation Rev. P. W. Tribble as pastor of Hightower Church for the coming year. Rev. E. G. Rich, Mod. P., Linton Wyatt, C.C.

Sep. 16, 1939, Rev. P. W. Tribble. 5. Granted letters of dismission to the following: Bro. Clarence Padgett, Bro. R. T. Nuckols, Sister Lily Mills Chumbler, Sister Geneva Cronan Hobgood. The church received a letter of confession from Bro. Buren Little and he desires prayers of this church. Rev. P. W. Tribble, Mod., Linton Wyatt, C.C.

Alto, Ga, Sept. 13, 1939

Dear Hightower Church and Members

As I lie here in the Sanatorium with a pain in my heart, looking back over the past, we realize the happenings, both the likes and dislikes and as long as everything is to our likes, we don't stop to think, how Christ suffered on the Cross that we might live again, but when we get down hearted, and our friends turn us down, we then go to God for help. After listening to one of Bro. Roper's many sermons in which he shed tears and unnamable sweat drops, in a revival with which me and several other sinners was saved. Very sorry to say that I strayed off from his teachings, thought I could fool the Lord, but he showed me I couldn't do that. Let's not get in our minds that we can get by Him, for that all seeing eye is watching us. Just about a year ago, I began to think the way I was living, so I thought I would see if I could get in touch with the Lord, so after weeks of praying and shedding of many tears, and that I feel this morning that God has forgiven me, and I thank him for that, and for saving and keeping me through these days of trouble.

We have organized here among the patients a Sunday school class in which I try to attend each Sunday and each week we have Bible class or prayer services which we can learn more about God's work. I ask the praying people of this church to remember me and my loved ones in your prayer. Buren Little.

Buren Little, 1912-1956, Buried at HBC.

Oct. 14, 1939, P. W. Tribble [No business under any item]. Rev. P. W. Tribble, Mod., Linton Wyatt, C.C.

Nov. 18, 1939, Rev. P. W. Tribble. 5. Collected $5.36 for coal. Also collected $12.95 for the unfortunate. By motion and second selected Bro. Monroe McPherson to teach a ten nite singing school. Rev. P. W. Tribble, Mod., Linton Wyatt, C.C.

Dec. 16, 1939, Rev. P. W. Tribble. 5. Granted Sister Dimple O'Bryan Greene letter of dismission. Rev. P. W. Tribble, Mod., Linton Wyatt, C.C.

Jan. 20, 1940, Rev. P. W. Tribble. 3. Received acknowledgements of a brother for intoxication. Rev. P. W. Tribble, Mod., Linton Wyatt, C.C.

Feb. 1940, Rev. P. W. Tribble. 3. Deferred action until next conference against two brethren. 5. Granted Sister Lizzie Wyatt a letter of dismission. Rev. P. W. Tribble, Mod., Linton Wyatt, C.C.

Mar. 16, 1940, Rev. P. W. Tribble. Taken up the charge against two brethren and withdrew fellowship from same. Rev. P. W. Tribble, Mod., Linton Wyatt, C.C.

Apr. 20, 1940, Rev. P. W. Tribble. 4. Received by letter Bro. O. F. Hitt and Sister Mae Hitt. Also received acknowledgement of a brother. Rev. P. W. Tribble, Mod., Linton Wyatt, C.C.

May 18, 1940, Rev. P. W. Tribble. 4. Received by letter Bro. Robert Lee Milford. 5. Granted Bro. H. G. Wilkie [Jr.] a letter of dismission. Collected $34.41 for lighting the church. Rev. P. W. Tribble, Mod., Linton Wyatt, C.C.

Jun. 15, 1940, Rev. P. W. Tribble. 4. Received by letter Bro. Clamor Roland and Sister Bessie Roland. 5. Granted letter of dismission to Bro. Gene Holcombe and Sister Myrtle Blackwell. Elected messengers to union meeting, appointed Linton Wyatt, Clemor Roland, R. E. West, Oss White, J. A. Heard. Also to the Hightower Association to meet with Cross Roads Baptist Church, the messengers are: H. G. Wilkie, W. M. Cowart, Monroe McPherson, R. B. Buffington, S. S. Wyatt, Newt Green. Rev. P. W. Tribble, Mod., Linton Wyatt, C.C.

Jul. 1940, Rev. E. G. Rich. [*No business under any item*]. Rev. E. G. Rich, Mod., Linton Wyatt, C.C.

From Cleo Heard Milford Diary: July 28, 1940: baptizing at Hightower. 33, 19 girls and 14 boys were baptized.

Aug. 17, 1940, Rev. E. G. Rich. 4. Received by letter Bro. Ira Cowart. 5. Granted Sister Eula Chadwick a letter of dismission. Went into the election of a pastor for the coming year. By motion suspended regular order of election and elected by acclimation Rev. P. W. Tribble as pastor of Hightower Church for the coming year. E. G. Rich, Mod., Linton Wyatt, C.C.

Sep. 1940, Rev. P. W. Tribble. 4. Received by letter Bro. Eugene White, Sister Floy White and Sister Ruth Ray. 5. Granted Bro. Elijah Dobson, Sister Lucinda Dobson and Bro. Egbert Roper letters of dismission.

Oct. 19, 1940, Rev. P. W. Tribble. 3. Received acknowledgements from two brethren. 5. Granted Sister Ruth Little and Sister Sadie Bruce letters of dismission. Rev. P. W. Tribble, Mod., Linton Wyatt, C.C.

Nov. 16, 1940, Rev. P. W. Tribble. 5. By motion and second decided to improve the heating system of the church with the deacons in charge. Rev. P. W. Tribble, Mod., Linton Wyatt, C.C.

Dec. 14, 1940, Rev. P. W. Tribble. 5. By motion and second, decided to make a contribution for Mrs. R. A. Roper, for Bro. R. A. Roper's monument. Collected $10.74. Rev. P. W. Tribble, Mod., Linton Wyatt, C.C.

Jan. 18, 1941, Rev. P. W. Tribble. [*No business under any item*]. Rev. P. W. Tribble, Mod., Linton Wyatt, C.C.

Feb. 15, 1941, Rev. P. W. Tribble. 3. Received acknowledgments from a brother. Rev. P. W. Tribble, Mod., Linton Wyatt, C.C.

Mar. 22, 1941, Rev. P. W. Tribble. [*No business under any item*]. Rev. P. W. Tribble, Mod., Linton Wyatt, C.C.

Apr. 19, 1941, Rev. P. W. Tribble. 5. By motion and second changed time of meeting from cnt. time to est. time. Rev. P. W. Tribble, Mod., Linton Wyatt, C.C.

May 17, 1941, Rev. P. W. Tribble. 5. Granted Bro. Cecil Smith a letter of dismission. Rev. P. W. Tribble, Mod., Linton Wyatt, C.C.

Jun. 14, 1941, Rev. P. W. Tribble. 5. By motion and second appointed messengers to the union meeting, Bro. Ira Cowart, Cleveland Wilkie, J. A. Heard, Linton Wyatt, H. G. Wilkie. Also to the Hightower Association, the messengers are: S. S. Wyatt, Elisha Cochran, Frank Wyatt, Emmett Cochran and Dewey Wyatt. Collected $1.50 for minutes. Rev. P. W. Tribble, Mod., Linton Wyatt, C.C.

July 18, 1941, Fri. "We have electric lights at church now," from Cleo Heard Milford diary.

Jul. 19, 1941, Rev. P. W. Tribble. 4. Received by letter Sister Ora Mae and Willene Rich, Brother Roy Balls, Sister Zular Balls, Sister Francis Turner. 5. Granted Sister Clara Perry a letter of dismission, and wrote Mr. John Wade letter.

Aug. 16, 1941, Bro. J. M. Richards. 5. Suspended the regular order of election and elected by acclimation, Rev. P. W. Tribble as pastor of Hightower Church for the coming year. By motion and second the church liberated Bro. Jim Richards to preach. Bro. H. G. Wilkie, Ast. Mod., Linton Wyatt, C.C.

Sep. 20, 1941, Rev. P. W. Tribble. 5. Granted Sister Atney Thompson a letter of dismission. Rev. P. W. Tribble, Mod., Linton Wyatt, C.C.

Oct. 18, 1941, Rev. P. W. Tribble. 3. Received acknowledgements from a brother. 4. Received by letter Mr. and Mrs. Earl Hill, also received letters of Mr. and Mrs. Roy Ball. 5. Dismissed by letter Bro. Frank Page. Collected $5.36 for lights exp. Rev. P. W. Tribble, Mod., Linton Wyatt, C.C.

Nov. 15, 1941, Rev. P. W. Tribble. [*No business under any item*]. Rev. P. W. Tribble, Mod., Linton Wyatt, C.C.

[*Cleo Heard Milford diary*: "Dec. 7, 1941: We went to Sunday school then to visit the Milford's. They had just got the news that Japan had bombed Hawaii, Honolulu and several islands. We went to Lathemtown Sunday nite and listened to war news with Mother and Dad. Dec. 8: Pres. Roosevelt in his 12:30 address declared we are in a state of war with Japan since yesterday. Congress pass the bill in short order. Dec. 9: Japanese planes near coast of California last nite…"]

Dec. 20, 1941, Rev. P. W. Tribble. 5. Collected $4.18 for lights, donated $35.95 in produce and $1.15 in cash to orphan home. Contributed to our pastor in 1941 - $140.53. Money in treasure $245.76. Rev. P. W. Tribble, Mod., Linton Wyatt, C.C.

Jan. 17, 1942, Rev. P. W. Tribble. 5. Collected $11.00 on new benches. Total in treasure $255.76, last month expenses for lights $1.00. P. W. Tribble, Mod., Linton Wyatt, C.C.

Feb. 14, 1942, Rev. P. W. Tribble. 5. Granted Sister Seary Jane Watkins letter of dismission. Collected last month $46.98. Last month exp. $1.00. Money in treasure $301.68. Rev. P. W. Tribble, Mod., Linton Wyatt, C.C.

Mar. 14, 1942, Rev. P. W. Tribble. 5. For the last month, collected $36.47, exp. $1.00, money in treas. $337.05. Rev. P. W. Tribble, Mod., Linton Wyatt, C.C.

Apr. 1942, Rev. P. W. Tribble. 3. Withdrew fellowship from a sister. 5 Granted Sister Myrtie May Williams letter of dismission. Collected last month $19.49, exp. for tools, lights $5.92, money in treasure $350.72.

May 14, 1942, Rev. W. H. Flannagan, appointed Bro. Flannagan, moderator 5. Collected last month $143. Expenses on benches $587.50, paid $473, indebtness of the church $114.50. Total Exp. $588.50. Rev. W. H. Flanagan, Mod., Linton Wyatt, C.C.

Jun. 20, 1942, Rev. P. W. Tribble. 5. Appointed messengers to the union meeting, names: S. S. Wyatt, R. B. Buffington, J. M. McPherson, Robert Milford, Linton Wyatt and Frank Wyatt, alternate. Also messengers to the association, names: R. E. West, Oscar Hitt, Elisha Cochran, O. F. Stewart, Lee Hester and H. G. Wilkie, alternate. Collected last month $11.04, Exp. $1.00 for lights. Rev. P. W. Tribble, Mod., Linton Wyatt, C.C.

Jul. 1942, Rev. P. W. Tribble. [*No business under any item*]. Rev. P. W. Tribble, Mod., Linton Wyatt, C. C.

Aug. 15, 1942, J. M. Richards, appointed Bro. Richards moderator. 5. Granted Bro. Amos Williams, Bro. Hoyt Williams and Sister Bertha Watkins letter of dismission. Suspended regular order of election and elected by acclamation Bro. P. W. Tribble for pastor of Hightower for the coming year. Collected $6.81, exp. $1.00. J. M. Richards, Mod., Linton Wyatt, C.C.

Sep. 19, 1942, Rev. P. W. Tribble. 5. Granted Bro. Grady Hendrix and wife [Vera] letters of dismission. Collected last month $29.13, exp. last month $11.14, money in treasury $24.18, indebtness $67.43. Rev. P. W. Tribble, Linton Wyatt, C.C.

Oct. 17, 1942, Rev. P. W. Tribble. 5. Granted Sister Maud and Essie Cannon and Bro. Robert Roper a letter of dismission. Collected last month $69.01, exp. $46.00. Donated to preacher last month $54.90. Rev. P. W. Tribble, Mod., Linton Wyatt, C.C.

Nov. 14. 1942, Rev. P. W. Tribble. 5. Collected last month $9.36. Expenses last month $37.43. Money in treasure 16.38. Rev. P. W. Tribble, Mod., Linton Wyatt, C.C.

Dec. 19, 1942, Rev. P. W. Tribble. 5. Collected Dec. $13.66. Exp 1.00, money in treasure 29.04.

Jan. 16, 1943, Rev. P. W. Tribble. 5. By motion and second pay for heater. Exp. last month for heater $12.50, light 1.00, total $13.50. Collected $17.07, money in treas. $32.60. Rev. P. W. Tribble, Mod., Linton Wyatt, C.C.

Feb. 20, 1943, Rev. P. W. Tribble. 5. Collected last month $8.54. Exp. $1.00. Money in treasurer $41.14. Rev. P. W. Tribble, Mod., Linton Wyatt, C.C.

Mar. 1943, Rev. P. W. Tribble. 5. Exp. last month $1.00. Money in treasure $40.14. Rev. P. W. Tribble, Mod., Linton Wyatt, C.C.

Apr. 1943, Rev. P. W. Tribble. 5. Collected last month $13.64. Exp. $1.00. Money in treasure $52.78. Rev. P. W. Tribble, Mod., Linton Wyatt, C.C.

May 15, 1943, Rev. P. W. Tribble. 5. Granted Bro. Grady Smith letter of dismission. Motion and second stated that would build a tool house. Collected last month $24.36, Exp. $16.26. Money in treasure $60.88. Rev. P. W. Tribble, Mod., Linton Wyatt, C.C.

Jun. 1943, 5. Appointed messengers to the association: W. M. Cowart, R. B. Buffington, Monroe McPherson, Linton Wyatt, Oscar Stewart, Garland Green. Also messengers to the union meeting: H. G. Wilkie, Robert Milford,

H. G. Wyatt, Lee Hester, Elisha Cochran and Frank Wyatt. By motion and second, appointed H. G. Wilkie, J. A. Heard and S. S. Wyatt committee to keep cemetery clean. Collected last month $21.38, Exp. $1.00 for lights, $.60 for Lord's Supper, Total $1.60, money in treas. $80.66. Rev. P. W. Tribble, Mod., Linton Wyatt, C.C.

Jul. 1943, Rev. P. W. Tribble. 5. Collected last month $164.94. Donated to pastor $50.00. Brother Cochran $65.00. Exp. for building supplies $13.93, total Exp. $128.93. Money in treas $116.73. Rev. P. W. Tribble, Mod., Linton Wyatt, C.C.

Aug. 1943, Rev. J. W. Richards. 3. Received acknowledgements of a brother. 5. No collections last month. Exp. $1.00, money in treasure $115.73. Suspended regular order of election and elected by acclamation Bro. P. W. Tribble for pastor of Hightower Church for the coming year. Rev. J. W. Richards, Ass't Mod., Linton Wyatt, C.C.

Sep. 1943, Rev. P. W. Tribble. 5. Granted Sister Fannie [*Lovelace*] Wilson and Sister Ada [*Hester*] Coker letters of dismission. No collection. Exp. $1.00, money in treas. $114.73. Rev. P. W. Tribble, Mod., Linton Wyatt, C.C.

Oct. 1943, Rev. P. W. Tribble. 5. Granted Sister Nettie [*White*] Aarons letter of dismission. Collected last month $21.10, exp. for supply house $50.00, for lights $1.00, Total exp. $51.00. Money in treas. $84.83. Rev. P. W. Tribble, Mod., Linton Wyatt, C.C.

Nov. 20, 1943, Rev. P. W. Tribble. 5. Donated the State Mission $15.00, also Orphan home $15.00. Collected last month $25.05. Expense for lights 1.00, gifts 30.00. Total expense $31.00. Money in treasurer $78.88. Collected for pastor last month $52.20. Total collections for pastor $98.20. Rev. P. W. Tribble, Mod., Linton Wyatt, C.C.

Dec. 1943, Rev. P. W. Tribble. 5. Collected last mon. $11.68, expenses $1.00, money in treas. $89.56, collected last month for pastor $45.00. Total collection for pastor $147.20. Rev. P. W. Tribble, Mod., Linton Wyatt, C.C.

Jan. 1944, Rev. P. W. Tribble. 5. By motion and second, hired a housekeeper. Collected last month $13.00, expense last month 1.00, money in treasurer 101.56. Rev. P. W. Tribble, Mod., Linton Wyatt, C.C.

Feb. 18, 1944, 5. Expenses $2.00: $1.00 for lights, $1.00 for housekeeper. Money in treasurer $99.56. Rev. P. W. Tribble, Mod., Linton Wyatt, C.C.

Mar. 18, 1944, Rev. McConnely [*likely W. Nelson McConnell*]. 5. Collected $11.90. Expense 1.50. Money in treasurer $109.96. Rev. McConnely, Ass't Mod., Linton Wyatt, C.C.

Apr. 15. 1944, Rev. P. W. Tribble. 3. Withdrew fellowship from a sister for fornication. 5. Granted a letter of dismission to Sister Corrine Hitt. Collected last month $51.48, Expense last month $1.50. Money in treas. $159.94. Rev. P. W. Tribble, Mod., Linton Wyatt, C.C.

May 20, 1944, Rev. P. W. Tribble. 4. Received by letter Bro. Elias Rich and Sister Eva Rich. 5. Granted Sister Blanche Swims, Sister Helen Wilkie, Sister Clara Mae Cochran and Bro. Joseph West letters of dismission. Collected last mo. $41.39, exp. lights 1.00, housekeeping .50, Baptist Hospital 20.00. Money in treas. 159.94, Total in treas. this month: 179.83. Rev. P. W. Tribble, Mod., Linton Wyatt, C.C.

Jun. 17, 1944, Rev. P. W. Tribble. 5. Appointed messengers to the association: R. B. Buffington, Amos Wilkie, Kile Bailey, Buck Pruitt, Cleveland Wilkie, W. M. Cowart. Also messengers to the union meeting: J. A. Heard, Linton Wyatt, Elisha Cochran, Lee Hester, S. S. Wyatt, Robert Milford. Also granted Sister Ruby [*Hester*] Milford a letter of dismission. Collected last mo. $22.61, Exp. lights 1.00, housekeeping .50, Lord's Supper supplies 2.43, Piano tuning 4.00. Total exp. 7.93. 194.51 + 14.68, Money in treas. $209.19. Rev. P. W. Tribble, Mod., Linton Wyatt, C.C.

Jul. 15, 1944, Rev. P. W. Tribble. 4. Received under the watchcare of the church Mrs. Lawrence Johnson, received by letter Lester Edwards. 5. Dismissed by letter Zed Padgett. Letters to the union meeting and association adopted. Collected last month $201.45. Donated to pastor $100.00, to Bro. Cochran $100.00. Lights 1.00, housekeeping .50. Total exp. $201.50. Money in treas. 209.14. Rev. P. W. Tribble, Mod., Linton Wyatt, C.C.

Aug. 19, 1944, Rev. Oscar Hitt, followed by J. W. Richards. 5. Suspended the regular order of election by ballots, and elected by acclimation, Rev. P. W. Tribble, for our pastor for the coming year. Granted Bro. Oscar Hitt, Mae Hitt, Eleanor Hitt, David Hitt, Doyle Wilkie, Ruby Dobson and Irene Majors, letters of dismission. Appointed R. B. Stewart housekeeper and pay the clerk $25.00 per year. No collection. Exp. lights $1.00, housekeeper .50, for pastor 35.00. Paid to churches destroyed by storm 25.00 (x 2) total exp. $51.50. Money in treas. $157.64. H. G. Wilkie, Ass't Mod., Linton Wyatt, C.C.

Sep. 16, 1944, Rev. P. W. Tribble. 5. Granted Sister Gemima [*Jemima*] Jane Hogan, Evalee Richards, Juanita Edwards, Ozell Blackwell, Celeste Holt, Moline Holt, Bro. Jim Richards, Rudolph Hogan and Lester Edwards letters of dismission. Exp. 1.00 for lights, .50 for housekeeping, Total exp. $1.50, col. for pastor $27.00, Treasure $183.44. Rev. P. W. Tribble, Mod., Linton Wyatt, C.C.

Oct. 1944, Rev. P. W. Tribble. 5. Granted Paralee Hendrix letter of dismission. Collected last month $25.11. Exp. last month $1.50. Money in treas. $207.05. Rev. P. W. Tribble, Mod., Linton Wyatt, C.C.

Nov. 18, 1944, Rev. P. W. Tribble. 5. Granted Mary Ellen McPherson letter of dismission. Collected for Mrs. R. M. Cantrell $23.65, for Mr. A. L. Blair $21.36. Exp. for light $1.00, housekeeper .50 total exp. $1.50. Money in treas. $207.05. Rev. P. W. Tribble, Mod., Linton Wyatt, C.C.

"Nov. 19, 1944. After Sunday School and preaching, Haygood boy and Gravley girl got married." Cleo Heard Milford diary.

Dec. 16, 1944, Rev. P. W. Tribble. 5. Motion and second to pay for stove pipe $2.20, window light [*pane*] $1.50, housekeeper $1.25, clerk $25.00. By motion and second, send GA Baptist Hospital $100.00, Orphans home $12.50, collected for hospital $67.68. Total Exp. $142.45. Money Treas. $130.78. Rev. P. W. Tribble, Mod., Linton Wyatt, C.C.

Jan. 20, 1945, Rev. P. W. Tribble. 5. Pay insurance on church house and furnishings. Collected last month $18.22. Exp. last month $18.16 for Bible fund, 1.25 housekeeper, lights 1.00, total exp $20.41. Money in treas. $128.53. Rev. P. W. Tribble, Mod., Linton Wyatt, C.C.

Feb. 17, 1945, Rev. P. W. Tribble. 5. Collected $9.57. Exp. for lights 1.00, insurance 79.00, housekeeper 1.25, Total Exp. $81.25. Money in treas. $56.85. Rev. P. W. Tribble, Mod., Linton Wyatt, C.C.

Mar. 17, 1945, Rev. P. W. Tribble. 5. Granted Olaine Roland a letter of dismission. Exp. for lights $1.00, housekeeper 1.25, Total exp. $2.25. Money in treas. $54.60. Rev. P. W. Tribble, Mod., Linton Wyatt, C.C.

Apr. 14, 1945, Rev. Gus Smith [*A. F. Smith*]. Appointed Rev. Sam Cochran, moderator. 5. Collected last month $28.22. Exp. for lights $1.00, for housekeeper 1.25. Total exp. 2.25. Money in treas. $79.57. Rev. Sam Cochran, Ass't Mod., Linton Wyatt, C.C.

May 19, 1945, Rev. P. W. Tribble. 5. Collected $66.49. Exp. For GA Baptist Hospital $66.45, lights 1.00, housekeeping 1.25, total exp. $68.70. Money in treasurer $77.36. Rev. P. W. Tribble, Mod., Linton Wyatt, C.C.

Jun. 16, 1945, Rev. P. W. Tribble. 5. Appointed messengers to the union meeting: Frank Stewart, Emmett Cochran, Linton Wyatt, Monroe McPherson, Garland Green, and Dewey Wyatt. Also messengers to the association: J. A. Heard, R. B. Buffington, H. G. Wilkie, S. S. Wyatt, Robert Milford, E. F. Cochran, and appointed a committee to place churches: Mr. and Mrs. Robert Milford, Mr. and Mrs. Cleveland Wilkie, and Mr. and Mrs. H. G. Wyatt. Exp. last month: Lights $1.00, housekeeper 1.25, Total exp. 2.25. Collected last month $23.71, Money in treasurer $97.82. Rev. P. W. Tribble, Mod., Linton Wyatt, C.C.

Jul. 14, 1945, Rev. P. W. Tribble. 4. Received by letter: Montaree Smith, Edna Smith, Louise Smith, Billie Smith. 5. Collected last month $186.71 for preacher, $2.50 for minutes. Paid Bro. Cochran $100.00, Bro. Tribble $86.71. Exp. for church $1.00 lights, 1.25 housekeeper. Total exp. $188.96. Money in treas. $95.57. Rev. P. W. Tribble, Mod., Linton Wyatt, C.C.

Aug. 18, 1945, Bro. H. V. Henderson. 5. Granted Bro. Garston Dobson and Eston Dobson and Glen Smith letters of dismission. Suspended regular order of electing by ballot and elected by acclamation Bro. P. W. Tribble for pastor of Hightower Church for the coming year. Collected last month for pastor $17.00, collected for church $16.58. Exp. last month: $1.00 for lights, 1.25 for housekeeper, 7.47 for plates. Total Exp. $9.72. Money in Treas. 102.43. H. G. Wilkie, Ass't Mod., Linton Wyatt, C.C.

Sep. 15, 1945, Rev. P. W. Tribble 4. Received by letter, Bro. Joe Wilkie, a deacon. 5. Exp. last mo. lights $1.00. No collection. Money in treasurer. $101.43. Rev. P. W. Tribble, Mod., Linton Wyatt, C.C.

Oct. 20, 1945, Rev. P. W. Tribble. 5. Collected for pastor $44.00, for church 38.00, total collection 82.00. Exp. 1.00, money in treas. $138.43. Rev. P. W. Tribble, Mod., Linton Wyatt, C.C.

Nov. 17, 1945, Rev. P. W. Tribble. 5. Collected last month $41.00. Expenses lights 1.00, home mission 20.00, foreign mission 20.00, total exp. $41.00. Money in treas. $138.43. Rev. P. W. Tribble, Mod., Linton Wyatt, C.C.

Dec. 1945, Rev. P. W. Tribble. 5. Granted Velvie Tatum a letter of dismission. No collection. Exp. for coal $4.45, lights 1.00, Total exp. 5.45. Money in treas. $132.98. Rev. P. W. Tribble, Mod., Linton Wyatt, C.C.

Jan. 19, 1946, Rev. P. W. Tribble. 5. Collected last month $48.59, Children's home 15.00, foreign missions 15.00, Bibles for foreign nation 18.50, lights 1.00. Exp. last mo. $49.50. Money in treas. $132.07. Rev. P. W. Tribble, Mod., Linton Wyatt, C.C.

Feb. 16, 1946, Rev. P. W. Tribble. 5. Collected last month $28.87, Exp. lights $1.00, housekeeping 1.25, Total exp. $2.25. Money in treasurer $158.69. Rev. P. W. Tribble, Mod., Linton Wyatt, C.C.

Mar. 16, 1946, Rev. P. W. Tribble. 5. Granted Dorothy Watkins a letter of dismission. By motion and second, draw from the treasurery $25.00 for clerk. Collected last month $48.74. Exp. last month: lights 1.00, housekeeper 1.25, children's home $10.00, foreign missions 10.00, clerk 25.00. Total $47.25. Money in treas. $160.18. Rev. P. W. Tribble, Mod., Linton Wyatt, C.C.

Apr. 20, 1946, Rev. P. W. Tribble. 3. Received acknowledgements from a brother. 5. Granted letters of dismission to Bro. Jess Thompson, Roy and Inez Baker. Motion and second to draw money from the treasurer to pay for song books. Collected last month $30.87. Exp. song books $15.00, housekeeper 1.50, lights 1.00. Total exp. 17.50. Money in treas. 173.55. Rev. P. W. Tribble, Mod., Linton Wyatt, C.C.

May 18, 1946, Rev. P. W. Tribble. 5. Collected last month $80.31. Expenses: GA B. Hospital $70.00, lights 1.00, housekeeping 1.25, Total exp. $72.25. Money in treas. $181.61. Rev. P. W. Tribble, Mod., Linton Wyatt, C.C.

Jun. 15, 1946, Rev. John Lummus. 4. Received by letter Sister Evalee Richards and under watchcare of the church Etta Grace Richards. 5. Appointed the following messengers to the union meeting: E. W. Cochran, H. G. Wilkie, Frank Wyatt, R. B. Buffington, Lee Hester, Robert Milford. To the association: J. A. Heard, Emmett Cochran, Newt Green, Kile Bailey, Roy Ball and Dewey Wyatt. Appointed a committee to keep cemetery clean: Emmett Cochran, Lee Hester and Joe Wilkie. Collected $20.39. Exp. housekeeper $1.25, lights 1.00, total expenses: $2.25. Money in treas. $199.75. J. J. Terry, Mod., Linton Wyatt, C.C.

Jul. 20, 1946 Bro. [John] Lummus ["In the beginning, God..." from Cleo Heard Milford diary]. By acclamation, appointed Bro. Lummus as moderator. 4. Received by letter Mr. J. W. [Jim] Richards, Cecil Wheeler, Bertha Voyles, Joyce Wyatt. Received under the watch care of the church, Mr. [Sylvester] and Mrs. [Mary] Lowe, Argie Wheeler, James Wilkie. 5. Collected $67.00 for Montaree Smith. Collected $2.90 for minutes. Total collection $68.90. (collected $231.00 for preacher). Expenses last month for lights $1.00, housekeeper 6.25, for Montaree Smith 67.00, Bro. Lummus 100.00, Bro. Cochran 100.00, Fred Carnes 25.00. Total expenses $299.25. Money in treas. $197.50. Bro. John Lummus, Ass't Mod., Linton Wyatt, C.C.

[*Cleo Heard Milford diary*: "July 27, 1946, at revival, a very touching service honoring service boys, about 30 there...Robert and Henry Milford, Fred Carnes and wife sang 'Camping in Cannan'..."]

Aug. 17, 1946, Bro. Jim Richards. 5. Elected by ballot Bro. John Lummus for our pastor for the coming year.

Granted Clemar Roland, Bessie Roland, Francis Roland, Mae Swims, Troy Jones and Raymond Jones letters of dismision. Collected for Bro. Tribble $123.00. Exp. lights $1.00, housekeeper 1.25, Bro. Tribble 123.00. Total exp. $125.25. Money in Treas. $195.25. Bro. J. W. Richards, Ass't Mod., Linton Wyatt, C.C.

"Aug. 17, 1946: Toy and Lura (Wyatt) went with us (Robert and Cleo), we met Dewey and Ruby (Cowart) at Oak Grove (Baptist Church) to see John Lummus. Dewey Cowarts brought John back. Aug. 18: John accepted church and preached to us after Sunday school. Sept. 13, 1946: Spent day at New Harmony Baptist Church, John Lummus ordained to preach." Cleo Heard Milford diary

Sep. 14, 1946, Rev. John Lummus. 5. Granted Claudie Mae Watkins a letter of dismission. Collected last month $12.00 for Dr.Tribble. Collected last month: $38.22. Total collection $72.72. Expenses lights 1.00, housekeeper 1.25, Foreign missions and Orphans home $22.50, Total expenses $24.25. Money in treas. $243.22.

Oct. 19, 1946, Rev. Fulton Roper. 5. Granted Minnie Heard letter of dismission. By motion and second the statement of a sister be rescinded. Collected $72.00 for Preacher Tribble. Exp. lights $1.00, housekeeper 1.25, coal 26.50, total expenses $100.75. Money in Treas. 214.47.

Nov. 15, 1946, Bro. Sewell. 3. Preferred a charge against a sister for fornication taken up the charge and withdrew fellowship from same. 4. Received by letter Holland, Bonnie, Winnie and Nettie Pearson. 5. Collected for Waleska Road Baptist Church $28.26. Exp. $28.26, Lights 1.00, housekeeper, 1.25, Total Exp. $30.51. Money in treas. $212.22. Rev. John Lummus, Mod., Linton Wyatt, C.C.

Dec. 14, 1946, Bro. Lummus. 5. Collected last month $31.17. Exp. last month: lights $1.00, housekeeper 1.25, Money in treas. $241.14. Rev. John Lummus, Mod., Linton Wyatt, C.C.

Jan. 18, 1947, Bro. Lummus. 5. Collected last month $12.55. Exp. last month: $4.95 heater repair, lights 1.00, housekeeper 1.25, Money in treas. $246.49. Rev. John Lummus, Mod., Linton Wyatt, C.C.

Feb. 15, 1947, Bro. Lummus. 5. Collected $49.05 for the pastor. Exp. $1.00 lights, 1.25 housekeeping, money in treasurey: $244.24. Rev. John Lummus, Mod., Linton Wyatt, C.C.

Mar. 15, 1947, Rev. John Lummus. 5. By motion and second to buy a portion of land from Mrs. R. E. Lovelace for $100.00 and by motion and second, draw from the treasurey for pastor $51.00. Collected last month: $41.53 for treas. Received of J. W. Richards $5.00 for land, Received of Tim Green $33.65. Total Collection $80.18. Exp., 1.00 for lights, 1.25 for housekeeping, pastor $51.00. Money in treas. $271.17. Rev. Johnnie Lummus Mod., Linton Wyatt, C.C.

Apr. 19, 1947, Rev. Fulton Roper. 5. Granted letters of dismission to Jim Richards, Evalee Richards, Etta Grace Richards, W. N. Dobson and Martha Bryant. Collected last month $32.79. Exp. Children's home and missions: $33.65, lights 1.00, housekeeper 1.25. Money in treas. $268.06. Rev. John Lummus, Mod., Linton Wyatt, C.C.

May 17, 1947, Rev. John Lummus. 5. By motion and second, pay the clerk $25.00. Collected $57.40. Exp. for clerk $25.00, lights 1.00, housekeeper 1.25, Money in treas. $298.21. Rev. John Lummus, Mod., Linton Wyatt, C.C.

Jun. 14, 1947, Rev. John Lummus. 5. Granted letters of dismission to: Wallace Wyatt, Mr. & Mrs. W. H. [William Harvey and Annie] Rainey, Denver Rainey, Margaret Dobson and Inez Dobson. Appointed the following messengers to the union meeting: S. S. Wyatt, H. G. Wilkie, Linton Wyatt, Dewey Cowart, Robert Milford and R. E. West. Also to the association: Robert Milford, Hallmon Roper, Dewey Wyatt, E. F. Cochran, J. A. Heard, R. E. West. Collected last month: $28.21. Exp: lights 1.00, housekeeper 1.25. Rev. John Lummus, Mod., Linton Wyatt, C.C.

Jul. 19, 1947, Rev. J. H. Boling, elected Preacher Boling moderator. 4. Received under the watchcare: Inez Hester, Mildred Cowart, Ruby Drummond, Mr. & Mrs.[*Saphronie "Fronie" Fife*] Hansel Cowart and Lurie Wilkie. 5. Granted letters of dismission to: John Wade, Eddie Jones, Clara Jones, Eugene Cochran and Mrs. H. L Scoggins. Collected last month $262.06. Expenses: Preacher Boling $100.00, Preacher Lummus 100.00, lights 1.00, housekeeper 1.25. Total exp: $202.25. Money in Treas. $383.98. Rev. J. H. Boling Ass't. Mod., Linton Wyatt, C.C.

Aug. 16, 1947, after a song by the choir, opened conference, elected H. G. Wilkie, Mod. 5. Suspended the regular order of election by ballot and elected by acclimation Rev. John Lummus for pastor of Hightower Church for the coming year. Collected for pastor $51.24, for cemetery cleaning $5.00. Exp. lights $1.00, housekeeper 1.25, Total expenses 2.25. Total collection $56.24. Money in treas. $437.97. Rev. John Lummus, Mod., Linton Wyatt, C.C.

Sep. 20, 1947, Rev. Fulton Roper. 4. Received by letter Frankie Wilkie. 5. Granted Tom Little, Georgia Haygood, Taylor and Mertie [*Myrtie Mae Scott*] Whidby letters of dismission and received the letter of Mrs. Weldon Wilkie. Collected last month $57.05 for church, for pastor 10.00, total collection $67.05. Expenses last month for pastor $51.24, light 1.00, housekeeper 1.25, total exp. 53.49. Money in treas. $441.53. Rev. John Lummus, Mod., Linton Wyatt, C.C.

Oct. 18, 1947, Rev. John Lummus. 5. Collected last month for pastor $135.50. Exp. last month $145.50 for pastor, lights 1.00, housekeeper 1.25. Total exp. $147.75. Money in treas. $429.28. Rev. John Lummus, Mod., Linton Wyatt, C.C.

Nov. 15, 1947, Rev. Thompson. 5. Granted Charles Watkins a letter of dismission and received the letter of Inez Hester. Collected last month $71.16. Expenses last month $48.66 to children's home, $22.50 to foreign missions, 1.00 for lights, 1.25 for housekeeper, for minutes .81. Total expenses $74.22. Money in treas. $427.03. Rev. John Lummus, Mod., Linton Wyatt, C.C.

Dec. 1947, Bro. Haygood followed by Rev. John Lummus. 3. Preferred charges against three sisters of the church for departing the faith, and withdrew fellowship. 5. Collected last month $21.43. Collected for pastor 5.00. Total collection $26.43. Exp. for pastor 5.00, lights 1.00, housekeeper 1.25, total exp. $7.25. Money in treas. $446.21. Rev. John Lummus, Mod., Linton Wyatt, C.C.

Jan. 17, 1948, Bro. Boles. 3. Preferred a charge against a brother and withdrew fellowship from him. 5. Granted Mr. and Mrs. S. S. [*Sylvester and Mary Ann*] Lowe and Margaret Green letters of dismission. Collected $17.66. Exp. lights 1.00, housekeeper 1.25, total exp. $2.25. Money in treas. $461.62. Rev. John Lummus, Mod., Linton Wyatt, C.C.

Feb. 14, 1948, Rev. John Lummus. 5. By motion and second, draw from the treasurer $50.00 to give to Harold Drummond. Collected last month $22.00. Exp. $50.00 for Harold, lights 1.00, housekeeper 1.25, song books 10.80, total exp. $63.05. Money in treas. $419.57. Rev. John Lummus, Mod., Linton Wyatt, C.C.

Mar. 20, 1948, Bro. Lummus. 5. Granted J. A. [*James A. "Marshall"*] McPherson and wife Leacie letters of dismission. Motion and second to renew insurance on the church. Collected last month $33.32. Exp. insurance, 109.60; 1.25 housekeeping; lights 1.00; money in treas. $341.04. Rev. John Lummus, Mod., Linton Wyatt, C.C.

Apr. 17, 1948, Bro. Lummus. 5. Granted G. W. Dobson letter of dismission. Motion and second to close the deal on land and appointed a committee to look after it. Names of committee Lee Hester and R. E. West. Collection last month $36.02. Exp. lights 1.00, housekeeper 1.25, total exp. $2.25. Money in treas. $374.71. Rev. John Lummus, Mod., Linton Wyatt, C.C.

May 15, 1948, Rev. P. W. Tribble. 3. Preferred a charge against a sister for departing from the faith, withdrew fellowship from her. 5. Granted Mrs. Collman Allen a letter of dismission. Collected last month $114.33. Exp. last month: children's home $18.75, foreign mission 18.75, lights 1.00, housekeeper 1.25, total exp. $39.75. Money in treas. $449.29. Rev. John Lummus, Mod., Linton Wyatt, C.C.

Jun. 19, 1948, Bro. John Lummus. 5. Granted Bro. Herbert Bruce and Sister Inez Nix letters of dismission. Suspended regular order of messenger by ballot and elected by appointment, messengers to union meeting: Elbert Cochran, Lee Hester, H. G. Wilkie, Halmon Roper, R. B. Buffington and B. V. Gilleland. Collected last month for Clyde Scott $88.92. Exp. last month: lights $1.00, housekeeper 1.25, for Clyde $88.92, total exp. $91.17. Money in treas. $447.02. John Lummus, Mod., Linton Wyatt, C.C.

Jul. 17, 1948, P. W. Tribble. 5. Granted Lewis Dobson a letter of dismission. By motion and second, draw from treas. $17.50 for piano tuning. Collected last month for preacher(s): $265.05. Exp. 1.00, 1.25, Dr. Tribble 132.53, Bro. Lummus $132.52. Total expenses 266.30. Money in treas. 444.77. Bro. John Lummus, Mod.

Aug. 1948, Elected Bro. H. G. Wilkie, Moderator. 5. Suspended regular order of election and elected Rev. John Lummus, pastor for another year. By motion and second, appointed messengers to the association: R. B. Buffington, Dewey Cowart, Robt. Milford, Lee Hester, Dewey Wyatt, and Grady Hester alternate. Granted Mr. and Mrs. Clinton Dobson letters of dismission. Motion and second to pay housekeeper $5.00 above regular payment, also pay clerk $25.00. Collected last month for pastor $98.85. Expenses: pastor $98.85, lights 1.00, housekeeper 6.25, clerk 25.00, piano tuning $17.50, total exp. $148.60. Money in treas. $411.52. H. G. Wilkie, Ass't Mod., Linton Wyatt, C.C.

Sep. 18, 1948, Rev. John Lummus. 5. Granted S. C. [*Samuel Clinton*] Wyatt, Turk Milford, J. S. Bowers and Mae Stiles letters of dismission. By motion and second, that a cemetery fund be set up, and draw $5.00 from treasurer for this fund. Collection last month for pastor $5.00, Robert Milford $72.79, children's home $15.00, foreign missions $15.00, cemetery fund $18.50, Total collection $126.29. Expenses: pastor 5.00, Robert 72.79, foreign mission 15.00, children's home 15.00, light 1.00, housekeeper 1.25, cemetery fund 23.50. Church treas. $404.27.

Oct. 16, 1948, Rev. John Lummus. 4. Received by letter Roy Glen Hester. 5. Collected $76.00 for Edd Mills. Collected for pastor $4.00. Total collection $80.00. Exp. $76.00, housekeeper 1.25, lights 1.00, total Exp. $78.25. Money in church treas. $402.02. Cemetery fund $24.50. Rev. John Lummus, Mod., Linton Wyatt, C.C.

Nov. 20, 1948, Rev. John Lummus. 5. By motion and second renew the coal supply. Collection $38.98. Exp: lights 1.00, housekeeper 1.25, total exp. $2.25. Money in treas. $438.75. Cemetery fund $24.50. Rev. John Lummus, Mod., Linton Wyatt, C.C.

Dec. 1948, Rev. John Lummus. 5. Pay for coal: $75.68. Collection $24.04. Exp. coal $75.68, lights 1.00, housekeeper 1.25, total exp. $77.93. Money in treas. $384.86, cemetery fund $24.50. Rev. John Lummus, Mod., Linton Wyatt, C.C

Jan. 1949, Rev. P. W. Tribble, elected Rev. P. W. Tribble, Mod. 5. Collected last month $39.20. Collected for preacher $2.00. Exp. last month: light 1.00, housekeeper 1.25, preacher 2.00, Total exp. 4.25. Total collection $41.20, money in treas. $421.81, Total Collection for pastor $109.85. Rev. P. W. Tribble, Ass't Mod., Linton Wyatt, C.C.

Feb. 19, 1949, Rev. John Lummus. 5. By motion and second, draw from the treasurer $100 for the pastor, and pay him $25.00 per month. Collected last month $78.70 for treas. collected for pastor $8.00. Total collection $86.70. Exp. housekeeper 1.25, lights 1.00, pastor 108.00. Total exp. $110.25. Money in Treas. $398.26, cemetery fund $24.50. Rev. John Lummus, Mod., Linton Wyatt, C.C.

Mar. 1949, Bro. Smith. 5. Granted J. M. [*James Monroe*] McPherson letter of dismission. Collected last month $78.23 for church, $5.00 cemetery fund, total collection: $83.23. Exp. lights 1.00, housekeeper 1.25, pastor 25.00, children's home 37.50, total exp. 64.75. Money in treas. $411.74, cemetery fund $29.50. Rev. John Lummus, Mod., Linton Wyatt, C.C.

Apr. 16, 1949, Rev. John Lummus. 5. Granted Lussie Fowler letter of dismission. By motion and second draw money from the treasurer for song books. By motion and second, moved to improve heating system and cover church. Appointed Robert Milford, Dewey Cowart, Grady Hester, Linton Wyatt, Emmett Cochran, Oss White and Buren Little as the fund committee. Collected last month $38.24. Exp. last month: lights $1.00, housekeeper 1.25, pastor 25.00, song books 14.60, Total exp. $41.85. Money in treas. $408.13, cemetery fund, $29.50. Rev. John Lummus, Mod., Linton Wyatt, C.C.

May 1949, Rev. John Lummus. 5. Motion and second draw from treas. $2.40 for wine. Motion and second appointed Oss White, Robt. Milford, Roy Ball building committee, with Oss White chairman. Collected last month: $70.45. Expenses last month: pastor 25.00, lights 1.00, housekeeper 1.25, total exp. $27.25. Money in treas. $451.33, cemetery fund 29.50, building fund $1118.35. Rev. John Lummus, Mod., Robt. Milford, Ass't. C.C.

Jun. 1949, Rev. John Lummus. 5. By motion and second, the building committee dispose of the coal, heaters, and pipe. By motion and second appointed messengers to the union meeting as follows: Grady Hester, Dewey Cowart, Amos Wilkie, Linton Wyatt, R. B. Buffington, H. G. Wilkie. Collected last month $43.34. Expenses: lights $1.00, floor paint 159.70, roofing and labor 325.00, wine 2.40, pastor 25.00, total exp. $513.10. Money in treas. $466.27, cemetery fund $30.50, building fund 849.65. Rev. John Lummus, Mod., Linton Wyatt, C.C.

Jul. 1949, Bro. Boles, elected Bro. Boles moderator. 5. Collected last month: $35.75 for treas., 215.94 for preachers, total collection: $251.69. Expenses last month: Bro. Lummus $132.47, Bro. Boles 107.47, lights 1.00, heating system 832.00, Total exp. $1072.94. Money in treas. $475.02, cemetery fund 30.50, building fund $17.75. Rev. Boles, Mod., Linton Wyatt, C.C.

Aug. 1949, Bro. Gus Smith. 3. Withdrew fellowship from a brother for departing the faith. 5. Elected Bro. John Lummus pastor for the coming year. Elected Dewey Cowart, clerk for the coming year and Robert Milford, assistant clerk. Elected Hallman Roper, Walter Roper, E. W. Cochran for cemetery committee. Also delegates for the association as follows: Lee Hester, E. F. Cochran, J. C. Pruitt, E. W. Cochran, H. G. Wilkie and Shelby Cornett. Collected last month $35.00. Exp: lights $1.00, underpinning 400.00, total exp. $401.00. Money in treas. $431.20. -55.00 = $406.20. Rev. Gus Smith, Ass't. Mod., Robt. Milford Ass't. Clerk.

Sep. 17, 1949, Bro. Sewell. 4. Received by letter Peggie Cochran and Bobbie Samples. 5. Appointed L. B. Wilkie to look after heat and church, ass't. Robert Milford. Paid Mrs. R. E. Lovelace $100.00 for land. Granted Mr. and Mrs. Henry Scott and Hazel [*Pearson*] Chadwick letters of dismission. Motion and second draw from cemetery fund to pay on land. Motion and second to pay clerk $25.00. Collection last month $48.44, paid for coal by Roy Ball $60.00. Expenses: land $100.00, pastor $25.00, clerk $25.00, light $1.00, bench and chair nobs $20.40, Total exp. $171.40. Money in treas. $435.96. Rev. John Lummus, Mod., Dewey Cowart, C.C.

Oct. 16, 1949, Rev. John Lummus. 5. Motion and second to have Bro. [*Paul*] Carmichael run Sunday school revival. Collection last month $58.09. Expenses: pastor $25.00, housekeeper 5.00, light 1.00, brooms 3.75, window paines 2.55, Total expenses $37.30. Money in treas. $455.75. Rev. John Lummus, Mod., Dewey Cowart, C.C.

Nov. 19, 1949, Rev. John Lummus. 5. Granted Faye Pearson Parris, Ruby Cantrell and Jessie Lee Scott letters of dismission. Collection: $39.75. Expenses: pastor $25.00, housekeeper 5.00, light bill for one year 12.00, Total expense: $42.00. Money in treasure $478.50. Rev. John Lummus, Mod., Dewey Cowart, C.C.

Dec. 17, 1949, Rev. John Lummus. 5. Granted Raul and Grace Green and Hazel Wyatt Hasty letters of dismission. Collection last month 22.25. Expenses: pastor $25.00, housekeeper 5.00, gas 28.00, total expense $58.00. Money in treasure $417.75. Rev. John Lummus, Mod., Dewey Cowart, C.C.

Jan. 14, 1950, Rev. John Lummus. 5. Motion and second for church to pay for song books, $15.60. Collection $23.00. Expenses: pastor $25.00, housekeeper 5.00, total expenses $45.60. Money in treas. 430.15. Rev. John Lummus, Mod., Dewey Cowart, C.C.

Feb. 18, 1950, Rev. John Lummus. 5. Granted Charles Green letter of dismission. By motion and second that Brother Carmichael teach Bible lessons. Collection last month for Winnell Cowart $57.91, for orphan's home $30.00, cemetery fund $5.00, Total collection $87.91. Expenses: pastor $25.00, housekeeper 5.00, Winnell Cowart $57.91, Orphan's home 30.00. Total expense $117.91. Money in treas. $400.15. Rev. John Lummus, Mod., Dewey Cowart, C.C.

Mar. 18, 1950, Rev. John Lummus. 5. By motion and second took the morning offering to use for cemetery funds. Collection $63.30. Expenses: work for cemetery 32.50, pastor 25.00, housekeeper 5.00, Total expense $62.50. Money in treasure $430.90. Rev. John Lummus, Mod., Dewey Cowart, C.C.

1939-1950 Book 5 Membership Roll

* Information found only in minutes

	Last name	First name	Middle name	How/when received, other info	How/when dismissed, other info	Remarks, items not listed in church roll (maiden name; spouse; birth-death; buried HBC; etc
5	Andrews	Myrtie		Bap Jul 1940	Death Jan 17, 2000	
5	Andrews	Willie	Mae	Bap Jul 1940	Death Oct 14, 2008	*Willie Mae (Andrews) Smith, 1928-2008*
5	Aarons	Nettie	White	Let Jul 1940	Let Oct 1943	
5	Andrews	Henry		Bap Jul 1942	Death Jan 28, 2000	
5	Allen	Colman, Mrs.		Bap Jul 1944	Let May 1948	
5	Blackwell	Myrtle		Bap Jul 23 1939	Let Jun 15, 1940	
5	Buffington	Kate	Edwards	Bap Jul 23, 1939	Death Oct 2013	*Kate (Buffington) Edwards*
5	Bannister	Evelyn		Bap Jul 1940		
5	Blackwell	Clarence		Bap Jul 1940		
5	Blackwell	Roy		Bap Jul 1940		
5	Boling	Forrest		Bap Jul 1941	Death Apr 24, 1963	*1908-1963, bur HBC*
5	Burtz	Junior		Bap Jul 1942	Death Mar 30, 1989	
5	Burtz	James		Bap Jul 1942	Death Jan 17, 1995	
5	Bailey	Kile		Bap Jul 1942	Death Apr 1954	*Kyle/K. E. Bailey, 1901-1954, bur HBC*
5	Bailey	Carolyn		Bap Jul 1943		
5	Bailey	Kile, Mrs.		Bap Jul 1944	Death 1961	*Maude Bailey, 1901-1960, bur HBC*
5	Bailey	Lois		Bap Jul 1944	Let Oct 1953	
5	Brooks	Pauline		Bap Jul 1945		
5	Brooks	Ralph		Bap Jul 1945		
5	Balls	Calvin		Bap Jul 1945	Let Jul 17, 1965	
5	Balls	Lavern		Bap Jul 1946		
5	Bettis	Alfred, Mrs.		Bap Jul 1946		
5	Brookes	Arah		Bap Jul 1946	Let Oct 1954	
5	Biddy	Virginia		Bap Jul 1947		
5	Bailey	Glenn		Bap Jul 1947		
5	Biddy	Earl		Bap Jul 1947		
5	Boling	Martha	Jean	Bap Jul 1947	Let Feb 1957	
5	Bowers	Moline		Bap Jul 1948	Let Jun 1950	
5	Ball	Roy		*Let Jul 1941	Let Jun 19, 1965 Licensed Minister	*1910-1972, bur HBC*
5	Ball	Zula		*Let Jul 1941	Let Jun 19, 1965	*1912-2002, bur HBC*
5	Cowart	Everett		Bap Jul 23 1939	Let Jul 14, 1956	
5	Cloud	Ercell		Bap Jul 1940	Let Aug 1946	
5	Chadwick	Eula		Bap Jul 1940	Let Sep 1940	

	Last name	First name	Middle name	How/when received, other info	How/when dismissed, other info	*Remarks, items not listed in church roll (maiden name; spouse; birth-death; buried HBC; etc*
5	Cowart	Ira		Let Sep 1940	Death May 3, 2004	*Ira William Cowart, 1912-2004*
5	Cochran	Gilbert		Bap Jul 1941	Let Aug 19, 1971	
5	Cowart	Dorothy	Kate	Bap Jul 1942	Let Apr 1952	
5	Cloud	Mamie		Bap Jul 1942	Death Apr 1978	
5	Cronan	Pauline		Bap Jul 1942	Let Sep 1959	
5	Cochran	Louise	McGaha	Bap Jul 1943	Death Dec 21, 2005	*Louise (Cochran) McGaha, 1931-2005, bur HBC*
5	Coleman	Fredda	Stewart	Bap Jul 1944	Let Feb 17, 1951	*Fredda (Coleman) Stewart*
5	Cowart	Evelyn	Little	Bap Jul 1944		
5	Cloud	Mary	Emma	Bap Jul 1945	Let Aug 1956	
5	Cowart	Loyd		Bap Jul 1946		
5	Cowart	Lorraine		Bap Jul 1946	Let Jul 1962	
5	Cannon	J.	D.	Bap Jul 1947	Death Mar 19, 2009	
5	Cowart	Marvin		Bap Jul 1947	Death Mar 31, 2009	
5	Cronan	Louise		Bap Jul 1947		
5	Cowart	Mildred		Let Jul 1947		
5	Cowart	Hansel		Let Jul 1947		*Marion Hansel Cowart, 1882-1961, bur HBC*
5	Cowart	Hansel, Mrs.		Let Jul 1947	Death Dec 1953	*Saphronie "Fronie" Fife, 1876-1953, bur HBC*
5	Cowart	Donald		Bap Jul 1948	Death Oct 7, 1986	*1935-1986, bur HBC*
5	Cornett	Betty		Bap Jul 1948	Let Jun 1964	
5	Coleman	Betty	Jean	Bap Jul 1948		*Or Bobbie Jean Coleman Beach?*
5	Cannon	Mattie	Laura Price	Bap Jul 1949		*Mattie Laura (Cannon) Price*
5	Cochran	Peggy		Let Sep 17, 1949	Let Jul 15, 1967	
5	Drummond	Grace		Bap Jul 23, 1939	Jun 1956; joined Methodist	
5	Dobson	Inez		Bap Jul 23, 1939	Let Jun 1947	
5	Drummond	Leroy		Bap Jul 1940	Death Dec 20, 2012	
5	Drummond	Christine	Wilkie, Grady	Bap Jul 1942	Death Feb 14, 2015	*1928-2015, Christine (Drummond) Wilkie, bur HBC*
5	Drummond	Harold		Bap Jul 1942	Death Nov 14, 1993	
5	Drummond	Betty	Jean	Bap Jul 1943	Let Aug 1965	
5	Dixon	Jr.		Bap Jul 1945		
5	Dixon			Bap Jul 1945		
5	Dixon			Bap Jul 1945		
5	Dean	Grace		Bap Jul 1945	Death Jun 11, 1965	
5	Drummond	Ruby		Let Jul 1947	Let Sep 1953	

	Last name	First name	Middle name	How/when received, other info	How/when dismissed, other info	*Remarks, items not listed in church roll (maiden name; spouse; birth-death; buried HBC; etc*
5	Edwards	Juanita		Bap Jul 1944	Let Sep 1944	
5	Edwards	Lester		Let Jul 1944	Let Sep 1944	
5	Edwards	J.	E.	Bap Jul 1945	Let Apr 15, 1967	
5	Gilleland	Edward		Bap Jul 23, 1939	Let May 16, 1953	
5	Gilleland	Sam		Bap Jul 23, 1939	Let Mar 14, 1964	
5	Goodwin	Lula	Bell	Bap Jul 23, 1939		
5	Gilleland	Dorothy		Bap Jul 1940	Let Aug 15, 1953	*Dorothy (Gilleland) Pruitt*
5	Green	Jack		Bap Jul 1940	Death Oct 29, 1989	
5	Green	Frankie	Edge	Bap Jul 1942		*Frankie (Green) Edge*
5	Gilleland	Mary		Bap Jul 1942	Let Apr 14, 1973	*Mary (Gilleland) Watkins*
5	Green	Charles		Bap Jul 1942	Let Aug 18, 1951	
5	Greene	Tommie	D.	Bap Jul 1943	Let Aug 18, 1951	
5	Gayton	Odell		Bap Jul 1943		
5	Gayton	Pauline		Bap Jul 1943	Death Jul 1958	*?Pauline (Boling) Gayton, 1908-1958, bur HBC*
5	Gayton	Hazel		Bap Jul 1943		
5	Gilleland	Bonnell	Mulkey	Bap Jul 1944		
5	Greene	Tyrus		Bap Jul 1944		*Tirus, Death Nov 18, 2014*
5	Graham	Earnest		Bap Jul 1944		
5	Gilleland	Walton		Bap Jul 1945 Deacon		
5	Greene	Wilma		Bap Jul 1945	Let Oct 18, 1952	
5	Gaither	Ralph		Bap Jul 1946		
5	Gilleland	Roger		Bap Jul 1949	Death Feb. 10, 2015	*1933-2015*
5	Greene	Glen		Bap Jul 1947	Let Oct. 20, 1962	
5	Greene	Loyd		Bap Jul 1947	Death May 25, 2004	
5	Gilleland	Edd, Mrs.		Bap Jul 1948	Let May 1953	
5	Gilleland	Atholine	Wilkie	Bap Jul 1948		*Atholine (Gilleland) Wilkie*
5	Gilleland	Hulon		Bap Jul 1948		
5	Heard	Grady		Let Apr 15, 1939	Death Jan 1940	
5	Heard	Minnie		Let Apr 15, 1939	Let Oct 19, 1946	
5	Hendrix	Grady		Let 1939	*Let Sep 1942	
5	Hendrix	Vera		Let 1939	*Let Sep 1942 Death	
5	Hill	Velma		Bap Jul 23, 1939		
5	Hamilton	Harold		Bap Jul 23, 1939	Death Sep 13, 1998	
5	Hamilton	Cooledge		Bap Jul 23, 1939	Death Aug 1972	

	Last name	First name	Middle name	How/when received, other info	How/when dismissed, other info	*Remarks, items not listed in church roll (maiden name; spouse; birth-death; buried HBC; etc*
5	Hester	Betty		Bap Jul 23, 1939		
5	Hester	Rupert		Bap Jul 23, 1939	Death Apr 2, 1978	
5	Hester	Grady	Lee	Bap Jul 28, 1940 Deacon	Let Oct 14, 1961	
5	Hitt	Eleanor		Bap Jul 28, 1940	Let Aug 1944	
5	Hogan	Rudolph		Bap Jul 28, 1940	Let Sep 1944	
5	Hogan	Jemina	Jane	Bap Jul 28, 1940	Let Sep 1944	
5	Hester	T.	P. Jr.	Bap Jul 28, 1940	Death 1943	*Thaddeus Pickett Hester Jr., 1924-1943*
5	Haygood	Georgia		Bap Jul 28, 1940	Let 1947	
5	Hitt	David		Bap Jul 1942	Let Aug 1944	
5	Hitt	Corrine		Bap Jul 1942	Let Apr 1944	
5	Holt	Celeste		Bap Jul 1942	Let Sep 1944	
5	Hill	Wilburn		Bap Jul 1942		
5	Hester	Betty		Bap Jul 1943		*Betty (Hester) Wallace*
5	Hutsey	Lily		Bap Jul 1943		
5	Holt	Moline		Bap Jul 1943	Let Sep 1944	
5	Hester	Herbert		Bap Jul 1944		
5	Hill	Helen		Bap Jul 1944	Let Sep 17, 1955	
5	Holloway	Jack		Bap Jul 1944	Death	
5	Hitt	Oscar		Let Apr 1940	Let Aug 1944	
5	Hitt	Mae		Let Apr 1940	Let Aug 1944	
5	Hester	Jack		Bap Jul 1945	Let Dec 1962	
5	Heard	Francis		Bap Jul 1946	Let Sep 18, 1965	*Francis (Lathem) Heard*
5	Hester	Inez		*Let Jul 1947	Let Oct 14, 1961	
5	Hester	Roy	Glenn	Let Sep 1948	Let Oct 19, 1963	
5	Howell	Herman		Bap Jul 1948		
5	Jones	Lois		Bap Jul 23, 1939	Let Aug 1954	
5	Jones	Barney		Bap Jul 23, 1939		
5	Jones	Bill		Bap Jul 1940	Death Aug 1982	*William Everett Jones, 1921-1982, bur HBC*
5	Johnston	Lawrence		Bap Jul 1943	Let Sep 1955	
5	Jones	Raymond		Bap Jul 1943	Let Aug 1946	
5	Jones	Troy		Bap Jul 1943	Let Aug 1946	
5	Jones	Dimple		Bap Jul 1943		
5	Jones	Jean		Bap Jul 1943		
5	Jones	Flora		Bap Jul 1949	Let Sep 1951	
5	Little	Elmer		Bap Jul 28, 1940		
5	Little	Weldon		Bap Jul 1941	Death May 1983	*George Weldon Little, 1925-1983, bur HBC*

	Last name	First name	Middle name	How/when received, other info	How/when dismissed, other info	*Remarks, items not listed in church roll (maiden name; spouse; birth-death; buried HBC; etc*
5	Lovelace	Imogene		Bap Jul 1942	Let Jul 1960	*Georgia Imogene Lovelace, 1929-2002, m. William Bursmith, bur HBC*
5	Little	Hayward		Bap Jul 1943		
5	Lovelace	Edna		Bap Jul 1945	Let Apr 1959	*Edna Lovelace, 1932-2005, m Virgil Chandler, bur HBC*
5	Lowe	S.	S.	Let Jul 1946	Let Jan 1948	*Sylvester, 1881-1965*
5	Lowe	S., Mrs.	S.	Let Jul 1946	Let Jan 1948	*Mary, 1886-1964*
5	Milford	Robert		Let May 18, 1940 Deacon	Death Aug 31, 1988	*Robert Lee Milford, 1915-1988, bur HBC*
5	Mills	Edgar		Bap Jul 29, 1940	Let Sep 18, 1976	
5	Majors	Irene		Bap Jul 29, 1940	Let Aug 1944	
5	Mills	Alline		Bap Jul 1941		
5	Mills	Lonnie		Let Jul 1942	Death 1948	*Lonnie C Mills, 1900-1947, bur HBC*
5	Mills	J.	T.	Bap Jul 1942		
5	Mills	Lillie		Bap Jul 1942		
5	Mills	Hazel		Bap Jul 1943	Let Aug 15, 1953	
5	Mulkey	Velvie		Bap Jul 1943	Let Oct 15, 1955	
5	Mulkey	Bernice		Bap Jul 1943	Death Dec 7, 1985	*Bernice D. Mulkey, 1905-1985, bur HBC*
5	Mulkey	Jim		Bap Jul 1943	Death Jan 9, 2010	*James P. Mulkey, 1929-2010, bur HBC*
5	Mills	James		Bap Jul 1944		
5	Mills	Sue		Bap Jul 1944		
5	Mulkey	Thelma		Bap Jul 1946	Let Jul 1960	
5	Mulkey	Sallie	Wilkie	Bap Jul 1946		
5	Milford	Turk		Bap Jul 1946	Let Sep 1948	
5	Millwood	William	Lee	Bap Jul 1946		
5	Mulkey	Susie	Allen	Bap Jul 1947	Let Dec 1953	
5	Mills	Estie	Mae	Bap Jul 1947		
5	Mills	Jessie	Lee	Bap Jul 1947		
5	McCord	Walter		Bap Jul 1949	Let Oct 1950	
5	McCord	Ruby	Dean	Let Oct 1949	Let Oct 1950	
5	Mulkey	Bill			Let May 1980	
5	Mulkey	Bill, Mrs.			Death	
5	Nix	Inez		Bap Jul 1944	Let Jun 1948	
5	Pope	Bill		Bap 1940		
5	Pruitt	J.	C. Buck	Bap Jul 1943	Death Mar 15, 1996	*1912-1996*
5	Phyfe	Paul		Bap Jul 1943		

	Last name	First name	Middle name	How/when received, other info	How/when dismissed, other info	Remarks, items not listed in church roll (maiden name; spouse; birth-death; buried HBC; etc
5	Phyfe	Hazel, Mrs.		Bap Jul 1944		
5	Phyfe	Winnie		Bap Jul 1945	Let Sep 1952	
5	Pruitt	Eugene		Bap Jul 1946		
5	Pearson	Mary	Lou	Bap Jul 1948	Let May 19, 1956	
5	Pearson	Holland		Let Nov 1946	Death Jan 1968	
5	Pearson	Nettie		Let Nov 1946	Death Nov 1950	*Nettie R. Boling Pearson, 1882-1950, bur HBC*
5	Pearson	Winnie		Let Nov 1946	Let Apr 1951	
5	Pearson	Bonnie		Let Nov 1946	Let May 18, 1957	
5	Roland	Clemar		Let Jun 1940	Let Aug 1946	
5	Roland	Bessie		Let Jun 1940	Let Aug 1946	
5	Roland	Olaine		Bap Jul 28, 1940	Let Mar 1945	
5	Roland	Francis		Bap Jul 28, 1940	Let Aug 1946	
5	Roland	Rubynell		Bap Jul 1949		
5	Ray	Corinne		Bap Jul 1942	Let Jul 1963	
5	Ray	Bill		Bap Jul 1942	Death Jul 11, 1999	
5	Ray	C.	J.	Bap Jul 1942		
5	Rich	Grant		Bap Jul 1943	Death Mar 8, 1979	
5	Rich	Donzie		Bap Jul 1943	Death Jan 11, 1985	
5	Rich	Ralph		Bap Jul 1943	Death Jun 21, 1973	
5	Rich	Wilma		Bap Jul 1944		
5	Richards	Jim			Let Sep 1944	*J. W. Richards, 1889-1966, bur HBC*
5	Richards	Evalee			Let Sep 1944	*1894-1979, Myra Evalee Fletcher m Jim Richards, bur HBC*
5	Roper	Bobby		Bap Jul 1945		
5	Raye	James		Bap Jul 1945	Let Jul 15, 1967	
5	Richards	Etta	Grace	Let Jul 1946	Let Apr 1947	
5	Richards	Jim		Let Aug 1946	Let Apr 1947	*J. W. Richards, 1889-1966, bur HBC*
5	Richards	Evalee		Let Jul 1946	Let Apr 1947	
5	Raye	Loujean		Bap Jul 1947	Let Jul 1951	
5	Raye	Eugene		Bap Jul 1947		
5	Rich	Junior		Bap Jul 1947	Let May 1957	
5	Rich	Pat		Bap Jul 1947	Let Jul 1959	
5	Rich	Loyd		Bap Jul 1947	Let Jul 1, 1973	
5	Rich	Angelina		Bap Jul 1947	Let Jul 1959	
5	Roper	Walter		Let Jul 1949	Death Dec 13, 1976	*Walter Rice Roper, 1888-1976, bur HBC*

	Last name	First name	Middle name	How/when received, other info	How/when dismissed, other info	*Remarks, items not listed in church roll (maiden name; spouse; birth-death; buried HBC; etc*
5	Roper	Walter, Mrs.		Let Jul 1949	Death Jun 19, 1980	*Bertha S. Roper, 1889-1980, bur HBC*
5	Roper	Ray		Let Jul 1949	Let Sep 14, 1968	
5	Roper	Dean		Let Jul 1949	Let Oct 15, 1966	
5	Strawn	F.	M.	Bap Jul 23, 1939	Let Mar 14, 1986	
5	Smith	Fannie		Bap Jul 1940		
5	Smith	Webb, Mrs.		Bap Jul 1940	Let Dec 16, 1967	
5	Satterfield	R.	C.	Let Jul 1942	Let May 17, 1958	*1904-1971, Rufus C. bur HBC*
5	Satterfield	Pauline		Let Jul 1942	Let May 17, 1958	*1911-2001, bur HBC*
5	Stewart	R.	B.	Bap Jul 1942	Let Feb 17, 1951	
5	Satterfield	Ethel		Bap Jul 1942	Let May 17, 1958	
5	Shoemaker	Ira		Bap Jul 1943	Death 1958?	
5	Smith	Louise		Bap Jul 1944		
5	Smith	Ralph		Bap Jul 1944	Death Aug 1971	
5	Smith	Lorene		Bap Jul 1944	Let Dec 1960	
5	Smith	Hoyt		Bap Jul 1944	Death Aug 1971	
5	Stewart	Helen		Bap Jul 1945	Let Jun 1954	
5	Smith	Montaree		Let Jul 1945	Let Nov 1950	
5	Smith	Edna		Let Jul 1945	Let Nov 1950	
5	Smith	Louise		Let Jul 1945	Let Nov 1950	
5	Smith	Billie		Let Jul 1945	Let Nov 1950	
5	Swims	Mae		Bap Jul 1946	Let Aug 1946	
5	Satterfield	Joe		Bap Jul 1946	Let May 17,1958	
5	Stewart	Bobby		Bap Jul 1947	Let Jan 2007	
5	Stewart	Charles		Bap Jul 1947		
5	Satterfield	Louise		Bap Jul 1948	Let May 17, 1958	
5	Samples	Willie	Dean	Bap Jul 1949		
5	Samples	Bobbie		Let Sep 1949		
5	Thompson	Atney		Bap Jul 1940	Let Sep 21, 1941	
5	Turner	Francis		Let Jul 1941	Death Apr 1, 1968	
5	Turner	Ida		Bap Jul 1948	Death Jan 7, 1983	*1904-1983, Ida Lee Turner, bur HBC*
5	Turner	Dorothy		Bap Jul 1948		
5	Voyles	Betty		Bap Jul 1946	Let Aug 16, 1952	
5	Voyles	Bertha		Let Jul 1946	Let Aug 17, 1974	
5	West	Sarah	Perkins	Bap Jul 23, 1939	Death Nov 6, 1996	*Sarah (West) Perkins, 1925-1996, Bur HBC*
5	Watkins	Dorothy		Bap Jul 23, 1939	Let Mar 1946	
5	Wallace	Loyd		Bap Jul 23, 1939		
5	West	Paul		Bap Jul 23, 1939	Death	

	Last name	First name	Middle name	How/when received, other info	How/when dismissed, other info	Remarks, items not listed in church roll (maiden name; spouse; birth-death; buried HBC; etc
5	Wilkie	Hubert		Bap Jul 23, 1939	Let Jul 1963	*Charlie "Hubert" Wilkie, 1925-2014, bur HBC*
5	Whidby	Taylor		Let Aug 19, 1939	Let Sep 1947	
5	Wheeler	Tom		Bap Jul 1940	Let Aug 16, 1952	
5	Wilkie	Grady		Bap Jul 1940	Death Jan 10, 2008	*1926-2008, bur HBC*
5	Wilkie	Homer		Bap Jul 1940	Death Dec 1, 1995	*1927-1995, bur HBC*
5	Wilkie	Helen		Bap Jul 1940	Let May 1944	
5	Wilkie	Bell		Bap Jul 1940	Death Sep 1973	*Flora Bell (Wyatt) Wilkie 1910-1973, bur HBC*
5	Wyatt	Ida		Bap Jul 1940	Death Jul 1961	*Ida (Hester) Wyatt, 1887-1961*
5	White	Edith		Let Aug 1940	Death May 20, 1990	*Edith (Smith) White, 1904-1990*
5	Wilkie	Herman		Bap Jul 1942	Let May 16, 1970	
5	Wilkie	Parnell	Gazaway	Bap Jul 1942	Let Aug 17, 1974	*Parnell (Wilkie) Gazaway*
5	Wilkie	Kathleen	Howell	Bap Jul 1942		
5	Wilkie	Leon		Bap Jul 1942	Death Oct 1, 1996 Deacon May 1965	*1929-1996, Amos James Leon, bur HBC*
5	Watkins	Grace		Bap Jul 1942	Let Feb 19, 1955	
5	Watkins	Bertha		Bap Jul 1942	Let Aug 1942	
5	Watkins	Charles		Bap Jul 1942	Let Jun 1948 *Let Nov 15, 1947	
5	Williams	Hoyt		Bap Jul 1942	Let Aug 1942	
5	Wheeler	Bonnie	Satterfield	Bap Jul 1943	Death Oct 27, 2009	*Bonnie (Wheeler) Satterfield*
5	Wilkie	Kathryn	Mills	Bap Jul 1943	Death Oct 11, 1991	*Ollie Kathryn (Wilkie) Mills, 1927-1991, bur HBC*
5	Watkins	Claudie	Mae	Bap Jul 1943	Let Sep 14, 1946	
5	Wheeler	Jimmie		Bap Jul 1943	Death	
5	Wilkie	Mary	Francis	Bap Jul 1944	Let May 18, 1963	
5	Wilkie	Betty	June	Bap Jul 1944		
5	Wheeler	Holland		Bap Jul 1944	Let Nov 1955	
5	White	Gerald	Pete	Bap Jul 1944	Death Sep 1, 2007	*Gerald "Pete" White, 1927-2007*
5	Wyatt	Delores		Bap Jul 1945	Let Apr 1955	
5	Wilkie	Evelyn		Bap Jul 1945	Let Oct 1957	
5	Wilkie	Flondell		Bap Jul 1945		
5	Wilkie	Eugene		Bap Jul 1945	Let Jul 1963	
5	West	Robert		Bap Jul 1946	Death Mar 2003 Deacon May 1965	*1920-2003*

	Last name	First name	Middle name	How/when received, other info	How/when dismissed, other info	*Remarks, items not listed in church roll (maiden name; spouse; birth-death; buried HBC; etc*
5	West	Edward		Bap Jul 1946		
5	Wheeler	Cecil		Let Jul 1946	Death May 24, 1984	*1906-1984, bur HBC*
5	Wheeler	Cecil, Mrs.		Let Jul 1946	Death Apr 28, 1991	*Beulah Argie Wilkie Wheeler, 1909-1991, bBur HBC*
5	Wyatt	Joyce		Let Jul 1946	Let Aug 1957	
5	Wyatt	Donald		Bap Jul 1947		
5	Wilkie	Elizabeth		Bap Jul 1947		*Roberts*
5	Wilkie	Myron		Bap Jul 1947		
5	Williams	Harold		Bap Jul 1947	Licensed Minister Nov 19, 1966 Let Jul 19, 1967	
5	Wilkie	Morris		Bap Jul 1947	Death Aug 10, 1988	
5	Wilkie	James		Let Jul 1946	Let Sep 1961	
5	Wilkie	Leroy		Bap Jul 1948	Death Apr 28, 2000	*1934-2000, Elmer Leroy Wilkie, bur HBC*
5	Wilkie	Alice	Howard	Bap Jul 1948	Let Aug 1970	
5	White	Edna		Bap Jul 1948	Let Dec 16, 1950	
5	Wheeler	Regina		Bap Jul 1949	Let Dec 16, 1950	
5	Wilkie	Lurie		Let Jul 1947	Let Aug 1968	
5	Wilkie	Joe		Let Sep 1945	Deacon Death Sep 30, 1980	*Joseph Henry Wilkie, 1900-1980, bur HBC*
*5	Baker	Inez			Let Apr 20, 1946	
*5	Blackwell	Ozell			Let Sep 16, 1944	
*5	Cochran	Clara	Mae		Let May 20, 1944	
*5	Cochran	Eugene			Let Jul 19, 1947	
*5	Dobson	Garston			Let Aug 18, 1945	
*5	Dobson	Margaret			Let Jun 14, 1947	
*5	Dobson	Clinton, Mrs.			Let Aug 1948	
*5	Dobson	Ruby			Let Aug 19, 1944	
*5	Green	Charles			Let Feb 18, 1950	
*5	Hendrix	Paralee			Let Oct 1944	
*5	Hill	Earl		Let Oct 18, 1941		
*5	Hill	Ollie	Pearl Milford	Let Oct 18, 1941		
*5	Holcombe	Gene			Let Jun 15, 1940	
*5	Johnson	Lawrence, Mrs.		Let Jul 12, 1944		
*5	Jones	Clara			Let Jul 19, 1947	
*5	Lathem	Travis, Sister			Let Aug 19, 1939	*1916-2003, m Lewis Hughes*

	Last name	First name	Middle name	How/when received, other info	How/when dismissed, other info	*Remarks, items not listed in church roll (maiden name; spouse; birth-death; buried HBC; etc*
*5	McPherson	J.	A.		Let Mar 20, 1948	*James A. "Marshall" McPherson*
*5	McPherson	Leacie			Let Mar 20, 1948	*Mrs. J A McPherson*
*5	Nuckols	R.	T.		Let Sep 16, 1939	*Brother*
*5	Page	Frank			Let Oct 18, 1941	
*5	Perry	Clara			Let Jul 19, 1941	
*5	Rainey	Annie	Hughes		Let Jun 14, 1947	*Mrs. W H Rainey*
*5	Rainey	W.	H.		Let Jun 14, 1947	*William Harvey*
*5	Ray	Ruth		Let Sep 1940		
*5	Rich	Elias		Let May 20, 1944		
*5	Rich	Eva		Let May 20, 1944		
*5	Rich	Ora	Mae	Let Jul 19, 1941		
*5	Rich	Willene		Let Jul 19, 1941		
*5	Roper	Egbert			Let Sep 1940	
*5	Scoggins	H., Mrs.	L.		Let Jul 19, 1947	
*5	Scott	Jessie	Lee		Let Nov 19, 1949	
*5	Smith	Glen			Let Aug 18, 1945	
*5	Stiles	Mae			Let Sep 18, 1948	
*5	Swims	Blanche	See bk 4, Blanche Green		Let May 20, 1944	
*5	Tatum	Velvie			Let Dec 1945	
*5	Wade	John			Let Jul 19, 1941 *Let Jul 19, 1947	*Requested a copy of letter on this date*
*5	White	Eugene		Let Sep 1940		
*5	White	Floy		Let Sep 1940		*Sister*
*5	Wilkie	Doyle			Let Aug 19, 1944	
*5	Wilkie	Frankie		Let Sep 20, 1947		
*5	Wilkie	Weldon, Mrs.		Let Sep 20, 1947		
*5	Williams	Amos			Let Aug 15, 1942	

Chapter 9: Beliefs and Worship Services

HBC was a founding member of the Hightower Baptist Association in 1835. An association consists of a group of churches geographically grouped, with similar beliefs, that work together to support the member churches. An association meeting is held yearly, and the persons elected or appointed to attend the meetings are the delegates or messengers. The association is subdivided into districts, consisting of a smaller geographical area and a district meeting is also held yearly and called the union meeting.

This chapter includes a quick glance of the beliefs of HBC and how worship services are conducted.

Membership and Organization

To become a member, one must confess a belief in Jesus Christ and ask to join by "experience of grace" as a candidate for baptism by immersion; by a transfer of a letter from another church of the same faith and order (Baptist); or "under the watch care" which means until a request for transfer of letter from another church of same faith and order (Baptist). In earlier years, members were also received by statement (profession of membership of another Baptist church where records are not available) or by restoration (after an event of exclusion, person could ask for forgiveness or state their acknowledgements and be received again into the membership).

HBC is not in possession of any document describing the constitution of the church from its earliest beginning. The date of 1840 is respected as the date of constitution; however, research now notes the church was organized earlier. It is inconclusive whether the date of 1840 is referenced by mistake, or if the constitution was indeed established about six years after the worship services began.

HBC is a member of the Hightower Baptist Association (HBA) and has been since the founding of that organization in 1835. The HBA belongs to the Georgia Baptist Convention and is a part of the Southern Baptist Association. The Abstract of Principles or Articles of Faith from the HBA apply to all member churches. A copy can be found at http://hightowerbaptist.org or in any yearly minute of the HBA and also in *Men and Missions, Vol. II, Churches*. Each church is then governed by their own rules of decorum or by-laws. The two particular ordinances of HBC are Baptism and the Lord's Supper.

For many years, HBC held services once a month. In February, 1898, HBC voted to have preaching two times per month. It is not known if the bi-monthly meetings continued from that date; however, for many years, HBC held services on the first and third Sundays before going "full time" in the 1980s. On the Saturday before the third Sunday, a preaching service followed by conference (business meeting) was held. On the third Sunday, a worship service consisting of singing and preaching was conducted. Sunday school was added and was consistently held each Sunday beginning in 1938 (additional information about Sunday school follows in this chapter). A summer revival followed by the baptizing was held yearly (if any potential members had joined to be baptized). If the revival was "going good," the services could continue past the established week and would become recognized as a protracted meeting. Yearly, usually the third Sunday in May, is an event known as May Meeting, the date for the observance of the Lord's Supper and for Foot Washing services. "Dinner on the ground" is included with this service. As mentioned, Sunday School became an important part of worship at HBC and other active groups and events such as Women's Missionary Union, Youth Groups, Choirs, Vacation Bible School, mid-week Bible Study classes, Spring Revival, Family Day and others have been added since 1950 and continue to provide worship and fellowship at HBC to sustain the strong and abiding faith in Jesus Christ.

Revival

William G. Hasty, Sr. wrote several entries about revival meetings in his book *Yesterday and More: Short*

Stories. William, also called Bill, served in numerous positions during his career including: Cherokee Co. School Superintendent and serving in the Georgia House and Senate. He wrote stories for the local newspaper prior to being published in several books. His wife, Hazel, was a descendant of the Wyatt's of the Hightower area. Bill wrote, "Numerous churches still have revival services during summer months particularly in July and August". For HBC, the third week in August was scheduled for many years and then moved to the third week in July in 1937 (Cleo Heard Milford Diary). Likely, the main reason the revival was scheduled in the summer was from the era when the country was rural and agriculturally based. The phrase, "We will have our revival after laying-by time," was referred to for many years. Laying-by time was noted as the last time to plow the rows, as the plant growth limited enough space for any additional plowing. By September, it was again time to return to the fields to begin the harvest; corn and cotton picking and fodder pulling time was a busy season. The revival meetings were not only for the spiritual blessing one could receive, but also for the social life. Young people met, dated, and later married after having attended revival meetings. In fact, summer revivals were the biggest social event in most rural communities until the automobile made its debut. This custom of summer revivals has not changed for many churches even though farming practices have not been a factor for many years.

Also, in the past, it was common for the pastor and the visiting preacher(s) or helper(s) to pack their clothing and leave their home for almost the entire week of revival meeting. They spent the night in the homes of various members of the church where revival was being held. Hasty added that: "during the earliest years, it is believed that a morning service (10:30) was held each day, followed by dinner on the ground, then the second service in the afternoon (1:30). The menu likely included string beans, cream corn, okra, tomatoes, squash, onions, lima beans, Crowder peas, breads, cakes, pies, chicken, salt cured ham, and other goodies which were enjoyed by all." Chores for the livestock made travel back and forth from home to church impractical for two services per day. After electricity became available and transportation became easier (cars rather than mules), the transition to a schedule of morning and nightly services became accepted. For a number of years, preachers were invited to partake of meals in the homes of members for dinner (noon meal) and supper (evening meal) between the morning and evening services. It was a special occasion for a family, complete with use of china and a desire to provide the best food that could be offered.

For many years, farming methods for HBC members were slow and methodical, and all family members were needed to help in the fields during planting and harvesting seasons. Therefore, schools followed the "agriculture calendar". After harvest, students attended school for five or so months, weather permitting. Summer school consisted of two or three months of class. When nearby churches held their week of revival, students could attend the revival meetings in lieu of staying at school. Mattie Heard Turner (personal interview) described how she volunteered to walk with her students from Macedonia School to Macedonia Church. Students did the same from Etowah School to Hightower for many years.

Frankie Green Edge (personal interview) remembered that: "In 1942, Etowah School dismissed the students from the 7th and higher grades, they would let us go to church (from school), and probably more than half of them on that list that were baptized come from Etowah school. Preacher Tribble was the preacher, and all us girls, we was talking while we were walking to the church and saying we're not going to go up for prayer, we all decided as a group we wouldn't go up. Well, Preacher Tribble was preaching, and he got to pointing his finger at us, he was bad to point his finger, and he pointed his finger all the time he was preaching right at us. I can't remember what he preached about that day, but I knew when he was pointing, I knew he was pointing at me. There was several of us saved that day. I'm sure glad we got out of school to go to church. I keep a list of the names of those baptized that year in my Bible. I think of all of them lots of times."

The Foxfire 40th Anniversary Book: Faith, Family and the Land summarizes the conversion experience this way: "In a person's life, being saved usually follows the period of conviction. Being under conviction is a time in a person's life when he or she realized that life is incomplete without accepting Christ and the teaching of Christianity. For some, it represents a time of worry and concern, as they are not one of the saved. God has already chosen each of us, each of us must choose Him back. Being saved means claiming the promises of God's Word. It means that one accepts Jesus as his or her personal Lord and Savior and believes the truth of His teachings."

In a written note, left for her family, Cleo Heard Milford (1917-2007) recorded this about her experience: "I was sitting with Auberine Roper (Rev. Robert Roper's granddaughter) and some other girls. Preacher Roper preached about the rich man and Lazarus. He also talked about fire and brimstone. I didn't know at the time how brimstone would burn, but I thought about a broom straw field. I knew how it would quickly burn and I felt like that was where I would be if I didn't believe in Jesus and claim him as my Savior. I prayed and lost touch with most that was going on. I remember hearing some old songs and Preacher Roper telling me to open my eyes. When I did, I had never seen before or since, so many beautiful people. All around Preacher Roper's head, there was a shining halo. On the way home with my mother and brother, Arch, even though it was stormy, everything still looked beautiful." Cleo joined HBC by experience in August 1929, and was a faithful member of her home church all of her life.

Baptizings

One way of becoming a member of HBC is by joining the church. The pastor announces that the door of the church is open. Joining by a profession of faith means that the individual steps forward, and at a designated time, speaks to describe their "experience". Common among the statements may be: "I was saved last night at revival, and I wish to join this church and live a Christian life." A member then states a motion to "receive the person as a candidate for baptism". A second to the motion would follow, then a vote of approval. Baptism is performed only for professing believers, and is done by complete immersion. HBC does not have an indoor baptistry. Throughout the history of HBC, all baptisms have taken place outside. In the earliest years, the baptizing was likely held at the nearby Etowah River. More recently, the location was in one of the two baptismal pools constructed by the church. The first was built on the property of Bro. Ed and Georgia Lovelace in August of 1918. On Oct. 19, 1918, HBC minutes state that the church had received on the pool $13.75. Details about the decision to build the pool or about the location seem to be missing. The following January 1919, minutes state that: "the church decides to borrow money and finish paying for the pool built in August, 1918." Descendants of the Lovelace's continue to own the property. Chris Chandler, a grandson, described Mr. Lovelace as an "engineer" of his day. He had installed a hydraulic ram near the stream to provide water for his home located "up the hill". The ram would supply enough power to pump water to a source at a higher elevation. Several natural springs were located near the stream and, no doubt, Mr. Lovelace provided the insight to construct the nearby cement baptismal pool. The pool would be filled with the spring-fed water in preparation for the baptizing event each year. Unanimously, all persons who described their baptismal experience at the Lovelace location have remembered the cold, cold water of that pool (Mattie Heard Turner, Glenn W. Wilkie, Hazel Wilkie Cook, Frankie Green Edge, E. W. Cochran, Atholine Gilleland Wilkie, Diane Cowart Martin, etc.). Also remembered was the long, long walk. Pictures confirm that it was only several hundred yards, yet the downhill terrain must have seemed much further. Even though the hillside provided a natural setting, easy for all to see, the elderly were not able to attend due to the walk on uneven ground. In September 1959, HBC made arrangements for a well to be drilled on the church property, which would allow a water source to fill a pool. In June 1960, a committee was formed to complete a baptismal pool adjacent to the church parking lot just west of the church. At the time of printing this book (2015), HBC continues to use that facility for baptisms. The following entry is from the Cleo Heard Milford diary: July 24, 1960: "Baptizing at new pool in church yard, 11 baptized, 11 saved."

The typical words spoken by the minister at time of baptizing: "In obedience to the command of my Father and upon the confession of your faith in Christ, I baptize you, my sister/brother in the name of the Father, the Son, and the Holy Ghost, Amen."

In the rare old photo shown following: Rev. Robert Roper, in 1924, baptized new believers in the pool built near the creek on the Lovelace property east of the church.

1924, Photo courtesy of Chris Chandler

Photo courtesy of Ken Wyatt, See full story including names in chapter 11, 1925 baptizing

In 1958, Rev. Paul Thompson is shown baptizing Broughton Cochran.

Edwin Cochran is pictured awaiting his baptism.

Photos above of the Cochran cousins courtesy of Brenda Curtis

Ruth Wilkie Pinyan is pictured in a dress with a lace collar, just to the right of the preacher in the last two pictures above. She shared this memory: "Some of my happiest memories as a young girl are of the times spent at worship services and other events at Hightower Baptist Church. The week of revival in 1958 was the best of all. Rev. Jay Bottoms preached that Monday night and I was ready to ask for forgiveness. It turned out to be a great week for many of us. I remember walking down the long hill to the baptismal pool and how overwhelmed I felt.

Mom brought a large safety pin to pin my dress together. I remember Rev. Paul Thompson, the pastor, so well. I also remember that a lady I did not know was baptized who was pregnant. All my other memories have faded over the years but I do recall the one that counts: That Monday night I was saved by grace."

1959 photos courtesy of Ken Wyatt.

The above four pictures are of the 1959 baptizing, believed to be the last year of use of the pool at the Lovelace farm. Rev. Paul Thompson is again the minister in charge. The young girl is believed to be Haney Green, and the boy (pictured just before and after immersion) is Jimmy Wyatt. According to Cleo Heard Milford Diary, entry on July 26, 1959: "Paul baptized 11, 14 saved."

Photo courtesy of Judy Northington

The photo on the left was taken, on the Lovelace property in 2015, of the old baptismal pool with remnants of the structure still visible. The natural terrain around the pool, just above the creek, allowed for great viewing from the crowds as shown in the picture. Many who still attend HBC in 2015 have fond memories of this very sacred place, mixed with the vivid memory of the cold, cold water.

Shouting

When one is filled with the spirit in a display of joy and rejoicing, shouting may take place. At HBC, this may be referred to as "getting happy." In the past, shouting was common at HBC as the men and women would start singing, chanting, waving their arms and shuffling their feet. As told by Frankie Edge: "I know mama (Hattie Turner Green, 1904-1997) told about when there was so much shouting (at HBC) that they broke the sleepers in the church. I don't know what year it was. They must have really been a jumping up and down. They used to be lots of shouting, but they don't do that much anymore." Inez Cowart Howard remembers the stories about the floor falling in during the time Bro. Rob Roper was pastor, the same event remembered by Hattie Green. It has been told that in later years upon the installation of central heat and air equipment beneath the floor, evidence was obvious of repairs that had been made after the shouting event. Glenn W. Wilkie (Chapter 11) tells of his mother shouting when he was saved.

May Meeting, Communion and Foot washing

At HBC, the third Sunday in May is designated for a celebration known as May Meeting. The events of the day include singing, preaching, communion, foot washing and dinner on the ground. The order of those events has varied throughout the years. Communion at HBC is a most reverent service with a minister giving an introduction (sermon) followed by the deacons assembling around the communion table to break the unleavened bread. No one partakes of the bread or wine freely, but must be served by a minister or a deacon. The recipe for preparing the bread has been passed down through the years and is usually the responsibility of a wife of one of the deacons. Many at HBC may remember the years before the church purchased communion trays with individual and disposable cups. Several water goblets were "passed around" during the mid-1900s and the plates and glasses were actually a depression glass pattern like those pictured below:

Another part of the service includes foot washing. Foot washing is a practice that shows an expression of humility, love and a servant's heart. The Bible depicts Christ again and again as a servant. At HBC, the date has not been determined when foot washing began as a service. Foot washing takes place between persons of the same gender. The ladies are assembled on one side of the altar area and the men on the other. Deacons place pans of water in front of pews that have been arranged for the service. Participation is optional. Each foot is placed one at a time into the basin of water and is washed by cupping the hand and pouring water over the foot, and dried with a long towel girded around the waist of the member performing the washing. The participants then trade places to continue the process. The service demonstrates love, gratitude and humility. Pictured below are some of the implements used for this service.

In *I Remember When and More*, Hasty (1994) states: "To me washing feet was one of the most humbling experiences a man could express to his fellow man. Members practicing this act believed they should follow Christ's teaching as He taught them in the 'upper room' the night before he was crucified. Of course, the men and women were separated in the church for this part of the service. I was always amazed at the work and preparation that went into the planning and carrying out of this mission of Christianity. There were dozens of long white starched towels stacked at the altar. Those beautiful white towels were draped around the waist of the person who was washing his brother's or her sister's feet. When the feet were washed he or she would tenderly dry them with the towel. They would then stand, shake hands or embrace. Afterwards, the partner would in turn, wash the other's feet. Indeed this was a very humbling experience as believers carried out the teachings of Christ."

Shown above is a view of what for many years was the last event of May Meeting, dinner on the ground.

Sunday school

Christian education was recognized many years ago as an important component of worship services at HBC. Sometimes called Sabbath Schools, it is apparent that HBC made numerous attempts from 1888 to 1938 to establish Sunday school. Likely, it was difficult to sustain the weekly services due to limited travel during the winter months or maybe even low attendance.

The list below taken from the HBC minutes shows the progression of Sunday school.

- March 17, 1888, HBC Organized Sunday school, Supt: J. B. Lawson, and Assist. Supt: H. K. Fletcher, other records note: J. B. Lawson, Supt., John Holcombe, Assist. Supt., H. K. Fletcher, Secty.

- Oct. 19, 1889, Elected to the Sunday School Association to be held at Friendship Church Saturday before the 1st Sunday in Nov. next: J. S. Wyatt and J. W. McGullion, H. K. Fletcher, alternate.

- Jun. 14, 1890, organized a Sabbath School and the officers elected were: G. B. Fletcher, Supt., J. S. Wyatt, Assistant Supt, J. W. McGullion, Sec.

- Oct. 18, 1890, organized Sabbath School and elected J. W. McGullion, Supt.; J. S. Wyatt, Assistant Supt.; A. H. Wilkie, Sec.

- Feb. 19, 1898, Organized a Sunday school. Elected Bro. John W. Holcomb, Supt., and J. H. Ellis Assist. Supt., Elected R. B. Pursell, Sec.

- 1903 from HBA minutes: R. A. Dunagan, S.S. Supt.; H. G. Wilkey, S.S. Sec.

- 1908 from HBA minutes: Glen Wilkie, S.S. Supt.

- 1909 from HBA minutes: R. L. Warren (Orange P.O.), S.S. Supt.

- 1914 (No HBC Sunday School information)

- Jan. 16, 1915, Motion carried to organize Sunday school at Hightower Church. Elected Bro. W. E. Pierce as Supt. and H. G. Wilkie as Sectary.

- 1915: S.S. Supt.: W. E. Pearse

- 1916: S.S. Supt.: W. E. Pierce;

- 1917: S.S. Supt.: Geo. Richards

- 1918: S.S. Supt.: W. E. Pierce

- Mar. 16, 1918, Motion carried to meet Sunday morning at 9:30 to organize a Sunday school.

- 1921-1924: no S.S. information

- 1925: SS Supt: R. E. Lovelace, Sec: H. G. Wilkie

- 1926: R. E. Lovelace, S.S. Supt.; H. G. Wilkie, Sec.

- 1927: R. E. Lawless, S.S. Supt.

- 1928 (No HBC Sunday School information)

- 1932: H. G. Wilkie, S.S. Supt. & Clerk, S.S. enrollment: 55

- *Feb. 27, 1938 "Organized Sunday school at Hightower. We had S. S. before that, but due to dirt roads, it was hard to have S.S. in winter, and of course the church was uncomfortable in cold weather" Cleo Heard Milford Diary.*

- 1940- 1949: H. G. Wilkie, S.S. Supt.

- 1950: Halmon Roper, S.S. Supt.

Chapter 10: Church Leadership-Pastors and Deacons

HBC recognizes two offices for leadership: pastors and deacons.

PASTOR

A pastor is elected for the purpose of the ministry of the word and as the shepherd of the flock. A pastor must be ordained and is responsible to serve as moderator in conference (business) meetings. Various titles used throughout the years at HBC include elder, preacher, minister or bishop, and these have been used interchangeably at HBC at various times. A preacher is a man "called from God" to preach the word, and after announcing the "calling" is licensed by his home church. Licensing ushers in a period when the church and the individual can evaluate whether the person is indeed suitable for pastoral ministry. C. B. Fowler was "liberated" at HBC on Aug. 15, 1896, which was another title for becoming licensed. If the person testifies to an internal calling by God through the Holy Spirit to the gospel ministry, evidences the biblical qualifications for the office and demonstrates the gifts necessary for effective pastoral ministry, the church may proceed with an ordination. Often this occurs when a church elects the licensed preacher to become their pastor. The ordination takes place at the person's home church.

A pastor of Hightower Baptist Church must be a member of a Baptist church and must be either an ordained Baptist preacher or a licensed preacher that would require an ordination upon being called or elected to serve as pastor of Hightower. Following tradition, the pastor announces during the last service of revival (usually during the Sunday service following the baptisms) the plans for the upcoming year. The message is usually similar to either: 1) God is leading me to resign from this church, or 2) God is leading me to make myself available to serve you for another church year if that agrees with the decision of the church. The next conference or business meeting (August) following the summer revival (third week in July) is known as preacher calling day. The congregation chooses a pastor (by secret ballot or by acclamation) for a one-year term.

The HBC minutes in the early 1890s show that J. R. Allen was elected in October for several years. By the late 1890s and continuing until 1937, preacher calling day was in the month of September. This indicates that the summer revival was likely in August during that time. Rev. Dr. P. W. Tribble was elected on August 21, 1937, the revival likely in July. Since 1937, it appears that HBC has held a yearly revival during the third week in July.

The following is a chronological list of the pastors of HBC, their years of service, biographical information, and pictures as available.

Who was the first pastor at HBC?

The names of the earliest pastors at Hightower Baptist Church remain a mystery, much the same as the precise beginning of the congregation itself. Hughes (1987) notes that Enon Church (later First Baptist of Woodstock) was constituted in 1837 but did not chose a pastor until 1840 even though the congregation was active. Did the same occur at HBC? For many years, it was thought that Alfred Webb was the first pastor even though the year that he began at HBC has not been confirmed. Further study indicates that HBC was a known congregation in 1834 and Webb did not likely arrive in Georgia until 1837. Therefore a few other possibilities now exist such as Duncan O'Bryant, Solomon Peek, L. J. Hudson, and F. M. Hawkins, followed by the lengthy tenure of Webb.

Pre-1834

Duncan O'Bryant, (born about 1785 and died in 1834 in eastern Oklahoma, then called Arcansaw) possibly met with a group of people in the Hightower area in the late 1820s and very early 1830s. He was a noted missionary to the Cherokee Indians. From 1821 to 1831 he taught "school" in the Cherokee territory in an area called Tinsawattee, later identified by Don Shadburn, local historian, as being in southwestern Dawson County, Georgia. He moved from Tinsawattee to Hickory Log, near present day Canton, Georgia. He was known for holding services in private residences near those areas. One particular location was at "Nelson's near Noochee's," thought to be near the Etowah River in eastern Cherokee County (Gardner, 1989). This suggests a possible early congregation near HBC even though no evidence has been found that either proves or disproves this possibility. Duncan O'Bryant may be the same as the Rev. Bryan listed as one of the first pastors at Mt. Tabor Baptist in Forsyth County (Collins and Collins, 1999), a nearby church with a similar history to HBC. O'Bryant was married to Martha "Patsy" Whitehead and had ten children: Wilson, Nancy, Fanny, Harriet, Sarah, Eliza Jane, Jacob, Hugh, Humphrey (likely named for the Baptist missionary Humphrey Posey) and Patsy. Rev. O'Bryant and most of his family left the north Georgia area with a number of Cherokee Indians by the early 1830s and moved to Oklahoma. He desired to continue with his mission work and to establish schools, but was cut short on his plan as he died there in 1834, just a few years after the move.

1834-1835

Solomon Walter Peak, (1771-1858) may have been the second pastor as he reportedly moved to Cherokee County in 1832 and was listed as pastor at Hightower from 1834-1835, as found in the Chattahoochee Baptist Association records. He was also listed as a delegate from HBC to the organization of the Hightower Association in 1835.

He was born in Surry County, North Carolina, and died in Cherokee County, Georgia, from typhoid. HBC joined the Chattahoochee Association in 1834, therefore the possibility exists that Peek was the pastor in prior years if the congregation, in fact, did organize prior to joining the association. Peek was ordained at Tesnatee Church (Habersham Co.) which was one of the original churches present at the organization of Chattahoochee Baptist Association in 1826. It is likely that his connection with the Chattahoochee Association was the impetus for HBC joining Chattahoochee in 1834. The Chattahoochee Baptist Association records state that in 1834, HBC had 15 members and were represented at the association meeting by delegates S. Peak, J. George, and H. Holcomb. In later years, churches where Peak was a pastor included Yellow Creek and Dewberry in the Chattahoochee Association, Timber Ridge, Enon (later Woodstock First Baptist) in Cherokee County and Concord in Cobb County. He was also the pastor of Boiling Springs Primitive Baptist Church in Milton County for nine years. His name is sometimes found with various spellings: Peak, Peatie, Peall, etc. He was married to Rachel Dunagan and together they had seven children including Elizabeth, Nancy, Margaret, Lindsey, Lucy, Solomon Jr., and Hannah.

Possibly from 1835 to about 1837

"L. J." Lemuel James Hudson, (born about 1790 and died after 1843) was a member of Brushy Creek Baptist Church in Taylors, South Carolina, was licensed to preach in 1822 and ordained in 1826. He was granted a letter of dismission in September 1833 from Brushy Creek and moved to Georgia. He was a delegate from HBC to the organizational meeting of the Hightower Association in 1835. Collins (1999, p. 88) suggests that since he was listed as a delegate for HBC, that he was probably a member of HBC also.

Could he also have been the pastor at that time and maybe the third for Hightower (*Men and Missions I*, page 213; Hightower Baptist Association, 1835)? He was the son of Pleasant Hudson and Sarah Kemp Hudson. He was married about 1815 to Mourning Raines, and together they had five children: William, Permilia, Lemuel James, Mourning and George W. E. Hudson.

Possibly from 1836 and 1837

"F. M." Frederick Marshall Hawkins (1811-1891) perhaps served as pastor at HBC either at the same time as L. J. Hudson or after Hudson and before Alfred Webb, possibly from 1836 and 1837 (*Men and Missions, Vol. I.*) F. M. attended school at Furman Theological Institute in South Carolina for nine months in 1834. A number of personal letters received by F. M. Hawkins and dated 1833 to 1842 are printed in "The Cottonpatch Chronicles" by Don L. Shadburn. These provide an insight to everyday life as well as references to many family members. F. M. was ordained in 1835 in South Carolina and settled in Cumming, Georgia, in 1836. He pastored numerous churches including Antioch, Bethlehem, Cumming, Cool Springs, Friendship, Haw Creek, Hightower, Hopewell, Island Ford, Macedonia, Mt. Zion, Sharp Mountain and others. He wrote several circular letters for the Hightower Baptist Association in which copies can be found in *Men and Missions, Vol. I.*

F. M. Hawkins

Photo from: *History of the Baptist denomination in Georgia: with biographical compendium and portrait gallery of Baptist ministers and other Georgia Baptists.*1881.

F. M. Hawkins was the son of William and Sarah Hawkins, and married first to Elizabeth Brannon. He and Elizabeth were parents to ten children. After her death, he married Samantha A. Brannon, the widow of his nephew Robert (killed in Civil War). Samantha was also a sister to his first wife, Mary Elizabeth. From Samantha's previous marriage she had five children and then F. M. and Samantha had twins which brought the number of children to seventeen.

Hawkins thought all ministers should get a sufficient education to enable them to preach the gospel intelligently. In recognition of his desire for education, a seminary to train new pastors was given the name F. M. Hawkins Theological Seminary in 1998 and was located at Friendship Baptist Church in Forsyth County, Georgia. The Hightower Association minutes of 1892 paid tribute to Hawkins after his death: "Whereas God, in his dispensation, has seen fit to remove from our midst our highly esteemed and much beloved brother Frederick Marshall Hawkins who was a faithful and able Minister of Christ and a wise counselor in this body, but now rests from his labors; and his works do follow him."

*1845 – 1876; 1876-1879

From **1835 to 1845**, one can only guess how the transitions occurred until the known listing in 1845 of Alfred Webb, pastor. The 1836 and 1842 HBA minutes do not list any data for HBC. For the years 1837-1844 (except for 1842), no HBA minutes have been located, so the exact data of who was pastor may be lost forever. Webb possibly began earlier than the noted 1845, but no proof has been found. One may question that the long respected date of HBC being constituted in 1840 may also be the beginning of Webb's tenure as pastor? A phrase that survived throughout the years says Webb was HBC pastor for upwards of forty years. If true, that would give reason to believe that Webb began in 1839 since his tenure ended in 1879. Other sources suggest service at HBC as either thirty-two years (*Men and Missions of HBA, Vol. I.*) or thirty-four years (Shadburn, 2003). During his tenure, according to the records of Hightower Association, two additional pastors served as co-pastors. One was McKinney Purcell in 1875. The other, Jefferson Barton, was likely listed by mistake as noted on the chart included in this chapter.

Alfred Webb (1800-1883), known as Elder Webb, earned respect as one of the most important early leaders of the Hightower Baptist Association and certainly was influential in the early years of HBC. It must be noted that Webb is often thought of as the first pastor of HBC. With the findings of the Chattahoochee Association, it is now believed that while he served as pastor of HBC for the longest term during the 1800s, he was not the first pastor. Regardless of the precise term at HBC, his influence was no doubt monumental. One example of his impact was the number of families that named a son for him. Those included Alfred Webb Hawkins (1849, son of Rev. Frederick M. Hawkins); Alfred Webb Ridings (1859); Alfred Webb Roberts (1844); Alfred Webb Holbrook (1858);

Alfred Webb Nation (1848); Alfred Webb Bowen; Alfred Webb Martin (1840); Isaac Webb George (1840); and likely many more.

Alfred Webb was born in Rutherford Co. North Carolina, on Feb. 1, 1800, to Robert and Emelia Clinton Webb. Alfred was the eleventh child of thirteen, and later his father also had two additional children with a second wife. One brother of Alfred was James Milton Webb, who apparently stayed in North Carolina and led a life that mirrored that of Alfred in Georgia. James M. Webb was an ordained minister and a leader in his local Baptist association. Gardner Webb University was named for his grandchildren, James L. and E. Yates Webb and Faye Webb Gardner. It was during Alfred's childhood that he first met the noted Baptist Missionary Rev. Humphrey Posey, who visited the Webb home in North Carolina. Perhaps Posey was supportive in Alfred's ministry and influential in his ultimate move into the North Georgia area.

Alfred Webb
Photo courtesy of HBA and HBC

In 1820 in Rutherford County, North Carolina, he married Arabella Hill (1898-1879), daughter of Reuben and Margaret Hill. While no children were born to this union, Alfred and Arabella raised several orphans and opened their home to nieces and nephews throughout the years. Webb was licensed (1822) and ordained (1825) in North Carolina. Exactly what prompted a migration from North Carolina to Georgia has not been determined. It is known that Alfred and Arabella settled in the southern area of then Lumpkin County, Georgia (later Dawson County), in the Barrett's district around 1837. Also in the area were Arabella's parents, the Hills. The nearby church was Mt. Vernon Baptist where Alfred pastored for many years and where both he and Arabella were buried. The occupation mentioned for Alfred in various census reports was Baptist Preacher, farmer and minister. Stories remain that he mastered Greek and Hebrew languages after he was a grown man, no doubt furthering his understanding and ability to communicate the Bible. He served as a delegate from Dawson County, GA, to meetings in Milledgeville, GA, just before the start of the Civil War.

Alfred Webb was the moderator of the annual meeting of the Hightower Baptist Association for forty-one years and the author of several circular letters published by the association (some are printed in *Men and Missions, Vol. I*). He pastored a number of churches in the North Georgia area, and a few for "upwards of forty years". Each church only met once a month, therefore he often served four churches during the same year. Notations in the HBA minutes indicate that during a few years, he was assisted by a co-pastor, also listed as co-supply. In addition to Hightower, his longest tenures were at Mt. Vernon, Mt. Tabor and Concord Baptist Churches. He pastored several churches in North Carolina and additional churches he pastored in Georgia include Cool Springs, Sharp Mountain, Cumming First, Four Mile, Dahlonega and Mt Olivet. The 1935 Hightower Baptist Association minute includes a summary of Rev. Webb. Mentioned is that he: "moved to Dawson County, Georgia in 1837, he pastored Concord 41 years, Mt. Tabor 42 years, Mt. Vernon 40 years and Hightower 34 years. Webb traveled in many states, from Virginia to Mississippi to work as a missionary and received little compensation for his missionary service. He resigned as moderator of the HBA in 1879." No doubt he was a wise and gifted minister who was a role model, counselor, and leader as noted in the special tribute found in the HBC minutes after his death on October 7, 1883.

In Memory of Bro. Alfred Webb.

Our church has never been called upon to mourn death of a brother more universally beloved than he whose name hereto this notice. He loved the church and the cause of Christianity. His intercession with his brethren in all the relations of life, and his communion with them illustrate his high appreciation of, and decoration to the cause of Christianity and the profession he made, in his daily walk and conversation he exhibited his high estimate of Christ Church her on earth, and added luster to its wisdom, strength and beauty. Honored and beloved by us, while living, let us while we record these lines, resolve to copy his virtues and embalm his memory in our hearts.

Resolved:

1st. That in the death of Bro. Alfred Webb, the Baptist church has lost one of its most useful and beloved ministers, the community one of its best citizens and the country a long tried urbane and faithful citizen.

2nd. That we bow submissively to the will of him who doeth all things well.

3rd. That having faithfully served this church as pastor for upward of forty years; that a blank page in our record book be inscribed to his memory.

This Nov. 17th, 1883.

John B. Richards, Church Clerk

A visit to Mt. Vernon BC in Dawson County, GA, in 2014 found the monument pictured above that continues to honor both Alfred and his wife Arabella. The following inscription was found on his tombstone:

"In memory of Alfred Webb, who was born the first day of Feb., 1880, and departed this life on the seventh day of Oct. 1883. Age 83 years, eight months, and seven days. Having spent more that sixty years of his life as a Baptist Minister in preaching the Gospel of Christ. But all his labor now are over and we shall here (sic) his voice no more - The dust lies silent in the tomb. He has gone to Heaven, his final home."

On the opposite side of the same tombstone is a tribute to his wife:

"Arabella Webb, Consort of Elder Alfred Webb, who was born in Rutherford County North Carolina, January the 1st, 1798 and departed this life June the 3rd, 1879, aged 81 years, 5 months and 2 days. United with the Baptist Church in the year 1826. After which she was always a faithful servant of Christ, having served the church as a preacher's wife for a period of 56 years, ever incouraging her husband to go and preach the gospel to others. Sleep on dear dead and take your rest. Till Christ shall rend the lamb, then from your grave ye shall ascend with all the ransomed throngs."

<u>1854</u> *error? Jefferson Barton. The 1880 Hightower Association summary lists the following pastors for Hightower Church: A. Webb 34 years, J. Barton, M. Purcell, and F. M. Hawkins. A careful review of the 1854 minute concludes that Barton was likely listed in error, as the chart shows the information was apparently misaligned.*

1876

James "McKinney" Purcell (1830-1905) possibly served as a co-supply pastor with Alfred Webb for one year. Brother McKinney, or "Mack" was born in Lumpkin County, GA, on June 24, 1830 and died in Gwinnett County on January 3, 1905. He was the son of James and Mary "Polly" Curry Purcell, early farmers near the Etowah River in current day Cherokee County. The Purcell family was likely located in the Hightower area in the early 1830s. It was reported that McKinney joined HBC about 1853 and was ordained at HBC in 1858. He was married to the former Mary Garrett Creamer and McKinney and Mary became parents to at least eight children. McKinney Purcell was only listed as a pastor for one year (1876) with Webb listed both before and after 1876. Since the date of Webb's death was 1883, those last years may have been too physically demanding for Webb to continue serving his churches alone and thus may have been the reason Purcell was listed as a pastor. Since no HBC records exist before 1882, this information is difficult to confirm. Other churches Purcell pastored include: Hopewell, Union Hill, Bethany, Mt. Zion, Shady Grove and Salem. Purcell was living in Milton County, GA, in 1870 and in Gwinnett County, GA, in 1880 and possibly remained in the Gwinnett and DeKalb area until his death. He was buried at Pleasant Hill Baptist Church in Tucker, Georgia.

J. McKinney Purcell

Photo courtesy Byron Burgess and *Men and Missions, Vol. I.*

In the HBC minutes of June 18, 1904, another "McKinney Purcell" is mentioned as New Harmony BC invited the eldership of HBC to be at the ordination of a Bro. McKinney Purcell on Friday before the first Sunday in August, 1904. This is likely T. M. (Thomas McKinney) Purcell listed in *Men and Missions Vol. I*, page 334.

About 1878-1879

C. S. (or C. L.) Hawkins – It was thought that a Preacher Hawkins "came in as supply" during the last of Webb's tenure, likely due to Webb's declining health. The 1880 HBA minute (summary) shows C. L. Hawkins as supply in 1878. C. L. Hawkins with a birthdate of 1877/1878 could not be this person. Further study found C. S. Hawkins, with either Street or Sterling for the middle name. C. S. Hawkins (1847-1928) known as Cicero Street Hawkins was a son of John and Manervia Kemp Hawkins. Some family information also lists a brother of Cicero S. to be Street Washington Hawkins. The record found and shown below was from information that preachers provided to a survey that was included in the publication. This record matches the supply information of 1879.

The Ministerial Directory of the Baptist Churches in U.S. of America (1899) lists the following: Hawkins, Cicero Starling, Heardsville, GA. Born Forsyth Co., GA. Lic. Nov. 18, 1869, Mt. Pleasant Ch. Ark., Ord. July '77, Hightower Ch., GA., P. Ophir, GA '78; S. Hightower '79; Mt. Pisgah, GA '94.

C. S. Hawkins was married to Eliza A. Pascoe (1848-1903), daughter of Samuel and Mary Pascoe. Sam and Mary are buried at HBC, which additionally connects C. S. Hawkins to HBC. Also a sister of C. S., Julia Hawkins, married John Samuel Wyatt.

About 1880-1881

Elder Francis Marion Williams (about 1828-1914) F. M. Williams was born to Wright and Rhoda Williams, the place of birth difficult to determine as sources disagree if it is in Georgia or a different state. Records indicate several men by the name Francis Marion are all likely named for the Revolutionary War hero Francis Marion from South Carolina in the 1700s. The date of birth of F. M. Williams is believed to be October 13, 1828, and the date of death July 13, 1914, with burial at Sharp Mountain BC in Ball Ground, Georgia. His fourth wife, Nancy, was buried beside him.

Williams was a church member of Conns Creek, Mica and Bethesda at various times, and was ordained in 1867.

Marion was wed to four different women and after the death of each one, he quickly remarried. With these marriages, he fathered at least eighteen children. First wife: Louise McHanon, eight children; second: Martha Jane Bruton, five children; third: Martha Louise Holcomb, four children and fourth: Nancy Azeliah Weaver, one daughter.

Elder Williams was described as a prominent Baptist preacher in North Georgia and pastored a number of churches in addition to Hightower including, New Harmony, Chalcedonia, Cool Springs, Conns Creek, Sharp Mountain, Hopewell, Mica and others. He was listed as the pastor of Sharp Mountain during the Great Revival of 1873, which legend says lasted for an extended time with over 100 eventually baptized, some of those in the icy Etowah River in December, 1873.

F. M. Williams

Photo from Roberts, Malinda. *The History of First Baptist Church Canton*, 1933. Also courtesy of Byron Burgess and *Men and Missions, Vol. I., Ministers.*

1882-1883; 1888

Elias Walter Allred (1824-1910), actually Elias Allred III, was born March 20, 1824, in Hall County, Georgia and died March 8, 1910 in Pickens County, Georgia. He was described as a highly honored, respected and powerful Baptist minister. He also served in roles as a tanner, hotel operator, senator, representative and tax collector. He married Martha "Patsy" Arthur in Cherokee County in 1848. No children were born to this union. Patsy died in 1904 and they both were buried at Cool Springs Baptist Church in Tate, Georgia. In addition to HBC, churches he pastored include Cool Springs, Goshen, Sharp Mountain, Macedonia, Mt. Zion, Mt. Tabor, Four Mile, New Harmony, Dawsonville and others.

Rev. Allred is the first minister listed in the minutes at HBC since the current records begin in 1882. E. W. Allred is listed numerous times as moderator of the church conference meetings.

1884-1885

Thaddeus Pickett (1845-1909) Elder Pickett, also known as Thad, was born on January 31, 1845, in Gilmer County, Georgia, to Joseph and Caroline Amanda Edney Pickett. He resided in Gilmer County until his early twenties. At age seventeen, he entered the Confederate army and was known to be a faithful soldier, always ready for duty. Interestingly, he is known to later serve in the Northern Army. After the war, he returned to Georgia, went to high school in Gordon County and worked to pay his own tuition and board. In 1866, he joined Talking Rock Baptist Church in Pickens County, and in 1868 was ordained to preach. His sermons were described as bold, earnest and original. Carver (2011) reprinted a May 18, 1888, article from the *Cherokee Advance* which said: "He says what he thinks, not caring who it hits, how it stings nor whose opinion it clashes with. Many conservative members did not agree with him, but it made no difference with him." The article was political in nature and printed during his candidacy for Congress. The strong viewpoints were also noted by Walker (1963) who described Pickett as "a very influential preacher; he was sought for revivals in the churches. Known as a man with firm views, on one occasion while pastor of the Canton First Church, when the newly redecorated church sanctuary revealed a cross painted over the pulpit, he refused to hold services until it was removed. Needless to say, this was done. He was a strong believer in foot washing and helped institute this in most of the

Thaddeus Pickett

Photo from publication of First Baptist Church, Canton, GA.

Photo from Roberts, Malinda. *The History of First Baptist Church Canton*, 1933. Also from Pickens County Historical and Genealogical Society. *Pickens County, Georgia Heritage.* Pickens County, GA: Pickens County Historical and Genealogical Society and Don Mills, Inc., 1998.

churches. Thad Pickett was known for his length as well as his depth in preaching. Three hours was never too long for one of the two or more sermons preached in revivals." In addition to HBC, churches he pastored include Friendship, Macedonia, Canton First, Cumming First, Jasper, Talking Rock and others.

His first marriage was to Ellen Stearns, and they had one daughter, Lilla. He later married Sarah E. Worley, and they were parents to Roscoe, Thaddeus Jr., Golden, Edney, Hillyer and Lenora. In addition to minister, other titles he held were merchant, hotel manager and ordinary of Pickens County. Thaddeus Pickett died on August 9, 1909 and was buried at Talking Rock Baptist Cemetery in Pickens County, Georgia. His tombstone reads: "Erected by the Jasper Baptist Association, In memory of Rev. Thaddeus Pickett, 1845-1909, a Baptist Minister 42 Years, A defender of truth." Both Ellen (1850-1880) and Sarah (1862-1947) are also buried at Talking Rock Cemetery.

Of local interest, family legend contents that Thaddeus Pickett Hester, Sr. (1886-1969), once a member at HBC and a descendant of the Hester families at Hightower, was named for Rev. Pickett. Thad Hester was born in 1886 following the tenure at HBC of Rev. Pickett from 1884-1885. The timing of his pastorate supports this family story.

1886-1887

Absalom H. Sheffield (about 1848 – 1900) lived in Lumpkin and Dawson County areas most of his life and was probably born on January 16, 1848 in Lumpkin County. The last name is sometimes found with the spelling of Shuffield, and his first name as Absolom or Abslum or Absolen. In 1850, his name was found in the U.S. Census in the home of Isham and Nancy Shuffield, possibly his parents.

In 1863, he married Caroline Jane Foster, and by 1870, they were living in Dawson County and he was listed as a farmer. They became parents to two sons, Charles and Joseph. Absalom served in the Confederate Army for the 65th Georgia Infantry. He was possibly ordained in 1874, and the 1880 U.S. Census showed the occupation of Absolum as "Minister of God". In the late 1880s, he was a landowner at Mazeppa, Big Creek district of Milton County, Georgia. Absalom died on May 19, 1900, in Pottawatomie County, Oklahoma, having moved there to live with or near their son Charles. Caroline was living there with Charles and family in 1910.

Additional churches he pastored were New Bethel, Amicalola, Bethel, Dawsonville, Goshen, Cross Roads, Shoal Creek, Macedonia, Friendship, Union Hill and others.

1889 – 1891; and 1899-1901 (1890-1891, Ingram was co-supply with E. Cochran, likely Elias Cochran)

Henry T. Ingram (about 1849 - 1921) was from Gaddistown in Union County, Georgia, and possibly born on May 24, 1849 or 1850. Sources disagree on his parents, but the death index completed in Forsyth County in 1921 stated that he was a son of Isaac and Sarah Hanes (Haynes) Ingram. He was believed married to Susanna Beard before 1870, as the census of that year showed he was living still in Union County Georgia with wife Susan, both are age twenty. He moved to the northern Cherokee County area before 1880, as he was licensed to preach at Four Mile Baptist Church in Pickens County and likely moved his membership to Conns Creek where he was ordained in June of 1878. In 1880 through 1910, he was listed as living in Cherokee County, Conns Creek District. He was credited for donating land and building the Conns Creek District Court House. It remained a polling location for the community until 1954. McConnell (1990) reported that Bro. Ingram traveled many miles in a one-horse buggy to his churches. In the winter months when weather was bad, he would spend the weekend with church members. A sad family story that was found in *Cherokee County, Georgia Heritage, 1831-1998* says that: "on one event when he was away from home as a circuit preacher, his wife, Susan was burned to death on April 1, 1918. She had built a fire to dry the clothes she had washed and her dress caught on fire." She is buried at Conns Creek BC. It is believed that after the death of Susan, he remarried to Lillian Bell Cochran. Henry passed away in 1921 and was buried at New Harmony BC in Forsyth County, Georgia.

Henry T. Ingram
Photo courtesy of HBC

He was a preacher for more than forty years. In addition to Hightower, he was also a pastor at Conns Creek, Four Mile, Hopewell, Zion Hill, Providence, Chalcedonia, New Harmony, Friendship, Ball Ground, Marble Hill, Concord and others.

1892-1894 and 1906-1908

James Robert Allen (1847-1915) was born in Gilmer County, Georgia, on August 27, 1847, to parents Samuel Denton and Terrecy Smith Allen. He lived in Gilmer throughout his childhood. After his marriage to Francis Elizabeth "Lizzie" Stephens in 1874, he was listed on the 1880 U.S. Census with his wife and young son in Pickens County, Jasper, Georgia as a dry goods merchant. At some point, he was also owner and operator of a hotel in Talking Rock and in the 1900 census was listed as a "preacher." James and Lizzie had eight children, four of whom reached adulthood: Bonnie, Kate, Edgar and Walter. He also was a state representative and senator from the Pickens County area.

In addition to HBC, other churches where he was pastor included Ball Ground, Jasper and Talking Rock. Some of these churches belonged to the Jasper Association where he served a few times as clerk and moderator. James Robert Allen passed away on March 3, 1915, and was buried beside his wife Lizzie at Talking Rock Baptist Church Cemetery.

1894-1895

Elias A. Cochran (1845-1931) On September 15, 1894, E. A. Cochran was elected to serve as pastor for the ensuing year. Elias was known as the man with the longest beard. No doubt, the biographical information that remains of Rev. Cochran is one of the most interesting and intriguing of all members of HBC. [For additional details, see Chapter 11: Hightower Highlights, Rev. E. A. Cochran]

Elias A. Cochran

Photo courtesy HBC

Elias was born August 8, 1845, a son of Terrell B. and Francis Nix Cochran, and either a brother or half-brother to Rev. Robert W. Cochran and others. Rev. Elias lived most of his life in Cherokee County, Georgia. He is listed as a member of HBC on the first roll book that began in 1882 and likely he had been a member for several years before. He had three marriages and his first two wives were sisters (Jane Fowler, Emma Fowler and Kansis Wheeler). No children were born in any of the marriages.

E. A. Cochran was ordained at HBC on October 20, 1884, the record can be found in this book in Chapter Four, minutes. His pastorate at HBC was only one year, yet he is listed numerous times as one of the preachers at the Saturday conferences and many times was elected to serve as moderator pro tem as needed. He also was appointed as a delegate from HBC to many union and association meetings. (The October 20, 1884, ordination date was recorded in the HBC minutes. The August 25, 1884 date listed below also agrees with the date on Rev. Cochran's tombstone at HBC cemetery.)

The Ministerial Directory of the Baptist Churches in U.S. of America (1899) lists "Cochran, Elias Alford, Creighton, Ga., Born Cherokee Co. Ga.: Lic. Nov. 1882, Canton Ch. Ga. Ord. Aug 14, 1884, Hightower Ch. Ga.: S. Hightower, Ga. '87-88; P. Yellow Creek, '88; Mt. Zion '89-90; Crab Apple '93-'96; Bethany, '97-'99, Corinth, Ga. '95-'99."

Rev. E. A. Cochran died on October 15, 1931, and was buried at HBC. His monument is one of the largest and most unusual in the entire cemetery. The lengthy inscriptions on the tombstone of his as well as of his three wives can be found in Chapter 12, Cemetery, Interments by Sections.

1896-1898

Claiborn Albert Wallis (1857-1945) was first elected as pastor at HBC October 20, 1895. The surname is also spelled "Wallace," and both spellings are found in the HBC minutes. Rev. Claiborn was born on September 1, 1857, to parents William and Martha Jane Harris Wallis. He spent many years of his life living in the Settendown district of Forsyth County, Georgia. He married first to Sarah "Sallie" Martin, and it is thought that they were parents to six children. After Sallie's death, he married Matilda Lawson. Claiborn was listed as a member at Mt. Tabor BC and later at Concord BC. While at Concord, he served as clerk and was ordained into the ministry in 1894. Other churches pastored include: Mt. Tabor, Mt. Pisgah, Four Mile, Ophir, Conns Creek, Birmingham, Haw Creek, Pleasant View, Hopewell, Liberty Grove and Yellow Creek.

C. A. Wallis

Photo courtesy of Byron Burgess, *History of Hopewell Church.*

1901-1905

Andrew Jackson Henderson (1849-1922) A. J. was born in Habersham County, Georgia, on April 9, 1849, to Albert Hines and Charlotte Black Henderson. He lived in Forsyth County, Georgia, during his youth and later in the Little River District of Cherokee County. He married first to Emily Thompson, and they became parents to four children. After Emily's death in 1880, he married Nancy Clayton, and together they were parents to six children. Tommy Henderson (1913-1998) who was a pastor at HBC in 1970 was a nephew of Rev. A. J. Henderson. A. J. joined Hopewell BC, was licensed to preach in 1893 and ordained into the ministry in 1895. On September 14, 1901, HBC elected Rev. Henderson as pastor. He was reelected three additional times and served as pastor for about four years. Rev. Andrew Jackson Henderson died July 14, 1922, and was buried at Hopewell BC Cemetery in Fulton County, Georgia. Other churches Rev. Henderson pastored include Beaver Ruin, Hopewell and Liberty Grove, Friendship, Sharp Mountain, New Harmony, and Shady Grove.

A. J. Henderson

Photo courtesy of HBC

1907 Error: ~~J. R. Cline;~~ The HBC minutes show that in September 1907, J. R. Allen was elected as pastor. The Hightower Association statistical chart shows <u>J. R. Cline</u> as pastor which is a probable typographical error. Interestingly, in some of the HBC records, his name is spelled "Aline," with the A possibly mistaken for a C, thus could that explain the name Cline? No person by the name of J. R. Cline has been found in records such as the U.S. Census or *Men and Missions, Vol. I.*; therefore it is most likely that J. R. Allen was the pastor until the election of J. R. Stone in 1908.

1909 – 1921

John Randall or Randle Stone (1855-1938). An index of *Georgia, Deaths, 1928-1938*, accessed Jun. 16, 2014, states that "John Randall Stone, born in 1855, died on Nov. 8, 1938, at age of 83 in Cumming, Forsyth, Georgia." Further study indicates he was most likely the son of David and Margaret E. McDonald Stone. Mrs. Margaret Stone was likely the daughter of Randle McDonald, a noted lawyer and statesman of Cherokee County in early 1830s. John R. Stone lived with his parents in the Northeast Cherokee - Southeast Pickens County area in his early life. In the early 1870s, he married his wife Mary, and they became parents to several children. In 1880, they were in Dawson County and John was listed in the census as a farmer. Later, his title included a miller. In 1920, he was living in Forsyth County and was recorded as a clergyman. Records show that he was licensed to preach in 1884 and was ordained before 1889. He was a great believer in missions and once wrote a circular for the Hightower Association about the subject. Rev. Stone was first elected as pastor at HBC in September 1908, and would serve consecutive years until 1921. His tenure of about twelve years was the most consecutive years since that of Albert Webb. He supplied a number of area churches as pastor including Corinth, Amicalola, Mt. Vernon, New Hope, Sweetwater, New Bethel, Juno, Concord, Liberty, Mt. Tabor, Conns Creek, Macedonia, Shady Grove, Sharon, Providence, New Harmony and Liberty Grove. During his ministerial work throughout the area, it is said that he baptized more than 1,250 people, a higher total than most any other minister in the HBA.

1921-1936

Robert "Rob" Amos Roper (1865-1939) was born on Feb. 3, 1865, in Pickens County, South Carolina to Rev. Samuel and Louisa Cassell Roper, and by 1880 he was living with his parents in Dawson County, GA. He married Martha Covington in 1886, and they lived in various homes in Pickens, Cherokee and Forsyth Counties during their lifetime while rearing their nine children. Children included: Walter, (Rev.) Fulton, Mary, Colman, Holman, Agnes, Emma, Maude, and Dewrey. He was a member of several Baptist churches throughout his career and was ordained into the ministry in 1910. He was first elected as pastor at HBC in October of 1921, and served faithfully for fifteen consecutive years (see note below about Rev. Anderson). During his pastorate at HBC, on Jan. 25, 1923, the following was recorded in the HBC minute: "Received by letter Rev. R. A. Roper and wife, Sister Martha Jane Roper and Sister Emma Roper as members in good standing with us. Also received under the watch care Bro. Hallmond and Colmond Roper."

J. R. Stone
Photo courtesy of HBC

Rev. Roper served the Hightower Baptist Association as moderator and committee member, and preached the Introductory Sermon in 1926.The churches he pastored include: Four Mile, Liberty Grove, Crabapple, Ball Ground, Bethlehem, Concord, New Harmony, Pleasant View, Amicalola, Macedonia, Friendship, Mt Pisgah, Mt. Vernon, Brookwood, Bethany, and others.

Brother Rob died on June 27, 1939, and was buried at Hightower BC beside his wife. Their tombstones read: Rev. R. A. Roper, 1865-1939, and Martha J. Roper 1867-1957.

1925 Error, **John M. Anderson,** listed in *Men and Missions Vol. I and II* was likely included as a mistake because HBC minutes do not show Anderson as moderator of any of the 1925 conferences, rather they show only Rev. R. A. Roper as moderator for 1925. No evidence of Anderson serving as co-pastor has been found, though that is a possibility. He was born April 4, 1858, and lived most of his life in Forsyth County, Georgia. He was a member of Friendship BC for over sixty years and was licensed to preach there in 1889 and ordained to preach in 1900. He married Ophelia Galloway in 1876, and they were parents to several children, including Hattie, Allie and Carrie.

R. A. Roper

Photo courtesy of Byron Burgess

1936-1946

Pledger Washington Tribble (1887- 1976). The Rev. Dr. P. W. Tribble was born on August 19, 1887, to William N. and Canzada Sams Tribble. He married on Christmas Day, 1907, to Myrtle "Myrt" Durham. He tried several jobs such as farmer and store clerk before deciding to go to medical school in Atlanta, Georgia, after the birth of his first four children. After medical school, he and his family lived for several years in Florida where he worked as a physician, before returning to his native Forsyth County. He "answered the call" to preach and was "liberated, also called licensed" in 1929, and ordained at Friendship BC in 1930. He and Myrt were parents to ten children: Fern, Fairy, Miriam, Ruth, P. W., Newton, Robert, Dorothy, Mata, and Lamar.

Dr. P. W. Tribble

Photo courtesy of Nancy Tribble Heard

Fondly known as "Doc," he is remembered by many HBC members not only for his preaching but for the medical care he provided to the community. House calls, especially to deliver that new family member, were common for his practice throughout the early 1940s. He experienced fatigue and an ensuing heart attack in the mid-1940s. Numerous factors, such as being a busy parent, physician, and preacher during the difficult era of WWII negatively influenced Pledger's health which was severe enough for him to "walk away" from his medical work for a period of about ten years. He returned to his medical practice about 1956 and continued until 1969. Many people from the Hightower area may remember riding in a car as their parents made the turn off State Highway Twenty onto Post Road to his medical office at his home. His footsteps by those days were slow, but the tunes he whistled let one know that he was about his business of providing appropriate medical care which often included doses of either penicillin (the dreaded injection) or paregoric.

Rev. Dr. Tribble continued his ministerial work for a number of years, serving as a leader for the Hightower Association as well as pastor at many churches such as Union Hill, Birmingham, Bethlehem, Crabapple, Sharp Mountain, North Canton, Mt. Tabor, Sharon, New Harmony, Friendship and others.

1946- 1951; 1966-1970; 1980-1983

John Hunter Lummus was born to Wes and Lille Mae Lummus in 1925. He grew up in the Holbrook Campground Community and attended New Harmony BC. He accepted Christ at age thirteen. His education endeavors carried him to achieve degrees from Canton High, Reinhardt College and later Oglethorpe University and University of Georgia. It was while attending Reinhardt as a teenager, John was called to preach. He served in the Navy during WWII and afterwards returned to his hometown and continued his role as preacher, with ordination in 1946. The next photo was taken about 1946 at the home of HBC members Robert and Cleo Milford.

As the story goes, by revival time at HBC in 1946, Rev. P. W. Tribble's health had weakened him to the point that he was unable to conduct revival services. Instead, Rev. Sam Cochran and a young man named John Lummus were asked to provide the preaching. On Sunday, July 28, 1946, seventeen were baptized and Preacher Cochran relayed the message that Dr. Tribble would not be able to pastor the church for the coming year.

As recorded in the diary of Cleo Heard Milford, on Saturday, August 17, 1946: "We went to Hightower. Jim Richards preached. We held voting for preacher with secret ballots, 111 people voted, and the majority was for John Lummus. Saturday night, Toy and Lura (Wyatt) went with us (Robert and Cleo Milford) to Oak Grove to see John Lummus. Dewey Cowart's brought John back. *Sunday, August 18, 1946. John (Lummus) accepted the church and preached to us after Sunday School. Rev. Lummus was a church member at New Harmony and that church agreed to ordain Lummus on September 13, 1946."* A few years later, she wrote on Sunday July 22, 1951. "John *baptized 20, then said his work (at HBC) was through, not to call him back. I couldn't help but cry."*

John Lummus went on to serve numerous churches as pastor for over a fifty-year period, traveled on several missionary trips, moderated at the HBA while also continuing his bi-vocational career in education. He has been a leader and mentor to many as he and his wife, Lois, served in their ministry throughout the years. It is with great appreciation that God saw fit for John Lummus to pastor at HBC on three different occasions.

.....

The following pastors served after the 1950 date however short biographical sketches are included of these more recent pastors.

1951-1953

Jack Sutton, (1897-1973) his full name was Walter Jackson Sutton. Brother Jack was born in Cleveland, Georgia, and moved with his family to Old Milton County, several years later. In 1918, he married Mattie Estelle DeVore, and they became parents to twelve children. Among those, three of his sons eventually became preachers: Harold, Jackson "J.D.," and James Edward "Bud". Rev. Jack was licensed in 1932 and ordained in 1935 at Providence BC. He pastored numerous churches throughout his lifetime and was reported to be a stern preacher who did not waiver in his beliefs under any circumstance (*Men and Missions, Vol. I.*). Walter Jackson Sutton passed away on November 2, 1973, and was buried at Providence BC in Alpharetta, Georgia.

John H. Lummus

1953-1956

Elbert A. Majors, (1914-1977) Rev. Majors was known as Brother Ebb or Eb. He held his church membership at Daves Creek BC in Forsyth County, Georgia, and was licensed and ordained there. He was married to Alline Williams. Some of the churches where he served as pastor were Oak Grove, Bethany, Mt. Zion and Providence. Rev. Majors was buried at Green Lawn Cemetery, Roswell, Georgia.

1956-1961; 1964-1966

Paul W. Thompson (1914-1994), was born to Govie and Agness Holbrook Thompson and lived in Forsyth County, Georgia. He was a member at Longstreet BC and ordained there in 1944. He married Grace Ridings, and they became parents to four children. He pastored numerous churches in Forsyth and Cherokee Counties.

1961-1964

Lealon Everett Ellis (1923-2005) was the son of William Henry and Lula Bell Carnes Ellis. He was a member of Mt. Pisgah BC in Forsyth County, Georgia, and ordained there in 1959. He was married to Edna Lee Dehart, and they became parents to two children. Lealon was a grandson of HBC deacon, John Henry Ellis (1863-1926). For a number of years, Brother Leland kept a collection of pictures and newspaper clippings of events that included his participation in weddings, funerals, and baptisms. His diligence in this project helped document a number of events at HBC in the early 1960s, and his efforts are appreciated. Brother Leland and Mrs. Edna lived in the Buffington Community of Cherokee County just behind the Skyline Café for many years. He and his wife were buried at Mt. Pisgah BC.

1970-1971

Thomas W. "Tommy" Henderson (1913-1998) was the last of fourteen children born to Albert Hines Jr. and Sarah Bates Henderson. He joined Hopewell BC in Fulton County Georgia and was licensed and ordained there in 1944. He married Demetra Wilson who lived near Holbrook Campground, and they became parents to one daughter. Tommy and Demetra made their home in Alpharetta, Georgia. He pastored numerous churches and also went on several missionary trips. Brother Tommy was a nephew of HBC pastor A. J. Henderson, who was at Hightower from 1901-1905. Rev. and Mrs. Henderson were buried at Roswell, Georgia.

1971-1973

Robert Quillen Martin was born in Forsyth County, Georgia to Buell and Edith Martin. His membership is at Coal Mountain BC where he was licensed (1963) and ordained (1964). Robert and his wife are parents to two children.

1973-1980; 1993-2013

Gerral B. Richards, a son of William McKinley and Ollie Mae Thompson Richards, joined Longstreet BC in 1952. In 1962, he was licensed to preach and was ordained in 1963, also at Longstreet. He and his wife are parents to three children.

1983-1986

Harold Edwin Thompson (1934-2003) was born to parents Rev. Hoyt E. and Clara Mae Wood Thompson and lived in the South Forsyth and North Fulton Counties in his early life. He married Joyce Vaughn, and they were parents to three children. Preacher Harold was licensed in 1956 and ordained in 1958. He was buried in Cumming, Georgia at Sawnee View Memorial Gardens.

1986-1992; 2013-

Ronnie Kenneth McCormick lives in Forsyth County, Georgia and became a member of New Harmony BC. It was there in 1981 he became a licensed preacher and was ordained there in 1984. He and his wife are parents to two children.

Hightower BC Pastors

Elected	Began HBC	End HBC	Last name	First/Middle	Birth/death	Other info.
	? <1832	?	? O'Bryant	Duncan	~1785-1834	Missionary to Cherokee Indians
	1834	1835	Peek	Solomon	~1771-1858	Chattahoochee Association records
	? 1835	? 1837	Hudson	L. J.	~1790-aft. 1843	HBA records
	*unk ? 1836	? 1837-1840	Hawkins	Frederick Marshall	1811-1891	Moved to Ga 1836; Listed in Men & Missions Vol I as pastor at HBC, but no date(s)
	? 1837-1840	? 1845				Webb was pastor at Mt. Tabor in 1837, no record for HBC
	1845	1875	Webb	Alfred	1800-1883	HBA records, likely began before 1845

Elected	Began HBC	End HBC	Last name	First/ Middle	Birth/ death	Other info.
?	1853	1854	*~~Barton~~	~~Jefferson~~	1801 - 1862	*This is likely an error in the HBA minutes
	1875	1876	*Purcell	James "McKinney"	1830-1905	Ordained at HBC, 1858; possibly a co-supply with A. Webb; *HBA only listed Webb…
	1876	1879	Webb Hawkins	Alfred C. S. (likely listed as C. L. by mistake)	1800-1883	1878; A Webb, Supply? C L Hawkins, came in as Supply, 1878
	1879	1881	Williams	Eld. Francis Marion	1828-1914	Ordained in 1867
1881- Nov 1882	1881	1883	Allred	Elias Walter	1824-1910	Pastor listed in 1st minute of HBC, June 1882
Sep 1883; Remained 1884	1883	1885	Pickett	Thaddeous	1845-1909	
Oct. 1885 Remained 1886	1885	1887	Sheffield	Absalom H.	1848-1900	
Sep. 1887	1887	1888	Allred Cochran	Elias W. E.	1824-1910 1845-1931	Allred supply, Elias A. Cochran as joint supply
Dec 1888 Oct 1889 Sept 1890	1888	1891	Ingram Cochran	Henry T. C. E. (likely E. A. Cochran)	Unk – 1921 1845-1931	By Dec 1888, Ingram listed as pastor; Cochran as joint supply
Oct. 17, 1891- Oct. 14, 1893	1891	1894	Allen	James Robert	1847-1915	
Sep. 15, 1894	1894	1895	Cochran	Elias A.	1845-1931	
Oct. 20, 1895- Sep. 18, 1897	1895	1898	Wallis	Claiborn Albert	1857-1945	
Sep. 1898 - Sep. 15, 1900	1898	1901	Ingram	Henry T.	Unk - 1921	
Sep. 14, 1901- Sep. 17, 1904	1901	1905	Henderson	Andrew Jackson	1849-1922	
Oct. 1905 Sep. 15, 1906 Sep. 17, 1907	1905	1908	Allen	James Robert	1847-1915	

Elected	Began HBC	End HBC	Last name	First/Middle	Birth/death	Other info.
1907?			~~Cline~~	~~J. R.~~		error
Sep. 19, 1908- Sep. 18, 1920 *Sep. 17, 1921	1908	1921	Stone	John R.	1855-1938	*elected, but did not serve another year
Oct. 1921- Sep. 14, 1935	1921	1936	Roper	Robert "Rob" Amos	1865-1939	
?	1925	1925	~~Anderson*~~ Recorded in error?	~~John M.~~	1858-1934	Men & Missions, Vol I, p 8; Vol II, p 186
Sep. 19, 1936; Aug. 21, 1937- Aug. 18, 1945	1936	1946	Tribble	Pledger Washington "Doc"	1887-1976	Revival likely moved to July in 1937?
Aug. 17, 1946- Aug. 1949	1946	1951	Lummus	John	1925	
	1951	1953	Sutton	W. Jack	1897-1973	
	1953	1956	Majors	Elbert	1914-1977	
	1956	1961	Thompson	Paul W.	1914-1994	
	1961	1964	Ellis	Leland Everett	1923-2005	
	1964	1966	Thompson	Paul W.	1914-1994	
	1966	1969	Lummus	John	1925	
	1969	1970	Henderson	Tommy	1913-1998	
	1970	1973	Martin	Robert Quillen	1936	
	1973	1980	Richards	Gerral	1940	
	1980	1982	Lummus	John	1925	
	1982	1986	Thompson	Harold Edwin	1934-2003	
	1986	1992	McCormick	Ronnie	1963	
	1992	2013	Richards	Gerral	1940	
	2013		McCormick	Ronnie	1963	

Deacons

HBC deacons are selected on an as needed basis. When the Church feels that it needs more deacons, usually three to five men are chosen to be ordained. Once the number of men has been decided, the Church members, at a subsequent conference, are asked to list the names of the men desired as deacons. Those men receiving the most votes are then ordained. The third chapter of First Timothy is used as a basic guideline for choosing deacons. At HBC, deacons are elected for life and serve as long as able. The duties are taking care of the business of the church along with seeing that the Church holds onto the teachings of the Bible....Submitted by Randy Wilkie

A concise list of previous deacons at HBC is difficult to create since the earliest church records begin in 1882. A review of the delegates from HBC appointed to attend both the association and union meetings in the 1800s reveals some names that are listed numerous times. A HBC member can be a delegate without being a deacon, however deacons are often among those selected to represent the church at those meetings. Additionally, early written records did not clearly identify names of persons, but often listed initials instead of first and middle names. Three early deacons were found listed in other church records, and were believed to be accurate. Any errors or omissions found in this list of deacons are unintended and it is desired that amendments be made as appropriate.

About 1852

Moses Ledbetter (1813 – ca 1855) HBC delegate 1853 and 1854. Joined as a deacon by letter from Beaver Ruin BC (family information in *The Heritage of Cherokee County, 1831-1998,* page 381).

Mid-1800s Ordination or letter unknown

Jonathan L. Coggins, (1815-1890) listed in 1877 Ophir BC minutes as J. I. Scoggins, a deacon from HBC served on presbytery for constituting Ophir. A HBC delegate 1867 and 1868.

James Purcell, (1797-1882) listed in 1877 Ophir BC minutes as a deacon from HBC who served on presbytery for constituting Ophir. A HBC delegate many times from 1848-1860s.

Late 1800s Ordination or letter unknown

Joseph Wyatt, (1831-1910), first wife (Mary Catherine Pascoe Wyatt, 1837-1884) buried at HBC; Joseph Wyatt listed in Sep. 14, 1877 constituting of Ophir BC as an ordained as deacon to serve. Joseph Wyatt served on presbytery as a deacon, at the 1890 deacon ordination at HBC, not sure where Joseph was a member. Possible Joseph Wyatt was a deacon at HBC before moving letter to Ophir?

HBC minutes begin in 1882

Nov. 1884 Ordination

Thomas N. Smith (1857-1919) Thomas Nathan Smith, buried HBC.

J. L. Williams (1835-1913) John Lewis Williams, Dismissed by letter Dec. 14, 1889. Joined again by letter Aug. 1894. Dismissed by letter Mar. 16, 1912.

May 1890 Ordination

G. B. Fletcher (1862-1932) George Barto "Bart" Fletcher, buried HBC.

J. S. Wyatt (1856-1929) John Samuel Wyatt, buried HBC.

Aug. 14, 1900 by letter as ordained deacon, **Bro. D. M. B. Dobson** (1851-1909) David Miles Berry? Dobson, and dismissed by letter, Nov. 15, 1902.

Oct. 20, 1900, by letter as ordained deacon, **J. S. Andrews** (1840-1902), John Andrews.

July 19, 1904 Ordination

    J. H. Ellis (1863-1926) John Henry Ellis, buried at HBC.

    G. B. Haygood (1848-1925) Samuel Green Berry "Bud" Haygood, buried at HBC.

    H. G. Wilkie (1877-1956) Hiram "Glen" Wilkie buried at HBC.

1911 by letter as ordained deacon, **G. W. Wehunt** (1847-1915) George W. Wehunt, buried at HBC.

Oct. 16, 1920 Ordination

    R. M. Cantrell (1879-1940) Raymond Marion Cantrell, buried at HBC.

    H. T. White (1881-1940) Henry "Turner" White, dismissed by letter May 20, 1934, buried at Rome, Ga.

    Jess L. Wilkie (1893-1947) Jesse Lee Wilkie buried HBC.

Apr. 17, 1926, Ordination

    R. E. Lovelace (1886-1938) Robert Edgar "Ed" Lovelace, buried HBC.

    R. Fulton Roper (1893-1985) Robert Fulton Roper, also licensed preacher at HBC 1930, dismissed by letter, Jul. 15, 1934.

    S. S. Wyatt (1886-1974) Samuel Septamus Wyatt, buried HBC.

January, 1939 Ordination

    Elisha Cochran (1884-1970) buried HBC.

    Joel Heard (1886-1968) buried Coal Mountain BC.

    Lee Hester (1889-1987) buried Macedonia Cemetery.

    R. E. West (1892-1965) Robert "Emory" West, Sr., buried HBC.

1945, by letter **Joseph "Joe" Henry Wilkie** (1900-1980) buried HBC.

November, 1950 Ordination

    Dewey Cowart (1908-1979) buried HBC, licensed and ordained preacher.

    Grady Lee Hester, dismissed by letter Oct. 14, 1961.

    Robert Lee Milford (1915-1988) buried HBC.

    Amos Wilkie (1908-1972) buried HBC.

    Linton Wyatt (1914-2008) buried HBC.

April, 1965 Ordination

    Elbert Cochran

Robert West (1920-2003) buried Macedonia Memorial.

Gene Wheeler

Leon Wilkie (1929-1996) Amos James "Leon" Wilkie, buried HBC.

Frank Wyatt (1914-1984) buried HBC.

<u>April, 1981</u> Ordination

Walton Gilleland

John Heard (1921-1991) buried Sawnee Gardens.

Carl Hill (1922-1981) buried Oakdale BC.

Edsel Smith (1926-1992) buried Sawnee Gardens.

Randy Wilkie

<u>December, 1981</u>, by letter **Toy Allen**

<u>January, 1995</u> Ordination

Coy Cochran

Thomas Heard

Billy Hill

Ronny Price

Lanny Wilkie

<u>February, 1998</u>, by letter **Weymon Cook**

<u>September, 1998</u>, by letter **Hubert Wilkie** (1925-2013) buried HBC.

<u>March, 2010</u>, by letter **Kent Cochran**

Pictures of deacons (as available):

John Lewis Williams (courtesy of Chad Williams) Seated: John Lewis Williams and Mary Ann Williams; Standing L-R: Johnny Zebulon, Mary Azilee and Green Berry Williams; picture ca 1892.

G B Fletcher

(courtesy of Rebecca Bannister)

John Henry and Mary Catherine Ellis

(courtesy of Larry W. Ellis)

John Samuel Wyatt

(courtesy of Ken Wyatt)

Hiram "Glenn" and Lula Wilkie

(courtesy of Darrell Cook)

Robert Edgar "Ed" Lovelace
(courtesy of Scott Bursmith)

Samuel and Leola "Pearl" Wyatt
(courtesy of Ken Wyatt)

Fulton Roper
(courtesy of Byron Burgess,
Men and Missions Vol. I)

Elisha and Jennie Cochran
(courtesy of Brenda Cochran Curtis)

Joel A. and Birddie Heard

R. Emory West

(courtesy of Tim Perkins)

Lee and Emma Hester

(courtesy of Regina Groover)

Joe and Ida Wilkie

Dewey, Ruby and Marvin Cowart

Robert and Cleo Milford, picture ca 1946

Grady Lee Hester

(courtesy of Regina Groover)

Amos Wilkie

(courtesy of Mitzi Chambers)

Linton and Winnie Wyatt

(courtesy of Ken Wyatt)

Leon Wilkie

(courtesy of Mitzi Chambers)

Robert and Claudine West

(courtesy of Gail Burtz)

Frank and Geneva Wyatt

John Heard

(courtesy of Thomas Heard)

Carl and Hazel Hill

(courtesy of Billy Hill)

Edsel Smith

L-R front: Gene Wheeler, Walton Gilleland, Leon Wilkie, Randy Wilkie; back: John Heard, Robert West, Elbert Cochran, Edsel Smith and Linton Wyatt
(photo courtesy of Brian Wallace)

Deacons at HBC, Alphabetical Listing

Last Name	First/Middle	Birth-death	Year Became a deacon at HBC	Ordination or Letter	Other info.
Allen	Toy	1925-1986	1981	Letter	
Andrews	J. S. John?	1840-1902	1900	Letter	
Cantrell	Raymond Marion	1879-1940	1920	Ordained	Bur HBC
Cochran	Coy		1995	Ordained	
Cochran	Elbert		1965	Ordained	
Cochran	Elisha Franklin	1884-1970	1939	Ordained	Bur HBC
Cochran	Kent		2010	Letter	
Coggins	J. L.	1815-1890	?		
Cook	Weymon		1998	Letter	
Cowart	Dewey Leonard	1908-1979	1950	Ordained	Also ord. preacher Bur HBC
Dobson	D. M. B.	1851-1909	1900	Letter	
Ellis	J. Henry	1863-1926	1904	Ordained	Bur HBC
Fletcher	G. Bart	1862-1932	1890	Ordained	Bur HBC
Gilleland	Walt		1981	Ordained	
Haygood	G.B.	1848-1925	1904	Ordained	Bur HBC
Heard	Joel	1886-1968	1939	Ordained	Bur Coal Mt.
Heard	John	1921-1991	1981	Ordained	Bur Sawnee M
Heard	Thomas		1995	Ordained	
Hester	Grady Lee		1950	Ordained	Dismissed by letter
Hester	Lee	1889-1987	1939	Ordained	Bur Macedonia
Hill	Billy		1995	Ordained	
Hill	Carl	1922-1981	1981	Ordained	Bur Oakdale
Ledbetter	Moses	1813-ca1855	1852/53		
Lovelace	Robert Edgar	1886-1938	1926	Ordained	Bur HBC
Milford	Robert Lee	1915-1988	1950	Ordained	Bur HBC
Price	Ronny		1995	Ordained	
Purcell	James	1797-1882	?		
Roper	Fulton	1893-1985	1926	Ordained	Also Ord. preacher
Smith	Edsel	1926-1992	1981	Ordained	Bur Sawnee Gardens
Smith	Thomas N.	1857-1919	1884	Ordained	Bur HBC
Wehunt	G. W.	1847-1915	1911	Letter	Bur HBC
West	Robert Earnest	1920-2003	1965	Ordained	Bur Macedonia Mem.
West	Robert "Emory"	1892-1965	1939	Ordained	Bur HBC
Wheeler	Gene		1965	Ordained	
White	Henry "Turner"	1881-1940	1920	Ordained	Dis. By letter, 1934 Bur Rome Ga
Wilkie	Amos Felton	1908-1972	1950	Ordained	Bur HBC

Last Name	First/Middle	Birth-death	Year Became a deacon at HBC	Ordination or Letter	Other info.
Wilkie	Amos James "Leon"	1929-1996	1965	Ordained	Bur HBC
Wilkie	Charlie "Hubert"	1925-2014	1998	Letter	Bur HBC
Wilkie	Hiram "Glen"	1877-1956	1904	Ordained	Bur HBC
Wilkie	Jessie L.	1893-1947	1920	Ordained	Bur HBC
Wilkie	Joseph Henry, Joe	1900-1980	1945	Letter	Bur HBC
Wilkie	Lanny		1995	Ordained	
Wilkie	Randy		1981	Ordained	
Williams	John Lewis "Jack"	1835-1913	1884	Ordained	Bur Macedonia BC
Wyatt	Arthur "Linton"	1914-2008	1950	Ordained	Bur HBC
Wyatt	J. Frank	1914-1984	1965	Ordained	Bur HBC
Wyatt	John Samuel	1856-1929	1890	Ordained	Bur HBC s/o Joseph and Mary C Pascoe Wyatt
Wyatt	Samuel Septamus	1886-1974	1926	Ordained	Bur HBC

Chapter 11: Hightower Highlights, Family Connections, Places and Events

Burns, Coffee, Wilkie and Leonard families.

The above families, connected by marriage have links to HBC.

Dr. John Burns (1794-1858), his wife Lucy (1796-1877), and several of their children are buried at HBC. Catherine Burns (1766-1849), the mother of Dr. John is also buried at HBC. Catherine's grave is marked by large stacked stone. Nearby, and with a similar stacked stone marker, is the grave of John Edward Coffee (1836-1852). John E. Coffee was the son of James Calton Coffee and Adaline Burns Coffee. Were Dr. John Burns and Adaline Burns siblings? If so, Catherine Burns and her presumed grandson have similar and unique stacked stone grave markers. Because of the stacked stones, these three graves are among the most unusual in the entire cemetery. One could guess that the third stacked stone grave, in the same vicinity but with no identification, may also be connected with the Burns/Coffee families, and likely a burial about 1850.

According to a family sketch found in *Heritage of Cherokee County*, James Calton Coffee (1819-1913) and Adaline Burns Coffee (1801-1889) had the following children:

John Edward Coffee (1836-1852) – buried HBC

James Alexander Coffee (1838-1918) m. Eliza Johnson

Louisa Catherine Coffee (1840-1926) m. Hiram Wilkie

Winifred Caroline Coffee (1842-1927) m James Lafayette Leonard

Texas Ann Coffee (1846-1897)

Hiram Wilkie (1836-1900) and James Leonard (1832-1888) were from families that lived near HBC. It is reported that in 1868 or 1869, Hiram and James joined their father-in-law James C. Coffee as he led a large number of families, possibly as many as twenty-one (including his children and their spouses), on a wagon train journey from Cherokee County, Georgia to northern Arkansas. Other Leonard families reportedly had moved to the Arkansas country in 1867. Much like the earlier migration to North Georgia, these people continued their quest for a better way of life by moving westward.

Cannon

On November 23, 1843, in Gilmer County, Silas F. Cannon (1817-1897) married Sallie Davis (1827-1903). Their children were Neta (Chastain), Rebecca "Rilla B." (Hester), Isaac, John, William, James, George, Huggins and Joseph. According to U.S. Census records, this family moved from Gilmer County, to Cherokee County, between 1860 and 1870. Silas served in the Civil War Company A, Cherokee Legion Infantry Regiment, Georgia State Guards. Pictured below is the grave marker for Silas and Sallie Davis Cannon, which is one of the most noticeable in section two, and one of the most unusual in the entire cemetery.

Photo courtesy of Judy Northington

Rev. Elias A. Cochran

Elias A. Cochran (1845-1931) was an unusual person. If it is thought that the average man was clean-shaven, married to one wife and father to many children, then E. A. Cochran would definitely not be considered average. Rather, he became known as the man with the longest beard, was married three times, and did not father any children. His life bore many drastic events and changes. He was born to Terrell B. and Francis Nix Cochran; apparently his mother died before he was ten years old as his father married a second time to wife Sarah Elizabeth Nix in 1855. In 1860, Elias was fifteen and living in the Cross Roads District, Cherokee County, GA, with his father (who was born in North Carolina), his step-mother and five siblings (including Robert W. Cochran, age eight). Duty called, and Elias went into a challenging world of the War Between the States. He enlisted in the Confederate service in 1864 and served as a prison guard at Andersonville. Near the end of the war, he joined with other guards to escort Union prisoners to Mississippi. While on the trip back, his group was captured in Alabama. He was released as a prisoner of war in Alabama in May of 1865. As found in *Men and Missions, Vol. I*, Elias joined New Harmony BC in September of 1865. His tombstone; however, states that he joined the Baptist church in 1867. This may suggest the date he joined HBC. In 1868, he married Jane Fowler, daughter of James and Sarah Fowler of HBC. About 1881 or 1882, he was called to preach. The HBC minutes begin in June of 1882 and on that date, E. Cochran was selected to serve as a delegate to the HBA yearly meeting. No record in the church minutes describe issuing Cochran a license to preach, yet he was one of the preachers of record at the conference meeting in August of 1882 and at many subsequent conference meetings. The date of his ordination was either August of 1884 or November of 1884. The August date is listed in a ministerial directory and on Cochran's tombstone; however, the October 19, 1884, minutes state that Bro. E. Cochran would be ordained at the next regular meeting. He was elected pastor at HBC for a term of one year in 1894 but served as co-supply on other occasions. In addition, he was mentioned in numerous HBC conference minutes as the moderator pro tem and many, many times as a delegate from HBC to both union and association meetings. His wife, Jane, died in September of 1888 and early in 1889, he married Jane's sister, Emma Fowler. His second marriage was cut short upon Emma's death in June of 1901. Soon he married for a third time to Kansas (Kanse) Wheeler, daughter of James and Rosa Davenport Wheeler of Forsyth County. According to the tombstone at HBC, E. A. Cochran died October 15, 1931. The large grave marker (shown left) notes information for Cochran and all three wives. The lengthy inscriptions for all four persons are detailed in Chapter 12 of this book, Cemetery: Interments by sections. It is believed that Kansas is indeed buried beside him, but the graves of both Jane and Emma Cochran are actually in another section of HBC cemetery although the headstone of Cochran describes memorials to him as well as all three wives. Also, located next to this monument are stones inscribed for Rev. Robert W. Cochran (brother of Elias) and Robert's wife Matilda. (Additional information can be found in Chapter 10 of this book, Pastors and Deacons.)

Photo courtesy of Judy Northington

Contributing sources: *Men and Missions, Vol. I.*; Shadburn, Don L. *Pioneer History of Forsyth County Georgia;* Shadburn, Don L. *The Cottonpatch Chronicles;* Lasher, George W. *The Ministerial Directory of the Baptist Churches in the United States of America.*

E. W. Cochran

Notes from a conversation on June 27, 2014, with one of HBC's oldest members.

E. W. Cochran was born on April 22, 1922, to Elisha and Jennie Cape Cochran at Orange, Georgia (now Macedonia Community). Soon the family moved to Ball Ground and by 1929, they relocated to Free Home. At age 92, E. W. lives with his wife on Highway 372 just north of the 372 and 20 intersection. He married Edith Hester, and they raised their five children on their farm at this same location. A World War II veteran, farmer and long time member of HBC, his vivid memory and willingness to share his thoughts brings a wealth of information about a century just passed.

Photo courtesy of Regina Cochran Groover

E. W. tells, "When we moved to Ball Ground, we lived at the Amos Wilson place, and then moved here when I was six years old. My family had a mule or horse and buggy and an old farm wagon, then Dad and Mama had their car. Dad had a T model, a '28, and Dad would drive to the corn mill over in Lathemtown when I was twelve years old, but Dad let me drive on the way home." Driver's license weren't required then. "Then we had an A model, then I bought a '34 roadster, it was about used up, I had to put oil in it all the time, then I got a '38 Ford. I started to school at Ball Ground, and then later went to Free Home. If someone got through nine grades at Free Home, they were in pretty good shape. I remember going to church in a buggy or wagon as a little boy. The parking lot was a small area; the rest of it was for mules, buggies and wagons. It was growed up in bushes and such and folks would hitch the mules and horses there and the trees were around the cemetery in front of the church. There were also big oak trees, no such thing as pavement. There were always two roads that led from the main road down toward the church, when you came off the main road. The oldest church burned, didn't it? I remember the one that is there now, but it was much smaller then, because we have added on to it since. I helped Roy Ball build the Sunday school rooms. I don't remember how long it was from when I started going to HBC until we started the improvements. The front steps were old rock, then we got marble later on. We only went to church once a month back then, and if you didn't pay a nickel a month, you might get turned out of the church (ha ha).

Inside the old church, there was potbellied stoves, burned coal. They wouldn't get warm until you were about ready to go home. The choir area was not there until later. The stove had a sand box around the bottom of it, some folks were known to spit it in during service, and a few would spit their chewing tobacco juice in the ashes at the bottom of the stove (ha). Later, they put in floor furnaces. My daughter, Regina, fell on one of those one time and still has a scar on her leg from the burn. Back in the day, when you went to church you knew you were going to stay a while. We used to have the hour and a half preacher. When he got through, then another one would get started preaching.

I was baptized down at the old pool, there was a good many when I was baptized, maybe 20 or 25 or more." The Association minutes of 1934 shows 35 baptized that year. "Mr. Lovelace had a water pump, called a ram. He used it to pump water to his house before they got electricity. Us boys didn't know what it was, and we were curious. We would go down there and try to figure out what made it work. We were eight or ten years old or so. The first preacher I remember was 'Robbbbb' Roper. I think he was there about twelve or fifteen years. I also remember old preacher Lias Cochran." (See Ch. 11, Rev. E. A. Cochran) "Us kids called him the old grey mare; he had the long grey beard you know. He is a distance relative, Dad called him a cousin, I don't know how much it was, 2nd or 3rd or what. He lived out there where Edsel Smith lived. My Grandpa Cape lived on the Franklin Gold Mine Road and every year when we had a reunion, Preacher Cochran would always ride by, and that's what I remember most about him.

I remember once, I was paid 10 cents an hour for work. I picked cotton and got paid nothing. I worked on the Jess Nelson place, the Tom Westbrook place, then sometimes Emory West sawmill till dinner time, then come home and pick cotton there about our place. I picked 100 pounds in an afternoon one time. Lots of pretty cotton, that's when I was a young boy at home, so we didn't get paid. Jess Nelson's wife was Lula Gilleland, she was Sam Gilleland's sister. Jess and Lula had a boy named Emmett, he married Clara Bailey, Kile Bailey's sister. They had a child named Max and then moved off to Marietta. I think Jess Nelson conducted singing school up there at Hightower in the early years. If he didn't, he went. My Daddy knew his Do Re Mi's, when he'd get in the spirit, he could sing the Do Re Mi's pretty good. He enjoyed it so well. Monroe Mac (McPherson) taught singing school, he belonged at HBC for a while. Mrs. Argie Wheeler would play the organ; the pump organ, she did. Before the piano, we used to have one of those organs. I don't know when they got the first piano. If we had a piano or organ, Argie played it. I don't remember not having a musical instrument of some kind.

Edith and I got married on November 14, 1943 at Sam Cochran's house, down the hill down there on the creek at Nelson. That was the marrying place. I don't remember any weddings at the church. Some would go to John Fossett over here; he was a Justice of the Peace. I was in the Army when we got married, and was stationed for a time in Grenada, Mississippi. Edith and I lived there until August of 1944 when I went overseas. I went back and forth across the English Channel three times. I wound up with frost bite on my feet and went to England for 87 days. After that, I went back to France and helped gasoline up the convoys. There were many dreadful hours, days and months. I think everyone needs to know what we had to deal with." E. W. received an honorable discharge on January 7, 1946.

E. W. was asked about other memories of HBC. He replied, "Nothing more than people love the old church place and haven't ever let it go down, they just kept improving it. We have lots of land down there, but I still appreciate the old stomping place. I know lots of people would like newer things, but the old church is where I feel at home. To me, it is a very beautiful church. I probably didn't tell you anything you didn't already know, but it has done me good, when you ask a question, it makes me think of something else. My memory ain't as good as it once was. I am thankful though, they all tell me my memory is pretty good. One more thing I remember, it was in more recent years, but during revival we had a thunderstorm and the lights went out. Regina (Groover) was playing the piano, Gerral Richards was the pastor. They opened the front doors, and moved the cars and shined the car lights in the front doors so they could have some light in the church. We had a real good service. I think Tabitha, my granddaughter and Staci Wheeler were saved that night." *Cleo Heard Milford diary, Friday, July 24, 1981: "Young people in charge of service, Kris Wheeler. Lights went out. Lots people up for prayer including Brantley Floyd, Stacie Wheeler, Brian Wilkie, Angie Cline, Tabitiha Price, Allison Thacker, and 4 people from Macedonia."*

E. W. concludes: "There's one more thing, I want you to hurry up and get the book made because I want to read it and I may not have long to be here."

It is with sadness that shortly after this visit, Edith Cochran passed away on July 20, 2014. Several months later, E. W. also passed on January 24, 2015. They are buried side by side at HBC, a church they knew so well and loved. Their marker reads: "Wed 70 years, Nov. 13, 1943. Our children, Ed, Regina, Rilla, Coy, Stanley." It is with honor for this family that this entry is included in this book!

Elisha and Jennie Cochran

Elisha Franklin Cochran, born March 22, 1884, was the son of Wiley Franklin and Eliza Jane Howell Cochran. Elisha married Jennie Cape on November 9, 1913. Jennie was born on August 12, 1895, to William and Mary Hawkins Cape. Elisha became a member of HBC in 1929, listed in the membership roll as Elishy Cochran. Elisha was ordained as a deacon of HBC in 1939. Elisha and Jennie became parents to eight children: Emmett Broughton (Mary Lee Cochran); Florence Geneva (Frank Wyatt); unnamed child (died at birth); Bonziel Oziel (died in infancy); Edward Watson, "E. W." (Edith Hester); Elbert Valentine (Izelle Holbrook); Elisha Gilbert (Audrey Roper); and Mirtie Louise (Cecil McGaha).

Both Elisha (death: December 27, 1970) and Jennie (death: May 3, 1971) are buried at HBC. Their child, Bonziel, is buried beside them. According to Cochran descendants, the unnamed infant of Elisha and Jennie is buried in section one near the graves of Nevels and Altiney Griffin Cochran.

Elisha, Jennie, and son Emmett
Photo courtesy of Brenda Curtis

Shown in the pictures below are Cochran siblings,

Photos courtesy of Brenda Curtis

L-R: Elbert, Gilbert, E. W., Louise, Geneva, and Emmett.

L-R: E. W., Gilbert, Elbert, Elisha, Louise, Jennie, Mary Lee, Emmett, and Peggy Cochran, Louise, E. J. and Frank Wyatt, and Elisha's brother Wiley Cochran.

Rev. Sam and Eunice Ellis Cochran

Rev Sam and Eunice (with infant Mary Lee),
front Jeanette and Ozell

Picture courtesy of Larry Waylon Ellis. Information from personal interview and with permission from: Ellis, Larry Waylon. *A Family History of John Henry Ellis and Mary Catherine Haygood Ellis*. 1997.

John Samuel Cochran (1897-1984) was a son of Thomas Govan and Leo Sarah Moody Cochran. Sam joined Conns Creek BC in August 1913 and later moved his membership to Bethesda BC. He was called to preach in the summer of 1930 and was later ordained at Bethesda.

Emma Eunice Ellis (1895-1971), daughter of John Henry and Mary Catherine Haygood Ellis, lived near HBC during much of her youth. She attended Creighton School near Andrews Chapel. She joined HBC by experience and was baptized in August of 1909; her name is listed as Euness Ellis in book three of HBC membership.

Sam and Eunice were married on August 16, 1914. They became parents to: Eva Jeanette (Homer Pinyan), Emma Ozell (Henry Milford), Mary Lee (Emmett Cochran), Carrie Inez (Clarence Coltrane), Eulon Samuel (Sara Hawkins), and Luther Eugene (Colleen Bagwell).

For many years, Sam and Eunice lived in Nelson, and called their farm Cedar Holler. In 1943, they moved to their home in Free Home community. Sam performed numerous weddings through the years, and perhaps was known as Marrying Sam. Stories as told by his family remain that the children and grandchildren of the Cochran's were often called to be witnesses to the weddings.

From those listed above, the following are buried at HBC: Sam and Eunice Cochran, John H. and Mary C. Ellis, and Mary Lee and Emmett Cochran.

Picture of Cedar Hollow, L-R: Sam Cochran, sons Gene and Eulan.

Photo courtesy of Brenda Cochran Curtis.

Hazel Cook remembers grandparents and revival at HBC

Photos courtesy of Darrell Cook

Pictured above is Floy Hazel Wilkie, about age ten and as a young adult.

Miss Hazel Wilkie joined HBC by experience in July 1936. She was dismissed by letter in 1950. Shortly before her death, Floy Hazel Wilkie Cook (1923-2013) wrote the following information for her son about her times at Hightower with her grandparents, Samuel Pascoe Porter (named for his grandfather Samuel Pascoe) and Emma Day Porter. Samuel and Emma Porter are buried at HBC near the graves of Wash and Francis Wilkie. Hazel Cook is buried at HBC in section four near her parents, Harrison (1900-1985) and Ruby Lee Porter (1905-1999) Wilkie.

"I loved to go visit them in the summer when school was out. I spent a week with them usually in August when the crops were laid by and revival meeting was going on. I remember we would stay with her friend Lula Cantrell and her husband. We went to meetings twice a day, morning and night. There were no screens in the windows and fans were passed around as it was real hot in the church. We made several trips to the water bucket that some of the boys kept full of fresh spring water with a gourd for drinking.

He (Samuel Porter) loved to go to Hightower Church. They only had services every third Sunday. Grandpa loved children and always kept Juicy Fruit chewing gum in his pocket. The children soon learned this and would always crowd around him in the yard after church and he would give them a stick of gum. I guess they knew him as the chewing gum man.

I quit going when I was about twelve years old but not until I was saved and baptized at Hightower Church during a revival meeting. The water was cold as it came from a spring and a lady kept watch over us and pinned our dresses with a safety pin between our legs to keep it from floating up to the top and exposing us. I was afraid of the water and was glad when it was over.

Most of my relatives are buried at Hightower and someday I will join them. My brother Hiram, mother and dad (Ruby Porter Wilkie and James Harrison Wilkie) and grandparents (Samuel and Emma Porter; Hiram "Glenn" and Lula Jones Wilkie) are there also."

Story contributed by Darrell Cook

Jewell Wilkie Cotton: "Homemaking: It Was Rough in the 1900s, Women Folk Worked Hard"

Moore, U. G. (1976, January 29). Homemaking: It Was Rough in the 1900s, Women Folk Worked Hard. *The Cherokee Tribune*, pp. 18-19.

Oza "Jewell" Wilkie was born on October 5, 1898 to parents Hiram "Glenn" and Lula Payne Wilkie. She was the oldest of eight children and grew up in the community near Old Hightower Church. She joined HBC by experience in August 1919. She married Robert Orren Cotton and lived much of her married life in the Macedonia Community, Cherokee County, Georgia. The following excerpts are from the above listed article.

(1976) Mrs. R. O. Cotton lives in a lovely quiet country home that is as comfortable and is equipped with as many modern conveniences as a home anywhere but when she was Jewell Wilkie, a little girl in the early 1900s living with her parents out near Old Hightower Church things were quite different.

"It was rough then...women folks had to work hard and I don't mean pecking on a typewriter or answering the telephone. I sure wouldn't want to go back there again. My mother had to spin cotton thread on a spinning wheel to use to knit our sox. Took six to eight hours to spin enough thread for one pair of long soxs. We made all our clothes...mother was lucky; she had a sewing machine. Not many folks had one. She bought wool and cotton material for the men's pants. Folks without a machine just had to do the best they could.

We went to church every Sunday; (*Hightower only had services on the third Sunday of the month, but it was common for families to attend neighboring churches on other Sundays*) had a good house but goodness, it was cold.

...Houses didn't have rugs, floors were cleaned by scrubbing with a shuck mop and sand. When you rinse them off, the planks would be real white. Sometimes a room without an outside door would have a hole in the corner for the water to run out. They would scrub the church floors about once a year...was a real community affair and took all day to get those benches out, scrub, rinse, and put the benches back.

We worked hard but enjoyed life more than folks do today. Used simple things...made what we had...never bought anything hardly...a real good life...but I wouldn't want to do it again...too used to modern day conveniences. No sir! I sure wouldn't want to go back." (See additional quotes from Mrs. Cotton in Chapter 11)

Cowart

Diane Cowart Martin reported this on Jan. 2, 2015, about her aunt, Inez Cowart Stewart Howard – a daughter of William and Toma Cowart – still living in Jan. 2015, age 96, born 1918, saved in 1931 or 1932. Inez remembers being 13 years old, there were 51 or 52 baptized that year, Rob Roper was the pastor. During the revival, there was such celebration and shouting that the pillars of the floor broke "through" and before revival could continue, the men of the church had to repair the floor. She remembers she thought she was going to freeze to death when baptized in the cold water at the pool on the Lovelace place.

William "Will" Edward Cowart (1889-1973) and Toma "Tomie" Cara Cornett Cowart (1891-1982) lived for many years in the Hightower District of Forsyth County, and attended Mt. Tabor BC and later Hightower BC. They are shown below. In the second picture with their family, the picture was taken just before one of the sons was scheduled to leave for military service. Many of the Cowart family are buried at HBC.

Inez Cowart Stewart Howard

Will and Tomie Cowart

Pic of family, standing L-R: Ira, Hubert, Clay, Dewey, Inez, Harley, Everett, and M. H. seated: Tomie, Dorothy and William

Photos courtesy of Diane Cowart Martin

Ira Cowart: "I Can Hear Them Singing Over There"

L: Ira Cowart, R: Ronnie Price

Photo courtesy of Regina Groover

Photo courtesy of HBC

One of Ira's favorite songs, the title listed above, blessed many who attended HBC throughout the years. Those who knew Ira Cowart would agree that he answered and fulfilled God's calling as a Church Song Director. A tribute recognizing Ira and his tireless work as a church leader is noted below. Ira was born on November 24, 1912, to William and Toma Cowart. He lived with his parents and farmed in the Hightower district of Forsyth County, Georgia and attended Mt. Tabor BC as a young boy. He met Effie Hester and they were married about 1935. Effie joined HBC in 1931 with a transfer from Liberty BC and Ira joined HBC by letter July 1940.

Ira and Effie were blessed with many years of marriage. Although no children were born to this union, they were fondly known to many youngsters as "Uncle Iree and Aunt Effie," whether as blood relatives or just church families. They lived for many years off State Highway 20 on "Smithwick Hill," Canton. Ira Cowart passed away on May 3, 2004, and Effie passed on Dec. 23, 2012. They are both buried at Cherokee Memorial Park, Canton.

In a wonderful celebration of Ira's many years as a song leader, Ira was recognized at a church service and presented with a plaque that is now displayed in the HBC fellowship hall. The plaque reads: "In appreciation and love to Ira Cowart, a faithful servant of our Lord Jesus Christ for devoting his love and service for over 50 years to Hightower Baptist Church as a faithful member and Church Song Director. Presented in love by Hightower Baptist Church November 1, 1998." For additional information about Ira and Effie Cowart, see Chapter 7.

Frankie Green Edge

L-R: Cindy, Frankie, Barry and Raymond Edge

Born to Tom and Hattie Bell Turner Green, Frankie has lived in the HBC community most all of her life. Among Frankie's ancestors are the names Green, Turner, Hawkins, Wyatt and Pascoe. Frankie remembers going to HBC as a child and seeing many horses and wagons "tied up" in the church yard. There were a few big trees, where the men loved to stand around and talk both before and after service.

Frankie graciously shared many memories with this writer in 2014. In no particular order, she remembered: "We always heard that way down on the cemetery out by the road, that slaves were buried there… My Grandmother Turner's father was married three times. Her mother died when she was about eight years old. Her father remarried right off, 'cause he needed somebody to look after the kids. She said her step-mother was real good to them. You know back then, men just got out and hunted a new wife….It sure is sad to think about the way the Indians were treated and the way they were run out…When I was young, the front of the church was just plain, and the steps were wooden I think and they just went right into the church…We went to church one time in the wagon, it had rained and rained and the roads were so bad. We lived down yonder on Julius Bridge Road, on the farm. That road was impassible and Papa Turner hitched up the mule and wagon and we all went to revival. Several families came in their wagons because the roads were so bad…It wasn't uncommon to cancel church if the weather was bad, especially in the winter…during the old days, if there was going to be a funeral at HBC, my Daddy always went and helped dig the graves…Nowadays, you can't imagine the school letting the kids out of class to go to church…My daddy drove a mule and wagon when he was about 8 or 9 years old, he hauled pyrite to Ball Ground, his dad had 8 wagons, I don't know if he owned them or if they belonged to the company, but dad would be right behind his daddy's wagon and they would drive them to Ball Ground and back….My Daddy went to Creighton School over there near Yellow Creek Road. He said he was in the 4th grade and the school burned down…I know that Nettie Lee [Lovelace] went to Tate to high school. There wasn't a bus in those days. It was hard to get an education. If you finished the 9th grade at the elementary school, you had done pretty good. High school was just two more years, but it was hard to get to Canton or elsewhere to high school…I remember the old wood or coal burning heaters in the church, up in the front. Also, there was a table with a water bucket on it and I think back and say, they Lord, the kids would go up there and get them a drink out of the dipper, and maybe they wouldn't drink it all and then they would put the dipper back in the water, my Mama didn't want us to drink out of it…I wish my family had more pictures from the early days. Not many people had a camera. Myrtie Wilkie was one of the first ones to have a camera that I knew anything about…I met Raymond in Canton. I was working at Jones Store and staying with my brother who was working at the cotton mill. In those days, if you went to Canton on Saturday, the streets would be full of people walking and shopping and all of them would be dressed up…After we married, we both worked at the cotton mill and for a while, we lived in the village. We had a nice, big, four room house. We lived on Jay Street, they call it Juniper now. There were big shade trees in our yard, the kids had tricycles and bicycles. I enjoyed living there…When I was little, gypsies would come around in an old truck of some kind, peddling dishes, pots and pans. Mama was afraid of them. Our house was off the road a bit and she always warned me to run home if I saw the gypsies coming.

Rumor was they would steal the children."

Frankie was baptized at HBC in 1942. Her story is told in Chapter 9 of this book, "revivals." She also shared that a few years ago she obtained a list of the people who were baptized that year. She keeps the list in her Bible and often thinks of those persons and their families. They are: Henry Andrews, Junior Burtz, James Burtz, Kile Bailey, Dorothy Kate Cowart, Mamie Cloud, Pauline Cronan, Christine Drummond, Harold Drummond, Frankie Green, Charles Green, Mary Gilleland, David Hitt, Corine Hitt, Celeste Holt, Wilburn Hill, Imogene Lovelace, J. T. Mills, Lillie Mills, Corinne Ray, Bill Ray, C. J. Ray, R. B. Stewart, Ethel Satterfield, Herman Wilkie, Parnell Wilkie, Kathleen Wilkie, Leon Wilkie, Grace Watkins, Bertha Watkins, Charles Watkins, and Hoyt Williams. Frankie demonstrates that HBC members continue to have a strong and abiding faith in Jesus Christ.

John Henry and Mary Catherine Haygood Ellis

This family reunion photo of the Ellis Haygood family was taken in the early 1920s. It was not unusual for families to spend the day together and have dinner on the ground. Also, for this particular event, the family hosted Rev. Elias A. Cochran, local preacher and it is presumed that he was given an opportunity to preach to the attendees. In the family photo, he is pictured third row (from front), sixth person from left to right, the fellow with the beard. Likely, the extended length of his beard was tucked into his shirt, as was his custom, since he was known as the man with the longest beard for his day (see additional story of E. A. Cochran in Chapter 11).

Picture and information courtesy of Larry Waylon Ellis from personal interview and with permission from: Ellis, Larry Waylon. *A Family History of John Henry Ellis and Mary Catherine Haygood Ellis*, 1997.

John Henry Ellis was born on October 27, 1862/1863, to John and Mary Jane Pinson Ellis. Mary Catherine Haygood was born on April 16, 1866, to Samuel Greenberry and Susannah Mosteller Haygood. Samuel Greenberry (G. B. on grave marker), known as Bud, and Susannah (Suseana) were baptized at Conns Creek in 1885 and transferred their church membership letters to HBC on November 14, 1896. On July 19, 1904, J. H. Ellis and G. B. Haygood (along with H. G. Wilkie) were ordained as deacons of HBC. G. B. (1848-1925) and Suseana A. (1844-1922) are both buried at HBC. (A picture of John Henry and wife Mary Catherine Ellis is included in Chapter 10, Deacons, of this book.)

John Henry Ellis and Mary Catherine Haygood were married on December 7, 1882, by Rev. H. T. Ingram. John Henry and Catherine Ellis joined HBC by letter on March 20, 1897. John Henry and Catherine became parents to ten children: Mary Rosanna (Pruitt), John Barry, James Elbert, Belsoney, Robert Lee, Oma Mae (Porter), Emma Eunice (Cochran), Daisey, William "Bill" Henry, and Carrie Irene (Sams). J. H. Ellis (1862/1863-1926) and Mary C. Fllis (1866-1948) along with several descendants are buried at HBC.

Larry W. Ellis also notes that the following are probable burials at HBC, but unmarked:

Littleberry Holcomb, Sr. (1764-1855), Elias/Eli Mosteller, and Carolyn Holcomb Mosteller (1805-1855).

Mira (Myra) Brady Fletcher Hogan

Mira Brady, born in 1821, married John Nelson Fletcher and lived in Lumpkin County Georgia and they became parents to eight children. After the death of John, Mira and the two youngest sons (H. K. and G. Barto) moved to the Franklin Gold Mine area in the 1880s. It has been told that Bart could knit the wire cables back together that pulled the pyrite up from the mines; a gift only a few people could do. Bart was ordained as a Deacon at Hightower Baptist Church in 1890. Mrs. Brady and her sons lived near Rev. Elias Cochran. Rev. Cochran was providing a home for a young lady, Sarah "Sallie" Azalee Ledbetter, who later married Bart Fletcher. After Sallie's death, Bart married Rhoda Spear. Hezekiah "Kelly," also called Kel (pronounced Cal) Fletcher married Augusta "Gussty" Hester. Barto and Kelly both raised large families in the Hightower area.

Family stories remain that Mira was skillful as a midwife and also quite proficient in speaking Dutch and in teaching children Dutch songs. She was very religious, studied the Bible and prayed often. Mira B. Fletcher married late in life to William Hogan, who lived in the area of Hogan's Pond off Gilmer Ferry Road. Mira B. Fletcher Hogan died in 1908 and was buried at HBC. Other family members of Mrs. Hogan that were also buried at HBC include Bart, his two wives, three of their children and also Kelly, his wife and one daughter.

HBC, as well as the community, were blessed by the contributions of Mrs. Mira B. Fletcher Hogan and her sons. No doubt many were pleased that they decided to move to the Hightower area.

Photo courtesy of Rebecca Bannister

Contributing to this story: Rebecca Bannister, with records from Era Fletcher Tribble of Cumming Georgia, daughter of Kelly Fletcher and Augusta Hester Fletcher.

Hezekiah Kelly and Augusta Fletcher

Back row, L-R: George Barto Fletcher, Ethel Jane Fletcher, Sarah Azalee Ledbetter Fletcher, holding a son, either Alfred Royston or Austin Barto Fletcher. In front is Myra Evalee Fletcher.

James Fowler

James Fowler (1797-1876) and wife Sarah Smith (1804-1875) were among the first settlers to the community near HBC. It is believed that James was a farmer, miner, and also a builder. James was possibly the builder of the Fowler home, still standing (2015), in nearby Forsyth County, and was thought to be built circa the 1830s, about the same time as the Stephen's log home (see Hightower Highlights, Daniel Stephens) as well as some of the mill structures near Pool's Mill. The record of James and Sarah Fowler found in *Forsyth County, GA Heritage, 1832-2011* notes that James obtained a forty acre land lot in the 1832 Gold Lottery, and later purchased additional acreage. Also reported was that James and Sarah were once members at Bethlehem Baptist Church before transferring their membership to HBC. They had eight children: Caroline, Lette, Elizabeth, Jane, Sarah Emma, Phillip, William Thomas, and General G. W. Several of their children as well as James and Sarah Fowler were buried at HBC. Daughter Jane Fowler married Rev. Elias Cochran, and upon her death, Rev. Cochran married another daughter of James and Sarah, Sarah Emma Fowler.

Photo courtesy of Ken Wyatt and Annabel Ballew

Mary Franklin

In the oldest portion of HBC cemetery, two of the largest monuments are those of Mary Franklin (1782-1858) and her son, Dr. Bedney L. Franklin (1815-1844). Pictured to the left is the marker of Mary Franklin, and nearby is a similar one for Bedney. Much has been written about this interesting family even though the details, such as Mary's ride on a mule from Athens to the HBC community to check on her forty-acre gold lot, leave one to wonder just what is true. Regardless, the Franklin Gold Mines were established by this woman, and at some point her son Bedney joined her. Few records have been found to determine how many other children may have lived and worked at the mines in the family business.

Mary Graves Cleveland, mentioned above, was likely the wife of Abednego Franklin (1776-1816), and they became parents to six sons and a daughter. A number of years after Abednego's death, "Widow Franklin" won the Cherokee land in the gold lottery in Cherokee County in 1832 and discovered gold there. In addition to her son Bedney Jr., she was also aided by her son-in-law, Charles McDonald. At one point, the company was named the Franklin and McDonald Mine. Her daughter, Ann McDonald, died in 1835, and later Charles would become a governor of Georgia. The 1844 date of death for Bedney Jr. is the oldest date of death noted on a monument in the HBC cemetery. Some records indicate that he drowned in the Etowah River. Other details, as told by a Pascoe descendant, relay that a tragic mining accident took the life of Bedney. The exact cause of death may never be known. Mary Franklin, founder of the Franklin Gold Mines, died in 1858, cause unknown. She is buried next to her son Bedney at HBC. Their monuments, quite elaborate for the era, leave a bit of information about their lives. Details of the inscriptions can be found in Chapter 12 of this book. One

Photo courtesy of Judy Northington

interesting item on Mary's marker states that she was a member of the Baptist Church for 51 years. No record exists to confirm a possible transfer of membership to HBC upon her move to the community. It is believed that the Franklin family continued to operate the mining company for another decade or so after Mary's death. Soon after the Civil War, the family sold their interest in the business, although the name Franklin Mines as well as Franklin Gold Mine Road have left a mark on this community, likely forever.

Additional information along with Mary's picture can be found on page 258, "Franklin, Cleveland, McDonald" in *Cherokee County, Georgia Heritage, 1831-1998.* Canton, GA: Cherokee County Historical and Genealogical Society and Don Mills, Inc., 1998.

Also information from page 62, Shadburn, Don L. *Pioneer History of Forsyth County 1832-1860, Vol. I.* Roswell, GA: Wolfe Associates, 1981.

Gilleland

Bunion Vester Gilleland (1886-1968) of Dawson County, Georgia, married first to Lavada Mae Redd, and they became parents to six children: Esco, L. J., Vester, Ithane, Etna and Helen Grace. When the youngest was about two years old, Levada passed away. Bunion was left with this large family and had a need for a new wife. The one chosen was Lilly Green (1898-1989). Bunion and Lilly became parents to an additional eight children: Ed, Sam, Mary, Dorothy, Walt, Roger, Atholine and Gene. Bunion and Lilly attended HBC for many years along with their children. Bunion and Lilly are buried in Section 4 at HBC.

Pictured above, probably before Gene was born, L-R: Bunion, Lilly holding Atholine, Sam, Ed, Dorothy, Mary, Roger and Walton.

Photo courtesy Mitzi Chambers

Newt and Rossie Hester Green (e)

Rossie Hester, daughter of Andrew and Elizabeth Hester, married Henry Newt Green. Rossie's father, Andrew Hester, was born to Thomas and Mary Hester on December 4, 1847 in Pickens Co., South Carolina. After his father's death, Andrew was just a young lad when his mother moved to Cherokee Co., Ga. He married Elizabeth Davis in 1874. Andrew Thomas Hester (death 1910) and Elizabeth Davis Hester (death 1932) are buried at HBC. They were parents to the following: John Robert Hester (Alice Gertrude Lathem), William Andrew Hester (Dora Holcomb), Mary E. Hester (John Green), Christopher Columbus "Lum" Hester (Mattie Freeze), Lula Viola Hester (Raymond Marion Cantrell), Rossie Lee Hester (Henry Newton Green), Mattie A. Hester, Oscar Franklin Hester (Jewell May Porter and Maud unknown), and Thomas Edgar Hester (Flora Augusta Wilkie).

Rossie Lee Hester (1886-1938), mentioned above, married Henry "Newt" Green and had the following children: Thomas William, Donzie, Edward, Winnie Maude, Bonnie, Frank, Jesse Lee, Agatha, and Mary Blanche. At her mother's death, Agatha Green wrote the following which was found in a clipping from the *North Georgia Tribune*:

Death Saddens Greene's Home (Rossie Lee Hester Greene)

Death saddened the home of Mr. Newt Greene and children January 18, 1938, when it took from them a loving wife and a sweet mother. She had lived 1 year and 2 months after her first stroke of paralysis and Sat. Jan. 8th, she suffered the second stroke. And after 10 days of suffering Jesus called mother to "come." All was done for mother that loving hands could do.

The pearly gates were opened and a gentle voice said "come." God knew best and called her home, to live on the golden shore where partings come no more. We know that she is at rest but our home is sad without her.

Funeral services were held Wednesday, Jan. 19, 1938, at Hightower Baptist Church, with Rev. P. W. Tribble and Rev. Sam Cochran conducting the services. Her body was laid to rest in Hightower Cemetery. She is survived by her husband and nine children, as follows: Tom W. Greene, Edd Greene, Frank and Lee Greene, Mrs. Bowman Roper, Mrs. W. G. Rich, Miss Bonnie, Miss Agatha and little Miss Blanche Greene and 3 sisters, Mrs. R. M. Cantrell, Mrs. Mat Hester and Mrs. Mary Greene, 4 brothers, Judge, Will, Lum, and [Oscar Franklin] Hester, and a host of other relatives and friends who mourn with these survivors in their great loss.

William Green

It is believed that in Cherokee County, Georgia, on December 4, 1844, William Green married Martha White. William was born about 1820 and Martha about 1818. They were listed on the U.S. 1850 census as living in the HBC area. Both the Green and White families likely were living in Cherokee County before William and Martha married. William and Martha Green became parents to: Emerly (Ambrose Worley), Mary Jane (J. W. Fitts), Thomas E. (Elizabeth Arwood), Francis Ann (George "Wash" Wilkie), Samuel W. (Martha Jones), Elizabeth A. and Joseph P. (Nancy Ashworth) Green. (Also see story of daughter Francis Ann with husband George Washington Wilkie, Chapter 11). While it is unknown where William (1820) is buried, a marker is located at HBC for Martha Green (no dates) and adjacent to her son Samuel and his wife Martha Jones Green. The inscription says: "Grandmother Green, placed by Newt and Tim Green."

Pictured below is the family of Thomas Edward I and Elizabeth Arwood Green, photo believed circa 1916/1917.

Photo courtesy of Diane Cowart Martin (daughter of Ruby Green Cowart)

Back row, L-R: Hoyt Green, Thomas Edward Green II, Bessie Hall Green, Lucille Green Davis, Mollie Elizabeth Parker Green, Lillie May Green Gilleland, Ella Green Cornett, Lawrence Green

Front row, L-R: Wilburn Quill Green, Lee Barry Green, Mildred Green, William Edward "Will" Green, Thomas Edward Green I., Elizabeth Ann Arwood Green and Ruby Elizabeth Green Cowart

Many of the William and Martha Green family were members at HBC, buried there, and many descendants continue to worship there into the 2000s.

HBC siblings, cousins and extended families

Cochran Ladies: L-R: Geneva Cochran Wyatt, Mary Lee Cochran Cochran, Jennie Cape Cochran, Edith Hester Cochran, Louise Cochran McGaha, Audrey Roper Cochran, Izelle Holbrook Cochran

Photo courtesy of Brenda Cochran Curtis

Cochran Men: Standing L-R: Frank Wyatt, Elbert Cochran, E. W. Cochran, Emmett Cochran, Gilbert Cochran, Cecil McGaha, seated: Elisha Cochran

Photo courtesy of Brenda Cochran Curtis

Cochran: L-R: Brothers E. W. and Elbert

Photo courtesy of Regina Cochran Groover

Hawkins' and Pascoe's

Photo courtesy of Ken Wyatt

Haygood, G. B. and family

Photo courtesy of Larry W. Ellis

Lovelace Sisters: L-R: Nettie Lee Lovelace, Edna Lovelace Chandler, and Imogene Lovelace Bursmith

Photo courtesy of Chris Chandler

Milford family: L-R Joe, Judy, Cleo (Heard), Robert, Joyce and John

Smith and West families, Back L-R: Emory West, Homer Smith, Myrtie West, Velma Smith, Gus Smith; Front: Bob West and Jack Smith

Photo courtesy of Tim Perkins

West family: about 1945, L-R: Jake, Robert, Emma, Walker, Herbert and Edward West

Photo courtesy of Tim Perkins

West family, about 1945, L-R: Odell West, Ilah West Burns, Emma West, Imogene West Cannon and Merle West

Photo courtesy of Tim Perkins

Wilkie Sisters, L-R: Georgia Ann Wilkie Lovelace, Viola Wilkie Sandow, and Myrtie Wilkie

Photo courtesy of Chris Chandler

Wilkie cousins. L-R: Lanny Wilkie, Stanley Cook, and Randy Wilkie

Photo courtesy of Mitzi Wilkie Chambers

Wilkie, Four of the children of J. Harrison and Theodocia Wilkie, Standing L-R: Clara, Annie, and Argie. Seated: Spencer

Photo courtesy of Joyce Wilkie Odom

Wyatt, Sons of Samuel and Pearl. L-R: Cleveland, Clinton, Dewey, Grady, Linton and Toy

Photo courtesy of Ken Wyatt

Family reunion at the home of John Samuel WYATT c. 1922.

Wyatt, John Samuel Family Reunion, ca. 1922

Photo courtesy of Ken Wyatt

Joel and Birddie Heard

Joel Augustus Heard (1886-1968) and Birddie Julie Godfrey Heard (1887-1972)

Joel was born in Forsyth County, Georgia to John Arch and Sallie Harrison Heard. At the age of sixteen, Joel assumed the role of family patriarch upon his father's untimely death. Being the oldest child, Joel felt the need to help guide his younger brothers and sisters and developed a leadership role that has been modeled by numerous descendants. He did not waste time on many words, and his handshake, or his word, was worth as much as any signature. He went on to become an entrepreneur of his day with the horse and mule business and settled in Lathemtown, Georgia, in the early 1920s. Prior to moving from Forsyth County, he married the former Birddie Julie Godfrey, daughter of Elbert Cisney and Martha "Mattie" Carolyn Rives Godfrey. Together they became parents to seven children: Arch (Arah Harbin), Tom (Ruby Holbrook), Jessie (J. C. "Buck" Pruitt), Lee "Bud" (Frances "Pete" Lathem), Cleo (Robert Milford), John (Geneva Wilson) and Mattie (Robert "Bob" Turner). In keeping with the "few words", none of their children were given middle names. Joel and Birddie transferred their membership to HBC from Coal Mountain BC in February of 1931. Joel and Birddie attended HBC faithfully, Birddie taught classes for children at Sunday school and Joel became an ordained deacon in January of 1939. Joel always wore a hat, entered the church "on the men's side" and sat in the Amen Corner. This writer cannot recall ever seeing her grandparents, Joel and Birddie, sit beside each other at church, as Birddie always sat on the women's side opposite the Amen Corner. Joel and Birddie are buried at Coal Mountain BC Cemetery, Forsyth County, Georgia.

Pictured ca 1922, L-R: Arch, Jessie (Pruitt), Birddie, Bud, Tom, John, Joel and Cleo (Milford)

Pictured about 1945, L-R: Tom, Jessie (Pruitt), John, Cleo (Milford), Bud, and Mattie (Turner)

Lee and Emma Hester

Lee H. Hester was born on September 22, 1889, to parents John H. "Jack" and Rebecca B. "Rilla" Cannon Hester. John H. "Jack" (1844-1920) and Rilla Cannon (1847-1902) Hester were buried at HBC. Lee was a grandson of Thomas and Mary Williams Hester. The Hester family first came to Cherokee County early in the 1850s when the newly-widowed Mary moved with her children to be near her brother, Zebulon Williams. Lee met and married Emma Mae Whitfield, who was born on February 26, 1896, a daughter to Caleb and Rozella Whitfield. Lee joined HBC by experience on August 8, 1910. Emma joined HBC by letter on Dec. 20, 1913 and they were faithful members of HBC for all their lifetime. Lee and Emma had eight children. Irene died as an infant. The remaining seven, identified in the picture below, also became members at HBC.

Shown below L-R: Grady Lee, Ruby, Edith, Mr. Lee, Toy, Mrs. Emma, Jack, Effie and Roy at the 50th anniversary celebration of Mr. Lee and Mrs. Emma Hester.

The extended family of Lee and Emma Hester at their 50th anniversary, with their home pictured in the background

Photos courtesy of Regina Groover

Jack Hester, the youngest child of Lee and Emma, wrote in a booklet for a recent family reunion, that he and other descendants were fortunate to have Lee and Emma Hester as their ancestors. Now over 80 different families appreciate the love and legacy of Lee and Emma and are proud that they were brought together as a blessed extended family.

Jack remembers:

- Being told that Dad courted Mom in their surrey

- Mom and Dad took us to church at Hightower in the wagon when it rained real hard because we couldn't get the 1937 Ford up the hill in back of the Scott's home place; the 1937 Ford had 60 horsepower and a stick shift

- Spending the night with Toy (his brother) and Cliffie and that riding in their 4-door A-model Ford was quite an experience!

- Hoeing corn and raising cotton, plowing with a mule and getting lifted off the ground

- Cutting the cane and hauling it by wagon to Scott's syrup mill to make syrup for the family

- Scott's Steam Engine coming up the road with sparks coming from the wheels when it would hit the rocks along the dirt road. The Scott's would saw logs on our farm into lumber that Dad would sell or use on the farm.

- My brother Grady and I walked four miles to school at Coker's Chapel and later Macedonia. My Dad was a Trustee at Coker's Chapel.

- Grady and Roy being drafted into the Army in the early 40's and Mom crying because they had to go

- Mom and Dad had the first chicken house in the community

- It was a great day when Mom and Dad asked me if I would like to go to Reinhardt College. Along with many others, I helped pour the cement for most of the walkways near the administration building there.

- Dad was a Deacon at Hightower for many years. He died without having a single enemy. He told me many times, it is better to have the good will of a dog, than to have ill will.

- Receiving $25.00 from Ira and Effie (his sister) for learning to play the piano

- Great home cooked meals by sisters Effie, Ruby and Edith

- Grady and Inez provided great home cooked meals when Jackie and I were newly married

- Helping Dad cut wood and going with him with a wagon load of stove wood that he sold in Ball Ground. Sometimes we bought necessities at Hubbard's General Store with money earned. He also sold butter that Mom made from milk and sold other farm products we didn't need ourselves.

Jack provided this summary: "HBC has been a steady influence on the well-being of the entire community for many, many years; a light on the hill for all our lives." Many thanks to Jack Hester for his memories of the Hester family and for this example of a family with a strong and abiding faith in Jesus Christ!

Moses Ledbetter: Was He a HBC deacon?

In 1837, Moses Ledbetter joined the Forsyth Co. Militia and volunteered to fight in the Florida Seminole War to put down an Indian rebellion; he served for about a year before being discharged. In 1839, he volunteered a second time for the same reason, being discharged after a few months active duty. Once again he resumed his civilian life working as a lumberman and farmer; he would later become a goldminer.

Moses and his wife Mary were members of Beaver Ruin BC in Forsyth Co. for about ten years. Moses was a deacon and representative of that church at several Hightower Baptist Association Meetings. His name was no longer listed in the church records after 1845. He evidently left the Cumming area for Hightower, several miles to the west, relocating around Settendown Creek near the Cherokee/Forsyth Co. line. If he transferred his membership to HBC, he was likely received as an ordained deacon. In 1853 and 1854, M. Ledbetter was a delegate from HBC to the HBA meetings.

In 1850, it is thought that Moses was in California, looking for gold. He is presumed to have left Georgia in 1849. His family is not found in the 1850 census; they may have moved away while he was gone or may have joined him. In late 1851, Moses returned from California with a small fortune in gold and began buying property in both Forsyth and Cherokee Co. on Dec. 3, 1851. He purchased a 40 acre lot, #652 in the 3rd District of Section #1 in Forsyth Co, near Ducktown. Moses died in 1855. At that time, six of the children were under age of 14.

Most information for the above story found at: "Moses Ledbetter, the Forty Niner." *Cherokee County, Georgia Heritage, 1831-1998.* Canton, GA: Cherokee County Historical and Genealogical Society and Don Mills, Inc., 1998.

Ed and Georgia Ann Lovelace

Pictured to the left is the young family of Robert "Edgar" and Georgia Ann Wilkie Lovelace, along with daughter Fannie and son George. As the story goes, Georgia Ann Wilkie was born on April 27, 1890, to parents Wash and Fannie Wilkie. Mr. Wash Wilkie was a large landowner and ran a store in the "Ophir" community and just west of HBC. Even though the gold mining was beginning to falter, a young man named Edgar Lovelace (born Oct. 8, 1886), with some experience with the mining industry, moved to the area from Lumpkin County. He met and married Miss Georgia Ann. They lived on their farm just east of HBC and soon became parents to five children: George Hallman, Francis/Fannie (Wilson), Nettie Lee, Imogene (Bursmith) and Edna (Chandler). While farming was a necessity, Mr. Lovelace was considered quite the engineer of his day. Not only did he install a pump to provide water in his home long before electricity was available, it is also told that he provided the plan for HBC to add the extension for the choir section in January of 1938. Unfortunately, his life was cut short before that year ended.

An original newspaper clipping from *North Georgia Tribune* reads as follows:

R. E. Lovelace, Canton GA, Dec. 12, 1938 – Rites for R. E. Lovelace, 52, prominent Cherokee Countian, who died at his home near here Thursday after a long illness, were held Saturday in Hightower Baptist Church. The Rev. P. W. Tribble officiated, assisted by the Rev. M. J. Williams and burial was in the Hightower cemetery. Mr. Lovelace, a native of Gainesville, was educated at the North Georgia Military Academy. He is survived by his wife, one son, G. H. Lovelace of Wilmington N.C., four daughters, Mrs. C. L. Wilson and Misses Nettie Lee, Imogene and Edna Ann Lovelace, one granddaughter Janis Carole Lovelace, a brother, C. C. Lovelace of Ponca City, Okla., and an aunt, Mrs. W. B. Harris, of Paso Robles, Cal., and Gainesville.

Photo courtesy of Chris Chandler

Left a widow, Georgia Ann continued to live on the farm and instilled in her children a love for education coupled with hard work. Pictured to the right are L-R Georgia, Imogene (top) Edna and Nettie Lee. This family continued to attend and support HBC for many years. Edgar, Georgia, all their children and the spouses of the married ones are all buried at HBC.

Photo courtesy of Chris Chandler

Nettie Lee Lovelace

Mary Helen Cissell, local author, conducted numerous interviews with area persons just before 2008 for her book *Living, Laughing, Loving in Old Lathemtown*. She included an entry from an interview with Nettie Lee Lovelace of HBC, but the following excerpt was extra material. With Mrs. Cissell's kindness and permission, portions of this additional interview are shared here for publication in this book.

Nettie Lee Lovelace

"I was born on December 15, 1919, to parents Robert E. Lovelace and Georgia Ann Wilkie Lovelace at this farm and have lived here all of my life. It was known for many years as the Hightower area of Cherokee County. My grandfather, George Washington Wilkie, owned a lot of property here. He had eleven children and all of them inherited a farm except one who took money instead. My father's family, the Lovelace's, came from Lumpkin County and Dawson County. They were originally from England.

I had one brother and three sisters: the birth order was my brother George, my sister Frances, myself, and sisters Imogene, and Edna. I enjoyed my childhood growing up on the farm. Back then, our purchases were few; even the stores didn't have much to buy, just baking soda, salt, flour and sugar, for example. We grew all of our own food and my mother would can vegetables and dry the fruit. To dry apples you would put them on a wire screen in the sun. The county had a cannery in Canton and we would take our vegetables there to be canned. They would put them in tin cans with no labels. That would have been in the 1930s and '40s.

We were one of the first families in the area to get a car; however, we still walked to Hightower Baptist Church most of the time because it was so close. When we went on trips in the car, we would go to the mountains in the fall and to the State Fair in Atlanta and to Canton. Going to Atlanta or Canton was a big event. When I was a teenager, I attended Orange Church in Lathemtown occasionally for a singing. I often spent the night with Cleo Milford, she was Cleo Heard then. She was good at keeping records. She kept a record of who preached every service and the scripture taught. I was also a close friend with Cleo's sister, Mattie.

Creighton School

My brother and sisters and I went to Creighton School until 1933 when it was consolidated with Etowah School. Creighton was located near the Creighton (Franklin) Gold Mine. It was a two room school but only had one teacher for grades 1-8. That was a great school and we had a great time! We would begin with a big enrollment in the summertime when the crops were finished, or laid by. Winter would come and enrollment would dwindle. My teacher, Mrs. Pearl McClure, was the wife of our family doctor. Dr. George McClure moved here when the mines were active. He was the kind of doctor that would make house calls. When someone in our family became sick, daddy would go get him in his car.

At Creighton, everybody had to buy their own school books. If they couldn't afford them, they would get used books, or the teacher would arrange for somebody to give them books. We went to school from 8:00 a.m. until about 5:00 p.m. or until the teacher got ready for us to go home. She taught all day long. We had recess and played tag, jump rope, hopscotch and town ball. Our teacher demanded respect and she got it. I think she used a switch. I used a switch too when I started teaching. Here's the difference in the parents then and now: parents used to come to a teacher and say, 'If they don't behave, you punish them and then let us know and we will punish them also when they get home.'

I actually started teaching when I was in the third grade at Creighton. I could read pretty well and the teacher would put me in an extra room with students who couldn't read or work their math problems and I would teach them. We did that in the summertime, because in the winter it was too cold to be in a room without a stove.

Drive-By Weddings

My Dad was a Justice of the Peace. Many couples came to our house to get married. People would stop by any time of the day or night and show my dad their wedding license and Daddy would marry them and Mama would witness. My dad never did charge them.

He also served as a judge in the Justice of the Peace Court. It was in a little one-room courthouse called Crossroads, just before the 4-way stop near here. Nothing serious was ever presented there. When anything happened in our community, people would come to him for advice. He was a deacon in the Hightower Church. He died when he was only 52 years old of extremely high blood pressure which damaged his kidneys and heart.

Girl Farmers

After my father's death, my mother was left with the three younger girls to raise. She had to be strong! I dropped out of school for a short time when Dad was real sick and helped out at home. My mother built chicken houses and managed the farm. She bought a new tractor, an International Harvester, with new equipment. My two younger sisters and I learned how to operate that tractor. Our brother had already left home. That year we had more fun with that tractor! We made nice straight rows and raised oats, corn, and lots of hay. We did the plowing, planting and cultivating because we thought it was so much fun. By the next year, the newness of the tractor was over and the fun was gone!

My Parents: Love at First Sight

During the days of our youth, not many people went to college. However, in our family, there was an understanding that we would go to college. My dad went to college in Dahlonega at the North GA Agricultural School. After he finished there, he worked for the newspaper offices in Dahlonega and Gainesville. He used to set the type by hand. His father, William James Lovelace, was a mining engineer. He helped open the mines in Dahlonega. When the pyrite mines were opened on Creighton Road, my father and grandfather came here to work. Pyrite is used for making gunpowder and ammunition. My mother told me about the first time that she ever saw my dad. He was wearing his uniform from North GA College. She thought that he was the most handsome man that she had ever seen! My dad said that when he first saw my mother, he exclaimed, 'She's mine!' My mother was living in the big white house with her parents, the Wilkie's. They had a general store, a cotton gin, and a warehouse. The community was originally called Ophir and the Ophir post office was in the store. The family home is still there today (on Hwy. 369).

Going Away to High School

I went to Etowah School through 9th grade. There were no buses in the area for transportation to a regular high school; therefore I went to Reinhardt High School at the same location as the college in Waleska. I had a little apartment with some girls. We had the same teachers as the college students and our classes were in the college buildings. Later I went to Tate High School, because I had a cousin that lived in Tate that needed my help. She had some health problems and her brother offered me free board if I would help her get through high school. The marble building was the high school. We both graduated from Tate. The next year, I went back to Reinhardt to attend college for two years. Then I went to North GA and graduated there. My oldest sister had heart problems and rheumatoid arthritis and wasn't able to go to college, but the remainder of my siblings and I did attend college.

Etowah and Free Home Schools

My first teaching job was at Etowah School where I had attended. It was a 4 room school with 4 teachers. It was built in 1934 and consolidated Creighton and Oakland Schools. It was located off Hwy. 369 near Hightower Baptist Church. It was the first school in the state to be built by the WPA, Works Project Administration. Opening day was a huge event attended by families in the community and the State Superintendent of Schools. In the 1940s, a school lunchroom was added on to the building. Parents brought fresh vegetables from their gardens and chickens to be prepared to feed the entire student body. The school was closed in 1956 when it was consolidated with Free Home. Consolidation was necessary at the time because of a severe drop in enrollment. However, there was much community opposition to it, and the community lost a lot of its spirit. In the meantime, I began teaching at Free Home in 1949. At one time, I had 52 students in grades 5 and 6, but an average number would be 35 or 40. Each teacher taught a combination of 2 grades in each classroom. Yes, I had discipline! At the old Free Home School, we didn't have a library, and there was no central heating. Teachers had to build fires in the wood burning heaters and take out the ashes. When the new school was built in 1956, it was a nice brick building with central heat and a nice library. We thought we were on "Cloud 9"!

After about twenty years in the classroom, I received a nice surprise. I was asked to become the curriculum director for Cherokee County. I talked to my mom and she encouraged me to accept the position. I worked an additional twenty years as curriculum director and later as assistant superintendent in charge of instruction. I retired when I was 58 years old. I was teased that I was the youngest person to retire with 40 years of service! Of course I started teaching at a young age, as I said, in the third grade! Actually, the year that I started teaching was 1939, before my 19th birthday. I had not completed my college degree at that time, which was common during that era."

After retirement, Nettie Lee spent her time traveling, working on her farm (she continued driving her tractor), spending time with family and attending church functions at her beloved HBC. She was a valued member of the choir and the unofficial church historian. A major project on her farm was the restoration of a log cabin (pictured below) for which she was most proud. The cabin dates back to the 1830s and was believed to be the home of the Daniel Stephens family. Many are grateful for her many contributions to HBC as well as the community and for her life well-lived.

Nellie Lee Lovelace
Photo courtesy of Mary Helen Cissell

Sam and John Pascoe

Samuel Pascoe (1810-1887) and wife Mary Jackson Pascoe (1817-1889) are buried at HBC. Also believed buried nearby is Virginia "Little Ginny" Mourning Victoria Pascoe (1861-1862). No evidence exists to determine whether John and Mary Pascoe were HBC members as they are not found in membership book one. Perhaps the choice to bury Little Ginny at HBC also led to the parent's burial there in later years. The Pascoe's were parents to fourteen children. Several of those were HBC members, as well as numerous descendants continue to attend HBC.

Samuel Pascoe was reportedly born in Cornwall County, England, where his family was associated with the tin and copper mines. In 1826, it is thought that Samuel and two brothers, John and James, immigrated to America in pursuit of the gold mining industry. Family stories conclude that James settled in Pennsylvania and later died in a coal mine disaster. John and Samuel made their way into North Georgia. After struggles in the Dahlonega area, John moved to the Etowah River and Settendown Creek District. With the financial help of a local landowner, Major Wiley Petty (HBC member), John was able to lease land from the Leonard family and begin business as a gold miner. John had some measure of success with gold, and built a fine home in anticipation of arranging for his wife-to-be, still in England, to join him (not sure if they were married or just engaged). Most sources believe the "Pascoe-McClure-Leslie-Rainey" home was built between 1847-1853, taking some four years to complete. John imported a carved oak floor-to-ceiling mantel and other furnishings from England. A carriage drive was located in front of the house and a road led to the ferry crossing. Tragedy struck in 1853, and John's death was attributed to mercury poisoning. A process using mercuric acid to separate gold from other minerals, led to breathing this substance which caused his death. His fiancé never occupied the home. Instead, while on her way to America, she got the news of John's death and went back to England. John was buried at Andrew's Chapel Cemetery, located in the vicinity near HBC.

Mary and Sam Pascoe - Photo courtesy of Ken Wyatt

Meanwhile, Samuel Pascoe had an expertise with explosives and was hired to help with construction of a dam in Athens, Georgia. While there, he was injured during an explosion by a rock hitting his forehead. He was nursed back to health by a young woman named Mary Jackson. They eventually married and lived in Putnam and Heard Counties for a period of time, later moved to Lumpkin County and eventually to Cherokee County. Among the children of Samuel and Mary were twin sons born after John Pascoe's death, and named: Samuel Washington "Poodle" and John Jackson "Pug" Pascoe. Samuel W. (wife, Effie Stephens) and John (wife, Ella Stephens) were all four HBC members (HBC membership books one and two). Another child of Sam and Mary Pascoe, their daughter Mary Catherine, married Joseph Wyatt. Descendants of the Wyatt's have attended HBC for many years.

After John Pascoe's death in 1853, Samuel Pascoe became the owner of the Pascoe home, and lived there for the remainder of his life. His youngest child, Little Ginny, was his prize. When she was born, the story remains that Samuel said, "Here is the most beautiful babe of all. She is the blossom of my last seed. I am blessed beyond all measure." Again, tragedy struck this family and in July, 1862, Little Ginny died. Samuel was reportedly away on a business trip in South Georgia, and the family attempted to preserve her body until Samuel returned home. Her body was wrapped in camphor and salt and kept in the cellar of the house for several days. A group of men made an unsuccessful attempt to find Samuel, but the child was buried one day before he returned home. He changed her name to Mourning Victoria after her death. While over time, the tombstone carvings have made identification difficult, it is believed that Mourning Virginia Victoria, Little Ginny, Pascoe is buried at HBC in a grave like the one pictured to the right.

Photo courtesy of Judy Northington

Wiley Petty (1805-1892)

If one person could be chosen for a conversation "back in time" that would likely have many answers to the history of Hightower Association, it would be Rev. Alfred Webb. However, for the history of HBC, the person of choice would be Wiley Petty. Several documents, including old newspaper articles, left active footprints of Petty, yet in many ways he must have been quite illusive. If he was the same Wiley Petty as listed in the 1830 U.S. Census, he was living in Pickens County, South Carolina, before his move to Georgia. Cherokee County, Georgia land records show that Petty made numerous land purchases (and sales) throughout the years; one as early as 1833. A Cherokee County deed book notes that on August 22, 1834, a statement was recorded to identify his stock mark that could be found on his animals: a crop off the left ear, a swallow fork in the right ear. This early date placed Petty in the vicinity of HBC. Since the church was listed as a member of Chattahoochee BA in 1834, was Petty a charter member of HBC? No record has been found to prove or disprove this idea, but Petty continued to own land in area near HBC and upon his death, was buried in the church cemetery.

Wiley Petty married Martha Bailey Nix (1811-1871), the wedding possibly took place before leaving South Carolina. Martha's father, Charles Nix, was also listed in the 1830 SC census. Wiley and Martha did not have any children. Upon Martha's death, she was buried at HBC. Next, Wiley married Atlantic Harris. Wiley Petty and A. Petty are listed in HBC's membership book one, which begins in the year 1882. At Wiley's death in 1892, he was buried at HBC beside his first wife, Martha. Also found in book one membership roll is Pheba Petty. According to the 1880 U.S. Census, Cross Roads District of Cherokee County Georgia, a female named Pheby Petty (listed as black, and house servant) was living in the Wiley Petty household. Recorded by Pheba's name in the church roll is that she died on February 3, 1889. No record of burial has been found, but one could guess that she may be among those persons of color believed to be buried in an unmarked area of section one of HBC cemetery.

Wiley Petty not only bought and sold property; he was also a witness as recorded on deeds numerous times. He is credited with helping John Pascoe obtain his property from the Leonard family in the early 1840s, which led to the Pascoe Mining Company. He is listed in the local newspaper (*Cherokee Advance*) a few times in the late 1800s. In a July, 1885 article, Wiley Petty recalls names of many early settlers to the Cherokee area, a list that includes several HBC people, (Mary Franklin, Henry Holcomb, James Purcell, William Boling, Dr. John Burns, Edward Porter, Zebulon Williams, Nevels Cochran and Daniel Stephens)! One article from 1886, titled "A Talk With Major Petty," tells that "he settled here in 1834; that he nearly sheds tears at times when he speaks of his red-skinned friends, who were compelled to leave their heritage in this rich and lovely region; of old Aunt Thebe (Pheby) whom he brought with him from South Carolina and is still living with his family." Petty was a Civil War veteran, but the records found to date only list him as a private, therefore, the origin of the name or title Major is unknown.

Wiley Petty lived in the home located on the now named Logan Lane, also the former home place of Glenn W. Wilkie (long time HBC clerk). Legend also tells that during a particular dry summer (date unknown), Wiley Petty invited HBC to baptize new members in a pond on his property. This would have been long before the baptismal pool was constructed on the Lovelace property. The local area must have suffered a devastating drought if the water level in the Etowah River was too low to use for a baptizing.

Apparently, Petty had some wealth when he moved to Georgia as he quickly became a large landowner. How he weathered the stormy years of the Civil War, how he became to be named Major, to what extent, if any, was he involved in the mining industry as well as many other questions may remain unanswered. For the items of interest that were left behind, thank you Wiley Petty.

July 22, 1892, local newspaper reported: "We were saddened to hear of the death of **Major Wiley Petty** at his home near Ophir last Monday. He was in his 88th year and was one of the first settlers of Cherokee, having moved here before the Indians left" (Local Lines; Page 3 col 2).

In the next picture, Leon Wilkie (1929-1996), grandson of the above mentioned H. Glenn Wilkie was standing near the Petty home shown to the left. Also visible in the background is one of the farm buildings that may have been present during the lifetime of Wiley Petty.

Photo courtesy of Mitzi Wilkie Chambers

Bobby Roper

Bobby Roper lived in Atlanta as a young boy and visited his Roper family in the Free Home and Hightower communities on weekends. Bobby was born to parents Henry "Holman" and Bertie Turner Roper, his grandfather was Robert A. Roper, long time HBC pastor.

Photos courtesy of Bobby Roper

Bobby as a baby

Bobby Roper

Holman Roper, about 1927

View of HBC and funeral of Rev. R. A. Roper in 1939

Roper Family Reunion

Thomas Nathan Smith

Thomas Nathan Smith, HBC member and deacon, was the son of James W. and Rebecca Hester Smith. T. N. was born November 24, 1857, and died June 14, 1919. He first married Joanna Angeline "Angie" (last name unknown 1861-1889), and they had three children: Augustus Franklin, Okta Angeline, and Nettie Joanna. After Angie's death, T. N. married a widow Sarah "Jane" Sandow Lathem (1859-1899). T. N. and Jane became parents to Homer Spurgeon, Maggie Alice, and Myrtie Estelle (Robert Emory West). Thomas N., Angie, Jane, Myrtie and Emory are buried at HBC.

Shown below are five of the children of T. N. Smith. Front, L-R: Myrtie West, and Nettie Williams. Back, Homer Smith, Okta Smith and Gus Smith.

Photo courtesy of Tim Perkins

Julius Turner

John Julius Turner (1883-1962) married Dora Wyatt (1882-1968), daughter of John Samuel and Julie Hawkins Wyatt. A son, Paul was born in 1918, the picture below was likely taken before his birth. Their other children are shown in the picture.

L-R: Ruby Turner, Julius Turner, Estee Turner, Hattie Turner, Dora Wyatt Turner, and Leo Turner

Julius Turner is mentioned in Chapter 11, in the section labeled "Names of Local Roads and Places" because the Julius Bridge Road is named for him. Julius and Dora are buried at HBC. Also, among others interred at HBC are: Hattie Bell Turner Green and Thomas Edward Green; and Leo Turner Boling and Forrest Boling.

The West Family

The George W. West family moved to the Hightower area of Forsyth County, GA from the Union County/ Spartanburg County area of South Carolina in about 1853. While the West family has long been associated with Hightower Baptist Church, from historical records and gravesites, it seems likely that the family, which consisted of George W., his wife Jennet (Cowen) West, six sons and four daughters, attended Concord Baptist Church in Forsyth County at least until the 1890s.

A letter from Jennet (Cowan) West to her second son Paschal West in 1888 mentions going to meeting. This is an excerpt from the letter:

"Well, this is Sunday but I don't go to meeting often. I have sutch a bad way of getting along. I can't get in a wagen by myself. They set me in a chair and lifts me in and I can't get in the steps withoute help, but I recon it is all right. I have been very well waited on ever since I have been crippled. The nabers is all very kind to me. They come after me when I say I will go."

Through the lens of history, the West family's affiliation with Hightower Baptist Church can almost be seen as the result of series of tragedies that befell the family. We must always keep in mind that it's sometimes easier to see sadness and tragedy when researching our ancestors because war, death and illness left records while celebrations and other happy times often did not. We can be sure that the good times the Wests of Forsyth and Cherokee County, Georgia, had outweighed the sad facts we find in old historical records. That said, the George W. West family was first struck with tragedy in 1863 when their eldest son, Lightner West, a private in Company D of the 56th Georgia Infantry, died in October 1862 at Tazewell, Tennessee.

Lightner West left behind a widow, Sarah E. (Moore) West. His only son, Lightner Leander West, was born the January after his death. This son was the patriarch of the first West family to attend and be buried at Hightower Baptist Church.

As a child, according to Census Records, he lived with his mother and her second husband John A. Whitmire in Dawson County, Georgia. But in the 1880 United States Census, he was shown as living on his grandfather's farm in Hightower, Forsyth County, GA. He married Josephine L. McDaniel in 1882. They were probably still living on the Forsyth County side when this image was taken c. 1896. (There's another half of this image, which features the George W. McDaniel family.)

The 1890s brought more tragedy for the West Family. Lightner's grandmother and the family matriarch, Jennet (Cowen) West, died in about 1888 after a long decline that left her able to walk only on crutches. During 1891, flu or other illness decimated the area, and four of George W. West's children (Lightner West's aunts and uncles) passed away within the year. In 1895, George W. West, who had remarried the widow Nancy (Bagwell) Clayton, also passed away. His farm in the Hightower District of Forsyth County was sold off. Lightner West's only three remaining aunts and uncles on his West side had all migrated to Arkansas by the mid-1890s. The West family of Forsyth County, Georgia had effectively moved on.

In the 1900 census, the Lightner and Josie (McDaniel) West family is living in the Hightower District of Forsyth County, along with all of their 7 children. But about 1906, they began construction of what is now the West Milford

Farm near Free Home in eastern Cherokee County, Georgia. It is believed the family began attending Hightower Baptist Church around this time.

Family lore has it that Josie (McDaniel) West was a skilled carpenter in her own right, and also "the meanest woman you ever stepped across" when it came to being strict with children, grandchildren and great-grandchildren!

All of Lighter and Josie West's 7 children lived to adulthood. Their eldest, Walter Linton West (called Linton), married Emma Elizabeth Hester in 1905. Linton and Emma's fifth child, Olin, died as an infant and was the first West buried at Hightower Baptist Church. The children included Linton, Amattie Ella, Carl Roan, Nettie (Thaddeus Pickett Hester), John Martin, Robert Emory (Myrtie Smith) and George Ernest.

The names of those pictured above as labeled on the photo, front row L-R: Carl, Lightner, John, Josephine, Linton with Ilah; back: Mae, Ella, Nettie, Emory, Ernest and Emma.

The late 1920s brought more tough times for the West Family. The elderly Lightner L. West and his wife Josie both passed away and were buried at Hightower in 1927 and 1928 respectively. Their sons, Walter Linton West and John M. West, also passed away in 1928. My great-grandfather, Walter Linton West, died of pneumonia, exacerbated by a heart condition, after searching for missing members of the Millwood family after a tornado raged through the area in April 1928. And though his death certificate says he was "struck by lightning," family lore has it that John M. West died of electrocution at his home near downtown Ball Ground when changing a light bulb.

Newspaper account of the Millwood Tornado:

"The tornado which struck Cherokee County last Monday night at about 10:00 o'clock near Lathemtown and Orange, was probably the most appalling disaster that has visited our county. Five persons were hurled to death and a score of others injured, houses and barns blown away, cattle hogs and chickens disappeared and vehicles demolished, is the toll that this brutal tornado exacted. Coming on this little community while they slept and striking with viciousness and without warning, the windstorm carved a path of quarter of a mile wide and four miles long of the countryside, leaving uprooted trees, demolished homes and death and destruction in its wake. The tornado struck first at the home of William J. Millwood in the Orange Community, and after killing four members of this family and injuring five others, and scattering the Millwood home over a lot of land, traveled east to Lathemtown and destroyed four more houses."

- From the *Cherokee Advance*, March 28, 1928

The West family continued to attend Hightower Baptist Church and has celebrated weddings and Baptism there, and mourned their dead with funerals and burials in the churchyard.

Other Wests who have been part of the Hightower legacy include all of the children of Walter Linton West and their families: Ilah West Burns, Imogene West Cannon, Joseph L. (Jake) West, Walker West, Herbert West, Frank West, Robert West, Paul West, and Edward E. West.

Edward E. West is my, grandfather. At 89 years old, he's the only surviving child of Walter Linton West, and he still attends services at Hightower when his health allows.

The West family is proud to be a part of the Hightower Church legacy for over 100 years.

For more information about the West family, you can contact Jennifer Dunn at jenngenlandia@gmail.com or 770-596-5399.

Article and photos submitted by Jennifer Dunn.

Emory West

In addition to the Walter Linton West family, another son of Lightner Leander West made a contribution to HBC and the community. Robert "Emory" West (1892-1965) was a veteran of WWI as pictured in Chapter 6 of this book. He married on Feb. 7, 1921, to the former Myrtie Estelle Smith (1897-1977), daughter of Thomas Nathan Smith (HBC deacon) and Sara Jane Sandow Lathem Smith. Emory was ordained as a HBC deacon in 1939. Mr. Emory was the owner of Free Home Store, later known as West and Perkins, when his son-in-law became a partner. When Mr. Emory took over the store, he also helped friends fund and build chicken houses and sold them the chickens and feed from the store. The operation was a great example of general merchandise. Emory and Myrtie suffered much sadness with the death of several infants. Roy, Ray and Jack are buried at HBC in the area near the highway. A daughter, Sarah Josephine West (1925-1996), graduated from Canton High and Bessie Tift College and became a schoolteacher. She married R. B. Perkins on July 24, 1953. Another son, Robert "Bob" Emory West, Jr. was born to Emory and Myrtie in 1935. Bob married Mary Jean Manous in 1959. Several grandchildren of Emory and Myrtie continue to live in the Free Home community and attend HBC. Emory, Myrtie, R. B., Sarah and Bob are buried in the section behind the church at HBC. T. N. Smith is buried near the front of the church by his first wife, Angie. Jane Smith is also buried near the highway and across the drive from the three West infants.

Many who still attend HBC may share the following memories of Mr. Emory. Trips to the Free Home Store for a few necessities and a few treats are remembered well. His generosity with the penny candy is a memory for a lifetime! An extra nickel could buy the smallest bottle of Coca-Cola from the drink box with the coldest water ever. A Coke never tasted any better than from that cold water. Thank you, Mr. Emory, for always smiling and welcoming the children of the community to the store.

Information and Photos courtesy of Tim Perkins

Emory (holding grandson Tom Perkins) and Myrtie West

Young Sarah West and her brother Bob at play near the home now known as the West Milford Farm.

R. B. and Sarah West Perkins

John M. White

John M. White (born about 1845) was 85 years old as noted on the death certificate completed by the informant W. A. White when he died on Feb. 26, 1930. He was buried at Hightower; the "undertaker" was Jones Mercantile Co. Mary J. Evans White, wife of John M. (1841-1911) was also interred at HBC. Perhaps the photo shows John M. White as the elderly one (with crutches) in this photo thought taken in 1927, and to his right, likely W.A. White (1868-1940) followed by Mary Wyatt White (1877-1961). W.A., or William, and wife Mary are also buried at HBC. John and Mary were also parents to other children including Rosey, Julius and Henry Turner White. Others in the picture are not identified but likely are family members of the White's.

Photo courtesy of Ken Wyatt

George Washington (1889-1950) and Rosetta E. Cape Wilkie

George Washington Wilkie was born March 12, 1889, to Henry Lee and Jeulyne Richards Wilkie. George was named for his grandfather George Washington "Wash" Wilkie (1850-1917) who married Frances Green. George (1889) married Rosetta E. Cape, who was born Nov. 20, 1889, daughter of William J. and Mary F. Cape. George Washington Wilkie died May 9, 1950, and Rosetta Cape Wilkie died on Feb. 19, 1978, and they, along with three of their seven children, (Hurle, L. B. and Hoyt) are buried at HBC. Their children were: (1) Starling Hurle, 1908-1909 (2) Laura Myrtle Ruby, 1910-1996 (3) William Lee Broughton "L. B.," 1912-1988 (4) Hoyt, 1915-1917 (5) Weldon, 1917-1996 (6) Glenn W., born 1921 and (7) David Aaron, born 1924.

George worked at the Tate Marble Mill, as a farmer and later at the Canton Cotton Mill. Their son, Glenn W., provided insights about this family and also about "growing up in the shadows of HBC" for this writer on July 3, 2014. Glenn said, "My mother told me many times, that they were debating about what to name me, and they had thought about naming me for an uncle. We had a home birth, you know, and the doctor suggested why not name me Glenn W. and the W. would not stand for a name, just the initial to distinguish me from Mr. Hiram Glenn Wilkie."

Glenn W.'s vivid memories of having his burden lifted during revival services 1934, hearing his Mother shouting in celebration, followed by the baptizing at the "old pool" in the "coldest water surely," speaks of the spirit felt in and around HBC in the 1930s. Glenn W. freely described his testimony as follows: "I recall the summer I was baptized, the pool, it was way down the hill. They had a weekly revival service, I can't remember if it was July or

Photo courtesy of Glenn W. Wilkie

August, it was changed at some point – a visiting preacher would be invited to help run the revival, it began on Saturday and had a Sunday service, then went into the revival week. Some of my friends my age, I can't recall their names, except I do remember E. W. (Cochran). Monday and Tuesday we had morning and evening service, and as those days passed, I believe I was 13 years old, seeing some of my friends go up for prayer, be converted, and join the church, it began to bear on me dramatically. I felt a loneliness and emptiness, something was wrong! I think it was on a Wednesday, when the invitation was given, I was standing there with some of my friends, or family or something. I had a very dear old aunt sitting on the women's section, all of a sudden, one way or another, my eye caught her, she got up out of her seat, most everybody was already standing up of course, but she started walking across in front of the pulpit, walked across and down the aisle toward where I was sitting. I knew without a doubt she was coming to me, and she did. She put her arm around my shoulder and I felt so condemned, she never said a word, but I knew exactly what she had come over there for. I was sitting on the end of the bench. I moved a little bit, she was standing out in the aisle, I walked out and down to the altar I went. Ola Wilkie was her name. She was married to Clyde, my Daddy's brother. I came to the altar, bowed my head, got down on my knees and cried out to God to forgive me of whatever sins I may have committed; even today, it strikes me very deeply. I knew I was on the wrong track, my buddies, I believed they had gotten on the right track, and I wanted to get on the same track they were on. Anyway, I pleaded my case to God. My Bible, the King James Bible, says repent, repent and be baptized. Not at that point, but since then I've looked at it many times and in the dictionary, Webster, and in that big college dictionary I've got out there, what does repent mean? To feel pain or sorrow, for something done, or something left undone, especially for sin committed. That's the meaning of repent. After a period of time, [while at the altar] I felt like I had great relief and ever sin I had ever been guilty of, I felt like God had forgiven me. My mother, she was usually very reserved, but I set out and hollered, other people were shouting all around, I wasn't the only one converted at that time, my mother came over there with tears in her eyes and running down her cheeks, it wasn't tears of sadness it was tears of happiness. She shouted, you could hear her all the way outside the church, if you could have heard her over the other people, that's the kind of revivals we had. Sometimes we stayed in the night until midnight a few times with people. Anyhow, the weekend came, and I joined the membership, and was baptized on Sunday."

The following list of those baptized in 1934 was read to Glenn W. and his responses are included in quotes. E. W. Cochran, Roy Cannon, Rudolph Corn, Winnie Grace Buffington, Cinderella Bowers, Clay Cowart, George Dean, Mark Dobson, Magadalene Edwards, Maynard Edwards, Bonnie Green, ?? Cornett, Clarence Hawkins, Hunter Hawkins, Jewell Hawkins, Roy Hester, John Heard, Bloomer Little, Nettie Lee Lovelace, Catherine Little, Richard Lathem, Rade Phyfe, Paul Patterson, Balem Reece, Joe Rich, Myrtie Scott, Billy Turner, Brooke White, Toy Wyatt, Walton White, Samuel Wyatt, Jewell Wyatt, Glenn W. Wilkie "I knew that rascal," Alvin Wilkie, "my cousin," Clara Wilkie,"she was Alvin's sister," and Frank West.

This family is another example of the strong and abiding faith of HBC people. Pictured below are Glenn W. and his wife Katherine.

Glenn and Lula Wilkie's family

Contributors: Darrell Cook, Ruth Ann Wilkie Pinyan, Mitzi Wilkie Chambers, etc.

(photo courtesy of Darrell Cook and others)

Pictured above is the Glenn Wilkie family about 1924/1925. The location of the picture is believed to be at the Glenn Wilkie home place, which was the former home of Wiley Petty, member of HBC in the early and mid-1800s. Last name Wilkie, unless listed otherwise: <u>Back row</u>, L-R: Harrison, Dennis, Amos, Cleveland, Thad Wallace, Orrin Cotton, Jewell Wilkie Cotton, and Pearl. <u>Front row</u>, L-R: Ruby Porter Wilkie, Hazel, in her lap, Glenn, Lula Pearl Jones Wilkie, Annie Belle Wallace, w/Edith Wallace, Annie Maude Wallace, H.G. Jr, Hiram Samuel.

Hiram "Glenn" Wilkie (b. Jun. 4, 1877 – d. Sep. 30, 1956) was a son of George Washington "Wash" and Frances Ann Green Wilkie. Glenn married on December 24, 1896, to Lula Pearl Jones (b, Apr. 5, 1879 – d. May 31, 1962). The children of Glenn and Lula were: Oza Jewell (1898-1985 m. Orren Cotton); James "Harrison" (1900-1985 m. Ruby Lee Porter); Annie Belle (1903-1990 m. Henry Thad Wallace); Edwin "Dennis" (1905-1994 m. Callie Mae Wheeler); Amos Felton (1908-1972 m. Flora Belle Wyatt); George "Cleveland" (1910-1997 m. Edith Pauline Drummond); Alice Pearl (1912-2007 m. L. J. Gilleland); Ruth Ann (1917-1917); and Hiram Glenn Jr. (1919-1975 m. Lera Irene Bryant).

On September 20, 1956, the fifth Sunday of the month, Mr. Glenn Wilkie went to church at Hightower like he usually did every Sunday. As remembered by some of those in attendance, he was sitting in the choir area near the door on the side next to the Amen Corner. Quietly, he slumped in his seat and passed away. It was a dreadful day for those in attendance. As written in 1956 by Cleo Heard Milford in her daily diary, "We all at Hightower were very sorry to lose Mr. Wilkie. He has meant much to all of us, both at Sunday school and church." His funeral and burial at Hightower followed on Tuesday, October 2, 1956.

Glen and Lula Wilkie

Date of photo reported to be summer, 1956 of Mr. Glenn Wilkie sitting on the porch of his beloved HBC.

Photos courtesy of Ruth Ann Wilkie Pinyan

Wash and Frances Wilkie

The Wilkie Family - Circa 1898
TOP ROW, LEFT TO RIGHT: EDDIE FOREST, MYRTIE JEWEL, MATTIE JOSEPHINE, ALICE, VIOLA MINERVA
BOTTOM ROW, L TO R: GEORGE WASHINGTON, FRANCIS GREEN, GEORGIA ANN, FLORA AUGUSTA, HARRISON
NOT PICTURED: LEE, GLENN, HENRIETTA

Pictured ca 1898-1900 with Wash and Frances Wilkie are eight of their eleven children.

Front row, L-R: George Washington Wilkie, Frances Ann Green Wilkie, Augustus (Gussie) Wilkie Hester, Harrison Wilkie

Second row, L-R: Myrtie Wilkie, Georgia Ann Wilkie Lovelace

Third row, L-R: Edward, Viola Wilkie Sandow, Alice Wilkie Holcomb, Mattie Wilkie McGullion.
(Other family members not pictured: Lee, Glenn and Henrietta Wilkie Richards.)

Photo above courtesy of Darrell Cook and Ruth Ann Wilkie Pinyan.

Many Wilkie descendants in the Hightower area can claim as their ancestors George Washington Wilkie (1850-1917) and Frances Ann Green (1850-1919). George and Frances were married on December 30, 1866, just as the dust was settling from the War Between the States. No doubt this was a rugged time and many were looking for a return to a settled family way of life (note that both George and Frances were sixteen years old at the time of marriage). The 1870 U. S. Federal Census lists George (farmer) and Frances with an Ophir post office, believed to be nearby the Hightower Church. On the Appointments of U.S. Postmasters, 1832-1971, George W. Wilkie was listed as the postmaster at Ophir, Cherokee as of April 13, 1888. Wash and Frances are buried at HBC.

The grave marker for Wash and Frances Wilkie is one of the most unique in the cemetery; the space between the large vases resembles a chair.

Photo courtesy of Judy Northington

Zebulon Williams

The Williams family, that were members of Hightower Baptist Church, settled in the Cross Roads District of Cherokee County in 1843 when Zebulon and Ollie Barker Williams moved their family from rural Pickens, South Carolina. Zebulon and Ollie had both been raised in South Carolina, with Zebulon being born in 1799 in current day Pickens County to Joseph and Rebecca (Bowen) Williams and Ollie being born in 1806 in Greenville County to Gray and Mary (Tankersley) Barker. Having just settled his father's estate, Zebulon chose to venture to new lands that had in just the prior decade been opened to settlement with the removal of the Cherokee Indians. There was talk of gold and fertile land that would make for great farming. Zebulon bought 40 acres that is currently located near Newt Green Road in Free Home community. As his farm prospered and his sons grew into manhood, he was able to acquire additional land nearby. The first mentioning of the Williams family at Hightower is on October, 1845 when Zebulon is listed as a delegate from the church for the Hightower Baptist Association's yearly meeting. An interesting political side note from an Augusta Chronicle newspaper article from 1853 is when Zebulon is listed as saying that in August 1852 the Honorable Hershel V. Johnson, in Canton stated, "he had no confidence in Union Democrats, that they could not be trusted, that they stunk, and that they would be dead and eat up by the buzzards before the dog days were out." It seems that politics have not changed a bit over time.

Though not certain, it is quite possible that Ollie Barker Williams' parents were members of Hightower and were possibly buried there also. Gray and Mary Barker both died in the area in the 1850s (his inventory stated he had land that would currently correspond with lots along Highway 372 and Newt Green Road also).

By 1860, Zebulon's farm was valued at $1,000, and he had two young slaves to help with the work there. The Civil War hit the family hard. Three of Zebulon's sons fought in the Confederacy (Joseph, John, and Joel), all enlisting in Company D of the 56th Regiment on May 12, 1862. Within four months, Joel died in a hospital in Chattanooga, and before the end of the war, both Joseph and John both had been captured twice (Joseph in Vicksburg and near Nashville; John in Vicksburg and in Kentucky). The war was terribly detrimental to not only the Williams family, but the entire membership of Hightower and the surrounding community. Many sons, husbands, brothers, and fathers were killed or disabled by the war, and the properties they had worked so hard for were often left in spoils. This can be seen in a comparison of the 1860 and 1870 agricultural censuses which shows that Zebulon had 40% more land, yet it was worth ½ the value and he had much less in livestock and in the amount of crops produced. In 1872, Zebulon sought $165 in restitution from the US government since Sherman's army had stolen his horse on their march to the sea in 1864. He received $100 for this. It is worth noting that a condition of receiving restitution was the applicant had to be loyal to the Union Army during the war. This is extremely doubtful since three of his sons served in the Confederacy. Despite the war, Zebulon and his family continued to live on their farm in Cross Roads before he died of dropsy in 1879. An article in the Cherokee Advance in 1885 quoted octogenarian Major Wiley Petty as stating that Zebulon, his wife, and (his brother) Abel were among the early settlers of the county, whose bodies now rest calmly in the Lap of the Earth.

Though Zebulon was the first of his family to settle in the area, he was not the only one. He was followed in the 1850s by his brother Abel and sister Mary Williams Hester, both of which lived near Hightower. Mary owned land along Old Mill Road, while Abel lived just west of Hester Road and McClure Drive. They, along with many of their children, were longtime members of this community.

In looking at the offspring of Zebulon and Ollie, we find a family very devout in their Christian walk, which was centered around Hightower Church. Every one of their children and many of their grandchildren were members of Hightower. So strong was their faith, that eight of their twelve children moved in 1884 to Arkansas and later Oklahoma, where they served as Baptist Missionaries to the Native Americans (On Oct. 19, 1884, James, Rebecca, Sarah, Abi, T. Jefferson and his wife Margaret were all dismissed by letter from Hightower as found in the HBC minutes). The family of Zebulon and Ollie Williams included:

- Henry Briggs (1827-1910) and wife Sarah Adeline Jones

- Mary Ann (1830-1926), husband Thomas Perry Shelley, and their twelve children

- Rebecca Caroline (1836-1917), never married

- Sarah Elizabeth (1839-1905), never married

- Eliza Catherine (1843-1931), husband Joseph Fowler, and their four children (two children were born in Arkansas)

- James Madison (1849-1927), never married

- Thomas Jefferson (1849-1935), wife Margaret Elizabeth Jones, and their four children

- Altzeany Abi (1852-1932), she met her husband, James C. Caughron in Gravette, Arkansas and they had six children

Photo courtesy of Chad Williams

Pictured above, front, L-R: Anna Caughron, Altzeany Abi Williams Caughron, Zelda Caughron, Thomas Jefferson Williams, Margaret Jones Williams (wife of TJW); back, L-R: Ida Lee Caughron, Ollie S. Caughron, Martha C. Williams, James Madison Williams and Ollie Jones Williams.

Abi, Thomas J. and James M. were siblings of John L. Williams. They moved to Oklahoma to serve as Baptist Missionaries to the Indians in the 1890s.

Of the three remaining (Joel had died in the war), Joseph remained in Cherokee Co. until his death in 1910 (being buried at Holbrook Campground); John stayed in Cherokee until around 1911 when he moved to Cobb Co. to live with his son, where he died in 1913 (buried at Macedonia); Little Berry moved to Bartow Co. around 1905, where he died in 1940 (buried at First Baptist of Emerson).

Photo courtesy of Chad Williams

Shown in picture from circa 1892 are back row, L-R: Johnny Zebulon, Mary Azilee, and Green Berry Williams; front row, L-R: John Lewis and Mary Ann Wooten Williams.

Zebulon's third son, John Lewis Williams "Jack" was born Feb. 16, 1835, in Pickens County, South Carolina, and moved with his family to Cherokee when he was 8. He married Miss Mary Ann Wooten in 1854. Though it hasn't been proven, Mary Ann may be the daughter of Henry and Martha Wooten of Lumpkin County (later Atlanta). They spent their entire married life in the Cross Roads and Orange communities and were faithful members of Hightower and Macedonia, with John being ordained a Deacon at Hightower in 1884. John's farm was on both sides of Coker's Chapel Road going down to Henry Scott Road and including Smithwick Creek. He also had land that included what is now the neighborhood at Holly Trace Lane on the west side of State Highway 372. John applied for and received a Civil War pension for his service in the Confederacy. He stated, in 1897, that he suffered from kidney trouble and was broken down because of "age and expansion". Besides his pension, John supplemented his farm income by serving as superintendent of the Cherokee County Home (home for the elderly indigent).

John and Mary Ann had 9 children and over 73 grandchildren, some of which are still known in the parts around Hightower today (Hawkins, Humphrey, Smithwick). Of their children, two remained in Cherokee for the rest of their lives Roxian (1859-1940, wife of Abraham M. Smithwick and buried at Oakdale) and Laura Jane (1860-1934, wife of John Humphrey and buried at Macedonia). Two moved to Gordon County: Georgian Elizabeth (1855-1926, wife of Clairborn Augustus Hawkins) and Ancil Monroe (1867-1915, husband of Cordelia Henderson). Son Joel Wesley (1864-1932, husband of Newell Louella Pruitt) settled in Grundy County, Tennessee. Their remaining four children all moved and died in Cobb County, several of which worked at the Marietta Knitting Mill: Malendia Caroline (1862-1934, wife of Thomas Gibbs Smithwick), Green Berry (1869-1960, husband of Genie Lou Verda Young of Salacoa), Johnny Zebulon (1873-1937, husband of Mary Rosalee Mullinax), and Mary Azalee (1876-1951, wife of William Alonzo Franklin).

Well into the middle of the 20th century, descendants of Zebulon and Ollie Williams (particularly the descendants of Joseph and John) met for an annual reunion. Now the descendants are spread far and wide across the great land. In the 172 years that the Williams family has been part of the community surrounding Hightower, the area has evolved from a pioneer area of farmers into a part of the metropolitan Atlanta area, but the core values and hard Christian work ethic that was there in 1843 is still there and thriving today. God's hand will always be on Hightower and the community as long as the fellowship of the people work hard to share God's word and serve Him to the fullest.

Written in 2015 by descendant, Chad Williams.

John Samuel Wyatt

Pictured to the left is John Samuel Wyatt, his wife Octavia, daughter Gennie and son Franklin.

John Samuel Wyatt was an ordained deacon at HBC and served in that capacity for many years. John was born on April 20, 1856, to Joseph and Mary Catherine Pascoe Wyatt. He married in 1874 to his first wife, Julia P. Hawkins, and they became parents to John, Mary, Joseph Aaron, Emma Theodocia, Dora Louisa, Julia Elizabeth, Samuel Septamus (the seventh child), Bartow Barton, Webb Hawkins, Rosa Victoria and Bessie. John Samuel married second to Sara T. Tollison who had a son, J. W. Wyatt. His third marriage was to Octavia Smith, and they became parents to Myrtle Eugenia "Gennie" and Roscoe "Franklin" as shown above. Julia Hawkins Wyatt, Sarah Tollison Wyatt, John Samuel Wyatt and Octavia Wyatt are all buried at HBC. The young Franklin Wyatt succumbed to a disease and died about 1908. It is unknown where Franklin is buried.

Contribution of this story from Ken Wyatt.

Photo courtesy of Ken Wyatt

Joseph Wyatt 1831-1910

When writing about the Wyatt family and their contribution to Hightower Baptist Church and its community, all roads lead back to the life of Joseph Wyatt.

Joseph was born September 22, 1831, in St. Austell, Cornwall, England. His parents were John and Mary Elizabeth Pauls? Wyatt. His father was a copper miner and Joseph, at the age of 19, was also listed as a copper miner in the 1851 England Census in St. Andrews Bridge, Tywardreath, Cornwall, England. He was the youngest of 8 boys. Three other brothers immigrated to Georgia. They were Solomon Wyatt (1820-1893), Abraham Wyatt

(1825-1903) and Capt. Francis "Frank" Wyatt (1828-1883) who died in Silverton, CO, where he was working as a mine blacksmith while his family resided in Cobb County, GA.

Joseph immigrated in 1854 to Georgia most likely due to the expansive gold mining operations occurring in the area. During a bad storm while crossing the Atlantic, he promised God that he would join a church if he landed safely. He was saved at Shiloh Methodist camp meeting located near Ophir soon after.

Joseph married into the mining family of the Pascoe's. He married Mary Catherine Pascoe June 7, 1855, one year to the day after coming to America. They were married by Rev. Alfred Webb. Mary Catherine was the daughter of Samuel and Mary Elizabeth Jackson Pascoe. The Pascoes, who also were from Cornwall, England, operated their own Pascoe Mines, adjacent to the Franklin Mines, from 1840-1852. The Pascoe homeplace was located on the banks of the Etowah and still stands today. Family legend states that Mary Catherine would go out of the house and work the ferry across the Etowah as travelers needed to cross. On one foggy day, Mary Catherine came out of the house to help a passerby. Despite not being able to see the traveler clearly, she ended up falling in love just based on the sound of Joseph's voice. No doubt, Joseph's accent would have been similar to her father's since both were from Cornwall, England.

L-R: John Samuel, James Lewis, and Joseph Wyatt
Picture and story courtesy of Ken Wyatt

Joseph and Mary Catherine's farm was located near present day Ophir Baptist Church. While every census in Cherokee County lists Joseph's occupation as a farmer, his brothers are listed as and worked as miners.

Joseph and Mary Catherine had 14 children. They were John Samuel, Joseph Henry, Sarah J, William Jackson, Rev. James Lewis, Emma Victoria, Robert Franklin, Mary "Ella," Charles Hansel, George Washington, Nathaniel, and 3 others not named that died in infancy.

Mary Catherine died July 10, 1884. Joseph then married Louisa Hendrix in 1885. They had 7 children. They were Lula Bell, Thomas Harrison, Alma Pearl, Truman, Annie O., Dona Mae, and Lillie Day.

Joseph Wyatt died on October 3, 1910. The following article was published in *The Cherokee Advance* on November 4, 1910, as the first article on the front page.

An Unshaken Faith

By Furman T. Williams

A few weeks ago I was invited to assist Brother Theo Willis in a protracted meeting at Ophir, a church located on the Eastern hills of Cherokee County.

On arriving I was introduced to a man of tottering frame and weight of years by the name of Joseph Wyatt. I noticed the intense interest he had in church work and the bold stand he would take for what he thought to be right. On the 3rd instant I was invited to attend the funeral of this same brother whom I met only a few weeks since, who had passed into the undiscovered country from whose bourne no traveler returns.

After the service a member of the family gave to me the following paper which was written by Brother Joseph Wyatt and which was found in a book after his death:

"Joseph Wyatt was born September 22, 1831, left Liverpool, England the 2nd day of May, 1854 landed in New York June 7, 1854 and June 7, 1855 married Mary Catherine Pascoe a noble little woman and when she died I am satisfied she died in the full triumph of a living faith in the blessed Jesus who hath died for us, and that I shall join hands with her at that day when He calls His children home. For I know in whom I have believed, and am persuaded that He is able to keep that which I have committed to Him against that day. Yea blessed Lord, I am fully satisfied of the fact and when I am gone, tell the living that I was a sinner saved by grace."

The following paper prepared by a member of the family was read at his funeral: "Joseph Wyatt professed a hope at Shiloh camp ground and united with the church about 39 years ago. He joined the Baptist Church and was a charter member of Ophir Church and was ordained a deacon serving in that capacity. He was very faithful, contending for what he thought to be right. He has had 21 children born unto him, fourteen by his first marriage, 6 of whom died in infancy. The other eight were raised and all embrace Christ, 7 of whom are still living. He has seven by his second marriage, 5 of them still living, and most of them have accepted Christ. He now dies saying it will be a happy exchange with me. Praise the Lord for his goodness. He was the youngest one of 8 boys and the last one to leave this world. One brother died in England, two in Australia, one in Colorado, two in Georgia, one lost.

We, the family, bow in submission to God's will feeling that the Lord has been very good to us in sparing our dear father to such a good old age, and for the bright Christian evidence, feeling that this is God's way, and trusting that after a while we will all meet in the happy beyond where congregations never break up and Sabbaths never end, but where the redeemed of the Lord shall walk with Him by day for there is no night there. Let us rejoice and be exceedingly glad and be ready to go with Him to the marriage of the Lamb. Sleep on dear father we believe we will meet you after a while by the grace of God."

I recall after the first service of the meeting at Ophir (the last one that Bro. Wyatt attended) how he came to me with tear dimmed eyes and said that the seed had been sown which would bring forth a harvest in the future and how he encouraged us in the ministry.

The funeral services were conducted by Bro. Theo Wills and J. R. Stone in the presence of a large congregation. What better evidence could a man leave to the world than to write before his death that he knew in whom he believed and whose faith could not be shaken by the turmoils of life.

We feel sure that this saint of Israel who has fallen, died fully assured of the fact that the God of all grace was sufficient for him, and is now resting from his labors. Truly he loved his church and its work, and we trust that the unshaken faith he had in his Lord will be the evidence of others who are striving to win the prize.

The Cherokee Advance

It is uncertain whether or not Joseph was a deacon at Hightower or was ordained at the same time as Ophir was being constituted. It is known that he was one of the original charter members of Ophir in 1877 and served as a deacon. There are several instances where church members of Hightower branched off to help establish other local churches. Mary Catherine Pascoe Wyatt is buried among many of her children and her parents in the Hightower Cemetery, while Joseph is buried at Ophir.

Submitted by Kenneth R. Wyatt

Places

Free Home

Hightower BC was in the Ophir community and Cross Roads District which predates the community of Free Home. After the mining industry declined and after the closure of Etowah Elementary School, the local school for residents was **Free Home**. While the name of Cross Roads district remains, no one is exactly sure where the original "Cross Roads" was located. Kenneth Wyatt remembers a building once was located on the now named Hightower Trail that was the designated Cross Roads Polling Station for voting in the 1950's.

Reflections on Free Home: Cleo Milford, 82, a lifelong resident, looks out at her land. She attended the old two-story school, which was heated by wood stoves.

The Atlanta Journal-Constitution

In 1999, Cleo Heard Milford (HBC member) was interviewed for an article in the *Atlanta Journal and Constitution* titled "Some things don't change at Free Home". She claimed, as legend does, that Captain Delevan Lively, a Civil War veteran was responsible for the name Free Home. Seems he had a plan to attract families to the area by offering free land to anyone willing to build a home, thus the name Free Home. If they moved, the home and property would revert back to Lively. Captain Lively was a teacher in the community at the school, then called Chestnut Log.

In later years, the cross roads (known in 2015 as Free Home, intersection of Highways 20 and 372) became a new center of the community. Mr. Emory West became the owner/operator of the Free Home Store at the location as shown in the picture below. Mr. Emory would eventually move that original store and construct the still existing brick building currently housing an antique store. Across the way, in the location of the current Publix shopping center, Mr. Emory and his wife Myrtie Smith West (both HBC members and both buried at HBC) built a fine brick home which stood for many years.

Photo courtesy of Tim Perkins

Names of Local Roads and Places

Newt Green Rd.

George McClure Lane

Glen Wilkie Trail

Lovelace Lane (R. Edgar Lovelace and family)

Pools Mill (Dr. M. L. Pool)

Julius Bridge Rd. (John Julius Turner)

Franklin Gold Mine Rd. (Mary Franklin)

Hester Drive (descendants of Mary Williams Hester)

All those who have a road or place named for them listed above are buried at HBC with the exception of Dr. M. L. Pool and Mary Hester. It is believed that Dr. Pool was a member at HBC as he was a delegate to association meetings several times in the mid-1800s. Numerous family members of Mary Hester have and continue to be associated with HBC.

Frankie Green Edge told: "The name for Julius Bridge Road, it is for my grandfather, but back when everybody was raising cotton. That's the way he went to Lathemtown to take cotton to the gin, and the bridge washed away. He was a feller that didn't have no patience, he just stayed on the road commissioner, stayed on them trying to get them to build the bridge back, they kept putting him off to where he just went and built the bridge back himself. And so when they were naming the roads, you know they didn't have names back then, but when they started naming roads, they named it Julius Bridge Road. You take this little road back down toward 369, it used to, there was a road goes straight you can come out on 369 –it used to go on through to Macedonia, but that bridge also washed away, and they never did build it back. He was the kind of fellow that could build about anything, so he built the bridge."

Homes

The J. A. and Birddie Godfrey Heard home in Lathemtown. The Heard's lived at this home from the 1920s until 1970s.

R. Edgar and Georgia Ann Wilkie Lovelace occupied this home just east of HBC. It is to this house that Mr. Lovelace devised his water pump (ram) which led to the location of the nearby baptismal pool for HBC along the creek. Mr. Lovelace's success for running water was many years before electricity became available in the area.

Photo courtesy of Chris Chandler

Shortly after the turn of the century in 1900, Lightner Leander and Josephine McDaniel West purchased property on what is now Ball Ground Road in Free Home. Legend remains that Mr. West was a skilled carpenter and that Josephine was rather adept with building skills as well. The Milford family told that Mr. West was working at the marble mill in the Ball Ground/Tate Georgia area and had access to wood working equipment and completed the carving of the balusters himself. After the death of Mr. West in 1928, the property was soon sold by the West family. After ownership changed a few times, Robert and Cleo Heard Milford moved into the home in 1939. The home remains in 2015 in the Milford family.

George Washington "Wash" and Frances Ann Green Wilkie lived in this home in what was then known as the Ophir community. The location of the still surviving home (2015) is just a short distance west of HBC on State Highway 369. The Wilkie's also owned and operated a store and cotton gin nearby. The current homeowners are descendants of Wash and Frances Wilkie.

The home pictured to the left was a common design found in the area in the late 1800s and was the home of John Lewis (deacon at HBC) and wife Mary Ann Wooten Williams. Also pictured is their daughter Azalee. This picture was taken about 1897 (see additional information: Chapter 11, Zebulon Williams).

Photo courtesy of Chad Williams

Pascoe/McClure/Leslie/Rainey Home

Photos courtesy of Ken Wyatt

This lovely home, one of the few remaining structures from the gold mining days near HBC, was built circa 1847 – 1853, by John Pascoe (additional information, Chapter 11: Sam and John Pascoe). It is believed to be the oldest structure still surviving from the gold mining days. The second picture above shows a building adjacent to the home, believed to be the original kitchen that was moved to another location at some point in time. The home is situated a short walk from the Etowah River and in the early years a ferry was located nearby. After John Pascoe's tragic death in 1853, his brother Samuel and wife Mary became residents of the home. After Samuel's death (he and Mary are buried at HBC), several employees of various mining companies lived in the home. Many HBC families are descendants of the Pascoe's. Eventually, the home was purchased by Dr. George McClure and later, Samuel Leslie. The home is currently (2015) occupied by the Rainey family, who are descendants of both the Pascoe and Leslie families. With the Pascoe connection, the current family is delighted that the original home is back in the family.

The history of the home on land lot #328 (Pascoe Homeplace, Ball Ground, GA) includes the estimated dates of ownership below:

Pascoe's 1847-1891 (44 years)

Various mining companies owned the property

McClure's 1919-1955 (36 years)
Leslie's 1955-1998 (43 years)

At present, the home is owned by the Rainey family.

Poole's Mill

Poole's Mill Bridge Park, a scenic area containing a covered bridge and shoals was converted from private ownership to a county-owned park in the late 1900s. The picturesque recreation area near HBC in Forsyth County is named for Dr. M. L. Pool/Poole (1825-1895), likely a member of HBC if indeed he is the same person as the delegate "M. L. Pool" who represented HBC at the association meetings in 1869-1872, 1874, and 1877. Dr. Pool was married to Lucy Caroline Mangum Pool (1826 - 1883). They became parents to eleven children and three of their daughters are believed to be buried at HBC, Martha (Jane Poole) Fowler, 1845-1863; Eliza (Adeline) Poole, 1854-1856; and Laura (Theodocia Poole) Lipscomb, 1859-1875; and at least one granddaughter, Nancy G. Lipscomb (1875-1876). Dr. and Mrs. Pool are buried in a private cemetery in Forsyth County.

Personal photos of July 5, 2014

As noted in the picture, the historical sign located adjacent to the bridge reads: "Cherokee Chief George Welch constructed a grist mill here on his extensive home place about 1820. An uncovered bridge was later added. With the 1838 removal of the Cherokees, the land was sold to Jacob Scudder. Dr. M. L. Pool purchased it from Scudder´s family in 1880. Abandoned in 1947, the mill burned in 1959. The original bridge washed away in 1899 and was replaced with the present 96-foot structure, (the "covered bridge") in 1901. Constructed in the town lattice design by Bud Gentry, the bridge's web of planks crisscrossing at 45 to 60 degree angles are fastened with wooden pegs or trunnels at each intersection."

Researchers have documented a relationship between Jacob Scudder and George Welch. It is believed that Scudder married Diana Jones in Jackson County, Georgia. By 1814, he had moved to the Cherokee Nation with his young family. A few years later, George Welch known to be a Cherokee Chief married Diana Scudder's sister, Margaret Jones.

In *Cry of the Eagle,* Forest Wade describes the old covered bridge that crosses Settendown Creek in Forsyth County. "Just below the bridge on the right side of the creek is a portion of the stone foundations where a water-powered grist mill and sawmill once stood." Wade adds further that a cotton gin was built beside the mill house and great numbers of citizens of Forsyth County and the surrounding area patronized it during the 1920s and later. No doubt the Poole's Mill area was a destination for many HBC members of yesteryear for business and in more recent years, for recreation. The shoals and old foundations, as well as the covered bridge, provide a wonderful glimpse into the livelihood of the past.

Schools

Hightower School. In the earliest of days, HBC had a "meetinghouse" as listed in the 1845 deed between Daniel Stephens and HBC. Possibly this log structure served both for school and church functions. A school called Hightower likely existed before the organization of a number of area schools that are listed below. It is thought that at some point in time, the Hightower school building was located "across the road" from the current HBC building and graveyard and was possibly also used for church services after the believed loss of the church building due to fire about 1879. Later, the school building also burned and the students then attended Andrews Chapel/Creighton School. Eugene Croy wrote in *Pine Top Fox* that "Old timers of the Hightower community whose forefathers were of the first white people in this community tell me that there was once a school at Hightower Church many years ago. Some think it may very well have been one of the mission schools that were built in the Hightower community for the Indians in the early 1800s" (page 7).

Also found at http://www.cherokeecountyga.org/1876.htm, under the listing for Ophir, Georgia, 1876.

Ophir was a post village of Cherokee County 12 miles from the county seat, 30 miles from Marietta, and 30 miles from Gainesville. The population of Canton was 100. The following business was found in the 1876-1877, Georgia State Directory.	
▪ High Tower School, R. B. Allen, teacher	

From *Public Education in Cherokee County, 1982*:

Andrews Chapel School, located in east Cherokee County just north of current Ga. Hwy. 369 and east of Boardtree Creek. Andrews Chapel Methodist Church was on the same property. Only a cemetery remains today; tombstone dates are from the 1830s to 1900. The church burned and was not rebuilt. The school was also destroyed by fire some years later. Past students remember the beloved Professor Norton who was also a minister. He became ill with mumps and died while he taught at Andrews Chapel and was buried at HBC. After the school building burned, the students were moved into two dwelling houses belonging to the Creighton Mining and Power Company. It is thought that about 175 students and two teachers were at Andrews Chapel School at one point in time ... Written by Nettie Lee Lovelace.

Creighton School, located in the northeast corner of the Cross Roads district near the old Creighton (Franklin) Gold Mines and also near the Thomas Holcomb home place. The school was in operation in 1907. Nesbit D. Penn was the teacher at that time. In 1933, Creighton was consolidated with Etowah School. Flora Turner and Pearl Wofford Doss also taught at Creighton. Some of the families who attended there were: Holcomb, Buffington, White, Satterfield, Nelson, Boling and Andrews....Written by Marjorie T. Bobo.

Photo courtesy of Ken Wyatt

The above photo is believed to be from a school near HBC and taken about the year 1915. Most likely it was of the Oakland School, described below. Identification of individuals is unknown; however, Linton Wyatt is thought to be among the students pictured.

Oakland School was located on Highway 369 about one-fourth mile east of the Ball Ground-Free Home Road and Highway 369 intersection. The school was in operation in [until] 1933. Some of the teachers were Cliffie White, Jewell Wilkie Cotton, Winnie Garrett Lathem, Vera Bell Williams, Bell White (1908) and C. W. Smithwick (1907-1908). Family names of some who attended Oakland were Wyatt, Wilkie, Little, Nelson, Dean, McPherson, Hogan, Wehunt, Andrews and Green... Written by Marjorie T. Bobo

Etowah School 1953 - Photo of post card, source unknown

Etowah Elementary School, for grades one through nine was built in 1934 and held its first graduation in spring of 1935. It was a consolidation of the Creighton and Oakland Schools. Liberty School was supposed to be a part of the consolidation but because of community objection, school continued there for two more years then moved to Etowah. Etowah was located in east Cherokee Co. and just west of HBC. The school was named for the Etowah River which is about a mile from the school. Land for the site was donated by Myrtie Wilkie and Joe Wyatt. It was the first school in the state to be built by the laborers furnished through the Works Project Administration (WPA).

Photo courtesy of Mary Helen Cissell

Because of the WPA, the opening was a big event with the State Superintendent of Schools, M. D. Collins, and all local members of the County Board of Education in attendance. The auditorium was filled with parents and children followed with lunch on the grounds. It was a day filled with pride and excitement. The first trustees of the school were R. E. Lovelace, chairman, H. G. Wilkie, Sr., and S. S. Wyatt. Teachers included Mr. and Mrs. T. J. Land, Annie Laura Doss, and Gladys Holcomb. The school remained open until 1956 when it was consolidated with Free Home and Holbrook and the new school was built at Free Home. A decline in enrollment contributed to the consolidation decision but community opposition was evident and the consolidation caused a loss of community spirit….. Written by Nettie Lee Lovelace.

A common practice during the Etowah Elementary days included an agricultural calendar; attendance for five winter months and two summer months with "vacation" aligned for farming chores of planting and harvesting. After the crops were "laid by," the summer revival season began at local churches. For HBC, the revival was held during the third week in August for many years and later changed to July. The students at Etowah could opt to walk with a designated teacher to the nearby services at HBC. Whether by desire to attend or just to get out of school, many students were afforded an opportunity to hear the gospel and accepted Christ during their break from school.

(*Those mentioned above who are buried at HBC include Myrtie Wilkie, R. E. Lovelace, H. G. Wilkie, Sr., S. S. Wyatt, Gladys Holcomb and Nettie Lee Lovelace.*)

Shingle House on Yellow Creek Road

A two storied building, covered in vines, still (2015) remains on Yellow Creek Road less than one mile away from HBC to remind those who pass by of a life in another era of time. According to Johnston (2011) the "Shingle House" was built during the 1880s and is the last remaining structure from the Creighton/Franklin Gold Mine Complex. The building served as a commissary, offices, post office, boarding house and a small stamp mill where local residents could sell gold ore.

Stephens and Lovelace Log Cabin

Daniel Stephens and family settled on land between HBC and Board Tree Creek. In 1845, HBC secured a deed to the church property from Stephens (see appendix, Deed 1). Legend remains that the Stephens family met a tragic fate in 1852 as over a period of four months, Daniel and Sela Stephens and three adult children succumbed to the deadly typhoid fever. The grave markers of the Stephens family in section one of HBC cemetery still denote sadness of an era when sickness and lack of medical care often meant death was eminent. Names and dates of those mentioned above can be found in Chapter 12 of this book.

Legend remains that Daniel Stephens and his wife lived in the log cabin near HBC. It is fortunate that the rough-hewn log structure still remains and was restored by recent landowner Nettie Lee Lovelace. While a few comforts have been added (electricity), the home reflects an era of a simple, yet rugged way of life. Many thanks to a Lovelace descendant, Chris Chandler and photographer, Judy Northington for the following pictures of this glimpse into the past.

Photos of log cabin courtesy of Judy Northington

West home

Mr. Emory West and his wife Myrtie Smith West built a lovely red brick home near the crossing of Highways 372 and 20 in Free Home. Pictured in the buggy above is believed to be their son, Bob. In the recent years, the home was removed from the site for the construction of the Publix Grocery and Shopping Center.

Events

Funerals and burials, practices and customs

The Foxfire 40th Anniversary Book, Faith, Family and the Land, gives the following description of funerals in rural Georgia, likely similar to customs at HBC prior to 1940. "When anybody died, the neighbors would go in and help out and wash the body. A lady in the community would make the burial clothes. The men would make the casket and also the men would dig the grave at the cemetery. They made the caskets out of wood and sometimes would line it with some kind of cloth. The service was usually held at the cemetery. In early days, they didn't take 'em to the church. They just took 'em to the cemetery. People would mourn and carry on. They would let the casket down with ropes into the grave, they didn't have any vaults. Sometimes they would bury 'em near their home, it depended on what the family wanted to do. There were lots of graves in family cemeteries near homes" (page 30).

Sosebee Funeral Home was one of the first in Canton, Georgia and opened for business in 1940. Death certificates from the 1920s record the name of the undertaker, but are more likely just the name of the businesses where the caskets were bought, such as B. F. Coggins Dept. Store, Canton; W. A. Lathem and Sons, Orange; Jones Mercantile Co., Canton and Lovelady Duncan Co., Ball Ground.

Likely, most funerals were their own separate event. Nevertheless, at least once at HBC, the service was held in conjunction with the regular worship service. On Sunday, January 18, 1942, Cleo Heard Milford wrote in her personal diary, "Old Lady Little (Georgia Little's Mother) was buried at Hightower, funeral during preaching hour." Further study found the name and dates as follows: Margaret "Millie" Cagle Little, 1858 - Jan. 1942.

While the earliest graves were marked with simple rocks or stones, numerous cemeteries throughout northern Georgia and particularly in the Etowah River basin area have graves marked with markers, likely carved from materials such as sandstone or soapstone to exactly fit the pieces together. These "slot and tab tombs" are thought to have been a popular choice during the era of 1840s-1890s of persons with English and Scotch-Irish descent and of those predominantly Baptist. The decorative stone grave shelters are found in the shape of a box with an oblong horizontal lid (ledger stone) of local stone with two slots cut into it, through which the vertical head and foot stones are fitted. The bodies of the deceased persons were presumably underground. It is thought that the stone grave shelters prevented wandering open-range livestock from stepping into the softer dug earth of a human grave; also used to prevent predators and scavengers from digging up a buried human body, especially in shallow graves dug into rocky ground.

The picture to the left shows two graves at HBC that are examples of the slot and tab design. The headstone with "head and shoulders" shape and on the right in the picture is engraved with E. S. Poter, Sept. 20, 1805, Aug. 26, ?, possibly between 1870-1878. Family descendants report that this is the grave of E. S. Porter not Poter. The other adjacent one with the peak shape is illegible but reported to be Cynthia Porter the wife of E. S. Porter.

There are also two additional slot and tab markers at HBC which are smaller and are likely the graves of children. One is believed to be the grave of Virginia Victoria "Mourning" Pascoe (1861-1862). Additional family information about Virginia and a picture of the grave marker can be found in Chapter 11: Sam and John Pascoe.

Photo courtesy of Judy Northington

Illness Tragedy and Death

While many tragedies likely surrounded the deaths of those buried at HBC, a few noted here are:

Henry "Grady" Fowler, age 30 was killed in the same tornado that killed Mr. and Mrs. William Millwood and 2 children, in Orange Community. Grady died Wednesday morning from the results of Monday's tragedy. March 29, 1928.

William Hester (1879-1905) is believed to be the one from the Hester family that died as a result of a head injury suffered when he was kicked by a mule.

Charlie Loggins, death May 24, 1921. Law officer murdered while in line of duty.

Martin Prince, buried in an unmarked grave, was killed in a pyrite mine accident as published in the November 1915 edition of the *Cherokee Advance*.

Daniel Stephens family, typhoid. 1852 was an especially difficult year for friends and neighbors living near HBC. Oral stories have survived over time to describe how devastating this disease was for at least one particular HBC family. Daniel Stephens, his wife and three adult children succumbed to this dreadful disease. As noted on the tombstones that still remain just in front of the current church building, side by side the markers show dates of death Mrs. Sela on March 4th, Mr. Daniel on March 11, Miley J., on March 24 (age 17), William on March 25th (age 21) and then Samuel on July 4th (age 20). Typhoid fever was one of the most tragic epidemic diseases of the 1800s. The intestinal infection is spread by ingesting the bacteria from contaminated food or water. It can be prevented and now treated with antibiotics, but knowledge of prevention as well as the discovery of antibiotics was not available, unfortunately for families like the Daniel Stephens' family.

Photo courtesy of Judy Northington

Wars and Rumors of Wars...

A few of the earliest settlers to the Hightower area knew more than desired about the American Revolution. At least eleven persons buried at HBC have markers showing birthdates in the late 1700s. One of the earliest birthdates noted was Catherine Burns. From death date and age on marker, her birth was Feb. 11, 1766. She was ten years old when the Declaration of Independence was written. James White was born in 1776 and was just a few months old by July 4, 1776. Two popular choices for naming sons were George Washington and Francis Marion. The War of 1812 would soon follow. If fathers, brothers, grandfathers or uncles were engaged in those fights, the families had their faith tested, and those born during this era would have heard stories. The renewed strength with the assurance of life, liberty and the pursuit of happiness sustained these families as they migrated into Georgia from the Carolinas and elsewhere.

Gold and fertile farmland enticed many to North Georgia. Although records such as the census are scarce before 1850, evidence abounds that many relocated to Cherokee and surrounding counties before the Civil War began. The Franklin's and Pascoe's had established mining operations and neighboring families were selling goods (wheat, meat, etc.) to the Franklins to support the workers in the mines. Mrs. Franklin's ledger book showed payment to workers and slaves that were owned by Mrs. Franklin to work the mines.

Alfred Webb, the pastor at HBC (and other surrounding churches) made a trip to Milledgeville, the state capital, to vote for succession from the Union. One must wonder if that had an impact on his sermons at HBC. Many, many families were called upon to supply soldiers for the cause. Some returned home and to their known way of life. Many were devastated by the effects of the war: George Wilkie (1827-1863) was killed in Vicksburg, Mississippi; Phillip Fowler (1837-1913) likely suffered post-traumatic stress syndrome, though not called that at the time. Recorded in *The Heritage of Cherokee County Georgia, 1831-1998*, page 250, "Fowler, a story typical of the men of Cherokee County whose date of birth destined them to leave their families and fight battles over causes remote to their existence. The War of Northern Aggression had a devastating effect on Phillip. Although he would survive with minor injuries, their lasting effect would stay with him until he died." Injured, sick, hungry and tired, they returned to find a community in turmoil as the reconstruction years were difficult. Many buried at HBC were veterans of the war (see appendix, list of veterans). Only one in this cemetery has a gravestone noting "a faithful Union Soldier." The Hightower Association cancelled services for a couple of years during the war and many churches suspended activities.

Vicksburg, Mississippi

The Civil War took its toll on the people in and around HBC. Many boys and men, young and old alike, found themselves assembling to fight the war. The older ones often became assigned to the home guard groups. These were compared to the National Guard as we know today, but were assigned to help keep peace in the community. For their service, they were also veterans of the war and often applied for and received veteran pensions on into the early 1900s. Many of the younger men found themselves in the midst of battles. An interesting process for organization for this wartime era was the philosophy of grouping together men from the same geographical area, which were acquainted and often blood related, so perhaps an element of trust was already in place. While possibly a good idea from a military standpoint, it often fractured and splintered many families when numbers were killed in the same battles. Such was true of the Co. D., 56th Regiment, Infantry and also Co. E., 36th Regiment. Numbers of northern Cherokee and northern Forsyth area boys were sent with these groups to fight in Vicksburg.

Winnie Grace Wyatt: "It was just pitiful times: HBC during the American Civil War of 1861-1865."

Pictured above front, L-R: Maude Pearson Buffington, George Spurgeon Pearson, and Eliza Wilkie "Granny" Pearson. Back: Walter, Junior, and Oscar Pearson. (Other family members not pictured, Fred, husband of Eliza and son Edgar)

Pictured above, L-R Linton Wyatt and Winnie Grace Buffington Wyatt

Photos courtesy of Ken Wyatt

Winnie Grace Buffington Wyatt (1918-2007) was quite a story teller. She likely "got that" from her Granny, Eliza Wilkie Pearson (1854-1932). Winnie said, "that's all I know and that was handed down from Granny. Lord I wish my Granny had been living, you'd got a kick out of that. She could just talk and tell you everything." Due to the foresight of grandson Ken Wyatt, this information was extracted from a recorded oral interview between Ken and his grandparents, Linton (1914-2008) and Winnie Wyatt. The conversation took place July 16, 1996. Much gratitude is extended to Ken for his generosity in sharing this valuable record as well as the pictures. [Linton and Winnie Wyatt, Robert B. (1891-1952) and Maud Pearson (1891-1985) Buffington, and Fred (1850-1922) and Eliza Wilkie Pearson are all buried at HBC.]

Winnie said, "Them was pitiful times, it was just pitiful times." Flinchum describes that Cherokee County was on the periphery of the fighting and that some writers and experts have noted over the years that nothing of any importance happened in Cherokee County during the war. However, Winnie's account agrees most with Yates: "The citizens of Cherokee County saw plenty of war." Canton suffered losses due to the partial burning of many of the town's buildings in 1864 (Flinchum p. 83). Union cavalry (Flinchum) arrived in the spring of 1864 and "added to the local misery in carrying out their foraging raids, seizing property and farm goods from hard-pressed families in Cherokee County. The people of Cherokee County suffered deprivations from both sides of the conflict, which was remembered for many years to come" (p. 75). The references from Flinchum concur with Winnie's stories.

Murder During Conference

On a 3rd Saturday in October, possibly in the year of either 1864 or 1865, the women and children and a few old men had met at HBC for the monthly conference meeting. It was during that event that shots were fired and church members soon discovered the murder of a young man whose body was left just across the road from the church. It was told the young man had been working on a farm down near Orange.

"Granny said they were having conference, it was the third Saturday in October, in 1860 something I guess, when that boy was killed across the road. Granny said there wasn't no men there, just a few that was real old men, that weren't able to go you know [to the war], and it just like to have scared everybody to death. Granny, she told me how long they waited about leaving the church and going over there to see what had happened, but I don't know now how long they waited, but they were scared to death, afraid they'd [the scouts] come on over to the church, but they didn't I reckon they just kept a going. Somebody did go across the road, I guess some of the men that was able to walk, and they found him and they dug the grave, right there and I reckon after they seen that the scouts had moved on, Nettie Lee [Lovelace] said she had heard some of her folks say that when they put the boy down in the grave, they's a woman, I don't know who the woman was, said she took her handkerchief out and spread it over his face. But I've been over there where he's buried. They used to be just a great big old pile of rocks on the other side of the highway, in the pasture there. They may have moved the rocks now, since it's in a pasture....

They picked him up down here at Orange, he was a-minding cattle, they didn't have a pasture [fence] and he was minding cattle. He wasn't a part of the family there, he was working and staying with them for what he could eat, the little he got to eat, and the scouts came through and they would take anything they wanted or that was better than theirs, those scouts, they just went about stealing. I don't know where they were from, never heard. They just called them scouts. I don't know what they done with the cattle he was minding, but they picked him up and brought him up here across the road from the church, and killed him. And in his shirt pocket he had a piece of a ham bone or shoulder bone or something with a little piece of meat on it and a piece of cornbread, and that was going to be his lunch, and they killed him, and I don't know why, 'cause he didn't have anything. The boy was just a poor boy that was a working for what little bit he got to eat. Now, he didn't belong to the family he was a working with, he wasn't related to them, I don't know where he was from, they just took him in and worked him, that's what they done, he'd work and all he ever got out of it was a little bit of food. He was down at Orange with some family, that's all I know.

I don't guess the people he was working for ever come to look for him or anything. If the scouts didn't take their cows, I guess they probably went back home you know when night come. He hadn't eat no dinner, the boy hadn't and Granny said he had a piece of what she called a ham bone and a piece of cornbread, and that was gonna be his dinner. That just killed me when she'd tell about that you know. I guess the boy was hungry. By the way she talked, he might have been about sixteen, fifteen or sixteen years old. I don't know how they found out where he come from. I don't know how, or who the people were that he was living with or where he come from or nothing. Don't guess she knew, I don't doubt it. It was a pitiful thing."

Dr. William H. Dean, a resident of Woodstock and one of the few doctors in the area, wrote this about Enon Baptist Church. *"There was no meeting at Enon from the meeting in May until December (1864) following in the meantime this portion of the country was overrun by the Federal forces. The country literally desolated, nearly all of last year's crop destroyed by the army. The stock nearly all killed or carried off and the people caused to suffer for bread and many made dependent upon the government for rations. Nearly all the Baptist churches in the neighborhood closed. There were regular meetings held at Enon from December up to the present time although there was no record kept or preserved until February, 1865"* (Flinchum, p. 77).

Foragers

"I don't know how old Granny was but her and her Mother lived over there on the river just about where the old bridge crosses the river, right in that area somewhere or another, that's where her and her Mother lived in a little two room house because her Daddy was in the war and her Mother's folks lived up yonder what we call the bend of the river after you cross Settendown, and go around up there to them houses you come to, that's where her parents, the Francis' lived. I don't know how come Granny and her mother were living by theirselves or what, now, but they were. And the scouts come through; Granny and her Mother would go up to her grandparents every weekend and they come through and they poured every bit of flour they had in the dough tray and worked it up and left it, they'd eat cornbread, they had a little bit of flour, Granny said, they'd save to make pies once in a while, but these scouts dumped every bit of it in the dough tray, worked it up in a big wad of dough and went off and left it. And they thought Granny, or her mother would cook that, it had something in it that would have killed them, I guess and they didn't eat it but some of the neighbors fed it to, as Granny said, their sow, which was their hog, and I don't know if it killed their hog, or almost killed it or something. I don't know, but I reckon Granny and her Mother had a cow and I don't know if they took their cow, if they did, I don't ever remember hearing Granny tell about it.

Ultimate Sacrifice in Vicksburg

Granny's daddy, (*George W. Wilkie, 1827-1863*) she was an only child, she didn't have no brothers nor sisters, and she was about 10 year old when he had to go, (*Elizabeth A. Wilkie Pearson, 1854-1932*) and all his brothers, there was four of 'em, and they all had to go, their last name was Wilkie. They was in Vicksburg, Mississippi."

Marlin (1932, page 211) list the following in Georgia Volunteer Infantry, Company E, 36th Regiment: Francis M. Wilkie, George W. Wilkie, J. C. Wilkie, and W. Wilkie.

"Uh huh and Granny's daddy got up one morning and the fort where they slept, it had little peep holes you know ever so often, I guess it was built out of logs, now I don't know. And he got up and started across the courtyard, they called it, and a bullet came through one of them holes and it went in here, went all the way through him, and dropped out in his coat pocket, so his brothers brought that bullet home. Granny had it, I don't know what went with it. And I reckon his 3 brothers all come back but he got killed and he's buried out there in the Confederate Cemetery in Vicksburg, Mississippi. And Granny was 10 years old. He come home one time after he went, he was drafted into the war, and he come home one time. He got real bad sick and they sent him home, I guess to die, but he got well and when he got well, he had to go back.

If they was any fighting around through this area I don't know about it, and I don't reckon they was any buried around here anywhere except that boy, if there was anybody else buried, I never did hear it. It was just pitiful times. Wasn't worth what lives that was lost. Granny's Daddy that was buried out yonder, if you go to his grave, you don't know if that'd be him or not cause I guess they put a monument up, a little marker up with his name on it. I don't know even know what his name was but George Wilkie, George Washington if I had to guess, cause that was the name that had been handed down, years and years and years. Mama had a brother named George, and one of her brother's boys was named George, so it was just in the family and on down.

Plowing in Disguise

And Granny said there was a man that lived right down here, do you know where the bridge is down here on the creek after you go down the old rocky hill and turn out to the creek? The bridge used to be there but it's been tore out now and they's a bottom across the creek. Granny said that man made a crop one whole year and gathered it and he wore a dress and a bonnet so people would think he was a woman that was a plowing – you see, if they knowed it was a man, they would have come and got him and thowed him into the war you know…

Close Call Cutting Broom Straw

One day Granny and her little friend, her name was Rebecca Coffee that's where Becky got her name, and they had been up here, up this creek down here somewhere, getting broom straw to make straw brooms with, you know, and Granny said this little old waggin and one old scout was in it, she said his leg smelt so bad they couldn't hardly stand it. But anyway, he stopped and made her and Becky Coffee, it was a flat bed waggin, he made them get in the waggin. They laid their broom straw up there, Granny said his leg smelt so bad you couldn't hardly stand it. And she said her mama had always told her, don't you never get in a wagon with nobody, 'cause that was the only way of travelling they had. And Granny said, I don't know how far they'd go, she said he just kept on beating his old horse or whatever he was a driving, making him get faster, and Granny said, me and Becky, we just rez up she said and we just jumped off of that waggin and left our broom straw and run. Cause he would have carried them with him cause he had intentions you see. And Granny would just say, Becky and me, we just rez up and jumped up over out of that waggin and run, we just run just as hard as we could run and the way she talked now, they had got a way on down, I don't know how far up the creek here they was a getting broom straw, but they had got a way on down, and they seen he wasn't a gonna stop where they thought they should get off at, so that's where Granny said we just rez up and jumped off of that waggin. Yea, it was sure pitiful times…"

1925 HBC Baptizing at Etowah River

Photo courtesy of Donald Wilkie

Front L-R: Rev. Robert A. Roper, pastor, Jabe Holcombe, Otto Rich, Carl Green, Hoyt Green, Oscar Stewart, Truman Hester, Hubert Rich, Emmett Nelson, Ed Green, Jake West, and Ervin Woodall

Back L-R: Marie Eubanks (Cloud), Fannie Lovelace (Wilson); V. D. Crow, Winnie Green, Ollie Wilkie, Pearl Wilkie, Lillie Green Gilleland, Thelma Adams, Evie Cronan, and Hazel Yother. Not pictured: *Edith Drummond (Wilkie)

* On July 16, 2014, Herman Wilkie reported that his mother, Edith Drummond (Wilkie) was also baptized in 1925 with the group pictured above. On that Sunday morning, the family car had a flat tire, and she arrived too late for the picture. Edith is listed in membership book number four as joined by experience, August 1925.

Even though the baptismal pool near the church was built in 1918 on the Lovelace property, 1925 was a year of extreme drought thus the baptizing was moved to the Etowah River. The spring which fed the baptismal pool dried up that year. A second baptizing was held that same summer, reports are not clear if at the pool or also at the river, but in total it was reported that 33 were baptized during that summer and early fall (listed in 1926 HBA records). Another big baptizing occurred in 1930 (recorded by HBA as 1931) in which 51 were baptized. Stories through the years have referred to these large numbers for both events. Regardless, there was much celebrating for the newly saved souls. The thought exists that due to the severe weather conditions, many had become weary and were especially seeking trust that better days were ahead; their faith was certainly being challenged. A further explanation was found online, www.aboutnorthgeorgia: "The drought that struck in 1924 – 1927 affected a wider area than simply North Georgia, affecting the Coosa River and Altamaha Basin as well at the Chattahoochee River. The Weather Bureau reported the lowest stream levels ever recorded in north Georgia in July-September, 1925, stating that the drought not only affected agricultural operations, but industrial operations as well. Combined with the ongoing devastation from the boll weevil, migration from rural Georgia to urban Georgia reached epic proportions. The impact of this drought, plus other natural events, sent the Georgia economy into a depression well before the rest of the United States."

Church bus of 1930s

While not exactly designated as a church bus, Mr. Joel Heard of Lathemtown was known to provide transportation for area people in his mule truck, particularly for the young folks and especially during summer revivals at HBC.

Gene Pruitt, HBC member and a grandson of Mr. Joel remembers the late 1930s or early 1940s when "Pap" drove that old Studebaker mule truck. In 2014, Gene described the following: "I guess Pap and Uncle Bud (Lee Heard) would clean out the back of the truck and put in some hay, because we had either hay or benches to sit on. Pap would also put a drape or curtains around the wheels to help protect the people from the dust and the mud. We would climb up in there and away we would go. Anyone that was out by the road could jump on board and we'd be off to church." It is believed that many were afforded an opportunity to attend church because of Mr. Joel Heard's effort to provide transportation.

Additional information about the truck, found in the personal diary of Cleo Heard Milford, a daughter of Mr. Joel and Birddie Heard. The entries describe revival time in 1934:

<u>Tuesday nite, July 31, 1934</u>. we went to meeting in the truck, we had 36 on it.

<u>Wednesday nite, Aug.1, 1934</u>. Went to meeting. Roy Hester was converted, but as it was rainy and we had 43 on the truck, we came home before meeting broke.

<u>Thursday nite, Aug. 2, 1934.</u> John [Heard] was converted, Also Richard Lathem, Billie Turner, Gilleland Turner, Roy Cannon, a Scott girl, a Wilkie girl and a Wilkie boy. There were about 13 in all. We had 42 on the truck.

<u>Friday, Aug 3, 1934</u>. Went to meeting. There were about 7 converted. Among them, Mark Dobson, Bloomer Little, Rade Phyfe and Winnie Grace Buffington. Preachers that came home with us for dinner were Roper, Rich,

Cochran and Tribble.

Friday nite, Aug. 3, 1934. We went to church on the truck. We had 51, I think.

Sunday, August 5, 1934. I helped Mother prepare dinner and then went to the baptizing at Hightower There were 34 baptized, 24 boys and 10 girls. …after we got back from the pool, we sat in a car until time for us to give the newly baptized ones our hands….We went in the church and stayed until Preacher Roper ended his service.

……

The following statement was from an interview with Cleo Heard Milford and recorded on June 4, 1995: "When we married, we didn't have a vehicle (car or truck), just 2 mules and a "waggin" and the mules was Daddy's. We married in October of 1939 and moved here to the West house in December of 1939. On the weekends, Daddy (Joel) stopped and we rode to church with him in his truck. He took everybody to church, you know. Robert (Milford) bought a second hand truck a little later."

Attire from the Early to Mid-1900s

Frances Ann Green Wilkie, pictured to the left, was born August 9, 1850. It is not known what year this picture was taken, but the dress shown would have been common for middle-aged women in the early 1900s. She died on August 19, 1919, and was buried at HBC.

While Frances Ann Wilkie had a number of children, the following two pictures of two of her daughters were offered for inclusion in this book. The young Myrtie Wilkie (1887-1977) is shown with a bouquet. Flora Augusta "Gussie" Wilkie Hester (1892-1966) is shown wearing a two-piece suit complete with hat. Both sisters are also buried at HBC.

Photos above courtesy of Chris Chandler

Sarah West Perkins (1925-1996) was the only daughter of HBC family Emory and Myrtie West. Pictured below in the nice dress is Sarah in 1946.

Photo courtesy of Tim Perkins

W. H. Ellis, tells that "Hightower Once a Booming Gold Town"

Thompson, Chuck. "Hightower Once a Booming Gold Town." *The Forsyth County News*. December 7, 1983: 8A.

Excerpts from an article describing an interview with W. H. Ellis, age 80, son of John Henry Ellis, grandson of Greenbury Haygood (J. H. Ellis and G. B. Haygood are both buried at HBC).

At one time, Hightower was a "pretty good sized town" with "lots of Indians and stores." W. H. Ellis lived in Hightower until he was 16 years old and claims to know every trail and "short cut" in the area. He knows a lot about the area's history, through stories passed down from generation to generation. Ellis' father worked in the Pyrite Mine and died at age 62 in the 1920s. His grandfather lived to be 90.

The Creighton Mine began as the Franklin Gold Mine and was later purchased by the Creighton Mining Company. The "Shingle House" served as an office for both the Franklin and Creighton mines, and at one time it also served as a post office. The shaft of the Creighton Mine went deep into the ground and under the Etowah River. Miners dug in a northerly direction and after reaching a certain point, headed east and west. The shaft reached to one of the richest gold veins ever struck and reportedly a "brick of gold" was derived from the mine each month. One day the good fortune of the Creighton mine came to an end. It was lunchtime, and all the miners had left the shaft when suddenly it collapsed under the Etowah River. Water was drawn into the shaft and for a brief period the river was dry. Once all the tunnels inside the mine were filled, the river resumed its westward flow, sealing the mine for good.

Located nearby the Creighton Mines was the Andrews Chapel Methodist Church and school. It was destroyed by fire, and the Creighton Mine donated a building across Settendown Creek as a replacement.

Like the Creighton Mine, the Pyrite Mine was also successful. It was equipped with a mill three stories high and a rock crusher. Carts of ore were pulled through a steep shaft to the surface. Steps descended into the mine about 10 feet and the water was continually pumped out of the tunnels inside. While no one was killed in the Creighton Mine disaster, Ben Fowler lost his life in a dynamite explosion inside the Pyrite Mine.

Also referenced are Pool's Mill, New Harmony and Hightower Churches.

South of Hightower were two settlements by the name of New Harmony. Ellis tells that this resulted in mail often going to the wrong New Harmony. To remedy the situation, the U.S. postmaster requested that New Harmony in

Forsyth County find another name. A man in the town owned a large number of ducks and thus the inspiration for the name "Ducktown". New Harmony Baptist Church elected to keep its name and is still called by that name today.

Included in the original article was a hand drawn map of the HBC area. Below is a portion of that interesting map.

[Original newspaper article shared by Larry Waylon Ellis, July 2014]

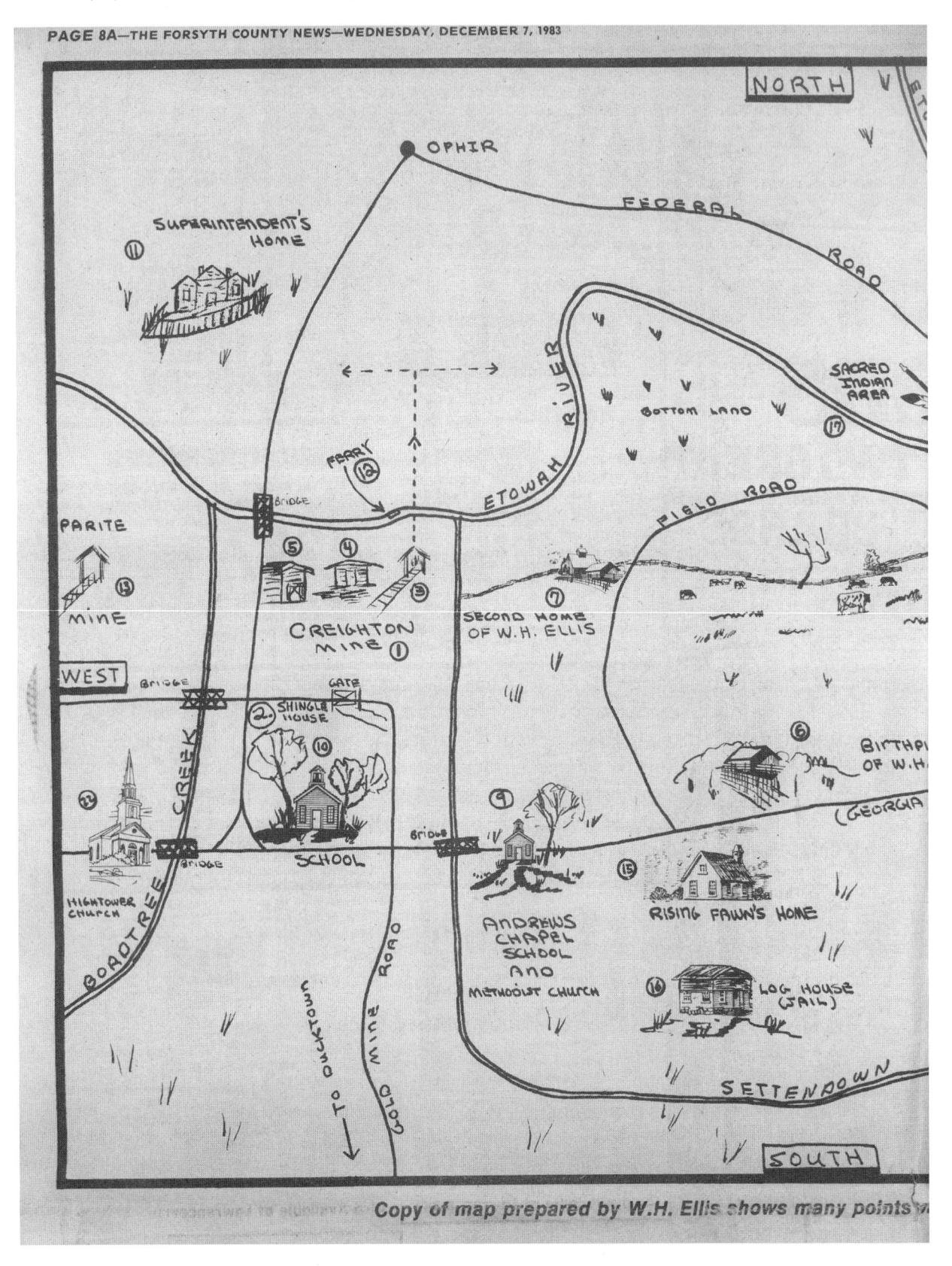

First wedding and memories of HBC

Photo courtesy of Brenda Curtis

Early in the evening of August 31, 1956, Peggy Cochran and C. W. Smith were married at HBC by Rev. Elbert Majors. It is believed that this was the first wedding held at HBC as a special event. (Prior weddings at HBC were conveniently held after regular church service, and records of those are scarce.) Peggy remembers Rev. Majors as "a special man". Pictured back row, L-R: Randall and Bill Cruice, Doris Smith, Mary Lee Cochran, Montaree Smith, Johnny Smith, and Grady Smith. Front row, L-R: Emmett Cochran, Broughton Cochran, Keith Magnee, Peggy Cochran Smith, C. W. Smith and Janice McClure.

Other memories from Peggy:

We always had good singing at HBC.

For several years, we had what would be called "pot-bellied stoves" for heat.

There was an A-Men side and an A-Women side at the front of the church.

It was nice when Sunday school rooms were built so that each age class had their own special room.

I always enjoyed the Christmas programs, usually on the 3rd Sunday afternoon in December, when a huge evergreen tree was cut fresh and brought in to be decorated for the church wide Christmas program that night – we always worked for many weeks practicing for the Christmas program. Santa always brought in a sack of "goodies" for the children, mainly oranges and apples. He came in the church when we started singing "Jingle Bells."

I remember playing the piano for a baby's funeral; I was only 12 years old and very nervous.

I remember hearing about slaves being buried "way down" on the lower side of the cemetery.

May meeting was always special, maybe because of such wonderful food. Sometimes we called it "meeting on the ground."

Revival was always the 3rd week in July – for a long time it was services mid-day and evening. People visited from other churches.

I have lots of special memories of Hightower. It is still special to me.

Peggy Cochran Smith. August, 2014.

Friends

Below are some examples of HBC families and friendships.

Friendships founded at Hightower often last throughout one's lifetime. Attending church was an opportunity not only for worship but also for social interaction. Church events have provided a time for meeting friends as well as renewing old friendships. After Sunday service, many impromptu plans were made to spend the afternoon together.

Three friends from HBC,

L-R: Cleo Heard, Nettie Lee Lovelace, Ruby Hester

On a particular Sunday afternoon likely in the late summer of 1935 or 1936, Cleo, Nettie Lee and Ruby were invited as guests to the home of Ira and Effie Cowart. While visiting, the three girls had their picture taken as they enjoyed a watermelon cutting. Ruby, in 2014, tells that the location was at the "Cowart farm down near the river and that Mr. William Cowart had grown some fine melons that year." The location was believed to be near the present day Preserve at Etowah Subdivision; the old road turned by a home and went down toward the Etowah River where Mr. William and Mrs. Toma Cowart and family lived. Ira and Effie (Cowart) were renting a home and lived near his parents in the same area. Also of interest is the period barn, with notched logs, and attached ladder outside for access to the barn loft. Many farms of this era had similar structures built of the notched log style.

(Personal interview with Ruby Hester Milford, July, 2014)

Sarah West and Mattie Heard at Heard home in Lathemtown

Courtesy of Tim Perkins

Standing, L-R: Effie, Ira, Ruby, with Donald, Dewey, and Marvin Cowart

Sitting, L-R: Ruby Hester, Nettie Lee Lovelace

Photo courtesy of Diane Cowart Martin

These young boys were likely returning chairs to the church after a baptizing event. Note the unpaved parking area and windows before stained glass.

L-R: unknown, Ed Cochran, Carol Ball, and Broughton Cochran

Diane Cowart and Judy Milford have an after church visit at the Milford home.

Back row, L-R: Donald Cowart, Gene Pruitt, Middle, L-R: Frankie Pruitt, J. L. Cowart, Joe Milford, Billy Pruitt, and front: John Milford

The Pruitt and Milford boys are cousins and added church friends for an afternoon of football fun.

Pictured above, L-R: Cleveland Wilkie, Nettie Lee Lovelace, Robert Milford and Henry Milford. While not an officially named quartet, these four friends (two were brothers) were among several singers who grouped together to sing at church functions. Likely, Cleveland sang the "lead," Nettie Lee was alto, Robert sang tenor and Henry was the bass singer. Singing schools, "all day church singings," and other events featured quartets such as the one shown above.

John. Heard: A WWII Story

Many verses in the Bible could match the following story, but maybe none any better than Romans 12:12. "Rejoicing in hope, persevering in tribulation, devoted to prayer." Many, many prayers for the safety and welfare of the WWII soldiers were lifted up during those tumultuous years of the early 1940s. Perseverance to survive the Battle of the Bulge in the cold winter of 1944 led one young soldier to eventually rejoice in hope. That hope of a return to a healthy life was aided with rehabilitation by playing golf at Augusta National Golf Course, not a highly publicized opportunity. The following is a story of HBC member John Heard (1921-1991) published in 2013 and reprinted with permission from the managing editor at turner.com. Photo from *PGA.COM April 8, 2013*.

http://sports.yahoo.com/news/wounded-war-ii-veteran-john-183807973--golf.html

Wounded WW II veteran John Heard had a unique rehab assignment - play Augusta National.

John Heard, a member of the 308th Engineering Combat Battalion assigned to the 8th Army at the Battle of the Bulge, was the lone member of his unit to survive a land mine blast in 1944.

Tom Heard had never heard his father, John, talk about golf, and he had never seen him play. John was a farmer and poultry inspector in rural Georgia, and he spoke occasionally about his days playing baseball. But golf never came up.

Then in 1975 Tom and his brother sat in the living room to watch an epic final round of the Masters as Jack Nicklaus won over Tom Weiskopf and Johnny Miller. As the CBS cameras showed panorama shots of the 13th hole with azaleas and dogwoods in full bloom, Tom said, "Wow that is beautiful."

He was shocked when his father said, "Yeah, that is a pretty place, but it's a tough hole."

The boys looked at their father and asked, "You've been to Augusta National?"

John said, "Sure. I played it every day I was there."

Tom said, "I never knew you played golf."

His father said, "I don't. Augusta National's the only place I ever played."

The fact that John Heard played the only golf of his life at Augusta National, not once but numerous times, came as almost as big of a shock to his sons as the fact that he had never mentioned it before. But men of that generation kept a lot of things locked away. More often than not, it was for good reason.

John Heard was with the 308th Engineering Combat Battalion assigned to the 8th Army at the Battle of the Bulge in the winter of 1944. On a snowy December morning, a member of their unit tripped a large German mine buried in the French countryside. An entire squad was blown to bits. John was the only survivor.

With shrapnel in his shoulder, back and hip, he was medically evacuated to Paris, and then flown to England for several weeks. When he was strong enough to travel, John returned stateside on the Queen Mary and was transported by train to the Army's Camp Gordon Hospital in Augusta for rehab.

Physical therapy wasn't much of a science in the 1940s, so John's rehab consisted of whatever calisthenics he could do, followed by golf in the afternoon at a local club, Augusta National, which opened its doors to wounded veterans.

John played the National almost every day for six months. He had never played the game before and never played it after. Like most parts of the war, he put that piece of his life away never to be visited again.

Those who knew Bob Jones and Clifford Roberts personally would not be surprised by John's story. Roberts discovered Augusta and the old Berckman's Nursery during his time in the Army at Camp Gordon (now Fort Gordon), and Bob Jones was a captain in the Army Air Corp and landed in Normandy on D-Day plus one.

For years Roberts and Jones allowed any uniformed serviceman free admittance to the grounds for the tournament. That was how Arnie's Army got its name. And for decades the club provided aid and support to military families in the area.

But Augusta National members kept quiet about the good deeds they did for wounded heroes like John Heard, just as they remain silent to this day on matters big and small. You won't hear anyone at the National speak about the extraordinary charity work the club does, not just in Augusta but throughout the country, nor will the men in green jackets utter a peep about their ongoing support for wounded veterans and their families.

The best charity is always the quietest. That is something to remember when the lazy criticisms of Augusta National are trotted about again this year. The privacy they so jealously protect does not conceal some nefarious conspiracy.

Sometimes, as in the story of John Heard and the wounded heroes of World War II, it is for the good.

Christmas

Records of Christmas celebrations in the 1800s are scarce for the Hightower community. What is known is that in the early 1900s, little commercialization existed surrounding the Christmas holiday. If the weather was "just right" the week of Christmas was one of the hog-killing times for many families. On Christmas Eve, the children would hang one of their socks on the mantle in hopes of some fruit or candy. Christmas day included a meal, often with extended families (aunts, uncles and cousins,) and the menfolk would go hunting in the afternoon.

The third Sunday worship service was likely attended, weather permitting, and Luke 2 was probably read most years. After Sunday school was firmly established, a yearly Christmas celebration included a program on the Sunday night before Christmas where children sang and acted out the story of Mary, Joseph and Baby Jesus, along with shepherds, wise men and angels. The script was often written by someone in the church. The evening began with everyone singing "Oh Come All Ye Faithful," and the drama portion ended with "Jingle Bells" that always produced a visit from Santa. Members of Sunday school classes drew names and gave presents to each other as well as their teacher(s).

Serenading, also known as "Sernating"

A serenade is an event when one sings or plays an instrument, such as a fiddle, to entertain someone. In the community near HBC, the term was fondly called sernating and pronounced SIR-nating. In the early 1900s, and probably even before, the young folks would go sernating especially at Halloween or even at New Year's. The event was likely replaced with trick-or-treating in later years.

Frankie Edge remembers, "When Bob and Maude Buffington lived there in the shingle house and we would go sernating over there and we would have the biggest time with them, it was probably Halloween, we had the most fun, we lived over there on the farm on Julius Bridge Road, that road was named later for my grandfather, but at the time it didn't have no name, none of the roads were named until lots later. We would start out down there where we lived and we would go around and the Gilleland's went with us, Mary, Dorthy and Sam and I think it was just Sam, but the others were too little, went on around to the Rays, over there at that farm, when they moved up here, it was on Dr. Jones farm, not the Dr. Jones from Canton, but from Atlanta, a big ole 2 story house over there, he hired Mr. Ray to look after the farm and the horses, they just come part time. We started out and everybody joined us and we went on to Nettie Lee's, we walked of course and at the church cemetery, you know the big old monument that has the shape of a chair? I think it is Wash and Frances Wilkie's monument. Well, we would dare everybody to go up there and sit down, and the rest of us would stand down there in the road, some were afraid to go into the cemetery in the dark. We dressed up in old clothes and things, and some of us would take ashes out of the fireplace and darken our faces, we would go house to house and some places you might get parched peanuts, some places an apple, some you wouldn't get nothing, but we had fun."

Box Suppers

A box supper is a social gathering usually at a local school for a fund-raising effort. The girls would prepare a meal, place it in a box or bag, and then the boys would bid in auction fashion for the prize box and the opportunity to eat the meal with the girl.

Frankie Edge recalled, "We'd have box suppers, I remember the only one I went to, it was up at Etowah School, that kind of thing wouldn't be allowed at church because the bidding was too much like gambling. The girls had to fix two sandwiches, 2 cookies or 2 pieces of cake, then the boys would bid on them. Anyway, this boy bought mine, I sure didn't want to eat dinner with him and oh I hated it so bad, and you know you had to eat with him, and I said I'd never do that again. I don't guess he give over a dollar because nobody had much and I guess it wasn't more than a dollar. There wasn't nothing much for any kind of entertainment, so if anything was going on at the school, everybody went. I played basketball on the team at Etowah, we won the tournament one year. Wilma Green was on our team…"

Jewell Wilkie Cotton (1918-1985) told it this way: "We had a lot of fun back then but our social life was a lot different from now. We used to have pound suppers where everybody brought a pound of something to eat and we'd all eat together, sorta like a covered dish supper now. Then we had box suppers where all the girls would fix a box of food with enough in it for two people. They would be auctioned off and the boys would bid on the boxes. Whoever bought the box would get to eat supper with the girl that brought it. Sometimes the rest of the boys would get together and run the price way up when a boy would be bidding on his best girl's box. That was mean, wasn't it?" (Moore, 1993)

Fourth of July

Mrs. Cotton also stated: "On the Fourth of July, everybody went to an all day frolic up at Franklin Gold Mine. That's where I drank my first glass of lemonade. There wasn't a bridge over the river; had to cross over on a flat bottom ferry, pulled a rope to get across. We looked forward to this all year."

Marriages

Courting, or dating followed by marriages was common place for the young people of the Hightower community. For many years, especially throughout the 1800s, ladies were afforded an opportunity to meet potential suitors while attending church services. Many young men dated by attending church services and activities and then walking his "date" home.

Atholine Gilleland Wilkie remembers: "My older half-sister told me, that after her mother died, Dad was left with five very young kids. He (Bunion Gilleland) was living in Dawson County at the time, but he talked with Dr. McClure who told him that he thought old man Green had a daughter that was available. Mother (Lillie Green) wrote letters to Dad, and Esco wrote the letters for Dad, and after a short few months, my Mother and Dad married."

A widow or widower with children was quite desperate for a mate for survival. In a number of cases, if a man's wife died, he would then propose and marry a sister of his first wife. In other situations, often brothers married sisters. There were quite a few families that shared a common surname, but were from a different "set".

Weddings in the early days were simple events. As was often the case, the couple would speak to the preacher or justice of the peace, and upon presenting the marriage license could marry at the home of the official. One story told of a couple traveling to the preacher's house and upon a surprise meeting on the roadway, simply stopped and exchanged their vows at that very spot.

The story of the wedding of Ira and Effie Hester Cowart is included in Chapter 7 of this book.

Winnie Grace Buffington and Linton Wyatt were united in marriage at the home of the bride. Interestingly, Robert and Maude Buffington were living in the Shingle House, a well-known surviving vestige of the gold mining years and located on current Yellow Creek Road about one mile from HBC.

"Nov. 19, 1944, After Sunday School and preaching, Haygood boy and Gravley girl got married," as noted in the diary of Cleo Heard Milford.

Pictured below are two of the children of Elisha and Jennie Cochran from their prospective wedding days. Mr. and Mrs. Elisha Cochran, as well as both couples pictured are all buried at HBC.

Emmett and Mary Lee Cochran were married in 1937 and Cecil and Louise Cochran McGaha were wed in 1954.

Photos courtesy of Brenda Cochran Curtis

Another wedding photo is that of HBC's Gene and Barbara Tippens Wheeler, wed in 1958. The wedding location believed to be at Chalcedonia BC.

Photo courtesy of Kris Wheeler

Old Timer's Day

HBC has celebrated its history by a glimpse into the past with this event including attire from days gone by. A few examples include the following:

E. W. Cochran told: "I have an old hat, that big black one that I wore on old timers day at HBC, my granddad got it at Old Orange Store down there, it's probably 150 years old."

Pictured L-R: Tabitha Price, E. W. Cochran, Deidre Groover and Tonya Price

Transportation of days gone by

L-R: Effie Cowart, Rilla Price and Edith Cochran

Photos courtesy of Regina Groover

Scruggs Controversy

This story is mentioned here to provide some details for future researchers about the association records from the 1880s. The association minutes during those years are confusing. For a few years, the association actually had a division and each group had their own association meeting complete with minutes. One group continued to use the HBA name while the other became the Old HBA. While searching for the yearly data for HBC in the 1883 association minute, early efforts found the data for HBC was missing. Later, it was discovered that the initial list of churches was actually from the Old HBA. No prior knowledge was known of the two different associations. In further study, the HBA records were located. Diligent research is needed to locate all records of this decade or so of unfortunate turmoil. Hopefully future researchers can be spared confusion by acknowledging that the association suffered a split for this period of time.

Prompting the confusion, as was learned, was the credibility of a particular minister. As the story goes, credentials of a minister were not likely investigated in the mid to late 1800s. A man that professed to be a preacher was trusted on good faith, and usually that was enough. A situation occurred; however, with the person of Elder Henry J. Scruggs. It seemed the new preacher to the area was worthy, successfully leading revivals and baptizing new converts. It was later learned that Mr. Scruggs had a questionable background with leaving a wife and taking another woman for a new wife. This behavior was greatly frowned upon, and thus came into question whether those he had baptized were indeed credible members of their perspective churches. This issue led to a major controversy within the existing association as well as a number of churches. Eventually this led to a split in the association to form the "Old HBA" with about ten of the churches. The thirty or so churches that stayed as HBA contended that it was appropriate for individual churches to recognize the validity of the Scruggs baptism, as those persons had been baptized in good faith and it was not a new member's fault for the minister to later be found unworthy. Some churches believed that it was necessary for those persons to be baptized again. The churches (thirty or so) that stayed with the association became known as "Scruggites," and the others (about ten) were labeled "Slab-offs". No record has been found to indicate that Henry Scruggs conducted or assisted with any revivals at HBC. During the controversy, a spokesperson for the association was Rev. Thaddeus Pickett. Interesting to note, Rev. Pickett was pastor at HBC in 1884-1885, so likely HBC was informed of the issue.

As with many disputes, accounts are chronicled or remembered according to the perspective of those involved. Additional information was found in the following sources:

Hightower Baptist Association History Committee. *The Men and Missions of Hightower, Volume I: Ministers.* Hightower Baptist Association History Committee, about 2005. Page 322.

Hightower Baptist Association History Committee. *The Men and Missions of Hightower, Volume II: Churches.* Canton, GA: Doss Printing Services, Inc. 2013. Page 97 and 477-479.

"Twenty Years' Strife Between Baptist Factions in North Georgia." *The Weekly Constitution*, 28 Dec. 1886. Accessed http://atlnewspapers.galileo.usg.edu/atlnewspapers.

Chapter 12: Cemetery Records

Photo courtesy of Ken Wyatt

This picture (date unknown) with the cemetery in the background was taken at HBC of three of the children of Samuel and Mary Jackson Pascoe. L-R, believed to be: Josephine Pascoe Cox, Samuel W. Pascoe, and Grace Pascoe Gilstrap. One can note the five markers on the left of this picture show graves of the Daniel Stephens family, as well as the tall monuments of the Franklins.

HBC Cemetery, an introduction

The rolling hillsides of northern Georgia finds many country churches with adjacent cemeteries. In the northeastern portion of Cherokee County, Georgia, Hightower BC was chosen as the resting place for many loved ones. A valuable contribution to any church history is an in-depth study of the burial grounds like the one found at HBC. Here one will find the tradition of headstones facing eastward; a practice that is linked with spiritual beliefs of the resurrection. It is estimated that some nine hundred burials have taken place at HBC since the early to mid-1800s. There are a number of sites with unidentifiable stones or assumed burial sites with no stones or markers remaining. The materials used for grave markers that range from simple stones and marble to granite and brick is a history unto itself. Many headstones depict a name, dates of birth and death, as well as other decorative and informational inscriptions.

Whether legend or fact, stories remain that the first grave in the Hightower Baptist Church Cemetery may have been that of a young child. While the year is unknown, it was told to this writer by Nettie Lee Lovelace that in the 1820s or so, a family or group of families that were migrating westward through the north Georgia area experienced a tragic event. Maybe they had purposely taken the Old Alabama/Downing Ferry route as it veered westward from the Old Federal Road and found a place to stop for the night near a spring on the Boardtree Creek just east of the current church. While at this site, a child succumbed to an illness and died. The family looked upward to the hilltop and chose the location for the burial of the child's remains. This story has survived the years as the likely beginning of the Hightower Church Cemetery.

It is yet to be determined whether this burial ground began before or after the beginning of the church or the assembly of a worship group at this location. Perhaps a meeting house was erected nearby only after the burials began. Perhaps the Native Americans, the Creeks and later the Cherokees, had already established the knoll for burials. Legend says that the grounds are home to not only those unfortunate travelers, but also many white settlers, African-American slaves and Native Americans. A few graves are noted to be members of the Methodist denomination. From the Civil War era, one grave is marked as a union soldier while several are noted as C.S.A., Confederate States of America. Particular sites are often selected by survivors of the deceased; however, the decision to be buried at Hightower was sometimes noted in one's last will and testament, as the examples found in the wills of James Pursell and Samuel Pascoe.

"…State of Georgia, Cherokee County Last will and testament of **James Pursell** written 9 November 1875. I desire to be buried in the family burial ground at Hightower Church in Cherokee County …."

"…State of Georgia, Cherokee County Last will and testament of **Samuel Pascoe,** deceased, written 4 March 1882. *Item one:* I desire that my body be laid away in a decent Christian like manner in the family burial ground at Hightower Church in Cherokee County under the Masonic Order, my soul I give to God"….admitted to record at May term 1887 of Cherokee County Court of Ordinary…….

Many sources are available for cemetery research, some more accurate than others. In an effort to provide the most helpful and precise record of HBC, the two lists that follow provide careful studies of both burials by location and an annotated alphabetical list.

The first list is titled: **Hightower Baptist Church Cemetery: Interments by Section.** The names and/or dates as well as tombstone inscriptions (without annotation) are listed as best as can be determined. Some of the listings were noted before 2000 and are now illegible. (Many thanks are extended to Ken Wyatt for his work on the original list.) Also included is a code for finding the general location for section-row-grave. Many of the rows are not aligned therefore the numbering system will lead a researcher to an area rather than an exact gravesite. A study of early graves may provide hints of relationships for genealogists. In some areas, copings denote family sections where several of the same lineages are buried. A walk through the cemetery shows a history of family links and a history of trends and available materials for gravestones matching the era within which the section was most frequently selected. For identification purposes for this publication, the burial grounds are labeled by sections 1-5. The numbering follows a chronological pattern of when property was obtained by the church. An introduction is included with each section describing property deeds, the common materials used for marking graves in that era, and other information.

The second list is **Hightower Baptist Church Cemetery: Alphabetical List of Interments**. This table also gives the section-row-grave where the graves are located (unless unmarked) as well as other identifiable information, such as middle or maiden names in italics. Included are names of people thought to be buried at HBC, with no present identifiable marker. Some of these were reported by descendants or records found on death certificates and other public records. Best efforts have been made to verify the information; however, any omissions or mistakes that are found are certainly unintended.

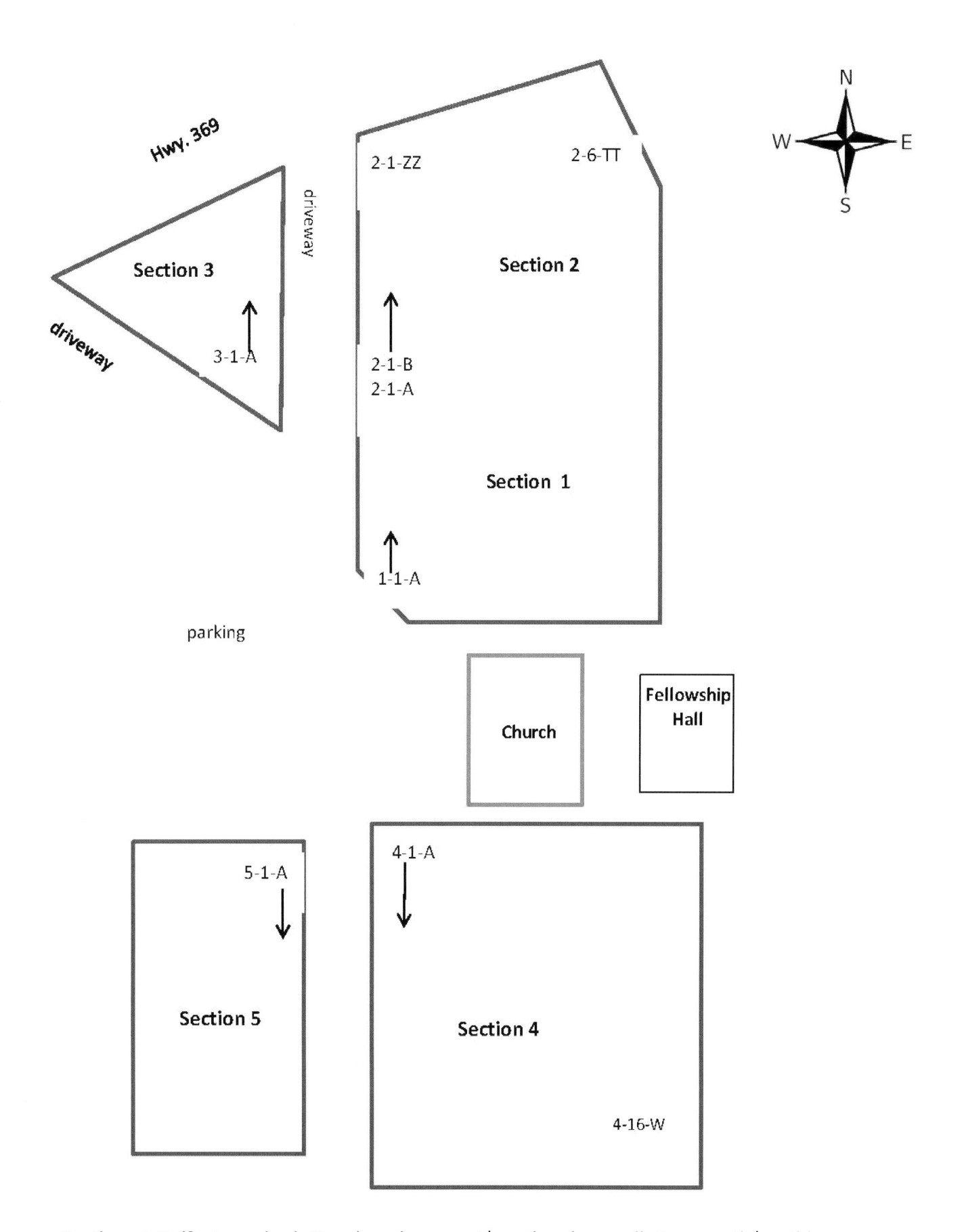

Sections 1-5, (first number) **Row** (numbers, east/west) and **grave** (letters, north/south).
The starting point for each section is corner grave closest to the parking lot.

Hightower Baptist Church Cemetery Interments by Section.

Section 1.

This section includes land purchased from Daniel Stephens in 1845. This area is likely where burials in this cemetery first began earlier than 1844 and likely on private property. There is evidence of numerous unmarked graves, and some with stones without inscriptions. While stone of various types were most common, a few markers are marble. This section includes a few graves with the unique stacked stone enclosures and also a few with slot and tab designs. These are among some of the most unusual or unique in the entire cemetery. A custom from this early era shows many markers inscribed with the years, months and days that the person lived.

Tragedies for HBC

Early deaths occurred in the Franklin, Stephens and Pascoe families. Dr. Bedney Franklin's grave marker at HBC notes his death in 1844 and is the oldest date of death found in the HBC cemetery. Additional information about some of the early deaths can be found in Chapter 11: Illness, Tragedy and Death.

Location: Section-Row-Grave, use the cemetery diagram in this chapter as a guide for the information in the column labeled location.

Location	Last Name	First, Middle, or Maiden	Date of Birth	Date of Death	Inscription
1-1-T	Lonard	Leeane	Dec. 23, 1824	Nov. 6, 1913	Asleep in Jesus. (At bottom of marker: From National Marble Co. Ball Ground Ga.)
1-1-V	Leonard	M. E.	Sep. 20, 1848	Jun. 18, 1918	"Mother"
1-1-W	Leonard	J. B.	Mar. 27, 1850	Mar. 13, 1909	Happy are they whose hope is in the Lord. Father
1-1-Y	White	Mary M.	Jul. 22, 1877	Nov. 13, 1961	
1-1-Z	White	William A.	Jun. 22, 1868	Jul. 24, 1940	
1-1-AA	White	J. M.	1845	1930	CSA Co E 1 Ga St Troors
1-1-BB	White	Mary J.	Apr. 5, 1841	Mar. 8, 1911	"Come Ye Blessed; Asleep in Jesus" Wife of J. M. White Age 69 yrs. 11 mo. & 3 da.
1-1-DD	Nelson	Gilleland	Aug. 13, 1909	Apr. 13, 1910	
1-1-EE	Nelson	Nancy Elizabeth	Mar. 15, 1921	Mar. 28, 1921	Dau. of Mr. & Mrs. M. Paul Nelson, Budded on earth to bloom in heaven
1-1-GG	Green	Martha E.	Jun. 22, 1859	Oct. 12, 1938	
1-1-HH	Green	Samuel L.	Mar. 8, 1855	May 15, 1917	Gone but not forgotten
1-1-II	Green	Martha	(no dates)		Grandmother Green; By Newt & Tim Green. (In lot with Samuel & Martha E. Green.)
1-2-E	Cochran	Nevils Holcomb	1815	Dec. 26, 1863	One large marker with wife & children Married Sep. 10, 1840
1-2-E	Cochran	Altiney J. Griffin	1818	1855	Wife of Nevels Cochran
1-2-F	Cochran	Infant			Child of Elisha and Jennie Cochran
1-2-U	Pursell	James	Dec. 3, 1797	Aug. 30, 1882	Was born : departed this life:
1-2-V	Pursell	Mary	Oct. 5, 1805	Oct. 8, 1876	Was born: died:

Location	Last Name	First, Middle, or Maiden	Date of Birth	Date of Death	Inscription
1-2-W	Fowler	C. M.	(no dates)		
1-2-FF	Purcell	B.	Sep. 21, 1827	May 11, 1899	In memory of: age 71 yrs. 7 mo. 21 days
1-2-JJ	White	James	Mar. 10, 1776	Oct. 28, 1848	In memory of, departed this life
1-2-KK	White	Mary		Oct. 29, 1853	Marker on ground
1-3	?				
1-4-D	Lipscomb	Nancy G.	May 12, 1875	Jun. 13, 1876	Dau. of Dr. T. L. and Laura T. Lipscomb; Age 1 yr, 1 mo, 1 day
1-4-U	Pursell	Susan T.	Aug. 6, 1844	Apr 6, 1889	Was born: Died: Aged 44 years 8 mo & 20 days
1-4-Y	Burns	Lucy	Nov. 8, 1796 (calculated)	Mar. 13, 1877	Aged 80 yrs 4 mos 5 days
1-4-Z	Burns	Jefferson D.			J. D. B.
1-4-AA	Burns	Dr. John	Apr. 26, 1794	Oct. 11, 1858	Sacred to the memory of: Age 64 years 5 months & 15 days
1-4-BB	Burns	W. Melmoth W.	Dec. 20, 1833 (calculated)	Jan. 13, 1847	Sacred; In memory: Who departed this life: aged 13 yrs 24 days,
1-4-CC	Burns	Warren M.	Feb. 28, 1831 (calculated)	Jun. 5, 1847	Departed this life:16 yrs 3 m 7 days
1-4-DD	Burns	Josepsun	No dates		
1-4-EE					Large stacked stone tomb near Burns and Coffee
1-5-D	Fowler	Martha J.	Nov. 2, 1845 (calculated)	Jan. 27, 1863	Daughter of Dr. M. L. & L. C. Pool; Age 17 yrs, 2 mo, 25 days
1-5-E	Pool	Eliza A.	Nov. 14, 1854	Apr. 17, 1856	Daughter of Dr. M. L. & L. C. Pool
1-5-G	Lipscomb	Laura T.	Nov. 2, 1859	Jul. 4, 1875	Wife of T. L. Lipscomb
1-5-J					stone
1-5-L	Boling	F. T.	Jan. 17, 1842	Feb. 2, 1862	In memory of: born and departed this life: aged 20 years 15 days He died a volunteer in the army at Richmond Virginia
1-5-T					stone
1-5-BB	Burns	Catherine	Feb. 11, 1766 (calculated)	Jun. 24, 1849	(Stacked stone tomb) In memory of; who departed this life; 83 yrs, 4 months, 13 days
1-5-DD	Coffee	John E.	Dec. 10, 1836	Aug. 23, 1852	(Stacked stone tomb) Relations and friends as you pass by Remember as you are now so once was I. And as I am now so you must be So prepare for death and follow me. Age 15 yrs 8 mos 13 days

Location	Last Name	First, Middle, or Maiden	Date of Birth	Date of Death	Inscription
1-5-EE	Montgomery	Polly			In memory of:
1-6	?				
1-6-C	Boling	James A.	Sep. 23, 1827	Feb. 18, 1853	In memory of: aged 25 years 4 months & 26 days. Departed this life
1-6-D	Pursell	Elizabeth	Feb. 15, 1831	Feb. 6, 1853	Dau. of William & Mary Boling, was born… departed this life… Age 21 yrs, 11 mo. 24 days
1-6-E	Boling	John R.	Nov. 18, 1832	Feb. 1853 No "day" on marker Calculated Feb. 2	In memory of: Aged 20 years 2 months & 14 days
1-6-F	Jones	Sarah Ann	May 31, 1851	Jul. 31, 1852	In memory of: Aged 1 Y. 2 M.
1-7-					stone
1-7-F	Springer	Nicey	Dec. 11, 1839	(no date)	
1-7-G	Springer	Dempsey	Jan. 2, 1804	Aug. 3, 1899	
1-7-H	Springer	Infant			Infant son of Demsy & M. E. Springer
1-7-J	?				stone
1-7-K	Boling	Mary	Apr. 4, 1808	Jun. 27, 1853	Sacred to the memory of: who was born and departed this life, aged 45 years, 2 months and 23 days."
1-7-KK	Williams	Zebulon	1799	1879	*Flat marker*
1-7-LL	Williams	Ollie Barker	1806	1882	
1-7-NN	McGullion	Mattie J.	1874	1951	
1-7-OO	McGullion	James W.	1853	1905	Mason
1-8-J					
1-8-N					Stone
1-8-O	Chambers	Elizabeth Jane	1840	Jun. 6, 1848?	
1-8-P	Chambers	William			
1-9-B	Boling	H. C.	Oct. 15, 1839	Oct. 25, 1910	A noble Christian gentleman has gone to his rest. "CSA"
1-9-C	Boling	Emily R.	Oct. 20, 1847	Oct. 5, 1909	
??					stone
1-9-F	Stephens	Samuel	Mar. 24, 1832	Jul. 4, 1852	In memory of: Aged 20 y 3 m and 10 d
1-9-G	Stephens	William	Nov. 19, 1930	Mar. 25, 1852	In memory of: Aged 21 y 4 m and 6 d
1-9-H	Stephens	Miley	Sep. 2, 1834	Mar. 24, 1852	In memory of… Age 17 yrs, 6 mo 22 days
1-9-I	Stephens	Daniel	Nov. 11, 1802	Mar. 11, 1852	In memory of: Aged 49 Y. 4 M.
1-9-J	Stephens	Selah	1799	Mar. 4, 1852	In memory of: Aged about 54 Y.
1-9-P	Freeze	C. Julius	Jan. 1850	Jan. 28, 1929	

Location	Last Name	First, Middle, or Maiden	Date of Birth	Date of Death	Inscription
1-9-Q	Freeze	Eliza J.	Jan. 30, 1846	Oct. 1, 1912	A devoted wife and loving mother
1-10-B	Hester	A. T.	Dec. 4, 1847	Sep. 22, 1910	He will not fail thee. Resting till the resurrection morn.
1-10-B	Hester	Eliza Davis	Dec. 1, 1854	Dec. 17, 1932	
1-10-F	Franklin	Mrs. Mary G.	Mar. 15, 1782	Jul. 31, 1858	Front/West: In memory of : Relict of Col. Bedney Franklin, Deceased of Morgan Co Ga, Daughter of John and Catherine Cleveland, Granddaughter of Col Ben Cleveland of the Revolution North: Devoted mother, ascend to heaven. East: Eminent of energy, Decision and fortitude, under great calamities South: 51 years a member of the Baptist Church in Georgia. She left no duty undone
1-10-G	Franklin	Dr. Bedney L.	Feb. 25, 1815	Jul. 11, 1844	Front/West: Erected to the memory of Dr. Bedney L. Franklin, born; died; Aged 29 years, 4 months, and 17 days Back/ East: This monument was erected by a Mother's love to the memory of one who was all a Mother's heart would wish. Peace to the soul, Dear Bedney.
1-10-DD					Stone
1-11-C	Holcombe	Lucy C.	Jan. 4, 1827	Sep. 8, 1858	Sacred to the memory of: She was a very orderly member of the Methodist Episcopal Church for 16 years before her death. Aged 31 years 8 month & 4 days. Her sparkling eyes and blooming cheeks, withered like the rose and died. The arms that once embraced me round, lie mouldering under the cold ground. I have a hope that cheers my breast, to think my love has gone to rest; For while her dying tongue could move, She praised the Lord for pardoning love.

Location	Last Name	First, Middle, or Maiden	Date of Birth	Date of Death	Inscription
1-11-F	Burton	Edward	Jun. 5, 1800	Jun. 18, 1851	Sacred to the memory of: Aged 51 years and 3 days. He was a very orderly member of the Methodist Episcopal Church for many years before his death. Sleep on my loving husband sleep This marble shall my memory keep But deeper in my heart is graven the thought that we shall meet in heaven
1-11-G	Holcombe	Robey	Nov. 14, 1848	Oct. 18, 1853	
1-11-H	Holcombe	Mary R.	May 27, 1825	Dec. 2, 1848	Sacred to he memory of: Aged 23 years, 6 months, 6 days. Remember relations and friends as you pass by. As you are now so once was I. As I am now so you must be Prepare for death and follow me.
??					Unmarked of Littleberry Holcombe??
1-11-I	Burton	Margarett Jane	Sep. 14, 1836 (calculated)	May 16, 1848	In memory of: Daughter of Edward & Sarah Burton. Aged 11 years 8 months & 2 days
??					Unmarked of Ransom Burton??
??					Unmarked of James Ransom Holcomb??
1-11-O	Petty	Major Wiley	Oct. 5, 1805 Or 1806	Jul. 18, 1892 Jul. 3, 1892?	In memory of: Aged 86 yrs, 8 mo, 13 days His last words, The Lord giveth and the Lord taketh. Blessed be the name of the Lord.
1-11-P	Petty	Martha B.	May 20, 1811	Mar. 21, 1871	In memory of: Aged 59 years 10 months & 1 day
1-11-AA	Thacker	Emma V.	Nov. 6, 1867	Jun. 7, 1923	Mother; She was a kind and affectionate wife, a fond mother and a friend to all.
1-11-BB	Wyatt	Julie P.	Jan. 11, 1858	Mar. 29, 1893	Sacred to the memory of: Wife of J. S. Wyatt, Departed this life, Aged 35 yrs. 2 mos. 18 days
1-11-CC	Wyatt	Sarah J.	Sep. 15, 1860	Sep. 9, 1897	Sacred to the memory of: Age 36 yrs., 11 months, 24 days
1-11-DD	Wyatt	Mary C.	Feb. 25, 1837	Jul. 10, 1884	Sacred to the memory of: Wife of Joseph Wyatt, was born, departed this life: Our mother here lies underground, The dearest friend we ever found. O, let us think of all she said, and all the kind advice she gave.
1-11-LL	Poter/Porter	E. S.	Sept. 20, 1805	Aug. 26,?	And departed this life August 26;Slot and tab tomb. Family confirms last name: Porter

Location	Last Name	First, Middle, or Maiden	Date of Birth	Date of Death	Inscription
1-11-MM	Porter	Cynthia			Unmarked; Slot and tab tomb; family reported as wife of E.S. Porter
1-12-M	Cochran	Sarah F.	Mar. 27, 1857	Apr. 3, 1857	??
1-12-N	Cochran	Sarah	Mar. 19, 1824	Sep. 15, 1853	Age 29 years, 5 months, 9 days. A member of Hightower Ch.
??					Stone
??					Stone
1-12-X	Pasco	Virginia Mourning Victoria?			??dates

1861-1862 (family records)

A small slot and tab tomb |
| 1-12-Y | Pasco | Samuel | Mar. 4, 1810 | Mar. 26, 1887 | Sacred to the memory of:

Born in Cornwall England

Age 77 years 22 days.

He was a member of Baptist Church for 44 years.

Hark I hear a soothing voice say Father is dead. He is not dead but only fallin asleep in Jesus. |
| 1-12-Z | Pasco | Mary | Sep. 7, 1817 | Sep. 15, 1889 | Wife of Samuel Pasco, Sacred to the memory of: Aged 82 years 8 days. She was a member of the Baptist Church 25 years

Mary hath chosen that good part, which should not be taken away from her. |
1-12-AA					stone
1-12-BB	??				Small slot and tab tomb
1-12-CC	Porter	John Henry	Jul. 26, 1878	Aug. 26, 1878	
1-12-DD	Porter	Amanda L.	Aug. 2, 1842	Nov. 4, 1887	Wife of E. T. Porter
1-12-EE	Porter	Edward	Mar. 9, 1882	Jan. 19, 1897	
1-12-FF	Porter	Mary J.	Feb. 23, 1870	Sep. 21, 1887	??
1-12-HH	Ellington				
1-12-II	Ellington	Annie P. Jenkins	Mar. 29, 1885	Jul. 7, 1957	
1-13-A	Smith	Thomas N.	Nov. 24, 1857	Jun. 14, 1919	Asleep in Jesus blessed sleep From which none ever wake to weep
1-13-B	Smith	Angie	Apr. 18, 1861	Dec. 10, 1889	Wife of Thomas N. Smith
??					Stone
??					Stone

Location	Last Name	First, Middle, or Maiden	Date of Birth	Date of Death	Inscription
1-13-H	Hawkins	Sarah M.	Jan. 20, 1847	May 28, 1852	In memory of: Daughter of J. S. & S. M. Hawkins
1-13-I	Kemp	M. L.	Mar. 8, 1826	Nov. 5, 1851	In memory of: son of Aaron & Sarah Kemp
1-13-J	Kemp	Harry	Mar. 28, 1821	Jun. 24, 1849	???
1-13-K	Taylor	Martha	Apr. 2, 1824	Oct. 16, 1846	Member of the M E Church South
1-13-L	Kemp	Aaron	Mar. 2, 1779	Sep. 24, 1865	???
1-13-M	Kemp	Sarah	Jan. 27, 1785	Mar. 25, 1863	
1-13-N	Chastaine	Bassel	Feb. 10, 1906	Jul. 2, 1907	Infant son of Silas & Maggie Chastaine. Gone but not forgotten
1-13-HH	Ellington	Frank H.	May 20, 1913	Aug. 9, 1972	
1-13-II	Ellington	Mildred J.	Apr. 21, 1909	Sep. 30, 1986	
1-14-A	Haygood	John Sullivan	Aug. 29, 1878	Dec. 7, 1944	
1-14-B	Haygood	Tommy Etta	Aug. 4, 1884	Oct. 18, 1923	
??					stone
1-14-H	Haygood	Pledger Wilborn	May 16, 1928	Feb. 2, 1931	
1-14-J	Haygood	G. B.	Apr. 21, 1848	Jan. 15, 1925	
1-14-K	Haygood	Suseana A.	Dec. 24, 1844	Nov. 5, 1922	Wife of G. B. Haygood, Our loved one
??					Lot edged with stacked stone
1-14-N	Haygood	Mae	Jan. 29, 1896	Jun. 10, 1952	
1-14-O	Haygood	James E.	Apr. 17, 1881	Oct. 10, 1931	
1-14-P	Haygood	Annie	May 24, 1881	Jan. 28, 1913	
1-14-Q	Purcell	J. H.	Aug. 21, 1883	Oct. 13, 1884	"J. H. P." Budded on Earth to Bloom in Heaven
	Martin	Josiah			
1-15-P	Strickland	Harriett		Died Jan the 3rd	Sacred to memory of: Age 65 years
	McMeken		Unmarked		
??	Several slaves and servants....				In 2015, area is near a metal stake near dogwood tree
??	Native Cherokee ??				
1-16-G	Kelley	Emiley	Jun. 22, 1818	Mar. 2, 1909	Member of the Baptist Church...
1-16-H	Sheffield	Wade	Jun. 11, 1912	Nov. 10, 1918	Son of J. D. & Mary Sheffield

Location	Last Name	First, Middle, or Maiden	Date of Birth	Date of Death	Inscription
1-16-I	Fowler	Charley B.	Apr. 30, 1855	No date	He joined the Baptist Church in August 1888 by experience at Hightower
1-16-J	Fowler	Georgian Caroline Cammel	Aug. 29, 1853	Apr. 27, 1924	She joined the Baptist church of Hightower in the year of 1887 by experience
1-16-K	Fowler	Walter E.	1922	1945	Son. Prepare to meet me in heaven
1-16-L	Fowler	Henry G.	Dec. 17, 1889	Feb. 14, 1958	Gone to rest.
1-16-M	Fowler	Ellar G.	May 20, 1894	Jun. 15, 1983	
1-17-C	Jameson	Infant Son	Sep. 3, 1891	Jul. 22, 1893	Infant son of J C Jameson
1-17-D	Holcombe	J. A.	Nov. 29, 1886	Oct. 26, 1905	Son of J. J. and L. D Holcombe. A precious one from us is gone A voice we loved is stilled A place is vacant in our home which never can be filled.
1-17-E	Holcombe	J. J.	Jun. 11, 1864	Jul. 27, 1937	Father
1-17-F	Holcombe	Louise	Oct. 26, 1862	May 31, 1927	Mother. A precious one from us has gone, A voice beloved is stilled, A place is vacant in our home, Which never can be filled. 64 yrs. 7 mo. 5 days
1-17-G	Wehunt	George W.	Jan. 26, 1847	Aug. 16, 1915	He was a faithful Union soldier
1-17-H	Wehunt	Avey E.	Jun. 4, 1854	Aft. 1910	
??	Fowler	Unknown			Stone
??	Fowler	Unknown			stone
1-17-M	Fowler	Harrison H.	Jul. 11, 1892	Sep. 10, 1948	GA WAGONER 36 INF 12 DIV WWI
1-18-D	Loggins	James H.	Jun. 2, 1844	Dec. 6, 1939	Father. Kind father of love, Thou are gone to thy rest.
1-18-E	Loggins	C. F.	1876	May 24, 1921	Age 45 years. As an officer, he died in the discharge of his duties. Erected by Cherokee Co. Grand Jurors, February Term of Court, 1921
1-18-F	Loggins	Georgia B.	Oct. 17, 1915	Aug. 22, 1922	
1-18-G	Loggins	Julie C.	May 11, 1880	May 14, 1961	
1-19-C	Loggins	Samuel L.	Jan. 14, 1907	Dec. 2, 1945	Gone but not forgotten
1-19-D	Emory	Miranda	Jul. 24, 1878	Feb. 4, 1949	
1-19-E	Emory	David T.	Dec. 18, 1881	Jul. 17, 1968	
					stone

Section 2

Section 2 includes land area purchased from Daniel Stephens in 1845, but located closer to Highway 369 from current church. Findings from dates of death suggest that this area became the second burial ground. It is possible that an early church building was located near or in this section.

	Last Name	First, Middle, or Maiden	Date of Birth	Date of Death	Tombstone Inscriptions
2-1-					stone
2-1-					Marked lot
2-1-M	Drummond	G. M.	Dec. 15, 1885	Sep. 25, 1892	
2-1-N	Drummond	James B.	1830	1890	Father of George Wesley Drummond
2-1-S	Thompson	Mrs. Jane		Jun. 17, 1883	Stone is broken
2-1-T	Drummond	Essie Jane	Aug. 14, 1900	Nov. 24, 1901	2nd stone "E. J. D."
2-1-GG	Little	George W.	1856	1913	Farewell my wife and children all, from you a father, Christ doth call.
	Little	G. W.	June 1857	Dec. 25, 1913	A footstone or older marker, believed to also be for George W. Little at 2-1-GG
2-1-HH	Little	Margaret	1858	1942	
2-1-II	Little	Dock L.	Oct. 15, 1886	May 7, 1961	
2-1-JJ	Little	Lillie M.	Mar. 6, 1883	Aug. 15, 1979	
2-1-NN	??				stone
2-1-OO	Drummond	Infant			Infant of G.W. and Texie Drummond
2-1-PP	Drummond	Texie Ann	Jan. 11, 1874	Jun. 9, 1913	Gone but not forgotten
2-1-QQ	Howard	Elijah	1812	1913	
2-1-TT	Howard	John	Mar. 30, 1866	May 26, 1914	Although he sleeps his memory doth live
2-1-VV	Collett	Litha	Aug. 17, 1874	Mar. 10, 1938	Mother
2-1-WW	Collett	Steve	Apr. 12, 1872	May 12, 1955	Father
2-1-ZZ	Little	H. L.	1837	1908	
2-1-AAA	Little	Mary J.	1837	1921	
2-2-E					stone
2-2-F	Hester	Howell Bell	Apr. 3, 1911	Apr. 25, 1913	Age 2 years 22 days, To him we trust a place is given, Among the saints with Christ in heaven
2-2-AA					stone
2-2-BB	Cannon	James M.	Mar. 3, 1856	Dec. 27, 1937	We will meet again
2-2-CC	Cannon	George W.	Mar. 3, 1858	Nov. 7, 1936	An honest man's the noblest work of God.
2-2-EE	Cannon	Lizzia	Jan. 20, 1870 or 1872	Jul. 13,?	Wife of James M. Cannon; date of death missing
2-2-FF	Cannon	Infant	Jul. 13, 1896	Jan. 14, 1897	Son of James M.& Lizzia Cannon

	Last Name	First, Middle, or Maiden	Date of Birth	Date of Death	Tombstone Inscriptions
2-2-HH	Floyd	Amanda			Stone on ground, no dates found, only name
2-2-JJ	Croy	Lillie	Sep. 27, 1904	Mar. 28, 1913	Dau. of L. O. and Lydia Croy "Darling we miss thee"
2-2-PP	Wallace	Nina	Mar. 2 (no birth year on marker)	Mar. 17, 1903	Infant of Jesse & Janie Wallace
2-2-QQ	Wallace	Linton Eugene	Sep. 28, 1901	Feb. 12, 1902	Son of Jesse & Janie Wallace
2-2-RR	Wallace	Grady	Dec. 2, 1898	Feb. 10, 1899	Baby Son of Jesse & Janie Wallace
2-2-UU	Wallace	Martha Jane	Feb. 5, 1879	Jan. 11, 1907	Wife of J. W. Wallace, "I Came to Jesus"
2-2-VV	Holcomb	Canzady	Dec. 23, 1844	Jan. 1, 1927	
2-2-WW	Holcombe	John W.	Dec. 11, 1842	Mar. 8, 1917	A sinner saved by grace.
2-2-XX	Price	Manervia	May 30, 1823	Aug. 16, 1896	"Farewell" Erected by Dr. J. M. & Mrs. Georgia Price
2-2-AAA	??				unmarked
2-2-BBB	??				unmarked
2-3-H	Fowler	W. T.	Jun. 15, 1841	Jun. 12, 1869	He has gone from us dear ones, his children his wife whom he willingly toiled for and loved all his life, O God, how misterious are thy ways to take from us this love one in the least of his days
2-3-I	Fowler	S. A.	Apr. 15, 1839		shared stone with W. T. Fowler
2-3-L	H. Unknown	John			Footstone: J.E.H.
2-3-CC	Cannon	Harvey "Huggins"	Abt. 1862	Mar. 1893	
2-3-DD	Cannon	Lenora Wheeler	Aug. 23, 1859	Nov. 18, 1951	
2-3-II	Gaddis	Johnie	Aug. 20, 1912	Sep. 5, 1912	
2-3-JJ	Croy	Almer	Feb. 12, 1910	Jan. 30, 1912	Dau. of L. O. and Lydia Croy "Darling we miss thee"
2-3-KK	Croy	Elmer	Nov. 24, 1906	Apr. 24, 1909	Son of L. O. and Lydia Croy "Darling we miss thee"
2-3-LL	Priest	Worth	Mar. 12, 1849	Jul. 5, 1900	Son of G. W. & Ella Priest
2-3-RR	Eaton	Andrew Jackson	Jan. 7, 1833	Dec. 5, 1890	Pvt Co. F 28 Ga. Inf. Confederate States Army (flat stone)
2-3-SS	Eaton	Leone	Apr. 6, 1904	May 21, 1904	Dau. of J. A. & Cora Eaton
2-3-UU	Cantrell	M. D.	1863	1935	
2-3-BBB	??				Stone, unmarked
2-4-B	Fowler	James	1797	Aug. 14, 1876	Born in S. C. A member of the Baptist church for 31 years.
2-4-C	Fowler	Sarah	Feb. 23, 1804	Aug. 28, 1875	Wife of James Fowler. A member of the Baptist church for 30 years.

	Last Name	First, Middle, or Maiden	Date of Birth	Date of Death	Tombstone Inscriptions
2-4-D	Fowler	Phillip K.	Jul. 14, 1832	Mar. 3, 1913	Pvt. Co. A 3 Ga. Sharpshooters CSA *possibly a memorial marker only
2-4-BB	Hester	William H.	Jul. 8, 1879	Feb. 26, 1905	He was faithful to every duty
2-4-CC	??				
2-4-DD	Hester	Rilla B.	May 17, 1847	Jun. 4, 1902	Wife of J. H. Hester
2-4-EE	Hester	J. H.	Feb. 22, 1844	Dec. 15, 1913	69 years, 9 mos, 23 days
2-4-FF	Cannon	S. F.	Sep. 26, 1817	Jul. 21, 1897	Father, The precious ones from us hath gone, the voices we loved are stilled, The place – vacant in our home which never can be filled.
2-4-HH	Cannon	Sallie	Aug. 10, 1827	Feb. 13, 1903	Mother, wife of S. F. Cannon
2-4-KK	Pierce	Ella	Jan. 6, 1906	Jun. 4, 1907	??
2-4-LL	Pierce	Bennie	Sep. 12, 1915	Sep. 12, 1915	
2-4-MM	Pierce	Henry Linton	Jun. 26, 1904	Aug. 1905	
2-4-TT	Wallace	Starlin Paul	Mar. 13, 1909	Mar. 27, 1909	Infant son of J.T. & E.J. Wallace. Age 2 weeks
2-4-WW	Hester	John E.	Dec. 31, 1877	Jan. 17, 1879	John, Joseph and Eliza, same marker
2-4-XX	Hester	Joseph	Dec. 8, 1846	Jul. 4, 1906	A light from our house hath gone, A voice we love is stilled. A place is vacant in our hearts That never can be filled.
2-4-YY	Hester	Eliza Jane	Jan. 24, 1849	Dec. 13, 1936	
2-4-CCC	Collett	John	Dec. 7, 1911	Feb. 16, 1935	Gone but not forgotten
2-5-A	Fair	Infant Children	Oct. 24, 1871	Oct. 24, 1871	Children of A. & C. Fair
2-5-F	Ingram	Martha R.	Nov. 12, 1847	Dec. 28, 1885	Wife of W. A. Ingram. In love she lived in peace she died, her life was craved but God denied.
??					Marked grave, unknown name
??					Marked grave, unknown name
2-5-R	Smith	Jane	Jan. 18, 1859	Dec. 10, 1899	Wife of Thomas N. Smith. Asleep in Jesus, peaceful rest whose wa-hing is supremely blest.
2-5-T	Sandow	John	Aug. 1, 1819	Mar. 29, 1890	Born in Cornwall England
2-5-V	Sandow	Sherman M.	May. 16, 1868	Feb. 27, 1901	Aged 32 yrs 11 ms & 11 days
2-5-II	Nix	Cynthia	Mar. 30, 1822	May 16, 1896	
2-5-JJ	Nix	Valentine	Jun. 23, 1822	Feb. 12, 1894	Age 72 years, 7 months, 9 days ?? In Memory of D. D. F. or D O E ???

	Last Name	First, Middle, or Maiden	Date of Birth	Date of Death	Tombstone Inscriptions
2-5-OO	Norton	(Rev.) William Samuel	Apr. 16, 1866	May 5, 1903	Born in Cobb Co. Ga. His was beauty, truth and love. When Christ who is our life shall appear, then shall ye also appear with him in glory.
2-5-UU	Wilkie	Hurle S.	Sep. 2, 1908	Jul. 6, 1909	Son of Mr. & Mrs. G. W. Wilkie
2-5-YY	Herring	Josephine J.	Sep. 22, 1861	Nov. 16, 1906	
2-5-DDD	?				Red brick double lot
2-5-EEE	?				Red brick double lot
2-6-F	Chastain	Perle M.	May 4, 1881	Nov. 13, 1881	Gone but not forgotten
2-6-G	Chastain	John William	Jun. 17, 1871	Aug. 1, 1872	
2-6-J	Hosey	Infant	Nov. 3, 1878	Nov. 3, 1878	Infant son of Mrs. E. L. Hosey
2-6-K	??				stone
2-6-L	Nix	Little Son	Mar. 4, 1877	Mar. 4, 1877	A Little Son of F. C. and H. A. Nix
2-6-O	Nix	Huldaha	Feb. 19, 1846	May 21, 1902	
2-6-P	Nix	Francis	May 16, 1845	Dec. 3, 1924	His words were kindness his deeds were love, his spirit humble he rests above
2-6-Q	Dooley	Claud	Mar. 20, 1896 (calculated)	Aug. 7, 1896	Age 4 mos. and 18 days, s/o Dave and Mary Dooly
2-6-R	Dooley	Mary	Jun. 2, 1870	Aug. 13, 1896	Wife of Dave Dooley, Aged 26 yrs 2 mo 11 days. Mary was a member of the Baptist church 11 years. She hath chosen that good part which shall not be taken away.
2-6-S	Dooley	D. L.	May 1, 1872	Jan. 13, 1899	Masonic Tribute; Short pains short grief, Dear Brother were thine. Now joys, eternal and divine.
2-6-KK	Wilkie	E. Viola	Jul. 28, 1911	Dec. 31, 1911	Dau. of Mr. & Mrs. J. H. Wilkie
2-6-OO	Mulkey	Harold E.	Apr. 5, 1949	Apr. 24, 1996	SP4 US Army
2-6-PP	Collier	Sallie Rich	May 26, 1873	Oct. 7, 1909	
2-6-QQ	Mulkey	Jesse M.	Jun. 15, 1908	Feb. 6, 1999	We will meet in heaven
2-6-RR	Mulkey	Bernice D.	Jul. 3, 1905	Dec. 7, 1985	
2-6-SS	Mulkey	Jessie Leon	Jul. 29, 1944	Mar. 7, 1988	What we keep in memory is ours unchanged forever.
2-6-TT	Mulkey-Byess	Edna Louise	Feb. 14, 1929	Jan. 24, 2001	
2-7-B	Porter	Homer	Mar. 29, 1920	Oct. 7, 1932	
2-7-I	Odum	Elizabeth	Jan. 4, 1822	Apr. 9, 1907	A tender mother
2-7-L	Nix	W. C. M.	Apr. 18, 1887	Dec. 11, 1887	Dau of F. & H. A. Nix
2-7-M	Nix	Mary E. D.	Oct. 16th, 1878	Jan. 31st 1887	Dau of F. & H. A. Nix

	Last Name	First, Middle, or Maiden	Date of Birth	Date of Death	Tombstone Inscriptions
2-7-P	Nix	J. B.	Mar. 2, 1853	Jun. 4, 1913	Father. Earth has no sorrow that heaven cannot heal
2-7-Q	Nix	Annie	Sep. 12, 1857	Jul. 8, 1923	Mother. Earth has no sorrow that heaven cannot heal
2-7-R	Nix	Mary Ethel	Nov. 18, 1888	Apr. 30, 1889	Aged 5 mos 12 days. Dau of J. B. & A. Nix
2-7-S	Stephens	Mary	Feb. 7, 1823	Apr. 3, 1902	Known as Aunt Polly, Aged 79 yrs 1 mo & 24 days
2-7-V	Jones	Lizzie Wright	Apr. 11, 1873	Nov. 2, 1918	At rest
2-7-W	Jones	Jerry	1906	1919	Son of William and Lizzie Jones. The Lord is my refuge. At rest
2-7-X	Jones	William T. W.	Jun. 7, 1865	Jul. 13, 1948	At rest
2-7-					stone
2-7-CC	Speer	Mirtle Lee	Apr. 15, 1900	Jun. 24, 1900	
2-7-DD	Speer	Ida Belle	Apr. 24, 1879	Jun. 14, 1900	Wife of Willie Speer
2-7-EE	Speer	Ethel	1898 / Sep. 4, 1898	Jan. 6, 1901	?? Infant daughter of Willie and Bell Speer
2-7-FF	Speer	Mary Inez	Jan. 15, 1912	Feb. 22, 1912	??
2-7-GG	Speer	Little Pearl	Jan. 29, 1906	Aug. 17, 1908	??
2-7-PP	Rich	Little Jeptey	Aug. 23, 1909	Dec. 26, 1913	Son of L. D. & Ora Rich, "Not dead, only asleep"
2-8-E					Red Brick Lot, unnamed
2-8-F					Red Brick Lot, unnamed
2-8-AA	Dowda	J. F.	Mar. 16, 1865	Sep. 24, 1902	Shares stone with Bell Dowda
2-8-BB	Dowda	Bell	Mar. 7, 1862	Feb. 23, 1901	
2-8-DD	Dowda	Clyde F.	Sep. 14, 1908	Oct. 24, 1908	Son of W. D. & Julia Dowda, Budded on earth to bloom in heaven
2-8-FF	Dowda	Ruby Lee	May 12, 1910	Jun. 30, 1912	Dau. of W. D. & Julie Dowda. God called thee home, he thought it best. Sleep on sweet little one.
2-8-GG	White	Manervia	Jan. 14, 1824	Sep. 3, 1913	Gone but not forgotten, At Rest.
2-8-HH	Richards	Henrietta *Wilkie*	1869	1892	Mother
2-8-JJ	Richards	Mary	Dec. 25, 1839	Apr. 11, 1901	Wife of J. M. Richards
2-8-KK	Richards	J. M.	Jul. 15, 1840	Nov. 24, 1927	Mason
2-9-A	Fletcher	James Sanford	Sep. 18, 1911	Jul. 29 1913	
2-9-B	Fletcher	William Herbert	Mar. 30, 1909	Aug. 26, 1911	??
2-9-C	Fletcher	Sarah Azalee	Jun. 18, 1869	Nov. 18, 1903	Wife of G. B. Fletcher
2-9-D	Fletcher	Mary Maybell	Jun. 5, 1892	Jul. 18, 1892	??
2-9-E	Hogan	Myra B. *Fletcher*	Jan. 18, 1821	Aug. 3, 1908	??
2-9-F	Cochran	Mrs. Jane	Jul. 13, 1830	Sep. 1, 1888	

	Last Name	First, Middle, or Maiden	Date of Birth	Date of Death	Tombstone Inscriptions
2-9-H	Cochran	Emma	Feb. 14, 1834	Jan. 30, 1901	Dau of James and Sarah Fowler
2-9-L	Green	Maudie	Sep. 22, 1886	Jul. 7, 1913	Dau. of T. E. and E. P. Green
2-9-M	??				stone
2-9-N	Green	Sarah	1875	1909	
2-9-O	Green	Will	1874	1956	
2-9-P	Green	Mollie	1884	1967	
2-9-T	Boling	E. Ester	Apr. 6, 1903	Mar. 8, 1907	
2-9-U	Boling	W. T.	Mar. 23, 1868	Oct. 31, 1929	
2-9-DD	Bryant	George Mansel Thomas	Jul. 19, 1905	Aug. 27, 1908	
2-9-EE	Bryant	J. T.	Oct. 15, 1871	Jul. 27, 1914	God's Finger touched him and he slept. Weep not. He is at rest. Mason
2-9-FF	Wilkie	Flonnie M.	Apr. 17, 1907	Nov. 19, 1918	A rose in God's garden; dau of Ed and Mattie Wilkie
2-9-GG	Wilkie	Elsie I.	Nov. 16, 1909	Feb. 4, 1910	Asleep in Jesus; dau of Ed and Mattie Wilkie
2-9-LL	Gayton	Franklin D.	Dec. 22, 1934	Oct. 29, 1954	
2-9-MM	Gayton	Mary G.	Jul. 26, 1948	Sep. 5, 1956	
2-10-BB	Kelley	Evie Leo	Apr. 1, 1908	May 17, 1911	Dau. of R. E. & S. E. Kelley 3 yrs 1 mo 17 days
2-11-GG	Shoemaker	Vonnie "Runt"	Apr. 26, 1948	Jan. 1, 1982	SP4 US Army Vietnam; We Love You Daddy
2-11-HH	Shoemake	Mamie Lerlene	Apr. 15, 1945	Aug. 15, 1945	Our Little Darling
2-11-II	Shoemake	Roy	Jan. 1, 1912	Sep. 30, 1982	
2-11-JJ	Shoemake	Ila	Feb. 5, 1914	May 16, 2004	
2-11-KK	Jones	Michael Dwayne	Aug. 22, 1962	Aug. 22, 1962	Infant
2-11-LL	Boling	Buman Boot	Aug. 6, 1909	May 4, 1983	
2-11-MM	Gayton	Hershel L.	Apr. 14, 1902	Mar. 8, 1969	
2-11-NN	Gayton	Maggie P.	Sep. 8, 1908	Sep. 29, 1958	Gone but not forgotten
2-11-OO	Mulkey	James P.	Jul. 23, 1929	Jan. 9, 2010	Go Rest High on that Mountain
2-11-RR					J.L.M. footstone
2-12-Z	Jones	Carrie E.	1897	1988	
2-12-AA	Jones	Grover C.	Aug. 19, 1890	Jan. 9, 1969	Georgia PFC 327 Infantry World War I
2-12-BB	Wehunt	Larry J.	1949	1968	
2-12-CC	Jones	Robert W.	Mar. 1, 1952	Oct. 27, 1968	
2-12-DD	Jones	William E.	Oct. 20, 1921	Aug. 28, 1982	US Army World War II
2-12-EE	Jones	Estelle F.	Aug. 6, 1931	Aug. 10, 2015	
2-13-A					

	Last Name	First, Middle, or Maiden	Date of Birth	Date of Death	Tombstone Inscriptions
2-13-B	West	Michael Paul	Feb. 4, 1966	Jun. 16, 1984	
2-13-C	Norrell	Willard J.	Feb. 17, 1933	Aug. 3, 1990	CPL US Army "Gone but not forgotten"
2-13-D	Norrell	Emma Jo	Sep. 11, 1937		??
2-13-E	Norrell	Nealurs	Feb. 26, 1906	Dec. 23, 1980	
2-13-F	Norrell	Ruby	Apr. 11, 1910	May 19, 1997	
2-13-G	Cronan	Edgar L.	Dec. 26, 1900	Aug. 21, 1985	"Beyond the Sunset"
2-13-H	Cronan	Minnie A.	May 12, 1903	Jul. 22, 1980	
2-13-J	McGhee	Michale Shane	Apr. 18, 1971	Apr. 18, 1971	
2-13-N	Cosby	John C. "Chris"	Jun. 17, 1960	Sep. 24, 1976	We will meet again
2-13-R	Green	Hoyt A.	May 15, 1907	Jun. 14, 1978	Asleep in Jesus
2-13-S	Green	Vester G.	Mar. 30, 1914	Mar. 31, 1991	
2-13-V	Jones	Willie C.			Together forever; Married: Sep 11, 1951
2-13-W	Jones	Bonnie G.	Apr. 16, 1937	Sep. 27, 1998	Our children: Gracie, Linda, Jimmy, Shirley, Michael
2-14-CC	Jones	Pamela Anne	Nov. 3, 1971	Nov. 3, 1971	

Section 3

Property was purchased from John Howard in 1914 and a remaining portion from Mrs. John Howard in 1920. This section is often referenced as the triangle. Date of death for this area begins in 1915. (Exception: some memorial markers show earlier date, but actual burial is elsewhere, such as Jane and Emma Cochran)

	Last Name	First, Middle, or Maiden	Date of Birth	Date of Death	Tombstone inscriptions
3-1-A	Nix	E. L.	Aug. 20, 1884	Nov. 6, 1931	
3-1-B	Fletcher	G. Barto	Feb. 3, 1862	May 28, 1932	Fond memory points our hearts to thee.
3-1-C	Fletcher	Rhoda J.	May 7, 1876	Jul. 25, 1951	
3-1-D	Pearson	Walter C.	Jul. 24, 1886	Jan. 12, 1925	
3-1-E	Pearson	Susie M.	May 26, 1888	Apr. 21, 1963	
3-1-F	Cannon	Elmer C.	Jun. 15, 1887	May 23, 1957	Father
3-1-F	Cannon	Billy Byron	Jan. 1, 1924	Jun. 16, 1926	
3-1-G	Cannon	Herman K.	Mar. 16, 1925	Jan. 4, 1977	Son
3-1-G	Cannon	Dorothy Evans	Sep. 14, 1918	Jun. 12, 1919	
3-1-H	Pearson	Eliza	Jun. 10, 1854	Oct. 25, 1932	Mother

	Last Name	First, Middle, or Maiden	Date of Birth	Date of Death	Tombstone inscriptions
3-1-I	Pearson	Fred	Jun.15, 1850	May 15, 1922	Father
3-1-J	Fowler	Charlie	No dates		?? also in 1-16-I
3-1-K	Wilkie	Hoyt	Feb. 18, 1915	May 28, 1917	Son of Mr. & Mrs. G. W. Wilkie
??					unmarked ; R. J. F.
3-1-N	West	Roy	Nov. 9, 1921	Nov. 20, 1921	Jesus gathers the buds for Heaven. Son of Mr. & Mrs. Emory West
3-1-O	West	Ray	Mar. 4, 1924	Mar. 9, 1924	Safe in the arms of Jesus. Son of Mr. & Mrs. Emory West
3-1-P	West	Jack	Dec. 9, 1931	Dec. 9, 1931	Gone so soon. Son of Mr. & Mrs. Emory West
3-1-S	Pugh	Ellar *Hawkins*	1877	1915	
3-1-T	Pugh	James V.	1873	1938	
3-1-U	Fowler	Odis			??
3-1-V	Fowler	Myrtle			??
					Unmarked
3-1-Y					Unmarked; 2 small graves, likely children
3-1-Z	White	Ronald & Donald	May 1, 1951	May 2, 1951	Twins of Charles & Dot White
3-1-AA					Unmarked; stone
3-1-DD	Smith	Katherine R.	1949	1949	(temporary marker)
3-1-EE	Little	Andrew	Nov. 11, 1891	Jan. 15, 1921	At rest. His toils are past his work is done, He fought the fight the victory won.
3-1-GG	Dobson	Dock G.	Mar. 21, 1907	Oct. 10, 1948	
					Unmarked
					Unmarked
3-1-JJ					Unmarked
3-1-KK					Unmarked
3-1-LL	Ellis	J. H.	Oct. 27, 1863	Aug. 26, 1926	Asleep in Jesus
3-1-MM	Ellis	Mary C.	Apr. 6, 1866	Jul. 5, 1948	Sweetly sleeping
3-1-NN	Porter	Luther D.	Feb. 24, 1892	Oct. 19, 1917	
3-1-OO	Porter	Oma Mae	Oct. 10, 1893	Dec. 28, 1974	
3-1-PP	Collier	Hiram P.	Jul. 17, 1873	Mar. 15, 1941	Father
3-1-QQ	Collier	George Ann	Feb. 20, 1876	No death date listed	Mother
3-1-RR	Norrell	Franklin Odell	Jun. 10, 1930	Jun. 10, 1930	Son of Mr. & Mrs. N. N. Norrell. A little time on earth he spent till God for him his angel sent.
3-2-A	Howard	Flara	Jul. 14, 1895	Sep. 19, 1930	
3-2-B	Wilkie	Infant Children	Jan. 29, 1927	Jan. 29, 1927	Children of Mr. & Mrs. Joe Wilkie, "Asleep in Jesus"
3-2-C			May 19, 1928	Jun. 2, 1928	
3-2-D	Howard	Anner	Feb. 11, 1860	Jan. 16, 1940	

	Last Name	First, Middle, or Maiden	Date of Birth	Date of Death	Tombstone inscriptions
3-2-E	Howard	W. L. D.	May 12, 1857	Dec. 19, 1928	
3-2-F					Unmarked; stone
3-2-H	Pearson	Bertha Pope	Feb. 7, 1899	(no date)	Mother ??
3-2-I	Pearson	Oscar H.	Sep. 28, 1883	Sep. 15, 1918	Father ??
3-2-J	Smith	Lula	Oct. 23, 1875	Mar. 16, 1934	Mother:
3-2-K	Smith	A. J.	Aug. 14, 1876	Nov. 28, 1932	Father: Yes, God took you home, it was his will, and in our hearts, your memory liveth still
3-2-L	Smith	Edward Jasper	Sep. 8, 1832	Apr. 18, 1916	In thee O Lord Have I put my trust. Age 83 yr. 7 mo. 10 days
3-2-M	Smith	Sarah Elizabeth	1835	(no date)	
3-2-Q	Green	Thomas E.	1848	1922	
3-2-R	Green	Elizabeth A.	1853	1928	
3-2-S	West	Olin F.	Jan. 25, 1914	Jun. 20, 1915	
3-2-T	McClure	Thomas N.	Dec. 10, 1941	Dec. 23, 1941	Son of Mr. & Mrs. George McClure
3-2-U	McClure	Charles F.	Apr. 24, 1933	Jul. 25, 1933	Son of Mr. & Mrs. George McClure
3-2-Y	Green	John R.	1876	1915	
3-2-Z	Green	Mary E.	1878	1940	
3-2-AA	Green	Joseph P.	1858	1916	
3-2-BB	Green	Mrs. Nancy L.	1850	1928	
3-2-CC	Long	Nancy	Sep. 14, 1833	Mar. 22, 1915	Joined the Baptist church at Bethlehem, Union Co. Ga. In 1854
3-2-DD	Pearson	Edd H.	May 31, 1880	Oct. 27, 1935	
3-2-EE	Pearson	Nettie R.	Aug. 4, 1882	Nov. 27, 1950	
3-2-GG	Bryant	Clifton	Feb. 13, 1908	Oct. 4, 1919	"Thy Will Be Done" Twas but a flower too good for earth transplanted into heaven.
3-2-HH	Williams	Amanda	Nov. 18, 1849	Mar. 7, 1916	??
3-2-II					Unmarked Stone in lot with Joe and Lillie Williams
3-2-JJ					Unmarked Stone in lot with Joe and Lillie Williams
3-2-KK					Unmarked Stone in lot with Joe and Lillie Williams
3-2-LL	Williams	Joe	1886	1935	
3-2-MM	Williams	Lillie	1884	1928	
3-2-NN	Faulkner	Robert	Mar. 30, 1888	Dec. 26, 1917	Gone but not forgotten.
3-2-OO	Ellis	James Elbert	Aug. 12, 1888	Jan. 3, 1932	At rest.
3-3-A	Cochran	Rev. J. Samuel	Feb. 9, 1897	Aug. 8, 1984	

	Last Name	First, Middle, or Maiden	Date of Birth	Date of Death	Tombstone inscriptions
3-3-B	Cochran	Eunice Ellis	Dec. 3, 1895	May 31, 1971	
3-3-C	Ramsey	Rice A.	Jul. 16, 1850	Dec. 17, 1925	
3-3-D	Ramsey	Susan A.	1856	Dec. 10, 1939	
3-3-F	Porter	Edward M.	Jun. 21, 1916	Nov. 13, 1918	Son of Mr. & Mrs. S.P. Porter,
3-3-G					Unmarked stone
3-3-I	Hester	Jewell May	Aug. 14, 1900	Apr. 16, 1918	Come Ye Blessed. Wife of Oscar F. Hester. Gone home, Safe in the arms of Jesus.
3-3-L	Wilkie	George W.	Apr. 1, 1850	May 14, 1917	Mason. Farewell my wife and children all, from you a father Christ doth call.
3-3-M	Wilkie	Frances Ann	Aug. 9, 1850	Aug. 19, 1919	Her words were kindness, her deeds were love. Her spirit humble, she rests above.
3-3-O	Wilkie	Ruth	May 31, 1917	Jul. 6, 1917	Dau. of Mr. & Mrs. H. G. Wilkie, Gone So Soon
3-3-Q	Green	Joseph Frank	May 18, 1876	Jun. 16, 1960	
3-3-R	Green	Pearl Smith	Feb. 23, 1904	May 16, 1994	
3-3-S					Unmarked Broken stone
3-3-T	Bryant	Thomas	Jul. 3, 1851	Jun. 27, 1923	Father. Dear parents, though we miss you much, we know you rest with God.
3-3-U	Bryant	Lucy Ann	Nov. 12, 1856	May 13, 1922	Mother.
3-3-GG	Hester	John	1867	1916	??
3-3-HH	Hester	Dora	1866	1937	??
3-3-II	Cochran	Rev. Robert W.	(no dates)		
3-3-JJ	Cochran	Rev. E. A.	Aug. 8, 1845	Oct. 15, 1931	Joined the Baptist church in the year 1867. Ordained to the work of the ministry at Hightower Baptist Church Aug. 14, 1882. A preacher of the gospel. 42 years I have fought a good fight, I have finished my course, I have kept the faith. Henceforth there is laid up for me a crown of righteousness which the Lord the righteous judge shall give me at that day. A SINNER SAVED BY GRACE.
3-3-KK	Cochran	Kansas	Sep. 18, 1859	Dec. 23, 1938	Joined the Baptist church while quite young, living a true Christian life ever since. She perceived that her merchandise is good. Her candle goeth not out by night. Tis sweet to dwell in love divine, To know that Christ the Lord is mine.

	Last Name	First, Middle, or Maiden	Date of Birth	Date of Death	Tombstone inscriptions
3-3-LL	Cochran	Jane	Jul. 13, 1830	Sep. 1, 1888	2nd marker in 2 N She patiently bore all her suffering, like Job of old. She professed a hope in Christ Aug. 28, 1950. She said "The Lamb which is in the midst of the throne shall feed them and shall lead them unto living fountains of water and God shall wipe away all tears from their eyes. Asleep in Jesus, blessed sleep. From which none ever wake to weep.
3-3-MM	Cochran	Emma	Feb. 14, 1834	Jun. 30, 1901	2nd marker in 2 N She joined the Baptist Church of Christ about 50 years ago. She was a faithful Christian living her religion every day of her life. A true devoted wife. She cannot come back here but we can go where she is. Shall we gather at the river where bright angel's feet have trod?
3-3-NN	Cochran	Matilda L.	(no dates)		
3-3-OO					Unmarked Stone
3-3-PP					Unmarked Stone
3-4-G	Porter	Emma D.	Mar. 7, 1883	Feb. 8, 1962	
3-4-H	Porter	Samuel P.	Dec. 8, 1875	Jun. 19, 1937	
3-4-N	Wilkie	Henry Lee	Nov. 11, 1867	Sep. 14, 1936	(same inscription as on Jeulyne's marker)
3-4-O	Wilkie	Jeulyne	Apr. 4, 1868	May 8, 1949	A precious one from us is gone, a voice we loved is stilled. A place is vacant in our home, which never can be filled.
3-4-R	Wilkie	Pearl Elizabeth	Apr. 15, 1924	Jun. 9, 1924	
3-4-T					Unmarked Stone
3-4-U					Unmarked Flat stone
3-4-V	Green	Olin	Apr. 26, 1907	Apr. 14, 1918	
3-4-W	Hardin	Harold	Jul. 13, 1915	Jun. 5, 1917	"Nothing we miss more" son of Mr. & Mrs. E.T. Hardin
3-4-X	Hardin	Larkin T.	Sep. 2, 1877	Sep. 21, 1916	"Gone to a bright home where grief cannot come." Woodsman of the World Footstone: L. T. H.

	Last Name	First, Middle, or Maiden	Date of Birth	Date of Death	Tombstone inscriptions
3-4-Y	Rich	Winnie M.	Oct. 3, 1843	Mar. 2, 1933	Wife of J. P. Rich, "She was the sunshine of our home"
3-4-Z					Stone in lot with Rich and Eubanks
3-4-AA	Rich	Ab	No dates		Stone in lot with Rich and Eubanks
3-4-BB	Rich	Joanna Russell	May 8, 1870	Jan. 30, 1934	
3-4-CC	Eubanks	H. E.	Jul. 2, 1894	Nov. 13, 1916	??
3-4-DD	Eubanks	Maggie R.	Feb. 18, 1896	Feb. 22, 1985	Wife of H. E Eubanks
3-4-EE	Hamilton	Maynard Henry	Sep. 6, 1895	Aug. 21, 1976	Loving husband of Maggie Rich Eubanks
3-4-GG	Hester	Johnie Lee	May 18, 1920	Sep. 21, 1920	Our darling: Asleep in Jesus. Son of Boy and Zenie Hester. From Mother's arms to the arms of Jesus.
3-4-HH	Hester	Infant Son	May 9, 1918	May 9, 1918	Our darling: Asleep in Jesus. Son of Boy and Zenie Hester.
3-4-JJ	Hester	H. L.	Dec. 31, 1925	Nov. 13, 1932	Our darling: Asleep in Jesus
3-4-KK	Hester	Zenie C.	Oct. 22, 1900	Apr. 29, 1995	
3-4-LL	Hester	Boy	Jun. 7, 1893	Feb. 5, 1969	
3-4-MM	Hester	Herbert	Mar. 12, 1929	Mar. 14, 1971	"Georgia: SP 6, US Army"
3-5-C	Hester	Eddie Frank	May 27, 1919	Jul. 21, 1981	
3-5-D	Hester	George Lee	Sep. 9, 1924	Nov. 14, 1995	
3-5-E	Hester	Flora Augusta	Sep. 19, 1892	Dec. 2, 1966	"Gone Home"
3-5-F	Hester	Thomas Edgar	Sep. 6, 1895	Aug. 28, 1936	"Gone Home"
3-5-G	Fowler	William			
3-5-H	Fowler	Doshie			
3-5-I	Sandow	John A.	Feb. 9, 1863	Dec. 13, 1918	"Gone but not forgotten"
3-5-J					Stone?
3-5-K	Sandow	Annie B.	Jan. 24, 1893	Feb. 18, 1920	"Her spirit smiles from that bright shore, and softly whispers weep no more."
3-5-R					Unmarked stone
3-5-V	Nix	Landrum R.	Jul. 31, 1895	Mar. 28, 1925	
3-5-X	Green	Marie	Feb. 1916	Nov. 1919	
3-5-Y	Pearson	Bertha	Jul. 26, 1900	May 26, 1927	
3-5-Z	Pearson	Preston	Jan. 29, 1903	Sep. 22, 1930	
3-5-AA	Wallace	William C.	Jul. 4, 1856	Sep. 28, 1944	
3-5-BB	Wallace	Jossie R.	Jul. 21, 1857	Sep. 4, 1920	"Gone but not forgotten" Wife of W C Wallace
3-5-CC	Wallace	Mary			
3-5-DD	Herring	Emma	Apr. 20, 1890	Feb. 29, 1919	"Mother"
3-5-EE	Herring	Walter	Feb. 10, 1889	Dec. 20, 1935	"Father"
3-5-FF	Herring	Holbert	Apr. 27, 1912	Oct. 8, 1929	

	Last Name	First, Middle, or Maiden	Date of Birth	Date of Death	Tombstone inscriptions
3-5-HH	Dobson	Effie Viola	Mar. 14, 1915	Nov. 11, 1918	"Our darling is gone but not forgotten"
3-5-JJ	Woodall	Riley	1879	1954	
3-5-KK	Woodall	Minnie	1882	1924	
3-6-I					Unmarked stone
3-6-J					Unmarked stone
3-6-K					Unmarked stone
3-6-L	Pierce	W. E.	Oct. 10, 1880	Apr. 8, 1921	??
3-6-N	Andrews	Oscar	1902	1968	
3-6-O	Andrews	W. J.	May 31, 1880	Oct. 25, 1926	
3-6-P	Andrews	Mattie	Aug. 27, 1880	Dec. 24, 1951	
3-6-Q	Andrews	Herschel	1914	1935	
3-6-R	Rich	Hulon M.	Apr. 5, 1939	Jun. 9, 1939	`
3-6-T	Fletcher	H. K.	Feb. 6, 1860	Oct. 29, 1926	"Father, At Rest"
3-6-U	Fletcher	Augusta	Apr. 21, 1870	Nov. 21, 1947	" Mother, At Rest"
3-6-V	Fletcher	Janie Belle	Jun. 8, 1910	Feb. 22, 1922	"Weep not Father and Mother for me, for I am waiting in glory for thee."
3-6-W	Wyatt	Herbert	Sep. 3, 1923	Sep. 3, 1923	Burial location reported by family. Infant of Samuel S. & Pearl Wyatt, unmarked,
3-6-X					Unmarked stone
3-6-Y	Green	Mildred	1915	1921	
3-6-DD	Wade	Gertrude	1890	1923	
3-6-EE					Unmarked stone
3-6-KK	Wheeler	Bud		Mar. 1925	"Loving Respects to Bud Wheeler"
3-7-G	Cochran	Emmett	Jan. 21, 1915	Jun. 23, 2003	
3-7-H	Cochran	Mary Lee	Aug. 15, 1921	Jan. 23, 2012	
3-7-I	Cochran	Elisha F.	Mar. 22, 1884	Dec. 26, 1970	
3-7-J	Cochran	Jennie C.	Aug. 12, 1895	May 3, 1971	
3-7-K	Cochran	Bonziel Oziel	Mar. 11, 1921	Jun. 3, 1921	Gone but not forgotten
3-7-Q	Boling	Mary P.	1877	1924* (Dec. 3, 1922 on death certificate)	"Our Loved Ones"
3-7-R	Boling	John F.	1873	1926	"Our Loved Ones"
3-7-V	Buchana	Jewell	Jul. 14, 1920	Jul. 17, 1971	
3-7-W	Buchanna	Charlie	Jul. 7, 1913	Dec. 31, 1948	"Asleep in Jesus"
3-7-X	Wilson	Infant	Jan. 17, 1925	Mar. 8, 1925	Infant of J.H. and C.A. Wilson
3-7-Y	Turner	Ida Lee	Dec. 31, 1904	Jan. 7, 1983	
3-7-Z					Unmarked Stone
3-7-AA					Unmarked stone

	Last Name	First, Middle, or Maiden	Date of Birth	Date of Death	Tombstone inscriptions
3-7-BB	Turner	Mary J.		Jan. 17, 1923	
3-8-L	Fowler	Grady	(no dates)		
3-8-M	Chumbler	James M.	(no dates)		
3-8-N	Chumbler	Emma L.	(no dates)		
3-8-O	Boling	Clyde M.	Aug. 23, 1901	Sep. 9, 1934	"Beloved one, farewell"
3-8-Q	Wheeler	Clifford G.	Aug. 22, 1902	Nov. 8, 1942	
3-8-R	Boling	George C.	Aug. 4, 1906	May 18, 1945	"He was loved by many. He is at rest with Jesus."
3-8-S	Boling	J. Lowery	Apr. 16, 1872	Jan. 29, 1926	
3-8-T	Boling	Julia S.	Jan. 30, 1875	Mar. 21, 1931	
3-8-X	Coleman	Edwin	Dec. 22, 1922	Feb. 16, 1935	"Gone but not forgotten"
3-8-Y	Coleman	Charles H.	1893	1953	
3-8-Z	Coleman	Myrtle L.	1894	1978	
3-8-AA	Coleman	Ted	Oct. 2, 1925	May 3, 1975	
3-9					Empty row
3-10-J	Parker	Fannie Josephine	Sep. 23, 1917	Jan. 6, 2008	
3-10-K	Parker	Edward Harris	Jul. 3, 1917	Dec. 27, 1941	
3-10-L	Parker	Mildred Josephine	Dec. 11, 1938	Dec. 11, 1938	
3-10-M	Parker	Edna Joyce	Jul. 3, 1942	Nov. 10, 1944	
3-10-N	Mills	Thompson	1861	1931	
3-10-O	Mills	Loma C.	1892	1985	
3-10-P	Hester	Joseph L.	Jan. 13, 1876	Jun. 26, 1955	"Resting till the resurrection morn"
3-10-Q	Hester	Willie D.	May 27, 1881	Mar. 26, 1926	
3-10-V					Stone, no inscription
3-10-X	Rich	Alice E.	1907	1929	"At Rest"
3-10-Y	Rich	James O.	Dec. 22, 1938	Jun. 24, 1939	"At Rest"
3-11-P	Stewart	Ruby	Sep. 6, 1926	Sep. 6, 1926	"Gone So Soon" Inf. Dau. O. F. Stewart
3-11-Q					Lot with blocks; no name
3-11-R					Lot with blocks; no name
3-11-S	Speer	Emory			
3-12-O	Cannon	John W.	Nov. 13, 1852	Dec. 1, 1940	"Father"
3-12-P	Cannon	Laura McGinley	Nov. 28, 1862	Jun. 8, 1928	"Mother"
3-12-Q	Cannon	Mattie McGinley	Oct. 9, 1898	Sep. 21, 1927	"Sister"
3-12-S	Hester	Augustus	Jun. 8, 1895	Oct. 26, 1982	U S Army World War I
3-12-T	Hester	Jessie L.	Apr. 9, 1901	Feb. 12, 1987	

	Last Name	First, Middle, or Maiden	Date of Birth	Date of Death	Tombstone inscriptions
3-13					Empty row
3-14-N	Wheeler	Ozelel	Mar. 5, 1918	Sep. 3, 1941	
3-14-O	Wheeler	Victoria	Jun. 2, 1861	Nov. 24, 1928	
3-14-P	Wheeler	Ernest F.	Sep. 27, 1893	Nov. 3, 1985	
3-14-Q	Wheeler	Martha L.	Apr. 28, 1891	Sep. 6, 1978	

Section 4

Property was purchased from Mrs. Georgia Lovelace, ½ acre just south of the church in 1923, an additional ½ acre in 1949. Oldest date of death on marker: 1927. This section is located behind the church.

	Last Name	First, Middle or Maiden	Date of Birth	Date of Death	Tombstone Inscriptions
4-1-F	Wilkie	Ida L.	Sep. 20, 1904	Jan. 9, 1995	
4-1-G	Wilkie	Joseph H.	Jul. 15, 1900	Sep. 30, 1980	
4-1-H	Wheeler	C. H.	Jan. 10, 1906	May 24, 1984	
4-1-I	Wheeler	B. Argie	Dec. 4, 1909	Apr. 29, 1991	
4-1-J	Wheeler	D. Lanier	Jan. 20, 1943	Aug. 11, 1947	
4-1-M	Wheeler	Brenda Sarah	Jul. 20, 1962	Jul. 21, 1962	
4-2-F	Wilkie	Annie F.	Sep. 23, 1905	Feb. 6, 1968	Meet me in heaven
4-2-G	Wilkie	Theodocia	Feb. 22, 1873	Jan. 1, 1957	A Loving Wife and a good Mother
4-2-H	Wilkie	J. Harrison	Dec. 2, 1871	Mar. 21, 1949	A True Husband and a faithful Father
4-2-I	Wilkie	Clara J.	Oct. 2, 1907	Sep. 14, 1963	Asleep in Jesus
4-2-J	Wilkie	Gladys B.	Jul. 2, 1907	Nov. 24, 1996	There is Rest in Heaven
4-2-K	Wilkie	Charlie M.	Dec. 14, 1903	Jul. 22, 1964	
4-2-N	Gilleland	Pearl W.	Aug. 6, 1912	Jun. 10, 2007	
4-2-O	Gilleland	L. J.	Nov. 24, 1910	Apr. 4, 1963	Mason emblem; There is Rest in Heaven, God's Will Be Done
4-2-P	Turner	Dora	Mar. 15, 1882	Jun. 26, 1968	
4-2-Q	Turner	John J.	Apr. 21, 1883	Mar. 18, 1962	Mason emblem; At rest
4-2-R	Boling	Leo	Sep. 25, 1907	Aug. 27, 1988	At rest
4-2-S	Boling	H. Forrest	Mar. 5, 1908	Apr. 24, 1963	
4-2-T	West	Myrtie E.	Jan. 28, 1897	Sep. 1, 1977	
4-2-U	West	Robert Emory	Dec. 12, 1892	Jan. 27, 1965	
4-2-V	Perkins	Sarah W.	Aug. 25, 1925	Nov. 6, 1996	Wed July 24, 1953
4-2-W	Perkins	R. B.	Feb. 29, 1920	Feb. 13, 1994	In Heaven There Are Two Angels More

	Last Name	First, Middle or Maiden	Date of Birth	Date of Death	Tombstone Inscriptions
4-2-Y	West	Robert Emory Jr.	Oct. 19, 1935	Jan. 13, 2006	A heart of gold stopped beating, two shining eyes at rest. God broke our hearts to prove he only takes the best.
4-3-F	Wilkie	Homer L.	Sep. 14, 1927	Dec. 1, 1995	Meet me in heaven. US Army Korea
4-3-G	Wilkie	W. Morris	Jan. 22, 1931	Aug. 10, 1988	
4-3-H	Wilkie	W. Sam	1902	1973	
4-3-I	Wilkie	Kate E.	1900	1945	
4-3-J	Gaither	Ralph Lee Jr.	Jul. 3, 1945	Jul. 4, 1945	Our darling
4-4-F	Simmons	Barbara Anne	Sep. 10, 1946	Jul. 14, 1947	
4-4-G	Simmons	Dorothy W.	Jan. 5, 1928	Oct. 9, 1958	
					Unmarked stone, bricked single lot
4-4-J	Wilkie	Lula P.	Apr. 5, 1879	May 31, 1962	
4-4-K	Wilkie	H. Glenn	Jun. 4, 1877	Sep. 30, 1956	God Is and All Is Well
4-4-L	Ball	K. Carlous	Mar. 17, 1946	Apr. 4, 1946	
4-4-M	Ball	Zula Lee	Feb. 19, 1912	Feb. 20, 2002	
4-4-N	Ball	James Roy	Aug. 21, 1910	Feb. 25, 1972	
4-4-R	Buffington	Maude P.	Aug. 17, 1891	Oct. 25, 1985	
4-4-S	Buffington	Robt. B.	Nov. 15, 1891	Mar. 23, 1952	Dying Is But Going Home
4-4-T	Wyatt	Winnie G.	May 6, 1918	Jul. 29, 2007	
4-4-U	Wyatt	Arthur Linton	Nov. 22, 1914	Nov. 20, 2008	
4-4-X	Richards	Aaron I.	Jul. 8, 1922	Aug. 2, 1960	GA CPL CO D 504 PRCHT IFT WWII BSM-PH
4-4-Y	Richards	Myra Evalee	May 5, 1894	Apr. 25, 1979	
4-4-Z	Richards	"Jim" James W.	Oct. 16, 1889	Feb. 3, 1966	
4-4-AA	Burns	Esco G.	Apr. 23, 1908	Jul. 1, 1978	Book of Life
4-4-BB	Burns	Vernon L.	Apr. 9, 1904	Jun. 14, 1977	Memory Lane
4-5-F	Green	Susie Carol	Oct. 13, 1934	Jan. 8, 1940	Our darling. Asleep in Jesus
4-5-G	Green	Wilburn Q.	Nov. 3, 1911	Nov. 24, 1987	
4-5-H					Unmarked
4-5-I					Unmarked
4-5-J	Hill	Kenneth E.	Apr. 6, 1940	May 13, 1941	
4-5-K					Unmarked
4-5-L	Drummond	Geo. Wesley	Mar. 8, 1877	Sep. 2, 1941	The Way of the Cross Leads Home.
4-5-M	Drummond	Cora Bell	Feb. 2, 1888	Jun. 4, 1964	
4-5-N					
4-5-O	Cowart	Harley R.	Aug. 3, 1915	Feb. 9, 1950	
4-5-P	Cowart	George Edwin	Apr. 15, 1943	Jan. 30, 1992	Beloved Son, Daddy, and Grandpa

	Last Name	First, Middle or Maiden	Date of Birth	Date of Death	Tombstone Inscriptions
4-5-Q	Hill	Earl E.	Oct. 25, 1896	Feb. 1, 1961	
4-5-R	Hill	Ollie M.	Jul. 25, 1900	Jan. 26, 1982	
4-5-U	Gilleland	Samuel Allen	Nov. 20, 1951	Nov. 20, 1951	Safe in the arms of Jesus
4-5-V	Gilleland	Lillie M.	Jul. 28, 1898	Nov. 13, 1989	
4-5-W	Gilleland	Bunion V.	Feb. 1, 1886	Feb. 21, 1968	
4-5-X	Wilkie	Shelia June	Oct. 6, 1952	Jun. 27, 1953	Gone to be an Angel
4-5-Z	Wilkie	James Leon	Jan. 27, 1929	Oct. 1, 1996	Our children: Shelia, Randy, Lanny, Mitzi, Melody
4-5-AA	Wallace	Annie Belle	Feb. 20, 1903	Jan. 13, 1990	
4-5-BB	Wallace	H. Thad	Feb. 17, 1898	May 19, 1965	
4-5-CC	Wilkie	Flora Belle	Jul. 3, 1910	Sep. 11, 1973	
4-5-DD	Wilkie	Amos Felton	Mar. 16, 1908	Jan. 19, 1972	
4-6					
4-6-G					Unmarked head and foot stone
4-6-H	Bailey	Maude	Mar. 20, 1901	Nov. 29, 1960	
4-6-I	Bailey	K. E.	Jun. 1, 1901	Apr. 2, 1954	
4-6-J	Wilkie	Martha Sue	Oct. 18, 1942	Dec. 13, 1942	daughter
4-6-K	Wilkie	Gennie O.	Mar. 18, 1907	Oct. 30, 1985	Mama
4-6-L	Wilkie	Robert L.	Mar. 12, 1905	May 5, 1984	Daddy, Gone but not forgotten
4-6-M	Cowart	John H.	Jun. 2, 1863	Oct. 28, 1943	Gone but not forgotten
4-6-N	Cowart	Mary E.	Dec. 2, 1858	Jan. 24, 1945	
4-6-O	Cowart	Toma C.	Jan. 1, 1891	Apr. 14, 1982	Mother
4-6-P	Cowart	William E.	Jan. 2, 1889	Dec. 24, 1973	Father
4-6-R	Cowart	Fronie F.	Jan. 15, 1876	Dec. 25, 1953	
4-6-S	Cowart	M. Hancel	Dec. 22, 1882	Mar. 22, 1961	We will meet again
4-6-T	Cowart	Nola M.	Feb. 13, 1911	May 23, 2003	
4-6-U	Cowart	William Guy	Mar. 21, 1902	Jul. 17, 1954	Thy will be done
4-6-V	Cannon	Fannie Louise	Jun. 28, 1941	Mar. 6, 1999	Shared stone
4-6-V	Cannon	James D.	May 21, 1933		You can not tell from where the wind comes or where it goes. John 3:8
4-6-V	Cannon	Lisa Ann			
4-6-Y	Bise	Alexander H.	Sep. 5, 1879	Jan. 20, 1956	Father, At Rest
4-6-Z	Davis	Lucille	May 27, 1916	Oct. 17, 1980	Dying is but going home
4-6-AA	Davis	Hershel	Jan. 6, 1905	Oct. 7, 1966	Georgia PVT 3441 Ordnance MAM CO WWII
4-6-BB	Williams	G. W.	Jul. 2, 1868	May 15, 1958	
4-6-CC	Green	Billy H. "Smiley"	Jun. 30, 1945	Jan. 17, 1964	Son
4-6-DD	Green	Velma M.	Dec. 16, 1920	Apr. 29, 1978	Mother

	Last Name	First, Middle or Maiden	Date of Birth	Date of Death	Tombstone Inscriptions
4-6-FF	Green	Willie H.	Nov. 15, 1919	Feb. 25, 1981	US Navy WW II
4-7-E	West	George E.	May 20, 1896	Nov. 7, 1950	GA Pvt. 122 Infantry 31st Div WW I
4-7-F	West	Josephine L.	Oct. 21, 1857	Jul. 5, 1928	A tender Mother and faithful friend
4-7-G	West	L. L.	Jan. 16, 1863	Nov. 30, 1927	He was beloved by God and Man
4-7-H	West	Mrs. Emma E.	Jul. 24, 1884	Jan. 18, 1950	Farewell my children all, From you a mother Christ doth call.
4-7-I	West	W. Linton	Feb. 28, 1883	Apr. 17, 1928	At rest in Heaven. Farewell my wife and children all, From you a father Christ doth call.
4-7-J	West	Ella	Oct. 27, 1884	Sep. 28, 1962	
4-7-K	Wilkie	John L.	1897	Oct. 1, 1940	Pvt. US Army
4-7-L	Jenkins	Grace K.	1901	1982	In Lot with Wilkie headstone
4-7-M	Wilkie	Keith	1932	1997	Shared stone with John L. and Grace Wilkie
4-7-N	Wilkie	Rosetta E.	1889	1978	
4-7-O	Wilkie	George W.	1889	1950	We will meet again
4-7-P	Crenshaw	Francis Evelyn	Sep. 7, 1932	Sep. 27, 1968	Our dear mother and companion. Rest in peace.
4-7-Q	Crenshaw	M. T.	Jul. 6, 1917	Jan. 2, 1985	US Navy
4-7-S	Roper	Ruby B.	Oct. 29, 1915	Jan. 6, 1995	
4-7-T	Roper	V. G.	May 24, 1910	Sep. 20, 1974	
4-7-U	Roper	Betty Jane	Oct. 23, 1937	Jun. 14, 1954	Daughter
4-7-W					Unmarked stone
4-7-X	Cowart	Cora D.	Nov. 11, 1906		
4-7-Y	Cowart	Isaiah	Jul. 15, 1904	Aug. 4, 1959	
4-7-BB	Cowart	Ruby E.	Dec. 18, 1913	Dec. 10, 1991	
4-7-CC	Cowart	Dewey L.	May 15, 1908	Jan. 27, 1979	
4-7-DD	Cannon	Fannie Lee	1914		
4-7-EE	Cannon	Jonnie	1909	1962	
4-7-FF	Cannon	Mattie M.	1874		
4-7-GG	Wheeler	Billy N.	Apr. 6, 1947	May 7, 1970	Sgt US Army Vietnam
4-7-HH	Wheeler	Agatha G.	May 8, 1922	Feb. 11, 2009	
4-7-II	Wheeler	Bill	Feb. 11, 1922	Sep. 22, 2002	T Sgt US Army WWII
4-8-F	Roper	Martha J.	1867	1957	Mother
4-8-G	Roper	Rev. R. A.	1865	1939	Father; Just a Sinner Saved by Grace
4-8-H	Dobson	Eston Lee	Jul. 8, 1931	Jul. 8, 1931	At rest with Jesus
4-8-I	Hendrix	Vernie Lee	Apr. 12, 1929	May 12, 1929	Asleep in Jesus
4-8-J	Unmarked				

	Last Name	First, Middle or Maiden	Date of Birth	Date of Death	Tombstone Inscriptions
4-8-K	Dobson	Martha	May 25, 1869	Mar. 17, 1940	Mother
4-8-L	Dobson	William M.	Jan. 2, 1861	Oct. 25, 1950	Father
4-8-M	Dobson	Thomas Kim	Feb. 7, 1887	Mar. 11, 1949	Son
4-8-N	Garrett	Jane Dobson	May 16, 1909	Oct. 18, 1983	Mother
4-9-F	Roper	Bertha S.	Jul. 26, 1889	Jun. 19, 1980	Mama
4-9-G	Roper	Walter R.	Nov. 28, 1888	Dec. 13, 1976	Daddy
4-9-H	Cloud	Infant	Mar. 24, 1946	Mar. 24, 1946	
4-9-I	Cloud	Marie	Oct. 10, 1914	Feb. 17, 1998	
4-9-J	Cloud	Carl	Nov. 5, 1907	Mar. 24, 1995	
4-9-K	Allen	Evelyn	Oct. 8, 1930	Dec. 29, 1995	Here Lies My Mama. Gran Gran to My Children. A Sister to Seven and Now Forever with 'God.' Your Son
4-9-N	Mills	Lonnie C.	1900	1947	Your devoted family
4-9-O	Roper	Flossie P.	Jan. 20, 1910	Apr. 1, 1999	Mother, Memory Lane, Book of Life
4-9-P	Roper	Samuel A.	Jan. 31, 1907	Feb. 25, 1951	Father, Book of Life
4-9-U	White	Floy E.	Apr. 1, 1895	Apr. 9, 1960	Red Brick Lot
4-9-V	White	Eugene D.	Jul. 2, 1893	Dec. 31, 1963	
4-9-Y	Cowart	Donald K.	Nov. 18, 1935	Oct. 7, 1986	SP4 US Army WWII
4-9-Z	Roper	Winnie G.	May 17, 1912	Apr. 7, 2001	
4-9-AA	Roper	Bowman G.	Oct. 3, 1910	Feb. 10, 1961	
4-9-BB	Green	Emma Roper	Feb. 1, 1905	Apr. 3, 1969	
4-9-CC	Green	Tom W.	Oct. 12, 1904	Dec. 28, 1984	
4-9-DD	Green	Bonnie G.	Mar. 2, 1918	Jan. 20, 1983	
4-10-G					Unmarked head stone and foot stone, (Baby?)
4-10-H	Dobson	William Lee	Feb. 12, 1924	Feb. 19, 1933	
4-10-I	Haygood	Inez F.	Apr. 25, 1904	Mar. 11, 1998	
4-10-J	Haygood	Joe D.	Apr. 25, 1917	Oct. 8, 1959	In my Father's House are many Mansions
4-10-K	Haygood	Inf. Dau. Edith	Apr. 1, 1938	Apr. 1, 1938	
4-10-P	Southern	Lillie	Oct. 6, 1875	Jun. 17, 1964	At Rest
4-10-Q	Southern	G. W.	Sep. 19, 1872	Apr. 11, 1942	
4-10-R	Phyfe	Lou Vennie	Jun. 26, 1882	Mar. 4, 1957	Mother
4-10-S	Phyfe	James Samuel	Sep. 27, 1872	Aug. 14, 1955	Father. Death is only a shadow across the path to heaven
4-10-T	Phyfe	Rade	Apr. 18, 1917	Jan. 19, 1975	
4-10-V					Unmarked Stone, Baby?
4-10-X	Cannon	Nora S.	Apr. 15, 1884	Nov. 30, 1964	Mother
4-10-Y	Cannon	Harvey D.	Nov. 23, 1886	Apr. 26, 1973	Father, We Will Meet Again

	Last Name	First, Middle or Maiden	Date of Birth	Date of Death	Tombstone Inscriptions
4-10-Z	Cannon	George H.	Jun. 9, 1923	Apr. 12, 1958	Son, Georgia, Pvt Co F. 351 Infantry, W W II BSM
4-10-BB	Cannon	Jewell I.	Oct. 6, 1916	Mar. 23, 2003	
4-10-CC	Cannon	Toy M.	Oct. 22, 1917	Oct. 20, 1958	Sunrise tomorrow, together forever
4-10-DD	Cannon	Virgil Toy	1943	1983	
4-10-EE	Holbrook	Myrtie Mae	Sep. 16, 1918	Jun. 9, 2010	
4-11-F	Dobson	Shirley Ray	Dec. 23, 1939	Sep. 16, 2001	
4-11-G	Dobson	Lonnie Herbert	Mar. 30, 1917	Dec. 21, 2006	
4-11-H	Dobson	Helen W.	Aug. 22, 1892	Aug. 19, 1975	
4-11-I	Dobson	Lemar W.	Mar. 27, 1894	Mar. 29, 1983	
4-11-J	Haygood	Mattie J.	Feb. 14, 1889	Feb. 9, 1974	
4-11-K	Haygood	Green Seldon	May 1, 1876	Jun. 24, 1935	Picture of two persons on headstone
4-11-M	Sewell	James P.	Apr. 14, 1937	Aug. 21, 1937	
4-11-N	Sewell	Bertha M.	Sep. 17, 1912	Nov. 11, 1995	
4-11-O	Sewell	James H.	Mar. 20, 1914	Jul. 20, 1995	
4-11-Q					Unmarked
4-11-R					Unmarked
4-11-S	Satterfield	Margie M.	Nov. 1, 1881	Nov. 23, 1963	
4-11-T	Satterfield	M.C.	Apr. 21, 1885	Dec. 19, 1957	
4-11-U					Cement block lot, no headstone
4-11-V	Reynolds	Debbie Odessa	Jul. 21, 1966	Jul. 24, 1966	
4-11-Z	Pearson	Toy	Mar. 15, 1911	Jan. 8, 1958	Georgia PVT CO L 121 Infantry WWII
4-11-AA	Wilkie	Myrtie	Oct. 27, 1887	Jul. 6, 1977	She's Safe at Home
4-11-BB	Sandow	Oscar Harrison	Jul. 7, 1900	Dec. 18, 1882	
4-11-CC	Sandow	Viola M.	Dec. 9, 1879	Jun. 19, 1969	We will meet again. Mother
4-11-DD	Holcomb	Weldon J.	May 18, 1909	Jan. 20, 1975	PFC US Army
4-11-EE	Holcomb	Alice W.	Aug. 20, 1884	Mar. 20, 1968	Mother
4-11-FF	Holcomb	S. D. "Bud"	Mar. 15, 1878	Jan. 9, 1962	Father
4-11-GG	Holcomb	Gladys Elberta		Mar. 13, 1993	A Dedicated Teacher
4-11-HH	Satterfield	Pauline	Jan. 6, 1911	Dec. 20, 2001	
4-11-II	Satterfield	Rufus C.	Mar. 27, 1904	Aug. 15, 1971	
4-12-D	Green	Henry Newton	Aug. 31, 1883	Jul. 29, 1968	Father. How Beautiful Heaven Must Be
4-12-E	Green	Rossie Lee	Dec. 4, 1886	Jan. 18, 1938	Mother
4-12-F	Wyatt	John S.	Apr. 20 1856	Jan. 25, 1929	Masonic Emblem; His Toils are past, his work is done. He fought the fight, the victory won.

	Last Name	First, Middle or Maiden	Date of Birth	Date of Death	Tombstone Inscriptions
4-12-G	Wyatt	Octavia Smith	Feb. 19, 1861	Mar. 18, 1946	Third wife of John W. Wyatt; Asleep.
4-12-I	Wyatt	Pearl L.	Jul. 2, 1885	Aug. 4, 1971	Mother. Book of Life
4-12-J	Wyatt	Samuel S.	Feb. 11, 1886	Nov. 26, 1974	Father. Memory Lane
4-12-K	Wyatt	Billie Buren	Jan. 21, 1940	Apr. 25, 1941	
4-12-L	Wyatt	Bobbie Grace	Feb. 20, 1917	Nov. 22, 2002	
4-12-M	Wyatt	Mathel "Dewey"	Mar. 13, 1909	Apr. 17, 1995	
4-12-O	Cannon	Jane C. McCurry	May 4, 1912	Feb. 6, 1999	Mama
4-12-P	Cannon	Roy	May 26, 1914	Oct. 31, 1942	Daddy
4-12-R	Little	Michael L.	Dec. 2, 1941	Feb. 15, 1967	
4-12-T					Unmarked stone, no name
4-12-U					Unmarked stone, no name
4-12-V					Unmarked stone, no name
4-12-W	Mulkey	Clarinda I.	Jan. 1, 1874	Jan. 6, 1963	Gone but not Forgotten
4-12-X	Bohannon	Mandy M.	1894	1988	(temporary marker)
4-12-Y	West	Jed Hunter	Oct. 5, 1954	Feb. 9, 1955	Infant Son. How Soon Fades the Tender Flower
4-12-Z	West	Ellabell D.	Jan. 20, 1935	Dec. 22, 2012	Loving Mother
4-12-DD	Shelton	Kimberly Sue	Oct. 18, 1969	Oct. 18, 1969	
4-12-II	Wilkie	Callie			
4-12-JJ	Wilkie	Hiram Samuel	Feb. 1, 1921	Jul. 17, 1973	Georgia Tec 5 US Army WWII
4-13-A					
4-13-B	Rich	Rev. E. G.	Jun. 17, 1869	May 2, 1941	
4-13-C	Lovelace	Mary Elizabeth	Aug. 11, 1909	Aug. 14, 2002	
4-13-D	Lovelace	George H.	Oct. 19, 1909	Aug. 5, 1973	
4-13-E	Lovelace	Georgia Ann Wilkie	Apr. 27, 1890	Aug. 24, 1965	
4-13-F	Lovelace	Robert Edgar	Oct. 8, 1886	Dec. 8, 1938	
4-13-G	Little	S. G.	Feb. 14, 1932	Feb. 29, 1932	Our Darling is Gone
4-13-J					Unmarked (red brick lot)
4-13-K					Unmarked (red brick lot)
4-13-L	Hester	Mattie J.	Jun. 8, 1883	Jun. 28, 1965	
4-13-M	Hester	Christopher C.	Aug. 26, 1881	Feb. 17, 1946	
4-13-N	Cantrell	Lula V.	Feb. 24, 1883	Jul. 23, 1954	Resting
4-13-O	Cantrell	Raymond M.	Nov. 30, 1879	Mar. 28, 1940	Resting
4-13-R	Pace	Charlie Carwell	1865	1946	
4-13-S					Unmarked
4-13-T	Little	Donnie Hugh	Nov. 25, 1947	Jun. 9, 1968	Our Only Son. "Georgia Cpl Co A 1 MT BN 1 MAR DIV Vietnam PH"
4-13-U	Little	George W.	Oct. 12, 1925	May 12, 1983	
4-13-V	Little	Evelyn C.	Dec. 13, 1929	May 10, 2013	

	Last Name	First, Middle or Maiden	Date of Birth	Date of Death	Tombstone Inscriptions
4-13-X					Unmarked stone, no name
4-13-Z	Mills	Ollie Kathryn Wilkie	Dec. 20, 1927	Oct. 11, 1991	
4-13-AA	Wilkie	Oler Lee	Feb. 12, 1905	Nov. 11, 1969	
4-13-BB	Wilkie	Henry Clyde	Apr. 5, 1903	Dec. 14, 1979	
4-13-FF	Cook	Hazel W.	Jun. 20, 1923	Mar. 1, 2013	Mother
4-13-GG	Wilkie	Ruby Lee	Aug. 12, 1905	Jan. 3, 1999	
4-13-HH	Wilkie	Harrison	Nov. 16, 1900	Jul. 12, 1985	
4-14-A	Pearson	Laura	Mar. 16, 1878	May 21, 1954	
4-14-B	Pearson	Jack	Aug. 29, 1878	Sep. 17, 1948	
4-14-D	Lovelace	Nettie Lee	Dec. 15, 1919	Apr. 18, 2010	
4-14-E	Wilson	Fannie	Jun. 13, 1912	Feb. 16, 1955	
4-14-F	Wilson	Chester Lee	Jul. 31, 1902	May 17, 1961	
4-14-G	Wilkie	Maggie P.	Nov. 14, 1895	Feb. 11, 1980	
4-14-H	Wilkie	Jessie L.	Nov. 5, 1893	Aug. 3, 1947	The Way of the Cross Leads Home
4-14-I	Rich	Donnie H.	May 3, 1938	Jan. 15, 1939	
4-14-J	Green	Kenneth E.	Feb. 11, 1939	Feb. 14, 1939	
4-14-L	Wilkie	Martha L.	Apr. 27, 1888	Mar. 30, 1945	
4-14-M	Wilkie	Eddie F.	May 3, 1882	Nov. 1, 1954	Where the Flowers Bloom Forever
4-14-N	Wilkie	Ernest	Jun. 30, 1912	May 25, 1940	Not dead, only asleep
4-14-O	Cloud	Mattie Doris	Apr. 24, 1940	Apr. 24, 1940	
4-14-P	Cloud	William Herbert	Mar. 24, 1941	Mar. 24, 1941	
4-14-Q	Little	Ruby Jane	May 25, 1912	Oct. 19, 2004	Mother
4-14-R	Little	Broughton Henry	Mar. 19, 1910	Apr. 9, 1969	Daddy, Thy Will Be Done
4-14-S	Little	Maudie Alice	Apr. 12, 1890	Mar. 16, 1949	
4-14-T	Little	George Henry	Mar. 13, 1882	Apr. 3, 1962	
4-14-X	Bell	Dessie Little	Oct. 3, 1913	Dec. 17, 1983	
4-14-Y	Little	Buren	May 2, 1912	Dec. 4, 1956	He Has Gone to the Mansions of Rest
4-14-Z	Little	J. B.	Dec. 3, 1914	Aug. 4, 1959	
4-14-BB					Small stone, no name
4-14-DD	Page	Michael Brian	Aug. 20, 1967	Nov. 6, 1984	Budded on earth to bloom in heaven
4-14-EE	Dobson	Lucinda E.	Jan. 29, 1880	Nov. 12, 1953	There are no partings in heaven
4-14-FF	Dobson	Elijah W.	Jul. 24, 1878	Oct. 3, 1958	
4-14-HH	Cronan	Fred J.	Sep. 17, 1908	Oct. 1, 1993	Father
4-14-II	Cronan	Hilda F.	Oct. 7, 1918	Jul. 19, 1966	Mother
4-14-II	Martin	Lisa Angela	Aug. 19, 1971	Aug. 19, 1971	
4-14-KK	Martin	Leonard Eugene	Oct. 28, 1962	Jul. 17, 1992	What We Keep in Memory is Ours Unchanged Forever
	Cronan	Evelyn	Feb. 5, 1945		
4-14-MM	Martin	Leonard Davis "Dock"	Apr. 25, 1943	Feb. 24, 2014	What We Keep in Memory is Ours Unchanged Forever

	Last Name	First, Middle or Maiden	Date of Birth	Date of Death	Tombstone Inscriptions
4-15-C	Chandler	Virgil Clements	Aug. 1, 1933	Aug. 31, 2011	US Army
4-15-D	Chandler	Edna Lovelace	Aug. 22, 1932	Sep. 14, 2005	
4-15-E	Bursmith	Georgia Imogene	Apr. 26, 1929	Nov. 24, 2002	
4-15-F	Bursmith	William F.	Jul. 20, 1917	Mar. 5, 1976	S1 US Navy, WWII
4-15-I	Cronan	Edith			No dates
		George Grady???			Unmarked?
		George Eugene??			
4-16-G	Andrews	Robert Gerald	Jul. 12, 1941	Nov. 23, 2005	
4-16-H	Andrews	Roy Hurley	Sep. 17, 1944	Sep. 16, 1990	
4-16-I	Andrews	Etta Lou	Jan. 14, 1905	Jun. 18, 1982	Married May 11, 1924, Beyond the Sunset. Mama
4-16-J	Andrews	Homer D. "Peg"	Feb. 2, 1899	Jun. 13, 1982	Married May 11, 1924, Beyond the Sunset. Daddy
4-16-K	Andrews	Lula	Aug. 5, 1880	Sep. 14, 1968	Mother
4-16-N	Andrews	James Carl	1913	1949	Brother
4-16-R	Dean	Sarah M.	Jun. 23, 1876	Jan. 18, 1948	
4-16-S	Dean	Steve D.	Aug. 24, 1870	Mar. 10, 1952	At Rest With Jesus
4-16-T	Collier	Gennie	Mar. 24, 1915	Nov. 8, 1999	
4-16-U	Collier	W. L.	Sep. 6, 1901	Sep. 23, 1965	At Rest
4-16-V	West	Joseph L.	Nov. 28, 1908	Jan. 7, 1973	In My Father's House are Many Mansions
4-16-W	West	Hessie M.	May 3, 1920	Aug. 14, 1983	

Section 5

Property located SW of church, and South of baptismal pool. For Rows 1-7, begin at corner closest to church and continue West, Graves A-? begin at north side of each row and proceed south.

Oldest date of death on marker is 1978.

	Last Name	First, Middle, or Maiden	Date of Birth	Date of Death	Tombstone Inscriptions
5-1-A	Wilkie	Levi Chase	Jul. 14, 1999	Jul. 14, 1999	Our Little Angel
5-1-B	Milford	Cleo Heard	Jan. 3, 1917	Aug. 11, 2007	Our Children: Joe, John, Judy and Joyce
5-1-C	Milford	Robert Lee	Jun. 6, 1915	Aug. 31, 1988	
					spaces
5-1-O	Wilkie	Heath Frank Allen	Feb. 25, 1993	May 3, 2005	Our Sunshine. Beloved Son, Brother and Grandson, Loved by All
5-1-X	Gilleland	"Becky" Rebecca Leslie	Sep. 26, 1940	Mar. 26, 2005	Married Jun. 6, 1962

	Last Name	First, Middle, or Maiden	Date of Birth	Date of Death	Tombstone Inscriptions
5-2-A	Wilkie	Callie Mae	Aug. 19, 1909	Sep. 8, 1983	
5-2-B	Wilkie	Edwin Dennis	Nov. 13, 1905	Feb. 11, 1994	
5-2-D	Wilkie	Ira. B.	Jun. 28, 1942	Dec. 24, 1990	
5-2-E	Cloud	Mattie Grace	Feb. 19, 1920	Apr. 20, 1999	
5-2-F	Cloud	William Hoyt	Jan. 9, 1917	Oct. 4, 1983	
5-2-H	Green	Hattie	Sep. 27, 1904	Dec. 30, 1997	
5-2-I	Green	Thomas E.	Oct. 4, 1900	Jan. 6, 1984	
5-2-J	Wilkie	Christine O.	Dec. 4, 1933	Feb. 2, 1985	
	Wilkie	J. T.			
5-2-M	Rollins	Dewey	1928	1993	
5-2-O	Wilkie	Winnell			
5-2-P	Wilkie	Lewis	Jun. 17, 1936	Jun. 24, 1995	Daddy; Memory Lane
5-2-Q	Wilkie	Bertha M.			
5-2-R	Wilkie	Rupert	May 5, 1938	May 11, 2007	Daddy; Married Dec. 20, 1958
5-2-S	Hamilton	Cindy J.	Jan. 24, 1958	Nov. 28, 2003	Married Sep. 24, 1977
5-2-Y	Gaddis	Leslie Lee III	Jul. 14, 1950	Sep. 11, 2000	Married Jul. 18, 1970
5-3-A	McClure	George Calvin	Jun. 16, 1934	May 12, 2009	
5-3-B	McClure	Mattie Ruth	Aug. 16, 1914	Nov. 27, 1993	
5-3-C	McClure	George Lipscomb	Aug. 19, 1910	Apr. 19, 1979	
		Henrietta			
5-3-E	Wyatt	Geneva C.	Dec. 15, 1916	Feb. 8, 1982	
5-3-F	Wyatt	J. Frank (Deacon)	Jun. 1, 1914	Jun. 23, 1984	
5-3-I	Green	Alice I.	Nov. 6, 1911	Aug. 1, 2004	
5-3-J	Green	Garland L.	Aug. 7, 1910	Oct. 31, 1992	
5-3-L	Wilkie	Henry Grady Jr.	Jul. 27, 1950	Sep. 1, 2009	
5-3-M	Wilkie	Christine	Jun. 24, 1928	Feb. 14, 2015	
5-3-N	Wilkie	Henry Grady Sr.	Jul. 8, 1926	Jan. 10, 2008	Pvt. US Army, WW II Married Aug. 5, 1945
5-3-O					unmarked
5-3-P	Wilkie	Charlie "Hubert"	Apr. 12, 1925	Jun. 30, 2014	US Navy, WW II
5-3-Q	Harber	Richard J.	Aug. 2, 1946	Mar. 29, 2013	US Marines

	Last Name	First, Middle, or Maiden	Date of Birth	Date of Death	Tombstone Inscriptions
5-4-A	Wilkie	Arminda	Apr. 5, 1939	Sep. 11, 2012	Arminda J. Pendley; Wife of John C. Pendley, Isaiah 41:10. Fear not thou; for I am with thee.
5-4-B	Wilkie	Randall	Aug. 29, 1938	Dec. 20, 1978	
5-4-D	Wilkie	L. B.	Jul. 14, 1912	Mar. 24, 1988	
5-4-E	Wilkie	Maggie Lee	Dec. 5, 1911	May 26, 1995	
5-4-G	Watkins	Delmer	Nov. 6, 1924	Nov. 22, 2009	
5-4-I	McGaha	Louise	Mar. 22, 1931	Dec. 21, 2005	
5-4-J	McGaha	Cecil R.	Feb. 26, 1931	Nov. 10, 2009	
5-4-L	Pruitt	Vic	Oct. 11, 1959	Jun. 11, 2013	Our children: Mitchell and Derick
5-5-A	Crenshaw	Terri Leigh	Dec. 25, 1955	Aug. 28, 1985	
5-5-B	Teal	Les H.	Jul. 18, 1966	Mar. 30, 1995	
5-5-I	Waldrop	Tina Gayton	Sep. 4, 1971	Jun. 8, 2011	
5-6-					
5-7-A	Boling	Bobby	Apr. 26, 1939	Jan. 3, 1989	
5-7-B	Boling	Julian P.	Apr. 23, 1941	Sep. 23, 2009	
5-7-C	Cipriani	Chad Edward "Cip"	Jul. 27, 1978	Aug. 4, 1997	
5-7-F	Heard	Cheyenne Gabrielle	Jan. 11, 1996	Sep. 13, 2013	"Smile, God Loves You" Loving Daughter and Cowgirl of Nichelle & Tim Stewart and Jason & Debra Heard
5-8-A	Burch	Robert H. Jr.	Sep. 23, 1920	Mar. 26, 1989	US Army, WW II
5-8-B	Burch	Jesse James	Mar. 23, 1925	Jan. 12, 1995	Daddy; Gone Home
5-8-F	Wilkie	Elmer Leroy	Dec. 31, 1934	Apr. 28, 2000	US Army Infantry Our Children: Tim, Deree
5-8-G	Cochran	Edith Hester	Nov. 22, 1922	Jul. 20, 2014	Nov. 13, 1943; Wed 70 years
5-8-H	Cochran	E. W.	Apr. 21, 1922	Jan. 24, 2015	Our Children: Ed, Regina, Rilla, Coy, Stanley
5-9-C	Parrott	Steven Lee	Oct. 19, 1955	Jan. 21, 2015	

Hightower Baptist Church Cemetery: Alphabetical List of Interments.

Interesting facts:

Earliest date of <u>birth</u> calculated from tombstone information: Catherine Burns, 1766-1849 (Ten other stones note birth years in the 1700s).

Earliest date of <u>death</u> recorded on a tombstone: Bedney Franklin, 1815-1844.

Oldest person at date of death as recorded on tombstone: Elijah Howard, 1812-1913.

Information gathered from: HBC cemetery, obituaries, death certificates and families.

Location: Section-Row-Grave, use the cemetery diagram in this chapter as a guide for the information in the column labeled location.

Location in Cemetery: section-row-grave	Last Name	First Middle (Former/Maiden)	By = buried beside or nearby; other information	Date of Birth	Date of Death
4-9-K	Allen	Evelyn *Margaret Evelyn Cloud*		Oct. 8, 1930	Dec. 29, 1995
4-16-I	Andrews	Etta Lou *Thompson*	By Homer D. Andrews	Jan. 14, 1905	Jun. 18, 1982
3-6-Q	Andrews	Herschel		1914	1935
4-16-J	Andrews	Homer D., "Peg" *David*	By Etta Lou Andrews	Feb. 2, 1899	Jun. 13, 1982
4-16-N	Andrews	James Carl		1913	1949
4-16-K	Andrews	Lula *Pinyan*		Aug. 5, 1880	Sep. 14, 1968
3-6-P	Andrews	Mattie *Martha Green*	By W.J. Andrews	Aug. 27, 1880	Dec. 24, 1951
3-6-N	Andrews	Oscar *William*		1902	1968
4-16-G	Andrews	Robert Gerald	By Roy Andrews	Jul. 12, 1941	Nov. 23, 2005
4-16-H	Andrews	Roy Hurley	By Robert Andrews	Sep. 17, 1944	Sep. 16, 1990
3-6-O	Andrews	W. J. *William Jackson*	By Mattie Andrews	May 31, 1880	Oct. 25, 1926
4-6-I	Bailey	K. E. *Kyle/Kile Ethern*	By Maude Bailey	Jun. 1, 1901	Apr. 2, 1954
4-6-H	Bailey	Maude	By K. E. Bailey	Mar. 20, 1901	Nov. 29, 1960
4-4-N	Ball	James Roy	By Zula and Carlous	Aug. 21, 1910	Feb. 25, 1972
4-4-L	Ball	K. Carlous	By Zula and Roy	Mar. 17, 1946	Apr. 4, 1946
4-4-M	Ball	Zula Lee	By Roy and Carlous	Feb. 19, 1912	Feb. 20, 2002
4-14-X	Bell	Dessie Little	By Buren Little	Oct. 3, 1913	Dec. 17, 1983
4-6-Y	Bise	Alexander H.		Sep. 5, 1879	Jan. 20, 1956
4-12-X	Bohannon	Mandy Victoria M.	By Clarinda Mulkey	Sep. 6, 1894	Jun. 17, 1988

Location in Cemetery: section-row-grave	Last Name	First Middle (Former/Maiden)	By = buried beside or nearby; other information	Date of Birth	Date of Death
5-7-A	Boling	Bobby	By Julian Boling	Apr. 26, 1939	Jan. 3, 1989
2-11-LL	Boling	Buman Boot		Aug. 6, 1909	May 4, 1983
???	Boling	Clifford	Obit; death certificate	Aug. 10, 1898	Aug. 26, 1934
3-8-O	Boling	Clyde M		Aug. 23, 1901	Sep. 9, 1934
2-9-T	Boling	E Esther		Apr. 6, 1903	Mar. 8, 1907
1-9-C	Boling	Emily R Rebecca *Green*	By H. C. Boling	Oct. 20, 1847	Oct. 15, 1909
1-5-L	Boling	F. T., Floyd T.	Possibly a memorial marker, died in Richmond, VA, CSA	Jan. 17, 1842	Feb. 2, 1862
3-8-R	Boling	George C.		Aug. 4, 1906	May 18, 1945
1-9-B	Boling	H. C. Henry Clay Sr.	By Emily Boling	Oct. 15, 1839	Oct. 25, 1910
4-2-S	Boling	H. Forrest Henry Forrest	By Leo Boling	Mar. 5, 1908	Apr. 24, 1963
3-8-S	Boling	J. Lowery	By Julia S. Boling	Apr. 16, 1872	Jan. 29, 1926
1-6-C	Boling	James A.		Sep. 23, 1827	Feb. 18, 1853
???	Boling	James Allen	Obit, N Ga Tribune?	Dec. 1884	Jun. 1943
3-7-R	Boling	John F. Franklin	By Mary P. Boling	1873	Dec. 16, 1926
1--E	Boling	John R.		Nov. 18, 1832	Feb. 1853
3-8-T	Boling	Julia S. *Jones*	By J. Lowery Boling	Jan. 30, 1875	Mar. 21, 1931
5-7-B	Boling	Julian P. Paul		Apr. 23, 1941	Sep. 23, 2009
4-2-R	Boling	Leo *Turner*	By H. Forrest Boling	Sep. 25, 1907	Aug. 27, 1988
1-7-K	Boling	Mary	1st w/o William Boling	Apr. 4, 1808	Jun. 27, 1853
3-7-Q	Boling	Mary P. Mary Prude *Green*	By John F. Boling	1877 *Apr. 27, 1877*	1924 (on marker) *Dec. 3, 1922 on death certificate*
2-9-U	Boling	W. T. William Thompson		Mar. 23, 1868	Oct. 31, 1929
3-2-GG	Bryant	Clifton	Grandson of Amanda Williams	Feb. 13, 1909	Oct. 4, 1919
2-9-DD	Bryant	George Mansel Thomas		Jul. 19, 1905	Aug. 27, 1908
2-9-EE	Bryant	J. T. John Thomas		Oct. 15, 1871	Jul. 27, 1914

Location in Cemetery: section-row-grave	Last Name	First Middle (Former/Maiden)	By = buried beside or nearby; other information	Date of Birth	Date of Death
3-3-U	Bryant	Lucy Ann *Garrett*	By Thomas Bryant	Nov. 12, 1856	May 13, 1922
3-3-T	Bryant	Thomas	By Lucy Ann Bryant	Jul. 3, 1851	Jun. 27, 1923
3-7-V	Buchana	Jewell	By Charlie Buchanna or Buchanan	Jul. 14, 1920	Jul. 17, 1971
3-7-W	Buchanna	Charlie	By Jewell Buchana or Buchanan	Jul. 7, 1913	Dec. 31, 1948
4-4-R	Buffington	Maude *Pearson*	By Robt. Buffington	Aug. 17, 1891	Oct. 25, 1985
4-4-S	Buffington	Robt. B, *Robert Brown*	By Maude Buffington	Nov. 15, 1891	Mar. 23, 1952
5-8-B	Burch	Jesse James		Mar. 23, 1925	Jan. 12, 1995
5-8-A	Burch	Robert H. Jr. *Harris*		Sep. 23, 1920	Mar. 26, 1989
??	Burgess	Shirley Christine	Obit, infant d/o M/M Charles Burgess		Dec. 1941
1-5-BB	Burns	Catherine B.		Feb. 11, 1766 (calculated)	Jun. 24, 1849
1-1-AA	Burns	Dr. John		Apr. 26, 1794	Oct. 11, 1858
4-4-AA	Burns	Esco Gilleland	By Vernon Burns	Apr. 23, 1908	Jul. 1, 1978
1-4-Z	Burns	Jefferson D.		Unk	Unk
1-4-DD	Burns	Josepsun		unk	unk
1-4-Y	Burns	Lucy		Nov. 8, 1796 (Calculated)	Mar. 13, 1877
4-4-BB	Burns	Vernon Lee	By Esco Burns	Apr. 9, 1904	Jun. 14, 1977
1-4-BB	Burns	W. *Melmoth W.*		Dec. 20, 1833 (calculated)	Jan. 13, 1847
1-4-CC	Burns	Warren M.		Feb. 28, 1831 (calculated)	Jun. 5, 1847
4-15-E	Bursmith	Georgia Imogene *Lovelace*	By William Bursmith	Apr. 26, 1929	Nov. 24, 2002
4-15-F	Bursmith	William F.	By Imogene Bursmith	Jul. 20, 1917	Mar. 5, 1976
1-11-F	Burton	Edward		Jun. 5, 1800	Jun. 18, 1851
1-11-I	Burton	Margaret Jane	Dau of Edward and Sarah Burton	Sep. 14, 1836 (calculated)	May 16, 1848
3-1-F	Cannon	Billy Byron	s/o Elmer & Minnie Cannon; Cert 19448	Jan. 1, 1924	Jun. 16, 1926
3-1-G	Cannon	Dorothy Evans		Sep. 14, 1918	Jun. 12, 1919
3-1-F	Cannon	Elmer Cranston		Jun. 15, 1887	May 23, 1957
4-7-DD	Cannon	Fannie Aza Lee	By Jonnie Cannon	Jun. 12, 1914	Mar. 6, 1983

Location in Cemetery: section-row-grave	Last Name	First Middle (Former/Maiden)	By = buried beside or nearby; other information	Date of Birth	Date of Death
4-6-V	Cannon	Fannie Louise	By James D. Cannon and Lisa A. Cannon	Jun. 28, 1941	Mar. 6, 1999
4-10-X	Cannon	George Harvey	By Nora S. and George H. Cannon	Jun. 9, 1923	Apr. 12, 1958
2-2-CC	Cannon	George W.		Mar. 3, 1858	Nov. 7, 1936
2-3-CC	Cannon	Harvey "Huggins"	By Lenora W. Cannon	About 1862	Mar. 1893
4-10-Y	Cannon	Harvey D.		Nov. 23, 1886	Apr. 26, 1973
3-1-G	Cannon	Herman K.		Mar. 16, 1925	Jan. 4, 1977
2-2-FF	Cannon	Infant	Son of James M.& Lizzia Cannon	Jul. 13, 1896	Jan. 14, 1897
4-6-V	Cannon	James D.	By Fannie L. and Lisa A. Cannon		
2-2-BB	Cannon	James M.		Mar. 3, 1856	Dec. 27, 1937
4-12-O	Cannon	Jane McCurry	By Roy Cannon	May 4, 1912	Feb. 6, 1999
4-10-BB	Cannon	Jewell I.	By Toy M. Cannon	Oct. 6, 1916	Mar. 23, 2003
3-12-O	Cannon	John W.	By Laura Cannon	Nov. 13, 1852	Dec. 1, 1940
4-7-EE	Cannon	Jonnie Hunter	By Fannie A. Lee Cannon	Jan. 29, 1909	Dec. 6, 1962
3-12-P	Cannon	Laura McGinley	By John Cannon	Nov. 28, 1862	Jun. 8, 1928
2-3-DD	Cannon	Lenora Wheeler	By Harvey Huggins Cannon	Aug. 23, 1859	Nov. 18, 1951
4-6-V	Cannon	Lisa Ann	By Fannie L. and James D. Cannon		
2-2-EE	Cannon	Lizzia Jones	Wife of James M. Cannon	Jan. 20, 1870 or 1872?	Jul. 13, ?
??	Cannon	Marvin		1917	1958
4-7-FF	Cannon	Mattie Matilda	By Jonnie and Fannie Cannon	Aug. 12, 1874	Jun. 5, 1967
3-12-Q	Cannon	Mattie McGinley	Dau of John & Laura McGinley Cannon	Oct. 9, 1898	Sep. 21, 1927
4-10-X	Cannon	Nora Scott	By "Son: George H. Cannon"	Apr. 15, 1884	Nov. 30, 1964
4-12-P	Cannon	Roy M.	By Jane Cannon- McCurry	May 26, 1914	Oct. 31, 1942
2-4-FF	Cannon	S.F. "Silas"	By Sallie Davis Cannon	Sep 26, 1817	Jul. 21, 1897
2-4-HH	Cannon	Sarah "Sallie" *Davis*	By S.F. Cannon	Aug. 10, 1827	Feb. 13, 1903
4-10-CC	Cannon	Toy M.	By Jewell Cannon	Oct. 22, 1917	Oct. 20, 1958
4-10-DD	Cannon	Virgil Toy		May 18, 1943	Mar. 10, 1983
4	Cannon-McCurry	Jane Epperson	By Roy M. Cannon	May 4, 1912	Feb. 6, 1999
??	Cantrell	Ida Alice Smallwood	w/o M. D. Cantrell	Mar. 16, 1865	unk
4-13-N	Cantrell	Lula Viola	By Raymond Cantrell	Feb. 24, 1883	Jul. 23, 1954
2-3-UU	Cantrell	M. D. Memory Jefferson Davis	s/o Hiram Cantrell, death certificate, age 74?	1863	Mar. 8, 1935
4-13-O	Cantrell	Raymond Marion	By Lula Cantrell	Nov. 30, 1879	Mar. 28, 1940

Location in Cemetery: section-row-grave	Last Name	First Middle (Former/Maiden)	By = buried beside or nearby; other information	Date of Birth	Date of Death
1-8-O	Chambers	Elizabeth Jane	By William Chambers	1840	Jun. 6, 1848
1-8-P	Chambers	William	By Elizabeth Chambers		
4-15-D	Chandler	Edna *Lovelace*	By Virgil Chandler	Aug. 22, 1932	Sep. 15, 2005
4-15-C	Chandler	Virgil Clements	By Edna Chandler	Aug. 1, 1933	Aug. 31, 2011
1-13-N	Chastain	Bassel		Feb. 10, 1906	Jul. 2, 1907
2-6-G	Chastain	John William	By Perle Chastain	Jun. 17, 1871	Aug. 1, 1872
2-6-F	Chastain	Perle M.	By John W. Chastain	May 4, 1881	Nov. 13, 1881
3-8-M	Chumbler	Emma L.	Same marker as James Chumbler. No dates on marker	Jan. 1873 ?	Unk
3-8-N	Chumbler	James M.	Same marker as Emma Chumbler. No dates on marker	Unk	Jul. 16, 1947 ?
5-7-C	Cipriani	Chad Edward "Cip"		Jul. 27, 1978	Aug. 4, 1997
4-9-J	Cloud	Carl	By Marie Cloud	Nov. 5, 1907	Mar. 24, 1995
4-9-H	Cloud	Infant	By Carl and Marie Cloud	Mar. 24, 1946	Mar. 26, 1946
4-9-I	Cloud	Marie	By Carl Cloud	Oct. 10, 1914	Feb. 17, 1998
4-14-O	Cloud	Mattie Doris	Dau of William & Mattie Cloud	Apr. 24, 1940	Apr. 24, 1940
5-2-E	Cloud	Mattie Grace *Wilkie*	By William Hoyt Cloud	Feb. 19, 1920	Apr. 20, 1999
4-14-P	Cloud	William Herbert	Son of William & Mattie Cloud	Mar. 24, 1941	Mar. 24, 1941
5-2-F	Cloud	William Hoyt	By Mattie Grace Cloud	Jan. 9, 1917	Oct. 7, 1983
??	Cloud	Winnell		Dec. 1928	Feb. 27, 1929
3-3-II	Cochran	(Rev). Robt. Wiley	Husband of Matilda Cochran	Abt. 1852	Aug. 24, 1937
3-3-JJ	Cochran	(Rev.) E. A.		Aug. 8, 1845	Oct. 15, 1931
3-3-A	Cochran	(Rev.) John Samuel "Preacher Sam"	By Eunice Cochran	Feb. 9, 1897	Aug. 8, 1984
1-1-E	Cochran	Altiney Jane *Griffin*	By Nevels Cochran	1818	1855
3-7-K	Cochran	Bonziel Oziel	By Elisha and Jennie Cochran	Mar. 11, 1921	Jun. 3, 1921
5-8-H	Cochran	E. W. Edward Watson	By Edith Cochran	Apr. 21, 1922	Jan. 24, 2015
5-8-G	Cochran	Edith *Hester*	By E. W. Cochran	Nov. 22, 1922	Jul. 20, 2014
3-7-I	Cochran	Elisha Franklin	By Jennie Cochran	Mar. 22, 1884	Dec. 26, 1970

Location in Cemetery: section-row-grave	Last Name	First Middle (Former/Maiden)	By = buried beside or nearby; other information	Date of Birth	Date of Death
Buried 2-9-H Additional marker: 3-3-MM	Cochran	Emma *Fowler*	2nd wife of Rev. E.A. Cochran; buried by Jane Fowler Cochran and Elizabeth F. Odum	Feb. 14, 1834	Jun. 30, 1901
3-7-G	Cochran	Emmett B.	By Mary Lee Cochran	Jan. 21, 1915	Jun. 23, 2003
3-3-B	Cochran	Eunice *Ellis*	By J. Samuel Cochran	Dec. 3, 1895	May 31, 1971
1-2-F	Cochran	Infant	Child of Elisha & Jennie Cochran; Cert 7382	Jun. 22, 1919	Jun. 22, 1919
Buried: 2-9-F Additional marker: 3-3-LL	Cochran	Jane *Fowler*	1st wife of Rev. E.A. Cochran; buried by Emma Fowler Cochran and Elizabeth F. Odum	Jul. 13, 1830	Sep. 1, 1888
3-7-J	Cochran	Jennie *Cape*	By Elisha Cochran	Aug. 12, 1895	May 3, 1971
3-3-KK	Cochran	Kansas *Wheeler*	3rd wife of Rev. E. A. Cochran	Sep. 18, 1859	Dec. 23, 1938
3—7-H	Cochran	Mary Lee	By Emmett Cochran	Aug. 15, 1919	Jan. 23, 2012
3-3-NN	Cochran	Matilda *Leonard*	Wife of R. W. Cochran; 63 years cert 29340	Abt. 1862	Nov. 7, 1925
1-2-E	Cochran	Nevels Holcomb	By Altiney Cochran	1815	Dec. 26, 1863
1-12-M	Cochran	Sarah F.		Mar. 27, 1857	Apr. 3, 1857
1-12-N	Cochran	Sarah Nix	1st wife of T. B. Cochran	Mar. 19, 1824	Sep. 15, 1853
1-5-DD	Coffee	John Edward	Possible grandson of Catherine Burns	Dec. 10, 1836	Aug. 23, 1852
3-8-Y	Coleman	Charles Henry		1893	Sep. 17, 1953
3-8-X	Coleman	Edwin		Dec. 22, 1922	Feb. 16, 1935
3-8-Z	Coleman	Myrtle L.		1894	1978
3-8-AA	Coleman	Ted		Oct. 2, 1925	May 3, 1975
2-4-CCC	Collett	John		Dec. 7, 1911	Feb. 16, 1935
2-1-VV	Collett	Litha	By Steve Collett	Aug. 17, 1874	Mar. 10, 1938
2-1-WW	Collett	Steve	By Litha Collett	Apr. 12, 1872	May 12, 1955
4-16-T	Collier	Gennie D.	By W. L. Collier	Mar. 24, 1915	Nov. 8, 1999
3-1-QQ	Collier	George Ann, Georgia	By Hiram Collier	Feb. 20, 1876	Aug. 18, 1952 Buried here??
3-1-PP	Collier	Hiram P.	By George Collier	Jul. 17, 1873	Mar. 14, 1941
2-6-PP	Collier	Sallie Loura *Rich*		May 26, 1873	Oct. 7, 1909

Location in Cemetery: section-row-grave	Last Name	First Middle (Former/Maiden)	By = buried beside or nearby; other information	Date of Birth	Date of Death
4-16-U	Collier	William Lincoln	By Gennie Collier	Sep. 6, 1901	Sep. 23, 1965
4-13-FF	Cook	Hazel *Wilkie*		Jun. 20, 1923	Mar. 1, 2012
2-13-N	Cosby	John C. "Chris" Christopher		Jun. 17, 1960	Sep. 24, 1976
4-7-X	Cowart	Cora D.	By Isaiah Cowart	Nov. 11, 1906	Nov. 27, 2001
4-7-CC	Cowart	Dewey Leonard	By Ruby Cowart	May 15, 1908	Jan. 27, 1979
4-9-Y	Cowart	Donald Kenneth		Nov. 18, 1935	Oct. 7, 1986
4-5-P	Cowart	George Edwin		Apr. 15, 1943	Jan. 30, 1992
4-5-O	Cowart	Harley R.		Aug. 3, 1915	Feb. 9, 1950
4-7-Y	Cowart	Isaiah	By Cora Cowart	Jul. 15, 1904	Aug. 4, 1959
4-6-M	Cowart	John H.,	By Mary Cowart	Jun. 2, 1863	Oct. 28, 1943
4-6-S	Cowart	M. Marion Hancel	By Fronie Cowart	Dec. 22, 1882	Mar. 22, 1961
4-6-N	Cowart	Mary E. *Chumley*	By John H. Cowart	Dec. 2, 1858	Jan. 24, 1945
4-6-T	Cowart	Nola *Mills*	By Wm. Guy Cowart	Feb. 13, 1911	May 23, 2003
4-7-BB	Cowart	Ruby Elizabeth *Green*	By Dewey Cowart	Dec. 18, 1913	Dec. 10, 1991
4-6-R	Cowart	Saphronie "Fronie" Evelyn *Fife*	By M. Hancel Cowart	Jan. 15, 1876	Dec. 25, 1953
4-6-O	Cowart	Toma "Tomie" Cara *Cornett*	By William E. Cowart	Jan. 1, 1891	Apr. 15, 1982
4-6-P	Cowart	William Edward	By Toma Cowart	Jan. 2, 1889	Dec. 24, 1973
4-6-U	Cowart	William Guy "Wm."	By Nola Cowart	Mar. 21, 1902	Jul. 17, 1954
4-7-P	Crenshaw	Frances "Evelyn" *Wilkie*	By M. T. Crenshaw	Sep. 7, 1932	Sep. 27, 1968
4-7-Q	Crenshaw	Martin T., Jr.	By Frances Crenshaw	Jul. 7, 1917	Jan. 2, 1985
5-5-A	Crenshaw	Teri Leigh		Dec. 25, 1955	Aug. 28, 1985
??	Cronan	Anner/ Lee Anna		Jun. 2, 1875	Mar. 6, 1937
??	Cronan	Arnel			
2-13-G	Cronan	Edgar Lee	By Minnie Cronan	Dec. 26, 1900	Aug. 21, 1985
4-15-I	Cronan	Edith Lourance *Boling*	w/o George Grady Cronan	Jan. 9, 1904	Sep. 9, 1947
4-14-HH	Cronan	Fred Jackson	By Hilda Cronan	Sep. 17, 1908	Oct. 1, 1993
??	Cronan	George Eugene	"Age 2 months" s/o George & Edith Boling Cronan	Apr. 1937	Jun. 27, 1937
??	Cronan	George Grady	h/o Edith Cronan	Jun. 22, 1895	Mar. 30, 1983
4-14-II	Cronan	Hilda Francis	By Fred Cronan	Oct. 7, 1918	Jul. 19, 1966

Location in Cemetery: section-row-grave	Last Name	First Middle (Former/Maiden)	By = buried beside or nearby; other information	Date of Birth	Date of Death
??	Cronan	Johnnie Lee	s/o E. L. and Minnie Cronan; cert 29446	Aug. 1925	Dec. 12, 1926
2-13-H	Cronan	Minnie Pearl *Andrews*	By Edgar Cronan	May 12, 1903	Jul. 22, 1980
2-3-JJ	Croy	Almer	Dau. of L. O. and Lydia Croy	Aug. 12, 1910	Jan. 30, 1912
2-3-KK	Croy	Elmer	Son of L. O. and Lydia Croy	Nov. 24, 1906	Apr. 24, 1909
2-2-JJ	Croy	Lillie	Dau. of L. O. and Lydia Croy	Sep. 27, 1904	Mar. 28, 1913
4-6-AA	Davis	Hershel	By Lucile Davis,	Jan. 6, 1905	Oct. 7, 1966
???	Davis	Mary	Age 86 years	Abt 1852	Apr. 11, 1938 Obit Apr. 15, 1938
4-6-Z	Davis	Mattie "Lucille"	By Hershel Davis	May 27, 1916	Oct. 17, 1980
??	Dean	Cebren	s/o Felton & Lucille Loggins Dean; Unmarked, Cert 11269	May 1, 1921	May 1, 1921
??	Dean	Linton William		Sep. 29, 1892	Apr. 1, 1932
4-16-R	Dean	Sarah Matilda *Crow*	By Steve Dean	Jun. 23, 1876	Jan. 18, 1948
4-16-S	Dean	Steve D.	By Sarah M. Dean	Aug. 24, 1870	Mar. 10, 1952
3-1-GG	Dobson	Dock Garston		Mar. 21, 1907	Oct. 10, 1948
3-5-HH	Dobson	Effie Viola		Mar. 14, 1915	Nov. 11, 1918
4-14-FF	Dobson	Elijah W.	By Lucinda Dobson	Jul. 24, 1878	Oct. 3, 1958
4-8-H	Dobson	Eston Lee		Jul. 8, 1931	Jul. 8, 1931
4-11-H	Dobson	Helen *Wilkie*	By Lemar Dobson	Aug. 22, 1892	Aug. 19, 1975
??	Dobson	Infant son of Stephen		May 11, 1951	May 12, 1951
??	Dobson	Laura Bell		Jan. 10, 1926	Dec. 1, 1928
4-11-I	Dobson	Lemar W.	By Helen Dobson	Mar. 27, 1894	Mar. 29, 1983
4-11-G	Dobson	Lonnie Herbert	By Shirley Dobson	Mar. 30, 1917	Dec. 21, 2006
4-14-EE	Dobson	Lucinda E.	By Elijah Dobson	Jan. 29, 1880	Nov. 12, 1953
4-8-K	Dobson	Martha *Blackwell*	By William M. Dobson	May 25, 1869	Mar. 17, 1940
??	Dobson	Ruffus Cleon		Nov. 14, 1929	May 27, 1930
4-11-F	Dobson	Shirley Ray	By Lonnie Dobson	Dec. 23, 1939	Sep. 16, 2001
4-8-M	Dobson	Thomas Kim	By William M. & Martha Dobson	Feb. 7, 1887	Mar. 11, 1949
Unmarked Cert23597	Dobson	Virgil Clay	s/o R. O. & Effie Dobson	Jul. 11, 1926	Oct. 21, 1926
4-10-H	Dobson	William Lee		Feb. 12, 1924	Feb. 19, 1933
4-8-L	Dobson	William Monroe	By Martha and Thomas Dobson	Jan. 2, 1861	Oct. 25, 1950

Location in Cemetery: section-row-grave	Last Name	First Middle (Former/Maiden)	By = buried beside or nearby; other information	Date of Birth	Date of Death
2-6-Q	Dooley	Claud		Unk	Aug. 7, 1896
2-6-S	Dooley	D. L.; Dave	By Mary Dooley	May 1, 1872	Jan. 13, 1899
2-6-R	Dooley	Mary	By D. L. Dooley	Jun. 2, 1870	Aug. 13, 1896
2-8-BB	Dowda	Bell *White*	By J. F. Dowda	Mar. 7, 1862	Feb. 23, 1901
2-8-DD	Dowda	Clyde	Son of W. D. and Julie Dowda	Sep. 14, 1908	Oct. 24, 1908
2-8-AA	Dowda	J. F.	By Bell Dowda	Mar. 16, 1865	Sep. 24, 1902
2-8-FF	Dowda	Ruby Lee	By Clyde Dowda	May 12, 1910	Jun. 30, 1912
4-5-M	Drummond	Cora Bell *Hester*	By George Wesley Drummond	Feb. 2, 1888	Jun. 4, 1964
2-1-T	Drummond	Essie Jane		Aug. 14, 1900	Nov. 24, 1901
2-1-M	Drummond	G. M.		Dec. 15, 1885	Sep. 25, 1892
4-5-L	Drummond	George Wesley	By Cora Drummond	Mar. 8, 1877	Sep. 2, 1941
2-1-OO	Drummond	Infant of G.W. and Texie Drummond			
2-1-N	Drummond	James B.		1830	1890
2-1-PP	Drummond	Texanna "Texie" *Hester*	1st wife of G. W. Drummond	Jan. 11, 1874	Jun. 9, 1913
2-3-RR	Eaton	Andrew Jackson		Jan. 7, 1833	Nov. 5, 1890
2-3-SS	Eaton	Leone	"dau. of J.A. and Cora Eaton"	Apr. 6, 1904	May 21, 1904
1-12-II	Ellington	Annie *Porter* Jenkins		Mar. 29, 1885	Jul. 7, 1957
1-13-HH	Ellington	Frank Henry	By Mildred Ellington	May 20, 1913	Aug. 9,1972
1-13-II	Ellington	Mildred J.	By Frank Ellington	Apr. 21, 1909	Sep. 30, 1986
3-2-OO	Ellis	James Elbert		Aug. 12, 1888	Jan. 3, 1932
3-1-LL	Ellis	J. H., John Henry	By Mary C. Ellis	Oct. 27, 1863	Aug. 26, 1926
3-1-MM	Ellis	Mary Catherine *Haygood*	By John H. Ellis	Apr. 6, 1866	Jul. 5, 1948
1-19-E	Emory	David T.	By Miranda Emory	Dec. 18, 1881	Jul. 17, 1968
1-19-D	Emory	Miranda	By David Emory	Jul. 24, 1878	Feb. 4, 1949
3-4-CC	Eubanks	H. E.		Jul. 2, 1894	Nov. 18, 1916
3-4-DD	Eubanks	Margaret Ruth "Maggie" *Rich*	By H. E. Eubanks and by M. H. Hamilton	Feb. 18, 1896	Feb. 22, 1985
2-5-A	Fair	Infant Children of A. & C. Fair	(Anthony & Caroline Fair)	Oct. 24, 1871	Oct. 24, 1871
3-2-NN	Falkner	Robert		Mar. 30, 1888	Dec. 26, 1917
??	Fife	Daisy	Age 11 months; cert 08736		Mar. 3, 1931
3-6-U	Fletcher	Augusta Azalee *Hester*	By H.K. Fletcher	Apr. 21, 1870	Nov. 21, 1947
3-1-B	Fletcher	George Barto "Bart"	By Rhoda Fletcher	Feb. 3, 1862	May 28, 1932
3-6-T	Fletcher	H. K., Hezekiah Kelly	By Augusta Fletcher	Feb. 6, 1860	Oct. 29, 1926

Location in Cemetery: section-row-grave	Last Name	First Middle (Former/Maiden)	By = buried beside or nearby; other information	Date of Birth	Date of Death
2-9-A	Fletcher	James Sanford		Sep. 18, 1911	Jul. 29, 1913
3-6-V	Fletcher	Janie Bell/Belle	Near H.K. and Augusta Fletcher	Jun. 8, 1910	Feb. 22, 1922
2-9-D	Fletcher	Mary Maybell		Jun. 5, 1892	Jul. 18, 1892
3-1-C	Fletcher	Rhoda J. *Spears*	By G. Barto Fletcher	May 7, 1876	Jul. 25, 1951
2-9-C	Fletcher	Sarah Azalee *Ledbetter*	1st wife of G. Barto Fletcher	Jun. 18, 1869	Nov. 18, 1908
2-9-B	Fletcher	William Herbert		Mar. 30, 1909	Aug. 26, 1911
2-2-HH	Floyd	Amanda	w/o Franklin Floyd	Abt. Dec. 1836	Aft. 1910
2-4-D	Fowler	(Pvt) Phillip K.		Jul. 14, 1832	Mar. 3, 1913
1-2-W	Fowler	C. M.			
1-16-I	Fowler	Charley B.	By Georgia Fowler	Apr. 30, 1855	?? Dec. 1925 Nov. 4, 1925
3-1-J	Fowler	Charlie			
3-5-H	Fowler	Doshie "Theodicia" TheoDocia *Smith*	By William Fowler d/o Edward & Sarah Smith cert 13457	Apr. 5, 1872	May 10, 1925
1-16-M	Fowler	Ellar G. *Gravitt*	By Henry G. Fowler	May 20, 1894	Jun. 15, 1983
1-16-J	Fowler	Georgian Caroline "Georgia" *Campbell*	Cert 10911; by Charley Fowler	Aug. 29, 1853	Apr. 17, 1924
1-17-M	Fowler	Harrison H.	s/o Charlie & Georgia Fowler	Jul. 4, 11, 12 1892 ??	Sep. 10, 1948
3-8-L	Fowler	Henry "Grady" Grady Fowler	Died from injuries suffered during a tornado	Ca 1898 or 1904	Mar. 28, 1928
1-16-L	Fowler	Henry Grady	By Ella Fowler	Dec. 17, 1889	Feb. 14, 1958
2-4-B	Fowler	James	By Sarah Fowler	1797	Aug. 14, 1876
1-5-D	Fowler	Martha J. *Pool*	w/o George Washington Fowler	Nov. 2, 1845 (calculated)	Jan. 27, 1863
3-1-V	Fowler	Myrtle	By Odis Fowler d/o Dock & Ella Hawkins Pugh Cert 23601	Jun. 17, 1903	Oct. 9, 1926
3-1-U	Fowler	Odis	By Myrtle Fowler	Abt 1899/1901	Dec. 1939 (obit)
2-3-I	Fowler	S. A., Sarah A. *Porter*	With W. T. Fowler	Apr. 15, 1839	Unk 9 Mar. 1924?
2-4-C	Fowler	Sarah Smith	By James Fowler	Feb. 23, 1804	Aug. 28, 1875

Location in Cemetery: section-row-grave	Last Name	First Middle (Former/Maiden)	By = buried beside or nearby; other information	Date of Birth	Date of Death
2-3-H	Fowler	W. T. "William Thomas"	With S. A. Fowler	Jun. 14, 1841	Jun. 23, 1869
1-16-K	Fowler	Walter E.		1922	1945
??	Fowler	Walter Grady	s/o Henry Grady & Louella Gravitt Fowler, Unmarked Cert 618	Jan. 3, 1926	Jan. 3, 1926
3-5-G	Fowler	William	By Doshie Fowler	1867 or 1865	1937 or 1940
1-10-G	Franklin	(Dr.) Bedney L.	Son of Mary Franklin	Feb. 24, 1815	Jul. 11, 1844
1-10-F	Franklin	Mrs. Mary Graves *Cleveland*	Owner of Franklin Gold Mines ca. 1830s -1858	Mar. 15, 1782	Jul. 31, 1858
1-9-P	Freeze	C. J. Cleophus Julius	By Eliza Freeze	Jan. 1850	Jan. 28, 1929
1-9-Q	Freeze	Eliza *Jane Johnson*	By C. J. Freeze	Jan. 30, 1846	Oct. 1, 1912
2-3-II	Gaddis	Johnie		Aug.12, 1912	Sep. 15, 1912
5-2-Y	Gaddis	Leslie Lee, III		Jul. 14, 1950	Sep. 11, 2000
4-3-J	Gaither	Ralph Lee Jr.		Jul. 3, 1945	Jul. 4, 1945
4-8-N	Garrett	Jane *Dobson*		May 16, 1909	Oct. 18, 1983
2-9-LL	Gayton	Franklin D.		Dec. 22, 1934	Oct. 29, 1954
2-11-MM	Gayton	Hershel L.	By Maggie Gayton	Apr. 14, 1902	Mar. 8, 1969
2-11-NN	Gayton	Maggie P.	By Hershel Gayton	Sep. 8, 1908	Sep. 29, 1958
2-9-MM	Gayton	Mary G.		Jul. 26, 1948	Sep. 5, 1956
4-5-W	Gilleland	Bunion Vester	By Lillie Gilleland	Feb. 1, 1886	Feb. 21, 1968
4-2-O	Gilleland	L. J.	By Pearl Gilleland	Nov. 24, 1910	Apr. 4, 1963
4-5-V	Gilleland	Lillie Mae *Green*	By Bunion Gilleland	Jul. 28, 1898	Nov. 13, 1989
4-2-N	Gilleland	Pearl W.	By L. J. Gilleland	Aug. 6, 1912	Jun. 10, 2007
5-1-X	Gilleland	Rebecca *Leslie* "Becky"		Sep. 26, 1940	Mar. 26, 2005
4-5-U	Gilleland	Samuel Allen		Nov. 20, 1951	Nov. 20, 1951
5-3-I	Green	Alice I.	By Garland Green	Nov. 6, 1911	Aug. 1, 2004
4-6-CC	Green	Billy H. "Smiley"		Jun. 30, 1945	Jan. 17, 1964
4-9-DD	Green	Bonnie G.		Mar. 2, 1918	Jan. 20, 1983
3-2-R	Green	Elizabeth "Lizzer" *Arwood*	By Thomas E. Green	1853	Dec. 20, 1928
4-9-BB	Green	Emma *Roper*		Feb. 1, 1905	Apr. 3, 1969
5-3-J	Green	Garland Luther	By Alice Green	Aug. 7, 1910	Oct. 31, 1992
5-2-H	Green	Hattie B. *Turner*	By Thomas Edward Green	Sep. 27, 1904	Dec. 30, 1997
4-12-D	Green	Henry Newton	By Rossie Lee Green	Aug. 31, 1883	Jul. 29, 1968
2-13-R	Green	Hoyt Axon	By Vester Green	May 15, 1907	Jun. 14, 1978
??	Green	Infant son of Frank Green		Unk	Feb. 14, 1939

Location in Cemetery: section-row-grave	Last Name	First Middle (Former/Maiden)	By = buried beside or nearby; other information	Date of Birth	Date of Death
3-2-Y	Green	John R.	By Mary E. Green	1876	1915
3-3-Q	Green	Joseph Frank		May 18, 1876	Jun. 16, 1960
3-2-AA	Green	Joseph P.	By Nancy L. Green	1858	1916
4-14-J	Green	Kenneth E.		Feb. 11, 1939	Feb. 14, 1939
??	Green	Mae			Mar. 9, 1955
3-5-X	Green	Marie	Mayree, d/o Henry Newton & Rossie Green, cert 17168	Feb. 17, 1916	Nov. 15, 1919
1-1-GG	Green	Martha E. *Jones*	By Samuel Green	Jun. 22, 1859	Oct. 12, 1938
1-1-II	Green	Martha *White*	"Grandmother Green; marker placed by Newt & Tim Green"	(no dates) *Abt 1820*	
3-2-Z	Green	Mary E.	By John R. Green	1878	1940
??	Green	Matty	d/o Tom W. & Mattie Roper Green, Unmarked Cert 11410	May 9, 1926	May 9, 1926
2-9-L	Green	Maudie	Dau of Thomas E. & Elizabeth P. Green	Sep. 22, 1886	Jul. 7, 1913
3-6-Y	Green	Mildred	Dau Lee B. & Bessie Green	1915	1921
2-9-P	Green	Mollie Elizabeth *Parker*	By Will Green	Dec. 1, 1884	Sep. 22, 1967
3-2-BB	Green	Mrs. Nancy L.	By Joseph P. Green	1850	Dec. 18, 1928
3-4-V	Green	Olin		Apr. 6, 1907	Apr. 14, 1918
3-3-R	Green	Pearl *Smith*		Feb. 23, 1904	May 15, 1994
4-12-E	Green	Rossie Lee *Hester*	By H. Newton Green	Dec. 4, 1886	Jan. 17, 1938
1-1-HH	Green	Samuel L.	By Martha E. Green	Mar. 8, 1855	May 15, 1916
2-9-N	Green	Sarah	By Will Green	1875	1909
4-5-F	Green	Susie Carol	By Wilburn Green	Oct. 13, 1934	Jan. 8, 1940
3-2-Q	Green	Thomas E.	By Elizabeth A. Green; s/o William and Martha White Green, cert 14346	Jan. 15, 1848	Jun. 21, 1922
5-2-I	Green	Thomas Edward	By Hattie Green	Oct. 4, 1900	Jan. 6, 1984
4-9-CC	Green	Tom W.		Oct. 12, 1904	Dec. 28, 1984
4-6-DD	Green	Velma Margaret *Cloud*	By Willie H. Green	Dec. 16, 1920	Apr. 29, 1978
2-13-S	Green	Vester *Gilleland*	By Hoyt Green	Mar. 30, 1914	Mar. 31, 1991
4-5-G	Green	Wilburn Q.		Nov. 3, 1911	Nov. 24, 1987
2-9-O	Green	William Edward "Will"	By Sarah and Mollie Green	Dec. 18, 1874	Jan. 25, 1956
4-6-FF	Green	William Harold "Willie H."	By Velma Green	Nov. 15, 1918	Feb. 25, 1981

Location in Cemetery: section-row-grave	Last Name	First Middle (Former/Maiden)	By = buried beside or nearby; other information	Date of Birth	Date of Death
2-3-L	H. Unknown	John			Footstone: J.E.H.
5-2-S	Hamilton	Cindy J. *Edge*		Jan. 24, 1958	Nov. 28, 2003
??	Hamilton	Lesley	s/o J. B. & Sarah Smallwood Hamilton, Unmarked Cert 6853	May 3, 1900	Apr. 1, 1925
3-4-DD	Hamilton	Margaret Ruth, "Maggie" *Rich* Eubanks		Feb. 13, 1896	Feb. 22, 1985
3-4-EE	Hamilton	Maynard Henry		Sep. 6, 1895	Aug. 21, 1976
??	Hammontree	Sallie Elizabeth Wheeler Price	obit	Feb. 19, 1883	Dec. 26, 1939
5-3-Q	Harber	Richard J.		Aug. 2, 1946	Mar. 29, 2013
3-4-W	Hardin	Harold	son of Mr. & Mrs. E.T. Hardin	Jul. 13, 1915	Jun. 5, 1917
3-4-X	Hardin	Larkin T.		Sep. 2, 1877	Sep. 21, 1916
1-13-H	Hawkins	Sarah M.	Dau John S. and Sarah Hawkins	Jan. 20, 1847	May 28, 1852
1-14-P	Haygood	Annie *Cochran*	1st wife, By James E. Haygood	May 24, 1881	Jan. 28, 1913
4-10-K	Haygood	Edith	By Joe and Inez Haygood	Apr. 1, 1938	Apr. 1, 1938
1-14-J	Haygood	G. B. Samuel Greenberry	By Suseana Haygood	Apr. 21, 1848	Jan. 15, 1925
4-11-K	Haygood	Green Seldon	By Mattie Haygood	May 1, 1876	Jun. 24, 1935
??	Haygood	Guy	s/o James & Annie Haygood	1910	?
4-10-I	Haygood	Inez *Foster*	By Joe Haygood	Apr. 25, 1904	Mar. 11, 1998
	Haygood	Infant, Ch. Advance March, 1911	Child of John Haygood		Mar. 1911
1-14-O	Haygood	James Elmer	By Annie Haygood and Mae Haygood	Apr. 17, 1881	Oct. 10, 1931
4-10-J	Haygood	Joe D.	By Inez Haygood	Apr. 25, 1917	Oct. 8, 1959
1-14-A	Haygood	John Sullivan	By Tommy Etta Haygood	Aug. 29, 1878	Dec. 7, 1944
1-14-N	Haygood	Mae *McClain*	2nd wife; By James Haygood	Jan. 29, 1896	Jun. 10, 1952
4-11-J	Haygood	Martha Jane "Mattie" *Wallace*	By Green Seldon Haygood	Feb. 14, 1889	Feb. 9, 1974
1-14-H	Haygood	Pledger Wilborn		May 16, 1928	Feb. 2, 1931
1-14-K	Haygood	Suseana, Susannah *Mosteller*	By G. B. Haygood	Dec. 24, 1844	Nov. 5, 1922
1-14-B	Haygood	Tommy Etta	By John S. Haygood	Aug. 4, 1884	Oct. 18, 1923

Location in Cemetery: section-row-grave	Last Name	First Middle (Former/Maiden)	By = buried beside or nearby; other information	Date of Birth	Date of Death
5-7-F	Heard	Cheyenne Gabrielle		Jan. 11, 1996	Sep. 13, 2013
4-8-I	Hendrix	Vernie Lee		Apr. 12, 1929	May 12, 1929
3-5-DD	Herring	Emma Elizabeth *Wade*	By Walter Herring	Apr. 20, 1890	Feb. 29, 1919
3-5-FF	Herring	Holbert		Apr. 27, 1912	Oct. 8, 1929
3-5-EE	Herring	John "Walter"	By Emma Herring	Feb. 10, 1889	Dec. 20, 1935
2-5-YY	Herring	Josephine J.		Sep. 22, 1861	Nov. 16, 1906
1-10-B	Hester	A.T., Andrew Thomas	By Eliza D. Hester	Dec. 4, 1847	Sep. 22, 1910
3-1-S	Hester	Augustus A. "Gus"	By Jessie Hester	Jun. 8, 1895	Oct. 26, 1982
3-4-LL	Hester	Boy Cranston	By Zenie Hester	Jun. 7, 1893	Feb. 5, 1969
4-13-M	Hester	Christopher Columbus "Lum"	By Mattie Hester	Aug. 26, 1881	Feb. 17, 1946
3-3-HH	Hester	Dora *Wheeler*	By John Hester	Nov. 25, 1866	Apr. 13, 1937
3-5-C	Hester	Eddie Frank	Son of Thomas & Flora Hester	May 27, 1919	Jul. 21, 1981
1-10-C	Hester	Eliza *Davis*	By A. T. Hester	Dec. 1, 1854	Dec. 17, 1932
2-4-YY	Hester	Eliza Jane *Jefferson*	By Joseph Hester	Jan. 24, 1849	Dec. 13, 1936
3-5-E	Hester	Flora Augusta *Wilkie*	By Thomas Hester	Sep. 19, 1892	Dec. 2, 1966
3-5-D	Hester	George Lee	s/o Thomas & Flora Hester	Sep. 9, 1924	Nov. 14, 1995
3-4-JJ	Hester	H. L.		Dec. 31, 1925	Nov. 12, 1932
3-4-MM	Hester	Herbert		Mar. 12, 1929	Mar. 16, 1971
2-2-F	Hester	Howell Bell		Apr. 13, 1911	Apr. 25, 1913
??	Hester	Infant Daughter		May 1, 1922	May 1, 1922
3-4-HH	Hester	Infant Son	Son of Boy and Zenie Hester	May 9, 1918	May 9, 1918
??	Hester	Infant Son of Thad		Apr. 27, 1931	Apr. 27, 1931
3-12-T	Hester	Jessie *Lathem*	By Gus Hester	Apr. 9, 1901	Feb. 12, 1987
3-3-I	Hester	Jewell May *Porter*	Wife of Oscar F. Hester	Aug. 14, 1900	Apr. 16, 1918
3-3-GG	Hester	John	By Dora Hester	1867	1916
2-4-WW	Hester	John E.	s/o Joseph Hester	Dec. 31, 1877	Jan. 17, 1879
2-4-EE	Hester	John H. "Jack"	By Rilla Hester	Feb. 22, 1844	Dec. 15, 1913
3-4-GG	Hester	Johnie Lee	s/o Boy and Zenie Hester, cert 25238	May 18, 1920	Sep. 24, 1920
2-4-XX	Hester	Joseph	By Eliza Jane Hester	Dec. 8, 1846	Jul. 4, 1906
3-10-P	Hester	Joseph Lafayette	By Willie Hester	Jan. 13 1876	Jun. 26, 1955
??	Hester	Lissie	Age 1 year	Abt 1929	Aug. 13, 1930
4-13-L	Hester	Martha "Mattie" J. *Freeze*	By Lum Hester	Jun. 8, 1883	Jun. 28, 1965
??	Hester	Mattie		Sep. 3, 1889	Jan. 8, 1968

Location in Cemetery: section-row-grave	Last Name	First Middle (Former/Maiden)	By = buried beside or nearby; other information	Date of Birth	Date of Death
??	Hester	Ottis	s/o Oscar F. & Maud Brackett Hester; Unmarked, Cert 17041	Jun. 9, 1920	Jun. 16, 1920
2-4-DD	Hester	Rebecca "Rilla" B. *Cannon*	By Jack Hester	May 17, 1847	Jun. 4, 1902
3-5-F	Hester	Thomas Edgar	By Flora A. Hester	Sep. 6, 1895	Aug. 28, 1936
2-4-BB	Hester	William H.	Son of Jack & Rilla Hester	Jul. 8, 1879	Feb. 26, 1905
3-10-Q	Hester	Willie D. Ardale Jean *Freeze*	By Joseph L. Hester; d/o C. J. & Jane Johnston Freeze Cert 5936	May 27, 1881	Mar. 26, 1926
3-4-KK	Hester	Zenie *Cloud*	By Boy Hester	Oct. 22, 1900	Apr. 29, 1995
??	Higgins	Harriett *Collett*	Info from Page 151 Heritage Forsyth	Nov. 1848	Sep. 3, 1929
4-5-Q	Hill	Earl Elijah	By Ollie Hill	Oct. 25, 1896	Feb. 1, 1961
4-5-J	Hill	Kenneth Edward		Apr. 6, 1940	May 13, 1941
4-5-R	Hill	Ollie Pearl *Milford*	By Earl Hill	Jul. 25, 1900	Jan. 26, 1982
2-9-E	Hogan	Myra *Brady* Fletcher		Jan. 18, 1821	Aug. 3, 1908
4-10-EE	Holbrook	Myrtie Mae		Sep. 16, 1918	Jun. 9, 2010
4-11-EE	Holcomb	Alice Dora *Wilkie*	By S.D. "Bud" Holcomb	Aug. 20, 1884	Mar. 20, 1968
2-2-VV	Holcomb	Canzady *Haygood*	By John W. Holcombe	Dec. 23, 1844	Jan. 1, 1927
4-11-GG	Holcomb	Gladys Elberta	By S. D. "Bud" and Alice Holcomb	Sep. 2, 1912	Mar. 13, 1993
??	Holcomb	Littleberry Sr.	Burial possible but not confirmed (L. Ellis, page 69)		
4-11-FF	Holcomb	Sherman D. "Bud"	By Alice Holcomb	Mar. 15, 1878	Jan. 9, 1962
4-11-DD	Holcomb	Weldon J.		May 18, 1909	Jan. 30, 1975
1-17-D	Holcombe	J. A.	Son of J J and Louise Holcombe;	Nov. 29, 1886	Oct. 26 1905
1-17-E	Holcombe	James Jackson "J.J."	By Louise Holcombe	Jun. 11, 1864	Jul. 27, 1937
2-2-WW	Holcombe	John W.	By Canzady Holcomb	Dec. 11, 1842	Mar. 3, 1917
1-17-F	Holcombe	Louise *Hogan*	By J. J. Holcombe; d/o Thos. W. & Susan Wooten Hogan cert 10555	Oct. 26, 1862	May 31, 1927
1-11-C	Holcombe	Lucy Cathryn *Burton*	2nd w/o Littleberry Holcomb	Jan. 4, 1827	Sep. 8, 1858
1-11-H	Holcombe	Mary Jane Robey Burton		May 27, 1825	Dec. 2, 1848
1-11-G	Holcombe	Robey		Nov. 14, 1848	Oct. 18, 1853
2-6-J	Hosey	Infant Son	s/o E. L. Hosey	Nov. 3, 1878	Nov. 3, 1878

Location in Cemetery: section-row-grave	Last Name	First Middle (Former/Maiden)	By = buried beside or nearby; other information	Date of Birth	Date of Death
3-2-D	Howard	Anner, Melissa A. Southern	By W.L.D. Howard	Feb. 11, 1860	Jan. 16, 1940
2-1-QQ	Howard	Elijah		1812	1913
3-2-A	Howard	Flara		Jul. 14, 1895	Sep. 19, 1930
2-1-TT	Howard	John		Mar. 30, 1866	May 26, 1914
3-2-F	Howard	W. L. D.	By Anner Howard	May 12, 1857	Dec. 9, 1928
2-5-F	Ingram	Martha Ruth *Boling*	w/o W.A. Ingram	Nov. 12, 1847	Dec. 28, 1885
1-17-C	Jameson	Infant Son	s/o J. C. Jameson	Sep. 3, 1891	Jul. 22 1893
4-7-L	Jenkins	Grace K. Wilkie	By John L. Wilkie	1901	1982
2-13-W	Jones	Bonnie G.	"Our children: Gracie, Linda, Jimmy, Shirley, Michael"; By Willie C. Jones	Apr. 16, 1937	Sep. 27, 1998
2-12-Z	Jones	Carrie E.	By Grover Jones	Oct. 12, 1897	Jun. 2, 1988
2-12-EE	Jones	Estelle F.	By William E. Jones	Aug. 6, 1931	Aug. 10, 2015
2-1-AA	Jones	Grover Cleveland	By Carrie Jones	Aug. 19, 1890	Jan. 9, 1969
??	Jones	Infant Daughter of Grover Jones		Mar. 3, 1928	Mar. 3, 1928
2-7-W	Jones	Jerry	s/o William and Lizzie Jones	1906	1919
??	Jones	John Darrell		Jun. 9, 1957	Jan. 11, 1958
2-7-V	Jones	Lizzie Wright	By Wm. T. W. Jones	Apr. 11, 1873	Nov. 2, 1918
2-11-KK	Jones	Michael Dwayne		Aug. 22, 1962	Aug. 22, 1962
??	Jones	Opal	"Age 9 years"	Abt. 1924	Jan. 9, 1933
2-14-CC	Jones	Pamela Anne		Nov. 3, 1971	Nov. 3, 1971
2-12-CC	Jones	Robert W.		Mar. 1, 1952	Oct. 27, 1968
1-6-F	Jones	Sarah Anne		May 31, 1851	Jul. 31, 1852
2-12-DD	Jones	William Everett	By Estelle Jones	Oct. 30, 1921	Aug. 28, 1982
2-7-X	Jones	William T. W.	By Lizzie Jones	Jun. 7, 1865	Jul. 13, 1948
2-13-V	Jones	Willie C.	By Bonnie Jones		
1-16-G	Kelley	Emaline "Emily"		Jun. 22, 1818	Mar. 2, 1909
2-10-BB	Kelley	Eveline "Evie" Leo	Dau. of Robert E. and Susan E. Kelley	Apr. 1, 1908	May 17, 1911
1-13-L	Kemp	Aaron	By Sarah Kemp	Mar. 2, 1779	Sep. 24, 1865
1-13-J	Kemp	Harry/Harvy/Harvey		Mar. 28, 1821	Jun. 24, 1849
1-1-I	Kemp	M. L.	Son of Aaron and Sarah Kemp ????	Mar. 8, 1828 Or 1825/26?	Nov. 5, 1851
1-13-M	Kemp	Sarah	By Aaron Kemp	Jan. 27, 1785	Mar. 25, 1865
??	Lancaster	John Herbert		Nov. 1, 1930	Dec. 17, 1930
1-1-W	Leonard	J. B. John Benjamin	By M .E. Leonard	Mar 27, 1850	Mar. 13, 1909

Location in Cemetery: section-row-grave	Last Name	First Middle (Former/Maiden)	By = buried beside or nearby; other information	Date of Birth	Date of Death
1-1-T	Leonard	Leeane (Lonard)		Dec. 23, 1824	Nov. 6, 1913 or 1918
1-1-V	Leonard	M. E. Mary E.	By J. B. Leonard	Sep. 20, 1848	Jun. 18, 1918
1-5-G	Lipscomb	Laura Theodocia *Pool*	Wife of T. L. Lipscomb	Nov. 2, 1859	Jul. 4, 1875
1-4-D	Lipscomb	Nancy G.		May 12, 1875	Jun. 12, 1876
3-1-EE	Little	Andrew		Nov. 15, 1891	Jan. 15, 1921
4-14-R	Little	Broughton Henry	By Ruby J. Little	Mar. 19, 1910	Apr. 9, 1969
4-14-Y	Little	Buren	By Dessie Little Bell	May 2, 1912	Dec. 4, 1956
2-1-II	Little	Dock Lee	By Lillie M. Little	Oct. 15, 1886	May 7, 1961
4-13-T	Little	Donnie Hugh	By George W. and Evelyn Little	Nov 25, 1947	Jun. 9, 1968
4-13-V	Little	Evelyn *Cowart*	By George W. and Donnie Little	Dec. 13, 1929	May 10, 2013
4-14-T	Little	George Henry	By Maudie Little	Mar. 13, 1882	Apr. 3, 1962
4-13-U	Little	George W.	By Evelyn and Donnie Little	Oct. 12, 1925	May 12, 1983
2-1-GG	Little	George W.	By Margaret Little	1856/ Jun. 19, 1857	Dec. 25, 1913
??	Little	Grace Lawson		Abt. 1909	Mar. 9, 1951
2-1-ZZ	Little	H. L. "Henry"	By Mary J. Little	1837	1908
4-14-Z	Little	J. B. "John Bloomer"		Dec. 3, 1914	Aug. 4, 1959
2-1-JJ	Little	Lillie Montana *Hester*	By Dock L. Little	Mar. 6, 1883	Aug. 14, 1979
2-1-HH	Little	Margaret	By George W. Little	1858	1942
2-1-AAA	Little	Mary J.	By H. L. Little	1837	1921
4-14-S	Little	Maudie Alice *Hester*	By George Henry Little	Apr. 12, 1890	Mar. 16, 1949
4-12-R	Little	Michael L.		Dec. 2, 1941	Feb. 16, 1967
4-14-Q	LIttle	Ruby Jane *Westbrook*	By Broughton H. Little	May 25, 1912	Oct. 19, 2004
4-13-G	Little	S. G.		Feb. 14, 1932	Feb. 29, 1932
4-14-X	Little Bell	Dessie Mae	By Buren Little	Oct. 3, 1913	Dec. 17, 1983
1-18-E	Loggins	C. F., Charles/Charlie F.	Age 45 Yrs. h/o Julia Higgins, s/o J. H. & Harrett Brackett Loggins cert 11268	1876	May 24, 1921
1-18-F	Loggins	Georgia Bell	d/o Charles F. & Julia Ann Higgins Loggins cert 19841	Oct. 17, 1915	Aug. 22, 1922
1-18-D	Loggins	James H. Jim		Jun. 2, 1844	Dec. 6, 1939

Location in Cemetery: section-row-grave	Last Name	First Middle (Former/Maiden)	By = buried beside or nearby; other information	Date of Birth	Date of Death
1-18-G	Loggins	Julie C.		May 11, 1890	May 14, 1961
1-19-C	Loggins	Samuel L.		Jan. 14, 1907	Dec. 2, 1945
1-1-T	Lonard	Leanne, see Leonard			
3-2-CC	Long	Nancy		Sep. 14, 1833	Mar. 22, 1915
4-13-D	Lovelace	George Hallman	By Mary E. Lovelace	Oct. 19, 1909	Aug. 5, 1973
4-13-E	Lovelace	Georgia Ann Wilkie	By Robert E. Lovelace	Apr. 27, 1890	Aug. 24, 1965
4-13-C	Lovelace	Mary Elizabeth	By George H. Lovelace	Aug. 11, 1909	Aug. 14, 2002
4-14-D	Lovelace	Nettie Lee		Dec. 15, 1919	Apr. 18, 2010
4-13-F	Lovelace	Robert Edgar	By Georgia Lovelace	Oct. 8, 1886	Dec. 8, 1938
1- ?	Martin	Josiah/Joseph		Unk	Unk Sep. 4, 1848?
4-14-MM	Martin	Leonard Davis "Dock"		Apr. 25, 1943	Feb. 24, 2014
4-14-KK	Martin	Leonard Eugene		Oct. 28, 1962	Jul. 17, 1992
4-14-JJ	Martin	Lisa Angela		Aug. 19, 1971	Aug. 19, 1971
3-2-U	McClure	Charles F.	Son of Mr. & Mrs. George McClure	Apr. 24, 1933	Jul. 25, 1933
5-3-A	McClure	George "Calvin"		Jun. 16, 1934	May 12, 2009
5-3-C	McClure	George Lipscomb	By Mattie R. McClure	Aug. 19, 1910	Apr. 19, 1979
5-3-B	McClure	Mattie Ruth *Hurt*	By George L. McClure	Aug. 16, 1914	Nov. 27, 1993
3-2-T	McClure	Thomas N.	Son of Mr. & Mrs. George McClure	Dec. 10, 1941	Dec. 23, 1941
4-12-O	McCurry	Jane C. Cannon	By Roy Cannon	May 4, 1912	Feb. 6, 1999
??	McDavid	Columbus	Ch Advance, 6-27-1913		Jun. 1913
5-4-J	McGaha	Cecil R.	By Louise McGaha	Feb. 26, 1931	Nov. 10, 2009
5-4-I	McGaha	Louise *Cochran*	By Cecil McGaha	Mar. 22, 1931	Dec. 21, 2005
2-13-J	McGhee	Michale Shane		Apr. 18, 1971	Apr. 18, 1971
1-7-OO	McGuillion	James W.	By Mattie McGuillion	1853	1905
1-7-NN	McGuillion	Martha "Mattie" Josephine *Wilkie*	By James McGuillion	1874	1951
5-1-B	Milford	Cleo *Heard*	By Robert Milford	Jan. 3, 1917	Aug. 11, 2007
5-1-C	Milford	Robert Lee	By Cleo Milford	Jun. 6, 1915	Aug. 31, 1988
3-10-O	Mills	Loma Catherine	By Thompson Mills	Jun. 16, 1892	Jan. 6, 1985
4-9-N	Mills	Lonnie C.		1900	1947
4-13-Z	Mills	Ollie Kathryn *Wilkie*		Dec. 20, 1927	Oct. 11, 1991
3-10-N	Mills	Thompson	By Loma Mills	1861	1931
1-5-EE	Montgomery	Polly		Unk	Unk
??	Moody	Allen	unmarked?? Info from Ch. Heritage p. 424	1792	1849
??	Moody	Nancy Murphy		1794	??

Location in Cemetery: section-row-grave	Last Name	First Middle (Former/Maiden)	By = buried beside or nearby; other information	Date of Birth	Date of Death
??	Mosteller	Carolyn Holcomb	Burial possible but not confirmed, (L. Ellis, page 69)		
??	Mosteller	Elias/Eli	Burial possible but not confirmed, (L. Ellis, page 69)		
2-6-RR	Mulkey	Bernice D.	By Jesse M. Mulkey	Jul. 3, 1905	Dec. 7, 1985
4-12-W	Mulkey	Clarinda Ingram	By Mandy Bohannon	Jan. 1, 1874	Jan. 6, 1963
2-6-OO	Mulkey	Harold E.		Apr. 5, 1949	Apr. 24, 1996
2-11-OO	Mulkey	James P.		Jul. 23, 1929	Jan. 9, 2010
2-6-QQ	Mulkey	Jesse M.	By Bernice Mulkey	Jun. 15, 1908	Feb. 6, 1999
2-6-SS	Mulkey	Jessie Leon	By Edna Mulkey-Byess	Jul. 29, 1944	Mar. 7, 1988
2-6-TT	Mulkey-Byess	Edna Louise	By Jessie L. Mulkey	Feb. 14, 1929	Jan. 24, 2001
1-1-DD	Nelson	Gilleland		Aug. 13, 1909	Apr. 13, 1910
1-1-EE	Nelson	Nancy Elizabeth	Dau. of Mr. & Mrs. M. Paul Nelson	Mar. 15, 1921	Mar. 28, 1921
2-7-Q	Nix	Annie	By J. B. Nix	Sep. 12, 1857	Jul. 8, 1923
2-5-II	Nix	Cynthia		Mar. 30, 1822	May 16, 1896
3-1-A	Nix	Enoch L.		Aug. 20, 1884	Nov. 6, 1931
2-6-P	Nix	Francis Calloway	By Huldaha Nix (1st wife); h/o Emmer Nix (2nd wife) s/o Valentine & Synthy Smith Nix cert 35526	May 16, 1845	Dec. 3, 1924
2-6-O	Nix	Huldaha *Coltrane*	By Francis C. Nix	Feb. 19, 1846	May 21, 1902
2-6-L	Nix	Infant Son	A Little Son of F. C. and H. A. Nix	Mar. 4, 1877	Mar. 4, 1877
2-7-P	Nix	J. B.	By Annie Nix	Mar. 2, 1853	Jun. 4, 1913
3-5-V	Nix	Landrum		Jul. 31, 1895	Mar. 28, 1925
2-7-M	Nix	Mary E. D.	Dau of F. & H. A. Nix	Oct. 16, 1878	Jan. 31, 1887
2-7-R	Nix	Mary Ethel	Dau of J. B. and A.Nix	Nov. 18, 1888	Apr. 30, 1889
2-5-JJ	Nix	Valentine		Jun. 23, 1822	Feb. 12, 1894
2-7-L	Nix	W. C. M.	Dau. of F. & H. A. NIx	Apr. 18, 1887	Dec. 11, 1887 or 1892
2-13-D	Norrell	Emma Jo	By Williard J.Norrell		
3-1-RR	Norrell	Franklin Odell	Son of Mr. & Mrs. N. N. Norrell	Jun. 10, 1930	Jun. 10, 1930
??	Norrell	Minnie Nancy	C. Milford Diary: Dec. 3, 1960, Mrs. Norrell's funeral	Aug. 19, 1884	Dec. 1, 1960
2-13-E	Norrell	Nealurs	By Ruby Norrell	Feb. 26, 1906	Dec. 23, 1980
2-13-F	Norrell	Ruby	By Nealurs Norrell	Apr. 11, 1910	May 19, 1997
2-13-C	Norrell	Willard James	By E Norrell	Feb. 17, 1933	Aug. 3, 1990

Location in Cemetery: section-row-grave	Last Name	First Middle (Former/Maiden)	By = buried beside or nearby; other information	Date of Birth	Date of Death
2-5-OO	Norton	(Rev.) Wm Samuel		Apr. 16, 1866	May 5, 1903
2-7-I	Odum	Elizabeth *Fowler*	Jane Fowler Cochran and Emma Fowler Cochran; Grave for Berry Odum ?? b 1813	Jan. 4, 1822	Apr. 3, 1907
4-13-R	Pace	Charlie Carwell		1865	1946
4-14-DD	Page	Michael Brian		Aug. 20, 1967	Nov. 6, 1984
??	Parker	Donald Eugene		Oct. 20, 1937	Dec. 13, 1980
3-10-M	Parker	Edna Joyce	Dau of Edward and Fannie Parker	Jul. 3, 1942	Nov. 10, 1944
3-10-K	Parker	Edward Harris	By Fannie Parker	Jul. 3, 1917	Dec. 27, 1941
3-10-J	Parker	Fannie Josephine *Wilkie*	By Edward Parker	Sep. 23, 1917	Jan. 6, 2008
??	Parker	George	Age 70 years??	Unk	Jun. 22, 1932
3-10-L	Parker	Mildred Josephine	Dau. of Edward and Fannie Parker	Dec. 11, 1938	Dec. 11, 1938
??	Parker	Missouri Lively	Age 85 Obit: 1943 N. Ga. Tribune Dec 1943	Jul. 26, 1858	Dec. 29, 1943
5-9-C	Parrott	Steven Lee		Oct. 19, 1955	Jan. 21, 2015
1-12-Z	Pascoe	Mary		Sep. 7, 1817	Sep. 16, 1889
??	Pascoe	Others – unmarked?			
1-12-Y	Pascoe	Samuel		Mar. 4, 1810	Mar. 6, 1887
1-12-X	Pascoe	Virginia Mourning Victoria	Dau. of Samuel & Mary Pascoe	Oct. 15, 1861	Jul. 1862
3-2-H	Pearson	Bertha *Pope*	By Oscar Pearson	Feb. 7, 1899	(no date)
3-5-Y	Pearson	Bertha *Wallace*	By Preston Pearson	Jul. 26, 1900	May 26, 1927
3-2-DD	Pearson	Edd H.	By Nettie Pearson	May 31, 1880	Oct. 27, 1935
3-1-H	Pearson	Eliza *Wilkie*	By Fred Pearson	Jun. 10, 1854	Oct. 25, 1932
3-1-I	Pearson	Fred	By Eliza Pearson; E.F., s/o Ephrom & Nancy Wattle Pearson cert 11458	Jun. 15, 1850	May 15, 1922
4-14-B	Pearson	Jack	By Laura Pearson	Aug. 29, 1878	Sep. 17, 1948
4-14-A	Pearson	Laura *Farmer*	By Jack Pearson	Mar. 16, 1878	May 21, 1954
3-2-EE	Pearson	Nettie R. *Boling*	By Edd Pearson	Aug. 4, 1882	Nov. 27, 1950
3-2-I	Pearson	Oscar H.	By Bertha Pope Pearson	Sep. 28, 1883	Sep. 15, 1918
3-5-Z	Pearson	Preston	By Bertha Pearson	Jan. 29, 1903	Sep.22, 1930
3-1-E	Pearson	Susie M. Green	By Walter Pearson	May 26, 1888	Apr. 21, 1963
4-11-Z	Pearson	Toy		Mar. 15, 1911	Jan. 8, 1958
3-1-D	Pearson	Walter C.	By Susie Pearson; s/o E. F. & Eliza Wilkie Pearson cert 662	Jul. 24, 1886	Jan. 12, 1925

Location in Cemetery: section-row-grave	Last Name	First Middle (Former/Maiden)	By = buried beside or nearby; other information	Date of Birth	Date of Death
5-4-A	Pendley	Arminda Wilkie	By Randall Wilkie	Apr. 5, 1939	Sep. 11, 2012
4-2-W	Perkins	Robert Bart "R.B."	By Sarah Perkins	Feb. 29, 1920	Feb. 13, 1994
4-2-V	Perkins	Sarah *West*	By R. B. Perkins	Aug. 25, 1925	Nov. 6, 1996
??	Petty	Larkin Newton	Ch Advance Nov 12, 1886	Abt. 1864	Nov. 1886
1-11-O	Petty	Major Wiley	By Martha Petty	Oct. 5, 1805	Jul. 3, 1892
1-11-P	Petty	Martha B.	By Wiley Petty	May 20, 1811	Mar. 21, 1871
??	Phillips	Infant	Child of Paul Phillips; 6 months		Jul. 1951
4-10-S	Phyfe	James Samuel	By Lou Phyfe	Sep. 27, 1872	Aug. 14, 1955
4-10-R	Phyfe	Lou Vennie	By James Phyfe	Jun. 26, 1882	Mar. 4, 1957
4-10-T	Phyfe	Rade		Apr. 18, 1917	Jan. 19, 1975
??	Pierce	Bennie		Sep. 12, 1915	Sep. 12, 1915
2-4-KK	Pierce	Ella	???	Jan. 6, 1906	Jun. 4, 1907
??	Pierce	Henry Linton		Jun. 26, 1904	Aug. 1905
3-6-L	Pierce	William Edward	s/o Henry & [Mattie] Wilkie Pierce, cert 8560	Oct. 10, 1880	Apr. 8, 1921
1-5-E	Pool	Eliza A.		Nov. 15, 1854	Apr. 17, 1856
1-12-DD	Porter	Amanda L. *Pascoe*	By Edward Porter, & John H. Porter, likely sons	Aug. 2, 1842	Nov. 5, 1887
1-11-MM	Porter	Cynthia	By E.S. Porter; slot & tab tomb, unmarked		
3-3-F	Porter	Edward M.	Son of Mr. & Mrs. S.P. Porter,	Jun. 21, 1916	Nov. 18, 1918
1-12-EE	Porter	Edward	By Amanda Porter	Mar. 9, 1882	Jan. 19, 1897
3-4-G	Porter	Emma D.	By Samuel Porter	Mar. 7, 1883	Feb. 8, 1962
2-7-B	Porter	Homer		Mar. 29, 1920	Oct. 7, 1932
1-12-CC	Porter	John Henry	By Amanda Porter	Jul. 26, 1878	Aug. 26, 1878
3-1-NN	Porter	Luther D.	By Oma M. Porter	Feb. 24, 1892	Oct. 19, 1917
1-12-FF	Porter	Mary J.		Feb. 23, 1870	Sep. 21, 1887
??	Porter	Patsy/Mrs. Joe	obit		Oct. 1943
3-1-OO	Porter	Oma Mae *Ellis*	By Luther Porter	Oct. 10, 1893	Dec. 28, 1974
3-4-H	Porter	Samuel P.	By Emma Porter	Dec. 8, 1875	Jun. 19, 1937
1-11-LL	Porter	E. S. Edward Sanders	marker says E.S. Poter; by Cynthia Porte (unmarked)	Sep. 20, 1805	Aug. 26, 1875
???	Price	Claton E.; Clayton	s/o Filmore & [Sallie] Wheeler Price, cert 3487	Jul. 30, 1909	Mar. 1, 1920
2-2-XX	Price	Manervia		May 30, 1823	Aug. 16, 1896
???	Price Hammontree	Sallie Elizabeth *Wheeler*		Feb. 19, 1883	Dec. 26, 1939
2-3-LL	Priest	Worth	Son of G.W. & Ella Stephens Priest	Mar. 12, 1899	Jul. 5, 1900

Location in Cemetery: section-row-grave	Last Name	First Middle (Former/Maiden)	By = buried beside or nearby; other information	Date of Birth	Date of Death
??	Prince	Martin May be Robert M. Prince	Unmarked; killed in pyrite mine accident; Cherokee Advance Nov. 1915	Abt. Jun 1879	Nov. 2, 1915
5-4-L	Pruitt	Victor Joey		Oct. 11, 1959	Jun. 11, 2013
3-1-S	Pugh	Ellar *Hawkins*	By James Pugh	1877	1915
3-1-T	Pugh	James V.	By Ellar Pugh *Aka James "Dock" Pew*	1873	Jun. 7, 1938
1-2-FF	Purcell	Benjamin		Sep. 21, 1827	May 11, 1899
1-6-D	Purcell	Elizabeth A. *Boling*	Buried near brothers James and John Boling; w/o Benjamin Purcell	Feb. 15, 1831	Feb. 6, 1853
1-14-Q	Purcell	J. H.		Aug. 21, 1883	Oct. 13, 1894
?? 1	Pursell	Ambusber/ James M.	Bur near James and Mary Pursell	Jul. 4, 1836	Sep. 7, 1857
1-2-U	Pursell	James	By Mary Pursell	Dec. 3, 1797	Aug. 30, 1882
??	Pursell	Lily M.		Feb. 15, 1831	Feb. 26, 1853
1-2-V	Pursell	Mary	By James Pursell	Oct. 5, 1805	Oct. 8, 1876
1-4-U	Pursell	Susan Theresa		Aug. 6, 1844	Apr. 26, 1889
3-3-C	Ramsey	Rice A.	h/o Ann Ramsey; s/o John & Sarah Martin Ramsey cert 31955	Jul. 16, 1850	Dec. 17, 1925
3-3-D	Ramsey	Susan A. Leonard		1856	Dec. 10, 1939
4-11-V	Reynolds	Debbie Odessa		Jul. 21, 1966	Jul. 24, 1966
3-4-AA	Rich	Ab, Abraham Lincoln		May 24, 1868	Feb. 28, 1928
4-13-B	Rich	(Rev.) Elisha Grant		Jun. 17, 1869	May 2, 1941
3-10-X	Rich	Alice E.		1907	1929
4-14-I	Rich	Donnie Huey		May 3, 1938	Jan. 15, 1939
3-6-R	Rich	Hulon Mager	grandson of W.J. and Mattie Andrews	Apr. 5, 1939	Jun. 9, 1939
3-10-Y	Rich	James Oliver		Dec. 22, 1938	Jun. 24, 1939
2-7-PP	Rich	Jeptha Joseph "Jeptey"	Son of L.S. & Ora Rich	Aug. 23, 1909	Dec. 26, 1913
3-4-BB	Rich	Joanna Russell		May 8, 1870	Jan. 30, 1934
??	Rich	Minnie		1844	May 5, 1933
?? 4-13-A??	Rich	Victoria *Sandow*	No marker at this site	Oct. 28, 1874	Aug. 1, 1954
3-4-Y	Rich	Winnie Margaret *Watkins*	"Wife of J. P. Rich"	Oct. 3, 1843	May 2, 1933
4-4-X	Richards	Aaron Isaiah		Jul. 8, 1922	Aug. 2, 1960
??	Richards	Alvin Buron		Apr. 19, 1930	Apr. 19, 1930

Location in Cemetery: section-row-grave	Last Name	First Middle (Former/Maiden)	By = buried beside or nearby; other information	Date of Birth	Date of Death
2-8-HH	Richards	Henrietta *Wilkie*		1869	1892
2-8-KK	Richards	J. M., James M.	By Mary Richards; h/o Martha J Richards; s/o James C & Mary Thomas Richards	Jul. 15, 1840	Nov. 24, 1927
4-4-Z	Richards	James "Jim" Washington	By Myra Richards	Oct. 16, 1889	Feb. 3, 1966
??	Richards	Jeneal	d/o J. M. & Verna Stafford Richards; Unmarked cert 19562	Jul. 4, 1925	Jul. 4, 1925
2-8-JJ	Richards	Mary	By J. M. Richards	Dec. 25, 1839	Apr. 11, 1901
4-4-Y	Richards	Myra Evalee *Fletcher*	By Jim Richards	May 5, 1894	Apr. 25, 1979
??	Ridings	James Eugene		Apr. 18, 1928	Apr. 18, 1928
5-2-M	Rollins	Dewey		1928	1993
4-8-G	Roper	(Rev.) R. A.	By Martha Roper	Feb. 3, 1865	Jun. 27, 1939
4-9-F	Roper	Bertha S.	By Walter Roper	Jul. 26, 1889	Jun. 19, 1980
4-7-U	Roper	Betty Jane	By V. G. and Ruby Roper	Oct. 23, 1937	Jun. 14, 1954
4-9-AA	Roper	Bowman G.	By Winnie Roper	Oct. 3, 1910	Feb. 10, 1961
4-9-O	Roper	Flossie P.	By Samuel Roper	Jan. 20, 1910	Apr. 1, 1999
??	Roper	Infant	d/o Carl & Josie Kent Roper; Unmarked cert 620	Jan. 21, 1926	Jan. 21, 1926
4-8-F	Roper	Martha J. Covington	By Rev. R. A. Roper	Aug. 4, 1867	Sep. 18, 1957
4-7-S	Roper	Ruby B.	By Vestus Roper	Oct. 29, 1915	Jan. 1, 1995
4-9-P	Roper	Samuel Alfred	By Flossie Roper	Jan. 31, 1907	Feb. 25, 1951
4-7-T	Roper	V. G. "Vestus"	By Ruby Roper	May 24, 1910	Sep. 20, 1974
4-9-G	Roper	Walter Rice	By Bertha Roper	Nov. 28, 1888	Dec. 13, 1976
4-9-Z	Roper	Winnie G.	By Bowman Roper	May 17, 1912	Apr. 7, 2001
3-5-K	Sandow	Annie B.		Jan. 24, 1893	Feb. 18, 1920
2-5-T	Sandow	John		Aug. 1, 1819	Mar. 29, 1890
3-5-I	Sandow	John Anthony Jr.		Feb. 9, 1863	Dec. 13, 1918
??	Sandow	Margaret Purcell Boling	Unmarked, assumed here??	Jun. 1828	Unk
4-11-BB	Sandow	Oscar Harrison		Jul. 7, 1900	Dec. 18, 1982
??	Sandow	Sarah E. Rillas "Sallie" Epperson		Sep. 21, 1869	Jun. 11, 1957
2-5-V	Sandow	Sherman M.		Mar. 16, 1868	Feb. 27, 1901
4-11-CC	Sandow	Viola Minerva *Wilkie*		Dec. 9, 1879	Jun. 19, 1969
??	Sanford	E. S.		Sep. 18, 1911	Jul. 23, 1913
4-11-T	Satterfield	M. C.		Apr. 21, 1885	Dec. 19, 1957

Location in Cemetery: section-row-grave	Last Name	First Middle (Former/Maiden)	By = buried beside or nearby; other information	Date of Birth	Date of Death
4-11-S	Satterfield	Margie M.		Nov. 1, 1881	Nov. 23, 1963
4-11-HH	Satterfield	Pauline		Jan. 6, 1911	Dec. 20, 2001
4-11-II	Satterfield	Rufus C.		Mar. 27, 1904	Aug. 15, 1971
4-11-N	Sewell	Bertha Mae Maggie Haygood	By James H. Sewell	Sep. 17, 1912	Nov. 11, 1995
4-11-O	Sewell	James Hoyt	By Bertha Sewell	Mar. 20, 1914	Jul. 20, 1995
4-11-M	Sewell	James Pledger	By James H. & Bertha Sewell	Apr. 14, 1937	Aug. 21, 1937
1-16-H	Sheffield	Wade		Jun. 11, 1912	Nov. 10, 1918
4-12-DD	Shelton	Kimberly Sue		Oct. 18, 1969	Oct. 18, 1969
2-11-JJ	Shoemake	Ila	By W. Roy Shoemake	Feb. 5, 1914	May 16, 2004
2-11-HH	Shoemake	Mamie Lerlene		Apr. 15, 1945	Apr. 15, 1945
2-11-II	Shoemake	William "Roy"	By Ila Shoemake	Jan. 1, 1912	Sep. 30, 1982
2-11-GG	Shoemaker	Vonnie "Runt"		Apr. 26, 1948	Jan. 1, 1982
4-4-F	Simmons	Barbara Anne		Sep. 10, 1946	Jul. 14, 1947
4-4-G	Simmons	Dorothy W.		Jan. 5, 1928	Oct. 9, 1958
??	Simons	Narsisia	Age 94 ? Unmarked cert 14220	Abt. 1826	May 20, 1920
3-2-K	Smith	A. J.	By Lula Smith	Aug 14, 1876	Nov. 28, 1932
1-13-B	Smith	Angie	By Thomas N. Smith	Apr. 18, 1861	Dec. 10, 1889
??	Smith	Betsy	Aunt Betsy Smith; Ch Advance may 1893		May 1893
3-2-L	Smith	Edward Jasper	By Sarah E. Smith	Sep. 8, 1832	Apr. 18, 1916
3-1-DD	Smith	Katherine R.		1949	Nov. 20, 1949
3-2-J	Smith	Lula	By A. J. Smith	Oct. 23, 1875	Mar. 16, 1934
3-2-M	Smith	Sarah Elizabeth	By Edward Smith; w/o Edward Jasper Smith; d/o Wm. & Sarah Fowler Young cert 20690	Jul. 3, 1835 (calculated)	Jul. 3, 1924
2-5-R	Smith	Sarah "Jane" Sandow	?? 2nd w/o T N Smith?	Jan. 18, 1859	Dec. 10, 1899
1-13-A	Smith	Thomas Nathan	By Angie Smith; Cert 7381	Nov. 24, 1857	Jun. 14, 1919
4-10-Q	Southern	Gatewood W.		Sep. 19, 1872	Apr. 11, 1942
4-10-P	Southern	Lillie Moore		Oct. 6, 1875	Jun. 17, 1964
3-11-S	Speer	Emory	??		
2-7-EE	Speer	Ethel		Sep. 4, 1898	Jan. 3, 1901
2-7-DD	Speer	Ida Bell		Apr. 24, 1879	Jun. 14, 1900
2-7-Ff	Speer	Mary Inez		Jan. 15, 1912	Feb. 22, 1912
2-7-CC	Speer	Myrtle Lee		Apr. 15, 1900	Jun. 24, 1900
2-7-GG	Speer	Pearl		Jan. 29, 1906	Aug. 17, 1908
1-7-G	Springer	Dempsey	By Nicey Springer	Jan. 2, 1804	Aug. 3, 1899

Location in Cemetery: section-row-grave	Last Name	First Middle (Former/Maiden)	By = buried beside or nearby; other information	Date of Birth	Date of Death
1-7-H	Springer	Infant of Dempsey & M. E. Springer		Unk	Unk
1-7-F	Springer	Nicey ? Mannissa ?	By Dempsey Springer	Dec. 11, 1839	Unk
1-9-I	Stephens	Daniel	By Selah Stephens	Nov. 11, 1802	Mar. 11, 1852
2-7-S	Stephens	Mary	w/o Larkin Stephens ??	Feb. 7, 1823	Apr. 3, 1902
1-9-H	Stephens	Miley J.		Sep. 2, 1834	Mar. 24, 1852
1-9-F	Stephens	Samuel		Mar. 24, 1832	Jul. 4, 1852
1-9-J	Stephens	Selah	By Daniel Stephens	1799	Mar. 4, 1852
1-9-G	Stephens	William		Nov. 19, 1830	Mar. 25, 1852
3-11-P	Stewart	Ruby		Sep. 6, 1926	Sep. 6, 1926
??	Stiles	Frank W.		Jun. 1, 1933	Jun. 1, 1933
1-15-P	Strickland	Harriet	Sacred Memory of Hairett Strickland, age 65 years	Jan.	unk
1-13-K	Taylor	Martha		Apr. 2, 1824	Oct. 16, 1846
5-5-B	Teal	Lesley Howard		Jul. 18, 1966	Mar. 30, 1995
1-11-AA	Thacker	Emma Victoria *Wyatt*	d/o Joseph & Mary Pascoe Wyatt cert 16550	Nov. 6, 1867	Jun. 7, 1923
??	Thacker	Infant Son	s/o Carl & Edna Cannon Thacker	Nov. 18, 1910	Nov. 18, 1910
2-1-S	Thompson	Jane		Unk	Jun. 17, 1883
4-2-P	Turner	Dora Louisa	By John J. Turner	Mar. 15, 1882	Jun. 26, 1968
??	Turner	Doria		May 11, 1876	Feb. 13, 1939
??	Turner	George W.		Feb. 16, 1931	Mar. 7, 1931
3-7-Y	Turner	Ida Lee		Dec. 31, 1904	Jan. 7, 1983
4-2-Q	Turner	John Julius	By L. Dora Turner	Apr. 21, 1883	Mar. 18, 1962
??	Turner	Mary	Unmarked? Dau of John & Dora Wyatt Turner; cert. 8871	Apr. 23, 1922	Apr. 23, 1922
3-7-BB	Turner	Mary J.	w/o John R Turner; d/o John & Christine Wright Holcomb cert 809	Jan. 17, 1843	Jan. 17, 1923
3-??	Turner	William Beaugard		Apr. 20, 1873	Jul. 2, 1945
3-6-DD	Wade	Gertrude	Mother of Forrest Wade; w/o John Wade; d/o Charley & Francis Bannister; cert 812	1890	Jan. 8, 1923
5-5-I	Waldrop	Tina Paulene *Gayton*		Sep. 4, 1971	Jun. 8, 2011
4-5-AA	Wallace	Annie Belle *Wilkie*	By H. Thad Wallace	Feb. 20, 1903	Jan. 13, 1990
2-2-RR	Wallace	Grady	Baby Son	Dec. 2, 1898	Feb. 10, 1899
4-5-BB	Wallace	H. (Henry) Thad	By Annie B. Wallace	Feb. 17, 1898	May 19, 1965

Location in Cemetery: section-row-grave	Last Name	First Middle (Former/Maiden)	By = buried beside or nearby; other information	Date of Birth	Date of Death
??	Wallace	John C.		Unk; age 72 yrs.	Apr. 24, 1958
3-5-BB	Wallace	Jossie R. "Josephine"	By William Wallace; d/o G. W. Redd cert 22566	Jul. 21, 1857	Sep. 4, 1920
2-2-QQ	Wallace	Linton Eugene		Sep. 28,1901	Feb. 12, 1902
2-2-UU	Wallace	Martha Jane	Wife of J. W. Wallace	Feb. 5, 1879	Jan. 11, 1907
3-5-CC	Wallace	Mary	Likely 2nd wife of W. C. Wallace	Unk	Unk
2-2-PP	Wallace	Nina		Mar. 2, 1903	Mar. 17, 1903
2-4-TT	Wallace	Starlin Paul	Mar. 13, 1909	Mar. 27, 1909	Infant son of J.T. & E.J. Wallace. Age 2 weeks
3-5-AA	Wallace	William C.	By Jossie Wallace	Jul. 4, 1856	Sep. 8, 1944
??	Warren	R. L.	s/o Henry Warren; Ch Advance: 6-26-1914	Apr. 1913	Jun. 1914
5-4-G	Watkins	Delmar E.		Nov. 6, 1924	Nov. 22, 2009
1-17-H	Wehunt	Avey Evaline *Kelly*	By George Wehunt	Jun. 4, 1854	Unk, aft 1910
1-17-G	Wehunt	George W.	By Avey Wehunt	Jan. 26, 1847	Aug. 16, 1915
2-12-BB	Wehunt	Larry James		Dec. 5, 1948	Oct. 27, 1968
4-7-J	West	Amattie "Ella"		Oct. 27, 1884	Sep. 28, 1962
4-12-Z	West	Ellabel *Duncan*	By Jed H. West	Jan. 20, 1935	Dec. 22, 2012
4-7-H	West	Emma Elizabeth *Hester*	By W. Linton West	Jul. 24, 1884	Jan. 18, 1950
4-7-E	West	George Earnest		May 20, 1896	Nov. 7, 1950
4-16-W	West	Hessie Mae *Moore*		May 3, 1920	Aug. 14, 1983
3-1-P	West	Jack	Son of Mr. & Mrs. Emory West	Dec. 9, 1931	Dec. 9, 1931
4-12-Y	West	Jed Hunter	By Ellabell West	Oct. 4, 1954	Feb. 9, 1955
4-16-V	West	Joseph L.		Nov. 27, 1908	Jan. 7, 1973
4-7-F	West	Josephine L. *McDaniel*		Oct. 21, 1857	Jul. 5, 1928
4-7-G	West	L. L. Lightner Leander	h/o Josephine West; s/o Lightner & Sarah Moore West, cert 26550	Jan. 16, 1863	Nov. 30, 1927
2-13-B	West	Michael Paul		Feb. 4, 1966	Jun. 16, 1984
4-2-T	West	Myrtie Estelle *Smith*	By Robert Emory West	Jan. 28, 1897	Sep. 1, 1977
3-2-S	West	Olin F.	Son of W. Linton & Emma E. West	Jan. 25, 1914	Jul. 20, 1915
3-1-O	West	Ray	Son of Mr. & Mrs. Emory West	Mar. 3, 1924	Mar. 9, 1924
4-2-Y	West	Robert Emory Jr. "Bob"		Oct. 19, 1935	Jan. 13, 2006

Location in Cemetery: section-row-grave	Last Name	First Middle (Former/Maiden)	By = buried beside or nearby; other information	Date of Birth	Date of Death
4-2-U	West	Robert Emory Sr.	By Myrtie West	Dec. 12, 1892	Jan. 27, 1965
3-1-N	West	Roy	Son of Mr. & Mrs. Emory West	Nov. 9, 1921	Nov. 20, 1921
4-7-I	West	W. Walter Linton	By Emma West	Feb. 28, 1883	Apr. 17, 1928
4-7-HH	Wheeler	Agatha G.	By Bill Wheeler	May 8, 1922	Feb. 11, 2009
3-14-N	Wheeler	Amanda Ozell or "Ozelel"	d/o Mr. & Mrs. Ernest Wheeler	Mar. 5, 1918	Sep. 2, 1941
4-1-I	Wheeler	Beulah Argie *Wilkie*	By C. H. Wheeler	Dec. 4, 1909	Apr. 29, 1991
4-7-II	Wheeler	Bill	By Agatha Wheeler	Feb. 11, 1922	Sep. 22, 2003
4-7-GG	Wheeler	Billy N.		Apr. 6, 1947	May 7, 1970
4-1-M	Wheeler	Brenda Sarah		Jul. 20, 1962	Jul. 21, 1962
3-6-KK	Wheeler	Bud William Newton??	s/o Cranston Wheeler?? and Eveline or Eliza Holland ?? cert 6848	Unk Abt. 1863	Mar. 1925
4-1-H	Wheeler	Cecil H.	By B. Argie Wheeler	Jan. 10, 1906	May 24, 1984
3-8-Q	Wheeler	Clifford G.		Aug. 22, 1902	Nov. 8, 1942
4-1-J	Wheeler	D. Lanier		Jan. 20, 1943	Aug. 11, 1947
3-14-P	Wheeler	Ernest Filmore	By Martha Wheeler	Sep. 27, 1893	Nov. 3, 1985
3-14-Q	Wheeler	Martha Ida *Land*	By Ernest Wheeler	Apr. 28, 1891	Sep. 6, 1978
3-14-O	Wheeler	Victoria		Jun. 2, 1861	Nov. 24, 1928
3-1-Z	White	Donald		May 1, 1951	May 2, 1951
4-9-V	White	Eugene David	By Floy White	Jul. 2, 1893	Dec. 31, 1963
4-9-U	White	Floy Estell Conn	By Eugene White	Apr. 1, 1895	Apr. 9, 1960
1-1-AA	White	J. M. John Milton	By Mary J. White	1845	Feb. 26, 1930
1-2-JJ	White	James	By Mary M. White	Mar. 10, 1776	Oct. 28, 1848
2-8-GG	White	Manervia	2nd w/o Hugh White	Jan. 14, 1824	Sep. 3, 1913
???	White	Mary E. Smith	1st w/o Elisha White	1860	Feb. 6, 1884?
1-1-BB	White	Mary J. Evans	By J. M. White	Apr. 5, 1841	Mar. 8, 1911
1-2-KK	White	Mary M. Barker?	By James White	May 14, 1780?	Oct. 29, 1853
1-1-Y	White	Mary M. *Wyatt*	By William A. White	Jul. 22, 1877	Nov. 13, 1961
??	White	Paul Outrell	Unmarked cert 19842; s/o Joel & Essie Tallant White	Aug. 25, 1921	Aug. 15, 1922
3-1-Z	White	Ronald		May 1, 1951	May 2, 1951
??	White	Sybil	Dau of Lewis and Pearl Green White; Ch Advance 12-28-1928	1923	Dec 1928
1-1-Z	White	William A.	By Mary M. White	Jun. 22, 1868	Jul. 24, 1940
4-5-DD	Wilkie	Amos Felton	By Flora B. Wilkie	Mar. 16, 1908	Jan. 19, 1972
4-5-Z	Wilkie	Amos James "Leon"		Jan. 27, 1929	Oct. 1, 1996
4-2-F	Wilkie	Annie Frances		Sep. 23, 1905	Feb. 6, 1968

Location in Cemetery: section-row-grave	Last Name	First Middle (Former/Maiden)	By = buried beside or nearby; other information	Date of Birth	Date of Death
5-4-A	Wilkie	Arminda	By Randall Wilkie	Apr. 5, 1939	Sep. 11, 2012
4-12-II	Wilkie	Callie E.	By Hiram S. Wilkie	Oct. 14, 1914	Jan. 18, 2009
5-2-A	Wilkie	Callie Mae *Wheeler*	By E. Dennis Wilkie	Aug. 19, 1909	Sep. 8, 1983
5-3-P	Wilkie	Charlie "Hubert"		Apr. 12, 1925	Jun. 30, 2014
4-2-K	Wilkie	Charlie Marvin	By Gladys Wilkie	Dec. 14, 1903	Jul. 22, 1964
5-3-M	Wilkie	Christine *Drummond*	By Henry Grady Wilkie, Sr.	Jun. 24, 1928	Feb. 14, 2015
5-2-J	Wilkie	Christine Onia *Jones*		Dec. 4, 1933	Feb. 3, 1985
4-2-I	Wilkie	Clara J.		Oct. 2, 1907	Sep. 14, 1963
4-14-M	Wilkie	Eddie Edward Forrest	By Martha L. Wilkie	May 3, 1882	Nov. 1, 1954
5-2-B	Wilkie	Edwin Dennis		Nov. 13, 1905	Feb. 11, 1994
2-6-KK	Wilkie	Elizabeth "Viola"	Dau of Mr. & Mrs. J. H. Wilkie	Jul. 28, 1911	Dec. 31, 1911
5-8-F	Wilkie	Elmer Leroy	US Army, Infantry	Dec. 31, 1934	Apr. 28, 2000
2-9-GG	Wilkie	Elsie Irene	Dau of Ed & Mattie Lou Wilkie	Nov. 16, 1909	Feb. 4, 1910
4-14-N	Wilkie	Ernest Edward		Jun. 30, 1912	May 25, 1940
2-9-FF	Wilkie	Flonnie Myrtle	Dau of Ed & Mattie Lou Wilkie	Apr. 17, 1907	Nov. 19, 1918
4-5-CC	Wilkie	Flora Belle *Wyatt*	By Amos F. Wilkie	Jul. 3, 1910	Sep. 11, 1973
3-3-M	Wilkie	Frances Ann *Green*	By George Washington Wilkie; Cert 10733	Aug. 9, 1850	Aug. 19, 1919
4-6-K	Wilkie	Gennie O. *Williams*	By Robert Lee Wilkie	Mar. 18, 1907	Oct. 30, 1985
5-4-B	Wilkie	George "Randall"	By Arminda Wilkie Pendley	Aug. 29, 1938	Dec. 20, 1978
4-7-O	Wilkie	George Washington	By Rosetta Wilkie	Mar. 12, 1889	May 9, 1950
3-3-L	Wilkie	George Washington "Wash"	By Frances Ann Wilkie	Apr. 1, 1850	May 14, 1917
4-2-J	Wilkie	Gladys Belle *Byers*	By Charlie Wilkie	Jul. 2, 1907	Nov. 24, 1996
4-13-HH	Wilkie	Harrison	James "Harrison" by Ruby Lee Wilkie	Nov. 16, 1900	Jul. 12, 1985
5-1-O	Wilkie	Heath Frank Allen		Feb. 25, 1992	May 3, 2005
4-13-BB	Wilkie	Henry Clyde		Apr. 5, 1903	Dec. 14, 1979
5-3-L	Wilkie	Henry Grady "Cotton" Jr.		Jul. 27, 1950	Sep. 1, 2009
5-3-N	Wilkie	Henry Grady Sr.	By Christine Wilkie	Jul. 8, 1926	Jan. 10, 2008
3-4-N	Wilkie	Henry Lee	By Juelyne Wilkie	Nov. 11, 1867	Sep. 14, 1936
4-4-K	Wilkie	Hiram "Glenn"	By Lula P. Wilkie	Jun. 4, 1877	Sep. 30, 1956
4-12-JJ	Wilkie	Hiram Samuel	By Callie Wilkie	Feb. 1, 1921	Jul. 17, 1973

Location in Cemetery: section-row-grave	Last Name	First Middle (Former/Maiden)	By = buried beside or nearby; other information	Date of Birth	Date of Death
4-3-F	Wilkie	Homer L.		Sep. 14, 1927	Dec. 1, 1995
3-1-K	Wilkie	Hoyt	Son of G. W. & Rosetta Wilkie	Feb. 28, 1915	May 28, 1917
2-5-UU	Wilkie	Hurle	Son of G. W. & Rosetta Wilkie	Sep. 2, 1908	Jul. 6, 1909
4-1-F	Wilkie	Ida Elizabeth *Wyatt*	By Joseph H. Wilkie	Sep. 20, 1904	Jan. 9, 1995
3-2-B	Wilkie	Infant Child; Joseph Brook	Child of Mr. & Mrs. Joe Wilkie.	Jan. 29, 1927	Jan. 29 1927
3-2-C	Wilkie	Infant Child; Buren Herbert	Child of Mr. & Mrs. Joe Wilkie	May 19, 1928	Jun. 2, 1928
5-2-D	Wilkie	Ira Bramlett		Jun. 28, 1942	Dec. 24, 1990
4-2-H	Wilkie	J. (John) Harrison	By Theodocia Wilkie	Dec. 2, 1871	Mar. 21, 1949
4-13-HH	Wilkie	James "Harrison"	By Ruby Lee Wilkie	Nov. 16, 1900	Jul. 12, 1985
4-14-H	Wilkie	Jesse Lee	By Maggie P. Wilkie	Nov. 5, 1893	Aug. 3, 1947
4-7-K	Wilkie	John L.	By Grace Jenkins	Jan. 1897 or Feb. 16, 1897	Oct. 1, 1940
4-1-G	Wilkie	Joseph Henry	By Ida Wilkie	Jul. 15, 1900	Sep. 30, 1980
3-4-O	Wilkie	Juelyne *Richards*	By Henry Lee Wilkie	Apr. 4, 1868	May 8, 1949
4-3-I	Wilkie	Kate Estell *Wood*	By W. Samuel Wilkie	1900	1945
4-7-M	Wilkie	Keith		1932	1997
5-4-D	Wilkie	L. B.	By Maggie L. Wilkie	Jul. 14, 1912	Mar. 24, 1988
5-1 A	Wilkie	Levi Chase		Jul. 14, 1999	Jul. 14, 1999
5-2-P	Wilkie	Lewis		Jun. 17, 1936	Jun. 24, 1995
4-4-J	Wilkie	Lula Pearl *Jones*	By H. Glenn Wilkie	Apr. 5, 1879	May 31, 1962
5-4-E	Wilkie	Maggie Lee	By L. B. Wilkie	Dec. 5, 1911	May 26, 1995
4-14-G	Wilkie	Maggie Pearl *Porter*	By Jesse L. Wilkie	Nov. 14, 1895	Feb. 11, 1980
4-14-L	Wilkie	Martha Lou "Mattie" *Wallace*	By E. Forrest Wilkie	Apr. 27, 1888	Mar. 30, 1945
4-6-J	Wilkie	Martha Sue	By Robert & Gennie Wilkie	Oct. 18, 1942	Dec. 13, 1942
4-11-AA	Wilkie	Myrtie Jewell		Oct. 27, 1887	Jul. 6, 1977
4-13-AA	Wilkie	Oler Lee *Bruce*		Feb. 12, 1905	Nov. 11, 1969
3-4-R	Wilkie	Pearl Elizabeth	d/o Gordon & Alice Mae Southerland Wilkie; cert 17352	Apr. 15, 1924	Jun. 9, 1924
4-6-L	Wilkie	Robert Lee	By Gennie Wilkie	Mar. 12, 1905	May 5, 1984
5-2-P	Wilkie	Robert "Lewis"		Jun. 17, 1936	Jun. 24, 1995
4-7-N	Wilkie	Rosetta E. *Cape*	By George Wilkie	Nov. 20, 1889	Feb. 19, 1978
4-13-GG	Wilkie	Ruby Lee	By Harrison Wilkie	Aug. 12, 1905	Jan. 3, 1999
5-2-R	Wilkie	Rupert Hugh		May 5, 1938	May 11, 2007
3-3-O	Wilkie	Ruth Ann	Dau of Mr. & Mrs. H. G. Wilkie	May 31, 1917	Jul. 6, 1917

Location in Cemetery: section-row-grave	Last Name	First Middle (Former/Maiden)	By = buried beside or nearby; other information	Date of Birth	Date of Death
4-5-X	Wilkie	Shelia June		Oct. 6, 1952	Jun. 27, 1953
4-2-G	Wilkie	Theodocia *Stancil*	By J. Harrison Wilkie	Feb. 22, 1973	Jan. 1, 1957
4-3-G	Wilkie	W. Morris		Jan. 22, 1931	Aug. 10, 1988
4-3-H	Wilkie	Walter Samuel	By Kate Wilkie	Mar. 8, 1902	Oct. 28, 1973
5-4-D	Wilkie	William Lee Broughton "L. B."	By Maggie Lee Wilkie	Jul. 14, 1912	Mar. 24, 1988
3-2-HH	Williams	Amanda Jane *Chumbley*		Nov. 18, 1849	Mar. 7, 1916
??	Williams	Andrew J.	Unmarked cert 3646; s/o Joseph J. & Lillie Little;	Jul. 2, 1924	Feb. 19, 1925
??	Williams	Edith Pearl	Unmarked cert 18934; d/o Joseph J. & Lillie Little	May 24, 1926	Aug. 7, 1926
4-6-BB	Williams	G. W.	By Hershel & Lucille Davis	Jul. 2, 1868	May 15, 1958
3-2-LL	Williams	Joseph Jackson "Joe"	By Lillie Williams	Apr. 8, 1886	Jul. 4, 1935
3-2-MM	Williams	Lillie	By Joe Williams	1884	1928
1-7-LL	Williams	Ollie *Barker*	By Zeb Williams	May 19, 1806	Jul. 10, 1882
1-7-KK	Williams	Zebulon	By Ollie Williams	Jan. 8, 1799	Jul. 6, 1879
4-14-F	Wilson	Chester Lee	By Fannie Wilson	Jul. 31, 1902	May 17, 1961
??	Wilson	E. T.		Jul. 7, 1865	Jul. 9, 1944
4-14-E	Wilson	Fannie *Lovelace*	By Chester Wilson	Jun. 13, 1912	Feb. 16, 1955
3-7-X	Wilson	Infant Katharine Vernelia	Child of J.H & Mary Wilson; cert 6847	Jan. 17, 1925	Mar. 8, 1925
3-5-JJ	Woodall	Alfred "Riley"	By Minnie Woodall	Apr. 7, 1879	Oct. 8, 1954
3-5-KK	Woodall	Minnie Bryan	By Riley Woodall	1882 or Aug. 7, 1884	Jun. 3, 1924
4-4-U	Wyatt	Arthur "Linton"	By Winnie Wyatt	Nov. 22, 1914	Nov. 20, 2008
4-12-K	Wyatt	Billie Buren	By M. Dewey and Bobbie G. Wyatt	Jan. 21, 1940	Apr. 26, 1941
4-12-L	Wyatt	Bobbie Grace	By M. Dewey Wyatt	Feb. 20, 1917	Nov. 22, 2002
5-3-E	Wyatt	Geneva *Cochran*, Florence Geneva	By J. Frank Wyatt	Dec. 15, 1916	Feb. 8, 1982
3-6-W	Wyatt	Hurbert	Unmarked cert 25545; s/o S. S. & Pearl Smithwick Wyatt, burial location reported by family	Sep. 3, 1923	Sep. 3, 1923
5-3-F	Wyatt	James "Frank"	By Geneva Wyatt	Jun. 1, 1914	Jun. 23, 1984
4-12-F	Wyatt	John Samuel	By Octavia S. Wyatt, Third Wife	Apr. 20, 1856	Jan. 25, 1929
1-11-BB	Wyatt	Julie P. *Hawkins*		Jan. 11, 1858	Mar. 28, 1893

Location in Cemetery: section-row-grave	Last Name	First Middle (Former/Maiden)	By = buried beside or nearby; other information	Date of Birth	Date of Death
1-11-DD	Wyatt	Mary Catherine *Pascoe*	1st wife of Joseph Wyatt	Feb. 25, 1837	Jul. 10, 1884
4-12-M	Wyatt	Mathel "Dewey"	By Bobbie G. Wyatt	Mar. 13, 1909	Apr. 17, 1995
4-12-G	Wyatt	Octavia *Smith*	By John S. Wyatt	Feb. 19, 1861	Mar. 18, 1946
4-12-I	Wyatt	Pearl Leola *Smithwick*	By Samuel Wyatt	Jul. 2, 1885	Aug. 4, 1971
4-12-J	Wyatt	Samuel Septmus	By Pearl Wyatt	Feb. 11, 1886	Nov. 26, 1974
1-11-CC	Wyatt	Sarah J.		Sep. 15, 1860	Sep. 9, 1897
4-4-T	Wyatt	Winnie Grace *Buffington*	By A. Linton Wyatt	May 6, 1918	Jul. 29, 2007
??	Young	Rebecca	Ch Advance; 11-20-1899	Abt. 1813	Oct. 1899

Appendix A: Membership Data

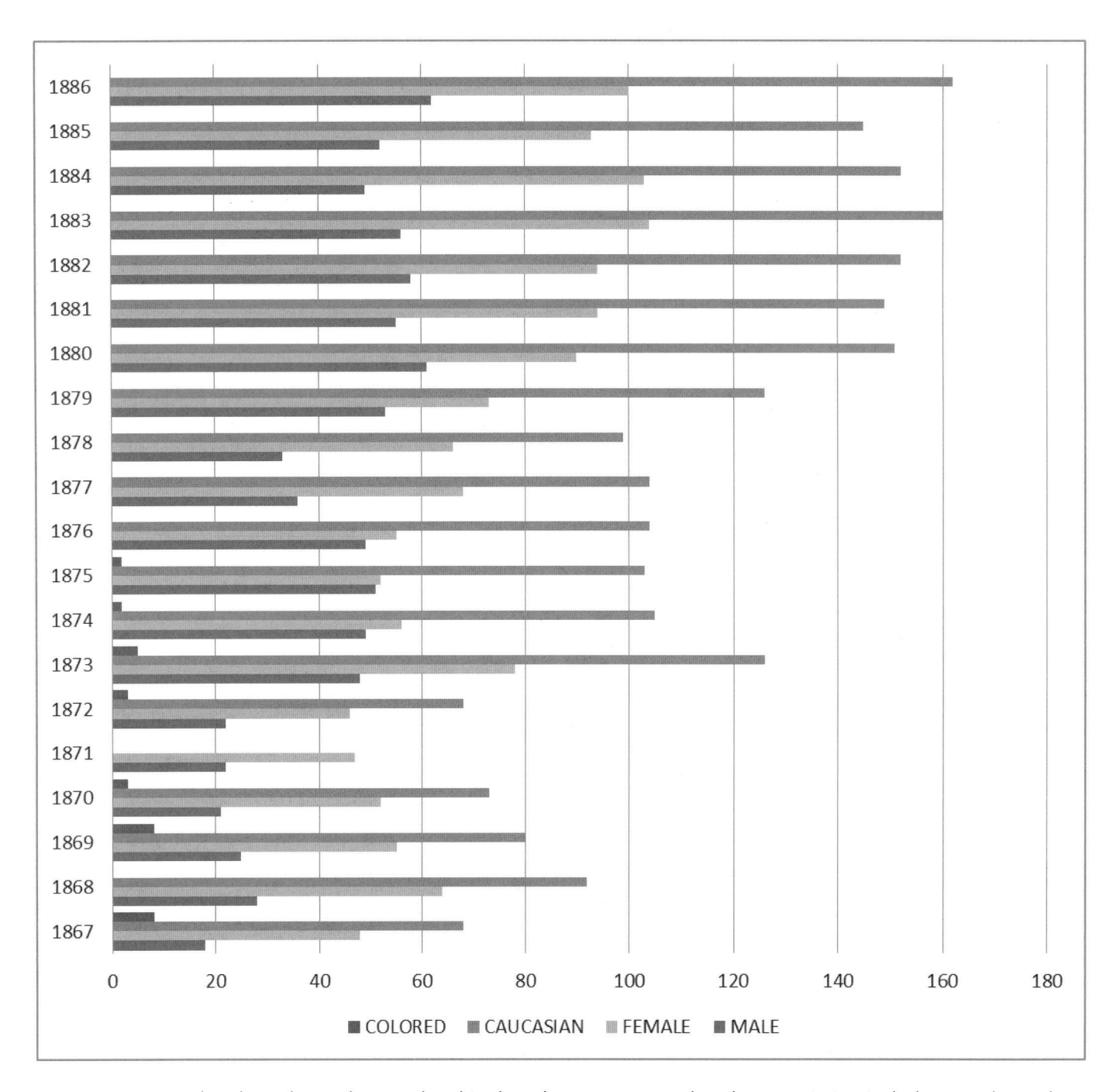

Beginning in 1867, this chart shows the membership data that was reported to the Association including gender and race. It is likely that African Americans were members at HBC from the earliest years, but no data is available to confirm that possibility. Phoebe/Phoeba Petty (listed as black on 1880 U.S. census) was HBC member as noted in membership book 1 (see additional information in Chapter 11: Wiley Petty).

Hightower Baptist Church Total Members

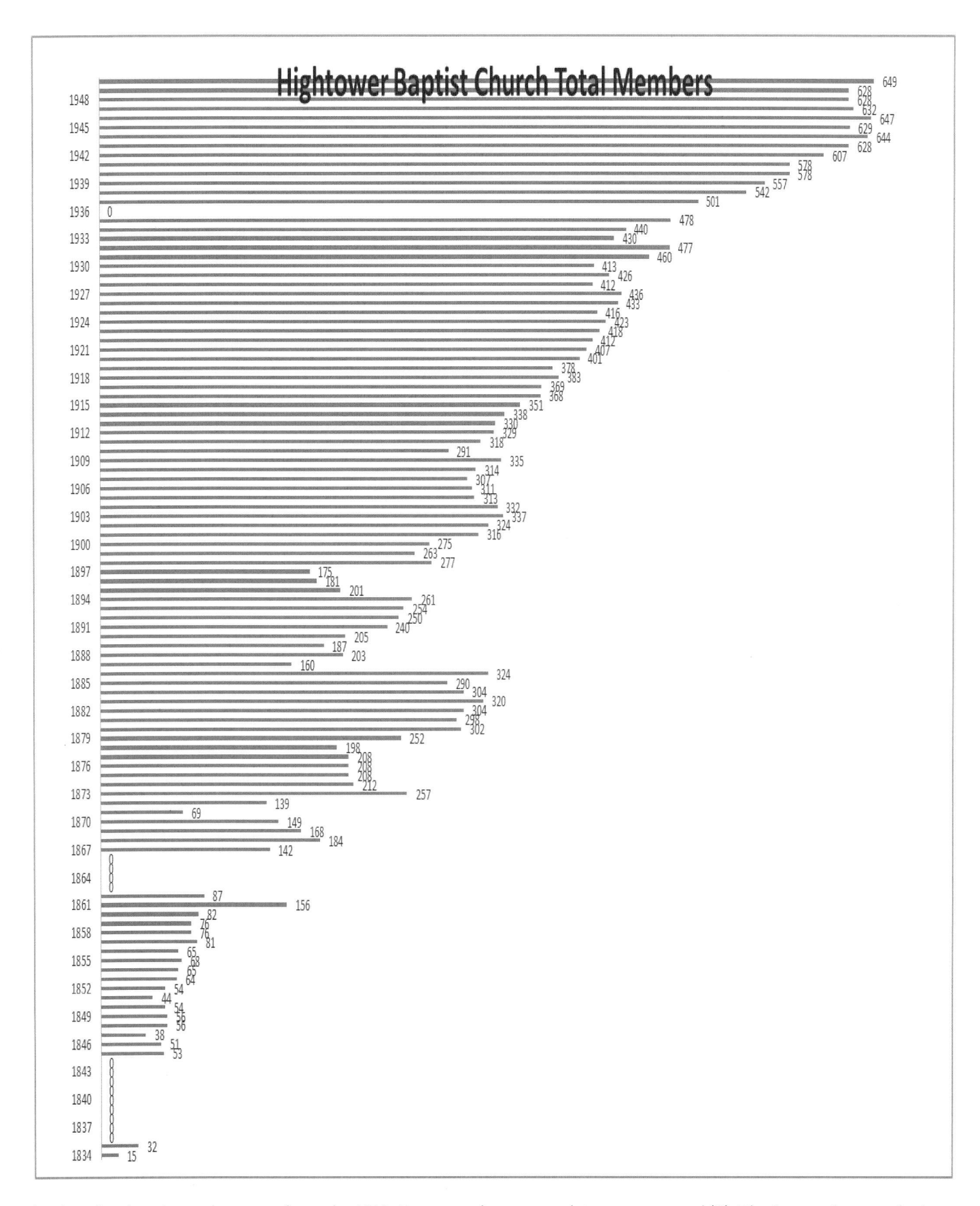

Year	Members
1950	649
1949	628
1948	628
1947	632
1946	647
1945	629
1944	644
1943	628
1942	607
1941	578
1940	578
1939	557
1938	542
1937	501
1936	0
1935	478
1934	440
1933	430
1932	477
1931	460
1930	413
1929	426
1928	412
1927	436
1926	433
1925	416
1924	423
1923	418
1922	412
1921	407
1920	401
1919	378
1918	383
1917	369
1916	368
1915	351
1914	338
1913	330
1912	329
1911	318
1910	291
1909	335
1908	314
1907	307
1906	311
1905	313
1904	332
1903	337
1902	324
1901	316
1900	275
1899	263
1898	277
1897	175
1896	181
1895	201
1894	261
1893	254
1892	250
1891	240
1890	205
1889	187
1888	203
1887	160
1886	324
1885	290
1884	304
1883	320
1882	304
1881	298
1880	302
1879	252
1878	198
1877	208
1876	208
1875	208
1874	212
1873	257
1872	139
1871	69
1870	149
1869	168
1868	184
1867	142
1866	0
1865	0
1864	0
1863	87
1862	156
1861	82
1860	76
1859	81
1858	81
1857	65
1856	68
1855	69
1854	64
1853	54
1852	44
1851	54
1850	55
1849	56
1848	38
1847	51
1846	53
1845	0
1844	0
1843	0
1842	0
1841	0
1840	0
1839	0
1838	0
1837	0
1836	32
1835	15
1834	

The data for the above chart was from the HBA. For several years, no data was reported (0). The interesting trends show above that from the beginning of 15 members in 1834 to the 649 members in 1950, HBC has been a church of steady growth in membership. Charts courtesy of Debbie Boles.

Appendix B: Land Lots and Deeds of Hightower Baptist Church

2015: total acreage = 22.71 acres, being portions of land lots 535 and 536 in Cherokee County, Georgia, 3rd district, 2nd section.

Even though a congregation in the name of Hightower Baptist met for worship in 1834 (membership in Chattahoochee Association) and likely a year or two earlier, the first official deed to the church was in 1845 of approximately two acres.

Deed 1: 1845.

Cherokee County, Georgia, Land Records, Book G, page 544

Daniel Stephens   Georgia

    To   Cherokee County:

Etower Baptist Church

Part of No. 536 - 3 - 2

    This indenture made this fifteenth day of March Eighteen hundred and forty five between <u>Daniel Stephens</u> of the one part and the <u>Baptist Church at Howtower</u> of the other part both of the same State and County aforesaid witness that the said Daniel Stephens for and in consideration of the sum of five Dollars to him in hand paid by the said Church the Receipt whereof is hereby acknowledged hath granted and sold and by these presents do grant bargain and sell unto the said Church and their successors all that Lot or tract of Land containing <u>two Acres</u> (2) more or less situate lying and being in Cherokee County and known by being a part of Lot No five hundred and thirty six (<u>536</u>) and in the third district and second section beginning at the north west corner of said Lot and Running south two hundred yard to a stake corner thence East seventy yards to a stake corner thence north Two hundred yards to a stake corner on the old line thence to the beginning inclosing the Meeting house and Grave yard to have and to hold the said tract of Land with all and singular the Rights members and appurtenances thereunto in any manner appertaining unto the said premises and the said Stephens for himself his heirs and assigns unto the said Church and their successors and assigns will warrant and forever defend in fee simple in witness whereof the said Stephens hath hereunto set his hand and seal the day and year above written and sign in presents of us.

William Boling   Daniel Stephens (LS)

James. C. Coffee, J. P.

Recorded this sixth day of January 1846

        James Jordan Clerk

.....

**Etower/Howtower – Since the church is recorded as Hightower in 1834 Chattahoochee Association minutes and also in 1835 in Hightower Association minutes, it is possible that the reference in the deed of Etower and Howtower were errors in spelling.

Another example of misspelling: Book G, Vol 7: LL 232 and 233, Cherokee Co, 3rd Dist.; 2nd Sect. Feb. 14, 1844, from Joseph Williams to Terrell B. Cochran of Cherokee Co, that land "that lies from the West bank of the Heytower River..." Signed Joseph Williams, Witness: Daniel Stephens and James Coffee, J. P.

Prior to Daniel Stephens' ownership, the following records pertain to Land Lot 536, 3rd District, 2nd Section of Cherokee Co. Ga.: <u>1832</u> Gold Lottery draw to: Uriah Hardman of Butts Co. Ga. (Lucas: 1832 Gold Lottery, p. 215); <u>1834</u> Uriah Hardman to: John Lofton (Cherokee Co. Deed Book D, p. 269-270); <u>1839</u> John Lofton to: Daniel Stephens (Cherokee Co. Deed Book D, p. 270-271)

....

(From HBC minute: Dec. 20, 1913: Moved and seconded to appoint a committee to see about getting more land for burying ground. Committee: T.N. Smith, L. L. West, Henry Ellis, R. W. Cochran.)

Deed 2: 1914.

Cherokee County, Georgia, Land Records, Book LL, page 150

State of Georgia, Cherokee County.

This indenture made this 17 day of March in the year of our Lord One Thousand Nine Hundred and Fourteen between <u>John Howard</u> of the State of Georgia of the County of Cherokee of the first part and <u>The Deacons of Hightower Baptist Church</u> of the State of Georgia of the County of Cherokee of the second part, witnesseth That the said party of the first part be and in consideration of the sum of Fifty Dollars in hand paid at and before the sealing and delivery of these presents, the receipt whereof is hereby acknowledged, has granted, bargained, sold and conveyed, and by those presents does grant bargain and sell, and convey unto the said party of the second part, and their successors in office, all that tract or parcel of land lying and being in 3 Dist. & 2nd Sec. of said State and County and known as part of lot of land No. Five Hundred and Thirty Five (535) containing one acre off of said lot and said hill to commence at the South West corner of said Church lot and running West to a set up rock, 76 feet, thence North to a certain road at the Canton road and there East to the original corner of the said Church lot.

To have and to hold the said bargained premises, together with all the singular the rights, members and appurtenances thereof, to the same being, belonging or appertaining, as the only proper uses, benefit and be of the Hightower Church or the Trustees and their successors the said party of the second part, heirs and of heirs and designees forever defend the right and title of the above described property unto the said parties of the second part, their successors and delivered in the presence of:

L L West	John Howard
H. K. Fletcher	Monia Howard
Newton White, NP & JP	

Recorded April 20, 1914, Robt. G. ?? Clerk

Records pertaining to Land Lot 535, 3rd District, 2nd Section of Cherokee Co. Ga., prior to ownership of John Howard: **1832** *Gold Lottery draw to: Michaelberry Holloway of Captain Williams District of Ware Co. (Lucas: 1832 Gold Lottery, p. 258);* **1840** *Mickelberry Holloway to: Michael Peterson (Book G, p 312);* **1846** *Michael Peterson to: Anthony Phillips; (others??);* **1910** *Franklin Pyrite and Power Company, a corporation, to John Howard*

.....

Deed 3: 1920.

Cherokee County, Georgia, Land Records, Book WW, page 562

Mrs. John Howard to Hightower Church

State of Georgia Cherokee County, This indenture made this 23 d day of July 1920, between Mrs. John Howard administratrix upon the estate of John Howard late of said County deceased of party of the first part, and Hightower Church or the Deacons of Hightower Church and their successors in Office of the County of Cherokee and State of Georgia as parties of the second part.

Witnesseth that for and in consideration of the sum of ten ($10) dollars in hand paid at and before the sealing and delivery of these presents the receipt whereof is hereby acknowledged has granted bargained sold and conveyed and by these presents does grant, bargain, sell and convey unto the said parties of the second part, all that tract or parcel of land lying or being in the third district and second section of said state and county and known as part of lot of land number (535 five hundred and thirty-five) one eighth of an acre more or less lying between the public road and the road leading to the church from the public road.

The said tract to be used as Church purposes and burying ground. The said Mrs. John Howard will hereby quit claim the said described property to the second party.

Whereof she has hereunto set her hand and affixed her seal the day and year above written.

Witness by: Mrs. John Howard L. S.

H. G. Wilkie

Newton White N.P. & J. P.

Filed in office April 10, 1936/ 1930?

Recorded April 10 1936/ 1930?

** *The property from John Howard (1914) and Mrs. John Howard (1920) also described in deed between J. S. Wyatt and S. S. Wyatt dated November 16, 1945..." Lot of land No. 535, lying south of the main road with the exception of two small tracts sold to church and described as follows: One-Eighth of an acre lying between the public road and the road leading to church from public road; also a strip of land 25 yards wide and 206 yards long, lying west of church beginning at rock corner west of the Church, and running North to original rock corner near public road, thence along road to starting point, being one acre more or less"....*

.....

HBC minutes: Feb. 1923, select committee to buy land. Mar. 1923, report on buying land and collected $14.90 on the same. Apr. 1923, collected money to pay off land and H. G. Wilkie to get deed and have it recorded.

Deed 4, 1923.

Cherokee County, Georgia, Land Records, Book PP, page 549.

State of Georgia, Cherokee County

This indenture made this 11th day of May in the year of our Lord, One Thousand Nine Hundred and twenty-three between Georgia A. Lovelace of the State of Georgia of the County of Cherokee of the first part and deacons, successors and members of Hightower Church of the State of Georgia and County Cherokee, of the second part. Witnesseth: That the said party of the first part, for and in consideration of the sum of twenty-five dollars, in hand paid at and before the sealing and delivery of these presents, the receipt whereof is hereby acknowledged, granted, bargained, sold and conveyed and by these presents was, grant, bargain, sell and convey unto the paid party of the second part their heirs and assigns all that tract or part of land lying and being in

3rd Dist. and 2nd section of County of Cherokee, State of Georgia, on half acre of land and no more on lot no. 536. Line commencing at the southwest corner of present church property at ____ lines running south 104# feet thence east 209 feet, thence north 104 feet to start at southwest corner of present church property, thence 209 feet west to starting point, said land containing ½ acre. ....

...In witness whereof the said party of the first part has hereunto set her hand and affixed her seal, the day and year first above written.

G. H. Sandow   Georgia Lovelace

Newton White

    N.P. & J. P.   Mack Sandow

May 14, 1923

.....

Mar. 1947. Motion and second to buy a portion of land from Mrs. R. E. Lovelace for $100.00. Apr. 1948. Motion and second to close the deal on land and appointed a committee to look after it. Names of committee: Lee Hester and R. E. West. Sep. 1949, draw on cemetery fund to pay for land.

Deed 5, 1949.

Cherokee County, Georgia, Land Records, Book 18, page 572.

State of Georgia, Cherokee County

This indenture, made this 16 day of September, in the year of our Lord One Thousand Nine Hundred and Forty Nine between <u>Mrs. Georgia A. Lovelance</u>, of the State of Georgia, of the county of Cherokee, of the first part and <u>Trustees Hightower Baptist Church</u> of the State of Georgia, of the County of Cherokee, of the second part, Witnesseth: That the said party of the first part, for and in consideration of the sum of One Hundred and No/100------ Dollars, in hand paid at and before the sealing and delivery of these presents, the receipt whereof is hereby acknowledged has granted, bargained, sold and conveyed by these presents does grant, bargain, sell and convey unto the said parties of the second part, their heirs and assigns, all that tract or parcel of land lying and being in the third district and second section of said state and county and being part of lot number <u>536</u> described as follows: Beginning at a made corner on original North and South line of lot 536 at other property of said church and running South along said original line 105' to a made corner, thence in an Easterly direction 210 feet to pine tree, thence in a Northerly direction 105 feet back to Church property, thence along the line of Church property and other property herein conveyed 210 feet East back to beginning point. Containing one half acres, more or less.

To have and to hold the said bargained premises, together with all and singular the rights, memers and appurtenures thereof, to the same being, belonging, or in any wise appertaining, to the only proper use, benefit and behoof of him the said party of the second part, his heirs and assigns, forever in fee simple. And the said party of the first part for her heirs, executors and administrators, will warrant and forever defend the right and title of the above described property unto the said party of the second part, his heirs and assigns against the claim of all persons whomsoever.

In witness whereof the said party of the first part has hereunto set his hand and his seal, the day and year first above written. Signed, sealed and delivered in the presence of

Robert L Milford   Mrs. Georgia A. Lovelace

Dewey L Milford *(incorrect last name...)*

John R. Fossett, J P.

Recorded 19th Sept. 1940 *(should be 1950)*   C M Holcomb, Clerk

.....

Deed 6, 1958.

Cherokee County, Georgia, Land Records, Book 47, page 100.

Warranty Deed

State of Georgia, Cherokee County

This indenture made this ___ day of October in the year of our Lord One Thousand Nine Hundred and Fifty Eight between Mrs. R. B. Buffington, Mrs. Winnie Grace Wyatt and Mrs. Kate Edwards

Of the State of Georgia and County of Cherokee of the first part and Hightower Baptist Church

Of the State of Georgia and the County of Cherokee of the second part

Witnesseth that the said parties of the first part, for and in consideration of the sum of One Hundred Fifty Dollars in hand paid at and before the sealing and delivery of these presents, the receipt whereof is hereby acknowledged has granted, bargained, sold and conveyed and by those present the ___ grant bargain sell and convey unto the said part ___ of the second part

…..

All that tract or parcel of land lying and being in original lot of land number 535 in the 3rd District, 2nd Section, Cherokee County, Georgia, containing one acre, more or less, being more particularly described as follows: BEGINNING at a marble marker on the South side of the Canton-Frogtown Public Road at the intersection of said road with the private road leading to the Hightower Baptist Church Road 80 feet, more or less, to the present West line of the Hightower Baptist Church property and which point is 80 feet West of the North and South original line on the East side of land Lot No. 535; thence south along the present line of Hightower Baptist Church property 300 feet, more or less, to the southwest corner of the present church property marked by a rock; thence East along the present church property line 80 feet to a rock corner on the original North and South line of the East Side of Land Lot 535; thence South the original line 210 feet to a rock ?? On said original line; thence West 160 feet to a marble maker thence North 515 feet to point of beginning.

This being part of the property conveyed by Grady Wyatt to R. B. Buffington on July 27, 1949 by deed recorded in Book 18 page 528, Cherokee County Deed Records, R. B. Buffington having ___ died ___, a resident of said County, leaving as his sole heirs at law, his widow, Mrs. R. B. Buffington, and two daughters, Mrs. Winnie Grace Wyatt and Mrs. Kate Edwards, all of who are his heirs. In administration ___ ___ the _____ of R B. Buffington deceased and _____as all debts of said estate are paid.

Signed:

Dewey Cowart ??

Linton Wyatt

Betty Wyatt, Notary Public

Mrs. R. B. Buffington, Winnie Grace Wyatt, Kate Edwards

Recorded Oct. 28, 1958

…..

Deed 7, 1986.

Cherokee County, Georgia, Land Records, Book 508, page 200,

Feb.3, 1986

Between Edna L. & Virgil C. Chandler to Hightower Baptist Church…

For .207 acre… of Land Lot 536

…..

Deed 8, 1998.

Cherokee County, Georgia, Land Records, Book 3407, page 330.

November 14, 1998: new survey of all previous deeds: portions of Land Lot 536 and land Lot 535 to equal 6.910 acres

…..

Deed 9, 2002.

Cherokee County, Georgia, Land Records, Book 5512, page 117-120.

September 10, 2002

Between Conrade Chang and Veronica Chang and Hightower Baptist Church, Inc. for parcel lying and being in Land Lots 535 and 546.

+ or – 15 acres.

….

Sources:

Cherokee County, Georgia, Court House records

Hightower Baptist Church Minutes

Personal notes from Linton Wyatt family and Leroy Wilkie

Appendix C: Military Veterans at HBC

HBC honors all who have served in the military over the years. Worship services near Memorial Day and Veterans Day often include recognition of veterans present. Cleo Heard Milford noted in her personal diary: "Sunday, March 17, 1946 – Sunday School, Special Program for Service Boys, Dr. Tribble preached." Included in this list are veterans who are/were members of HBC, those connected to HBC by family or friends or those buried at HBC. This list is not meant to be exclusive of any known veterans; apologies to any omitted. At least four persons were killed in action: F. T. Boling (CSA), George W. Wilkie (CSA), Thad P. Hester, Jr. (WWII) and Donnie Hugh Little (Vietnam). The last names listed below that are followed by an asterisk (*) note inclusion in a wonderful publication from 2001: *Honoring the Veterans of Hightower Baptist Church and Veterans of Hightower Church Families* by Regina Groover. More detailed information including many pictures is included in Groover's booklet. As stated well by Regina, "There is no way that we can express our gratitude to those who have served their country so that we may have freedom but please accept this heart-felt expression of our love and appreciation for all you did for our country!"

Last Name	First, Middle	Date birth/death	Military and Other information
Boling	F. T.	1842-1862	CSA; bur HBC
Boling	Henry C. Sr.	1839-1910	CSA; bur HBC
Burch	Robert H. Jr.	1920-1989	US Army, WWII; bur HBC
Bursmith	William F.	1917-1976	S1, US Navy; WWII; bur HBC
Cannon	George H.	1923-1958	WWII, bur HBC; Ga. Pvt. Co. F., 351 Infantry, BSM
Cannon	Silas F.	1817-1897	CSA; bur HBC
Chandler*	Virgil	1933-2011	US Army; bur HBC
Cochran	Elias	1845-1931	CSA; bur HBC, pastor at HBC 1894-1895
Cochran*	Edward Watson	1922-2015	US Army, WWII; bur HBC
Cochran*	Elbert	1925	US Army, WWII
Cook*	Weymon	1931	US Army
Cowart	Donald K.	1935-1986	US Army; bur HBC
Cox	Arnold	1939	US Army
Crenshaw	M. T.	1917-1985	US Navy; bur HBC
Curtis	Donald		National Guard, 1978-1984
Davis	Hershel	1905-1966	US Army, WWII; bur HBC
Day	Albert	1949	Sgt. E5; US Army; Vietnam
Dobson	Mark		WWII
Eaton	Andrew Jackson	1833-1890	CSA; bur HBC
Echols	Thedford "Ted" Dewey Jr.	1930-2015	US Air Force, Korea
Edge*	Raymond	1920-2007	US Army, WWII
Edwards*	James Hoyt	1929-1996	US Army
Edwards*	Jay	1923-2007	US Army
Fowler	Harrison H.	1892-1948	WW I; bur HBC
Fowler	Phillip K.	1832/37-1913	CSA, marker at HBC
Fowler	W. T.	1841-1869	CSA; bur HBC
Gaddis*	Leslie Lee, Jr.	1922-2004	US Naval Air Corp
Gilleland*	Edward William	1923-2012	US Navy
Gilleland*	Gene	1939	US Army
Gilleland*	Mark		US Army, Vietnam

Last Name	First, Middle	Date birth/death	Military and Other information
Gilleland*	Roger Benjamin	1933-2015	US Army
Gilleland*	Samuel Alonzo	1924-1997	US Army
Grant*	Jimmy		US Army
Green	Willie H.	1919-1981	US Navy, WWII; bur HBC
Griffin	Clinton		US Army, 1954-56; Army Reserves
Griffin	Ethan	1994	US Marines
Groover*	Earl	1948	US Air Force
Groover*	Rupert Carol	1919-1999	US Army, WWII
Hamilton*	Jimmie Harold	1924-1998	US Navy, WWII
Harber*	Richard J.	1946-2013	US Marines, bur HBC
Haygood	James Lowe	1843-1929	CSA
Heard*	John	1921-1991	US Army, WWII
Hester	Augustus	1895-1982	US Army, WWI; bur HBC
Hester	Gary	1952	Air Force; 12 years in Guam during Vietnam Conflict
Hester	Grady	1927	Army Air Corp; 1945
Hester	Herbert	1929-1971	US Army, bur HBC
Hester	J. H.	1844-1913	CSA; bur HBC
Hester	Roy	1920-1976	US Army paratrooper; WWII
Hester	Sam	1948	Air Force Reserves
Hester*	Thad Pickett Jr.	1924-1943	WWII; "Died in service to our country"
Hill*	Carl James	1922-1981	US Army, WWII
Holcomb	Weldon J.	1909-1975	PFC US Army; bur HBC
Holcombe	John W.	1842-1917	CSA; bur HBC
Jones	Grover	1890-1969	US Army, WWI; bur HBC
Jones	William E.	1921-1982	US Army, WW II; bur HBC
Little	Henry L.	1837-1908	CSA; bur HBC
Little*	Donnie Hugh	1947-1968	US Marines, Vietnam; Killed in action; bur HBC
Loggins	James H.	1844-1939	CSA; bur HBC
Lummus	John		US Navy; WWII; former pastor at HBC
Martin*	Harry James	1943-2010	US Army, Vietnam
McCleskey	P. J.	1943	US Army, Vietnam; 1963-69
McGaha*	Cecil R.	1931-2009	US Army, bur HBC
Mulkey	Harold E.	1949-1996	US Army; bur HBC
Mullinax*	Ronald Louis		US Army, Vietnam
Nix	Francis Calloway	1845-1924	CSA; bur HBC
Nix	Valentine	1822-1894	CSA; bur HBC
Norrell	Willard	1933-1990	US Army; bur HBC
Parker	Don		US Army; Vietnam; 1967-1968
Pascoe	James Henry	1835-1916	CSA
Pascoe	Samuel	1810-1887	CSA; bur HBC
Pearson	Toy	1911-1958	Pvt. Co. L 212 Infantry, WWII, bur HBC

Last Name	First, Middle	Date birth/death	Military and Other information
Perkins*	R. B.	1920-1994	US Army, WWII; bur HBC
Petty	Wiley	1805-1892	CSA; bur HBC
Pickett	Rev. Thaddeus	1845-1909	CSA and Union? pastor of HBC, 1884-1885
Pinyan	Oscar "Stanley"	1945	US Army (1966-1968)
Price	James Lanier	1925-2014	US Army
Price*	Ronny	1951	US Army, National Guard
Pruitt	Billy		US Navy
Pruitt*	Gene	1934	US Army
Purcell	B. Benjamin?	1827-1899	CSA; bur HBC
Ray*	C. J.	1924-1998	US Navy, WWII
Ray*	Johnny Charles	1947-1978	US Army, Vietnam
Ray*	W. C. (Bill)	1926-1999	US Navy, WWII
Richards	Aaron I.	1922-1960	US Army, WWII; bur HBC
Richards	J. M.	1840-1927	CSA; bur HBC
Rogers	Ray	1948	US Army, Vietnam; 1968-70
Rucker*	Horace William	1921-1993	US Navy, WWII
Sandow	John	1819-1890	CSA; bur HBC
Sheffield	Absolom H.	1848-1900	CSA; pastor of HBC,1886-1887
Shoemake	Vonnie "Runt"	1948-1982	US Army, Vietnam; bur HBC
Smith	Edward Jasper	1832-1916	CSA; bur HBC
Smith*	Edsel	1926-1992	US Army
Thompson	Bryce	1992	US Army
Thompson	John	1965	US Army
Turner*	Thomas Estee	1915-1989	US Army
Vecchione*	Mark	1946	US Army, Germany, 1968-69
Watkins	Lester J.	1933-2014	US Army, Korea
Watkins*	Delmar Edward	1924-2009	US Navy, WWII; bur HBC
Wehunt	George	1847-1915	Union Soldier; bur HBC
West	George Earnest	1896-1950	US Army, WWI; bur HBC
West*	Edward E.		US Army, WWII
West*	Frank B.		US Army, WWII
West*	Grady Earl	1950-2009	US Army
West*	Paul Hunter	1922-	US Army, WWII
West*	Robert	1920-2003	US Army, WWII
West	Robert "Emory" Sr.	1892-1965	US Army, WWI
Wheeler	Billy N.	1947-1970	US Army, Vietnam; bur HBC
Wheeler*	Gene	1937	US Army, National Guard
Wheeler*	Kurt	1963	US Air Force
White	J. M. (John M.)	1845-1930	CSA; bur HBC
Wilkie	George W. (William?)	1827-1863	CSA; killed and buried in Vicksburg, MS
Wilkie	Glenn W.		Army Air Corp., WWII
Wilkie	Henry Grady Sr.	1926-2008	Pvt. US Army; WWII; bur HBC
Wilkie	Hiram Samuel	1921-1973	TEC 5 US Army; WWII; bur HBC

Last Name	First, Middle	Date birth/death	Military and Other information
Wilkie	Homer L.	1927-1995	US Army, Korea; bur HBC
Wilkie	Ira B.	1942-1990	US Army; bur HBC
Wilkie	John L.	1897-1940	US Army; bur HBC
Wilkie	Justin	1980	US Army; Afghanistan; 2007-2014
Wilkie	Wesley Lamar	1968	Corp. US Marine Corp
Wilkie*	Charlie Hubert	1925-2014	US Navy, WWII
Wilkie*	Elmer Leroy	1934-2000	US Army
Wilkie*	Myron D.	1933	US Army, Korea
Wilkie*	Robert "Lamar"	1939-2012	US Army, Korea
Williams	Joel	1841-1862	CSA
Williams	John Lewis	1835-1913	CSA
Williams	Joseph Washington	1828-1910	CSA
Wright	Henry Fleming	1919-1983	US Army, WWII
Wolf*	Phillip Aubrey	1948-2013	US Marines, Vietnam

Appendix D: Identification of persons named on stained glass windows

HBC installed the beautiful stained glass windows in 1973. The windows are a wonderful addition to the atmosphere of the sanctuary and each has an inscription at the bottom with names of those honored or remembered at this church. The initial purchase included eight windows and two small transoms over the doors to the porch. Upon the extension of the church in the early 1990s, two additional windows were added to each side to total twelve.

On approach to the church on the front steps, entering the doorway on the left, the window above the door is noted in memory of "George David Wilkie." A walk down the aisle toward the altar finds windows from the left numbered one through six. Across the altar and proceeding toward the other entry door is number seven through twelve, with the window over that doorway labeled "Mr. and Mrs. J. H. Wilkie." An effort to identify the name of each person or family and locate their pictures proved difficult, but below is a brief sketch about each person or family and pictures that were submitted.

Left Doorway: **George David Wilkie**

Photo courtesy of Joyce Odom

"David" Wilkie was born on January 8, 1950 to George "Spencer" and Fayceil Victoria "Pete" Turner Wilkie. Due to a tragic auto accident, David lost his life on February 14, 1967. In addition to his parents, he was also survived by two sisters. His grandparents were John Harrison and Theodocia Stancil Wilkie, and Andrew Jackson and Harriet Victoria White Turner. David was buried at the Smith-Lathem Cemetery in Free Home.

1 **John Heard Family; Robert Milford Family**

Photo courtesy of Thomas Heard

John Heard Family

John Heard (son of Joel and Birddie Heard) was born January 30, 1921, married on September 7, 1946 to Alice Geneva Wilson. Their wedding was one of the first church weddings of the Lathemtown community and was held at Orange Methodist Church in a double ceremony with Mary Loyce Lathem and Hamrick W. Smith. John joined HBC by experience in July of 1934. Geneva joined HBC by letter in 1965. John and Geneva were parents to three children and lived most of their lives in either Lathemtown or Holbrook

Campground communities. John and Geneva are buried at Sawnee View Memorial Gardens in Cumming, Ga. The Heard's share the nameplate on this window with John's sister and brother-in-law, Cleo and Robert Milford.

Robert Milford Family

Robert Lee Milford (son of John and Mary Milford) was born June 6, 1915 and married on October 7, 1939 to Cleo Heard, born January 3, 1917 (daughter of Joel and Birddie Heard). The marriage was performed by Rev. J. Samuel Cochran at his home in Nelson, Georgia. Robert and Cleo lived with the John R. Milford family in Ball Ground, Ga. until Robert could "finish the crops that fall" and then moved into their home in Free Home, the former Lightner West family home. Cleo joined HBC in 1929 and after their marriage, Robert transferred his membership from Conns Creek BC in 1940. The couple became parents to four children. Robert died on August 31, 1988 and Cleo continued to live in the family home until her death on August 11, 2007. They are both buried at HBC.

2 **Elbert Cochran Family; Buck and Jessie Pruitt**

Elbert and Izell Cochran

Photo of Mr. and Mrs. Cochran, courtesy of granddaughter, Amanda Tomolavage

Elbert Cochran was born to Elisha and Jennie Cochran of Free Home on Feb. 14, 1925. He married Izell Holbrook. Elbert joined HBC and was baptized in August of 1938. Izelle Cochran later joined HBC by transfer of letter from New Harmony BC. Elbert and Izell are parents to four children and live in the Free Home community.

Buck and Jessie Pruitt

Jessie Heard, daughter of Joel and Birddie Heard was born March 23, 1914. She joined HBC and was baptized in 1928. She married J. C. "Buck" Pruitt who joined HBC in 1943. Buck and Jessie became parents to three sons and lived most of their lives on Highway 20 just east of Free Home School. Buck and Jessie are buried at Holbrook Campground Cemetery.

3 **LeRoy C. Pendley and Berline O. Pendley**

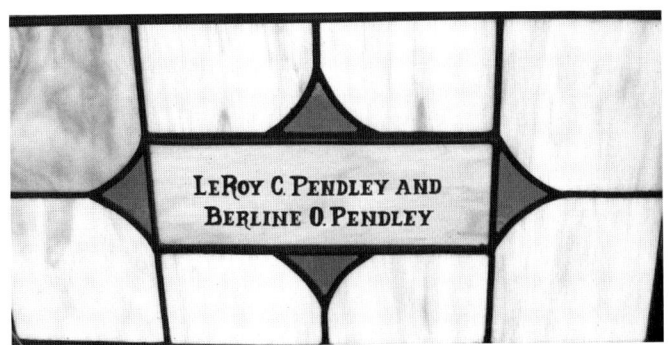

Leroy Pendley was born on August 12, 1916. He married Berline Orr who was born on April 7, 1919. LeRoy and Berline lived in the Free Home community for many years and became parents to one child. LeRoy died on July 7, 1972 and is buried at Haw Creek Cemetery in Cumming, Ga. His tombstone inscription says "He loved everybody." Berline passed away on July 18, 2003 and is also buried at Haw Creek.

4 **Elisha F. and Jennie C. Cochran**

Elisha and Jennie Cochran

Photo courtesy of Brenda Curtis

Elisha Franklin Cochran, born March 22, 1884, was the son of Wiley Franklin and Eliza Jane Howell Cochran. Elisha married Jennie Cape on November 9, 1913. Jennie was born on August 12, 1895 to William and Mary Hawkins Cape. Elisha and Jennie became parents to eight children. Elisha (death: December 27, 1970) and Jennie (death: May 3, 1971) are buried at HBC.

5 **C. H. Wheeler family**

C. H. and Argie Wheeler

Photo courtesy of Gene Wheeler

Cecil H. Wheeler was born on January 10, 1906 to General M. and Caroline "Callie" Purcell Wheeler. Cecil married Beulah "Argie" Wilkie daughter of J. Harrison and Theodocia Stancil Wilkie. Argie was born on December 4, 1909. Cecil and Argie became parents to five children, four sons and one daughter. Cecil passed away on May 24, 1984 and Argie died on April 28, 1991 and they are both buried at HBC.

6 **Joel A. and Birddie G. Heard; Lee and Emma Hester**

Joel A. and Birddie Heard

Joel Heard was born in Forsyth Co. on May 22, 1886 to John Arch and Sallie Harrison Heard. On September 13, 1908, Joel married Birddie Julie Godfrey. Birddie was born on December 19, 1887 to Elbert C. and Mattie Rives Godfrey. The Heard's moved to Lathemtown in the early 1920s where they raised their seven children and attended HBC. They transferred their church memberships from Coal Mountain BC to HBC in February, 1931. Mr. Joel passed away on February 18, 1968 and Birddie died on May 14, 1972. They are buried near their son, Arch (1909-1933) at Coal Mountain Cemetery in Forsyth County, Ga.

Lee and Emma Hester

Photo courtesy of Regina Groover

On September 22, 1889, Lee H. Hester was born to John H. "Jack" and Rebecca "Rilla" Cannon Hester. Lee joined HBC and was baptized in 1910. On February 26, 1896, Emma Mae Whitfield was born in Dawson County, Georgia. Lee and Emma married on April 17, 1912 in Cherokee County, Ga. She joined HBC by letter in 1913. They lived near Coker's Chapel and attended both Liberty and Hightower churches when their children were young. Lee and Emma were blessed with eight children, seven who lived into adulthood. Emma preceded Lee in death, passing away on January 26, 1977. Lee died on February 4, 1987 and both are buried at Macedonia Cemetery.

7 Robert Emory and Myrtie S. West

Robert Emory and Myrtie West

Photo courtesy of Tim Perkins

Robert "Emory" West Sr., born December 12, 1892 was the son of Lightner L. and Josephine McDaniel West. Myrtie E. Smith was born to Thomas N. and Jane Smith on January 28, 1897. Emory and Myrtie married and had several children, at least three who died in infancy. Mr. Emory was well known as the owner and operator of Free Home/West and Perkins General Store for many years. Emory died on January 27, 1965 followed by Myrtie on September 1, 1977. Both are buried in HBC cemetery.

8 Bunion Gilleland Family; Amos Wilkie Family

Bunion and Lillie Gilleland

Photo courtesy of Mitzi Chambers

The Bunion Gilleland and Amos Wilkie families were neighbors in their later years and a daughter of the Gilleland's married a son of the Wilkie's.

Mr. Bunion/Bunyon Vester Gilleland was born on February 1, 1886, in Dawson County Georgia. In 1906, he married Levada Mae Redd and they became parents to six children: Esco, L. J., Vester, Juanita, Lucille and Helen Grace. After Levada's untimely death in 1921, Bunion married on April 30, 1922, to Lillie Mae Green (born 1896), daughter of William and Mollie Green. Bunion and Lillie became parents to eight children: Ed, Sam, Dorothy, Mary, Walt, Roger, Atholine and Gene. Bunion died on February 21, 1968, and Lillie lived as a widow for 21 years before her passing in 1989. Both are buried at HBC.

Amos and Bell Wilkie

Photo courtesy of Mitzi Chambers and Eula McIntosh

Mr. Amos Felton Wilkie was born on March 16, 1908, in Cherokee County to Hiram Glenn and Lula Pearl Jones Wilkie. On January 28, 1928, he married Flora Belle Wyatt (daughter of Bart and Ida Hester Wyatt) who was born July 3, 1910. Amos and Belle had the following children: Leon, Frances, Leroy, Betty, Lamar, Eula, Effie and Linda. Amos died on January 19, 1972, and the following year, Belle passed away on September 11, 1973. Amos and Belle are buried at HBC.

9 Robert Edd and Georgia Ann Lovelace

Edd and Georgia Ann Lovelace

Photo courtesy of Chris Chandler

Robert Edgar Lovelace was born October 8, 1886 to W. J. and India Lovelace of Lumpkin County, Ga. Georgia Ann Wilkie, daughter of George Washington and Francis Green Wilkie, was born on April 26, 1890. These two were married on December 16, 1906 and became parents to one son and four daughters. The Lovelace home was just east of the HBC property. Edd Lovelace died on December 8, 1938. Georgia Ann lived in the family home until her death on August 24, 1965. They are buried at HBC.

10 Walter R. and Bertha H. Roper

Walter Rice Roper was born on November 28, 1888 to Rev. Robert A. and Martha Jane Covington Roper. Walt was one of nine children born to Preacher Roper and his wife, Martha. Preacher Roper served HBC as pastor for about fifteen years, 1921-1946. Walter married on August 23, 1909 to Bertha Holcomb (born on July 26, 1889). Walter and Bertha had at least six children including Ruby, Gladys, Wynelle, Robert, Clara Mae and Dean. In their later years, they lived on Ball Ground Road near Free Home. Walter died December 13, 1976 and Bertha on June 19, 1980 and both are buried at HBC.

11 Carl J. Hill Family; Ronald Mullinax Family

Carl Hill Family

Photo courtesy of Billy Hill

Carl James Hill and Hazel Reinhardt Hill transferred membership to HBC in 1969. Carl and Hazel were married in 1946 and became parents to three sons. Carl was born on October 1, 1922, and died on May 24, 1981. Hazel was born on August 24, 1928, and passed away on January 30, 2012. Carl and Hazel are buried at Oakdale BC Cemetery in Canton.

Ron and Carol Mullinax

Photo courtesy of Carol Mullinax

Ron and Carol transferred their membership to HBC in 1990s and are the parents of two children. They continue to be active members of HBC.

12 Edsel and Willie Mae Smith; Clinton and Gladys Griffin

Edsel and Willie Mae Smith

Photo courtesy of Gladys Griffin

Edsel Smith was born on November 29, 1926. Edsel joined HBC by a transfer of letter in 1952. Willie Mae Andrews was born on May 25, 1928 and joined HBC by experience and was baptized in 1940. Edsel and Willie Mae lived in Forsyth County, Georgia, and became parents to one daughter. Edsel passed away on September 28, 1992 and Willie Mae later died on October 15, 1998. Both are buried at Sawnee View Memorial Gardens in Cumming, Georgia.

Clinton and Gladys Griffin

Photo courtesy of Gladys Griffin

Gladys Andrews Griffin and her husband Clinton share the inscription on this window with Gladys' sister and brother-in-law Willie Mae Andrews and Edsel Smith. Gladys joined HBC and was baptized in 1951. Clinton joined by letter in 1975.

Right Doorway

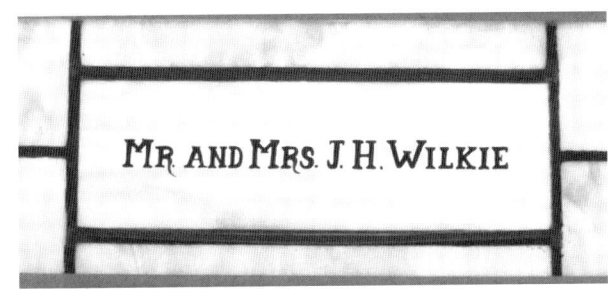

Mr. and Mrs. J. H. Wilkie

Records pertaining to the stained glass windows are scarce thus proper identification of J. H. Wilkie proved difficult. Possibilities include John Harrison Wilkie (1871-1949), Joseph Henry Wilkie (1900-1980) and James Harrison Wilkie (1900-1985). Descendants reported that likely Spencer Wilkie and Argie Wilkie Wheeler were responsible for the window in honor and memory of their parents, John Harrison and Theodocia Stancil Wilkie, who are pictured below. John "Harrison" was a son of Wash and Francis Wilkie. Harrison and Theodocia were parents to Jesse Lee (1893-1947), Glenn (1895-1896), Arthur (1899-1977), Joseph Henry (1900-1980), Walter Samuel (1902-1973), Charlie Marvin (1903-1964), Annie (1905-1963), Clara (1907-1963), Argie (1909-1991), Elizabeth Viola (1911-1911) and George Spencer (1913-1974).

Theodocia and Harrison Wilkie

Photo courtesy of Joyce Odom

Reference list

Bottoms, Roy E. "Saint Andrews Chapel Cemetery, Cherokee County, Georgia: Located Near the Old Franklin Gold Mine." *North West Georgia Historical and Genealogical Society, Vol nine; Number one*, January 1977.

Campbell J. H., *Georgia Baptists: Historical and Biographical.* Perry, GA: J. W. Burke ad Company, 1874. Digital Version; At various libraries (WorldCat).

Carver, John. *Bivouac of the Dead Confederate Soldiers of Cherokee County, Georgia.* 2008.

Carver, John. *Cherokee County, Georgia; In Days Gone By.* Jasper, GA: Wheeler Printing Co. 2011.

Cashin, Edward J. ed. *A Wilderness Still, The Cradle of Nature: Frontier Georgia.* Savannah Ga. 1994.

Chalcedonia Baptist Church Minutes, 1873-1893, R. T. Jones Memorial Library, Canton GA.

Chattahoochee Baptist Association Minutes, *1833-1980.* Chattahoochee Baptist Association, Gainesville, GA.

Cherokee County Civil War Sesquicentennial Committee. *Cherokee County Voices from the Civil War.* Canton, GA: Cherokee County Historical and Genealogical Society, 2014.

Cherokee County Heritage Book Committee. *The Heritage of Cherokee County.* Walsworth Publshing Co, 1998.

Cherokee County Historical Society. *Glimpses of Cherokee County.* Canton, GA, 1981.

Chupp, D. *History of First Baptist Church of Canton, Georgia 1833-1983.* Canton, GA: First Baptist Church, 1983.

Cissell, Mary Helen. *Living, Laughing, Loving in Old Lathemtown: A Collection of Oral Histories of Lathemtown, Free Home, and Orange, Georgia.* Canton, GA: Orange United Methodist Women, 2008.

Coal Mt. Baptist Church Historical Committee. *Building a Firm Foundation: History of Coal Mountain Baptist Church.* Roswell: Wolfe Publishing, 1989.

Collins, Mitchell A. and Wanda C. Collins. *Stepping Out on Faith: History of Mt. Tabor Baptist Church 1833-1999.* Fernandina Beach, FL: Wolfe Publishing, 1999.

Conns Creek Baptist Church Minutes, 1847-1900. Compiled by Carold Howell, Transcribed by David Scott Dingler. R. T. Jones Memorial Library, Canton, GA.

Croy, Eugene. *Pine Top Fox.* Cherokee Co. GA: Eugene Croy, 1976.

Dawson County Historical and Genealogical Society. *Dawson County, Georgia Heritage, 1857-1996.* Canton, GA: Dawson County Historical and Genealogical Society and Don Mills, Inc., 1997.

Deming and others. *Concord Baptist Church, Cobb Co. GA. 1982.*

Ellis, Larry Waylon. *A Family History of John Henry Ellis and Mary Catherine Haygood Ellis.* Ball Ground, GA: Larry Waylon Ellis, 1997.

Flinchum, Gerald W. *Crossroads, Creeks and Clashes: Civil War Skirmishes in Cherokee and North Cobb Counties: 1864.* Woodstock, GA: Gerald W. Flinchum, 2014.

Forsyth County News. Cumming, GA.

Gaddis, Elbert B. *Cherokee Days Gone By, 1993.* Self-published, 1993.

Gardner, Robert G., Charles O. Walker, J. R. Huddleston, and Waldo P. Harris III. *History of the Georgia Baptist Association, 1784-1984.* Atlanta, GA: Georgia Baptist Historical Society, 1988.

Gardner, Robert G. *Cherokees and Baptists in Georgia.* Wilkes Publishing Co., Washington, GA: 1989.

Goff, John H. *Place Names of Georgia.* Athens: University of Georgia Press, 1975.

Groover, Regina. *Honoring the Veterans of Hightower Baptist Church and Veterans of Hightower Church Families.* 2001. Self published.

Harrell, Bob. "Once They Mined Gold in Creighton." *The Atlanta Constitution,* 10 May 1977, page 2-B.

Hasty, William G. Sr., *I Remember When and More, Short Stories.* Canton, GA: William G. Hasty, Sr. 1994.

Hasty, William G. Sr., *Yesterday and More, Short Stories.* Canton, GA: Gilleland Printing.

Hawke, David Freeman. *Everyday Life in Early America.* New York: Harper and Row, 1988.

Hightower Baptist Association History Committee. *The Men and Missions of Hightower, Volume I: Ministers.* Hightower Baptist Association History Committee, about 2005.

Hightower Baptist Association History Committee. *The Men and Missions of Hightower, Volume II: Churches.* Canton, GA: Doss Printing Services, Inc. 2013.

Hightower Baptist Association Minutes, 1835-1998. Hightower Baptist Association, Cumming, GA.

Hightower Baptist Church Minutes, 1882-1950. Hightower Baptist Church, Ball Ground, GA.

History of the Baptist denomination in Georgia: with biographical compendium and portrait gallery of Baptist ministers and other Georgia Baptists. Reprint of original, published Atlanta, Ga.: Jas. P. Harrison & Co., 1881.

Huddelston, J. R., and Charles O. Walker. *From Heretics to Heroes: A study of Religious Groups in Georgia with Primary Emphasis on the Baptists.* Jasper, Georgia: Pickens Tech Press, 1976.

Hughes, Juanita. *Set Apart: The Baptist Church at Woodstock.* Published by First Baptist Church of Woodstock, 1987.

Johnston, Rebecca. *Cherokee County, Georgia: A History.* Canton, GA: Yawn's Publishing, 2011.

Krakow, Kenneth K. *Georgia Place-Names.* 3rd ed. Macon, GA: Winship Press, 1975.

Lasher, George William, ed. *The Ministerial Directory of the Baptist Churches in the United States of America.* Oxford, Ohio, Ministerial Directory Co., 1899.

Latty, John W. *Carrying off the Cherokee, History of Buffington's Company Georgia Mounted Militia.* CreateSpace, 2011.

Lawrence, Harold. *Methodist Preachers in Georgia: 1783-1900.* Tignall, GA: Boyd Publishing, 1984.

Marlin, Rev. Lloyd G. *The History of Cherokee County.* Atlanta: Walter W. Brown Publishing., 1933 reprint 1997.

McConnell, Reatha Sosebee. *Friendship is Reaching out: FBC Sesquicentennial Years.* 1990. Roswell, GA: Wolfe Publishing, 1990.

McRay, Sybil. *Sesquicentennial history of the Chattahoochee Baptist Association and it's affiliated churches.* Unknown Binding, 1976.

McRay, Sybil Wood. *This and That, History of Hall County Georgia, Volume I.* Gainesville, GA: Peeples Printing

Service, 1973.

Moore, U. G. "Homemaking: It Was Rough in the 1900's, Women Folk Worked Hard, Mrs. R. O. Cotton." *Cherokee Tribune*, 29 January 1976.

North Georgia Tribune. Canton, GA.

Pickens County Historical and Genealogical Society. *Pickens County, Georgia Heritage.* Pickens County, GA: Pickens County Historical and Genealogical Society and Don Mills, Inc., 1998.

Pierce, Alfred Mann. *A History of Methodism in Georgia, February 5, 1736- June 24, 1955.* Atlanta: North Georgia Conference Historical Society, 1956.

Public Education in Cherokee County. Canton: Cherokee County Board of Education, 1982.

Ragsdale, B. D. *Story of Georgia Baptist, Vol III: The Convention, Its Principles and Policies, Its Allies and Its Agencies, Its Aims and Its Achievements.* Atlanta: Foote and Davies Co., B. D. Ragsdale, 1938.

Reeves, Jeremiah Jr. File at Mercer Library – *Obituary, Reminiscences of Georgia Baptists, History of the Georgia Baptist Association and History of the Canton Baptist Church.*

Roberts, Malinda. *History of First Baptist Church of Canton, Georgia, Organized August 23, 1833: Centennial Celebration August 20-23, 1933.* [Place of publication not identified]: [publisher not identified], 1933.

Shadburn, D. L. and T. O. Brooke. *Crimson and Sabres: A Confederate Record of Forsyth County, Georgia.* Cumming, GA: Don L. Shadburn, 1997.

Shadburn, Don L. *Blood Kin: Pioneer Chronicles of Upper Georgia.* Cumming, GA: Don L. Shadburn, 1999.

Shadburn, Don L. *Cherokee Planters in Georgia 1832-1838.* Cumming, GA: Don L. Shadburn, 1989.

Shadburn, Don L. *Pioneer History of Forsyth County 1832-1860, Vol. I.* Roswell, GA: Wolfe Associates, 1981.

Shadburn, Don L. *Unhallowed Intrusion: A history of Cherokee Families in Forsyth County, Georgia.* Cumming, GA: Don L. Shadburn, 1993.

Shadburn, Don L. *The Cottonpatch Chronicles: Reflections of Cherokee History, People, Places, and Events in Forsyth County, Georgia.* Cumming, GA: Don L. Shadburn, 2003.

Sharp Mountain Baptist Church Minutes: 1839-1925. R. T. Jones Memorial Library, Canton, GA.

"Twenty Years' Strife Between Baptist Factions in North Georgia." *The Weekly Constitution*. 28 Dec. 1886. Accessed http://atlnewspapers.galileo.usg.edu/atlnewspapers.

U.S. Bureau of the Census, 1830-1940.

Wade, Forest C. *Cry of the Eagle: History and Legends of the Cherokee Indians and their Buried Treasures.* Phoenix, AZ: Betty Wade Tinsley, 1969.

Walker, Charles O. *Cherokee Footprints… Vol.1.* Canton, GA: Industrial Printing Service, Inc., 1988.

Walker, Charles, O. *Through the Years, 1848-1963: History of the First Baptist Church of Jasper.* Jasper, GA: First Baptist Church, 1963.

Walls, Louise. *A Walk Through Tyme: History of Concord Baptist Church.* Roswell, GA: Wolfe Publishing, 1997.

Watkins, Floyd C., and Charles H Watkins. *Yesterday in the Hills.* Athens, GA: University of Georgia Press, 1973 (reprint of 1963 edition).

Williams, David. *The Georgia Gold Rush: Twenty-Niners, Cherokees, and Gold Fever.* University of South Carolina Press: 1993.

Libraries, Archives, & Electronic Databases, Websites

Cobb County Library, Marietta GA

Dawson County Library, Dawsonville, GA

Hall County Library, Gainesville, GA

Lake Lanier Regional Library, Cumming, GA

Sequoyah Regional Library: R. T. Jones, Canton; Woodstock; Ball Ground

Georgia Baptist Convention

Mercer University Library, Mercer University, Macon, GA

GenForum website (http://genforum.genealogy.com)

http://worldconnect.genealogy.rootsweb.ancestry.com/

http://www.genealogy.com

http://home.ancestry.com/

https://familysearch.org/

http://historicforsyth.com/

https://archive.org/

http://www.findagrave.com/

http://billiongraves.com/

http://www.aboutnorthgeorgia.com/ang/Battle_of_Hightower

http://www.aboutnorthgeorgia.com/ang/North_Georgia_Droughts

http://sports.yahoo.com/news/wounded-war-ii-veteran-john-183807973--golf.html

http://ware.informationsmith.com/webb.htm

http://www.usgennet.org/usa/ga/topic/news/cherokeeadvance.htm

http://www.usgennet.org/usa/ga/county/hall/htmlpages/this_that.htm, ch. 2, parks and gold.

http://georgiainfo.galileo.usg.edu/histcountymaps/cherokeehistmaps.htm, 1830 Cherokee nation.

https://familysearch.org/pal:/MM9.1.2/QK31-VVK7 : accessed 16 Jun 2014, John Randall Stone, 1938; "Georgia, Deaths, 1928-1938", index and images, *FamilySearch.*

Gardner, Robert G. Baptist history and heritage http://www.baptisthistory.org/bhhs/digital-resources.html

Media

Wallace, Brian, Debbie and Randy Boles, Producers, Editors and Videographers. *Hightower Baptist Church: History and Memories [DVD]*. Ball Ground GA: 2010.

Other

Personal daily diaries of Cleo Heard Milford, 1934-2004.

Personal Interviews and contributors:

Rev. John Lummus, Don Shadburn, Frankie Green Edge, Herman and Atholine Wilkie, Ruth Ann Pinyan Wilkie, Ruby Hester Milford, Mattie Heard Turner, Mitchell Collins, Rev. Charles Jones, Carolyn Bates, Randy Wilkie, E. W. Cochran, Glenn W. Wilkie, Joey Wallace, Dr. Charles Ingram, Jennifer Smithwick, Donald and Shirley Wilkie, Larry W. Ellis, Byron Burgess, Rev. Ronnie McCormick, Rev. Gerral Richards, Annabel Ballew, Kenneth Wyatt, Ken Wyatt, Emily Wyatt, Darrell Rainey, Chris Chandler, Coy Cochran, Jack Hester, Darrell Cook, Billy Hill, Bobby Roper, Thomas Heard, Tim Perkins, Brian Wallace, Debbie Boles, Dr. Jimmy Orr, Earl Turpen, Clint Smith, Bobby Roper, Rilla Price, Edwin Wilkie, Jimmy McConnell, Chad Williams, Regina Groover, Brenda Curtis, Diane Martin, Mitzi Chambers, Karen Parrott, Joyce Odum, Gail Burtz, Jennifer Dunn, Whitney Wilkie and many, many others who gave holy hugs, encouragement and much help.

Special thanks to Judy Northington, personal friend and photographer and David Akoubian, professional photographer

Index

A

Aarons, 181, 188

Adams, 94, 113, 119, 160

Akoubian, 2, 7

Aline, 85-86, 216

Allen, 14, 27, 46-49, 85-87, 185,188, 192, 207, 215-216, 221, 225, 233, 296, 352, 359

Allred, 14, 39-41, 43-44, 213, 221

Amicalola BC, 114, 214, 217

Anderson, 39-40, 51-52, 56, 85, 88, 217,222

Andrews, 51-52, 55-56, 64, 88, 119,160, 188, 224, 233, 247, 297,346, 356, 359, 380, 407

Andrew's Chapel, 14, 34, 36, 81, 241, 269, 296. 309

Ararat BC, 12, 17, 20, 22

Arthur, 213

Arwood, 93, 251-252, 369

B

Bagwell, 157, 171, 241, 275

Bailey, 31, 40, 52, 57, 78, 160, 181, 183,188, 238, 247, 270, 350, 359

Baker, 44, 48, 50-51, 57-58, 84, 89, 160,183, 196

Ball, Balls, 179, 183, 186-188, 238, 314, 349, 359

Ballew, 249

Bannister, 160, 171, 188, 227, 248, 383

Barker, 31, 120, 284, 328, 385, 388

Barnwell, 44, 47, 57, 89

Barrett, 97, 114, 120

Barton, 209, 211, 221, 287

Bates, 7, 62, 220

Beard, 214

Beaver Ruin BC, 177, 216, 223, 264

Bell, 149, 355, 359, 375

Bennett, 86-87

Bethany BC, 212, 215, 217, 219

Bethesda BC, 212, 241

Bethlehem BC, Forsyth Co. Ga., 26, 36, 209, 217-218, 249

Bethlehem BC, Union Co., Ga. 342

Bettis, 188

Biddy, 39, 45-58, 83-85, 88-89, 119-120, 188

Birmingham BC 216, 218

Bise, 350, 359

Blackstock, 40, 56

Blackwell, 43, 123, 153, 155, 160, 178, 182,188, 196, 366

Blair, 182

Blalock, 172

Bloodworth, 58, 83, 89

Bobo, 39, 58-59, 78, 296-297

Bohannon, 354, 359, 377

Boles, 15, 185, 187, 391

Boling, 28, 32, 41, 43-47, 49-53, 55-58, 64, 72-73, 85-86, 88-90, 97-99, 107, 112, 119-120, 132, 138, 156, 158, 160, 170, 184, 188, 190, 193, 270, 274, 296, 327-328, 339, 346-348, 358-360, 365, 374, 378, 380-381, 392, 398

Bolles, 160

Bolling, 86, 107, 113, 116, 120, 153, 170

Bowen, 210, 284

Bowers, 157, 160, 186, 188, 280

Bowles, 120, 148, 160

Brackett, 116, 140, 372, 375

Brady, 57-58, 67, 72, 95, 98, 248, 373

Brannon, 209

Bredges, 57

Briggs, 285

Brooks, Brookes, Broks, 58, 85, 87, 89-90, 99, 102, 106-107, 120, 133, 188

Brookwood BC, 217

Bruce, 70, 160, 179, 185, 387

Bruton, 213

Bryan, O'bryan, 178, 208, 388

Bryant, Briant, 18-20, 50-51, 53, 57-58, 60, 62, 68,72, 87-91, 96, 106-107, 109-112, 114-116, 118-120, 147, 151-152, 184, 281, 339, 342-343, 360-361

Bryson, 124, 160

Buchanan, Buchana, Buchanna, 346, 361

Buffington, 12-13, 34, 120, 160-161, 177-178, 180-183, 185-188, 280,296, 302-303, 306, 318-319, 349, 361,389,395-396

Buice, 155, 160

Burch, 358, 361, 398

Burgess, 41, 57, 78, 212-213, 216-217, 228, 361

Burnes, 30

Burns, 29-31, 171, 235, 257, 270, 277, 301, 327, 349, 359, 361, 364

Bursmith, 192, 228, 255, 265, 356, 361, 398

Burton, 43, 45, 56-57, 330, 361, 373

Burtz, 188, 231, 247

Bushyhead, 20

Byers, 386

Byess, 337, 377

C

Cagle, 48-49, 59, 300

Callwell, Calwell, 153, 162

Campbell, Camel, 61, 63, 333, 368

Cannon, 28, 59-60, 85, 90, 106, 120, 159, 161-162, 171-172, 180, 189, 236, 257,262, 277, 280, 306, 334-336, 340, 347, 350-354, 361-362, 372, 376, 383, 398, 404

Cantrell, 53, 59-60, 67, 85, 90-91, 109-118, 120-121, 146-149, 151-154, 157-159, 162, 177, 182, 187, 224, 233, 242, 251, 335, 354, 362

Cape, 52, 60, 78, 91, 121, 138, 237-239, 253, 279, 364, 387, 404

Carmichael, 187

Carnes, 45, 58-59, 183, 219

Castleberry, 40-41, 59

Caughron, 285

Chadwick, 167, 178, 187-188

Chalcedonia BC, 36, 147, 157, 213, 215, 320

Chambers, 144, 230-231, 250, 258, 271, 281, 328, 362, 405

Chandler, 13, 81-82, 104, 192, 200-201, 255, 258, 265, 292, 298, 308, 356, 363, 396, 398, 406, 412

Chang, 397

Chastain, Chasten, Chasteene, 47-48, 50-51, 53, 59-60, 84-86, 90-91, 121, 146, 153, 236, 332, 337, 363

Chattahoochee Association, 12, 19-20, 24-25, 29-30, 208-209, 220, 270, 392

Christopher, 40, 52, 59, 78, 87, 91, 95, 121, 127, 147, 251, 354, 364, 372

Chumbler, Chumbley, Chumley, 113, 121, 129, 159, 161-162, 167, 177, 347, 363, 365, 388

Cipriani, 358, 363

Cissell, 7, 105, 266, 268, 298

Clark, 86, 91

Clayton, 56, 216, 275

Cleveland, 249-250, 329, 369

Cline, 216, 222, 239

Cloud, 85, 91, 121, 129, 161-163, 188-189, 247, 305, 352, 355, 357, 359, 363, 370, 373

Coal Mt. BC, 156, 220, 224, 233, 261, 404

Cobb, 64, 132

Cochran, 14, 32, 39-56, 58-59, 62, 66, 82-88, 90-91, 95, 97, 105, 107-116, 118, 120-121, 123-124, 140, 146-152, 154-159,161-162, 166, 175-177, 179-187, 189,196, 200, 202, 214-215, 218, 221,224-225, 228, 232-233, 236-242, 247-249,251, 253-254, 270, 280, 307, 311-312,314, 319-321, 326, 331, 338-340,342-344, 346, 358, 363-364, 371376-377, 388, 392, 398, 403-404, 412

Coffee, 31, 235, 305, 327, 364, 392

Coggins, 28, 30, 33, 223, 233, 300

Coker, 54, 87, 115, 128, 144, 181, 264, 286, 404

Cole, 65, 95

Coleman, Colmond, 157, 161, 189, 347, 364

Coletrane, Calltrane, Coltrane, 105, 152-153, 162, 241, 377

Collett, Collit, 106, 121, 162, 334, 336, 364, 373

Collier, 60, 90-91, 120-121, 163, 337, 341, 356, 364

Collins, 7, 12, 20, 44, 47, 59, 208, 298

Colwell, Calwell, 147, 162

Concord BC, 26, 36, 86-87, 150, 158, 210, 215-217, 274

Concord BC, Cobb Co., 208

Conn, 45, 385

Conns Creek BC, 31, 36-37, 39, 46, 48, 52-55, 83-84, 87, 111-112, 115, 147-149, 151, 153, 155, 212-217, 241, 247, 403

Cook, 84, 143, 172, 200, 225, 227, 233, 242-243, 258, 281, 283, 355, 364, 398

Cordell, 45, 59, 86, 91

Corinth BC, 154, 215, 217

Corn, 161-162

Cornelison, 45

Cornett, 126, 145, 156, 161-162, 164, 177, 187, 189, 244, 252, 280, 365

Cosby, 340, 364

Covington, 108, 111, 121, 134, 217, 381, 406

Cowan, 274

Cowart, 85, 123, 144-145, 149, 152-153, 155-156, 161-162, 164-165, 178-181, 184, 186-189, 200, 204, 218, 224, 230, 233, 244-247, 252, 280, 312-314, 319, 321, 349-352, 364-365, 375, 396, 398

Cowen, 274-275

Cox, 41-42, 56, 58-60, 121, 323, 398

Creighton, 28, 36,

Crenshaw, 41, 46, 58, 78, 351, 358, 365, 398

Cronan, 119, 150, 160-161, 177, 189, 247, 305, 340, 355-356, 365

Crow, 44, 59-60, 70, 83, 91, 161-162, 305, 366

Croy, 121, 158, 296, 335, 365

Cruice, 311

Curby, 162

Curry, 212

Curtis, 105, 175, 202, 228, 239-240, 242, 253, 311, 319, 398, 404

Cutts, 108

D

Daniel, 84

Darby, 128

Davenport, 54, 60-61, 91, 121, 237

Daves Creek BC, 219

Davis, 64, 76, 94, 100, 149, 236, 251-252, 329, 350, 355, 362, 366, 372, 376, 388, 398

Dawson, 51-52, 59-60, 91, 109, 121-122, 140

Dean, 30, 33, 43, 114-118, 122-123, 147, 153, 155-156, 162-163, 189, 192, 194, 280, 297, 304, 356, 366, 406

Dehart, 219

Dempsey, 153, 163, 172

Devore, 41, 219

Dispain, 110, 113-114, 122, 132, 135

Dixon, 189

Dobson, 47, 54, 60-61, 68, 84-85, 91, 102, 106, 115, 122-123, 140, 148, 154, 157, 162-163, 172, 177-178, 182, 184-186, 189, 196, 224, 233, 280, 306, 341, 346, 351-353, 355, 366, 369, 398

Donald, 27

Dooley, Dooly, 31, 57, 60, 91, 337, 366

Doss, 150, 172, 296, 298

Dowda, Dowdie, 42, 45, 51-56, 60-61, 86, 91, 122, 338, 366

Drummond, 28, 91, 117, 122-123, 155-156, 162-163, 184-185, 189, 247, 281, 305-306, 334, 349, 367

Dunagan, Dunigan, Dunnigan, 53, 56, 60, 84-87, 91, 102, 108-111, 117, 121-122, 139, 147, 150, 205, 208

Duncan, 384

Dunn, 277

Durham, 53, 57, 60, 218

E

Eason, 123, 155

Eaton, 43, 45-46, 61, 67, 74, 84-85, 91-92, 95, 335, 367, 398

Edwards, 71, 98, 107, 131, 147, 157, 160, 163, 181-182, 188, 190, 280, 395-396, 398

Ellington, 159, 163, 331-332, 367

Elliott, 45, 61

Ellis, 14, 39, 51-56, 61, 78, 83-88, 92, 98, 106-116, 118, 123-124, 132-133, 141, 147, 151, 158, 205, 219, 222, 224, 227, 233, 241-242, 247, 255, 309-310, 341-343, 364, 367, 373, 376, 379, 392, 408, 412; **Ellice**, 92, 123

Elrod, 29, 31

Emory, 129, 333, 367

Enon BC, 207-208, 304

Epperson, 163, 362, 381

Eubanks, 123, 134, 163, 305, 345, 367, 371

Evans, 41-42, 44, 46, 54, 61, 124, 146, 279, 340, 361, 385

F

Fair, 336, 367

Farmer, 66, 93, 124, 378

Faulkner, Falkner, 342, 367

Fife, 150, 173, 184, 189, 365, 367, Also See Phyfe

Fitts, 40, 42, 62-63, 92-93, 107, 124, 251

Flanagan, 180

Fleming, 19

Fletcher, 43-46, 48, 50, 52-54, 58, 62-63, 65, 67-68, 83-89, 92-93, 95, 106-113, 118, 124-125, 152, 159, 163, 168, 193, 205, 223, 227, 233, 248, 338, 340, 346, 367, 373, 381, 393

Flinchum, 303-304

Floyd, Floyed, 32, 62-63, 78, 83, 86, 92-93, 124, 134, 150, 172, 239, 335, 368

Ford, 41, 52, 62

Forrest, 152

Fossett, 238, 395

Foster, 163, 214, 371

Fowler, 20, 29-30, 32-34, 39-41, 49-53, 55, 59, 61-63, 74, 78, 83, 85-86, 92-93, 102, 108, 111, 118, 124-125, 135, 140, 150, 152, 159, 163, 172-173, 186, 207, 215, 236-237, 249, 285, 295, 301, 309, 327, 333, 335-336, 339, 341, 345, 347, 363-364, 368, 377, 382, 398

Francis, 304

Franklin, 11, 15, 20-22, 28, 31, 36, 113, 238, 248-250, 266, 270, 286, 288, 291, 296, 298, 301, 309, 318, 323, 326, 329, 359, 369, 393

Frasier, 28

Freeman, 62, 93

Freeze, 251, 328, 329, 369, 372-373

Friendship BC, 12, 36, 39, 45-55, 83, 113-114, 205, 209, 214-218

G

Gabrell, 88, 102

Gaddis, 110-111, 125, 174, 335, 357, 369, 398

Gaither, 190, 349, 369

Galloway, 217

Gardner, 19-20, 208, 210

Garrett, 57, 63, 89, 119, 212, 297, 352, 360, 369

Gayton, 190, 339, 358, 369

Gazaway, 164, 177, 195

Gentry, 295

George, 29-31, 208, 210

Gibson, 49, 63, 78, 94

Gilbert, 152-153, 164

Gilleland, Gilliland, 64, 73, 144, 151-152, 164, 171, 185, 190, 200, 225, 232-233, 238, 247, 250, 252, 281, 305, 318-319, 348, 350, 356, 361, 369-370, 398-399, 405

Gillstrap, Gilstrap, Gilstap, 41, 43, 49, 51, 64, 66, 70, 78-79, 93, 323

Gilmer, 78

Glover, 164

Godfrey, 22, 165, 261, 292, 404

Goff, 11-12, 19

Good, 126

Goodman, 164

Goodwin, 190

Goshen BC, 25, 213-21

Goss, 116

Graham, 190

Graves, 31, 249, 369

Gravitt, 368

Gravley, 182, 319

Green, Greene, 48-50, 52-53, 56-58, 62-64, 66-67, 73, 82, 87-89, 93-94, 99, 105-107, 117-119, 124-127, 132, 134-135, 144, 146, 148-154, 157, 161, 163-164, 168, 173, 176-178, 180, 182-185, 187, 190, 196-197, 199-200, 203-204, 246-247, 250-252, 274, 279-281, 283-284, 291, 293, 297, 305, 307, 318-319, 326, 339-340, 342-346, 349-353, 355, 357, 359-360, 365, 369-370, 378, 385-386, 399, 405-406

Greenlee, 27

Griffin, 32, 239, 326, 363, 399, 407

Grimes, 43, 64, 85, 94

Groover, 7, 64, 82, 93, 113-114, 116, 126, 144, 175, 229-230, 237, 239, 245, 254, 263, 320-321, 398-399, 404

Grover, 86

H

Hairson, 41

Hall, 96, 127, 128, 252

Hamby, 115, 140

Hamilton, 66, 94, 134, 165, 190, 345, 357, 367, 370-371, 399

Hammontree, 371, 379

Hanes, 214, **Haynes**, 214

Hanson, 114

Harber, 357, 371, 399

Harbin, 40-41, 49, 64-65, 79, 95, 127, 261

Hardin, 45, 50, 56, 66-67, 84, 88, 94-95, 115, 124, 126-127, 344, 371

Harden, 39, 41-42, 61, 65, 67, 79, 94-95, 113, 117, 128

Hardman, 392

Hardy, 39, 43, 46, 49, 65-66, 79, 95

Harris, 41, 44, 47, 49, 71, 86, 216, 265, 270

Harrison, 261, 404

Haskins, 27

Hasty, 171, 187, 198-199, 204

Haw Creek BC, 209, 216, 403

Hawke, 25

Hawkins, 29-30, 32-33, 41-42, 49-50, 52-53, 55, 64, 67, 76, 84-86, 95, 100, 107, 111-112, 115, 127-128, 165, 207, 209, 211-212, 220-221, 239, 241, 246, 254, 274, 280, 286-287, 332, 341, 368, 371, 380, 388, 404

Hayes, Hays, 41, 113

Haygood, 51-53, 59, 61, 66-67, 85, 92, 94, 108-109, 126-128, 166, 169, 182, 185,191, 224, 233, 241, 247, 255, 309, 319, 332, 352-353, 367, 371, 373, 381, 399; **Haggood**, 111, 115, 117-118; **Hagood**, 52-54, 56, 66-67, 84-86, 94-95; **Heggood**, 107, 109-110, 112, 115-116, 128,149-150, 155-156, 165-166, 173; **Heggwood**, 86; **Hegood**, 159; **Hegwood**, 87-88, 96, 113, 147; **Heygood**, 60, 91, 121, 149

Heard, 5, 22, 144, 149, 153-156, 158, 165, 175, 177-179, 181-184, 190-191, 218, 224-225, 229, 232-233, 261, 266, 280, 292, 306, 312-313, 315-317, 358, 371, 399, 402-404

Hembree, 53-55, 87

Hemphill, 79

Henderson, 14, 55-56, 83-85, 113, 116, 140, 149, 182, 216, 220-222, 286

Hendrix, 165, 177, 180, 182, 190, 196, 288, 351, 371

Hensley, 165

Henson, 41

Herring, 67, 87, 95-96, 118, 127-128, 136,337, 345, 371

Hester, 32, 42-43, 45-46, 50, 52, 60, 62-68, 72, 74, 76, 78, 91-92, 94-98, 100-102, 106, 110-111, 113-116, 118, 121-122, 124, 126-129, 131-132, 135, 137, 140, 143-145, 151-154, 156-158, 163, 165-166, 173, 175, 177, 180-181, 183-187, 191, 195, 214, 224, 229-230, 233, 236-237, 239, 245, 248, 251, 253, 262-264, 273, 276, 280, 283-284, 291, 301, 305-306, 308, 312-313, 319, 329, 334, 336, 343, 345, 347, 354, 358, 363, 367, 370, 372-373, 375, 384, 395, 398-399,404-405

Higgins, 67, 95, 373, 375

Hill, 166, 179, 190-191, 196, 210, 225, 232-233, 247, 349-350, 373, 399, 406

Hitt, 42-43, 52, 65, 79, 113, 147, 178, 180-182, 191, 247

Hobgood, 177

Hodges, 43; **Hodgeas**, 65

Hogan, 41, 61-62, 65, 67, 95, 126, 182, 191, 248, 297, 338, 373

Holbrook, 93, 116, 127, 153, 209, 219, 239, 253, 261, 353, 373, 403; **Holebrook(s)**, 147

Holcomb, 29-31, 33, 48-55, 66-67, 77-78, 83-87, 94-96, 101, 106-107, 114-115, 126-129, 147-149, 153, 165, 173, 205, 208, 213, 247, 251, 270, 283, 296, 298, 326, 330, 335, 353, 364, 373, 376, 383, 395, 399, 406; **Holcombe**, 42, 46, 64, 66, 94, 109, 111-112, 126-128, 140, 149, 156, 165, 178, 196, 205, 305, 329-330, 333, 335, 373, 399 **Halcombe**, 43

Holloway, 191, 393; **Holiway**, 165

Holt, 41, 65, 94, 138, 165, 182, 191, 247

Hopewell BC, 36, 155, 209, 212-213, 215-216, 220

Hosey, 49, 65, 95, 337, 373

Howard, 39-43, 45, 49, 52, 55-56, 64-67, 79, 85, 94-96, 107, 110-111, 126-128, 148-149, 196, 204, 244, 334, 340-342, 359, 373, 393-394; **Heywood**, (Possibly Howard) 148-149

Howell, 149, 191, 195, 239, 404

Huddleston, 19

Hudgins, 167

Hudson, 29, 31, 44, 207-209, 220; **Hutson**, 29

Hughes, 128, 196-197, 207

Humphrey, 46, 79, 286, Also See Umphrey

Hutsey, 191

Hyde, 44, 48, 79

I

Ingram, 14, 31, 37, 41, 44-46, 52-55, 84, 87, 96, 113, 129, 140, 153-154, 166, 173, 214, 221, 247, 336, 374, 377; **Ingraim**, 45, 52, 67

Island Ford BC, 209

J

Jackson, 268-269, 288, 323

Jameson, 333, 374

Jefferson, 64, 95, 37

Jenkins, 331, 351, 367, 374, 387

Johnson, 181, 196, 235, 284, 369

Johnston, 191, 298, 373

Jones, 18-20, 28, 36, 39-40, 44, 50, 67, 70, 78-79, 101, 106, 129, 137, 166, 184, 191, 196, 243, 251, 281, 285, 295-296, 317-318, 328, 338-340, 360, 362, 369, 374, 386-387, 399, 405,

Jordan, 392

Juno BC, 115, 217

K

Kelley, 57, 87, 89, 96, 332, 339, 374; **Kelly**, 57-58, 68, 85, 87, 89, 96, 129, 138, 148, 384

Kemp, 32, 67, 70, 96, 130, 208, 212, 332, 374

Kinsey, 129

Krakow, 11-12, 20

Kuykendall, 131

L

Lancaster, 166, 374; **Landcaster**, 131, 166

Lathem, 39, 41, 45, 53-55, 68, 74, 83, 130, 159, 166-167, 177, 191, 196, 251, 261, 273, 277, 280, 297, 300, 306, 372, 402; **Latham**, 21

Lawson, 43, 68, 205, 216, 375

Ledbetter, 29, 32, 50, 62-63, 68, 74, 93, 110, 124, 223, 233, 248, 264, 367

Lee, 47, 50, 68,

Lemby, 167

Leonard, 31, 46, 55, 68, 73, 96-97, 99-100, 106, 110, 120, 129-130, 134, 233, 235-236, 269-270, 355, 364, 374-376, 380; **Leonards**, 24, **Lenard**, 97; **Lonard**, 326, 374-375

Leslie, 269, 294-295, 356, 369

Liberty BC, Cherokee Co., 55, 83, 84, 85, 87, 108, 111, 144, 145, 147, 148, 149, 151, 153, 155, 156, 217, 245, 404

Liberty BC, Dawson Co., 17, 20, 22

Liberty Grove BC, 7, 115, 155, 216, 217

Lindsey, 39, 68, 79

Lipscomb, 33, 295, 327, 374

Little, 68, 87-88, 91, 96-97, 107, 113, 115-116, 118, 129-131, 151, 153, 156-158, 166-167, 177-178, 185-186, 189, 191-192, 280, 297, 300, 306, 334, 341, 354-355, 375, 388, 398-399

Lively, 36, 290, 378

Lofton, 392

Logan, 49

Loggins, 55, 68, 84, 86, 96-97, 109, 111, 113, 129-131, 140, 166, 301, 333, 366, 375, 399; **Logins**, 68, 118

Long, 68, 110, 114, 130, 342, 375

Longstreet BC, 219-220

Lovelace, 5, 7, 12-13, 16, 25, 77, 81-82, 101, 104, 106, 130-131, 143, 146-147, 149-150, 152, 155-159, 166, 175-176, 181, 184, 187, 192, 200, 203, 206, 224, 228, 233, 238, 244, 246-247, 255, 258, 265-268, 270, 280, 283, 291-292, 296, 298, 303, 305-306, 312-313, 315, 323, 348, 354-356, 361, 363, 376, 388, 394-395, 406; **Lawless**, 206; **Lovelance**, 395; **Loveless**, 116-117, 131, 148-151, 153-157

Low, 67, 96, 130, 141

Lowe, 183, 185, 192

Lummus, 5, 7, 14, 183-187, 218-219, 222, 399

Lyle, 43, 55, 68, 79

M

Macedonia BC, 36, 39, 44, 55, 84, 147, 151, 159, 199, 209, 213-214, 217, 239, 286; **Macedonie**, 45 **Masidonia**, 87, 148-149, 151, 153 **Massadonia**, 54, 110

Maddox, 40-42, 69, 72, 78, 98, 131; **Maddux**, 153

Magnee, 311

Majors, 14, 182, 192, 219, 222, 311

Mangum, 33, 295

Manning, 18, 20, 22

Manous, 277

Marble Hill BC, 147, 215

Marion, 301

Marlin, 18, 304

Martin, 14, 44, 49, 63, 66, 69, 92, 118, 131, 200, 210, 216, 220, 222, 244, 252, 313, 332, 355, 376, 380, 399

Mashburn, 41, 68-69

Mason, 41, 43-44, 46, 55, 69-70, 72, 79, 85, 93, 98, 102, 115, 122, 124, 128,131, 152, 173

McBrayer, 172

McClain, 371

McCleskey, 399

McCloud, 131

McCluney, 84

McClure, 31, 104, 109, 143, 266, 269,291, 294-295, 311, 319, 342, 357, 376

McConnell, 12, 27, 181, 214, **McConnely**, 181

McCord, 192

McCormick, 7, 9-10, 14, 220, 412

McCurley, 83; **McCurry**, 354, 362, 376

McDaniel, 65, 102, 131, 137, 275-276, 293, 384, 405

McDavid, 376

McDonald, 21, 28, 36, 69, 216, 249-250

McGaha, 189, 239, 253, 319, 358, 376, 399

McGee, 340, 376

McGinley, 347, 362

McGinnis, 177

McGuillion, 44-45, 68-69, 376, **McGullion**, 40, 44-47, 52, 69, 76, 131, 205, 283, 328

McGuire, 146, 173

McHanon, 213

McIntosh, 405

McMeken, 332

McPherson, 112-113, 131, 154-156, 158-159, 167, 177-178, 180, 182, 185-186, 197, 238, 297; **McFerson**, 118; **McFierson**, 131

McRay, 22

Mica BC, 114, 148-149, 151, 156, 212-213

Milford, 1, 5, 7, 35, 82, 143-144, 158-159, 165, 169, 172, 175, 178-184, 186-187, 192, 196, 199-200, 203, 206, 218, 224, 230, 233, 239, 241, 256, 261, 266, 275, 278, 281, 290, 293, 300, 306-307,

312, 314-315, 319, 356, 373, 376-377, 395, 398, 402-403

Miller, 111, 115, 147, 177

Mills, 151, 167, 170, 177, 186, 192, 195, 247, 347, 352, 355, 365, 376

Millwood, 192, 276-277, 301

Milton, 50

Montgomery, 328, 376

Moody, 155, 241, 376

Moore, 136, 243, 275, 318, 382, 384

Morgan, 48, 69

Mosteller, 28, 67, 94, 127, 247, 371, 376

Mt. Olivet BC, 210

Mt. Pisgah BC, 29, 32-33, 36, 50-55, 83-84, 111, 212, 216-217, 219; **Mt. Pisgee**, 151; **Mt. Pisgue**, 85, 147-149, 151, 153, 155-156, 158; **Mt. Puisgue**, 86-87

Mt. Tabor BC, 7, 12, 17, 20, 33, 36, 39, 44-45, 47-50, 52-53, 55, 83-84, 111, 145, 208, 210, 213, 216-218, 220, 244-245

Mt. Vernon BC, 36, 109, 210, 211, 217

Mt. Zion BC, 12, 35-36, 113, 209, 212-213, 215, 219

Mulkey, 85, 190, 192, 337, 339, 354, 359, 377, 399

Mullinax, 286, 399, 406

Murphy, 376

N

Nash, 69

Nelson, 20, 49, 53, 56, 60, 69-70, 79, 83, 91, 97, 102, 167, 238, 296-297, 305, 326, 377; **Nellson**, 134

Nesbit, 69

New Harmony BC, 7, 36, 39, 45-50, 52-55, 83-84, 87, 107, 111, 147-151, 153, 155, 156, 184, 212-218, 220, 236, 309, 310, 403

Newhouse, 42, 69

Nichols, 167

Nickleson, 69

Nix, 29-33, 41, 45, 47, 53, 69-71, 79, 84, 98, 132, 167, 185, 192, 215, 236, 270, 336-338, 340, 345, 364, 377, 399

Nooche, 20; **Noochee**, 208

Norrell, 167, 340-341, 377, 399

North Canton BC, 218

Northington, 7, 203, 236-237, 249, 269, 283, 298-301

Norton, 36, 54-55, 70, 110, 131, 296, 337, 377

Nuckols, 177, 197

O

Oak Grove BC, 155, 184, 218, 219; **Oak Grove BC, Milton Co.**, 113

Oakdale BC, 225, 233, 286, 406

O'Bryant, O'Briant, O'Bryan, 18-20, 25, 88, 132, 178, 207-208, 220

Odum, 43, 70, 74, 78, 122, 131-132, 337, 363-364, 377; **Odom**, 259, 402, 407; **Odem**, 50, 53, 84, 97, 108, 113

Ophir BC, 33, 36, 39, 45-50, 52-53, 55, 83-87, 111, 116, 145, 147-149, 151, 155-156, 216, 223, 288-289

Orr, 7, 403

P

Pace, 354, 378

Padgett, 109, 118, 133, 157, 177, 181; **Padget**, 167; **Pagett**, 148, 153; **Paggett**, 133

Page, 179, 197, 355, 378

Parham, 40

Parker, 87, 99, 107, 112, 115, 133-134, 141, 171, 252, 347, 370, 378, 399

Parris, 167, 187

Parrott, 358, 378

Pascoe, 21, 33, 71, 98, 212, 223, 234, 242, 246, 249, 254, 268-270, 287-289, 294-295, 300-301, 323-324, 326, 378-379, 388, 399; **Pasco**, 86-87, 331

Pass, 41, 42, 70, 79; **Pas**, 41, 383

Patterson, 167, 280

Payne, 133, 243

Pearson, 58, 71-72, 86, 94, 98-99, 102, 106, 110, 114-117, 125, 132-133, 147-148, 160, 167, 184, 187, 193, 302-304, 340-342, 345, 353, 355, 361, 378, 399

Peek, 29, 207-208, 220

Pendley, 358, 378, 386, 403

Penn, 296

Perkins, 104, 194, 229, 256-257, 273, 277-278, 291, 308, 313, 348, 378, 400, 405

Perry, 179, 197

Peterson, 393

Petty, 27, 28, 31, 34, 37, 49, 54, 70-71, 74, 99, 269-270, 281, 284, 330, 378, 390, 400

Phillips, 28, 379, 393

Phyfe, 167, 192-193, 280, 306, 352, 379; Also See Fife

Pickett, 14, 40-42, 85, 213-214, 221, 322, 400

Pierce, 23, 71, 98-100, 111-112, 114, 118, 132-133, 159, 167, 206, 336, 346, 379; **Pearce**, 86-87, 99, 102, 111, 113, 118, 134; **Pearse**, 110, 132, 206

Pinkerton, 160

Pinson, 37, 49, 53, 71-72, 98, 132, 247

Pinyan, 202, 241, 281-283, 359, 400

Pleasant Hill BC, 212

Pleasant View BC, 216, 217

Ponder, 149

Pool, 29-30, 33, 79, 291, 295, 327, 368, 374, 379; **Poole**, 295-296

Pope, 192, 342, 378

Porter, 39-40, 70-71, 79, 106, 114, 118, 123, 133, 147, 152-154, 167, 242-243, 247, 251, 270, 281, 300, 330, 331, 337, 341, 343-344, 367-368, 372, 379, 387; **Poter**, 300, 330, 379

Posey, 18-20, 208, 210

Price, 58, 69, 72, 84, 89, 98, 107-109, 111-113, 132-133, 153, 189, 225, 233, 239, 245, 320- 321, 335, 371, 379, 400

Priest, 58, 71-72, 74, 80, 98-99, 116, 132-133, 335, 379; **Pries**, 74

Prince, 133, 301, 379

Pruitt, 41, 52, 54, 61, 72, 83, 98, 113, 132, 143, 165, 181, 187, 190, 192-193, 247, 261, 286, 306, 314, 358, 379, 400, 403; **Pruett**, 42, 71; **Prewitt**, 71, 98

Pugh, 134, 341, 368, 380; **Pew**, 134, 380

Purcell, 24, 30, 32-33, 41, 47-53, 56, 62, 70-72, 83-85, 97-98, 113, 132, 209, 211-212, 221, 223, 233, 270, 327, 332, 380-381, 400, 404; **Pursell**, 29-30, 33, 39, 43-47, 52-56, 66, 70, 80, 87, 97, 106-107, 132-133, 205, 324, 326-328, 380; **Persell**, 29, 32

Q

R

Ragsdale, 5

Raines, 31, 159, 168, 208; **Rienes**, 159

Rainey, 168, 184, 197, 269, 294-295

Rainwater(s), 44, 72

Ramsey, 46, 73, 99, 134, 343, 380; **Ramsay**, 134

Ray, 41, 46, 47, 73, 162, 178, 193, 197, 247, 318, 353, 366, 400; **Raye**, 193

Redd, 250, 383, 405

Redmond, 71

Reece, 168, 280

Reeves, 18, 20, 22; **Reaves**, 41, 72

Reinhardt, 406

Reynolds, 72, 99, 353, 380

Rich, 40, 43, 46, 49, 72-73, 99, 117, 134, 143, 145-159, 168, 177-179, 181, 193, 197, 251, 280, 305-306, 337, 338, 345-347, 354-355, 364, 367, 371, 380

Richards, 6-7, 14, 30, 33, 39-47, 49-53; 55-57, 64, 72-73, 83, 85-88, 93, 99, 102, 108-109, 112, 118, 124, 134, 137, 141, 147, 151, 153, 158-159, 168-169, 173, 179-184, 193, 206, 211, 218, 220, 222, 239, 279, 283, 338, 349, 380-381, 387, 400

Richardson, 39, 80

Rider, 87, 99, 134

Ridings, 209, 219, 381

Ritchey, 167

Rives, 22-23, 261, 404

Roberts, 22, 30, 33, 196, 209, 213

Robertson, 99

Robinson, 42, 73

Roebuck, 167-168

Rogers, 73, 400; **Roggers**, 45

Roland, 168, 178, 182, 184, 193

Rollins, 357, 381

Roper, 12-14, 45-46, 51, 63, 73, 92, 116-117, 134-135, 143, 146-158, 167-168, 173, 177-180, 184-185, 87, 193-194, 197, 200, 204, 206, 217, 222, 224, 228, 233, 238-239, 244, 251, 253, 271-272, 305-307, 351-352, 369-370, 381, 406

Rucker, 400

Ruddell, 147

S

Salem BC, 212

Samples, 187, 194

Sandow, 21, 68, 73-75, 77, 92, 99, 104, 106, 118, 134-135, 258, 273, 277, 283, 336, 345, 353, 380-381, 394, 400; **Sando**, 62, 74

Sanford, 381

Sartor, 158

Satterfield, 111, 136, 151, 169-170, 173, 194-195, 247, 296, 353, 381; **Saterfield**, 136, 151; **Satifield**, 135-136, 146, 149, 151, 155, 169, 173

Scoggins, 184, 197, 223

Scott, 96, 122, 135, 158, 159, 169, 177, 185, 187, 197, 280, 306, 362

Scruggs, 322

Scudder, 42, 80, 295-296

Seabolt, 74

Sears, 74

Sewell, 54, 68, 74, 80, 87, 123, 149, 156, 158, 169-170, 177, 184, 187, 353, 381-382; **Sewal**, 52

Shadburn, 11, 19, 208-209, 237, 250

Shady Grove BC, 149, 212, 216, 217

Sharon BC, 217-218

Sharp Mountain BC, 24, 26, 36, 149, 151, 154, 209, 210, 212, 213, 216, 218,

Sheffield, 14, 42-43, 106, 214, 221, 332, 382, 400; **Shuffield**, 214

Shelley, 285

Shelton, 354, 382

Shipman, 169

Shoemake, 167, 169, 339, 382, 400; **Shoemaker**, 28, 194, 339, 382

Sikes, 112, 136, 153

Simmons, 349, 382; **Simons**, 382

Sissom, 113, 122, 135

Slaughter, 41, 80

Smallwood, 40-41, 50, 52, 73-74, 80, 99, 133, 135, 362, 370

Smith, 41-42, 44-50, 53-54, 68, 73-76, 84-88, 97, 99-100, 106-114, 116, 135-136, 138, 140, 149, 151, 158, 169, 173, 179-180, 182-183, 186-188, 194-195, 197, 215, 223, 225, 232-233, 238, 249, 256, 273, 276-277, 287, 291, 299, 311-312, 331, 336, 341-343, 354, 368, 370, 377, 382, 384-385, 389, 392, 400, 402, 405, 407

Smithwick, 286, 297, 388, 389

Southerland, 387

Southern, 39, 73, 74, 80, 99, 100, 110, 111, 116, 118, 135, 136, 141, 352, 373, 382

Sparks, 52, 62, 74, 135, 153, 169, 173

Spears, 124-125, 367; **Spear**, 248

Speer, 61, 74, 92-93, 99-100, 109, 117, 135, 338, 347, 382

Springer, 40, 71, 74, 80, 98, 328, 382

Staffice, 169

Stafford, 381

Stancil, 77, 101, 387, 402, 404, 407; **Stancel**, 137

Stanley, 5

Stearns, 214

Steavens, 112, 118, 135

Stephens, 15, 25, 29, 31-32, 43, 45-46, 66, 71, 74, 80, 94, 98-99, 132, 135, 215, 249, 268-270, 296, 298, 301, 323, 326, 328, 334, 338, 379, 382-383, 392

Stevens, 111, 127, 154

Stewart, 149-151, 154, 156-159, 163, 169, 180, 182, 189, 194, 244, 247, 305, 347, 358, 383

Stiles, 186, 197, 383

Stoyles, 45, 53, 74; **Stoyle**, 74

Strawn, 169, 194; **Strong**, 169

Strickland, 33, 72-73, 332, 383

Stripling, 47

Sutton, 14, 219, 222

Swims, 164, 181, 184, 194, 197

Swinford, 67, 74, 95

T

Tallant, 385

Tankersley, 284

Tatum, 183, 197

Taylor, 332, 383

Teal, 358, 383

Terry, 183

Thacker, 60, 90, 136, 239, 330, 383

Thomas, 75

Thompson, 5, 14, 75, 99-100, 110, 136, 179, 183, 185, 194, 202-203, 216, 219-220, 222, 309, 334, 359, 383, 400; **Tompson**, 147, 170

Thornton, 100

Thrasher, 67, 74, 84, 95, 100

Tidwell, 39, 80

Tippens, 75, 100, 320

Tollison, 287

Tomblin, 75, 100

Tomolavage, 403

Tribble, 14, 125, 144, 157-159, 175-186, 199, 207, 218, 222, 248, 251, 265, 307, 398

Turner, 41, 68, 75, 96, 100, 115, 126, 136, 146, 149, 152, 156, 158, 164-165, 170, 172, 176, 179, 194, 199-200, 204, 246, 261, 271, 274, 280, 291, 296, 306, 346-348, 360, 369, 383, 400, 402

U

Umphrey, 80, 100, 136; **Umptrey**, 40; Also See Humphrey

Underwood, 30, 32

Union Hill BC, 87, 112, 212, 214, 218

V

Vaughn, 136, 220

Vecchione, 400

Voyles, 183, 194

W

Wade, 40, 138, 139, 140, 179, 184, 197, 296, 346, 371, 383

Wadkins, 113, 116, 138, 141

Waldrop, 358, 383; **Waldrep**, 39, 75

Waleska Road BC, 184

Wallace, 7, 15, 51-52, 66, 77-78, 85-87, 92, 94, 100-102, 107-113, 115-116, 118, 123, 137-139, 148-149, 156, 170-171, 173, 184, 191, 194, 216, 232, 281, 335-336, 345, 350, 371, 378, 383-384, 387, 411-412; **Wallice**, 102; **Wallis**, 14, 50-55, 77, 216, 221

Warren, 42, 48, 51, 56, 76-77, 84-87, 101-102, 107-108, 110, 116, 130, 137, 152, 155, 171, 205, 384

Watkins, 125, 135, 138, 160, 180, 183-185, 190, 194-195, 247, 358, 380, 384, 400, 410

Watson, 57, 61, 75

Wattle, 378

Webb, 13-15, 19-20, 22, 26, 40, 67, 95, 127, 194, 207, 209-212, 217, 220-221, 270, 287-288, 301, 411

Webster, 48, 77

Wehunt, 108, 138, 224, 233, 297, 333, 339, 384, 400, **Weehunt**, 138, 147

Welch, 295-296

West, 44, 47-50, 55, 82, 85, 88, 102, 104-105, 108-113, 117-118, 128, 137, 139, 141, 144, 146, 148, 152, 154-156, 158-159, 171-172, 177-178, 180-181, 184-185, 194-195, 224-225, 229, 231-233, 238, 256-257, 273-278, 280, 291, 293, 299, 305, 307-308, 313, 340-342, 348-349, 351, 354, 356, 378, 384, 392-393, 395, 400, 403, 405

Westbrook, 39, 238, 375

Wheeler, 53, 67, 76-77, 95, 126, 138, 154, 183, 195-196, 215, 225, 232-233, 237-239, 281, 320, 335, 346-348, 351, 362, 364, 371-372, 379, 384-385, 400, 404, 407-408

Whidby, 177, 185, 195

White, 28, 31, 33, 39, 43-46, 48-49, 66-67, 70, 75-78, 80, 85-86,

95, 100-101, 104, 108, 112, 114-115, 127, 136-139, 146, 155, 167, 170-173, 178, 181, 186, 188, 195-197, 224, 233, 251, 279-280, 296-297, 301, 326-327, 338, 341, 352, 366, 370, 385, 393-394, 400, 402

Whitehead, 208

Whitener, 44; **Whitner**, 50, 76

Whitfield, 128, 144, 262, 404

Whitmire, 275

Wigginton, 101, 107, 137, 150, 173; **Wiginton**, 84, 101, 147, 150

Wilkie, 7, 13, 15-16, 27-28, 42, 44-45, 48, 53-54, 66, 68-69, 71, 73-78, 80, 82-88, 94, 98-102, 105-118, 130, 135-140, 143, 146-159, 162, 170-173, 175, 177-187, 189-190, 192, 195-197, 200, 202, 204-206, 223-225, 227, 229-235, 239, 242-243, 246-247, 251, 258-259, 265-267, 270-271, 279-283, 291-293, 297-298, 301-308, 315, 318-319, 337-339, 341, 343-344, 348-351, 353-358, 363-366, 372-374, 376, 378-381, 383, 385-388, 394, 397-398, 400-402, 404-407; **Wilkey**, 205

Williams, 29, 31-32, 39, 41-45, 47, 52, 54, 56, 68, 71, 75-78, 80, 84, 86, 96, 100-102, 109, 136-140, 148-151, 153, 155, 170-171, 173, 180, 195-197, 212-213, 219, 221, 223, 226, 234, 247, 262, 265, 270, 273, 284-288, 291, 293, 297, 328, 342, 350, 360, 386, 388, 392-393, 401

Williamson, 33

Willis, 288

Wilson, 44, 76, 80, 108, 155, 158, 166, 173, 181, 220, 237, 261, 265, 305, 346, 355, 388, 402 **Willson**, 75, 101, 148, 153, 171

Wimbish, 76, 111, 141

Wimpee, 114, 139

Wist, 33

Wofford, 46, 76, 80, 115, 139, 147, 170, 296

Wolf, 401

Woodall, 171-172, 305, 346, 388

Wooten, 42, 46, 77, 100, 286, 293, 373

Worley, 214, 251

Wright, 77, 94, 101, 106, 138, 338, 374, 383, 401; **Rite**, 94

Wyatt, 7, 13, 28-29, 33-34, 44-53, 56, 67, 76-78, 87, 95, 100-101, 105, 107, 111, 115, 117, 136-141, 143-144, 146-152, 154-160, 162, 166, 170-171, 177-187, 195-196, 199, 201, 203, 205, 212, 218, 223-225, 227-228, 231-232, 234, 239-240, 246, 249, 253-254, 259-260, 269, 274, 279-281, 287-290, 294, 297-298, 302-303, 319, 323-324, 330, 346, 349, 353-354, 357, 383, 385-389, 394-397, 405; **Waight**, 87; **Wight**, 87

X

Y

Yancy, 78

Yates, 303

Yother, 172, 305

Young, 61, 78, 286, 382, 389

Z

Zion Hill BC, 35, 215

Old T
Day